JOHN STOTT

THE MAKING OF A LEADER

A BIOGRAPHY
THE EARLY YEARS

Timothy Dudley-Smith

InterVarsity Press
Downers Grove, Illinois

InterVarsity Press
P.O. Box 1400, Downers Grove, IL 60515
World Wide Web: www.ivpress.com
E-mail: mail@ivpress.com

© *Timothy Dudley-Smith, 1999*

Published in the United States of America by InterVarsity Press, Downers Grove, Illinois, with permission from Universities and Colleges Christian Fellowship, Leicester, England.

InterVarsity Press® is the book-publishing division of InterVarsity Christian Fellowship/USA®, a student movement active on campus at hundreds of universities, colleges and schools of nursing in the United States of America, and a member movement of the International Fellowship of Evangelical Students. For information about local and regional activities, write Public Relations Dept., InterVarsity Christian Fellowship/USA, 6400 Schroeder Rd., P.O. Box 7895, Madison, WI 53707-7895.

The author has made every reasonable effort to obtain permission to reproduce letters and other material, including photographs, used in this book and is grateful for the cooperation he has received. Should any copyright holders have been inadvertently missed, they are asked to contact the publishers.

Photograph number 37 is taken from the Ashville Citizen, *December 29, 1956. Citizen photo—Glenn.*

Cover photograph: John Van Dorn

ISBN 0-8308-2207-0

Printed in the United States of America ∞

Library of Congress Cataloging-in-Publication Data

Dudley-Smith, Timothy.
  John Stott, the making of a leader: a biography: the early years/
  Timothy Dudley-Smith.
    p.   cm.
  Includes bibliographical references and index.
  ISBN 0-8308-2207-0 (alk. paper)
  1. Stott, John R. W.   2. Church of England—Clergy—Biography.
  3. Anglican Communion—England—Clergy—Biography.   I. Title.
  BX5199.S8344D83   1999
  283'.092—dc21
    [B]
                                                                    99-21813
                                                                       CIP

| 22 | 21 | 20 | 19 | 18 | 17 | 16 | 15 | 14 | 13 | 12 | 11 | 10 | 9 | 8 | 7 | 6 | 5 | 4 | 3 | 2 | 1 |

| 17 | 16 | 15 | 14 | 13 | 12 | 11 | 10 | 09 | 08 | 07 | 06 | 05 | 04 | 03 | 02 | 01 | 00 | 99 |

CONTENTS

Foreword

He would remind himself that the real leaders of English religious
thought and revival were never archbishops but were always the
simple priests, like a Wesley or a Keble or a Maurice.

Owen Chadwick on Archbishop Michael Ramsey[1]

The subject of this book is not a bishop or an archbishop, but has spent
over half a century as Curate, Rector and Rector-Emeritus of a London
parish. Among the significant aspects of 'religious thought and revival'
during this period – not simply in Britain and America – has been a
strong and maintained resurgence of a biblical and evangelical
Christianity. In and through this resurgence – again, not simply in
Britain and America – is woven inextricably the name, John Stott.

At the time of his ordination in 1945 it was difficult to see a future for
evangelicalism, in the Church of England at least, as anything more than
a faithful remnant, marginalized and all but excluded from the main
stream of church life. In this unpropitious climate All Souls Church
presented a platform of opportunity in the centre of London (then still to

some degree the centre of Empire) from which John Stott began to perceive and then to pursue his vision of a church apostolic in faith, alive in the Spirit, taught by the Scriptures and ready to respond in mission to the call of Jesus Christ.

This vision, as old as the New Testament, soon began to shape All Souls as a model of parochial life and organization, and especially of effective parochial evangelism, which was to inspire sister churches across the world. But the vision stretched far beyond the local church: it began to grasp the future, through new structures of evangelical thought, witness and strategy; and through Christian work and teaching with students and younger clergy. It embraced the historic evangelical ideals of the centrality of the Cross and the authority of Scripture, and invigorated them by a new, systematic and lifelong determination seriously to study and to teach the Bible; and to draw from it contemporary lessons in a rediscovery of the power of expository preaching.

High on the agenda as the movement gathered momentum was the place of the mind. True discipleship implied a thoughtful, informed and instructed church membership; as well as the urgent need for scholars of evangelical conviction and spiritual maturity to confront the long-accepted liberal climate of academic theology. Confrontation was unwelcome but inevitable; it was part of the task of leadership to be ready to defend as well as to establish and promote the gospel – but to do so with as little *odium theologicum* as possible, face to face, as brothers and sisters in Christ, with fairness and courtesy. So we find the writing and editing, the preaching and teaching, the London Lectures, the Institute for Contemporary Christianity, together giving expression to the conviction that Christ is Truth as well as Life, and that God is to be served and loved with mind as well as heart.

All this could not long remain a purely national or local vision. It began to embrace the cause of a world-wide evangelicalism, and notably the needs of students and pastors in other continents, not least in Third World countries and, more recently, in Eastern Europe. The Evangelical Fellowship in the Anglican Communion, the Langham Scholars programme and the Evangelical Literature Trust are indicative of the breadth of this involvement. Along with John Stott's global ministry, in a kind of symbiosis, has gone a recapturing of evangelical social concern, long recognized as the hallmark of such a faith. Through the Lausanne Movement he has helped commit his generation to a quest for world evangelization which seeks to give an undivided obedience both to the Great Commandment which includes the prophetic cry for justice, and to the Great Commission to make Christ known and to win disciples to his Name.

Such a task, still of course hardly begun and even then imperfectly realized, goes far beyond the work of any one man. But it is the story these pages attempt to recount through the very human struggles, with their human faults and foibles, of an individual life. John Stott will, I believe, come to be seen by history as among the world figures, 'the real leaders of religious thought and revival', of our time.

John Stott has been approached a number of times over the years by authors wishing to write his *Life*, or publishers seeking to commission an autobiography. David Edwards, for instance, wrote to him on behalf of Collins in 1977 during Christmas week, 'to raise with you the possibility that you might write an account of your ministry'. In his reply John Stott made it clear that this was not the first such approach and added, 'I still react negatively to the idea of an autobiography ... there is something slightly suspicious about anybody who presumes to write an autobiographical sketch'. He cited Peter Ustinov's revealing title, *Dear Me*; and James Agate's eight volumes of *Ego!* But he did not finally close the door on the possibility, 'ten years hence, when I am retired, although I still feel that if the story is worth writing up, it would be more impartial and much more valuable if written by somebody else'.

Twelve years went by without much evidence of the 'retirement' John Stott had mentioned; but they served as a reminder that a generation would not always be with us who had lived through and remembered the post-war years of evangelicalism; and also that biographies would certainly be written, whether he wished them or not. Christopher Catherwood's sketch in *Five Evangelical Leaders*, was an indication of what was sure to follow.[2]

Though I had been a friend of John Stott's since the 1940s, meeting him regularly and sharing with him in various projects, it was a surprise to receive a letter towards the end of 1990 asking if I would consider writing an authorized biography. The request came not from John Stott himself but from Prebendary Richard Bewes, the Rector of All Souls, on behalf of AGE, John Stott's 'Accountability Group of Elders', who advise him on his commitments and undertakings now that he is no longer in regular consultation with church wardens and a Church Council. Slowly the idea took shape. I could do very little until my own retirement just over a year later; but I talked at length with John Stott himself and, with his full encouragement and support, agreed at least to make a start on some of the interviewing and research. We had no fixed view on publication; John Stott hoped it might be only after his death. I wanted him to live long enough to change his mind – especially since I am only five years younger than he is himself.

From the start we agreed that any *Life* should also be to some extent a 'life and times', set against the story of the post-war period, the changing fortunes of Christian belief in an increasingly secular society, and of evangelicalism in particular. For my part, I have had to come to terms with the common objections against the publication of any biography in the lifetime of the subject. 'I really don't approve,' John Stott wrote to an old friend as recently as 1985, 'either of autobiographies or of biographies of the living. They are bound to lack objectivity and even integrity, it seems to me';[3] and for obvious reasons this is a view widely shared. As to the question of objectivity, I was helped by an essay of G. M. Trevelyan's, 'Bias in History', which suggests that the chief function of official lives is to 'supply material for judgment rather than to pronounce judgment', and defends the right of a biographer to be biased towards his or her subject. 'I once wrote three volumes on Garibaldi,' Trevelyan declares in his essay. 'They are reeking with bias. Without bias I should never have written them at all. For I was moved to write them by poetical sympathy with the passions of the Italian patriots ...'[4]

So my aim in these pages is that which Trevelyan here recommends, to supply information rather than to make judgments; and this means that what follows cannot be a definitive biography in the modern understanding of those words. It does not claim to be a measured assessment, nor can it present the subject in the kind of perspective that is only achieved with time. It does not generally attempt any probing of psychological dispositions as an explanation of why this happened and not that. John Stott has described those biographies as 'the most fascinating' which do not merely tell someone's story but 'uncover his secret'; by which he meant that they lay bare the direction and driving force of the person in question, 'to what he had dedicated his life and why'.[5] This, indeed, I could hardly fail to do, but I am very aware that what follows is a poor substitute for a portrait painted by that creative insight which sees beyond the surface to the inner being of the sitter, brought into clearer focus by the passing of the years. If nothing less than that is required of a biography, this book cannot claim to be one. It is rather the plain record of a longish life, not yet (thank God!) concluded as I write, set against the background of some of the events of which it was a part: in this instance, events of church and gospel. It seeks to recount within a firm chronological framework some of the movements of evangelical action, life and thought as touching, and touched by, an individual life central to evangelicalism, and especially to Anglican evangelicalism, both within and beyond the Church of England.

Counting on their fingers from the date of my retirement to the date of publication, there are those who will feel that this book has been a great while coming; even setting aside the fact that so far it contains only the first half of the story. I would remind them of Edward Carpenter's life of Archbishop Geoffrey Fisher, since I too have to report that 'the extent of the material was such as to be, for all practical purposes, almost inexhaustible'. Dr. Carpenter's book was referred to in Max Warren's autobiography as the 'forthcoming life of Geoffrey Fisher'; no doubt in their respective Westminster canonries they compared notes as to how their books were progressing. Max Warren published his in 1974, while Edward Carpenter's (admittedly much bigger) book did not appear until 1991. I feel I have therefore a few years in hand![6]

As it happens, about halfway through the original draft (in other words, about six years into the project) I read Owen Chadwick's *The Spirit of the Oxford Movement*.[7] One or two of the essays I had met before; much was new to me. As I read, I was astonished to find how closely I could relate what to Professor Chadwick were almost asides – statements of the obvious – on the work of a historian or biographer to the task I had in hand. The fact that his subject was in such contrast to my own was, for this purpose, irrelevant. He speaks, for example, of how Liddon, writing Pusey's biography 'with reverence, the reverence due to a great man', went on piling up detailed information at inordinate length until he 'succeeded in concealing Pusey's stature behind a pile of paper, and rendered the biography readable only by the student'.[8] My heart sank as I read. Again, in his essay 'Newman and the Historians', Owen Chadwick raises what he calls 'a puzzle about historical writing':

> Why is it that the history of a person, written while that person is still alive, never fails to discontent? The reason cannot be lack of perspective, for half a century has elapsed, and we see in a real historical perspective other events which happened less than half a century ago. The obvious reason is, that so long as the man lives, his private papers are not open to the inquirer. This is a good part of the explanation, but not all the explanation. Another part is the antagonism between the personal attachment which is necessary to private rapport, and the detachment or neutrality of mind which is necessary to public analysis.[9]

To this I can only say that John Stott's personal papers have been open to me from the beginning of the project. I have been fortunate that, in an age not given to letter-writing or to placing much value on correspondence, so much has survived. His practice has been in marked contrast with that of C. S. Lewis, for example, who wrote that 'it is my practice to consign to the flames all letters after two days'.[10] Sometimes there are drafts in his minuscule and abbreviated hand even when the actual letter (as in correspondence from Cambridge with his father) has been lost. Later there are sometimes carbons of letters, occasionally originals returned from among the papers of a recipient now dead, and letters still extant that I have been shown by others. Even so, I am conscious that much of his multifarious correspondence has gone beyond recall, though there is probably a higher proportion surviving from the earlier years than from the later – which is what one would prefer. Very little remains of any personal diaries kept by John Stott in his early days, though his own contemporary record of his conversion to Christ is quoted in chapter five. But from 1958 he has kept journals of his overseas visits, and I have been able to draw extensively on these.

When letters and first-hand accounts are available it has usually been my deliberate choice to prefer the words of original sources, contemporary observers or more experienced historians, to my own. Quotations from primary sources (memories of participants, original letters and so on) are clearly of unique value. But I have not hesitated to quote at length even from secondary sources (published accounts, contemporary histories) where this has lent authenticity or immediacy to the story I have to tell. Though ample notes will identify my sources for the student, the general reader is likely to find quotations of more interest than references. Because this is not an academic study I have felt able to expand abbreviations and correct hasty and obvious infelicities of grammar or style without invoking the accusatory 'sic'; just as in transcribing interviews I have occasionally smoothed over some of the characteristic repetitions, unfinished sentences and disordered expressions of conversational speech.

Perhaps the place where the shoe pinches, in Professor Chadwick's quotation above, is the tension between personal attachment and objectivity of mind. He continues:

> The historian has a little in him of the anatomist or dissector. A surgeon who cuts someone up does not wish to feel the body to be an object of his private affections: he must treat it as a thing, simply as an intellectual or physical problem to solve … A private bond is too strong for it to be possible to win a public detachment. On the contrary, a historian frigid in heart towards his theme can hardly ever write good history.[11]

I have already admitted – rather, claimed – a long-standing 'private bond' of friendship with my subject; and this would be a two-edged attribute in a conventional biography. But I hope in a story-teller the advantages outweigh the drawbacks. I have myself shared at first hand in a good deal of what I recount, at least in England, or am in touch with friends and correspondents who have done so. This is one of the most cogent reasons for writing such a study now, while those who experienced these events are, many of them (sadly, fewer than when I began), alive to remember them; and while John Stott's own recollections are available.

Sometimes, as with all of us, memories can prove with further research to be a little less than fully accurate, but without them some of the story, and many of the personal insights, would be beyond recall. Certainly future and better books about John Stott will be written: my hope is that this one will prove a quarry from which a few of their building-blocks may come.[12]

In telling the life story of any leading Christian, especially if he happens to be a teacher and a writer, there are bound to be references to his own understanding of the truth. In each of the decades that mark the divisions of this work there will be found an account of John Stott's publications; and every chapter, at least from the 1930s onward, contains pointers to his biblical and evangelical thinking. Beyond this, I have not tried systematically to set out his own theological position. This is partly because in his own words 'the evangelical faith is nothing other than the historic Christian faith'[13] and partly because it can be understood more clearly from his own writings, of which almost all the significant books are still readily available.[14] In the same way, references to John Stott's preaching ministry will be found throughout the text, including some of his insights into the preacher's task and his own approach to it. Since, however, he has himself written two books specifically on the subject of preaching, I have not sought to recapitulate their substance in any detail here.[15] I think the narrative itself will make clear what a large part of his ministry has always been devoted to preaching, and his conviction of the unique position given in Scripture to proclaiming the Word of the Lord.

When Owen Chadwick reminds us that 'a movement to canonise a man or woman cannot be a help to a true biography'[16] he utters a sentiment which I have had in mind – impressed on me as much by my subject as by anyone – from the beginning. Here, for example, is part of the letter John Stott provided for me to use when I approached his friends:

> I am anxious that you should have complete freedom in gathering material. Do not hesitate to ask my friends (or enemies!) any direct and personal questions you wish to ask. Your unfettered, uncensored enquiries have my full approval. I've no wish for a hagiographical book, but rather for an honest assessment of my 'life and times', – with 'warts and all'. So I hope *you* will feel free, and that those you approach will also feel free to cooperate with you in every way.[17]

I have not met the problems which confronted R. L. Megroz in his critical study of Walter de la Mare, who found his subject 'an adept, patient stone-waller' to the questions put to him;[18] nor have I had to contend with the embarrassment that caused Malcolm Muggeridge to abandon his projected biography of George Orwell, namely that 'he had found out too much about Orwell that he would rather not have known'.[19] On the contrary, wishing for everybody's sake to paint an honest picture, 'warts and all', I have been hard put to it to discover very many of them. Again and again those I have spoken to or corresponded with have had very little to place in the opposing scale, when compared with their almost universal, almost overwhelming, and – in repetition – almost wearisome expressions of appreciation and indebtedness: it would be fatally easy to compile, with the best intentions, a book which could, in Robert Runcie's devastating phrase, 'be consigned to the category of "Hagiographical Stocking Fillers"'.[20] And though many friends have been able to tell me something of their personal story, these are no more than the tip of the iceberg. They do little to convey this aspect of a lifetime's ministry. Owen Chadwick expresses just this of Edward King, Bishop of Lincoln, when he writes that 'King's influence was a personal influence over individuals, and therefore hidden in a way which the biographer can hardly touch'.[21] That must be true of any Christian minister: and certainly so of the subject of this book.

A small but important point that confronts biographers is what to call their subject. In childhood he is clearly John, and I have let that stand alone until on his leaving school it becomes less appropriate. 'Stott', alone, would then be possible, though his father Arnold Stott is an essential part of my story; and besides, I feel with Stevie Smith that the bare use of surnames for male contemporaries 'makes it sound as if they have all been raised to the peerage'.[22] From 1939, therefore, I have written 'John Stott', except of course when quoting from others, thankful that the name by which he is now generally known is conveniently succinct.

One further question which Owen Chadwick raises must be faced. Writing of Newman as a historian, he asks

> Was it really true that what he wanted out of history was not so much objective truth as the moral example which would help him? Was he in the stage of pre-modern history, where the purpose of history is to provide good and bad examples from the past?[23]

I have pondered this: and recognize that I would not have agreed to write this book solely out of a desire to record events for posterity. Because I owe much to Christian biography in my own discipleship, and because my calling is to be a minister of the gospel, I cannot escape the hope that this book may be of use within the purposes of God to inspire a reader here or there with the 'good example' it portrays. Without that hope (indeed, it has been more than a hope; it is a prayer) I would have used my time differently. But in saying this I utterly disclaim any suggestion that I have distorted the record for the purposes of edification. I believe the story will edify (that is, build up the reader in the faith) only insofar as it presents a faithful record of events, and of John Stott's place within them. At my insistence he has read the MS of each chapter and helped me to correct errors of fact. But it has been clear between us from the beginning, and proved in practice in many instances, that the final judgment is always mine.

Too many people have helped me with this book, including numerous librarians, for me to be able to thank them by name. John Pollock (often quoted in these pages) shared with me at the outset some thoughts on Christian biography; my daughter, Caroline Gill, has transcribed a thousand pages of recorded conversations; others have given interviews, written memoranda, supplied letters, or ransacked their files and diaries on my behalf. Some will be sad to see how little I have been able to find room to include of what they sent to me: others may be relieved! To all I am immensely grateful. Some of their names (by no means all) will be found in either the text or the notes which follow. I am conscious, too, that there are a great many people in all parts of the world who play, or have played, a significant part as colleagues, helpers or simply as valued friends in John Stott's life, but whose names do not appear in these pages. To them I offer my apologies and ask their understanding. Even in a biography such as this there is never space enough.

But I must find room at the end of this long Foreword to acknowledge a debt to my publishers, especially Colin Duriez of the Inter-Varsity Press; to Frances Whitehead who typed and revised the whole (and has begun on the second volume) and herself contributed to the story; and to John Stott whose friendship encouraged me at every stage and who contributed detailed memoranda, lengthy interviews and innumerable replies to my enquiries. More even than these, I thank my wife Arlette for whom this book has long been part of our daily life together: if it was the custom for those who cherish, support and sustain the writers of books to have their names printed on the title-page, hers would be in letters of gold.

TDS
Ford, 1998

The 1920s

ONE

—

Family Background:
Between the Wars

1

In the summer of 1929 the children using Park Square Gardens were getting out of hand. The gardens, a small square of slightly sooty green, carefully tended, lie at the north end of Portland Place in the centre of London, adjoining Regent's Park and half a mile from Oxford Circus. Subscribing key holders and their families (but not 'Servants during the absence from London of the family') could use the gardens on payment of a few guineas a year; and it was a valued privilege, open only to local residents, in a part of the West End where private gardens were few and far between.

Now, on 16th July, the Board of the Crown Estate Paving Commission received from their Clerk and Treasurer a report duly recorded in their Minutes in a neat copperplate hand:

Complaints having been received of the insolent behaviour of a lad named Stott aged 9 in Park Square Gardens the Board directed that a letter be written to his parents ...

The letter survives, and runs as follows:[1]

Complaints have been received from subscribers using Park Square and Crescent Gardens of the unruly behaviour of your son when he is in the gardens.

The Commissioners considered the matter at their meeting on the 16th instant and I am directed to request you to be good enough to take what disciplinary action you consider necessary to prevent in the future the lad in question annoying others using the gardens.

J. W. S. Appleton
Clerk

Dr. Arnold Stott, the recipient of this letter, was already a distinguished physician with consulting rooms in Harley Street, the most celebrated concentration of medical expertise in England. By now in his mid-forties, he was Consultant Physician at both the Westminster Hospital (then in Broad Sanctuary) and the London Chest Hospital in City Road, happily married and the father of two daughters (a third had died in infancy) and of a son John, the youngest and the most obstreperous.

'Every man is to a great extent the product of his inheritance', John Stott was to write fifty years later:

The most formative influence on each of us has been our parentage and our home. Hence good biographies never begin with their subject, but with his parents, and probably his grandparents as well.[2]

In a rare personal reference in one of his later books he described himself as descended 'from hard Norsemen and blunt Anglo-Saxons, with no spark of Celtic or Latin fire in my blood', and as 'one of those cold fish called an Englishman'.[3] Certainly the Stott family believe that their ancestors were cattle-breeding Vikings, who came from Scandinavia to Lancashire in about the tenth century, settling there after one of their raids. John Stott likes to claim piratical blood in his veins, and whenever he visits a Scandinavian country he asks to be received not as an alien but a native son come home. Authorities can be found to support the probability of such a claim, for example the *Genealogical Quarterly*, in an article on 'Stottiana for 1,000 years':

It is difficult to believe that all the Stotts in these islands have sprung from the same stock. It would seem much more likely they entered from more than one point and perhaps at widely different dates. But the undoubted Nordic nature of the name and the support given by the heraldry of the case make it reasonable to suppose that there was a numerous family or tribe of the Stoti in the Low Countries or Denmark, possibly both, in Viking days who were of a somewhat adventurous nature and set out as colonists … One must not exclude the possibility that some of the names Stote or Stot may have been nicknames (meaning strong as a bull or connected with cattle). From early times they may have been specially interested in sheep and weaving. If so they would eventually find Lancashire much to their liking.[4]

'Abraham' has been a common family Christian name; and at the start of the nineteenth century there were two Abraham Stotts in Lancashire, both born in Bolton, first cousins only some four years apart in age. Their common grandfather was John Stott of Rochdale. It was great-aunt Betty (so the family tradition goes) who found the money to enable Abraham the younger to establish a cotton-spinning factory; and it was he (John R. W. Stott's great-grandfather) who was always known as 'honest Abraham' or 'honest Abe'. The young John R. W. Stott used to tease his cousins by suggesting that this was obviously to distinguish him from their ancestor, the other Abraham (who had been an architect). In fact he acquired the name from the integrity with which he handled his financial affairs during the difficulties experienced by the cotton trade during the American civil war. 'Honest Abe' and his wife Elizabeth had eight children, though four died in childhood. Among the survivors were 'William Stott of Oldham, RBA' (so called to distinguish him from another painter, Edward Stott) a number of whose typical local landscapes, said to owe something to both Whistler and Manet, can be seen in Oldham Art Gallery today; and John Robert, John R. W. Stott's grandfather, who was known as 'the Napoleon of the Manchester Exchange' for his daring deals in cotton. He married Amelia ('Lily') Walmsley, daughter of Henry Walmsley, 'a man of means'.[5] They had one daughter and four sons, one of whom, Arnold, was John R. W. Stott's father. Arnold himself was born in 1885 a few miles from Oldham at Bardsley, Ashton-under-Lyme, but after school at Rugby he decided to stay south and study medicine at Cambridge and in London. He remained a director and shareholder in the firm of Abraham Stott and Sons, cotton-spinners, and took a strong family interest in the fortunes of the mill. Throughout the disastrous years of the cotton industry he regularly visited Oldham; and made it his policy to treat the employees more and more as partners in the business.[6] He had a strong sense of family loyalty and tradition, and was to give his father's names to his son John, together with the 'Walmsley' from his mother's family.

As a footnote to history, it seems that Percy, one of Abraham-the-elder's sons (not Abraham Stott the mill-owner, but Abraham Stott the architect), was vicar of St. Peter's Halliwell, Bolton, for thirty years. It was not until after his ordination (so Oliver, one of his sons, assured John R. W. Stott years later) that Percy Stott was led to a personal faith in Christ by William Haslam, that extraordinary Victorian parson who had himself been converted by his own sermon in his own pulpit, in Baldhu Church near Truro.[7] Percy and his wife Louise had ten children, all of whom became active evangelical Christians, with strong missionary concerns. The Oliver Stott mentioned above was one of the Executive Committee responsible for Billy Graham's remarkable Greater London Crusade at Harringay in 1954.[8]

Arnold Stott (John Stott's father) went from Trinity College, Cambridge to do his clinical studies at the Medical School of St. Bartholomew's Hospital, London. On qualifying as MRCS, LRCP in 1909 he became house physician, demonstrator in pathology, and chief assistant in the children's department: it was here that he began his life-long interest in cardiology, the study of the heart. The first electrocardiograph had recently been developed in Holland as a diagnostic tool, and demonstrated in London by Sir Thomas Lewis, the consultant under whom Arnold Stott served: Lewis's *The Mechanism of the Heart Beat, with Special Reference to its Clinical Pathology*, published in 1911, was a landmark in cardiac studies.[9] On the outbreak of war in 1914 Arnold Stott joined the Royal Army Medical Corps with a short-service commission, serving in France as a pathologist and eventually returning to civilian life with the rank of Major. It was not long before he was elected to the consultant staff at the Westminster Hospital, to establish his own department of electrocardiography. It was his pride, however, to describe himself as a consultant physician (and, if pressed, to admit to a 'speciality in heart and chest') rather than by the narrower and more specialized term of cardiologist.[10]

He was known as a meticulous teacher, if feared as an examiner. 'I remember particularly,' wrote a medical student of that period, 'that a candidate had stated that a patient might have a temperature: "No, he would have a pyrexia: all patients have a temperature which may or may not be raised".'[11] To those who worked under him he was a hard taskmaster, something of a martinet, always to be seen about the hospitals he served in the black coat and pin-striped trousers of his consultant status. He demanded the same standards from his housemen. One who appeared wearing a Crusader badge was told such an emblem was unbecoming on a hospital ward.[12] His hospital work, rather than his private practice from his Harley Street consulting rooms, was his consuming interest. He was punctilious, kind and correct to patients, painstaking with students but not one to overlook negligence or suffer fools gladly. He was a hard worker, an able administrator and a highly successful doctor, but he did not encourage his son to consider a career in medicine because it demanded such sacrifice of personal and family life and leisure.[13]

In outlook Arnold Stott was more a 'humanist' than a 'secularist', for though his intellectual position might be that of scientific secularism, he was genuinely committed to the betterment of humanity. He was a fervent believer in education, a child of the Enlightenment, with an almost naïve trust in the power of reason and the inevitability of progress to remedy the world's ills. His advice was much sought after both professionally and in the family circle. He was also a stickler for accuracy in the use of language. He once asked the houseman at the bedside of one of his patients what the man should be given to eat: 'A little fish, perhaps?' elicited the crushing response, 'Do you mean a sardine or a sprat?' Formidable, upright, able and public-spirited, he was not a man to be lightly crossed; but he was much loved by his grandchildren and was at his most human with them, or with his dogs and in his garden. His wife, Lily, for her part was unshakeably loyal, her strength of mind and character governed by a sweet and unselfish disposition. Though Arnold could be hurtful and sarcastic, she never responded in kind. They were devoted to each other and to their children; and, thanks largely to Lily the peacemaker, lived together in harmony and much happiness.[14]

If on his father's side John Stott is descended from Viking raiders, Lily's side of the family can be traced to the marriage of Mark Holland, who worked as a carpenter somewhere near what is now Waterloo Station, to Susannah Aldus; and to the marriage of Robert, one of their six sons, to Caroline Thatcher of Somerset. Robert and Caroline had four sons, and a daughter Emily Lorraine, a devoted evangelical Christian. A letter survives written by Emily in old age to her niece Louise (John Stott's Aunt Babe) with the gift of a Bible 'for your kind acceptance'. The letter continues:

It comes with *much* love, dearie, and many earnest prayers that this Holy Word of God may be a comfort and blessing to you as it *is* to me. I have read it through several times and as I still *daily* read in it I find God speaking to my heart by His Holy Spirit.

In the 14th Chapter of St. John's Gospel, you will read that Jesus has gone into Heaven to *prepare* a place for *you dear* and in the 43rd Chapter of Isaiah He says 'Fear thou not for I am with thee, (Louise). I have called thee (Louise) by thy name. *Thou art mine*'. God bless you as you read His message, my darling.

Emily's brother, Alfred Robert Holland (1851–1937) was John Stott's maternal grandfather, and he married Elizabeth Henrietta Stumm from Prussia. When John and his sisters were growing up they used to tease their mother at any sign of *Flussigkeit* (busy competence) or stern discipline, as derived from her Prussian blood. After their marriage, Alfred and Elizabeth Holland lived in Antwerp where he managed a hotel. John Stott's mother Emily Caroline – always known in the family as Lily – was born there, though her younger sisters Ella and Louise (nicknamed 'Babe') were born in London. Lily was always the strongest and most stable of the three sisters; Ella and Babe leaned on her advice and support. From Antwerp the Holland family moved to London, on Alfred's appointment as manager of the Grand Hotel on the corner of Northumberland Avenue and Trafalgar Square (since demolished to make way for redevelopment). One of the annual treats to which the young Stotts looked forward was a family luncheon at Frascati's, the famous restaurant in Oxford Street, of which Alfred was a Director.

Lily Holland and Arnold Stott met as students at a crammer's in Red Lion Square. He sat behind her and drew pictures of the back of her head! She had an ambition to become a medical missionary, but gave up medicine to look after her invalid mother and a much younger brother, Lance. Lily was five years older than Arnold and already thirty-one at the time of their wedding in 1911. Two daughters followed quickly, Joan in 1912 and Rosemary ('Tubby' to the family) in March 1914; she died suddenly of meningitis aged three, when her father was serving in France with the British Expeditionary Force. Even though they had her for so short a time – or perhaps because of it – 'Tubby' retained a special place in her parents' affections. Every spring, on the anniversary of her birthday, a little vase of Rosemary would be on each of their desks.[15] No further children were born for the period of the war; but Arnold had made little secret of his desire for a son, and in 1919 a third child was on the way – destined to be a third daughter, Joy. The last of Arnold and Lily's children was born on 27th April 1921, the long-awaited son, to be christened with the family names of John Robert Walmsley Stott.

Of his two sisters, Joan was, in childhood terms, almost of a different generation; nine years older than John, she was away at boarding school for much of his early years. Though at first she shared the day-nursery with the younger ones, she was inevitably very much the elder sister, finding her place in the family increasingly among the adults rather than with John and Joy. With Joy it was very different; she was barely more than a year older than John, small for her age so that they were often mistaken for twins, and his rival and companion in everything. Their childhood was punctuated – as in most families – with numerous rows, bickerings and nursery fights; the stormy waves on the surface of a settled, if sometimes exasperated, sibling affection which was to remain with them all their lives. It was with Joy that he would be taken regularly to 'the Gardens'; with Joy that he would go to parties, to church, to Sunday School; with Joy, later, that he would dance and make music in the family circle; and with Joy, at the age of seven or eight, that he would come to an agreement that 'we disapproved of prep schools' and that it was unnatural to take a child away from home and parents.[16]

In the early years of their marriage Arnold and Lily set up home in Addison Avenue, West Kensington, a quiet, wide, tree-lined street. Number 53 is one of a series of elegant identical semi-detached villas typical of many comfortable London family homes, built on four floors with a semi-basement kitchen, area steps for the tradesmen's deliveries, an attic for the maids and a footpath behind. Home was almost the last house on the west side of the Avenue, before the road is blocked by the large red-brick church of St. James, standing in what is still today an extensive grassy square. But by 1921, with the war behind him and increasing responsibilities at two London Hospitals, it was time for Arnold Stott and his family to settle in Harley Street. Dr. Stott had previously rented consulting rooms, first at 13 Harley Street and then at 30A Wimpole Street; now in May of that year, with John only a month old, he moved with his family to take up residence in his own home and his own consulting rooms, at No. 58, Harley Street.

It was not a convenient house from the family point of view. There were too many stairs, a conflict between family and patients over the joint dining-room and waiting-room; and in Lily's view it was too small for them. She always maintained that had she not been recovering from the birth of her baby (a longer process then than it is today) she would not have approved the purchase. Not far down the street was an ear, nose and throat surgeon, Walter Graham Scott-Brown. His young son Graham (later a medical missionary in Nepal) was befriended by John Stott as he followed in John's footsteps at Rugby and at Cambridge.

When the Stotts moved to Harley Street it had been the medical heart of London for over a hundred years. It takes its name from Edward Harley, second Earl of Oxford, who in 1713 married Henrietta, daughter of the Duke of Newcastle. She brought to him as part of her dowry a large part of the Cavendish Estate in Marylebone, known as Marylebone Fields, and it was on this land that Harley began to build. A church, 'The Oxford Chapel' was included in his new development and in 1721 building began of what is now St. Peter's, Vere Street.[17] Harley Street was planned by the Cavendish Estate to provide 'residences for nobility and gentry'. It was in 'Harley-street' that Jane Austen arranged for the Dashwoods to take 'a very good house for three months'.[18] In 1876 W. E.

Gladstone took No. 73 as his London home between his first and second periods of office as Prime Minister. It was considered important for those wanting 'a good address' to live at the Cavendish Square end of the Street, where house numbers were lower. Doctors drifted into Harley Street by ones and twos from about the 1830s onwards. Even by the middle of the century there were not much more than a dozen, and for many years the 'specialists' who practised from its consulting rooms and made their homes in its high elegant houses had not always been well-received by their colleagues in the profession. Thomas Addison, who gave his name to Addison's disease, 'dreaded becoming a specialist', and even in Arnold Stott's lifetime the consulting ophthalmic surgeon to St. George's Hospital was advising patients to avoid 'specialists' and 'to seek rather the advice of a physician or a surgeon who regards his calling as one and indivisible, and who recognizes that the whole is greater than any of its parts'.[19] It was an outlook with which Arnold Stott had some sympathy.

By the time that Arnold Stott had qualified, Harley Street 'had become a hallmark rather than an address':

> Harley Street's high noon, the golden age of consulting practice, was the first decade of the new century, when white spats were the insignia of medical eminence where formerly it was the gold-knobbed cane with the concealed pomander of sweet-smelling herbs; when frock coats and silk hats were 'the livery of the laborious week'; when the fixed fee was two guineas for the first consultation, three guineas for visits within four miles of Charing Cross; when there was a manservant at every other door, the surgeon's carriage-and-pair and the physician's one-horse brougham had not been finally displaced by the motorcar; and Sir Frederick Treves, Bart., GCVO, FRCS (1853–1923), of 6 Wimpole Street, was the great exemplar of medical authority and distinction.[20]

Just as Lister had travelled to Balmoral to operate on Queen Victoria, so Treves had added to the popular prestige of twentieth-century medicine when called to operate on the new King Edward VII for appendicitis (a term Treves avoided). The coronation was postponed; the king's condition and the bulletins of his medical attendants held the hourly attention of the Empire: the 'specialist' was now universally regarded as the head of his profession.

The post-war years, following the armistice of 1918, were not altogether an easy time to be a Harley Street consultant. Taxes were higher; the nation's health better than in the years before the war; medical standards in the provinces more than capable of treating disease or offering surgery for cases that in the earlier years of the century would have looked to London for help. There were fewer private residents in the Street; and it was becoming a minority of houses which served a single doctor or surgeon as both home and consulting rooms. Nevertheless, some medical families continued to make their homes in Harley Street, and to find in its immediate neighbourhood a social life which was the stronger for the presence of fellow professionals. Marylebone in the 1920s was still – as indeed in part it remains – one of the many 'villages' that make up London, and the proprietary chapel of St. Peter's, Vere Street, at the southern end of Wimpole Street, was known locally as 'the doctor's church' and attended by many medical families. Others (like the Stotts) chose the Church of All Souls, Langham Place; though young John was baptized in the parish church of St. Marylebone on 22nd July, soon after the move to their new home.

2

All Souls, Langham Place (the name derives from Sir James Langham of Northamptonshire) owes its existence to an Act of Parliament of 1818 for 'promoting the building of additional churches in populous parishes'. The parish of St. Marylebone had grown to some 75,000 inhabitants, of whom only 250 could be accommodated in the parish church; and the total capacity of that church, combined with the eight or nine Proprietary Chapels which had been built over the previous hundred years, could find seats for only a tenth of the local population. St. Marylebone was therefore much in the minds of the promoters of the Act; and in 1820 it was agreed that a new church should be built, financed by the parliamentary grant, to accommodate a substantial congregation. John Nash, the celebrated architect, from his offices on the far side of Oxford Street, was commissioned to design the new church. He was then at the height of his reputation, and had already made his mark on that part of London, laying out the plans for Regent's Park and much of Regent Street. Such was his reputation that he was soon afterwards entrusted with the enlarging of Buckingham House into what is now Buckingham Palace.

The commission to design the new church was not an easy one. There was some uncertainty about the plot on which it could be built; and a great number of interested parties. Nash had already in mind from his earlier designs a notably prominent spire, 'a fluted cone with its base encircled by a colonnade'. This he retained but modified his ideas to meet the particular needs of the site finally chosen, where the upper end of Regent Street would curve gently, by means of Langham Place, to meet the lower end of Portland Place. In a letter to the Church Building Commissioners (who were to pay the bills) dated 22nd May 1820, Nash wrote:

> From the nature of the bend of the street, the portico and spire will together form an object terminating the vista from the circus in Oxford Street – the spire (I submit) is the most beautiful of forms and is peculiarly calculated for the termination of a vista and particularly suitable to a Church. The portico I have made circular as taking up less of the passage of the street at the same time that it is most consonant to the shape of the spire.

He added that the proposed church would seat 1,820 people; and cost approximately £18,500, exclusive of architect's and surveyor's fees.[21] Work proceeded apace; the spire and portico, the most original and striking features of the building, were completed on Christmas Eve, 1823.

They were by no means universally admired. Questions were asked in the House of Commons as to how much this 'mass of deformity' had cost the taxpayer, with its uneasy combination of gothic spire and classic rotunda. Satirical verses were published in the *New Monthly Magazine;* and a cartoon entitled *Nashional Taste!!! (Dedicated without permission to the Church Commissioners)* was published in the following year, above the following couplets:

Providence sends meat	Parliament sends funds –
The Devil sends cooks –	But who sends the Architect? !!!

A striking feature of the interior, which has remained unchanged through the years, was the picture above the Holy Table by Richard Westall: 'his *Ecce Homo* (Langham Place) is an example of the late eighteenth-century revival of large religious paintings'.[22] It was presented to the church by King George IV (perhaps at the instigation of John Nash himself?) and has spoken eloquently to countless congregations ever since:

> It depicts Christ, handcuffed, thorn-crowned and in a purple cloak. Round his head are three hands, the hands of jeering priests and soldiers, who are all looking and pointing at him. Yet what they did in scorn and derision, we seek to do in faith, love and worship. Our whole ministry aims to be a testimony to him. And down the years thousands of worshippers have stood or knelt before this picture ... and prayed that, in response to his great love for us, we may live our lives for him.[23]

Meanwhile, as the day for the consecration of the church drew near, an Order in Council was published, dividing the over-large parish of St. Marylebone into districts (All Souls was not yet to have its own parish). It fell to the Vestry to choose not only the furnishings and appointments of the church, but also its dedication. The name 'All Souls' was thought 'highly appropriate … from the circumstances of its being erected to afford gratuitous accommodation to the poor inhabitants of this Parish …', and as expressing pastoral care for the living rather than commemoration of the dead. This was not so much pious rhetoric as bare realism. The Parish of St. Marylebone served a very mixed community. It included not only the 'good addresses' of Cavendish Square, Welbeck Street and Wimpole Street, but a considerable population from the other end of the social scale, a heterogeneous mix of races and nationalities as indeed can be found today in what has been called 'Soho north of Oxford Street'.

Finally, at Morning Prayer followed by Holy Communion, on Thursday, 25th November 1824, Bishop Howley dedicated the church as 'set apart to Thy service … to all generations'. The Bishop arranged for the new minister, the Reverend Dr. John H. Spry, to be the preacher. Howley, Bishop of London, and about to become Archbishop of Canterbury, was unlikely to have set for the church a high standard of pulpit eloquence. Owen Chadwick describes his preaching:

> Though eloquence would have been out of keeping with his character and countenance, he could rarely make a point with decision, his delivery was not only dull but embarrassing, his critics said that he drivelled. He perpetually lost the right words and visibly groped for the wrong, contrived to make a long speech sound interminable, and threw his hearers into a nervous fever. Making a speech at a girls' school, he could not think how to address the girls. 'My dear young friends – my dear girls – my dear young catechumens – my dear Christian friends – my dear young female women.'[24]

The service was attended by a hundred children from the Charity School, who were afterwards entertained to roast beef and plum pudding at a cost to the Vestry of £15.[25]

The evangelical tradition of the church seems to have been set by its second Rector, Charles Baring, an Oxford double First who had served his title at St. Ebbe's, Oxford, and was known as a friend of Lord Shaftesbury, the honoured evangelical reformer and philanthropist. It was a tradition continued faithfully by most (not all) of the succession of incumbents, not least by Prebendary F. S. Webster, who died in office the year before the Stott family became parishioners. Webster had been curate in Oxford under the celebrated Canon Christopher of St. Aldate's, Oxford, combining this with his work as first Principal of the Church Army Training Home. This was in Oxford until it moved to London in 1885.[26] Such pioneer mission work in downtown Oxford seems a far cry from the West-end ministry of All Souls and a Prebendal stall in St. Paul's Cathedral, but Webster's gifts and character were equal to both. A former student at the Training Home remembered how one afternoon he went to the fair for an open-air meeting:

> The Principal's coat was torn, our tunics were soon in pieces, and our caps were treated like footballs. They spat in our faces, bad eggs were thrown and all kinds of refuse hurled at us, but by God's grace we were enabled to hold on; and here I learnt that I must have courage, endurance, and grit. It did us much good ...[27]

Webster moved to London with the Church Army Training Home; and then for ten years to a large parish in Birmingham. He was appointed Rector of All Souls in 1898: a surprising appointment of a man still under forty, popularly known in his Oxford days as 'Frisky Frank',[28] and with little experience of a fashionable congregation. It seems to have been an imaginative attempt on the part of the Crown (as patron) to recognise that All Souls was more than a West-end church and congregation, but the parish church of what was then a considerable residential area of poor and overcrowded property:

> Socially the parish was treated as two distinct districts, bisected by Portland Place. When visiting westwards the clergy wore frock coats and silk hats, which was also the approved attire for open air meetings held near Marble Arch on Monday evenings in the summer, but in the eastern part of the parish they appeared in lounge suits. This often meant a change of outfit two or three times a day![29]

Webster's life and ministry ended suddenly and unexpectedly in January 1920 at the age of sixty, with the work of the parish slowly returning to normality from wartime conditions: a firm believer in the value of a day off away from the parish, he was on his way to play golf at Chorleywood when, crossing Baker Street, he was knocked down by a car and died in hospital. He had served as Rector for over twenty years, through both the Boer War and the First World War: to his foresight the parish owes the present Rectory at No. 12, Weymouth Street and also the Foley Street premises of the Church School.

By the time the Stotts moved to Harley Street, All Souls was in the care of a new Rector, Arthur Buxton, who belonged to an altogether newer generation of clergy. Travelled, missionary-hearted (he was a strong supporter of CMS, rather than the newly-founded BCMS), a man of enterprise and initiative, he had served in the war as Chaplain with the Rifle Brigade, and then as Minister of the Embassy Church at Cologne. When in 1928 the houses to the north of the church were demolished to make way for Broadcasting House, and the home of the newly-constituted British Broadcasting Corporation was established almost on the steps of All Souls, it was Buxton who forged a continuing link between All Souls and the BBC. When the BBC began to look for central churches where, on a Sunday morning, they could 'reproduce' a congregation of substantial size and create the atmosphere of a church for what was a totally new (indeed, controversial) experiment, All Souls was an obvious possibility. Arthur Buxton 'was keen to help but on Sunday mornings, like many Anglicans, he wanted to broadcast his service of Sung Eucharist'[30] which was unacceptable to the BBC. Though the Corporation had held back from offering a Sunday service so as not to be in competition with the churches, the first broadcast of a daily service on a week-day had taken place in January 1924 from St. Martin-in-the-Fields (where Dick Sheppard had been quick to grasp an opportunity which both St. Paul's Cathedral and Westminster Abbey had declined).[31]

Now Arthur Buxton began regular broadcast talks at 10.15 on Saturday evenings: an early example of the wider ministry of this church in London's busy heart. Nor were the possibilities of new technology overlooked when it came to making the voice of the church heard in its immediate neighbourhood. Since his church had no full peal of bells to summon the faithful, and perhaps prompted by his association with the technical skills of Broadcasting House, Buxton installed loud-speakers in the spire of All Souls, playing vastly amplified recordings of the bells of St. Mary-le-Bow and of St. Margaret's, Westminster. He was no doubt delighted when asked one day how he managed to train his bell-ringers with such precision!

Arthur Buxton was an impressive figure, tall, slim, elegant and well dressed. As a Rector in London's West End, he cultivated friends drawn from the theatre; and was pleased to be able to invite them to his church. Chief among these were the celebrated husband and wife team of Jack Hulbert and Dame Cecily Courtneidge. Since 1913 they had played opposite one another in musical comedy, and in 1923 had established a joint management which gave them both star roles in a long run of successes stage-managed by Hulbert. They were considerable celebrities, renowned even in the 1920s for a stage partnership combined with a happy marriage (which was to continue for sixty-five years). At All Souls

Hulbert, then in his thirties, could sometimes be seen in his role as sideman in the north gallery; and in 1928 his wife presented the font-cover as a memorial to her sister. But though in all this Arthur Buxton sought to make his church up-to-date, relevant and attractive, he was also responsible for moving its theological position from the definite evangelicalism of his predecessors towards the less biblical and less Protestant 'Liberal Evangelicalism' which had been growing in influence since the start of the century.[32] It was under Arthur Buxton's ministry that the Stotts spent fifteen years as parishioners.

Buxton's aim, according to his farewell letter to the congregation, dated 16th August, 1936, was:

> ... to make All Souls a central Church and community in which all can feel at home. I have sometimes been urged to make it high in ritual, but I have considered that the 'Liberal Evangelical' position ... is what appeals to the majority of Churchgoers. I have introduced eastward position, coloured stoles, a facing-the-same-way attitude of body as well as mind in the Creed ... as helps to worship and devotion, so that everything is done, as far as possible, decently and in order. And now, as I look into the unknown future, I see great spiritual possibilities. Through a young and enthusiastic ministry it is my hope and belief that God will do great things.[33]

'Central' is a very fair description of All Souls' geographical position in London's West End; and it may have been in this sense that Buxton used the word. But given the general tenor of his statement, it seems more likely that his aim was to move away from the distinctive conservative evangelicalism that he had inherited, into a position which would be broadly 'central' theologically, less 'narrow' in its traditions and church-manship, neither High nor Low; though Buxton had numbered at least one high churchman among his many curates. Coloured stoles ('that badge of blameless mediocrity'[34]) had been, as far as the Church of England was concerned, one of the innovations which the 1928 Deposit-ed Prayer Book had sought to legitimatize in a new rubric added at the start of the Communion Service. When Parliament rejected the book, it nevertheless continued to be published and sold; and its use overlooked, if not encouraged, by many bishops. It was not only cynics who viewed it as an attempt to bring within the framework of Anglican order a range of unauthorized changes in the conduct of worship which their proponents had no intention of abandoning – 'a sort of attempt to suppress burglary by legalizing petty larceny'.[35] When Parliament refused to authorize the book, the bishops were seen as men who proposed to have their cake and eat it, 'quietly defying Parliament while retaining the state connection'.[36]

It seems probable that though the 1928 Book did not become the regular use at All Souls, yet Buxton would have found himself in considerable personal sympathy with its suggested changes, and its provision of a Eucharistic Rite which approximated more closely to the medieval service.[37]

3

The five years either side of 1921, the year of John Stott's birth and of the family's move to Harley Street, form together a momentous decade. On the world stage the Russian revolution of October 1917 had created the USSR, putting paid to all hopes of a liberal democratic Russia for seventy-five years. November 1918 saw the armistice which ended the First World War, a conflict waged at the cost of some ten million lives, and followed by a series of treaties re-drawing the map of Europe. In 1919 Benito Mussolini set up his Italian Fascist party; three years later 24,000 Black Shirts marched on Rome while he waited in Switzerland to be called home to form a government. January 1920 heralded the formal start of the new 'League of Nations', though without American participation; 'the beginning of a permanent international political order with institutions in principle independent of any particular government' which may yet come to be seen 'as one of the most significant dates in our era'.[38]

A year later a young Adolph Hitler was voted President of the Nazi Party, and in 1925 published *Mein Kampf.* In the world beyond Europe the British Empire was changing. Canada, Australia, New Zealand, South Africa and Newfoundland, each of whom had made their contribution to the support of England and her allies during the war, became self-governing dominions within the British Commonwealth of Nations.

In England, too, these were decisive years. Even in the midst of war, a new Education Act raised the school leaving age to fourteen. After fifteen years of militancy women began to vote in parliamentary elections ('Britain could now as a result for the first time be fairly termed a democracy'[39]) and by 1919 the House of Commons had in Nancy Astor its first woman member. In 1920 Oxford University awarded its first degrees to women;[40] and in the same year the inauguration of the Church Assembly (authorized by the Enabling Act of 1919) gingerly marked the start of a new process of self-government for the Church of England. In 1921, William Temple (whose untimely death twenty-three years later, after less than three years as Archbishop of Canterbury, 'seemed to shake the western world as if one of its pillars had been removed'[41]) was consecrated bishop. The British Communist Party was founded in 1920, and the first Labour Government elected in 1924. A short-lived post-war boom quickly gave way to economic depression when 'Britain suffered the fastest economic collapse in her history'.[42] With unemployment standing at over one million, post-war Britain was 'riven by class antipathies and violent industrial disputes'.[43] The General Strike of 1926 drew attention to the plight of the miners but did little more:

> The miners came off the worst. That summer many of them were reduced to a diet of home-grown lettuce and stolen mutton from the hills. The coming of winter gradually forced them back to work; groups of them sued separately for peace with the mine-owners. Numerous poorer pits closed down for good ...[44]

Nevertheless, even so enlightened a politician as Harold Macmillan, looking back on the period with the benefit of hindsight, recalled chiefly the underlying mood of confidence engendered by a belief in 'progress':

> The nineteen-twenties were a time of general optimism, and rightly so. In spite of the many baffling problems at home and abroad, there seemed no reason to doubt that the evolutionary processes which had served us so well in the past would continue to operate in the future.[45]

It was also a period of rapid advance in technology and scientific discovery. In 1919 at Manchester University Ernest Rutherford had fulfilled the ancient dreams of alchemy and ushered in the atomic age by the first artificial transmutation of matter – 'splitting the atom'. The introduction of the electrocardiograph, the isolation of insulin in Toronto in 1921, a programme of immunization against diphtheria in 1923, successful open-heart surgery in 1925 and the discovery of penicillin in 1928, were symptomatic of the spectacular advances being made by twentieth-century medicine.

The motor car was revolutionizing travel at home; by 1922 an Austin 7 could be bought for £165; meanwhile the aeroplane had begun to shrink the world. The Royal Air Force had been established as the war was coming to an end; the Atlantic was crossed in May 1919 by a United States Navy seaplane; while a month later Alcock and Brown completed the first non-stop Atlantic crossing at an average speed of 120 miles per hour.[46]

'Talking pictures' appeared in 1923; and in 1926 John Logie Baird demonstrated at the Royal Institution his pioneer system of transmitting moving pictures by radio. The BBC, which had first broadcast radio programmes in 1922 (125,000 people bought 10 shilling licences), by then numbered its audience in millions; but a regular BBC TV Service began only in 1936. By 1930 about one fifth of all homes in Britain were wired for electricity.[47]

In the realm of ideas, it seemed that there was 'no longer an incalculable dimension to life'.[48] It would be another decade before C. S. Lewis would begin to emerge as the popular Christian apologist of his generation: in 1925, at the age of twenty-seven, he was not yet a believer, though at last elected to his long-sought Fellowship at Magdalen College, Oxford. Meanwhile T. S. Eliot, still with Lloyds Bank, was working on *The Waste Land,* whose publication in 1922 'established him decisively as the voice of a disillusioned generation'.[49]

Little by little the process of secularization continued to eat away at the fabric of traditional religious belief. The Darwinian revolution of the previous century appeared finally to have discredited a religion based upon divine revelation, if not indeed the concept of the divine. Charles Raven, who was to become one of the leading figures of academic religion – Regius Professor of Divinity at Cambridge, Master of Christ's College, Vice-Chancellor of the University – was one of those who represented the fervent efforts of liberal-minded theologians seeking to come to terms with the post-war climate of thought when he declared in 1921 that 'the new physical sciences have rendered untenable the traditional ideas of authority, of the supernatural, of miracles, and in fact of the whole method of God's operation'.[50]

He was not alone. Many prominent in church life sought to meet the challenge by a steady departure from orthodoxy in the name of liberalism; but if the cracks in the foundations of some monolithic establishments were not immediately noticeable, a second world war would soon render the process unstoppable. Sixty years on, looking back over much of his lifetime, John Stott would himself reflect on the revolt against authority and the loss of confidence by the churches in the Christian gospel:

Seldom if ever in its long history has the world witnessed such self-conscious revolt against authority ... the twentieth century has been caught up in a global revolution, epitomized in the two World Wars. The old order is giving place to a new. All the accepted authorities (family, school, university, State, Church, Bible, Pope, God) are being challenged. Anything which savours of 'establishment', that is, of entrenched privilege or unassailable power, is being scrutinized and opposed.[51]

This was true not only in respect of the content of the faith, but of the structure of the church. World-wide Anglicanism had begun with chaplaincies on the American continent (John Wesley would be an example); but the creation of a Protestant Episcopal Church in the United States towards the end of the eighteenth century signalled a new departure. By the 1930s an Anglican Communion in the modern sense was coming into existence as a family of independent churches, loosely tied together by affection, loyalty, and the framework of a common liturgy; but under no authority from Canterbury or elsewhere. With power to alter their doctrinal formularies, some of them represented no very formidable bulwark against the prevailing flood. John Stott described the process:

> As we approach the end of the twentieth century we are conscious that the erosion of Christian faith in the West has continued. Relativity has been applied to doctrine and ethics, and absolutes have disappeared. Darwin has convinced many that religion is an evolutionary phase, Marx that it is a sociological phenomenon, and Freud that it is a neurosis. Biblical authority has for many been undermined by biblical criticism. The comparative study of religions has tended to downgrade Christianity to one religion among many, and has encouraged the growth of syncretism. Existentialism severs our historical roots, insisting that nothing matters but the encounter and decision of the moment.[52]

In all this, the 1920s were proving to be the threshold of the modern age. They were significant years, and London a fascinating place, in which to spend the formative years of childhood in a secure and happy home.

TWO

—

Home in Harley Street: A London Childhood

1

The home to which the Stott family moved in the early summer of 1921, with young John a few months old, was No. 58 Harley Street, standing almost on the corner where Harley Street crosses New Cavendish Street. It is a tall imposing house, with bow-fronted rooms on three of its six floors. The front entrance boasts a carved fanlight surmounting a stone portico, expressive of assured stability, confidence and class. Inside, the house is surprisingly narrow, having only two main rooms to a floor, with servants' hall and a rather dark kitchen and scullery in the basement. It was every inch a doctor's household. The dining-room (which also acted as waiting-room) was on the ground floor, immediately to the right of the front door. Patients would have appointments from 2.00 p.m. onwards; so that early arrivals, before the family had quite finished lunch, would have to wait on a chair in the hall until the room had been cleared and made ready for them. Behind the dining-room was a further consulting room, let (in the manner of Harley Street) to a distinguished orthopaedic surgeon, Arthur Bankart, whose patients would also use the dining/waiting-room. Dr. Stott's consulting room was on the first floor at the back of the house, separated from the drawing room by a glass door. The secretary-receptionist worked in the drawing room, so that it was not available to the family during the afternoon. The main bedrooms were on the second floor, the servants in the attic, while on the third floor were day-nursery, night-nursery, and Nanny's bedroom. Nursery meals had to travel to this third floor from the kitchen in the basement.

A number of nannies came and went, followed by a small succession of governesses when Joy was getting beyond the nursery. Some were French: the family had strong links with the continent; some were more successful than others. Family tradition remembers how a young John would kick the nanny of the moment when she had been particularly trying ... it seems that few of them stayed for long.

The one who stayed was Nanny Golden. She was much loved, and the family remained in touch with her long after she married and moved away. She was a devout Christian, and had the joy of learning from her 'Johnnie' of his conversion to Christ twelve or fourteen years after she had left. John's elder sister Joan, known as Joanna – nine years older than her brother – recalls how Nanny Golden would teach Joy and John children's hymns and CSSM choruses; and how it would amuse her parents to see the two of them, aged perhaps three and four and on their best behaviour, singing 'Though my sins are scarlet'.[1]

John Stott has described how he could 'still remember the exultation I felt on the day I first got out of my pram and was allowed to walk'.[2] In the early days it was by pram and push-chair that Joy and John were taken on fine mornings, and again in the afternoon, to 'the gardens' – Park Square Gardens, to which the family were key holders, only a few steps from the top of Harley Street. Beyond these lay the delights of Regent's Park, with its celebrated Rose Garden. There was the Botanical Garden with banana trees in a great conservatory, long since pulled down; while the scents and sounds of the Zoo, with occasional glimpses of giraffes or elephants, were reminders of a wider world. In winter the frozen lake would attract skaters, and in summer the two little princesses, Elizabeth and Margaret Rose, could sometimes be seen driving in the inner circle. But it was mainly in the more familiar Park Square Gardens that as they grew older the Harley Street children played and met their friends. There was a fascinating tunnel joining the two parts of the gardens, running under the Marylebone Road; shouts and yodelling noises would be gratifyingly amplified when running through the tunnel, leading the chase or in hot pursuit. Here John graduated from babyhood (when he had to be restrained from an urge to pick the flowers, a London park-keeper's cardinal sin) through sand pit and swings to tricycles and fairy cycles, from which he was pleased to manoeuvre Joy from the pillion into a well-placed puddle; and so in time to small-boys' gangs, often of doctors' children, bristling with toy guns and knives, and offering scope for early powers of leadership. Then it would be home towards tea-time; and back to the nursery. Joanna remembers Nanny Golden walking up the three flights of stairs with an infant under each arm; two or three years later home-comings would be accompanied by the repeated reminder to go quietly through the hall and up the stairs 'because your father has a patient'. It was impossible to forget for long that this was a doctor's household; the family used to tease young John by telling him that the first words he uttered on learning to talk were 'coronary thrombosis'.

Arnold Stott was by conviction a scientific secularist.[3] He had a strong social conscience, and was a freemason committed to the philanthropy which drew many highminded professional people (he was a member of a doctors' lodge) to freemasonry at that time. He was an early supporter of the National Health Service, believing that medical care should be available to everybody, irrespective of their ability to pay for it. His days were given to his hospital work and his consulting rooms: his evenings after dinner (even, at times, when there were guests) to working for his membership – he was to be elected Fellow of the Royal College of Physicians in 1927 – and later to medical records, paperwork and correspondence. But on days out, at weekends and especially on holidays away from London, he sought to interest young John in hobbies that he himself had pursued. He was a keen naturalist, an expert botanist, interested also in music, stamp-collecting, fly fishing and wine.

Attempts to interest John in stamp-collecting, the hobby of King George V, were unsuccessful. Probably, like many fathers, Arnold tried too soon and too hard. With music he was much more fortunate: a natural aptitude ran in the family. John was to be known for his singing voice both at his prep school and at Rugby. By then he had found a cello when staying in Freiburg during the school holidays and had written home for permission to buy it. He had lessons, and was soon playing in the school orchestra; while at home his mother would accompany him on the grand piano in the drawing-room. Sometimes, especially when visiting his mother's parents in Hampstead, there would be musical evenings. Granny Holland, like Lily, could play the piano and had a fine singing voice. Arnold played the violin, Joy the clarinet and John the cello for their family quartets. John and Joy used a double music-stand, facing each other; from time to time John would make faces at his sister across their music so that the clarinet would falter and fail into a fit of giggles … family music was one of the highlights of their London life.

But long before that, at quite an early age, Arnold had been more successful in enthusing his son with aspects of the world of nature. Living not far from the London Zoo, they would pay occasional delightful visits. But it was on walks together in the country that John first began to acquire an interest in natural history. 'Shut your mouth and open your eyes and ears' his father would say to him; and would teach him where and how to look, the names of plants and butterflies and birds, the interdependence of the natural order.

It was these early lessons in observation that led to butterfly collecting, and then to bird watching. There are photographs of John Stott with a butterfly net from a very early age: it was part of his luggage when he was sent to boarding school at the age of eight. His father must have had considerable trust in John's responsibility, having given him (at about this time) a prescription for a little cyanide to make a killing-bottle: John in later life was in no doubt that it was cyanide – and that, had he sniffed it himself, it might have killed him. During the summer holidays Arnold would take his son 'sugaring' on warm nights. Together they would make a sticky brew, based on beer laced with treacle; and then in the garden or orchard where they were staying they would paint a band, three or four inches wide, round the trunk of every tree. John would be woken by his father about midnight, and they would go into the garden to discover by torchlight what moths or night-time butterflies, attracted by the sweetness and inebriated by the beer, had fallen to the foot of the tree. The rarer specimens would be put quickly into the killing bottle, and from there transferred to the collection. There would sometimes be hawk-moths, yellow underwings and red underwings; and all with the added fascination of a midnight expedition. Staying in Fowey in Cornwall one summer holidays John was excited to capture a number of rare Comma butterflies (so-called from a small white 'comma' under the wing), visitors from the continent that year. They were among the last of his ill-fated collection:

> One day in the 'nursery' at home, when I was setting butterflies, my sister Joy (provoked by me, I have little doubt) threw a cushion at me, which landed in the butterfly box. If I have ever seen red in my life, I saw it then. I chased her round and round the circular table, and reckon I would have done her grievous bodily harm if I had caught her.[4]

Arnold Stott understood the magnitude of this loss. He took John to his consulting room and sat him on his knee; and then made ineffectual attempts to repair the worst of the damage with Seccotine, smelly fish-glue, slow drying, messy, and difficult to handle. But the collection was ruined. John Stott continues the story:

> ... so it was then that I turned to birds, and I have often used it as a good parable of the Providence of God because although I was

inconsolable then, of course I'm very glad now ... people think one is eccentric enough to go round the world with binoculars, but to have gone round the world with a butterfly net would have been too much to bear.[5]

It cannot have been an easy establishment for Lily Stott to manage. She herself had been brought up in a home which numbered footmen among the servants, so perhaps the domestic staff (consisting of Christmas, the parlour maid, who also answered the door to patients and acted as receptionist, together with a housemaid, a cook and a between-maid) were not too much of a problem. But in addition there was the doctor's secretary working in the drawing-room, a second consultant seeing patients on the ground floor, sometimes a chauffeur, and on the nursery floor a nanny or governess (after Nanny Golden, a succession of them) – and the children.

It had been made rather too plain to the daughters that their father's heart had been set on a son. John's sister Joanna remembers:

My real name is Joan, though I call myself Joanna because there were so many 'Joans' in my generation and I changed it at school. But all the nannies when Joy and John were little used to say 'Well, of course, your father wanted a boy to be called John, and therefore you were called Joan ...'

Indeed, in the then state of medical knowledge, there were times when Arnold would hold it against his wife Lily that it was her responsibility when (before John's final arrival) three daughters were born in succession. And if Joanna felt it, it was harder still for Joy.[6] Nannies, in the nature of the case, tend to favour the youngest; and John's arrival a month after Joy's first birthday meant she hardly knew the special attention and privileges accorded to 'the baby' in most nurseries. Lily, too, would be bound to give a good deal of her attention to John, both as the youngest and as the only boy; and this had its effect in making Joy closer to Joanna, her big elder sister, than to Lily. 'When Joy and I used to fight,' John Stott recalled, 'she would in the end run to Joanna as I would run to my mother.'[7] Add to this the fact that as they grew into childhood Joy remained small of stature, with a noticeable squint, while John was good-looking, good natured and an attractive child; and it is not surprising to find a sense of frustration, rebellion and rivalry which remained with Joy, not always far below the surface, for the rest of her life.

Lily managed all this equably enough. A strong character, high-principled like her husband, she had an air of calm competence not easily ruffled. She was creative, teaching her children to make things with their hands; musical, with a fine singing voice which John inherited (as also her high colour and rosy cheeks); concerned for the welfare of all her household. One expression of this was the 'Domestic Fellowship' she and a few others originated, to help servant girls new to London and having no friends there, to meet others whose free time coincided with their own. These were not only social occasions and expeditions, but opportunities for self-improvement. Young John would sometimes go with his mother to attend the talks and classes. It was a form of personal social service which Lily set much store by. It was Lily, too, who would teach the children to say their bedtime prayers. John later wrote of her:

> My mother had been brought up as a Lutheran and retained the piety of her childhood. So she taught my two sisters and me to go to church, read the Bible and 'say our prayers'. These things I continued to do until my mid-teens out of loyalty to my mother ...

although by then it seemed to him 'a largely meaningless routine'.[8]

Joy and John were so much of an age that these prayer-times would sometimes be for both together, sometimes individually. They tended to be based largely on set prayers from a little book, and the 'portion' from the Bible Reading Fellowship notes. Fifty years later John Stott was to describe his recollection of a time when, night after night, as his mother came to him (he was then about six or seven) he would say to her anxiously, 'Mummy, what am I going to be when I grow up?' The question obsessed him, even at that tender age: 'I did not see myself qualified to do anything.'[9] Very wisely, Lily would tuck him in and say 'Don't worry, Johnnie, it will be shown you what you will do.' But the anxiety was very real.

Exercising his 'doctor's prerogative', and because he had no Christian faith of his own, Arnold Stott went to church only rarely – perhaps two or three times a year to the Morning Service at All Souls. But Lily went with the children fairly regularly in the early years, or in their holidays from boarding school. They would sit in the front row of the North Gallery, always pleased when Jack Hulbert was there to take the collection. In their nursery days John and Joy would usually be separated, sitting one each side of Nanny to keep them out of mischief; but this did not prevent them making little pellets of any used bus tickets they could find in their pockets, and dropping them on the fashionable hats of the ladies below 'scoring several direct hits and then, of course, ducking back'.[10] Joy used to tell her friends of how she remembered sitting with John in All Souls, their big blue Nanny in between them as usual. During the Lord's Prayer an arm stole round behind Nanny's kneeling form with a school cap on the end of it, while John's voice, as deep as it would go, whispered 'Collection, please!'[11]

For a time John and his sister attended the All Souls afternoon Sunday School, run for a rather select group mainly of doctors' children, and led by the Rector's wife, Esmé, Mrs. Arthur Buxton. John and Joy would go together, John dressed for the occasion: 'I used to go, I remember, on Sundays armed to the teeth with knives or daggers stuck into my socks or stockings and even a revolver in my belt, and hold up the little girls!'[12] The School was held in Mrs. Buxton's rectory drawing-room at 12 Weymouth Street, the room that was one day to be John Stott's own first-floor drawing-room during his twenty-five years as Rector. The children would arrive at 3.00 p.m. and put their pennies for missions (the Buxtons were staunch supporters of the Church Missionary Society) into a special collecting box adorned with the papier-mâché figure of a small native child. John had an early reputation for obstreperous behaviour, sometimes stirred up by Joy; she was well able to manipulate him, 'winding him up' until he was 'like an angry bull',[13] and would then sit back demurely to see the effect of her work. Pert, sporting, jolly, ebullient, she was a gifted tease. John would be admonished and sent out of the room: and Joy would be able to carry home an account of just what the trouble had been on this particular afternoon. Certainly Joanna's sisterly recollection is that 'He spent more time outside the room than inside it'.[14]

2

When John had well turned six, it was time to leave the day nursery and follow Joy (and Joanna, though she had long since moved on) to his first school, King Arthur's, Kensington.[15] He began (mornings only, apart from games days; with handwork on Wednesdays) in September, 1927. Before this lessons had been at home. There survive (a hint of things to come?) a very recognizable drawing of a parrot in primary colours from the age of five, and of an owl two years later. Before he went to King Arthur's he was not only drawing but writing:

> John Stott
> I am five
> I shall be six in April
> I have a fireman's helmet.

Along with the parrot and the owl, other birds feature in these early exercises:

15th February, 1928

Have you ever fed the seagulls?
Yes, I have fed the seagulls.
Where have you seen them?
I have seen them in Regent's Park.

In the same month there is an alphabet exercise:

Kathleen has a kitten
Leonard has a lamp
Marjorie has a mat
Noel has heard a nightingale

... one feels the author's real interest lies with Noel!

For a seven-year-old, John was by this time beginning to be well-grounded in French, which he would later read at Cambridge. No doubt his mother's continental background, and the French governesses who came and went, had much to do with this. King Arthur's School must have found him a promising pupil:

John Stott. Age 7.

DEVINETTE

Devinez qui je suis.
Etes-vous un animal?
Oui, je suis un animal.
Avez-vous quatre pattes?
Oui, j'ai quatre pattes.
Etes-vous grand?
Oui, je suis grand.
Habitez-vous le Zoo?
Oui, j'habite le Zoo.
Mangez-vous du foin?
Oui, je mange du foin.
Aimez-vous les gâteaux?
Oui, j'aime bien les gâteaux.
Avez-vous une trompe?
Oui, j'ai une trompe.
Etes-vous un éléphant?
Oui, je suis un éléphant.

Often during the school holidays, both now and later, the household would be increased by the addition of a cousin, Tamara, much the same age as John and Joy. She was the daughter of Lily's sister Ella, who had married Albert Coates the celebrated conductor, half English and half Russian by origin, and at that time travelling widely. Tamara therefore shared the nursery for weeks at a time, and looked on Lily as a second mother, sometimes saying 'I wish you were my Mum'. Arnold was more distant, preoccupied with his practice, and finding it inconvenient to have yet more children in the house. Meal times in particular were difficult. Arnold could be sarcastic and say unkind things. As a gourmet and a connoisseur of wine, he was fussy about his food at the best of times and is remembered for having thrown an unsatisfactory breakfast out of the window; but Lily was adept at keeping the peace, and John and Joy did not share Tamara's awe of their distinguished father and used to mock and tease both their parents and each other in the give and take of family life.

Tamara remembers that once in the nursery the three children (Joanna was away at boarding school) got hold of some clay pipes (perhaps given them for blowing soap bubbles, a traditional nursery pastime) and John appropriated some of his father's tobacco so that they could all experiment. She recalls, too, how after lunch every day the children would be put to lie flat on their backs on the floor of the big drawing room 'so that our spines would grow straight',[16] perhaps the origin of the famous 'horizontal half-hour' for which the adult John Stott would later be known in every part of the world.

Like most professional families, the Stotts worked hard during the year, and took two months out of London in the summer; though Dr. Stott would probably return to his practice and his hospitals after a bare fortnight, leaving the family still in the country, and visit them for the weekends. It would be an immense upheaval when the three children were small. In those years they took houses at Woodbridge in Suffolk or perhaps on the south coast, and once at least at Totland on the Isle of Wight. The cots were parcelled up in sacking and sent ahead, with the pram and the heavy luggage, by train. Nanny and a couple of maids would also travel by train, leaving early enough to make the holiday house ready before the arrival of the family by car. John's birthday was in the spring, and when he was old enough it became something of a family tradition to take a picnic out of London, perhaps to Stoke Poges, to pick bluebells and listen for the first cuckoo and no doubt for other birds as well. It would be on one of these family holidays or expeditions to the countryside that John experimented with a toy air-pistol, peppering the flanks of grazing cows to see them jump and start.

Christmas brought its own magic. Like many families, the Stotts enjoyed the mounting excitement of mysterious packages on top of the wardrobe in the parents' bedroom, the nursery table cleared for the pasting of paper chains, the drawing and decorating of cards, the scented tree in the corner of the drawing-room. But along with these went the special fascinations of a metropolitan Christmas. Harley Street is only five minutes walk from Oxford Street and Regent Street, the heart of the shoppers' West End. Big stores like Selfridges would vie with one another to present the best illuminations, the most sumptuous window displays. Everywhere the tempo of life increased.

Because Granny Holland maintained the German traditions of her childhood, Christmas Eve was for her the focal point of Christmas. The Stott family would visit her, and admire the huge tree in her boudoir, at first in Kensington Palace Gardens and in later years in Hampstead; and there would be an early exchange of presents. Then came the waking to Christmas Day itself; the descent from the nursery floor to sing carols to sleepy parents, and the opening of stockings. There would be church at All Souls; followed by a family gathering in the great drawing room, Arnold Stott on hands and knees under the illuminated Christmas tree, distributing the presents one at a time. Christmas lunch was followed by a brief walk in Regent's Park. Joanna remembers:

> I can see John now: I should think he was only just walking and talking – he must have been about two – chasing a squirrel in the park with some bread. He fell over and the squirrel vanished. John picked himself up and said 'Poor bloody little squirrel' – having heard it somewhere and with no idea what it might mean![17]

In 1932 King George V made the first Christmas Day broadcast to the people of the British Empire. By then John would be on holiday from his prep school: and the King's speech at 3.00 became, as for so many households, a well-remembered part of every Christmas. There were other family traditions too: even when they were quite young, Arnold Stott would take his children at Christmastime to one or other of the hospitals where he had beds and introduce them to his patients. It was a bringing together of the two sides of his life, the personal and the professional; and a much-appreciated courtesy:

> We went with him to the Westminster Hospital, I think when we were still very young. He would give us a little case history of Mr. So-and-so: he was very polite. And then 'Mrs. So-and-so, who has this and that, and whom we are able to help in this sort of way'.[18]

This was the old Westminster Hospital opposite Westminster Abbey, on the site of the present Queen Elizabeth II Conference Centre:

> It was a rather old-fashioned, archaic building in those days, but a great hospital. Then I think we used to go on to the Royal Chest Hospital in City Road and see patients there. We only stayed a minute or two with each, of course, but it was quite an eye-opener to us, and was one of the things that made me want to be a doctor.[19]

John did in fact want to be a doctor from his earliest years, particularly a paediatrician, which would combine his love of children with the practice of medicine as he observed it in his father; but his father was not in favour. Those Christmas visits to the hospitals clearly began young: there is a family recollection of young John going missing on one of them, and finally being run to earth flat on his back on the floor of the dispensary, his mouth open beneath the tap of a vast stone jar of Cod Liver Oil and Malt (of which he was inordinately fond) which was slowly trickling into his mouth.[20]

Then, through the Christmas holidays, there were parties and pantomimes. Sometimes it would be *Peter Pan*; sometimes *Dick Whittington*; perhaps the newest favourite, *Toad of Toad Hall*;[21] and, almost every year, Bertram Mills' Circus at Olympia with clowns and elephants and bare-back riding, the star performers gathered from the length and breadth of Europe. Tamara's father Albert Coates, the celebrated pianist and conductor, would sometimes come to visit them in Harley Street and provide a personal link with the London musical scene. On one occasion he took John and Tamara to meet Bruno Walter who was conducting at the Albert Hall (which John in his earliest years had half-believed was named after his uncle). The children were taken back-stage to the Conductor's Room, and witnessed the two huge men embracing warmly 'like a couple of enormous bears'.[22]

Harley Street and its environs formed one of London's many 'villages', where neighbours met constantly in the streets and in the parks, used the same shops, the same lending-library, the same parish church. For a professional family with young children in such a community Christmas also meant children's parties. Occasionally there would be a party at No. 58 with balloons and games and a party tea; more often Joy and John would be taken by Nanny to a friend's house, coats and shawls over their party clothes. In his increasing excitement John would sometimes be in danger of fulfilling every nanny's worst fears and 'going berserk', hitting the little girls and losing all control.[23]

Nannies and servants, the sheltered life of an upper-class home, the park to play in, the zoo, the pantomime, the circus: it was by any standard a privileged childhood. It says much for Lily's good sense that for the youngest, the long-awaited and only boy, it was not a spoiled one. Nor was it without reminders, in those early years, that there is more to life than pantomimes and parties. The Christmas visits to his father's hospitals clearly gave pause for thought; he observed his mother's interest in the servant girls fresh from the country and friendless in London, and the constant pressures upon his father from patients to whom the magic words 'Harley Street' might mean the difference between life and death.

Something of the wonder of the natural world was also a real part of John's upbringing; and perhaps more seeds were sown by the services at All Souls, by Esmé's Sunday School, by the nightly devotions, than were apparent at the time. It would be clear before John's school days were over that he had an active social conscience: and it seems likely that this concern for others began with his parents and his home – and not least with Nanny Golden and her shining example of selfless disinterested love.

Meanwhile, the years were passing. Petticoat government was no longer enough. It was time something was done for John to begin to harness those wild energies, and to train that enquiring mind. King Arthur's little school had done what it could. Perhaps the letter from the Crown Estate Paving Commission about 'the lad named Stott' confirmed what Arnold and Lily had been intending for their youngest: it was time to think of boarding school.

The 1930s

THREE

Oakley Hall: A Love of Birds

1

Arnold Stott had been educated at Rugby, the public school made famous by Thomas Arnold in the first half of the nineteenth century. He wanted his son John to follow in his footsteps, and the usual preparation for entry to any public school was to start at a 'Preparatory' School or 'Prep' School at the age of about eight. The next five years would then offer a good grounding in the major subjects necessary for public school entrance. The majority of boys who attended prep schools went as boarders. In good homes they were sorely missed from the family circle, not least by their mothers, but it was fully accepted as being in the child's best interests, an essential preparation for life at the much larger public school for which he was destined.

There is now no evidence to show why Arnold and Lily chose Oakley Hall for their son. There seems to have been no family connection with the school: it was barely founded when Arnold Stott's school career began, and there was no question of John following his father there, as would happen at both Rugby and Cambridge. It does not seem an obvious choice: Oakley Hall in Gloucestershire was a little old-fashioned, even by the standards of its day. It prepared boys for a range of public schools, but other prep schools had closer connections with Rugby and sent more boys there. There were plenty of good prep schools much nearer London, whereas Oakley Hall was nearly 100 miles by road. Distance, however, was not a great consideration. In the 1920s and 30s parents were not much given to visiting their son's boarding school except on special occasions: 'leave out' once or twice a term, perhaps; Speech Day or Sports Day; an important school match. It appears that John's parents took trouble over their choice, perhaps seeking advice from Gabbitas Thring, the educational consultants, and visiting a number of schools before coming to a decision.[1] Most probably personal recommendation from some friend or patient whose boy had done well there would have influenced their choice.

Oakley Hall had been founded in Cheltenham (as Brandon House) some forty years before. In 1905 it had moved to Pelham House, Folkestone, on the Kent coast, and to Cirencester as a temporary expedient towards the end of the First World War, to be out of reach of German bombs. A large house was found, with extensive grounds and gardens; and within a couple of years it became clear that there was little point in moving back to Kent. Cirencester is less than twenty miles from Cheltenham: the school was returning to its original roots, and there it stayed.[2] In 1928 a senior master, Major C. F. C. Letts, who had already been on the staff for seventeen years, took over as headmaster. In September 1929 John Stott joined the school, among the youngest of the fifty or sixty pupils. He was eight-and-a-half years old, and must have been conspicuous among the five new boys arriving for the start of term by the fact that his luggage included a large butterfly net.

The main house was not built as a school but had been the private home of Lord Grantley. It is a gracious building of Cotswold stone, with large gables at each end, and two smaller ones between. A set of sepia postcards which (to judge by the spelling) John will have acquired very early in his time there, give a picture of what the place was like. There is 'front of the house', ivy-covered; facing a flower garden, carefully tended lawns, and a lily-pond and fountain. 'Another veiu of the front' shows the greenhouse, and the gable-end of the fine chapel, built as a memorial after the First World War. 'A bit of big circle' is a summer photograph of part of the grounds; gravel paths, trimmed edges, flowering shrubs and trees. There is one of the 'tenis court' and another of 'criquite' on a tree-lined meadow. Here is the dining room, eight or ten boys to a table, white tablecloths, tulips in vases (perhaps someone knew the photographer was coming).

There is one picture of a dormitory: seven or eight iron bedsteads, topped by comforting eiderdowns, with carpet on the floor and curtains at the window – by no means universal for boarding schools then.

There is a row of eight identical china wash-hand basins, which would be filled, and later emptied, twice a day by the domestic staff whom everyone took for granted. Dormitories were largely unheated. On winter mornings there would be ice on the boys' wash-basins. 'Big School' is a typical form room of the period; the 'Gim' looks a bit forbidding; there is one postcard of a large outdoor swimming pool, presided over by a master armed with a long pole, presumably for life-saving purposes. The quaintest picture to modern eyes – but one which could be paralleled in many if not most prep schools of the period – is 'Military drill'; fifty boys, mostly in rather long short trousers, all wearing shapeless felt sunhats, and carrying at the slope the wooden rifles with which the drill was performed under the watchful eye of Sergeant Doubleday.

It may not have been the most inspired choice of prep school: John was not uniformly happy there, but perhaps few boys can claim that of any school. But by the time he left he was head boy, he had won a good scholarship to Rugby, and he had settled into a love of ornithology that was to last throughout his life.

No doubt at first he missed his home. To the youngest in the family, a boy brought up with sisters, nannies and governesses, affectionate by nature and receiving much warmth and affection, any boarding school would be a shock at first. Major Letts, the son of a clergyman, was a kind and humane man, of a military cast of mind, frightening only because headmasters were generally thought to be frightening.[3] He still tended to think as the army had taught him, and the school was carefully ordered along military lines; history tended to be mainly about battles, supplemented with royal genealogies and the dates of kings and queens. Mrs. Letts was a more obviously powerful figure, brisk rather than motherly, intelligent, unpredictable, given to likes and dislikes among the boys and therefore not always popular even with her favourites: remembered – perhaps unfairly – in her worst moments as something of a dragon with a short fuse. They were supported by an assistant staff which varied from the able and professional to the engagingly eccentric.[4] G. M. Jackson, the second master, was a classicist who also taught modern languages: in collaboration with Major Letts he had written a Latin primer which was used in the school. Remembering how much our view of our early teachers influences our appreciation of the subjects they teach, perhaps the foundations he laid can be seen in John's degree course and double First. Equally, he must have owed to the kindly Gladys Beale something of the place that music enjoyed in his early life. She taught the younger forms and was responsible for all the music of the school. Teaching at Oakley Hall may have been a little dull, unimaginative and formal; but boys were well grounded when they left, the more able securing scholarships, or high marks in the national standard of Common Entrance.

To be called 'Stott' rather than John or Johnnie, to sleep in a dormitory, wake to a cold bath, live in a community which, however privileged, did not escape the rough and tumble of school life – with all this, like other new boys, he had to come to terms. It seems he did so with resolution. Not long after term had started Mrs. Letts wrote to John's mother:

> John has settled down most wonderfully well. He was slightly *piano* the first night but since then has been absolutely at home. He has eaten well all the time and does not appear to be at all homesick. His cold has quite gone now, but was very nasty for a few days.
>
> He has played games every day except Monday, and seems to be getting on quite well. He is well up to everything and doing quite well in work. He has made a very good start.
>
> The play will be on Nov. 2nd so if we do not see you before, we shall hope to see you then.[5]

A month later his first half-term report told the same story. He had been placed in Form 1; his spelling was 'excellent' (something must have been achieved since he wrote the captions on his postcards of the school[6]) and his Scripture 'satisfactory'. Not surprisingly his French teacher found that 'his previous teaching is a great help to him': riddles about elephants with a sweet tooth would be well in advance of anything Form 1 was likely to require. Latin was a different matter. Like many another boy beginning Latin, there was much about it which did not appear as self-evident to him as it did to Gladys Beale, his teacher. More than sixty years later John Stott was to confide to an American audience that it was Latin which launched him on a career of deceit:

> It began when I was the tender age of eight. I could not understand the difference between the nominative and the accusative, the subject and the object of a verb, or when to put *mensa* ('table' in the nominative) or *mensam* ('table' in the accusative). So I am ashamed to say that I used to put *mensam*, with a thin line through the m, so that my teacher could take whichever she preferred![7]

Nevertheless Major Letts, the headmaster, was pleased with him:

> He has made a very good start all round. His discipline is by no means perfect; but he is perfectly straightforward and such trouble as he gives is certainly no more than might be expected from a

healthy boy of his age with a good deal of energy to work off. I think he has the making of a first class boy.[8]

And indeed among his contemporaries he was seen as cheerful, outgoing and friendly, reasonably popular, ready to be naughty, living life at speed. Adults were attracted by a certain sparkle of eye and personality; and by a sweet shy smile which belied his nature, since to those who knew him he never appeared particularly shy. Though he was homesick at times, he put a brave face on it. Almost his earliest letter home carried the reassuring news, 'I am having a lovely time hear.'[9] If it was not always strictly true, it was certainly a message Lily would have been delighted to receive. Less welcome would be later letters telling of his brushes with authority: 'I got very very sore this morning in Big Dormy. I got 5 with the cane, that means 25 strokes since I've been here and 6 times ...' (this was only his third term). A few days later, no doubt in reply to his mother's questioning, there is the plaintive and ingenuous confession, 'I honestly don't know why I get caned such a lot.'[10]

Whether his parents did indeed visit the school in his first term for the school play, as Mrs. Letts' letter suggests, they certainly did so from time to time. Joanna, in her late teens or early twenties, came down on more than one occasion. Sometimes they would spend the weekend at a hotel near Cirencester; John would stay to dinner and be driven back afterwards to sleep at the school. The big Chrysler would glide smoothly along the empty roads, the headlamps piercing the blackness. John and Joanna both remember his schoolboy pleasure at attaching a tin can to a long length of string, and towing it behind the car, throwing up sparks where it hit the road: 'a sort of home-made firework' with John 'just crowing with delight, giggling at this tin'.[11]

To be leaving school behind for a few hours, eating hotel dinners rather than school food, and to be re-united with one's family after weeks of term, was cause enough for high spirits. But there were difficulties too; it was not always an easy transition from the world of school to the world of home, or vice-versa. Even after John had left Oakley Hall and was at Rugby, partings tended to be tearful on both sides. At Oakley Hall there was a particular incident which illustrates the confusion he found in these relationships:

> I remember very well my mother coming down to see me for some reason, and I was told that she was in the Headmaster's study, and as I came in and saw her standing there, next to the Headmaster and the Headmaster's wife, I couldn't quite grasp who she was or how to relate to her in this atmosphere. Automatically, without thinking what I was doing, I advanced towards her, in a rather

pseudo self-assured way with my hand outstretched to shake her hand and say, 'How do you do, Mrs Stott?'

What to me is interesting psychologically is that the Headmaster's wife burst out laughing and I hated her instinctively for that lack of understanding; while my mother, bless her heart, played along with me, and put her hand out to shake me, and said 'How do you do, Johnny?'[12]

As he grew older his parents would come down to see him act in the school play or sing in concerts. At the age of ten he played the Clown in *Twelfth Night*, a part which includes the famous songs 'O mistress mine, where are you roaming?', 'Come away, come away, death' and the plaintive finale,

> When that I was and a little tiny boy,
>   with hey, ho, the wind and the rain;
> a foolish thing was but a toy,
>   for the rain it raineth every day.

He was chosen more than once to sing the treble solo at the Christmas Carol Service – on one occasion the descant to 'Silent Night'; and in April 1933 at the school concert he sang in a quartet which included one of the newly-arrived young masters, Robert Bickersteth, whose presence at the school was to mean much to John. They sang items from Gilbert and Sullivan operas: 'Strange adventure, maiden wedded', from Act II of *The Yeoman of the Guard*, and 'Three little maids from school are we' (with John as Yum-Yum) and 'The sun whose rays are all ablaze' (Yum-Yum's solo at the start of Act II) from *The Mikado*. The following year John and Mr. Bickersteth sang together: folk-songs, nursery rhymes, 'Who is Sylvia?' and 'Sweet and low'. At the start of his final year John played the part of Mark Antony in 'Scenes from Julius Caesar' (including, no doubt, 'Friends, Romans, countrymen, lend me your ears ...') and though the account in the school magazine found him inclined to overact, it recognized him as 'always the best ... really superb ... a performance that can rarely have been equalled in this school'. Allowing for the euphoria of the moment, it is a verdict supported by similar accounts of John's acting at Rugby.

On the playing field, reactions were more mixed. He batted at No. 10 for his house, Wolfe, in his first summer term (the small 'houses' of a moderately-sized prep school would mean that almost every boy would play for his house team) but was out for a duck. He lost at boxing (the unpopular preserve of Sergeant Doubleday who taught PE), having 'greatly handicapped himself by using his right hand for guarding only'.

The following summer in the Parents' Match, Dr. Arnold Stott also batted at number 10, was also out for a duck, but made four catches. John himself was set down as 'not a certain catch' in the school's account of their 1933 season.[13]

In the winter he played football; left-half at soccer ('At times he was exceedingly good, at times equally bad') and gained his colours at rugger ('very good at falling on the ball'); by the time he left he had played in all the first teams. Travelling to away-matches afforded a glimpse of a wider world. He wrote home:

> Yesterday … we ought to have played The Downs but they had infectious colds and coughs so we played the public school Radley … When we arrived we went straight into dinner where we talked away until a gong went and we turned and faced the middle of the room where the head (I think), his wife (I think) and the warden (I think) walked in. – it was a dreadful quiet while the only thing we could here [sic] was their foot-steps and swearing from the kitchen. Then he said some latin grace and we sat down – 367 of us – and had lunch: –
>
> > Soup, potatoes
> > Cold Mutton (Beef), 'beatroot' (potatoes)
> > Apple Dumpling with piles of sugar
> > Cheese.
>
> Then the gong went and we stood up and turned towards the passage and the same thing happened after grace. Then the staff and prefects went out, then us – it was awful …[14]

Oakley Hall, like many of its kind, was a Christian foundation. Besides the school chapel services, the day began and ended with morning and evening prayers in Big School, boys and masters alike kneeling on the floor while Major Letts would read the prayers. But it was to a friend and contemporary, Gerard Irvine,[15] that John owed his most vivid recollection of religion. Gerard's home was at Wotton-under-Edge, only some twenty miles from the school. His father was a Brigadier-General, an Irish Presbyterian with a soldier's straightforward faith, his mother devoutly high-church. John would sometimes visit Gerard's home on Sunday leave, rather than make the much longer journey to London. From him (confirmed and communicant at the age of nine) John learned how and when to cross himself in the school chapel, how to genuflect, and 'how to use the name of Jesus when you are tempted'.[16] It was part of a complicated pattern of religious background and high ideals, searching for something he was unable to define, that

John carried with him, as perhaps many do, into adolescence. In return, it was from John, the Londoner, that Gerard began to learn about butterflies and birds and the natural life of his own countryside. The two boys moved up the school together, gaining their second XI colours for soccer in the same term.[17]

The grounds of Oakley Hall were a delight for a young naturalist. They combined areas of wilderness with formal gardens and magnificent specimen trees. It was said that Roman coins could be found there; and Mrs. Letts prided herself on a vast conservatory with vines and exotic plants. On his first summer holidays from boarding school John's father presented him with a substantial notebook, indeed a miniature ledger bound in half-leather, inscribed 'Johnnie from Daddy, 19th August 1930, Burton Bradstock, Dorset'. 'Nature Notebook'[18] John headed the flyleaf; and on page one wrote 'List of Birds seen'. It says much for the encouragement he received both at home and at school, and for his own persistence and enthusiasm, that by the time the last entry appears in 1939, 150 closely ruled pages have been filled. In the month the family stayed in Dorset, besides the more common Crows, Rooks, Blackbirds, Robins, Tits, Wrens and Thrushes, John was able to enter a Sparrowhawk, a Kingfisher, a Wheatear, a Green Woodpecker and (on a visit to Abbotsbury) a Cormorant.

In addition to the list of forty or so 'Birds seen' listed for August and September 1930, there are three short essays, one on the Grey Wagtail ('the rarest native Wagtail'), one on the Water Wagtail and one on the Marsh Tit. Though the notes record actual sighting and observation ('As I was out for a country walk with Daddy we watched ...') they depend for their information on one of John's first bird books, Edmund Sandars' *A Bird Book for the Pocket*[19] then in its second edition.

2

The bird diary seems to have been put to one side in the face of other interests during 1931, but this was soon to change with the arrival of the new master, R. L. Bickersteth, in January 1933. Robbie Bickersteth was one of a large family, his father being the last of four generations of Liverpool surgeons. Their family home was in the Westmoreland countryside, the early nineteenth-century Casterton Hall near Kirby Lonsdale. From Eton he had moved on to Trinity College, Cambridge (Arnold Stott's college, where John hoped to go one day) and so to schoolmastering. Robbie Bickersteth's time at Oakley Hall was comparatively brief, but coincided with John's last two years at the school; and (as with many of his pupils) Robbie became a personal friend not only of John but of his parents also. He was a big rugged kindly man, a natural schoolmaster, able to inspire enthusiasm and affection and to impart his own deep love of natural history, especially bird life. In 1934 he went on to a short-lived partnership at Winton House, Winchester; and from there to teach for only a few months in Strathspey at Aberlour House, the prep school for Gordonstoun, before enlisting the day before war was declared. He served in the Seaforth Highlanders and was killed in action in Normandy in June 1944 during the D-Day landings: a shell passed through the turret of a tank behind which he was sheltering and he died instantly.[20] It was ten years since he had been briefly at Oakley Hall, but his memory was still green:

> No man has ever more quickly made his mark ... a good athlete, a keen naturalist, he founded the Natural History Society here and his knowledge of birds, which he imparted to many boys, was very extensive. Had he been spared he would have made a splendid Head Master of any preparatory school ...[21]

The Oakley Hall Natural History Society was started in the Lent term 1934, with Major Letts as president and John Stott as secretary, Robbie Bickersteth being the moving spirit. That summer the report of the Society's activities in the school magazine records the garden as full of hedgehogs and green snakes, with 120 birds' nests found in the grounds, twenty-one different birds known to have nested, and forty nests kept under observation. It was here at Oakley Hall that John began to ring birds for future identification, enlisting the help of one of the matrons: 'He would put a trap down overnight, and first thing in the morning Sister and I would go down to let the sparrows out.'[22]

But it was not only in term-time that Mr. Bickersteth's enthusiasm was making itself felt. John's bird diary resumes in 1933 with 'Birds that I have seen or heard. Summer Holidays'. He was now the proud possessor of binoculars. Long lists of birds are recorded in and around the Cotswolds – perhaps as term was coming to an end – and in the Easter holidays at Kew Gardens, in St. James's Park, and at a wide range of places within reach of London: reservoirs at Brent and Tring, Fulbourne Fen near Cambridge, Mildenhall gravel pit, Thetford Meres. The note-book also contains short essays on the Treecreeper and the Goldcrest – but this time the opening words are different: 'Mr. Bickersteth and I were hiding in a fir-tree ...' and 'After breakfast, Mr. Bickersteth, Baggallay and I were looking for birds ...' As witness to this newly-inspired activity, the bird diary contains over 400 entries for the year.

By his second year at Oakley Hall, Robbie Bickersteth had become a friend of the family; and in the Easter holidays, 1933, he called at their

Harley Street home to take John out for the day. The bird diary gives a full account:

> Mr. Bickersteth arrived at about quarter to seven and we soon start-
> ed off. The first birds I saw were Plovers. Nothing more was seen by
> either of us until we arrived at Cambridge where we had breakfast
> at the Blue Boar. The waiter gave us some cream with our porridge
> and so Mr. Bickersteth had it changed. After breakfast we went into
> Trinity and called on Mr. Bickersteth's brother. Then out along the
> Newmarket Road, stopping at Fulbourne Fen about a mile and a
> half out. Leaving the car we walked to the far end of the marsh. On
> the way we saw a great many Snipe, they were all Common Snipe
> and I heard, and had a wonderful view of, a Snipe drumming. We
> saw Reed Buntings and found a nest with 4 eggs in it. We saw
> Coots, Mallard, Swallows, a Sedge Warbler, and then I thought I
> heard a Grasshopper. Mr. Bickersteth said: 'No it's a warbler! a
> Grasshopper Warbler!' And there it was not 20 yds away from us,
> perched on the top of a reed, in full view, warbling magnificently
> just like a very loud Grasshopper. 'Brrrrr' ... We were by now
> incredibly late, not having intended to stop here at all, but we saw
> so many wonderful things that it was well worth it. ... So on we
> went till we came to Thetford, where we bought some buns, which
> we ate on the way to the meres. ... After that since it was getting
> late and there was no time for the last mere, we went to some
> friends of Mr. Bickersteth, who had large woods and a lake with
> some duck on it. We saw Common Gulls, Black Headed Gulls, 1
> Herring Gull, Pintail, Shoveler, Mallard and others. We also saw
> different species of Tits in the nesting boxes. Then, – after a
> marvellous day, – we had to wend our way homewards. We ran out
> of petrol in Epping Forest and had to buy some at a Hotel. Again
> on we went and in Seven Sister's Road Mr. Bickersteth told me to
> look in the back, where in their glory lay the first two COWARD
> Books![23] After that I told Mr. Bickersteth that it was my birthday!

There were further expeditions with Mr. Bickersteth in the same year, including one to the Cambridge Sewage Farm (a favourite haunt of bird-watchers, and one where, as an undergraduate, John would introduce many friends to his favourite recreation) and to Scolt Head, the most northerly point on the Norfolk coast, not long acquired by the National Trust, which was to be the scene of a more prolonged bird-watching expedition the following year.

The Christmas holidays 1993/4 brought an exchange of letters; accompanied by a Christmas present, Grey's *The Charm of Birds*.[24] In the paradoxical way of bird-lovers, Bickersteth proposed to take John for two nights to a sea-marsh to shoot geese; a plan which, for whatever reason, was not fulfilled. John's father had given him a camera for Christmas:

> You are a very lucky fellow to have such a generous father – there is absolutely nothing that a camera like that won't do and now it depends on you ...'[25]

Robbie's letter went on to say that he would like to call and see the camera, and a 'museum' which John was creating; and that he had plans for a visit to Tottenham Reservoir and Epping Forest; and, later in the year, to Scolt Head. This was a more ambitious project, but one in which Dr. Stott was very ready to share.

It must not be thought that birds occupied every waking moment of John's life at Oakley Hall. He was being prepared for a Rugby scholarship and his final school report shows that he was working hard. Nevertheless, birds remained a continuing preoccupation. 'The Life Story of a King-fisher', written at the age of twelve, is clearly a child's work: the bird is shot, with a leg broken, and found and cared for 'by a small boy'. Caught and ringed, 'it fell in love with another kingfisher. Each year we increased the number of kingfishers by six or seven ...' until it dies one cold winter, is stuffed by the Natural History Museum, and taken home to the boy's drawing room: 'There I am and there I will be for ever'. By contrast, an 'Essay on Migration', written a year later, is a serious and informed discussion, looking forward to the day when 'the twentieth century may still see the solution of one of the greatest mysteries of science'.

In the Easter holidays of 1934, during John's last year at Oakley Hall, he went to stay with the Bickersteths at Kirby Lonsdale. They began with a visit to Bainsbank races ('we heard a willow-warbler – Mr. Bickersteth's first this year'); but soon made their way to a nearby marsh where birds would be more plentiful. The following day they overslept (Robbie had been to a dance the night before) but took the car over the moors towards Kendal, stopping for a picnic lunch ('I didn't like the custard pie!'). They saw a Buzzard at Bassenthwaite and another at Borrowdale; and on the way home glimpsed a Common Sandpiper on a rock in the middle of the Derwent, a very early sighting for a summer migrant:

> So we stopped – Mr. Bickersteth was in a fearful state of excitement
> – and slowly backed towards it, having a marvellous view, only
> about ten yards away. We then had to go on as we were very late ...

There were other friends who shared John's growing enthusiasm for birds, including Alfred Stansfeld, who looked on the Stotts almost as a

second family. Alfred's father had been a doctor on the staff of St.
Bartholomew's Hospital with Arnold Stott in the days before the war, but
had died in the influenza epidemic of 1918 leaving a wife and a young
family. Arnold and Lily did their best to help them; and Alfred (five years
older than John) was able to secure a foundation scholarship at Epsom
College.[26] Though Alfred was older than John, they were united in their
friendship and their love of 'birding'.

> The difference in our ages did not seem to matter and we were
> equals in terms of decision-making when holidaying together. The
> development of an interest in birds and birdwatching occurred to
> some extent independently in each of us, each influencing the
> other.[27]

Much of their bird-watching was in East Anglia. Alfred's mother was
headmistress of Centre Cliff in Southwold, a Girls' Prep School, and the
two boys sometimes stayed there together for part of the school holidays.
In the summer of 1934 the Stotts rented Tunstall Rectory in Suffolk on
the road to Orford Ness, not far from the River Alde, and a paradise for
bird-lovers; and here Alfred stayed with them for a week or so. The boys
would haunt the river banks, and wade into the reedy marshes, disputing
together about the less certain of their sightings, though they 'generally
reached a consensus, sometimes after much mirth'.[28] The bird diary for
that holiday records over a hundred sightings, ranging from an
unidentified 'mystery bird' (rare as a diary entry[29]) to 'Pigeon: one of the
Rector's tame ones nested on a ledge over the front door'.

3

The Scolt Head expedition, mooted during the Christmas holidays and
planned through the Easter term, is the longest single entry in the bird
diary. It seemed likely to be the last of the Robbie Bickersteth holiday
outings, as he was to leave Oakley Hall after the summer term; and it
began only ten days after John's return from Kirby Lonsdale. Scolt Head
is a narrow island off Brancaster in North Norfolk, some four miles
long and cut off from the mainland by treacherous marshes; it is famous
for its bird life, and is one of the three main nesting areas for Terns
along that coast. Dunes covered in marram grass and long shingle
ridges protect the tidal mud-flats and saltings, where seals rest at low-
tide.[30] Because it is open to the North Sea, Scolt Head can be very
exposed and inhospitable, but to lovers of bird life it will always be a
special place. It had been acquired for the National Trust in 1923 mainly
through the efforts of Dr. Sydney Long, Secretary to the Norfolk and

Norwich Naturalists' Society. The following year Miss Emma Turner, FLS, FZS, at the age of fifty-seven offered her services as voluntary warden (she had already spent twenty summers photographing bird life on an island in Hickling Broad). *The Times* of 31 March 1924 reported:

> *Protection of Wild Birds*
> *Woman's Vigil on Norfolk's Coast*
>
> An experiment which begins in Norfolk next week will be watched with interest by ornithologists … (Miss Turner) will reside in a bungalow which has been presented by Mr. A. W. Cushion of Norwich and erected on a plateau halfway up the highest group of dunes … Food, letters and newspapers will be taken daily to the island by boat from Brancaster Staithe, and Miss Turner will be able to devote her time to the observation, recording, photographing and protection of the birds that nest on the island.[31]

The 'bungalow' was in reality a wooden hut, with a sitting-room and kitchen combined, three small bunk bedrooms and a larder. Lighting was by oil-lamps and candles, and cooking by paraffin stove:

> Miss Turner's position was never more than a temporary one, and in 1925 a permanent successor was found in the person of Charles Chestney, a local man. One of seventeen children, he had an intimate knowledge of the marshes and dunes around Brancaster from the wildfowling and rabbiting necessary to keep such a large family fed.[32]

The following extracts are from John's own account, as it appears in thirteen pages of his bird diary. It was a week after his thirteenth birthday:

SCOLT HEAD 3rd – 6th May '34

> One day during the Christmas Holidays, while Joy, Mummy and I were going back from the Robinson's dance, Mummy said that Daddy was very keen, both to go to Scolt Head, and to spend the next Summer Holidays in Norfolk: I was thrilled!
>   Chestney, Daddy, Mr. Bickersteth and I were taken across by Winterbottom [the local boatman]. On the way over [to the island], we saw Dunlin, Ringed Plover and Oyster Catchers. We had one adventure:– Half way up the creek, we suddenly stopped … a sandbank! Winterbottom howled with laughter, while Chestney and Mr. Bickersteth got out and pushed us off. When we arrived at the

hut – after carrying all the junk across the saltings – we said 'good-night' to Chestney and Winterbottom and set to work with the cooking, while Daddy made himself comfortable with a glass (and bottle) of sherry. The Dinner consisted of chips – delicious – cooked by Mr. Bickersteth. At about 9.00 p.m. I retired to bed for a good night's rest in a bunk above Daddy's only to wake up in the morning and hear … RAIN! RAIN! RAIN!!!! HOW DREADFUL! …

They woke to gray skies and a wet world:

We wandered along the shore, – in howling wind and heavy rain – finding 2 Ringed Plovers' nests, and seeing Oyster Catchers, Redshanks, Ringed Plover, and several Shelduck. … Then the weather brightened, and Mr. Bickersteth and I went out, while Daddy had forty winks! We went up into the sand hills behind the hut and watched Skylarks! Then, we went for a short walk in the direction of the Ternery putting a Mallard off her nest, – which Chestney had thought was deserted! We also visited a Pied Wagtail's nest in the side of a bank; and just as we were going away, a Cormorant flew over our heads. We also saw several Redshanks and Oyster Catchers, and just at the foot of the hut hill, a Wheatear popped out of a hole! …

The next morning … we walked along the shore, seeing Dunlin and Ringed Plover … Mr. Bickersteth rigged up my camera in the hide and left me to take a photo. … He went behind the dunes facing the hide and watched. In about 15 minutes, I heard the well known piping-note of the Ringed Plover. I ventured to turn my head and look for the bird. At first I could not see it, but when I heard it again, I saw it running towards the nest; but instead of going straight to the eggs, she stopped and 'dipped', walked round the hide, and sat on the eggs. I let her get settled and then, with great bravery on my part, I clicked it! She jumped up and ran away. I brought the next film into place and reset the camera. In about 10 minutes, after she had performed the same 'dance', I got two more photos, without her minding at all!

Next morning we got up early, had breakfast, packed, cleared up the hut … We slowly wandered down to the beach, with most of the luggage littered on various parts of our bodies, – books, glasses, cameras, coats, food and clothes!

When the luggage was in the boat, I took a photo of Mr. Bickersteth, Winterbottom and Chestney standing in the water, with Daddy sitting in the boat. Chestney then carried me into the boat, and we were rowed in a howling gale to the motor-boat. While going over, water splashed and drenched us all over, but eventually, we reached the mainland. We said, 'Good bye' to each other and got into our respective cars. Mr. Bickersteth followed us for a few miles, but eventually the moment came, and we parted in opposite directions and cold blood, after a really superb few days of birding, together with, North East wind, hard rain, porridge, omelettes, mud, a Ring Plover, sand, and we three …

ALONE!

John Stott's bookshelves still contain a memento of that visit: a copy of Miss Turner's lavishly illustrated book, published a few years before, *Bird Watching on Scolt Head*[33] with this inscription:

John from RLB, May 1934

Two days of North East wind and hard rain, porridge, omelettes, mud, a Ring Plover, sand and we three alone …

Back at Oakley Hall for his last summer term, John used his new camera to advantage to win the photographic competition 'with a delightful photograph of a Whitethroat feeding her young': she had been photographed nesting in a huge bed of nettles, from a ramshackle hide built by John and Robbie Bickersteth out of old sacking. That summer saw family holidays in Suffolk, with Norfolk excursions; and then in the Lake District. In September John returned to Oakley Hall for the last time, as head prefect and head of the school. Robbie Bickersteth found time to write to him from his new school, Winton House, Winchester (signing himself 'Robbie' for the first time as a gesture of adult friendship on equal terms) with advice for the Natural History Society, and for John to give himself to his work and 'be the best of prefects'.[34]

In November he sat the scholarship examination for Rugby and received a telegram a few days later: '23 November 1934: Heartiest congratulations on getting among the first three love Mummy and Daddy.' His final report from the school expressed the hope that he would 'become a really good French scholar in time'; and Major Letts wrote: 'He has made an excellent Head Prefect. I am very sorry to lose him and wish him every success at Rugby.' It was a wish amply fulfilled. Rugby brought John not only academic success, responsibility and recognition; but also a personal faith in Christ and the beginnings of a sense of the call of God to a life's work.

*   *   *

Meanwhile, in the middle of John's time at Oakley Hall, E. J. H. Nash, a school chaplain in his early thirties, was joining the staff of the Scripture Union:

> He graduated at Trinity College, Cambridge and did his theological training at Ridley Hall. From there, after serving two curacies, he was appointed chaplain at Wrekin School. His zeal to evangelise, which he could neither conceal nor restrain, clashed with his duty to instruct, and caused uneasiness. *Conversion* was a dangerous word, as indeed it still is. There was an agreement that he should apply his gifts elsewhere. In 1932 he was appointed by the Scripture Union to work among public schoolboys. His brief experience in a public school had shown him the field in which his work was to lie. It had also shown him the peculiar difficulties of this branch of Christian work.[35]

Eric Nash – 'Bash' as he was universally known – was to become a crucial figure in John Stott's life before many years had passed. 'Conversion' may indeed be a dangerous – indeed, a revolutionary – word, but to the end of his life John Stott would say that he owed his conversion, under God, to this one man.

FOUR

Rugby 1935–37: Growing Up

1

To read today the history of the 1930s is to be aware of little else but the relentless movement of Europe towards war. It cannot always have looked quite like that in the day-to-day life of the time. Voices summoning Britain to prepare to defend herself and her allies went largely unheeded until the eleventh hour. The English Channel, as so often in the past, seemed symbolic of British isolation from what was happening on European soil. And there were always preoccupations at home. Unemployment stood at 17% and had topped the three million mark by 1932; the stability of the monarchy, unquestioned at the Jubilee Celebrations of May 1935, with four generations of the royal family sharing in the service in St. Paul's Cathedral, was shaken by what seemed to many the end of an era when, six months later, Stuart Hibberd, the BBC's chief announcer, reported to a listening nation that 'the King's life is moving peacefully to its close'.[1]

The new king flew from Sandringham to London the morning after his father's death, the first time a British sovereign had travelled in an aeroplane. An older generation were conscious that the change of monarch symbolized the passing of an era, the coming of a bewilderingly unfamiliar 'brave new world'.[2]

Anxiety over Germany had been steadily mounting. She had withdrawn from the League of Nations as far back as 1933, and proclaimed Adolph Hitler as Head of State a year later. In 1935, Jubilee year, in flat defiance of the treaty of Versailles, Germany set herself to raise a conscript army of half a million. In the same year Mussolini invaded Abyssinia. Two months after King Edward's accession Hitler's troops entered the Rhineland; and a new fighter aircraft was seen in public for the first time at Southampton, the earliest 'Spitfire'.

It was against this background that Dr. and Mrs. Stott watched, no doubt with increasing anxiety, their son's life at prep school and then, from January 1935, at Rugby. Arnold Stott had served in France in the war of 1914–18; and must sadly have contemplated John growing up to be part of the inevitable conflict which was slowly engulfing Europe.

*　　　*　　　*

'The best story of a boy's school days ever written' is the large claim put forward by the editor of the Everyman edition of *Tom Brown's School Days* by Thomas Hughes.[3] Hughes denied that it was an autobiographical account; though he had himself been a boy at Rugby under the legendary Thomas Arnold. Arnold, more than any other man, raised Rugby to the rank of a great public school, and during his fourteen years as Head Master 'was changing the face of English education'.[4] He was by no means the first of Rugby's great headmasters, and the school was well past its 250th anniversary before his time. Founded as a Free Grammar School for local boys in 1567, it then suffered a century of legal and financial insecurity. But even before the close of the seventeenth century it was taking boarders from across the country; and in the early eighteenth century was a school of a hundred boys. Before Arnold's time it had moved from the 'Mansion House' of the original endowment to its present site, and a complete rebuilding had recently been completed. Nevertheless, it was Thomas Arnold's headmastership that put Rugby in the forefront of the developing concept of the English public school. His aim was not merely scholarship; his genius was to be pastorally concerned in every aspect of his pupils' lives, seeking to produce 'first religious and moral principle; secondly, gentlemanly conduct; and thirdly intellectual ability'; and by this means he made Rugby – and by a kind of educational osmosis the whole public school system – 'more earnestly Christian (and more humane and scholarly)'.[5]

By the time *Tom Brown's School Days* was written Dr. Arnold had been dead for fifteen years; Hughes dedicated the book to his widow. In it, 'he depicted, with a didactic purpose, schoolboy cruelties and loyalties, and considerably influenced English ideas on public schools.'[6] A famous passage in the book describes Squire Brown thinking hard about what should be his parting words as young Tom leaves home for the unknown world of boarding school:

> To condense the Squire's meditation, it was somewhat as follows: 'I won't tell him to read his Bible, and love and serve God; if he don't do that for his mother's sake and teaching, he won't for mine ... Shall I tell him to mind his work, and say he's sent to school to make himself a good scholar? Well, but he isn't sent to school for that – at any rate not for that mainly. I don't care a straw for Greek particles, or the digamma, no more does his mother. What is he sent to school for? Well, partly because he wanted so to go. If he'll only turn out a brave, helpful, truth-telling Englishman, and a gentleman, and a Christian, that's all I want.'[7]

Rather more than a hundred years later, these would no longer be entirely the sentiments with which Arnold Stott would despatch his son to Kilbracken House, Rugby, his own old house and school. Lily would have wanted John to continue to read his Bible – as indeed he did – and Arnold may (like Squire Brown) have wanted it for her sake. But he would have no doubts that his son was going to Rugby in pursuit of scholarship. With his German grandmother, John was already on the way to becoming a proficient Modern Linguist; medicine was not part of Arnold's hopes for him; even at this early stage he may have had his paternal sights set on a career in some branch of the Diplomatic Service. 'A brave, helpful, truth-telling Englishman, and a gentleman', certainly; but to Arnold Stott the idea that a father trained in scientific studies should hope to see his son turn out to be a Christian, in more than a formal and conventional sense of the term, would have seemed to belong firmly to Squire Brown's generation rather than his own.

Rugby in the mid-thirties was enjoying considerable prestige. Its name had long been a household word through 'Rugby' football, invented in a moment of inspired madness when in 1823 William Webb Ellis 'with a fine disregard for the rules of football as played in his time' picked up the ball and ran with it 'thus originating the distinctive feature of the Rugby game'.[8] Moreover, the name and reputation of Thomas Arnold still lingered, perpetuated in part by the phenomenal influence of *Tom Brown's School Days* which, if it was not being widely read by prep school boys of the 1930s, was fondly remembered by their fathers, especially fathers who were themselves Old Rugbeians. School House could still display (as it does today) the original fireplace where Tom Brown was 'roasted' as part of his initiation to Rugby life.

Arnold Stott had been there at the turn of the century, from 1898 to 1904. Ten years after that Rugby still retained a reputation for making few concessions to human weakness. Kenneth Grahame's son Alastair, for example, entered School House in 1914 and was 'desperately unhappy there'. His father took him away after six weeks.[9]

But the ruthlessness of style and pace experienced by Alastair Grahame was already in process of change. The Rugby of 1935 was not the Rugby of 1914, nor even Arnold Stott's Rugby of 1900, let alone Tom Brown's. Schools do change in the course of a hundred years. A term before John Stott became head of school a boy called Alan McLintock entered Rugby, later to become its chairman of Governors. These are his impressions, recollected in tranquillity, half a lifetime later:

> I went to Rugby in the summer term of 1939. War clouds were gathering but we in the School, especially the younger of us, were too pre-occupied with the routine of our life ... to worry much about events outside Rugby. Strains of 'Deep Purple' and 'Love walked in' could be heard across the Close on warm summer evenings.
>
> I had been happy at a well-ordered prep. school. We were warned there to expect much tougher conditions when we got to Rugby and there were dark rumours of fagging, beatings and general discomfiture. Our apprehensions were quickly laid to rest. Rugby under Hugh Lyon ... was already a very civilised place. And how could it have been otherwise? A school, like most other organisations, derives its tone and ethos from the top. Hugh Lyon was a man of great integrity, kind, wise and sensitive. I was lucky to be at the school during the middle and thus arguably the vintage years of his headship. Discipline was tight. It had to be because there was a war on and, greatly to our benefit then and later, we had to adhere to the rules. But it was by no means harsh. Hugh Lyon would never have allowed it to be. It was not within his temperament. We respected him for the example he set, for his sense of justice, for the strength of his Christian ideals and for his genuine interest in our activities and, above all, in us as individuals.[10]

McLintock's tribute to Hugh Lyon is not misplaced. After war service (and an MC) Lyon had taught at Cheltenham for five years and became Rector of Edinburgh Academy at the age of thirty-three. Five years later, still under forty, he returned to Rugby, his own old school, as headmaster. Contrary to the optimistic predictions of a decade before, the economic depression of 1929 and the declining birth-rate at the end of the First World War were making life difficult for independent schools. Numbers at Rugby remained reasonably stable, however, and indeed rose to a high point of 650 in the year that John Stott entered the school. Growing numbers made the later 1930s a time of much projected building, including plans for the new Kilbracken, designed to provide a gas-proof shelter in the basement – a commentary on the darkening world situation as Europe moved towards September 1939. Part of the 'civilizing' influences that Hugh Lyon brought to bear was the abolition in 1936, John's second year, of early school before breakfast – no light matter to boys on dark winter mornings in boarding houses some distance from their form room. An anonymous jingle celebrated the change:

> Let us hymn the Headmaster in suitable rhyme,
>   Whose pupils are having a halcyon time.
> For 'We rise up too early', they cried in New Zion –
>   So what could he say to them other than 'LYON'.[11]

Among much else, Thomas Arnold is credited with having invented the idea of the housemaster, in place of the earlier 'Dames' Houses' where boarders had simply lodged. As a matter of course, Arnold Stott entered John for Kilbracken, his own old house, a stone's throw from the Close (the main school campus), diagonally opposite the main gates, on the corner of Hillmorton Road and Little Church Street.[12] The house was built of brick round a central quadrangle and offered a fairly spartan existence. It was possible to travel in the same corridor right round the square. New boys were quickly introduced to 'fagging' – doing chores for the senior boys in the house. A cry of 'fag' would be heard: there would be a race around the long corridor; and the last to arrive would have to do the fagging. It might be something to fetch from the school shop; shoes to be cleaned; books to be carried; or (with great regularity) brass buttons to be polished to a military shine on the uniform of the school 'Officers Training Corps' which paraded weekly through the term.

F. W. Odgers was something of a character in the school (he had been teaching there since ten years before John was born) and was coming to the end of his fifteen-year tenure of the house. He took a form of middle school boys; and for the brighter entrants this could be their first introduction to teaching at Rugby. One such, a year older than John, realized that he had entered a new world when his form master the first day, sitting on a dais in the formroom, announced 'My name is Frank William Odgers. I live at No. 1 Hillmorton Road and I go to the lavatory twice a day.'[13] His successor, F. C. Slater, a Modern Linguist and a francophile, was already known to Arnold Stott; they shared a love of French wines and 'the good things of life'.[14] John Stott wrote of him, 'He and father got on well, and I can see them – vividly – after dinner, pipe in one hand and large brandy glass in the other, swilling the sacred liquid round and enjoying the bouquet.'[15] 'Porky' Slater (to use his school nickname) was not cut out to be a housemaster. He was ineffective and not generally popular. Parents he could manage, but the boys sensed that he was not seriously interested in them. The high reputation Kilbracken enjoyed in the school began to decline once Odgers' boys had left.[16]

Meanwhile, Robbie Bickersteth continued to correspond, the more freely since John was growing older, and was no longer his pupil. The letters begin to be couched in terms of warm affection – indeed, in terms that today would inevitably give rise to some suspicion, as between a bachelor schoolmaster in his thirties and a boy of fourteen. There is, however, with Robbie (as with other older friends who feature in this story) no hint whatever of impropriety. There was clearly mutual attraction and affection; letters begin 'My dearest Johnnie' and end 'Your loving Robbie', but this was not unacceptable in the 1930s. Robbie was a highly respected professional schoolmaster, and a valued family friend of the Stotts, to whose care they readily entrusted John. Arnold Stott was not a person likely to have been deceived, and it is clear that Robbie's warmth of affection was acceptable to John and his parents, totally free of any physical expression beyond normal friendship, and under careful open-eyed control. Robbie's letters show him as well aware that schoolmasters, however well-intentioned, could come to grief if they allowed their feelings for their younger friends to run away with them: the trust the Stotts felt for him was not misplaced. He writes in March, half-way through John's first term, in reply to John's account of himself:

> I am so happy, Johnnie, about Rugby, that you are really happy there and finding it all so exactly what you longed for and did so badly want …[17]

By this time John was beginning to be well settled into life at school. It was a busy existence. Besides the rugger of Webb Ellis's legacy there were fives and squash, with tennis, cricket and swimming in the summer term. School Certificate, the gateway to the 'Twenty' – the form below the Sixth – was looming on the horizon but still comfortably distant; progress through the lower forms was rapid and uneventful. His father watched with satisfaction, re-living his own school-days of nearly forty years before. Surviving letters show an almost pathetic eagerness to be accepted as his son's friend and confidant. His pride in John was immense: 'You are already a form higher, at least, than I was at your age, and nothing in the world will please me more than your beating me at *anything* …'[18]

'Birding' had taken a back seat during John's first term. Perhaps winter in a midlands town was not a very propitious setting. But his interest revived in the Easter holidays with a visit to the Lake District and the first of three family holidays in Ireland. On 4th May there is a reference in the bird diary to Swifts seen when 'riding in Gymnkana' (*sic.*) at Stanmore; and a week later comes the first term-time entry, noting Swifts, Chiffchaff and Jackdaws.

At the same time (perhaps helping to account for this revival of interest) the diary records: 'Was tested and became a member of the Ornithological Section of the Natural History Society !!!' It may well have been from this first summer term that John Stott retains a vivid recollection of sitting in his formroom in the New Block, where he could look out of the window on summer afternoons, and seeing the Swifts nesting in the eaves, 'little posses of birds circling the building with their high-pitched screams'.[19] For a short period he was able to keep in his study a baby Magpie, trying to feed it and give it time to fledge and fly. It had to be kept secret from the authorities, no easy task since it was far from house-trained. John built a ramshackle cage, but let it out from time to time with disastrous results...[20] There were expeditions to a nearby lake to see varieties of duck, a Lesser Spotted Woodpecker nesting in part of the school grounds to be photographed, and on at least one occasion a visit by the Natural History Society to Fawsley Park, where they watched a pair of Great Crested Grebes build their nest.

2

Besides the Natural History Society, one other Society deserves mention in any account of John's first year or so at Rugby – 'the ABC Society'. It was to a large extent his own invention; and the Minute and Account Book survives among his personal papers. It was a remarkable mixture of the wholly juvenile[21] with something more mature. It was not quite the passing schoolboy craze of an idle afternoon, but an attempt to give shape and substance, however amusingly and misguidedly, to a genuine and deeply-felt idealism. The Society sprang from the desire of John and two close friends, also fifteen-year-olds, to find a way to do good to the community. It has remained a notable characteristic of John Stott throughout his life that vision and aspiration are seldom allowed to run into the sand without an attempt to harness them to some form of organization. The particular way in which the 'ABC' wished to benefit the community was by giving baths to tramps, as a first step on the road to their rehabilitation. John was to describe it as 'a very general social desire, with a very unspecified programme':[22] though in fact the baths (had they happened) seem specific enough.

We then had to decide what to call it, and hit on 'ABC' because it would be easy for uneducated tramps to remember; and then had to find words to fit the initials. We came up with two: 'Always Be a Christian' and 'Association for the Benefit of the Community'. We then had to find things to do to benefit the community.[23]

They did find one or two small things to do in the context of life at school: anonymously posting the Test Cricket scores on the house notice board, for example, above the signature 'ABC'.[24]

The Minute Book (in John Stott's familiar hand) gives a list of MEMBERS (the three founders, Stott, Champness and Hargreaves) followed by the RULES: the Society is to be private; membership is by election and cannot be bought; donations shall be welcome; there shall be an entrance fee of 5s. (a substantial part of the termly allowance of a boy of John's age, when Mars bars were 2d and a three-course dinner in a Lyons Corner House could be had for 1s. 6d) and a subscription of 1s. per month.

Rules 6 and 8 ran as follows:

6. That membership does not compel any special friendship between members, but that members are encouraged to meet as often as possible, and to discuss their activities as far as each considers it wise, practical and necessary.
8. That the Treasurer shall report the present capital to the Secretary bi-annually.

The Committee (guided, one suspects, from the chair) knew that to bath and rehabilitate tramps would cost money; and they provided accordingly for the accumulation of the Society's funds as capital in the hands of the Treasurer. Sadly, though the Society survived for four or five terms, before it had been able to rehabilitate its first tramp the Treasurer mislaid the funds (there was some question of his having lent them to a brother who spent them and was unable to repay) – and the 'ABC' foundered.

It is not the only hint we have that some kind of pre-Christian social conscience was at work in John, stimulated by the example of his parents. Like many children, he had not only a strong sense of fair play, but also of outrage when the world did not live up to his standards. 'It isn't fair' is a cry from the heart that most people remember from the days of childhood. A particular example, tiny in itself, comes from a family holiday in the Oakley Hall days at Saundersfoot, near Tenby, on the South Pembrokeshire peninsular. Following an expedition to Caldy Island to see the ancient church and modern monastery, the Stotts were returning by boat and the boatman was bringing the island's letters to be posted on the mainland. John watched as the boatman peeled open a poorly-sealed envelope and began to read the letter. He remembers his mother's astonishment at his degree of indignation over something 'so incompatible with elementary standards of justice'.[25] Again, on one occasion a gang of workmen were digging a trench outside Kilbracken. Their lot seemed particularly hard, by contrast with the privileged position of the boys who were passing by. John felt acutely sorry for them; and with some embarrassment engaged one of them in conversation. Anxious that this should be more than mere social intercourse, he offered the man a prayer book, inviting him to use it to say his prayers. The man was an Irish navvy, probably a Roman Catholic, certainly one of nature's gentlemen. He accepted the book, and hoped John would understand if he did not use it himself, but he had a friend to whom he would like to pass it on.[26]

Such impulses of idealism among young people are not uncommon, hindered in nine cases out of ten by shyness or convention; but none the less real. Unbearably priggish from most adult standpoints, it is not difficult to see that they were courageous and costly at the time. Is it fanciful to compare John's Irish navvy, and his 'ABC' Society (which however laughable was yet an expression of compassion) with the well-known experience of Lord Shaftesbury (then Lord Ashley), the great Christian social reformer, at much the same age? His first biographer writes:

It was while he was at Harrow, and when he was between fourteen and fifteen years of age, that an incident occurred which, simple as it was in itself, influenced his whole after-life. He was one day walking alone down Harrow Hill when he was startled by hearing a great shouting and yelling in a side street, and the singing of a low Bacchanalian song. Presently the noisy party turned the corner of the street, and to his horror he saw that four or five drunken men were carrying a roughly made coffin, containing the mortal remains of one of their fellows, for burial. Staggering as they turned the corner, they let their burden fall, and then they broke out into foul and horrible language. It was a sickening spectacle. No solitary soul was there as a mourner. A fellow-creature was about to be consigned to the tomb with indignities to which not even a dog should be subjected. Young Ashley was horrified, and stood gazing on the scene spell-bound. Then he exclaimed, 'Good heavens! can this be permitted, simply because the man was poor and friendless!'

Before the sound of the drunken songs had died away in the distance he had faced the future of his life, and had determined that, with the help of God, he would from that time forth devote his life to pleading the cause of the poor and friendless.[27]

An altogether more realistic contact with the lives of the working class came in the summer of 1936. Unemployment in the early 1930s had reached epidemic proportions; and inspired by the example of the Duke of York[28] there were many ventures which aimed to bring together public schoolboys or undergraduates with men on the dole, so that the former might have a chance to see beyond the bare statistics and the newspaper accounts, and gain some personal and emotional insight into what it meant for a man and his family to be out of work. John experienced this in some degree at a Rugby camp at Whitehaven, an industrial and mining community on the north-west coast, and a major port until the rise of Liverpool docks. It was probably not entirely his decision ('a list was given out' at school[29]) and in fact the experience proved disappointing. The gulf was too wide to be easily bridged; the boys spent much of their time digging allotments; and in consequence they dozed heavily through the evening lectures on the causes and evils of unemployment. Though the statistics had improved since the start of the decade, these evils were still very real. In the same autumn, from the opposite side of the Pennines, the Jarrow Protest March set off for London. With two hundred marchers drawn from the closed shipyards and ironworks it was not the largest of the 'hunger marches' of the 1930s, but a figure of 68% unemployment in their community ensured massive local support. Stanley Baldwin, the Prime Minister (like Ramsay MacDonald two years before), refused to receive them; and they returned home by train.

Music continued to be a source of pleasure. John had been given singing lessons from quite an early age. Tamara remembered him describing his visits to Mark Raphael, his teacher in London, 'having to make frightful gestures and wave your hands about and not mind being stupid'.[30] From him he learned settings of *A Shropshire Lad* by Sir Arthur Somervell – 'Loveliest of Trees', 'On the Idle Hill of Summer', 'In Summertime on Bredon'; and a setting by Raphael himself of William Blake's 'Little Lamb, who made thee?' From him, too, possibly he learned the 'italianate style of pronunciation' against which Marcus Beresford, a music master at Rugby, was later to advise him. John's voice had broken about the time he left Oakley Hall, so that singing at Rugby had to wait a year or two. Then, with a strong clear baritone, he was again in demand as a soloist in Rugby Chapel, and for school concerts. Marcus Beresford led a double octet; and for a time this would gather at the end of morning school, snatching fifteen minutes before lunch to practise madrigals and part-songs in the Music School. John played the cello in the school orchestra before he possessed an instrument of his own.[31] On Saturday evenings there would be concerts in the Speech Room; and these, with the octet and chapel choir practice and Sunday Services (together with singing at house concerts and house suppers) meant that music continued to play a considerable part in John's life at school, as it did at home. Hugh Lyon, John's headmaster, was a poet who had won the Newdigate Prize at Oxford and had published verse; the boys rather liked him for it.[32] Marcus Beresford set to music one of his best known short poems, 'Envoi' for John Stott to sing; and as an undergraduate John made a recording under Beresford's direction for the BBC.[33]

3

John's home moved in 1936 during his early years at Rugby. 58 Harley Street had never seemed to Lily large enough for all that went on in it; and when No. 65 came on the market, she urged her husband to buy it. They did not have to move far: No. 65 is just across the road from No. 58, but with its main entrance facing north into New Cavendish Street. It is an imposing house, six storeys high, Georgian in style, in mellow brick with stone facings to the ground floor. Steps lead to a stone portico under a high semi-circular roof, supported by elegant classical columns and surmounted by carved and decorative stone urns. There was a mews for the chauffeur and the doctor's car. Every evening, when he was at home, John and his father would change into dinner jackets, his mother and sister into evening gowns; after dinner John and Joy would sometimes roll back the carpet in the great drawing room and dance together to the radio-gramophone, foxtrots and waltzes to the dance music of the day. Twice a year there would be more formal dinner-parties for Arnold Stott's housemen from the Westminster and the Royal Chest Hospitals. They would be on their best behaviour, calling him 'Sir', while Lily would charm them and put them at their ease. Patients and juniors alike would be conscious that Dr. Stott was now in the highest ranks of his profession; and from 1936 a Physician to the Royal Household. His son's telegram from Rugby must have meant a lot to him: 'HEARTIEST CONGRATULATIONS SIMPLY GRAND BRAVO–JOHN'.[34] One of his guests remembered Dr. Arnold (a few years later, just after the Second World War) as

> a somewhat awe-inspiring figure … a small grave determined man with half-moon spectacles … He acted and spoke with deliberation – rather an old-world consultant, a type now extinct. My impression at the dinner table was that he liked his guests not to be prolix, to consider carefully what contribution they made to the conversation, and to express it concisely. After dinner he retired to his study – a regular procedure.[35]

Besides his books, and the ever-present birds, there was much to entertain John in the school holidays. 'The Gardens' were still a good place to visit, perhaps for tennis, but now on roller-skates rather than by push-chair, racing along the pavements scattering pedestrians. There was swimming most days in the Marshall Street baths, just south of Oxford Street, or at the Regent Street Polytechnic, five minutes' walk away. As a member of the London Otters Club, John would regularly take part in team races and the occasional game of water polo.

It seems to have been at the end of one of these school holidays that he acquired the second of two minor scars which have remained with him all his life. The first was much earlier: John was a toddler, barely walking. On a family picnic, presumably in or near a farm, a cock showed interest in the party. John staggered towards it with his hand out to give it some bread; the cock took fright and caught him with its spur just under his eye. Much later, home from Rugby, John was being driven back to Harley Street by his mother on the South Carriage Drive through Hyde Park. It was dark; the lighting was poor; and Lily failed to see a bollard in the middle of the road and drove straight into it, so that John pitched forward and put his chin through the windscreen. He remembers little beyond lying on the pavement and coming to in the Westminster Hospital, his parents much relieved to find the damage no worse: Lily had believed for a moment or two that she had killed him. It secured for John a brief stay in hospital, a few days extra at home after the start of term, and a scar beneath his chin, inches from his jugular vein.[36]

Much of the school holidays was spent out of London. In 1936 John spent Easter with friends on the Norfolk-Suffolk borders, staying in Southwold and visiting broads and marshes in search of birds. Walberswick, Blythburgh and Breydon Water were happy hunting grounds; and Minsmere, long before it became the RSPB reserve it is today, was the scene of many recorded sightings. Near Dunwich, on 2nd April 1936, the bird diary breaks into capital letters: 'BITTERNS! 3!!! One female, one male and one immature (probably)'.

For two summers the family borrowed a house at Hertford Heath from one of the housemasters at Haileybury, secluded in the Hertfordshire countryside but within easy reach of London, and with the use of the school swimming pool. Arnold Stott, when he was free to join them, took the chance to introduce John to fly-fishing. Like many doctors, he was a keen fisherman, and listed it as his only recreation in *Who's Who*; he had recently been elected to the Flyfishers' Club.[37] John would be encouraged to put a saucer on the lawn and practise casting, trying to land the fly cleanly and gently in the saucer. Arnold had a rod on the Beane, a Hertfordshire trout stream, and would take John with him for a day's fishing, when the 'catch' often included sightings of Kingfishers.

Fishing was one of the attractions that led the family to pay two or three visits on holiday to Co. Galway, on the west coast of Ireland. In 1935 and again in 1936 they stayed at a small hotel near Moyard in what is now the Connemara National Park, a lush countryside of fine hills and grassy wetlands, with coastal inlets washed by Atlantic surges. Here, one holiday, John had mumps, and it took a year for the infection to pass right through the village.[38] The fishing was mainly wet fly rather than dry; and John would accompany his father in the boat with the gillie on Lake Ballynakill or Lake Fee. It was here too that he saw his first Choughs – birds which were later to be his frequent companions at the Hookses[39] – and had his first girlfriend. She was the fifteen-year-old daughter of another doctor staying in the same hotel and he thought her very beautiful:

> There was nothing immoral, though I think it was when I was first awakening to sexual desire and found her very attractive. I rode, I remember, on the same pony with her, so that I sat behind and had my arms round her … I'm not sure that I didn't ask her to marry me.[40]

One of his father's Irish friends, a radiologist who was with them on holiday, used to tease John in a not unwelcome way 'for having an eye for the girls'.

Robbie Bickersteth had written to John the year before, asking if there was 'any hope of booking you next summer for an expedition down the Danube by canoe'.[41] This attractive prospect did not materialize; but in the summer holidays of 1936 John was able to join him for a bird-watching holiday in the Outer Hebrides, staying with crofters where possible but ready to 'camp when we must'. His mother wrote from Weymouth, 'I should love to be able to have a glimpse of you both. Blue shorts and sweaters, wind-swept hair, shining eyes and glowing faces!'[42] Their destination was South Uist thirty miles west of the Isle of Skye. Much of the island is a flat and treeless landscape of lonely moors and small lochans under a wide sky, the sandy western seaboard indented and fretted by the Atlantic breakers; bird-life is plentiful along the shoreline with Turnstones and Oystercatchers. John and Robbie travelled north by car. At Loch Etive, on their way to catch the 6.00 a.m. boat at Oban, John noted Eiderduck and Oystercatchers: while crossing the Sound of Mull he recorded sightings of Kittiwakes circling round the boat, Cormorants holding their 'councils' on the rocky shore, plunging Gannets, two or three pairs of Puffins, and a good many Manx Shearwaters in flight.

Towards the end of their holiday they visited the tiny Isle of Eriskay between South Uist and Barra. Back in May Robbie had written to John with his plans for the holiday:

Far away in the Western Isles lies Eriskay – a tiny island not more than 3 miles long and one mile wide. It rises at one point to about 600 feet and has two little lochs on it and a large bay.

There – just south of South Uist in the Outer Hebrides is where I plan to spend our holiday. There are no roads and only one or two tiny crofts and cottages. South Uist – which is only a mile away is a maze of little lochs and heather and *must* be alive with birds, even so late as that.

We sail from Oban and it takes about 12 hours – are you a good sailor?!

I wrote to your mother on getting your letter and gave her *all* the dates ...[43]

In 1745 Eriskay was where Prince Charles Edward first set foot on Scottish soil. So to complete the story they spent a day on Benbecula to the north, home of the Greylag Goose, from which the Prince sailed with Flora MacDonald 'over the sea to Skye'. The diary notes Corn Buntings ('singing – rattle of a bunch of keys') and Rock Pipits everywhere along the shore. In all about fifty sightings are recorded of a great variety of species: though it was not until the last day of December that the diary was able to record a Great Northern Diver – on Tottenham Reservoirs!

No sooner had John returned home from Scotland than it was time to set off for Germany. He had taken School Certificate in July; it was already clear that his academic future would lie with Modern Languages. But beyond that ... ? Arnold Stott had some personal contact with Lord Vansittart ('whose forte' – at Eton – 'was modern languages'[44]), then permanent under-secretary in the Foreign Office; and it is probable that he wrote to him for advice. John's mother's mother was German, his command of languages was already convincing, so the idea of a career in the Foreign or Diplomatic Service was a natural one. It may well have been on Vansittart's advice that his father arranged for John to spend a few weeks in a *Pension* on the continent, twice in Germany and twice in France, during successive summer holidays from Rugby. In 1936 he stayed in Bendorf-am-Rhein, near Koblenz, where the bird diary is continued in Herr Pfarrer's garden, the names of the early sightings being entered first in English, then in German: 'Goldfinch – der Distelfink; Swallow – die Dorfschwalbe'. But after a dozen such bi-lingual entries, the diary reverts to English. Writing home, he told his parents that he had bought himself a cello. 'You had some nerve,' Lily wrote in reply, 'to go and unearth a professor of music to vet the instrument!'[45] Lily adds that she had looked up in Whittaker's Almanack the duty on musical instruments; and allowing for this, thought he had secured a bargain.

Even with such excitements, and with affectionate letters from home, such a stay in a foreign country would be a lonely experience for a fifteen-year-old: we find him writing to Robbie Bickersteth, no doubt to thank him for the Hebridaean holiday together, but also to ask his advice over a friendship with an older member of Kilbracken that was troubling his mind. The friendship seems to have been one-sided – a schoolboy 'crush' – and Robbie replied in a wise and lengthy letter giving sensible advice.[46] It seems to have been advice that John was unable or unwilling to follow even from Robbie, since a month later he wrote again[47] suggesting (sensibly but not very helpfully) that John should talk to Slater, who was housemaster to both boys, about it. Probably the friendship died a natural death as such things do; memories of his first 'girlfriend' in Connemara may have helped displace it; by the Christmas term Robbie writes to thank John for 'many a most welcome letter' and suggests that he should not pursue his idea of asking his older friend for a photograph.

The following year he stayed at Freiburg, north of Bremen, almost on the coast, and was aware of changes in the political climate:

> Everything seems much stricter in Germany than last year. Every foreigner now has to fill in a large form of where he lives etc., which has to be signed by his host, and himself – and this form is kept by the police. – I have a baby form which I have to carry about with me for use when I'm arrested![48]

The next summer, 1938, his father sent him not to Germany but to Paris, for a ten-day course in French language and literature at the Sorbonne.

John was now in the 'Twenty', the form below the Sixth, with a creditable School Certificate, sufficient to secure entry into Cambridge when the time came. Meanwhile pressures of serious study began to mount with Higher Certificate less than two years away. In the event John was to take this exam three times, in the summers of 1938, 1939 and 1940, with increasing distinction, even though he had passed satisfactorily in French and German, written and oral, with English Literature and Scripture Knowledge as subsidiary subjects, at his first attempt. The Easter holidays of 1937 saw John in the Lake District (perhaps with Robbie Bickersteth); then in the New Forest with his family; and finally for a week in Cheshire, bird-watching on the Dee before the start of the summer term. The sightings occupy six pages in the bird diary, almost the last substantial entries. Growing up was bringing with it, as it generally does, a new need to attend to the serious business of life.

FIVE

Rugby 1938–40:
Beginning with Christ

1

King George VI and Queen Elizabeth were crowned in Westminster Abbey on 12 May 1937. A fortnight after the coronation Baldwin resigned and Neville Chamberlain became Prime Minister. Mussolini and Hitler dominated the European scene, even while the International Brigade, communist formed and led, were fighting for the defence of Madrid in the Spanish Civil War. As 1938 began the drum-beat quickened. In February Anthony Eden resigned as Foreign Secretary in protest at the government's policy of appeasement; a month later Hitler annexed Austria. In October Hitler occupied Czechoslovakia as part of the notorious 'Munich Agreement' which brought Chamberlain home in triumph to announce to a cheering crowd from a first-floor window in Downing Street that it was to be 'peace with honour' and 'peace in our time'. Not everyone was deceived. In Cambridge F. L. Lucas of King's, always an outspoken opponent of totalitarianism, confided to his diary his impression of

the temporarily triumphant Prime Minister as resembling some country cousin whom a couple of card-sharpers in the train have just allowed to win sixpence to encourage him.[1]

Lucas was soon to be proved right. In March 1939, six months later, Chamberlain recalled the British ambassador from Berlin; May saw the 'Pact of Steel' between Hitler and Mussolini pledging mutual military support in time of war; on September 1st Germany and Russia invaded Poland; and two days later Britain was at war with Germany.

*   *   *

At the end of the Christmas holidays in January 1938 Arnold Stott arranged for John to be assessed by the Vocational Guidance Department of the National Institute of Industrial Psychology. Though he was now a firmly committed Modern Linguist, due to take his Higher Certificate in French and German next July, there was some remaining doubt as to the exact career for which he would be most fitted; perhaps it was a matter of a choice between the Foreign and the Diplomatic Services. If, in spite of his father's misgivings, medicine had ever been a serious possibility, that was now well in the past.[2] John was sixteen years, eight months. The six-page report provides a snapshot of this stage of his development.

The Institute found the result of the intelligence test 'distinctly good, though not exceptional'. They recognize a flair for languages, but are less certain of a future scholarship or a high-class degree. (John was in fact to become a Senior Scholar of Trinity, Cambridge, and a double First.) In performance tests and mechanical aptitude they found no marked talent.[3]

In character the Institute described him as friendly and open, markedly sociable, emotional and sensitive, particularly over the question of personal relationships. They speak of 'some initiative and driving power and considerable perseverance' and of 'promising qualities of leadership', which would be best employed in positions where he had to exercise a less thrustful and more constitutional authority. They speak of a very high standard of behaviour and ideals and of how 'an opportunity for service would appeal to him more than one which was purely self-seeking'. But they cannot advise direct social work: 'he feels deeply and too much contact with the seamy side of life would be likely to cause too much worry.' Even for a career in teaching, otherwise very suitable and one to which he had admitted himself attracted, 'his tendency to take a very personal view of things might make the life a rather strenuous one for him.'

They make a number of alternative suggestions as to a suitable life's work. The Civil Service or the Foreign Office; work with a Town Clerk or Borough Treasurer's Department; secretarial work in connection with the social services or hospital administration; law; or the secretarial side of business. They conclude, 'Since his education is likely to be prolonged for some time it would perhaps be unwise to make too definite a decision at the moment; his interests and aims may change considerably when he is older.' It was a prediction amply fulfilled. Within a month of this report John had experienced the most far-reaching change of any in his life: his conversion to Christ. And six months later, still only seventeen, he was sure of his future calling to the ordained ministry of the Church of England.[4]

John Stott has told the story of his conversion, as a schoolboy at Rugby, on many occasions in person and in print.[5] In the following pages it seems best to allow him to tell it, as far as possible, in his own words. The framework is mainly taken from his account in 'The Counsellor and Friend' but supplemented from other published sources and from personal interviews.

Religion played a considerable part in the life of Rugby, as it did with most public schools in the 1930s, and does in differing degrees today. The school grounds and the Close are dominated by the tower of the great Chapel, itself partly extended from and partly replacing an earlier chapel which proved to be too small. It is built on the grand scale, lofty with slender pillars in the polychromatic masonry typical of William Butterfield's High Victorian style. The pews face inwards, as in many college chapels at Oxford and Cambridge, and some of the furnishings (including the pulpit from which Dr. Arnold preached) are from the first chapel. There are memorials to some notable figures, among them Arnold himself; his son Matthew Arnold; 'Lewis Carroll', whose tablet is adorned with a border of lively characters from *Alice*; and the young poet Rupert Brooke who died in 1915, still under thirty, and is commemorated with a bas-relief profile and his sonnet 'If I should die …'

Attached to the chapel, but distinct from it, is the Memorial Chapel, a smaller but dominant and impressive building with a floor plan in the shape of a Greek cross, the four huge windows portraying the passion, crucifixion, rising and ascending of Christ, and containing (in all but one) images of the school. On the walls are Rolls of Honour to 686 boys from the school who died in the 1914–18 war.[6] It was consecrated the year after John was born, thirteen years before he entered the school.

At this time, the school day included a brief Chapel service conducted by one of the three chaplains, house prayers each evening led by the housemaster, and (in Kilbracken, at least) a time of silence in the dormitories to allow boys to say their prayers. Senior boys in Kilbracken had the daytime use of a small study to themselves, but all slept in dormitories. Sundays would include Holy Communion, and there were special arrangements for Lenten series, confirmation preparation and the like; including an informal Bible Study group known as 'Conference' under the benign eye of the chaplains. John himself was confirmed, after a series of six classes, in the autumn term, 1936.

What part this system of organized religion played in John Stott's own conversion to Christ it is of course impossible to say. Certainly, according to his own recollection, confirmation meant little to him. It is clear, too, that the formal religious life of the school cannot have been a sufficient or even a significant cause in the dramatic conversion of a fellow-pupil, Hugh Montefiore (later Bishop of Birmingham) in the same term as that in which John was confirmed. The two boys' experiences are in striking contrast; they were of different ages and school years, in different houses, and so hardly known to one another. Hugh's family were devout and practising Jews, John had been brought up as a churchgoer in a Christian tradition. Hugh's encounter was dramatic and visionary, untaught in Christian belief and unaided by any word of Scripture; John's was through praying friends, and the careful exposition of the biblical gospel. Perhaps one could add that while Hugh's experience was largely unrecorded until his life came to be written, John Stott by contrast has generally been ready (as the extracts following will show) to illustrate and commend the gospel he preaches from his own experience of how he found Christ and was found by him.

Here, first, is Hugh Montefiore's account, in his own words:

I was sixteen years old at the time, and it happened to me about 5 pm one dark wintry afternoon in 1936. I was sitting alone in my study in School House at Rugby School – all older boys had studies of their own: pillboxes, really. What happened then determined the whole future pattern of my life. I was, as I remember indulging in a rather pleasant adolescent gloom. I suddenly became aware of a figure in white whom I saw clearly in my mind's eye. I use this expression because I am pretty sure that a photograph would have showed nothing special on it. I heard the words 'Follow me'. Instinctively I knew that this was Jesus, heaven knows how: I knew nothing about him. Put like that it sounds somewhat bare; in fact it was an indescribably rich event that filled me afterwards with overpowering joy. I could do no other than to follow those instructions. I found that I had become a Christian as a result of a totally unexpected and most unusual spiritual experience, although that was not how I would have put it at the time. I was aware of the living Christ, and because of that I was aware of God in a new way. People ask me why and when I decided to convert. I did not decide at all; it was decided for me.[7]

Up to that time he had never in his life attended a Christian service of worship, either in a church or in chapel at school.

Adolescence is typically a time when many young people experience some sense of searching for the divine, and John Stott was no exception:

> As a typical adolescent I was aware of two things about myself, though doubtless I could not have articulated them in these terms then. First, if there was a God, I was estranged from him. I tried to find him, but he seemed to be enveloped in a fog I could not penetrate. Secondly, I was defeated. I knew the kind of person I was, and also the kind of person I longed to be. Between the ideal and the reality there was a great gulf fixed. I had high ideals but a weak will.[8]

Something of those high ideals has been illustrated already in John's story. There was a desire to be the best, a wish to serve, an active if uneducated social conscience; and perhaps too a personal pride which was wounded when the gulf between the ideal and the reality became too plain. A faith which would satisfy continued to elude him: religion there was in plenty; but not a religion which could meet his needs:

> Convinced that there was more to religion than I had so far discovered, I used on half-holiday afternoons to creep into the Memorial Chapel by myself, in order to read religious books, absorb the atmosphere of mystery, and seek for God. But he continued to elude me ...[9]
>
> What brought me to Christ was a sense of defeat and of estrangement, and the astonishing news that the historic Christ offered to meet the very needs of which I was conscious.[10]

No doubt other factors had been at work in God's good providence long before these solitary periods of divine discontent in Memorial Chapel, a little oppressed by its solemnity, its atmosphere of stillness and silence, the half-light from stained glass windows, the little books of devotion put out by the chaplains for the boys to read. Here John would come, seeking God:

> I think I can say it was that. I had no doubt that he existed, and I was never troubled with that kind of doubt, but I also knew that I didn't know him ... I had this sense of alienation and separation. There was a voluntary service every Wednesday or Thursday evening for about half an hour and I went regularly to that ... but although I could work up some sort of religious feeling it was with a

sense of great disappointment, I think I can say of disillusionment, that I couldn't find what I was wanting: either a mystical relationship on the one hand or power on the other.[11]

Talking to students twenty years later these experiences were still vivid. By then, John Stott was aware that they are a good deal more common than he could have imagined at the time; and often a true reflection of spiritual reality:

> I can still remember my own perplexity when as a boy I said my prayers and tried to penetrate into God's presence. I could not understand why God seemed shrouded in mists and I could not get near him. He seemed remote and aloof. I know the reason now.
>
> We are tempted to say to God, as in the Book of Lamentations, 'Thou hast wrapped thyself with a cloud so that no prayer can pass through.' But in fact God is not responsible for the cloud. We are. Our sins blot out God's face from us as effectively as the clouds do the sun.
>
> Many people have confessed to me that they have had the same desolate experience. Sometimes, in emergencies, in danger, in joy or in the contemplation of beauty, God seems to them to be near, but more often than not they are aware of an inexplicable awayness from God, and they feel abandoned. This is not just a feeling; it is a fact. Until our sins are forgiven, we are exiles, far from our true home. We have no communion with God. In biblical terms we are 'lost', or 'dead through the trespasses and sins' which we have committed.[12]

The New Testament is clear that any harvest will depend upon seeds sown long before.[13] It also makes clear that it is God himself who shapes the individual characters and destinies of his children.[14] It is not difficult to trace something of this divine providence at work in John Stott's early life, leading up to the Lent term, 1938. Consider that careful upbringing, with Lily's Lutheran piety; the prayers and 'Scripture portion' from the nursery onwards; the choruses and simple stories of Nanny Golden; Great-Aunt Emily, a true believer, who prayed for him; All Souls and its Sunday School; Gerry Irvine and Oakley Hall; the love of nature and of music; immortal longings in the Memorial Chapel; and perhaps (though it did not seem so at the time) confirmation eighteen months before.

And there was one further factor, even more clearly decisive, in the person of John Bridger:

It was John Bridger, one year ahead of me in the Modern

Languages department, who invited me to attend what today would
be called the 'Christian Union'. It had no name then and was
usually referred to anonymously as 'the meeting', though in my
diary I called it rather disrespectfully 'Bridger's Affair'.[15]

2

John Richard Bridger was a year older than John Stott, and a year senior
to him in the school. They were in different houses (Bridger was in
Sheriff) but both on the 'B' (or modern languages) side, and occasionally
in the same form. Bridger was a remarkable all-round sportsman, playing
cricket for the school at the age of fifteen,[16] hockey a year later, and in the
rugger XV for his last two years. His later record at Cambridge was even
more remarkable. He played five games and would undoubtedly have
been awarded his blue for three of them;[17] and at the same time secured a
triple First – in French, German and theology.

John Bridger, then about seventeen, had become a Christian some two
years before, through a Scripture Union holiday houseparty. He returned
to Rugby to start, or perhaps to revive, what in those days would usually
have been called a Christian Union. In fact, in the language of the school,
it tended to be called 'the meeting' and it was something over a year later
when John Bridger invited John Stott to come to it. It met on Sunday
afternoons straight after lunch in the rather inhospitable atmosphere of
one of the classrooms of the New Quad. John Bridger would lead, and to
John Stott's astonishment would himself give talks from time to time (he
was then about seventeen): 'I thought how extraordinary that a boy was
able to give a talk.'[18] But there were also visiting speakers; and among
them, in the Lent term of 1938, that same E. J. H. Nash at whose
holiday party in Eastbourne John Bridger had come to a personal faith in
Christ.

'Bash' as E. J. H. Nash was known to all his friends, young and old,
was then just forty. His background is documented in the memoir
published by some of his friends a year after his death in 1982:

> After leaving school, he started work with an insurance firm in
> London and it was in 1917, on his way home to Maidenhead by
> train, that he finally faced and responded to the claims of Christ
> upon his life. It is not known how soon after this great turning-
> point he began to think of Ordination; and certainly for some little
> time he continued his work in the city, while at the same time
> helping with the work at St Mary's Church, and taking an active
> part in the Scout Movement attached to it.

Then in 1922, encouraged by the Bishop of London, Dr Winnington-Ingram, and supported by grants at his disposal, Bash went up to Trinity College, Cambridge, and then proceeded to Ridley Hall ... he joined the Staff of the Scripture Union in 1932, and his real life's work began ...'[19]

He had originally applied to the Scripture Union in 1929, but had been told 'there was no vacancy where his gifts could be well used'. He therefore became Chaplain of Wrekin for three years, applied again, and was accepted.[20] How far his spell as a school chaplain had clarified and sharpened the vision God had given him is uncertain. But he now had no doubt of the work to which he felt called to dedicate his life:

> His conviction was that he must evangelise the leading public schools of this country. Others had done Christian work among schoolboys. Grenfell of Labrador had run camps in Anglesey and in the Purbeck Hills, the Crusader movement was at work among the day schools, and the Scripture Union West Runton camps in Norfolk had got under way; but before long it was clear that Bash was beginning to put an entirely new stamp on boys' work ... in 1934 a regular pattern was established, which continued until the war, with the Easter camp at St. Cyprian's, Eastbourne and the summer camp at Beachborough Park, a few miles inland from Folkestone.[21]

'Camp' in these descriptions, though invariably used to refer to these houseparties, is something of a misnomer. Only at the very beginning were Bash's 'camps' under canvas. St. Cyprian's ('Kippers' in the vernacular) was a well-known prep school; Cecil Beaton had been there, and Gavin Maxwell and George Orwell and Cyril Connolly; Beachborough Park was more isolated, a prep school set in a romantic country house a few miles from the Kent coast, the centre of a sporting estate and surrounded by woods and downland. It was through these regular 'camps' for public schoolboys that Bash pursued his remarkable ministry for something like forty years. To the human eye he was far from being an obvious choice for the task to which God called him, as appears consistently in the descriptions of him by those who worked closely with him. John Eddison, in the memorial symposium already quoted, readily admits that, at first sight, there was nothing particularly impressive about him:

> He was neither athletic nor adventurous. He claimed no academic prowess or artistic talent. It is true that he possessed certain gifts

which would have been useful in any field – a remarkable intuition, a shrewd common sense, a degree of business acumen and a sense of humour. But the secret of his remarkable influence lay deeper than this.[22]

For with his unassuming personality and disarming simplicity went a remarkable gift, honed by years of experience and never taken for granted, to make the gospel real and relevant to his chosen audience:

> ... he was at his best with a group of intelligent sixth-formers or undergraduates. Given this 'platform', all the charm of his personality would be exercised to win attention and a fair hearing – with remarkable success. Indeed, to many it was his ability to do this which surprised most of all. There was no pretence of scholarliness, or of theological profundity – though he knew parts of his Bible intimately, and could apply them with disconcerting appositeness. ... There was, in fact, an engaging and reassuring winsomeness about Bash as he urged his familiar points, and few could hear him without the growing conviction that this was a man who could speak with relevance of the greatest issues of life.[23]

It was as part of his ministry to the boys (not, in his day, girls) of the leading public schools that Bash visited Rugby on Sunday, February 13th, half way through the Lent Term, 1938. Here is John Stott's recollection of the speaker at 'Bridger's Affair' that day:

> ... He was nothing much to look at, and certainly no ambassador for muscular Christianity. Yet as he spoke I was riveted. His text was Pilate's question: 'What then shall I do with Jesus, who is called the Christ?' That I needed to *do* anything with Jesus was an entirely novel idea to me, for I had imagined that somehow he had done whatever needed to be done, and that my part was only to acquiesce. This Mr. Nash, however, was quietly but powerfully insisting that everybody had to do something about Jesus, and that nobody could remain neutral. Either we copy Pilate and weakly reject him, or we accept him personally and follow him.[24]

In spite of the daily prayers, the Bible readings, the countless sermons to which John had been exposed, this was a new thought: 'In a way I can't quite express I was bowled over by this because it was an entirely new concept to me that one had to do anything with Jesus. I believed in him. I never doubted him. He existed. He was part of my mental furniture.'[25] John Stott's account continues:

When the meeting was over, I went up to ask our visiting speaker some questions, the nature of which I do not now recall. What I do remember is that he had the spiritual discernment to recognise in me a seeking soul. So he took me for a drive in his car, answered my questions and explained to me the way of salvation. To my astonishment his presentation of Christ crucified and risen exactly corresponded with the need of which I was aware.[26]

As was his custom, Bash exerted no pressure for any immediate decision. But through the rest of that Sunday John was coming to terms with what he had heard in the talk with its challenge of 'What shall I do with Jesus?', and with how Bash had applied it so accurately to his condition in their talk together:

> With the benefit of hindsight I can say that the correspondence between my need and Christ's offer seemed too close to be a coincidence. So that night at my bedside I made the experiment of faith, and 'opened the door' to Christ. I saw no flash of lightning, heard no peals of thunder, felt no electric shock pass through my body, in fact I had no emotional experience at all. I just crept into bed and went to sleep. For weeks afterwards, even months, I was unsure what had happened to me. But gradually I grew, as the diary I was writing at the time makes clear, into a clearer understanding and a firmer assurance of the salvation and lordship of Jesus Christ.[27]

The diary here referred to makes it clear that in his talk at 'the meeting' Bash had linked his theme of Pilate's question with the metaphor of the narrow gate and the broad way in Matthew 7:13; and that either in the talk or (perhaps more likely) in the conversation afterwards he had pointed John to the verse in the book of Revelation in which the ascended and glorified Lord Jesus, in the last of the Letters to the Seven Churches, pictures himself as knocking on the door of the human heart:

> 'Behold, I stand at the door, and knock: if any man hear my voice, and open the door, I will come in to him, and will sup with him, and he with me.'

> (Revelation 3:20, AV)

It is an image made famous by Holman Hunt's picture, 'The Light of the World',[28] which indeed Bash often used. John Stott himself was to point many others to the striking picture conjured up by this verse from Revelation. Writing twenty years later to those preparing for confirmation he described what these words brought home to him in the school dormitory that Sunday night, the lights out and the other boys in bed:

> The verse which made it clear to me (nearly eighteen months *after* I had been confirmed, I am sorry to say) is understandably a favourite with many Christians. In it Jesus Christ is speaking, and this is what he says: 'Here I am! I stand at the door and knock. If anyone hears my voice and opens the door, I will come in and eat with him, and he with me' (Revelation 3:20). Jesus depicts himself as standing outside the closed door of our personality. He is knocking, in order to draw our attention to his presence and to signify his desire to come in. He then adds the promise that, if we open the door, he will come in and we will eat together. That is, the joy of our fellowship with each other will be so satisfying that it can only be compared to a feast.
>
> Here, then, is the crucial question which we have been leading up to. Have we ever opened our door to Christ? Have we ever invited him in? This was exactly the question which I needed to have put to me. For, intellectually speaking, I had believed in Jesus all my life, on the other side of the door. I had regularly struggled to say my prayers through the key-hole. I had even pushed pennies under the door in a vain attempt to pacify him. I had been baptized, yes and confirmed as well. I went to church, read my Bible, had high ideals, and tried to be good and do good. But all the time, often without realising it, I was holding Christ at arm's length, and keeping him outside. I knew that to open the door might have momentous consequences. I am profoundly grateful to him for enabling me to open the door. Looking back now over more than fifty years, I realise that that simple step has changed the entire direction, course and quality of my life.[29]

In his student addresses already referred to, or at least in their book form,[30] John Stott quoted from the schoolboy diary that he kept at the time. His account of that Sunday is on one of the few pages that survive, written up on the following day:

Monday, Feb. 14th
   Yesterday really *was* an eventful day! ...
   After lunch I went to Bridger's affair (this is still yesterday) when Bash talked – very beautifully – about the straight gate, narrow way

and life, contrasted with the broad gate, wide path and destruction.

After this he took me for a drive in the car. – We had a grand talk. I told him everything about myself …

Up till now Christ had been on the circumference and I have but asked Him to guide me instead of giving Him complete control. Behold! He stands at the door and knocks. – I have heard Him and now is He come into my house. He has cleansed it and now rules therein. If Satan comes along and knocks at the door, *I* will not go and answer it, succumbing to the 'pleasures of sin', – but Christ will go to the door, at whose sight Satan will flee. If Christ is my Master, sin is dead under my feet.

A 'sense of being right with God and with the world', of which John spoke in a 'Ten-to-Eight' BBC radio broadcast, was at least in the very early stages, not long in coming. The diary records just such an experience on the following day:

Tuesday, Feb. 15th

I really have felt an immense and new joy throughout today. It is the joy of being at peace with the world, – and of being in touch with God. How well do I know now that He rules me, – and that I never really knew Him before.

Wednesday, Feb. 16th

I began my thesis on Jane Austen this morning, and, getting off 5th lesson this afternoon, theoretically to watch the XV v. the town, was luckily able to finish it this evening. I managed to cover 18 sides, but I'm afraid it was pretty bad, for I have only read 'Pride and Prejudice' and 'Sense and Sensibility'.

I really have been feeling the 'peace which passeth all understanding' these last few days.

Thursday, March 3rd

'When compromise creeps in, power wanes.' We MUST take sides.

Bash came down to-day, and we had our first grand Q.T. together, though I was a bit frightened praying at the end. We read Phil. IV.

Saw a Barn Owl flapping lazily about in a field, after Q.Ts with Bash.

'Q.T.' stands for 'Quiet Times',[31] a short period of Bible-reading and prayer, whether alone or (as here) together.

Bash was an unerring judge of spiritual sincerity; and it is clear that he had detected from the beginning that this 'rich young ruler'[32] was in earnest and must now be nurtured in the faith. He was beginning to see answered the prayer that was in his heart from their first meeting: 'O God, if you will give me this boy, I will never again doubt your power to save.'[33] John Stott has recounted how Bash began to write to him:

A few days later his first letter arrived, enclosing a booklet[34] and giving practical advice on how to go on and grow as a Christian. A correspondence then developed between us, and he must have written to me once a week for at least five years. I still marvel at his faithfulness. For often they were long letters, broken into paragraphs with sectional headings underlined. Some paragraphs were heavily theological, unfolding the doctrine of the Atonement or the three tenses of salvation. Others were ethical, expounding the principles of moral conduct or marshalling the arguments – a bit too rigidly, as I now believe – why a certain practice should be regarded as 'worldly' and therefore avoided. Other paragraphs contained pastoral guidance on how to read the Bible, how to pray, or how to practise the presence of Christ each day so that he became as real on the rugger field as in chapel. In yet other paragraphs he would give detailed advice on how to run the Sunday meeting (whose leadership I took over from John Bridger when he went up to Cambridge), how to help other boys who were young in their faith, and how to recruit for the holiday camps. There was personal counsel too, especially on the need to get ten hours' sleep every night. Then every letter would end with a 'best thought', some precious biblical text opened up and applied. Alongside the best thought, however, often as a postscript and perhaps always as a deliberate prophylactic against an excess of piety, he would add a joke, usually of the schoolboy howler variety ...

His expectations for all those whom he led to Christ were extremely high. He could be easily disappointed. His letters to me often contained rebuke, for I was a wayward young Christian and needed to be disciplined. In fact, so frequent were his admonitions at one period that, whenever I saw his familiar writing on an envelope, I needed to pray and prepare myself for half an hour before I felt ready to open it.[35]

Many of those Bash counselled will have similar recollections. What John did not know at the time, and only came to guess some years afterwards, was that he was in Bash's daily prayers;[36] and it was not long before Bash gave him a small pocket New Testament similar to the one that he himself always carried. The verse he chose to inscribe on the flyleaf below his initials, EJHN, was Philippians 4:13: 'I can do all things through Christ who strengtheneth me.'[37]

Light had broken upon John's soul with some immediate assurance; but all was not yet clear and open day. There followed weeks and months of uncertainty and slowly developing understanding: yet always with the confidence that something had really happened, that things were different since he had 'opened the door to Christ'. Later he was to put it like this, expounding Paul's teaching in Romans 6:

> I find it helpful to think in these terms. Our biography is written in two volumes. Volume one is the story of the old man, the old self, of me before my conversion. Volume two is the story of the new man, the new self, of me after I was made a new creation in Christ … My old life having finished, a new life to God has begun.[38]

Later, too, he was able to look back on three distinct aspects of his experience where things had decisively changed. First, walking down a street in Rugby, he was conscious of a new awareness of being in love with everybody – in love with the world. Schoolboy antagonisms and antipathies had dropped away: 'I had no enemies left.'[39] It was to him at the time an authentic moment of truth.

Secondly, he now sensed that he belonged to a bigger family. The moments of parting with his parents and sisters, agonizing and tearful (even if only briefly) at Oakley Hall, were still sad and emotional; so much so, that he sometimes thought it would be easier if they did not visit him at school. But now, after conversion, things were different. If his parental family were not with him, his new Christian family was. When he asked himself why he no longer minded so much when his parents left for home, his answer was (along with the fact that he was growing older) that he had Christian friends.

The third reason had to do with chapel, and Rugby religion. Words that he had sung for years like the *Te Deum* or the *Nunc Dimittis* were suddenly full of meaning, relevant to his situation, part of his personal inheritance. When the time came for him to speak at the meeting, he would sometimes urge members to be loyal to the school chapel, and to discover, as he had done, that what for years had seemed lifeless formularies could become personally meaningful and precious.

But there was a still more decisive difference between Volume 1 and Volume 2 – the Bible. Up to this time, John was a Bible-reader in a regular but superficial way with little real understanding, and open, almost without knowing it, to the sceptical prejudices of the day. A year or so before, to his embarrassment, he had found himself in conversation with a visiting clergyman when some reference was made to the Holy Trinity:

> With the invincible assurance of teenage omniscience I said to him, 'Nobody believes in the Trinity nowadays'. I had no sooner said it than I was ashamed of it. The fact is that I had never thought about the Trinity. Finding it difficult to understand, I jumped to the conclusion that it was an outmoded superstition which intelligent people had long ago discarded.[40]

Now that he began to read the Bible from a new standpoint, he was ready to receive its teaching with a humble mind. He no longer presumed to sit in judgment on the Scriptures, but allowed them to be his teacher. The change was dramatic. Preaching in Sydney Cathedral during the Australian Scripture Union week, 1958, he described the difference:

> Before I was converted I used to read the Bible every day but I did not begin to understand it. After I received Jesus Christ as my Saviour and Lord, one of the first ways in which I knew that something had happened to me was that the Bible became a new Book. As I read it God began to speak to me; verses became luminous, phosphorescent. It was as if I heard the very Word of God through the Scriptures.[41]

Twenty years later he recounted this experience in more detail, reminding his readers that it was by no means unique or even exceptional:

> William Grimshaw, one of the great eighteenth-century evangelical leaders, told a friend after his conversion that 'if God had drawn up his Bible to heaven, and sent him down another, it could not have been newer to him'. It was a different book. I could say the same myself. I read the Bible daily before I was converted, because my mother brought me up to do so, but it was double-Dutch to me. I hadn't the foggiest idea what it was all about. But when I was born again and the Holy Spirit came to dwell within me, the Bible immediately *began* to be a new book to me. Of course I am not claiming that I understood everything. I am far from understanding everything today. But I began to understand things I had never understood before.[42]

And preaching to his congregation at All Souls, he moved on from testimony to exhortation:

What a marvellous experience this is! Don't think of the Bible as just a collection of musty old documents whose real place is in a library. Don't think of the pages of Scripture as if they were fossils whose real place is behind glass in a museum. No, God speaks through what he has spoken. Through the ancient text of Scripture the Holy Spirit can communicate with us today freshly, personally and powerfully. 'He who has an ear, let him hear what the Spirit says' ('is saying' – it is a present tense – through the Scriptures) 'to the churches.' (Rev. 2:7, *etc.*).[43]

So he moved steadily into clearer light. He began to underline in red selected verses in the New Testament Bash had given him; over forty verses are so marked, from Matthew, Mark and John and from most of the epistles except the Pastorals. Acts too is an interesting exception which he had yet to discover. When fifty years later he came to expound it in the 'Bible Speaks Today' series, his opening words were 'Thank God for the *Acts of the Apostles* !'.[44]

Later in that Spring term of 1938 flu struck the school, and John had to spend some time in bed. There, quite quickly, he wrote six stanzas setting out his new experience of Christ. He had grasped the great truths of Christ's death for sinners; of justification by faith, 'not of works, lest any man should boast'; of freedom from the law of sin and death; of Christ's call and our response; and of a life consecrated to the service of a new and gracious Master:

> Behold the Lamb, the Lamb of God,
>> Jesus the Saviour, who died.
> My sins on Him, on Him were laid;
>> My deepest need is supplied.
>
> For no merit of mine could this freedom win;
>> I'm unworthy still, do what I may;
> But Jesus has died and borne all my sin;
>> So I'm free – if I take Him to-day.
>
> In gratitude, Lord, for Thine infinite love,
>> Which brought Thee to suffer for me,
> I yield Thee my life, and may I live ever
>> Wholly and only for Thee.[45]

In the Easter holidays following his conversion to Christ John turned seventeen. He had already been a year in the Sixth form, and was steadily making his way up the school, gathering prizes as he went.[46] In the summer term of 1938 he found himself co-opted to the Levée. This is an institution unique to Rugby, an oligarchy of heads of houses entrusted with a considerable role in the running of the school, reporting (by means of its Minute Book) directly to the headmaster. By its constitution it could contain only two co-opted members, and co-option was thus a signal honour for a boy not head of his house and only moderately distinguished as a games player: John ran regularly for the school in cross-country events; and once played rugby for a school XV. John Bridger was already a member of the Levée as head of Sheriff house; he would have warmly supported John's membership and may indeed have proposed it. As with many such groups and committees in the future, John's membership would in due course lead on to chairmanship.

Before the end of the summer term John had begun a new notebook; not a bird diary, this time, but a record of sermons, Bible studies, talks – a kind of magpie's nest of treasures new and old garnered from a variety of sources in the first months of his post-conversion life. There are fifty-three entries, ranging from quotations from R. A. Torrey to Dom Bernard Clements, from acrostics on the word B I B L E[47] to 'Necessary qualifications of Christian workers'. Some are evidently the bases of the talks he gave at the meeting in his later terms (sometimes with a pencil line through them, presumably to prevent repetition on a later occasion); but a very early entry is headed 'Life at its Best'. This first recounts, and then further develops, the way of salvation set out in the booklet that Bash had given him in February. To this simple teaching John clung, working to make it his own and to deepen the foundations, but wanting also to share what he had found.

In the study next door there was a contemporary, Philip Tompson, a few months younger than John, whose difficult home circumstances would sometimes make him appear unhappy and withdrawn. He was therefore the first friend whom John tried to bring to Christ, explaining things as best he could, with his own copy of *Life at its Best* conveniently to hand between the pages of the Bible from which he was pointing Philip to key verses.

He simply couldn't understand what I was talking about; it was double Dutch to him, so after a while of course I lapsed into silence because I didn't know what to do next. But I do remember that at that point I secretly turned to prayer. After about a ten minute silence, it seemed to me, in which neither of us had anything to say, a verse came in to my mind and I said to him 'I wonder if this would help you', and I read it, and it isn't an exaggeration to say that immediately he said 'Oh, I see'.[48]

During that summer term of 1938, John took the first of three sittings of his Higher Certificate and began the holidays as usual with a month on the continent working at his language skills. Bash had arranged with him that following his return from Europe he would come to 'camp', his schoolboys' holiday houseparty at Beachborough Park, in the second half of August. John Eddison remembers his arrival:

> It was at Beachborough that John and I have very clear recollections of meeting for the first time. It was late in the evening, and I stood at the top of the main staircase, in a blue silk dressing-gown while he, hot-foot from France came prancing up the stairs looking very pleased with life, and clutching, if I remember aright, a bottle of wine. Whether this was intended as a gift for Mr Nash, whom John may not yet have discovered to be a teetotaller, I can't say.[49]

3

John Stott returned to Rugby in September 1938 as head of house, and a member of the Levée in his own right. John Bridger was still leader of the meeting but training John to step into his shoes, since he was due to leave the following term. John had greatly enjoyed his time at camp and was on the look-out for friends whom he might invite to the houseparty at St. Cyprian's ('Kippers') the following Easter. So Peter Melly became another of what was an extraordinary group of senior boys in Kilbracken who, through Bash and 'Bridger's Affair', and now through John Stott, were finding a living relationship with Christ. Chatting with Melly in the changing room after games, he asked if he would be interested in going to this schoolboys' houseparty in the coming Easter holidays:

> I said straight away that I would like to come. He told me later that he was quite overwhelmed by this response. I was the normal hard-swearing school boy, I suppose, no faith at all, just going to chapel at school, which was compulsory, and my parents taking me to church occasionally at home. John had prayed about this approach to me and had been fairly certain that he would be rebuffed.[50]

Peter Melly went to camp and there found Christ for himself. Back at Rugby John was assiduous in helping him to become established and to grow as a Christian:

John took me in hand from the beginning and taught me the Christian way of life. He took me on one side more than once to tell me where I was going wrong, and did this in the most loving and helpful way. I have been impressed ever since of the necessity of following up those who have been converted and teaching them what is right and acceptable in the life of a Christian. Even in those days John had a real grip of the Scriptures.[51]

There were thirty-nine boys attending the meeting on the first Sunday of the summer term 1939;[52] including seven or eight from Kilbracken, Stott, Tompson, Melly and George Toplas among them, all of whom were, or were about to be, house prefects.[53] Something over a dozen boys from Kilbracken went with John to camp at Beachborough Park[54] that summer; and most of these would attach themselves more or less regularly to the Christian Union meeting on their return to Rugby. John himself, though still very young as a Christian, found himself acting not only as a leader and a recruiter for camp and for the meeting, but as teacher and pastor. The letters to him that remain from that period, though no doubt only the tip of the iceberg, tell their own story. These are from different correspondents:

> I would like to thank you for your help in 'sort of' changing my life … my only regret is that I have not been able to turn up to the meetings as much as I should have liked.[55]
> You can't imagine what it has meant to me. I'll tell you – a completely *new* outlook on life – Just when I need Him most, He's ready – This morning I woke up at 6.45 about and first thing committed the day to Him …[56]
> I would like to thank you for one point in your talk last Sunday, 'Prompt to Obey'. I've been following that point for the week and I've really found it makes a difference.[57]

Following camp that Easter holidays, one of those whom he had invited wrote from his home in Sussex to say what it had meant to him:

> Dear John,
> I must write and thank you very very much for having introduced me to camp – it is difficult for me to say how extremely grateful I am.
> Your action, as you probably know already, has had a very powerful effect on me. Besides being the best 10 days of my life, camp has succeeded in doing what I thought to be impossible – it has brought religion right into my life, and thereby changed me

completely. I now realize how pleasant life can be, and I am sure this makes all the difference to me. It is really marvellous what a different person camp has made me, and I am eternally grateful to you and Bash for all the help you have both given me.[58]

It was a remarkable time; but as with all Christian work it was by no means an unbroken success story. 'I am very sorry to say', one friend writes to him, 'that I have decided to discontinue my weekly visit to the Christian Union. To continue them would only be hypocritical, and that is the last thing I want to be ... my regular attendance has only been due to my deep admiration for yourself and George T.'[59] Writing to John a year later, his successor as leader of the Christian Union summed up the down-side as he experienced it:

So many people ... seem to enjoy things terrifically their first term at CU and again at the beginning of next term but then drop away ... If beaks [*i.e.* masters] see – and I know House Masters usually do get to know all about it – that people just go there and don't keep it up, they must inevitably feel that there is not much in it, and it also prejudices other boys who come.[60]

Certainly John Stott, and other young leaders with him, had their share of disappointments. One hopes that before 'beaks' and Housemasters were too quick to criticize the Christian Union as a place of shallow conversions and emotional decisions, they remembered the parable of the sower (so little seed, sometimes after promising beginnings, coming to fruition) and the sobering statistics of lapsed communicants after careful Confirmation preparation and compulsory chapel. No doubt mistakes were made: rapid growth in numbers was not achieved without cost. Younger boys from a different kind of religious background could (and did) find this very personal and informal approach to religion confusing and disturbing. An example would be David Jenkins, John's fag, who arrived in Kilbracken aged thirteen and a half in the summer of 1939 from a devout and mildly high-church Christian home. His recollections of John at that time reflect an understandable hero-worship: 'Gracious, charming, handsome, kind, good – everything anyone would want someone to be – overwhelming; a wonderful person.'[61] It was important to Jenkins that John, though a scholar and in one or two house teams, was not primarily an athlete; since this meant that it was possible to be a success at Rugby without being good at games. John invited David Jenkins to the meeting in his first term. He was not finding Rugby a happy experience; everything was new to him, and he was subject to some mild bullying from his contemporaries. By most of them the meeting was regarded as a holy huddle – those who went tended to be known as the 'Jeesemen' – and peer-group derision is hard to bear. Jenkins was uneasily conscious that some from Kilbracken would be looking out of the windows after Sunday lunch to see who was 'getting religion'. He stuck it for eighteen months, though finding it 'an entirely foreign approach to religion'; and one which, perhaps in consequence of his Rugby experiences, he was never going to find it easy to come to terms with, even after ordination and a lifetime of Christian ministry.

Rugby at that time was something of a nursery of headmasters; it was not unusual for staff trained under Hugh Lyon to move on to the headships of well-known schools.[62] Perhaps it is not too surprising that some of them were uneasy about Bash's camps, and about school Christian Unions or 'meetings'. This in turn bred a kind of reserve or secrecy which was not dispelled until, quite a number of years later, there was a responsible body of masters and school chaplains with personal experience of camp (often as helpers there themselves) and of the lasting quality of Bash's spiritual work, who could commend it with authority. Perhaps too, by that time, the traditional public school religion was becoming harder to promote and to defend in a more hostile secularist climate; so that the vitality and strength of a personal and evangelical religion, in movements as responsible and experienced as Scripture Union, began to be welcomed as an ally in the cause of faith by those who in earlier days would have dismissed it as shallow and even dangerous 'enthusiasm'.

By this stage, F. C. Slater was not only John's housemaster but also his form master. In his end-of-term report he spoke of 'an extremely busy and profitable term' and (in his role of housemaster) 'I feel he has plenty of ideas of his own, which he will endeavour to put into practice next year. I hope he will not be in too much of a hurry. He is far more tolerant of compromise now.'[63] The reference to next year suggests that Slater already knew Hugh Lyon had chosen John to be head of school in succession to Patrick Rodger.[64] The 'extremely busy' summer term that Slater speaks of embraced not only membership of the Levée, work on his French and German which would turn the Higher Certificate passes of the summer before into distinctions, the leadership of Kilbracken and of the meeting, but also the title role in the school play. John had already acquired favourable mention in his house play the year before, when Kilbracken House Dramatic Society performed a farce by J. B. Priestley, 'Bees on the Boat Deck'. The review in the *New Rugbeian Supplement* spoke of 'Hilda Jackson (J. R. W. Stott) who, despite her excessive height, gave a distinctly feminine performance'.[65]

Perhaps it was this dramatic flair that led to his being cast in the title role of Richard II the following year, soon after his eighteenth birthday:

he warned his parents to be prepared for the 'ghastly sight' of their son in a rich auburn wig![66] The local paper pronounced it 'probably the finest Shakespearean show ever produced in the school ... J. R. W. Stott's characterisation is one which is head and shoulders above even the efficient company the school provides'[67] and to the *New Rugbeian Supplement* it was a tour-de-force:

> There can be few more exacting parts in Shakespeare than that of *Richard*. J. R. W. Stott at once made a good impression by his pleasant voice, which was quiet yet always audible, except at the end of the play when he was speaking from the back of the stage. His performance was restrained throughout and succeeded mostly by the smallness of its compass, never rising to any great heights, yet always holding interest through a long and difficult part. *Richard's* vacillation and petulance, his sudden changes from optimism to despair, his pathetic belief in his own royal destiny – there is no doubt that he portrayed all these, yet not so much at the dramatic climaxes of the part, as by a quieter, subtler inflexion of voice or manner at the lesser moments. His greater outbursts of feeling were less convincing, chiefly because he seemed to rely for achieving a climax on the sudden breaking of a plate or mirror rather than a gradual sustaining of the dramatic tension: some of his gestures, too, were monotonous and unnatural, especially in the passages that follow the great lines –
>
> > For God's sake let us sit upon the ground
> > And tell sad stories of the death of kings.
>
> On the other hand, his acting in the Dungeon Scene was excellent, and his portrayal of *Richard's* death was really moving and had great dignity.[68]

The play was performed on three evenings, Wednesday, Thursday and Friday, June 14, 15 and 16 in New Big School. On the Monday following, Harold Jennings the producer wrote to John:

> I have never really congratulated you properly on your performance as Richard, which I hope you enjoyed as much as I did. I think the results more than justified what I said to you about 'being ambitious for a really big success'; for there is no doubt that that is what you achieved. Comments and congratulations that I have received from all quarters have all emphasized that. Nor do I want you to think that I am patting myself on the back in this letter; for apart from some advice and a few rude remarks at times, the credit for the success belongs not to me, but almost entirely to you, for the

enormous amount of work and trouble and sympathetic insight and depth, which you put into the performance. Allow me!'[69]

Perhaps it is not surprising, looking back on this heady experience, that John felt he learned from it both 'the fascination of the footlights' and 'the danger of pretending to be somebody other than who you are'.[70]

It is often said that the actor and the preacher have something in common, even though this may be little more than the power to hold and move their hearers. Bash discerned in John a gift for speaking in public, and in order to encourage and develop this he arranged for John to accompany him during the school holidays as assistant missioner for a week's mission at a small free church, somewhere in Staffordshire. This was a form of local-church evangelism for which Scripture Union staffworkers were always in demand. Here, night after night, often to a few village women and some servicemen from a nearby military base, John would gain increasing experience in public speaking and Bible exposition which would stand him in good stead as preparation for the future, beginning with his capable leadership of the Rugby meeting.

Later in the summer holidays John was again with Bash at Beachborough Park, one of fifteen Rugbeans in the houseparty out of a total just short of 200. They assembled on August 17 for exactly a fortnight: by the time they dispersed it was August 31 and within three days Britain was at war. During September John's parents were on holiday with relatives in Buckinghamshire when Arnold Stott received notification from the War Office that he was recalled to the RAMC with the rank of Colonel, having returned to civilian life as Major following the end of the 1914–18 war. His family were much amused at this promotion since they regarded him as quite unmilitary, and he had been out of touch with the army for the last twenty years. They arranged to sell the house in Harley Street (and never returned there) and moved the family home to Woodlands Farm House, rented from friends of Joanna, in Stoke D'Abernon, between Cobham and Leatherhead in Surrey. For Lily, it was a social revolution of a kind being faced by her generation all over England. In London she had been used to a cook, maids and a chauffeur; to shopping by telephone; to no real garden. Woodlands was a new world, and she rose to the challenge with enthusiasm. Joy described the house in a letter to her brother at Rugby:

This place is fine. I expect Mamma has tried to describe it to you.
There is masses of mud, and cows, and a cherry-coloured
staircarpet, and rooms foursquare ... I suppose you have heard that
this is where all the cows multiply [the house backed onto the cow

sheds of the adjoining farm]. Terrific din; and Mummy pauses, hand uplifted, and says 'Oh Joy, Hark! – another cow in labour.' It's very amusing – little angel-calves … Mummy is a marvellous cook and I'm a marvellous skivvy, and Daddy prowls around his 'thirst-parlour' (cupboard!), and occasionally lifts plates, and puts them down in the wrong place, and his spectacles are always at the end of his nose … Mummy waxes fatter and fatter; I have literally to roll her through the doorways! She is very happy, I think.[71]

Lily clearly thrived on rural domesticity after the years of London life. In November Dr. Stott, already in his mid-fifties, was posted to France.

John returned to Rugby for his final year as head of the school, to sit a Cambridge scholarship[72] and to face the new conditions of the home front in time of war. Rugby was an important railway junction and a significant manufacturing centre in its own right, on the eastern fringe of the industrial heartlands. Gas-masks had already been issued and had to be carried at all times; air-raid precautions – shelters, sandbags, wardens' posts, static-water tanks – were everywhere in evidence, though identity cards and ration books were still some months away. Before term was far advanced Britain had 150,000 men in France with the Expeditionary Force and German U Boats were regularly attacking allied shipping. Though the general call to arms was for men aged twenty and over, Rugbeians who had left school the previous term were already in uniform and others were wondering whether to cut short their final term and enlist.

The Levée, with John in the chair, was kept busy helping the school adapt to these new conditions. The early air-raid practices were 'a matter for joking rather than an inconvenience'. However:

The black-out did indeed cause difficulties as the days grew shorter, and the Levée had to make and enforce strictly rules for one-way pedestrian traffic on Barby Road and the Close to avoid collisions and confusion, particularly when boys were changing schools in the dark between afternoon lessons.[73]

A further duty falling to the head of the school was to edit the school journal, *The Meteor*. The first issue of the new school year appeared in mid-October, with the opening words of the editorial (otherwise a singularly inconsequential piece of writing) confessing to a proper sense of new responsibilities:

The new editor of a school magazine that is positively hoary with age must perforce feel somewhat timid. In his eagerness to be valiantly correct he studies the literary masterpieces of his lofty predecessors.[74]

However, before the term ended, the new editor found himself sufficiently embroiled in a domestic controversy to feel that he should seek reassurance from the school's Chairman of Governors, William Temple, then Archbishop of York. *The Meteor* had carried a lively correspondence, originating in a request for the continued use in the school chapel of the robustly-worded prayer for use 'In the time of War and Tumults' from the Book of Common Prayer. Correspondence in succeeding issues of the journal took sides (staff as well as boys), resulting in the following letter:

My dear Stott,

I am very glad that you wrote and have not myself any complaint to make about your action as editor, though I confess it would have been still wiser to demand a still more drastic pruning of language. Why do pacifists persist in creating the maximum degree of bitterness in their pursuit of universal good-will!

The freedom of the press does not, in other quarters, the least hinder the editor from saying to writers of letters, 'I will publish your letter if you modify such and such an expression, but I cannot let my columns be used for that expression because of my own judgment that it will do great harm in this direction or that'.

I do not think I need say anything further to the Governing Body. The times when people's feelings are most sensitive are of course the times when the greatest care is called for, both as a matter of policy and also as a matter of charity.

Yours sincerely,
William Ebor[75]

William Temple was a frequent visitor to the school, on governors' business, or as a visiting speaker or preacher. John dined with him in the headmaster's house on at least one occasion, recalling little beyond 'his geniality and his quite extraordinary laugh which was like a cataract ...'.[76] Of his preaching in chapel, John recalled in particular his clarification of sin as self-centredness, the revolt of the self against God and against our fellow-human beings. Later, when he came to read *Christianity and the Social Order*, John was to recognize Temple's treatment of this basic theme; and to make use of it (as indeed he uses many Temple quotations) in his preaching and writing:

Archbishop William Temple's definition of original sin perfectly describes this truth: 'I am the centre of the world I see; where the horizon is depends on where I stand ... Education may make my self-centredness less disastrous by widening my horizon of interest; so far it is like climbing a tower, which widens the horizon for physical vision, while leaving me still the centre and standard of reference.'[77]

4

A month into term, and therefore five or six weeks after the outbreak of war, a group of senior boys (John among them) was taken by the school to an army recruiting centre in Birmingham in order to 'attest'. This was in fact (though it seems to have been very inadequately explained) equivalent to enlisting. They would not be called on to report for duty until they reached the age of twenty: with the expectation that such enlistment would lead quickly to commissioned rank, for which service in Rugby School Officers' Training Corps was counted as useful preparation. John had gained the OTC qualification, 'Certificate A', a few terms before.

John was, however, beginning to take a distinctly pacifist position as a result of his Christian convictions: he was later to describe himself at this period as 'an instinctive pacifist'.[78]

I had read the Sermon on the Mount for the first time through Christian eyes, and I naturally was a literalist; and when I came to the end of chapter five of Matthew on 'turning the other cheek', not repaying evil, I simply could not begin to understand how it could be possible to be a Christian and to fight.

I was therefore an instinctive pacifist. Now I know Bash was a pacifist, and I sometimes ask myself whether he influenced me – but I'm almost certain I can remember telling him that I was a pacifist, when he asked me what my attitude to the war was, and he then expressed his joy or pleasure because he was too, and then probably our convictions reinforced one another but I think it is honestly true to say that I had become an instinctive pacifist, as it were, on my own; he certainly never brought pressure to bear.[79]

It was therefore a shock to discover some considerable time later that the process of 'attesting', which had included a medical examination, was not a mere preliminary towards a point of decision still in the future, but constituted enlistment in the Forces of the Crown, and would be expected to result in posting to a training unit as soon as he reached the age of twenty. That this did not in fact happen can be traced to Hugh Lyon's practice of talking briefly with his senior boys from time to time as to their thoughts on a future career. Six months before the war, and not long after his conversion to Christ, John had told his headmaster that his thoughts were firmly fixed on ordination to the ministry of the Church of England. Under the regulations then in force, a candidate for ordination (who could show to the satisfaction of the authorities that his intention pre-dated September 1939) was one of the comparatively few categories of student who could be exempted from the requirements of military service without having formally to register and appear before a tribunal as a conscientious objector. Though John was never posted, he remained on the books of the Royal Warwickshire Regiment throughout the war; only finally receiving his discharge in January 1946, 'his services being no longer required for the purposes for which he enlisted'.[80] But before this happened, the issue of war service and this unwitting enlistment was to cause him much unhappinesss.

The Easter holidays, 1940, saw Bash's camp at a new base, Clayesmore School, in the tiny Dorset village of Iwerne Minster. Schools on or near the coast were clearly unsuitable while a German invasion remained even a remote possibility; and at Clayesmore it would be possible to help the war effort by providing working parties for harvesting in the summer and forestry at Easter and Christmas. Though John was unaware of it, it seems likely that Bash was already training him for a key role in the administration and development of this specialized ministry of the gospel to public schoolboys. John Pollock, then aged sixteen and a boy at Charterhouse, remembers Bash introducing him to John with the words 'He is head boy of Rugby where they treat him as if he were a master.'[81]

For Lily it was an anxious summer. Her husband was in France, and though she could not have known it at the time, the retreat to Dunkirk was ordered on 19 May; by 31 May the troops on the coast were totally encircled. She wrote on 23 May to John at Rugby:

> I feel a bit worried about Daddy – the enemy seem to be so near Dieppe. Altho' it is a port, and I suppose evacuation might be possible, yet the doctors could not leave the hospitals unattended. Would the personnel all become prisoners-of-war? I hope we shall soon hear from him ...[82]

She was concerned too about the rapidity with which important decisions seemed to be looming in her son's life, with his father in France or (on his safe return to England a month later) posted away from home. John had told her, of course, both of his determination to be ordained, and of his doubts about whether he could in conscience fight for his country. Her Sunday letter to him at the end of June expresses her anxiety:

> I feel you must have some talks with men who are in the church –
> men of culture and wide views who would explain that many
> sayings of our Lord uttered two thousand years ago cannot be quite
> literally taken. There is a duty to the community as well as to
> ourselves and very often it has to be put first for the sake of the
> good of the majority. Daddy and I don't mind the conscientious
> objector so much in theory but in your case we feel you have not
> sufficiently explored the pros and cons. We are going to take the
> bull by the horns and think of going to Claygate to see the Padre
> there. I feel convinced that there is some argument that we have not
> thought of. All the churches pray for the fighting forces and
> countenance taking up the sword in good cause. Unsullied
> consecration is rather isolationist and mosaic isn't it? Altho' I was
> practically convinced after last holidays that you had chosen the
> career you are suited for and long to work in – I do now agree with
> Daddy that you ought not definitely to become an ordinand until
> you are 21 and have a good basis at Cambridge of a not absolutely
> theological education.
>
> When your time for military registration comes along – if your
> opinion has not changed – you will not now be allowed to continue
> at Cambridge after the next year but will have to do government
> work of some sort. Everyone has to ...[83]

Claygate was the evangelical church which John and a friend from Rugby, who also lived at Stoke D'Abernon, used to attend in the holidays. R. G. B. Bailey, the vicar, was the 'padre' to whom John's mother refers in her letter. He recalls talking to John in the porch after Service; but it does not seem that his advice was very formally sought by Lily Stott on behalf of her son.[84] By this time John was in sight of the end of his years at school:

> 'Between agriculture and A.R.P.,' wrote a House annalist in his
> comments on the summer term of 1940, 'between fire-squad
> practice, L.D.V. and armament work, this term can only be
> described as a muddle. ... The Corps faded more and more into the
> background as L.D.V. advanced in numbers and importance, and
> time grew shorter and shorter for any other activities.' The situation
> arising from the collapse of the Western Front led to the
> abandonment of Speech Day, and – a much more cheerful

development – owing to paper shortage, all examinations except the Certificates were cancelled.[85]

In a singularly busy final term, John paid a visit to Cambridge to sit the Modern Language Scholarship examination at Trinity, being made specially welcome by John Bridger, anxious for news of the school and of the meeting. The work of the Levée continued, desiring the Headmaster 'to explain why the butter ration has been limited to ¼ lb. as last term'; enquiring 'why members of the school are not allowed to play tennis on the hard courts on Sundays' and expressing the hope that 'for the duration of the war, they be definitely exempted from wearing, and therefore bringing back, evening dress'.[86] The Levée took seriously their responsibilities, keeping meticulous Minutes which were submitted as recommendations to the Headmaster. His response and comment would then be added by the chairman. In the Lent term of 1940, responding to a particularly persistent request from the Levée, Hugh Lyon's response appears (in John Stott's handwriting) as 'The Headmaster will not be bullied …'[87]

Nevertheless, emergency conditions in that first summer of the war often brought changes to the life of the school which demanded quick responses. In June, in the middle of a heat wave, the General Inspection of the OTC was summarily cancelled at less than twenty-four hours notice. A fortnight later Philip Tompson was writing home to his parents:

> This is, or rather would have been, Speech Day week-end. At first Speech Day was going to take place though shorn of much of its usual glory, but when on Monday France collapsed, the H. M. cancelled Speech Day altogether.[88]

In the same letter home he described how he had been helping the editor ('Stott in Kilbracken') with work on *The Meteor*, which had urgently to be reduced in size by four pages on the Bursar's orders – at a time when the usual sub-editor was away in Oxford sitting an examination.

At his final meeting of the Levée, after the appointment of members of the school to a variety of offices (Captains and Secretaries of various sports, School Treasurer, members of Chapel committee etc.) the Levée discussed and minuted a subject close to its chairman's heart:

> The Levée discussed the opportunities afforded to boys of saying their prayers. All were of the opinion that a time should be set aside after the final silence-bell to enable boys to say their prayers, if they so wish, and it appeared that this system was generally in existence. The suggestion that there should be a 'Close' Time when all boys

must be in their studies and when they can be quiet before going to bed and possibly read their Bibles, – was not accepted. The Levée were on the whole of the opinion that those who wish to read their Bibles will – and should be encouraged to – do so.

J. R. W. Stott[89]

Floreat Rugbeia ('May Rugby flourish') is the title of the school motto. It was a phrase with which John had had difficulty in his capacity as editor of *The Meteor*:

I once received a letter for publication from Pat Rodger, who preceded me as head of the school and has recently retired from being Bishop of Oxford. In his letter he bemoaned the decadence of the school and signed his letter *Florebat Rugbeia* (meaning, 'Rugby once used to flourish'). I immediately assumed that this was a misprint and changed his signature to the school motto, *Floreat Rugbeia* ('May Rugby flourish!'). I thus entirely missed the subtleties of the Latin language, much to Pat Rodger's chagrin.[90]

The words also serve as the title of the Rugby School song, printed (with an English translation) in the school hymn book, and sung in chapel at the end of the school year:

Thank heavens! the holidays are here;
Studies are over and we're ready to go home.
Home will be glad to see us as School to get rid of us.
Everyone sing Floreat Rugbeia![91]

If it was used to conclude the summer term of 1940, John would have made his farewell to Rugby singing:

... for the moment let us take a holiday.
We are not yet lawyers or bishops ...

The 1940s

SIX

Cambridge in Wartime: Iwerne Minster

1

The University of Cambridge expressed its preparedness for twentieth-century hostilities by the particularly English announcement that no more recruits would be accepted for the horsed troops of the OTC cavalry squadron.[1] In October 1939 the number of freshmen was the highest for twenty years;[2] war had been declared on 3 September, but for many months it seemed to the civilian population something of a phoney war. In the spring of 1940 Basil Willey, Fellow of Pembroke College, was on holiday with his family in Devonshire when he heard the news that Hitler had invaded Denmark and Norway:

> ... I suppose I was more innocent of world-politics and military strategy than most people of my age and education, for I received this news with blank astonishment. Denmark! and *Norway!* My amazement and horror were mingled with a touch of admiration for the audacity, the scope and the brilliance of our common enemy ...
>
> May and June 1940 were months of miserable foreboding. Holland, Belgium, and finally France collapsed; what next? What could be left except the invasion of Britain itself?[3]

There was considerable concern that Cambridge, one of the first of the smaller cities to suffer, might become a principal target for enemy air-raids. The summer term ended suddenly in the fear that imminent invasion might mean 'the mass capture of the undergraduate body':[4]

> ... Term came to an end with an abruptness probably unparalleled since the sixteenth century when the studies of the place were liable to interruption from intermittent visitations of the plague ... By Tuesday the Colleges were virtually empty except for their non-academic residents, and patient dons, wrestling with examination papers.[5]

These fears were by no means unfounded. Hard on the heels of the Dunkirk evacuation came the Battle of Britain:

> ... That summer and autumn the threat of invasion lay over England as it had not done since Napoleon's Grand Army camped on the French coast a hundred and forty years before. But it never came. Fighter Command won the Battle of Britain and the navy did not lose control of the Channel. The blitz would go on night after night through the first half of 1941 but it quickly ceased to be part of an invasion plan. Britain had survived the fall of France and, led by Churchill, was now obstinately committed as a nation to nothing short of victory – in the circumstances a superb but seemingly impossible goal ...[6]

It was therefore to a Cambridge very different from the pre-war University that John Stott was admitted among the reduced intake who went up in October 1940; in the 1930s less than 2% of eighteen-year-olds went to university: now it was even less.[7] War was being waged in earnest; numbers in residence were already declining (though supplemented by medical students and others from colleges and hospitals in the London area). The city itself received many evacuees, adding some 12,000 to its population.[8] Brooke Crutchley of the University Press described some of the new arrivals:

> ... Cambridge quickly filled with mothers and children from the East End of London, various fighting units such as the Northants Yeomanry (they had recently exchanged their horses for small armoured cars and took advantage of the similarity of front and rear ends to drive the wrong way down one-way streets), fighter pilots training at nearby airfields, Bedford and Queen Mary Colleges and the Bartlett School of Architecture from London, the staff of the

Royal Society and the Masters in Lunacy; in a short time the population of the town had increased by half.[9]

In the following months eight or nine colleges gave accommodation to the RAF Initial Training Wings: Queens' housed Bart's Medical School; Christ's the London School of Oriental Studies. There was an RAF Transport Unit in King's, and many other colleges – including Trinity – had civil servants and the regional officers of various ministries. As the war progressed, Cambridge was to become home, often for short periods at a time, to various detachments of Dominion, Colonial and American forces.[10]

By comparison with what was to follow elsewhere, bombing proved to be only slight. In June a four-hour raid demolished a row of houses on the east side of the town with some loss of life. At the start of the October term John Stott's friend Philip Tompson, who had just come up from Rugby to Emmanuel, wrote home to his parents in Surrey:

Cambridge has yet not been much harmed by raids. One or two bombs have been dropped near the station, but the varsity has so far escaped harm. We have a warning nearly every night, but they are usually of pretty short duration, with very frequently no planes at all to be heard. However the whole sky is full of every sort of machine, especially those used for training purposes, during the daytime, and the place is thick with RAF men, mostly undergoing training. It is they who occupy at least a portion of a great many colleges, and we are therefore provided with a civilian pass in case we want to visit any college where they are partly in occupation.[11]

In common with the rest of Britain the black-out meant that after dark very little could be distinguished: no street lamps or lighted windows, but sometimes enough welcome moonlight to reveal the paths across the cobbled courts and the shadowed doorways. Elaborate air raid precautions, including shifts of fire-watchers patrolling roofs against incendiary bombs, were in place in every college. ARP shelters and static water tanks could be found in unlikely places. Surface water mains ran along the pavements of King's Parade, with pumping engines by the Backs. A. S. F. Gow, a fellow of Trinity, had begun in September 1939 a series of 'letters from Cambridge' to members of the college away on war service. His letter dated a few days before the start of the Michaelmas Term recorded cement-mixers and piles of gravel outside Trinity Great Gate, sandbag defences around the Porters' Lodge giving way to concrete ('whereas it was previously believed that they could withstand high explosives, it now seems improbable that they can be removed without them'), and the changed appearance of King's College Chapel:

> ... King's, who have been gradually taking the stained glass out of their Chapel at a cost of £75 per window, have desisted, leaving only four out of twenty-six windows, the rest being partly plain glass but mostly boarding. I suppose they were wise though I sometimes wonder what they will do with the windows if the Chapel is demolished.[12]

At Trinity, John Stott was one of only 136 'freshers' taking up residence, as against over 200 the year before. Food was already rationed, the weekly butter ration 'the size of a domino', wrote Basil Willey, 'and the sugar about as much as some (such as I) would normally have used up in one day':[13]

> ... Colleges responded to food shortages by abolishing feasts, cutting dinner by a course, and charging students a lump sum for full board. At Trinity the charge was initially 30 shillings a week, 25 shillings if you breakfasted at lodgings on your own rations. By 1942 this had risen to 35 shillings. Staff were short by then, and the Steward was reduced to trying to recruit undergraduates to peel vegetables in the kitchen at 1s.3d. per hour (apron included). The response was predictably meagre.[14]

Trinity itself, the creation of King Henry VIII, was then (as it is still) the largest and wealthiest college in either Oxford or Cambridge. Great Court extends over two acres of ground, and the architecture of Chapel, Gatehouse, Hall, Master's Lodge and rows of staircases looks for the most part much as it did in Tudor times. To the newcomer, a first impression is overwhelming:

> The big first court of Trinity College – the great quad – is one of the loveliest sights in Cambridge, or any other university town for that matter. The gateway is pushed into the crowded jumble of Trinity Street, with shops, and neighbouring college fronts, and – in the 1930s – ordinary houses unevenly and bustlingly bundled together, so you aren't prepared for the sudden opening of the huge courtyard into sheer space, the great expanse of turf, the high, plain chapel facade on your right, the long, modest terraces of staff and student rooms making up the other three sides to the square.[15]

And there is more to come: hidden away in cloistered seclusion behind Great Court lies 'Wren's great library beside the river, with its cool colonnading and slender arches'[16], the Backs, Trinity Bridge, the Avenue and the Fellows' Garden. Even in wartime, it was a sight to lift the heart.

John Stott's rooms were not in Great Court, but across Trinity Street in F4, Whewell's Court. This consisted of three subsidiary courts, familiarly known as 'the billiard table', because of its rectangular open lawn; 'the Garden of Eden', because of its luxuriant fig-tree; and the 'spittoon' (where John Stott had his rooms) because of its central drain. Here, on the first floor of a small block, he had a bedroom and sitting room (with a tiny 'Gyp room' or kitchen) which, as a scholar, he was able to retain for the whole of his four years in Trinity. His immediate impressions were a little daunting. 'My room is on the first (top) floor of Whewell's Court as you approach from the Great Court end,' he wrote home:

> When I first went into it I was rather distressed at its darkness and rather drab atmosphere, but everything's looking much more cheery now that I've bought some furniture, pictures etc. Unfortunately the paint on doors and window-frames and skirtings is BLACK!! but the Clerk of the Works says the whole room will be redecorated during next vac. should I want to stay. He says the stonework (round the windows) will be painted white, cream or lemon as will all wood-work.
>
> Soon after I arrived I went to see the Clerk of the Works who, I was told, would supply me with any furniture I required. But he is an elusive gentleman, and it was only after my fourth call that he responded by coming to see me himself. While he was a prisoner in my rooms I wrung him dry of all he had practically, and I've managed to wheedle off him a settee, bookcase, pillow, carpet, standard lamp, curtains, dressing-table mirror – and 2 new arm-chairs (in exchange for my present ones which are crimson!). – When his promises become kind I should be well set up.[17]

Whewell's Court, in Anthony Salvin's Gothic style, dates from the 1860s and is one of those Courts best described in the words of a wartime guide to Cambridge as 'fortunately so situated that the sightseer can easily avoid looking at them'.[18] Life at Trinity, whose size and academic distinction had made it 'a university within the university' had been faithfully described by an undergraduate of 1891; and in its essentials did not differ greatly in the 1940s from his recollections of fifty years before:

Great social freedom reigned at Trinity; and this seemed to me to be less true of the smaller colleges, it was I suppose partly due to our size. By social freedom I don't of course mean freedom from reasonable college discipline, but that we were free from the social tyranny of any one set of people or of any one kind of tastes. The eminent cricketers and oarsmen did not rule the college; they were merely one set among others, whom many of their fellow undergraduates did not even know by sight. Conversely of course this was equally true of the future Prime Ministers and Astronomers Royal. There is another important respect in which Trinity differs from some other educational institutions, and that is in the preeminence enjoyed among us by young men of comparatively mature mind. The head boys of the great public schools came up to Trinity already better trained in mind, and with wider interests than many so called educated men. By the time they had reached their third or fourth year they were already making themselves felt as men of character and intellect, and were creating throughout wide circles of the college, something of the atmosphere of an adult society.[19]

At the time of this account J. J. Thomson, a fellow of Trinity, was Cavendish Professor of experimental physics. He became Master of his college as the First World War ended, the last to hold the post by life-tenure, 'and died in the Lodge when the Battle of Britain was raging overhead'.[20] Alone among Cambridge colleges, the Master of Trinity is appointed by the Crown, acting on the advice of the Prime Minister of the day. Contrary to expectations, and in the midst of his conduct of the war, Winston Churchill proceeded with the appointment and chose the historian G. M. Trevelyan. Trevelyan's daughter wrote:

> ... When the old Master, Sir Joseph Thomson, died, the Trinity dons had felt inclined to ask to have the mastership left in abeyance 'for the duration', as the Vice-Master, Winstanley, was perfectly acceptable to them as acting Master and Winston's choice might not be so. George [Trevelyan] agreed with this view, but 'wisest Fate said No'. Churchill absolutely refused to postpone an appointment, and after consulting with Baldwin offered it to George. The dons urged him to accept and he himself felt that it would be ungracious and even 'cowardly and lazy' to refuse.[21]

In the Easter vacation of 1941 (and again in 1942) Trinity acted as host to the IVF annual conference, which had been forced to change its venue at short notice when the Hayes, Swanwick, was commandeered as a prisoner-of-war camp. Oliver Barclay, himself an undergraduate member of the college at the time, provides this small footnote to history:

> Rationing created a rather hilarious scramble to feed 150 people in the Guildhall on a diet of vegetable Cornish pasties! [Dr. Martyn] Lloyd-Jones gave a memorable Presidential Address on the raising of Jairus's daughter (Lk. 8:41–56). He focused on verse 53: 'They laughed him [Jesus] to scorn, *knowing* that she was dead' (AV), emphasizing the limitations of human knowledge and the power of Christ. The Master of Trinity, the historian G. M. Trevelyan, who was not a believer, attended and greeted Lloyd-Jones at the end with: 'Sir, it has been given to you to speak with great power.'[22]

John Stott's tutor was Patrick Duff, a classical scholar whose subject was Roman Law: Duff's father had been a fellow of Trinity when Arnold Stott was an undergraduate. Though Duff came to be regarded by some as over-conservative, there was no disagreement over the acuteness of his critical faculties; *The Times* recorded that 'he served his college in due course as tutor, senior tutor, and dean of college with imperturbability, balanced judgment and conscientiousness'.[23] In John Stott's last year in Cambridge, Duff was appointed Regius Professor of Civil Law; and for twelve years was vice-master of Trinity: very little happened in the college of which he was unaware.[24] He was a strong supporter of the college Chapel, and a staunch friend through difficult times.

Lecturers, even in the early days of the war, presented an unusual variety. 'Thursday is a completely free day as far as *lectures* go,' John Stott wrote home after a fortnight of term:

> Apart from lectures, we are expected to do 2 essays (sometimes 4), 2 proses and 2 translations (one in each language) a week. The lecturers are a varied crew. There is a sweet, plump German master, scented and bombastic; a rather cheaply humorous stutterer; a sinister, beetle-browed scholar; a jovial, benevolent red-face, and a second-hand, very orthodox drawler, whose monotonous drone is soporific to the nth degree. They are, as I say, a varied crew, – entertaining and mostly good teachers.[25]

It was a very male society. Newnham and Girton were the only women's colleges of the University, though women students were also about in Cambridge from two Colleges of Education, Homerton and Hughes Hall, and from some London colleges in their wartime quarters.

John Stott's first letter home described how he had lost no time in joining the college First Aid squad – a particularly appropriate body for a conscientious objector from a medical family:

> It's a very select body (pom! pom!), and I'm lucky to get in. About a fifth of those living in college do some sort of war-work: fire-fighting, first-aid, stair-case marshals, roof-watchers or messengers. I was very lucky because I volunteered before we were asked to and consequently am a first-aid-post dresser (with no previous experience!) and not a common or garden stretcher-bearer! We have 2 lectures a week, but I don't think we are going to be made to report when sirens go, until bombs start dropping. We're on duty on alternate weeks.[26]

Later letters describe a stretcher-bearer practice under the eye of a St. John's sergeant 'very comic – a dapper little man with a chocolate-coloured moustache'; and 'a long lecture on the structure of the human body – blood circulation, digestive system, etc. and my mind is a chaos of capillaries, gut, kidneys, plasma etc.'[27] His father must have been amused.

Among John Stott's undergraduate contemporaries were many friends from Rugby or from camp. There was one in particular whom Bash had asked him to keep an eye on, John Sheldon, a professing Christian and son of a clergyman but in much need of help and encouragement. From Repton he had been once to camp, but seemed to be making little spiritual progress. On his first evening in Cambridge John Stott was outside Great Gate when he spotted someone in the dense blackout whom he thought (for no reason either can remember) might be this John Sheldon. It was a lucky guess, and the beginning of a strong and lasting friendship. In the freshers' tennis tournament – postponed until the first week of November because of bad weather – John Stott and John Sheldon were partners in the doubles. 'We beat our opponents fairly easily, largely (as you will have guessed!) because John Sheldon is quite a champion! Yesterday, however, we met our match ...'[28] At John Stott's suggestion they began to meet regularly once or twice a week to read the Bible together (just as with Peter Melly at Rugby) and to go together to meetings of the university Christian Union. Again, at John Stott's instigation, John Sheldon began to come to camp regularly as one of the undergraduate leaders ('camp officers' was the accepted term). In due course John Sheldon went forward for ordination; he and John Stott trained together at Ridley Hall and have maintained a lifelong friendship. John Sheldon's recollections of John Stott at Trinity convey something of the intensity of his developing discipleship during that first year in Cambridge:

He was always meticulously dressed, and very disciplined about time, always going over to Hall at exactly the right moment. I often sat with him in Hall, meeting at 12.55 and seeing him return to his books at 1.45 as regular as clockwork – he was working 9 or 10 hours exactly every day. We often read the Bible together in his rooms in Whewell's Court: 'This is what we find in this passage, isn't it?' he would say. Jesus Christ so captured John that almost everything he said and did even in those early undergraduate days pointed to Him. If I hadn't been able to laugh and 'hoot' with him I would have found his witness and his life too much for me, too convicting; I could never live up to that![29]

It was during these early days at Trinity that John Stott began to cultivate the habit of early rising that was to stay with him all his life. He would set his alarm for 6.00 a.m. (later in life it became 5.00 a.m.) giving himself an hour and a half for quiet time and Bible study before crossing Trinity Street and Great Court, his head buried in *The Times*, for breakfast in Hall at 8.00.

2

The university Christian Union, properly called the Cambridge Inter-Collegiate Christian Union, was always known by its initials, CICCU, pronounced 'Kick-you'. It traces its formal origin back to 1876, but its early roots to the ministry of Charles Simeon, an undergraduate of almost a hundred years before. As Fellow of King's and minister of Holy Trinity Church, Simeon spent his whole life in Cambridge, and his mark is on it still.[30] For most of its history the CICCU has been the largest and most vigorous of Cambridge's many religious societies. Firmly evangelical and interdenominational with a strong missionary emphasis, its biblical and theological principles became stronger and more distinctive as those of the Student Christian Movement 'became still more comprehensive, more inclined to accept liberal opinions, as much concerned with debate as with prayer'.[31] C. N. L. Brooke, the historian of the university, describes its early days:

... CICCU was always evangelical in spirit, but not narrowly so: it appealed to a wide variety of churchmen, and it related to a wide range of religious activity. Some of it found a home in the Trinity master's lodge, where Montagu Butler held highly successful Bible meetings, some in the Henry Martyn Hall, built for the University Church Missionary Union in memory of a great Cambridge missionary in 1886–7, soon the home of CICCU too.[32]

John Stott himself was to find the history of the CICCU, especially in its relationship to the SCM, sufficiently significant to recount some of the story in his book *The Cross of Christ*[33] (seeing in the centrality of the atonement, objectively understood, one of the great watersheds of Christian doctrine in every generation):

> ... CICCU members were conscious of standing in the tradition of Bilney, Tyndale, Latimer, Ridley and Cranmer, the great names of the Cambridge Reformation. They also looked back with pride and affection to Charles Simeon, who for 54 years (1782–1836) as Vicar of Holy Trinity Church had faithfully expounded the Scriptures and, as his memorial plaque testifies, 'whether as the ground of his own hopes or as the subject of all his ministrations, determined to know nothing but Jesus Christ and him crucified'. It is not surprising, therefore, that they were becoming increasingly disenchanted with the liberal tendencies of the SCM, and specially with its weak doctrines of the Bible, the cross and even the deity of Jesus. So when Tissington Tatlow, General Secretary of the SCM, met CICCU members in March 1910, the vote to disaffiliate the Union was taken. The following year Howard Mowll (later to be Archbishop of Sydney and Primate of Australia) became President of CICCU and helped to establish it on firm evangelical foundations from which it has never been moved.[34]

After the First World War ended in 1918, many ex-servicemen went up to Cambridge as students. CICCU by now was much smaller than the SCM. Yet the SCM leaders (notably Charles Raven, the Dean of Emmanuel) made overtures to the CICCU, hoping that they would re-join and supply the missing devotional warmth and evangelistic thrust. To resolve the issue, Daniel Dick and Norman Grubb (President and Secretary of CICCU) met the SCM committee in the rooms in Trinity Great Court of their secretary, Rollo Pelly. Here is Norman Grubb's own account of the crucial issue:

> After an hour's talk, I asked Rollo point-blank, 'Does the SCM put the atoning blood of Jesus Christ central?' He hesitated, and then said, 'Well, we acknowledge it, but not necessarily central.' Dan Dick and I then said that this settled the matter for us in the CICCU. We could never join something that did not maintain the atoning blood of Jesus Christ as its centre; and we parted company.[35]

By the time John Stott went up to Cambridge, membership of the

CICCU was less than 250 in a university of some 4,000 undergraduates, and was to drop still further as the war progressed. That shrewd observer Max Warren was vicar of Holy Trinity, Cambridge: looking back on those first months of the war, it was his later conviction that the country had 'trembled on the brink of a religious revival. It only just did not happen'.[36] Amid the difficulties of war-time Cambridge, the life of the CICCU continued, if not with any remarkable experience of revival, at least with 'the general position more secure than for decades past':

> ... The Union's work continued, quietly but with lasting effect. 'From my own generation,' wrote one wartime president ten years later, 'I can think of many converts doing first-class work now'; and the names he could list included those of three missionaries, six doctors, two university lecturers, a schoolmaster, two research scientists and two engineers, and three clergymen, 'all brought to Christ through the ordinary course of the CICCU's activity.'[37]

It was a life-style into which John Stott threw himself wholeheartedly from the first. He was to find that the issue of the centrality of the cross of Christ – and the offence of the cross – had not changed over the years; that 'no man can preach Christ crucified faithfully, and escape opposition and persecution':

> ... It was when I was an undergraduate at Trinity College, Cambridge. Only recently I had come to Christ myself, and now – clumsily, I am sure – I was trying to share the good news with a fellow student. I was endeavouring to explain the great doctrine of justification by grace alone, that salvation was Christ's free gift, and that we could neither buy it nor even contribute to its purchase, for Christ had obtained it for us and was now offering it to us gratis. Suddenly, to my intense astonishment, my friend shouted three times at the top of his voice, 'Horrible! Horrible! Horrible!' Such is the arrogance of the human heart that it finds the good news not glorious (which it is) but horrible (which it is not).[38]

Such rebuffs were bound to be daunting for one who was still comparatively young in the faith. Looking back from the vantage point of almost fifty years John Stott later paid tribute to what the fellowship of the Christian Union had meant to him as an undergraduate fresh from school:

I sometimes wonder on which particular scrapheap I would be today, if it had not been for God's providential gift of the UCCF. For I went up to Cambridge a very wobbly and vulnerable young Christian. I could easily have been overwhelmed by the world, the flesh and the devil. But the Christian Union brought me friendships, teaching, books and opportunities for service, which all helped me to stand firm and grow up. I am profoundly grateful.[39]

But Bash's weekly letters, and the opportunities of leading the Rugby meeting and sharing in the work of camp, had laid good foundations, and he found in Trinity a slightly older friend, Oliver Barclay, who was able to offer him some stimulus to his Christian thinking in fields where Bash and the camp circle had less to offer. Because they were members of the same college, they were often together:

> ... Oliver and I met frequently at college prayer meetings, sat next to each other for meals and both sang in the college choir. We often walked round and round the Great Court of Trinity or along the Backs or in the Trinity Fellows' gardens, 'trying to solve all the problems of church and state' ... We were both pacifists and had conscientious questions about Christian participation in war.[40]

Oliver Barclay was in no doubt about John Stott's contribution to the life of the college CICCU group:

> John Stott made an immediate impact when he came up as a Fresher. In the first term two of his contacts professed conversion and his contribution in the rather small College group of about ten was very helpful. He was a skilled personal worker in evangelism and in helping younger Christians.
>
> He was a very disciplined man of prayer and used to insist on leaving meetings early – I think it was 9.30 – so that he could get to bed and get up in time next morning for his Quiet Time. He would walk out of a lively discussion at the stroke of 9.30 ... He never dominated those he helped. He just took time to read the Bible and pray with them and give them friendship.
>
> At the same time he was beginning to go bird-watching. He and I used to go out some Saturdays on bikes to a sewage farm and elsewhere in the Fens and discuss theology. I do not remember that we saw many interesting birds but it got us out of doors with time to talk.[41]

Besides the bird-watching, music continued to attract him. Within two or three weeks of his arrival, he was taking part in the Freshers' Concert of the University Musical Club – their 1057th concert, arranged by Henry Chadwick[42] whom John Stott had met at camp, then in his second year reading Music at Magdalene. John again sang his favourite Somervell airs, with Chadwick accompanying him: 'Loveliest of Trees', 'White in the Moon', and 'On the Idle Hill of Summer'. Years later, looking back on this occasion, John Stott remembered it as his last concert appearance. Although he had sung solos regularly both at Oakley Hall and at Rugby 'my amateurish performance convinced me that I should no longer regard myself as an acceptable soloist'.[43] Nevertheless he continued to allow himself to be persuaded from time to time, but always in the cause of the gospel. Visiting local village churches during his training at Ridley Hall he would sometimes sing 'I heard the voice of Jesus say' or 'My song is love unknown'; and at camp too (perhaps with Henry Chadwick again accompanying him) he could be persuaded to sing 'sacred solos' on a Sunday afternoon. At St. Peter's during his curacy he followed the example of the senior curate, Geoffrey Lester (known as 'the singing parson': Bishop Hensley Henson gave guarded approval to his singing in the pulpit in Cromer Parish Church[44]) and occasionally sang a solo at Morning or Evening Prayer. He also bought a piano-accordion to accompany the singing at the open-air evangelistic services which were held in different parts of the parish on Sunday evenings. It took him a little time to discover that it is not only sacred music which can be sung to the glory of God; by the time he was curate, his camp-fire 'skits' and comic songs were an essential part of the weekend camps for parish youngsters, but he had had to think himself through to this position. At Iwerne, before his ordination, it was a different story:

> Mark Ruston and others tried to persuade me to sing an item during the 'Last Night entertainment'. I replied, prompted by Bash, and with horrid piety, 'Take my voice, and let me sing always, only, for my King', to which Mark justly retorted who I thought he and other performers sang for! I clearly hadn't yet got the dualism of sacred and secular sorted out.[45]

At Cambridge he continued to work at his cello through his first two terms and even to arrange lessons. 'I was very glad to hear that your lessons had started,' his mother wrote in January 1941 to a Cambridge frostbound under ice and snow, 'and that you think the man is good ... I hope you are managing to practice every day – with a tuning-fork it should be possible in your rooms without a piano.'[46] But he soon found that music had to give way to the pressures of study and Christian work. By the following term he had ceased to play the cello, and gave away his instrument to Rugby School – not without occasional later regrets.

With Oliver Barclay he would sing in the choir of Trinity College chapel on Sunday evenings before dining in hall and going on to the CICCU evangelistic sermon in Holy Trinity, Charles Simeon's old church. On Sunday mornings he would sometimes make his way down Hills Road to St. Paul's, and once or twice to sit under Graham Hobson at the 'Round' Church of the Holy Sepulchre. Academic life was interspersed with fire-drills, ARP training, and occasional night-long vigils on the roof of Trinity chapel. But the greater part of his time as an undergraduate was divided between reading for his degree (with the hopes of his tutor, his parents and himself set on a First), the help he could offer to and derive from the CICCU, and his work for camp. He took half-an-hour's brisk walk for exercise (he played almost no games) and allowed himself by way of recreation to skim briefly through *The Times*. John Collins, who was to become John Stott's first deacon, was in Cambridge fresh from Haileybury, doing a short course with the RAF. He had rooms in Clare Memorial Court, between the University Library and the Backs. Morning by morning he would watch John Stott make his way through the Court to the Library, striding purposefully, gown flowing behind him: 'One could set one's watch by him.'[47]

Sundays were different: and apart from church, college chapel and the CICCU, each term would include one or more visits to some school Christian Union, which had links with camp. Bedford was one such school which received regular visits, since it could be reached from Cambridge in time for a meeting before lunch, even on the much-reduced wartime Sunday train timetable. A sixth-former recalled one such meeting in June, 1941:

> I had only been a personally committed Christian for a few weeks. Like the other C.U. speakers I had heard, John [Stott] came over to me as one who seemed to know Jesus personally and who loved Him. They were all such happy, free men with a deep, sincere and very clear Christian message. I was drawn to them in a way that I could not have explained at the time. I knew instinctively that here at last was the Christian message as I had always felt it must be – somewhere ... All this hit me during those summer months at Bedford School as I recognised a common 'something' in the lives of certain boys at the school and, above all, in these C.U. speakers that we heard week by week. John Stott typified them all. He was real. He cared for us boys. He was honest about our questions. What struck me about him also struck my parents who one day invited him to lunch. They found him very attractive.[48]

Many undergraduates attended the meetings, Bible-readings and evangelistic sermons which CICCU organized without ever becoming members; and John Stott himself never accepted membership:

> My father said to me before I went up, 'When you get to Cambridge, you will find an organisation called ...' and then he fumbled, and I think called it the Cambridge Inter-Collegiate Christian Mission, or something like that – but went on to say 'Don't join it: a lot of anaemic wets', that was his phrase; so I said to him 'All right, I won't, if you don't want me to'. So I never did join the CICCU, but I went to most of their meetings.[49]

The technical matter of 'membership' could probably have been waived to allow for his leadership and guidance of the Union by attendance at its Executive Committee, but Oliver Barclay, President at the time, had the wisdom to see that while John Stott could always be available for consultation over matters of policy, choice of speakers and so on, his time was better spent out of committee rather than in it:

> John Stott was a student from 1940 to 1945 and already showed unusual gifts. The CICCU Exec., however, had the sense to send one of their number to tell him that they would not invite him to join the next committee as they believed he should be free from committee meetings. They wanted him to get on with the evangelistic and pastoral work in which he was exercising an outstanding ministry. As the Exec. met for a whole evening and a substantial time of prayer on Sunday morning each week, as well as involving members in a range of other obligations, this was a sensible policy. It illustrates the fact that the real work of the CICCU was often not carried out by officials or committees. The whole effectiveness of the CICCU depended on the fact that a high proportion of ordinary members, both then and in almost all periods of its history, were active in personal evangelism and in helping one another in every way. The committee were very much looked up to and their example was influential; but they were not the CICCU ...[50]

Oliver Barclay was two years older than John Stott. He came from a well-known evangelical family, and was himself the son of CMS missionaries. His father, J. Gurney Barclay, had worked in the family bank for a number of years, intended for fast promotion to a senior post, but had instead responded to the call to serve God on the mission field. After some years in Japan he returned home in 1926 to become Far East Secretary of CMS.

For his undergraduate years Oliver had rooms in Great Court; and then stayed in Cambridge to work for a PhD. Basil Atkinson regarded him as one of the great CICCU Presidents:

> No account of the CICCU in wartime would be complete without a reference to the presidency of Oliver Barclay ... He had come up in 1938 and was one of the few people in the country who obtained at the local tribunal absolute exemption from conscription, as a conscientious objector. I was present at the hearing of the tribunal and was able to note the respect paid by the chairman to his character and to his name, associated for so many generations with godliness, Quakerism and pacifism. He was left free to do what he liked in the certain knowledge, as the chairman actually said, that it would be something useful. And so it was. He went on after his degree to valuable scientific research.[51]

Although drawn to read English (from a love of modern poetry – Eliot and Auden – at school) in fact Oliver Barclay chose to read Natural Sciences with a Part II in Zoology, and for most of the four years that he and John Stott overlapped at Trinity he was working for his doctorate on the mechanics of walking in animals. His childhood faith had failed him in his teenage years; but he was brought back to a personal commitment to Christ in his last year at Gresham's School through Frank Houghton, the CIM missionary (and later bishop), the uncle of a school friend. But it was the CICCU that helped him towards a firmly conservative view of biblical authority through the Saturday night Bible-readings and the friendship of other CICCU men in Trinity:

> Before the first year was over I had been brought to a confidence in the reliability of Scripture (which had all sorts of practical consequences), the beginning of an understanding of Christ's death and the dawning of an ability to explain the gospel to my friends. In this process the college Bible studies and the Saturday expositions were very important.[52]
>
> By the time Stott arrived I was orthodox though I had to think hard before signing the Basis to join the CICCU Exec. I was at first amazed to meet very intelligent young people who believed the Bible to be fully inspired and reliable. I had thought that was only the old and unthinking.[53]

Another formative influence in the Cambridge of the 1940s was John Wenham, the remarkable curate of St. Matthew's. John Wenham was some eight years older than John Stott, and had been one of Bash's camp officers from the early days of the 1930s in the Isle of Wight. At this time he was working for a London BD, and serving as part-time curate of St. Matthew's, 'probably the ugliest church in Cambridge'.[54] John Stott would occasionally speak or preach in the parish. On one occasion he was asked to take as his theme the Last Things, working from the Scofield Reference Bible[55] which Bash had given him and which is marked by a strong emphasis on dispensational theology and the literal fulfilment of an earthly millennial kingdom: 'I gave a straight address: that Christ was coming in the clouds, that the Rapture would take place, there were the seven years of tribulation, a thousand years of millennium, and then the great White Throne ...' John Wenham, who had already read theology for part of his Cambridge degree, was horrified 'and showed me the error of my ways'.[56]

In his developed thinking, John Stott would later attribute to the dispensationalist teaching of J. N. Darby and others, popularized in the Scofield Bible, the emphasis on a future 'kingdom age' which contributed to the neglect by many evangelical Christians of a sense of Christian social responsibility wider than personal philanthropy. His *Issues Facing Christians Today* cites this as one of five reasons for 'the Great Reversal'[57] in which evangelical Christians 'mislaid their social conscience':

> Fourthly, there was the spread (specially through J. N. Darby's teaching and its popularisation in the Scofield Bible) of the premillennial scheme. This portrays the present evil world as beyond improvement or redemption, and predicts instead that it will deteriorate steadily until the coming of Jesus, who will then set up his millennial reign on earth. If the world is getting worse, and if only Jesus at his coming will put it right, the argument runs, there seems no point in trying to reform it meanwhile.[58]

It might well have been John Wenham who introduced John Stott to the massive two-volume biography of Hudson Taylor,[59] a missionary classic which proved formative in shaping the committed discipleship of many young men and women of the time. Bash himself was guarded in recommending this biography, finding its portrayal of overseas missionary work (when his own strategic vision was to this country) rather over-whelming; but of the influence of the book there can be no doubt. John Wenham himself sold the two volumes from the camp bookstall to a young David Bentley-Taylor, who was to become one of the most distinguished among the later generation of missionary leaders in mainland China.[60] It was after reading them during a vacation from Cambridge that Shirley Johnson of the Overseas Missionary Fellowship (later Mrs. Bill Lees) 'told the Lord I would be a missionary if that was what he wanted'.[61]

Fifty years later John Stott reflected on what he had learned from Hudson Taylor's life and work, portrayed in these 1,100 pages:

> I can still remember the impact which was made on me, as an undergraduate at Cambridge University in the forties, when I read *Hudson Taylor: The Growth of a Soul* and *The Man Who Believed God*. Hudson Taylor's example challenged me, then as a student, and later as a pastor, to a greater and a wiser faith. He has always seemed to me to exemplify a robust, reasonable and realistic faith. He taught me four important aspects of Christian faith.
>
> First, faith rests on God's faithfulness. I remember reading that Hudson Taylor liked to render Jesus' command 'have faith in God' (Mark 11:22) with the words 'reckon on the faithfulness of God'. This paraphrase, although not exegetically exact, is theologically correct ...
>
> Secondly, faith is the trust of a child. God is not only the Faithful One, but our Father too through Jesus Christ ...
>
> Thirdly, faith is as necessary in the material realm as in the spiritual, that is, when needing money as much as when seeking converts. One of Hudson Taylor's best-known aphorisms was 'God's work done in God's way will never lack supplies' ...
>
> Fourthly, faith is not incompatible with the use of means. On his first voyage to China in 1853, the vessel in which Hudson Taylor was sailing was caught in a severe storm, off the coast of Wales. He had promised his mother that he would wear a life-belt. But when the captain ordered passengers to wear them, he felt it would be a sign of unbelief and thereby dishonouring to God. So he gave his away. But as he reflected on his action, he came to see his mistake. 'The use of means,' he wrote, 'ought not to lessen our faith in God, and our faith in God ought not to hinder our using whatever means he has given us for the accomplishment of his own purposes.'[62]

John Stott's commitment to his academic work left all too little time for Christian reading, since even Sundays tended to be busy days with church, college chapel, and the CICCU. One reason why friendship with Oliver Barclay and a few others was important was the need to wrestle with the intellectual challenge of an uncompromising evangelical faith; in Oliver Barclay's case from the scientific standpoint at a time when science was widely believed to have discredited many aspects of biblical belief. Like many another, John Stott regularly visited the second-hand book shops of Cambridge, and especially David's Bookstall in the market-place, where there could sometimes be found out-of-print titles by more conservative scholars. Works of evangelical piety have never been in short supply; but studies whose primary appeal was to the mind in the expounding and defending of biblical evangelicalism were hard to find, even at a fairly popular level, in wartime Cambridge.

John Stott recalled his problems over this when addressing the Christian Booksellers' Association Convention in Dallas, Texas, in 1992. After a reminder of the Boston Tea Party of 1773, he paid tribute to the work of the Inter-Varsity Press and its strong and positive influence in the whole post-war resurgence of evangelical faith and life. He told them:

> When I was an undergraduate at Cambridge University in the early 1940s (a vulnerable and immature evangelical believer, beleaguered by liberal theologians), there was no evangelical literature available to help me. In those days one had to ransack second-hand booksellers for volumes like A. H. Finn's *The Unity of the Pentateuch,* James Orr's *The Problem of the Old Testament,* R. W. Dale on *The Atonement* or works of the Princeton divines. But there was virtually no contemporary evangelical theology and IVP had not yet come into existence.[63]

To say 'IVP had not yet come into existence' was technically correct, but the Inter-Varsity Fellowship had published its first booklet in 1928, and Ronald Inchley had been appointed as Literature Secretary (combined with other duties) in 1936. Astonishingly it was agreed in 1939 that he should seek other work since the funds of the Fellowship could not support a married man![64] The entire range of IVF publications up to that time comprised little more than a small series of booklets, a Bible Study course entitled *Search the Scriptures,* an early history of the Fellowship[65] and three or four other books, of which *In Understanding be Men* and *Why the Cross?* were to form the mainstay of the CICCU bookstall well into the post-war years.[66] But in the early 1940s, war-time paper shortages limited all book production, and the Literature Committee of the Inter-Varsity Fellowship was meeting only occasionally, with its sights chiefly set on plans and policies for after the war:

> The department as such was put into mothballs. Existing stocks were transferred to the CSSM and Scripture Union Bookroom which agreed to act as trade agent for the duration of the war. With paper likely to be severely rationed it was thought that little more than a holding operation could be attempted as far as production of new titles was concerned.[67]

When, in his final years John Stott moved from Modern Languages to Part I of the Theology Tripos, the need for evangelical academic research and scholarship was acute. A 'Biblical Research Committee', which included John Wenham in its membership, had been set up by the IVF in 1939. Four years later their work bore fruit in Cambridge with the purchase of Tyndale House (bought from a relative of Oliver Barclay's 'at a very reasonable price', and with help from John Laing) as a residential centre and library for biblical studies. J. N. D. Anderson (later Professor Sir Norman Anderson) was the first full-time warden on his demobilization at the end of the war.[68] When he arrived to take up residence, Henry Chadwick was chaplain of Queens' College and living in Tyndale House, where he had already begun to collect the nucleus of the library.[69] Not long after that Major W. F. Batt ('Bill Batt') was in Cambridge for a CICCU mission; he and Norman Anderson had not met before, and went for a walk together to get acquainted. The war was not long over; they were both still comparatively young; they naturally talked about what the future might hold for them. Norman Anderson recalled how for Bill Batt 'his future was quite clear; he was a big farmer but he did a great deal of Christian work. I told him – I was at Tyndale House – that I didn't know what the future held for me. He told me later that God gave him a burden of prayer for me, and he used to pray for me every day. Where I would be apart from that, I really don't know ...'[70]

John Stott sat the Preliminary Examination in Modern and Medieval Languages, Part I, in the summer of 1941, the end of his first year. Twenty-three 'Firsts' were awarded, with his name among them.[71] On the day the *Reporter* carried the class-lists, his tutor wrote to congratulate him:

From P. W. Duff
Tutor
Trinity College
Cambridge   14th June 1941

Dear Stott,
Congratulations on your First, with almost exactly the same marks in every paper. You got 83 for each French paper, 81 for German Translation and 84 for German Composition. I am afraid I do not know where the First Class line was drawn, so that I cannot tell how far you were above it.

Yours sincerely,
P. W. Duff

P. S. This entitles you to a college prize of £4 in books from Deighton's.

P. W. D.[72]

3

With the academic year so satisfactorily concluded, the Long Vacation provided a welcome opportunity to put aside his books for a little, and give his attention to opportunities for Christian outreach. Bash's camp had now found a permanent holiday location at Clayesmore School, originally the home of a wealthy ship owner, in the tiny Dorset village of Iwerne Minster between Shaftesbury and Blandford. But first, before camp started, there was the opportunity to gain a different kind of experience in Christian work under Bash's eye. In the summer vacation of 1941,[73] and again in 1942, John Stott (with Oliver Barclay and John Sheldon) agreed to join the team of helpers at the CSSM[74] 'Beach Mission' at Borth on the Welsh coast, a few miles north of Aberystwyth, before moving on together to prepare for the summer camp at Iwerne. Beach missions were the original means of outreach adopted by the CSSM. With a team of young and enthusiastic workers, they attracted children who were on holiday with their parents; and by means of 'Special Services' with a sand pulpit on the beach and a range of innovative holiday activities they sought to make the gospel of Christ a reality to children who might have no background of Bible teaching in church or Sunday School. Many Christian leaders have paid tribute to what they learned as helpers in such mission teams. Max Warren,[75] one of the most influential missionary statesmen of the century, summed up his own experience of a similar CSSM beach mission on the south coast:

> To that joyful comradeship of young men and women, overflowing with enthusiasm for Jesus Christ, I owe my life-long conviction that true religion is essentially joyful, precisely because it has for its basis the unwavering assurance of the utter trustworthiness of Jesus. That indeed was the heart of the message, communicated day after day from the beach pulpit at Eastbourne as at many another seaside resort. The message was given with great simplicity. No doubt the simplicity was often very naïve, yet it was completely sincere and behind its delivery lay a great deal of private and corporate prayer. On the basis of such a very simple evangelical religion my Bible reading acquired what it had so far lacked, 'the warmth of desire', a warmth and enthusiasm which have grown down the years.

Writing in 1927 from Nigeria to his future wife Mary (who had shared with him the leadership of the Eastbourne CSSM) he added: 'It's easy to think of the mission field as a C.S.S.M. It's absolutely nothing like it though the experience of C.S.S.M. is probably the best preparation in the world for the actual task ahead.'[76]

The Borth CSSM began in the first week of August. It was under the joint leadership of Bash and Oliver Barclay, the latter assuming sole responsibility for the closing days of the mission after Bash and John Stott had left for camp. The team of young 'missioners' found that the house next door to their lodgings was occupied by the writer J. B. Priestley, whose 'Postscripts' broadcast by the BBC following the nine o'clock news on Sunday evenings in the early days of the war, had made his name a household word and his voice, 'rumbling but resonant',[77] immediately recognizable. His daughter used to come to the Beach Services; and he could often be seen as the sun went down over the sea, smoking his pipe, deep in thought, walking back and forth on the edge of the tide.

From his final year at Rugby, and increasingly throughout his time at Cambridge, John Stott became Bash's right hand man in the administration of the camp work. Bash had been running such camps for ten years before the move to Iwerne Minster; but he was by no means the first in the field. Baden-Powell held his first trial camp for developing 'Scouting' in 1907; but camps for schoolboys – and perhaps particularly camps run under Christian auspices as a way of sharing the gospel of Jesus Christ – had been established long before that. The word 'camp' continued to be used even when such ventures were no longer under canvas. There was a Scottish 'camp' for girls in 1907 at a school near Lilithgow ('most comfortable inside and the playing fields are excellent'). 1908 saw the first Crusaders' Union camp, and a variety of camps for schoolboys helped to gather in the harvest during the First World War. Soon the CSSM was running a series of 'holiday' camps, some in tents and some in boarding schools; and in 1924 the title 'Varsities and Public Schools Camps' was formally adopted. Six years later, as chaplain of Wrekin, Bash ran his first camp under their auspices at Seaford, and not long afterwards became a regular member of the CSSM staff. From the first, his were seldom canvas camps, though at Eastbourne in the summer of 1930, the campers slept in bell tents in the grounds of St. Andrew's, a local prep school. Wilfred Burton, the Quartermaster, remembered that 'Bash, in true fashion soon obtained a bed locally!'[78] Equally, the 'semi-military discipline' of the early post-1918 days quickly faded; though remnants of it lingered in names and titles into the 1970s and 80s. 'Camp officer' was the accepted designation of the leaders; catering remained in the hands of a 'Quartermaster'; there was an Adjutant ('Adjy'), and Bash himself was often known as 'Commy' (for Commandant). Such jocular titles continued by force of habit and tradition, long after any military connotation was forgotten.

From 1930 onwards, Bash's camps were increasingly distinguished from other similar ventures to a degree that justifies Richard Rhodes-

James' description of him as a pioneer in the field, and lies behind the assessment that 'he was beginning to put an entirely new stamp on boys' work'.[79] There were several elements to this 'new stamp', or indeed, new vision. First, in Bash's thinking, was the conviction that the privileged young people whom he sought to win for Christ through his camps were the future leaders of the country. Secondly, he had seen at first hand the 'public-school religion' of his day, and was convinced that, no doubt with splendid exceptions, it was failing the boys it sought to serve. John Stott himself is a good example of how regular attendance at all the outward observances of a school which genuinely believed its chapel to be the centre of its life could still leave boys unevangelized, with no understanding of the call of Christ, or of how they might respond. Inevitably Bash's vision attracted opposition:

> Such reasoning is open to, and has been exposed to, much criticism from two quarters, from Christians and from egalitarians. The Christian response has often been: the gospel knows no class distinctions, every man is as valuable to God as any other. Indeed, to quote scripture, 'God is no regarder of persons'. To which Bash would reply with that quiet assurance that could at once mollify and frustrate, 'Yes. Of course ...'
>
> The egalitarians, and this included both Christians and non-Christians, attacked from another angle. Public schools were undesirable; they were divisive and bred arrogance. If you had to run camps for public schoolboys, why not mix them with boys of humbler origin so that they could see 'how the other half lived'? Bash stood absolutely firm on this. His camps were not a social exercise. They were a spiritual battleground in which a particularly difficult battle was in progress. The boys must be placed in an atmosphere in which they could feel at ease with people they understood, with a range of activities that caught their interest and imagination. It was a highly specialised operation whose success could be jeopardised by attempting to do too many things at once. Bash believed in concentrating on the spiritual objectives with a single-mindedness that not everyone could always understand.[80]

Bash therefore looked for an equally single-minded loyalty from his co-workers; he was prepared to take the long view, and to give his life to the building up of the work entrusted to him. He had come to see, with great clarity, the suitability of the camp principle as the best means, under God, to present the gospel to the public schoolboy of his day. It offered the chance, in place of random unconnected sermons, to set out in ordered sequence, and in language suitable to his hearers, the gospel of the Scriptures and their plan of salvation. Moreover the chance to do this took place under the leadership of young men, themselves committed to Christ, who exemplified in their own fellowship the truths they taught; and who in their assorted gifts and characters (not least as games-players, but also as musicians, naturalists, photographers and so on) were attractive role models to the campers. It is to be doubted if Bash ever read a work of sociology, or spoke of 'peer group pressures' and the like; but he knew very well from his own observation that the boys he served were most relaxed and open among their own friends; and that, however dearly they loved their families, personal religion was often easier to face squarely and consider seriously away from home and parents.

Not only did Bash seek to ensure a high proportion of officers to boys, but he developed a highly-systematized pattern of pastoral care. The leader of a dormitory group would be directly responsible to get to know and befriend the small circle of boys, all much of an age, who came directly under his responsibility. There would be older leaders, and Bash himself, ready to help and advise and to see that all went smoothly. Younger dormitory officers would serve an apprenticeship as assistants to the more experienced, speakers at prayers would be carefully groomed, ruthlessly criticized, and (above all) knew themselves prayed for as they stood up to give, for twelve or fifteen minutes, a 'camp talk' at the simple morning or evening prayers. Such talks followed a carefully ordered pattern, presenting within a Trinitarian framework the call of Jesus Christ as living Saviour, the sinfulness of the human heart, the meaning of the cross, the cost of discipleship, the way to discover 'life at its best' by turning to Christ as Saviour, Friend and Lord. Then in the second half of camp the themes would move from evangelization to nurture, to equip those who had received Christ to begin to follow him and to grow in their new-found life and faith.

It was to this work that John Stott's vacations (for camp took place at Christmas and Easter, as well as in the summer holidays) and his limited spare time at Cambridge were committed. Bash's standards were high, and it was no light task. Nigel Sylvester, International Secretary of the Scripture Union, offers a glimpse of the thoroughness which pervaded every aspect of the preparation and planning, a thoroughness increasingly attributable to John Stott himself:

The camps themselves were meticulously organised ... Bash insisted on a high ratio of officers to boys, so that every activity could be properly organised and every boy given suitable pastoral care. The officers were carefully recruited and thoroughly trained. Most of them had come through the camps as boys, others had been converted at university and first arrived as 'senior campers'. Those who did not reach his high standards or were not prepared to make Iwerne Minster their top priority were advised to use their talents elsewhere. Every part of the camp operation was finely tuned to achieve its purpose of attracting the boys and winning them for Christ. But the style was relaxed and informal. Bash had a horror of intensity, believing that spiritual commitments made in a highly-charged atmosphere, by teenagers at any rate, were unlikely to last. He knew the value of well-timed humour, and used it to help boys to relax and think through issues calmly. Perhaps that is one of the reasons why so many of them continued as Christians into adult life.

Another reason was without doubt the care Bash took for the boys who were converted ... This patient nurture continued after a boy left school and was part of a clear long-term strategy. If he showed leadership potential, a boy was invited back to camp as a 'senior camper' or junior officer, and was gradually given more responsibility. Those who went on to university were encouraged not only to join the Christian Union but to attend a weekly camp prayer meeting. Bash himself visited Oxford and Cambridge nearly every term.[81]

Oxford and Cambridge contained many of the leaders of the work – the 'camp officers', often themselves converted to Christ as schoolboys through the work of camp. But it was to the public schools that camp looked as its mission field. Bash was always quick to encourage suitable men to return to the schools as members of the teaching staff, ambassadors alike for Christ and for the camp work. The pattern was readily discerned by contemporary observers, sometimes critically, sometimes with respect:

> All the major public schools were reached by the careful, thoughtful and dedicated work of the Iwerne Minster Camps represented by 'Bash' and his assistants. Their follow-up work was outwardly very low-key but meticulous and yielded dividends in the number of committed Christians going into the Anglican ministry and into the professions, notably teaching ... They were not men of straw; by and large, their faith endured – and developed.[82]

It was not only in the pastoral ministry and in teaching that boys helped and converted through the work of camp found their Christian vocation; though their ranks included a number of these, with future headmasters, professors and bishops among them. Some went overseas, perhaps as missionaries; others became doctors, lawyers, politicians, industrialists, musicians, artists or writers. David Sheppard, due to become England cricket captain and later Bishop of Liverpool and life peer, was introduced to this fellowship soon after his own commitment to Christ as an undergraduate at Cambridge:

> ... Some weeks later I joined a Christian house-party for a week. I said to myself, 'I didn't know there were people like this.' I did not mean that they were perfect: they were ordinary young men of my own age who were sincerely trying to work out the friendship of Christ every day. Discussing problems of Christian living and simply sharing a common life with them, and with other Christians in Cambridge, particularly in the Christian Union, made the idea of the Church as the family of God come alive. I know that I would never have begun to grow up in the faith if I had not seen a great deal of other Christians.[83]

Sir Fred Catherwood is another who was introduced to camp as an undergraduate, 'having suffered for five years under the dead chapel religion at Shrewsbury'. Though not without criticism of Bash's attitudes to intellectualism and to 'the distractions of girl-friends', he pays tribute to the fact that in spite of limitations, 'Bash's strategy has been spectacularly successful':

> The success of Bash-Camp was not an accident. Under Bash's gentle, caring, courteous attitude was an iron will. Each camp, we were asked in turn to a tête-à-tête over eggs and bacon in an old-fashioned cottage in the village, while he probed our souls and our plans, and tried to turn them gently and unobtrusively to his own vision.[84]

The war years might well have meant the end of Bash's camp work. He and John Stott had been discussing the future together soon after the outbreak of war:

> ... It seemed that camp, his life's work for God and the Gospel, was at an end. We read Matthew 24 together: 'You will hear of wars and rumours of wars; see that ye be not troubled'. It seemed to be a word from God Himself, that even a major world war was not going to be permitted to disrupt His work ...
>
> So it proved. Far from being the end of camp, the war turned out to be a new beginning. The purely holiday camp became first a

forestry camp and then a farming camp, with parents and school-masters ready to recognise and encourage camp as a contribution which boys could make to the total war effort.[85]

But such changes imposed on Bash an administrative burden which could only hinder his real calling. Up till then the work had been shared among a number of more senior colleagues, but it was made much heavier by the exigencies of wartime, and the large increase in boys attending. To meet the needs of the hour, John Stott very soon began to take over from Bash and others the work of Secretary and Treasurer. His first camp as one of the leaders was summer 1940; aged nineteen and a first-year undergraduate, he was Bash's right-hand man. John Eddison remembers the very youthful Secretary setting about this task:

> ... There is no doubt that John Stott was God's answer to the movement at this time, and to a host of problems. But his immaculate efficiency, his eye for detail and his almost workaholic perfectionism never diluted his cheerful courtesy, a mischievous sense of humour, and above all the tone of his spiritual leadership.[86]

Something of the confidence that Bash reposed in his young lieutenant can be seen in a precautionary note that he wrote and lodged with John Stott at this time. John Stott was not yet twenty; he had been a Christian for just three years, and a camp officer for less than a year. Among Bash's team there were men very considerably his senior, including clergy, schoolmasters and public school chaplains. Nevertheless it was to John Stott that Bash wished, 'if anything should happen to me', to entrust the work to which he knew God had called him:

From The Rev E. J. H. NASH, 10 Craufurd Rise, Maidenhead
Phone 1034

If anything should happen to me, I wish that John Stott shall
assume full and absolute control of the Kippers – Beachborough –
Iwerne Minster Camp. He knows my mind and will guide and
appoint officers as he sees fit.

E. J. H. Nash
30 March 1941[87]

From time to time in the leaders' prayer-meetings at camp, Bash would pray that God would 'raise up a Wesley'.[88] Perhaps he lived long enough to feel that his prayer was being answered.

4

From his first-floor 'office' at Clayesmore, overlooking the lily pond and the croquet lawns, John Stott exercised a benevolent supervision of the administration of every aspect of camp. For much of the day, while forestry and harvesting, games and expeditions, went on around him, he wrestled with the details of accounts and insurance, pay sheets, inventories, lists and timetables. Later Secretaries would be able to do more before camp began and after it had ended: but with the pressures of academic work it was essential to do as much as possible during camp itself. Nevertheless his presence was felt at the daily officers' meetings for prayer and planning; campers who met him in the corridors or sat next to him at meals found that he knew their names (and probably their home addresses and telephone numbers as well). One fifteen-year-old, rather proud of his knowledge of British birds, found himself talking to the Camp Secretary, who quickly discovered a fellow-ornithologist. A moment later John Stott called his attention to bird-song in the distance: 'Listen, there's a Treecreeper'. Somewhat mortified, the boy realized in that moment that he had heard nothing, and that he would not have recognised the song of the Treecreeper had he heard it.[89]

As camp settled into Clayesmore as a permanent base, it fell to John Stott as Secretary to negotiate the use of a vast walk-in cupboard between two rooms as a store for the increasing quantities of camp equipment, and to arrange for the Trinity College workshops to construct vast wooden crates, ingeniously designed to fit the space available. Every activity of camp (games, farming, forestry, expeditions, catering, entertainment, the preparation of the library for prayers and the chapel for Sunday Services) was charted and described in a series of 'white papers' which were handed out at the start of camp to the officer responsible for each department. At the end of camp, they were to be returned to the Secretary, annotated with 'crits. and suggs.' – criticisms and suggestions – so that lessons learned by experience would not have to be re-learned, but could be handed on, and the necessary administration steadily improved. Recollections of John Stott's participation in the light-hearted team games that formed part of camp's recreation are scanty. Indeed, when finally persuaded to turn out and play 'Crocker' (a mixture of cricket and soccer, a kind of tip-and-run played with a baseball bat and a soccer ball) in the 'Camp v. Officers' match, he was forced to borrow a pair of tennis shoes from a colleague, Douglas Argyle. Distressed by their rather grubby condition, he returned them after the match, having cleaned one of the pair to a satisfactory whiteness, leaving the owner to choose between appearing piebald or having to tackle the other!

He was a valued speaker for camp talks and Bible readings, even if he himself recalls them with some embarrassment:

> ... I was a freshman at university when [Bash] first entrusted me with the privilege of giving the Sunday afternoon 'Bible Reading' to senior boys at camp. Though I blush when I remember some of the naïve and even downright erroneous notions I taught, I can never be thankful enough that Bash pushed me into the deep end to sink or swim.[90]

And again:

> ... It was Bash's genius to try and trust people whose gifts maybe he perceived, in order to give them opportunities to develop their gifts; looking back, he gave me responsibilities that were far beyond my maturity; I really hadn't begun to understand principles of interpreting Scripture, but God gave me through Bash a love for the Bible ... I got a Young's Concordance very early and I used to look up words and follow them through the Bible.[91]

Whatever may have been the shortcomings of those early expositions, some who heard them retain vivid memories of a room full of schoolboys who had chosen to attend the afternoon Bible reading; and of a youthful John Stott's 'outstanding gift for capturing and holding the attention of his hearers'.[92] After tea on Sunday afternoons Bash would invite a few older campers, and any officers who happened to be free, to an informal time of singing in the library, the room used for camp prayers. John would sometimes be persuaded to sing solo – perhaps 'My song is love unknown' or 'Down from his glory', the Salvation Army adaptation of the tune *O Solo Mio* to sacred words;[93] perhaps 'The Lord looked upon Peter' or some Sankey favourite from *Sacred Song and Solos*.[94]

Even while John Stott was still an undergraduate Bash came to lean heavily on his judgment and powers of administration in everything to do with the running of camp. After some long and rather indeterminate discussion at the daily officers' meeting when a variety of views would have been expressed, Bash would sometimes end the discussion with 'A few of us will get together and sort that out' – and the 'few of us' was well known to mean often just himself and the Secretary. Indeed, the Secretary's diplomatic skills were a byword among his colleagues; and very necessary to the smooth running of camp in wartime. Whether it was with anxious parents, harassed railway officials, short-staffed suppliers, irate groundsmen or temporary cooks, it was John Stott who was sent for when it became necessary to appease, cajole, persuade. One sketch at the last-night's entertainment, enjoyed even more by his colleagues than by the campers, had John Stott answering the telephone: 'Yes, this is the Secretary ... my name is John Stott ... yes, STOTT, S for sugar, T for Treacle, O for Olive-oil ...'[95]

It was not always easy to keep more than 250[96] physically active men and boys adequately fed in the midst of rationing and shortages. Bash's letters would urge his officers to 'buy sardines' (before all tinned food was on 'points' later in the war): while to keep the 'Old Firm' – camp's tuck-shop – supplied with buns involved not only the local baker, but daily cross-country transport by rural bus from a baker's in Bourne-mouth. These were a very popular mid-morning supplement to camp rations: the record for one day's consumption seems to have been thirty-six dozen buns among a total of seventy-five people![97] Fuel was another problem: to keep the big house warm during the Christmas camps the Secretary had to arrange for at least four different kinds to be ordered and delivered, including peat from Scotland. Bash wrote at the end of the summer of 1941: 'Camp is one long answer to prayer these days, isn't it?'[98]

When the time came for John Stott to hand over the task of Secretary, just before his ordination in 1945, he prepared a four-page memorandum for his successor divided into 'Before Camp', 'On Arrival', middle, end, and 'After Camp'. 'Before Camp' included such items as school bursar, domestic staff, boiler man, travel vouchers, petrol coupons, ration books, lorries for forestry, laundry, agricultural insurance, hire of chairs, cleaning of swimming pool, dates of arrival, bank facilities – and so on. 'After Camp' included payment of all bills, checking of inventories, thank-you letters, analysis of expenditure and a range of similar items. For a student at Cambridge reading for a First, it was a formidable assignment three times a year. It was not surprising that his father (who had himself failed to get a First) more than once urged him to relinquish camp, and concentrate on his studies.

But to John Stott this was not so much a contribution to the war effort, though the farming and forestry made it that; it was his Christian service. Camp by camp, year by year, he saw boys won for Christ, and built up in their faith. David Watson's experience (a few years later) is by no means untypical:

> Undoubtedly the most formative influence on my faith during the five years at Cambridge was my involvement with the boys' house parties, or 'Bash camps' as they were generally known. Over the five years I went to no less then thirty-five of these camps: two at Christmas, two at Easter and three in the summer of each year. They were tremendous opportunities for learning the very basics of

Christian ministry. Through patient and detailed discipling (although that word was never used) I learned, until it became second nature, how to lead a person to Christ, how to answer common questions, how to follow up a young convert, how to lead a group Bible study, how to give a Bible study to others, how to prepare and give a talk, how to pray, how to teach others to pray, how to write encouraging letters, how to know God's guidance, how to overcome temptation, and also, most important, how to laugh and have fun as a Christian – how not to become too intense, if you like. I also gained excellent grounding in basic Christian doctrines, with strong emphasis being placed on clarity and simplicity. All this was being constantly modelled by those who were much more mature in the faith, and I may never fully realise how much I owe to the amazing, detailed, personal help that I received over those five years. No Christian organisation is perfect, of course; and it would be easy to find fault with a group as powerful and as effective as this one. But if God has given me a useful ministry in any area today, the roots of it were almost certainly planted during those remarkable five years in the camps. It was the best possible training I could have received.[99]

Others were more critical, even while recognizing that what Bash was achieving through camp could not be gainsaid. To those evangelicals who were not members, the camp network of leaders and potential future leaders seemed a formidable structure, into which there was no real means of entry. You belonged or you did not. In that sense – but only in that one – it seemed to have certain of the characteristics of the 'inner ring' so perceptively analysed by C. S. Lewis.[100] John King, not a member of the circle himself, was one of the first to write of the 'Bash camp' group among contemporary evangelicals, paying tribute to some of its strengths. But he went on to say:

> Many 'Bash campers' went from school to Cambridge and became pillars of the Cambridge Inter-Collegiate Christian Union, so that it was possible when the movement was at its zenith for a boy to go from public school to Cambridge, to ordination, to a curacy and to a parish of his own without having encountered the kind of life lived outside those particular circles ...
>
> If the 'Bash camp' movement must be summed up in a word, it must be said that it is too spiritual. Like the IVF, it is based on an over-simplification. It does not give a place to the processes of argument, consultation and independent thought which are essential to any genuine co-operation, inside the Church or outside it.[101]

It was never, perhaps, a wholly fair criticism, as history has demonstrated; John King had just finished a demanding eight-year stint as editor of the *Church of England Newspaper*, and his editorial pen had not been slow to criticize what seemed to him the weaknesses of fellow-evangelicals. Nevertheless, to some at least the cap seemed to fit; camp was not without its critics, and he expresses what a number of them felt about Bash's movement, however much or little they might know about it from the inside.[102]

During term-time, in the half-hours that could be spared from reading for his first-year examinations, the task of Camp Secretary was a daily preoccupation. There was endless correspondence hammered out in his rooms on a portable typewriter; prospectuses had to be printed and circulated, and applications received and dealt with according to a complicated formula devised by the Secretary. This provided different paragraphs of welcome, depending on whether it was a boy's first camp, second, third ... and so on up to eighth ('He is quite an institution now'), ninth ('We look forward to having him – again!'), and tenth. Besides the usual problems of the Cambridge winters ('seagulls on the Backs, chilblains on my person' wrote Gow in March 1941[103]) an array of wartime measures made new demands on Fellows and undergraduates alike. Trinity specialized in ARP practices, with College Fire Parties, First Aid teams, and nightly fire-watching rotas to guard the roofs from stray incendiary bombs. Routine exercises involved dealing with an imaginary fire in Whewell's Court: Whewell's did in fact suffer slight damage from a bomb in Jesus Lane.[104] The Emergency Blood Transfusion Service came to Cambridge seeking donors. Plans were considered to transform the Great Court baths into a Gas Decontamination Station. Sandbags, water-tanks, parades, and queues for almost everything were the order of the day. Bed makers – and set-books – like so much else were in short supply. Clothing coupons were not required for the purchase of academic gowns; Gow wrote in his twenty-fifth letter: 'You will therefore hear with relief that freshmen this October (at any rate) will not be born naked into the academic world.'[105]

Food continued to be a problem. The exclusive Pitt Club in Trinity Lane was taken over early in the war as a 'British Restaurant':

> ... Here 300 war workers and students a day could lunch for a shilling on cold meat and vegetables followed by a simple sweet like date pudding. The city's four British Restaurants together served one and a half million meals before they closed in 1945. Half of these were at the Pitt.[106]

At Trinity, too, a British Restaurant was established, serving similar lunches in Hall to undergraduates from King's, Clare, and London University (with the exception, by special dispensation from the Regional Commissioner's office, of 'metropolitan females').[107] But amidst this turmoil, something of the old Cambridge life remained. Harold Nicolson had occasion to pay a visit:

> ... I go round to Trinity, and there to my surprise I find Gerry Wellesley and Anthony Powell. I sit next to the Vice-Master. The lights in hall are shaded but the portraits are still lit up and the undergraduates in their grey flannel bags are still there. Afterwards we adjourn for port and coffee to the Combination Room. I sit next to George Trevelyan, the Master. I look round upon the mahogany and silver, upon the Madeira and port, upon the old butler with his stately efficiency. 'It is much the same', I say to him. 'Civilisation', he replies, 'is always recognisable.'[108]

It was possible, too, even in the midst of John Stott's busy Cambridge life, to find time for his abiding interest in birds. The 'great news' of his letter home at the start of the summer term was not of lectures, examinations, first-aid courses, Camp or CICCU:

> The GREAT NEWS is that a Black Redstart is nesting either on the top of Trinity Chapel or on one of the John's buildings next door!! I gather that the Black Redstart was chosen as the Cambridge Bird Club tie-design because it only breeds very, very seldom in Britain though nearly always in Cambridge. The joke is that the pair which visits Cambridge is becoming more and more refined ... ! Four years ago it bred on Marks and Spencer's! The year after it rose to a local cinema. Last year it didn't come, but by a supreme effort it has selected one of the college buildings (I think it's Trinity Chapel) as its nesting site this year. It only breeds otherwise on Canterbury Cathedral, Westminster Abbey and one or two other places. It makes an amazing noise, like the rattling of stones together or the buzz of an electric machine when the current is suddenly turned on.[109]

In June 1942, the end of his second year and two months after his twenty-first birthday, John Stott was again among the fourteen Firsts in French for Part I of the Modern and Medieval Languages Tripos; but dismayed to find himself getting no more than a 2.1 in German: 'I took it badly because it was the first time I had ever failed anything in my life ... I was very upset about it.'[110] Nine Firsts were awarded. Patrick Duff wrote a letter of consolation:

Dr Stewart says he is quite sure you are really a First Class man, but that you have not enough self-confidence for examinations. You have not been elected to a Senior Scholarship, but your Entrance Scholarship has been prolonged.[111]

Perhaps the long hours as Camp Secretary had taken their toll: though only for someone confidently thought of by the college as 'a First Class man' could a 2.1 be reckoned a disappointment. By this time, however, it was clear that John Stott would not continue with the Medieval and Modern Languages Tripos, but would begin instead to read Theology.

SEVEN

Towards Ordination: 'An Instinctive Pacifist'

1

At the outbreak of war, 3 September 1939, John Stott was almost eighteen and a half and about to begin his final year at Rugby. By mid-October he had 'attested' at Birmingham, unaware that by this act he was technically enlisting in the army and committing himself to military service when he should reach the required age. He had been a Christian for a year and a half; and was moving, with very little instruction or advice, to a position he would later describe as that of an 'instinctive pacifist':

> When the war broke out I was a very immature Christian … I had now read the Sermon on the Mount for the first time, with its commands not to resist evil but rather to turn the other cheek and to love our enemies. It seemed to me impossible to reconcile these injunctions with war. Nobody introduced me to the 'just war' theory or helped me to balance the biblical arguments. Bash was a pacifist himself, more perhaps on pragmatic than on clear doctrinal grounds, but he was no propagandist and did nothing to influence me.[1]

At home for the school holidays, John Stott wrote to the War Office on Christmas Eve 1939, to try to clarify his position. As matters stood he knew that God was calling him to train for the ordained ministry; and also that in the normal course of events he would find himself called up to serve in the army before completing his first year at Cambridge. The War Office replied on the last day of 1939 to say that until such time as he was definitely committed to a course of studies as a theological student he would remain available for posting to a Training Unit at the age of twenty. They added 'If in the meantime you become a Theological Student your case will be considered afresh.'

It was clear to John that if he was determined not to fight, only two roads were open to him: and both were complicated by the fact of his attesting only three months before. The first, and by far the simpler, was to seek to secure exemption as someone already committed to train for ordination before the start of the war. But even here, at this early stage of the war, the exact regulations were not clear-cut or easy to determine. The other alternative would be to take advantage of the provisions made for conscientious objection. In the case of a young man not already enlisted this would mean going before a local tribunal as Oliver Barclay had done. Such a tribunal might dismiss his application, or register him as a conscientious objector either for non-combatant duties in the armed forces or for specified work of a civil character, often in a hospital or on the land. Though such conscientious objectors were in general treated with much more understanding than during the First World War, nevertheless in the public mind considerable stigma, however unjustified, attached to the conscientious objector. Some who had failed to convince an unsympathetic tribunal served prison sentences; and on release were liable once again to be conscripted, prosecuted for failing to comply, and again imprisoned.[2]

Grim though this prospect must have appeared, it was highly unlikely that even these provisions would be available in the case of a man who had once attested, and now sought exemption on conscientious grounds. He would be under military discipline and his position made – to say the least – extremely difficult. Following the letter from the War Office John arranged to visit Cambridge later in the school holidays to obtain an interview with the Principal of Ridley Hall, his chosen theological college. The Principal, the Revd. J. P. S. R. Gibson, advised him that to be an accepted ordinand he should be in touch with a bishop, and so under the wing of a particular diocese. Rugby, where John was still at school, was in the diocese of Mervyn Haigh, Bishop of Coventry, who had confirmed him at the school a few years before. Accordingly John wrote to Bishop Haigh at the start of the January term. Haigh replied, offering to see him, with a view to arranging his provisional acceptance for ordination in the Coventry diocese, but saying:

> ... It is news to me that candidates for Ordination (other than
> conscientious objectors and medical rejects) will be excused military
> service, unless they were already established in a course of training
> and accepted as candidates *at the time that war broke out*. I think
> that you must have been misled by somebody. It may be that the
> Government will take a different view, but as far as I know only
> those who were accepted as candidates and had started on their
> training at the time war broke out, will be excused.
>
> Further, there is of course the moral problem whether a young
> fellow who has not begun his training for Ordination ought to
> regard himself as justified in not doing military service at a time like
> this and in a struggle like the present.[3]

Haigh had himself been ordained less than three years before the start of
the First World War. His biographer says of him that during the early
years of that war 'like all young clergymen of the time, he was restive and
fretful to serve as an Army Chaplain'.[4] By 1916 he obtained diocesan
permission to do so, serving until 1919 in German East Africa. It was not
therefore surprising that he should want to confront this young Rugbeian
with 'the moral problem'.

Some further letter-writing, seeking advice both from Bash and from
Paul Gibson as to how best to respond to the bishop's letter, resulted in a
request to Haigh 'provisionally to accept me as a candidate for ordination
in your diocese', but at the same time asking if this could be understood
as something short of a distinct pledge to a particular diocese.
Ordination, after all, could hardly be less than some five years in the
future. The draft of John's reply continues:

> With reference to the moral problem you raise, I do fully under-
> stand what you mean. I have again considered and will continue to
> consider seriously the implications involved; but at the moment I
> am conscious of a very definite call to the Ministry, and in the light
> of this I conscientiously feel that I should go ahead with preparation
> for that, and believe that in the long run I can serve my country
> better in this way. I hope you will understand my position ...[5]

With commendable promptitude, Haigh arranged to see John in
Rugby, calling at the Headmaster's house to do so on the afternoon of
February 7th; the following day his secretary wrote to John saying that,
following the interview, the bishop wished to be in touch with John's
mother (his father was out of the country on active service); and also to

make further enquiries through the Bishop of Manchester[6] (acting for the bishops in negotiations with the government) about the possibility of exemption. It sounds as though John had been able to impress upon Haigh the sincerity of his conviction. On the same day Haigh wrote to Lily saying that he had seen John and was fully prepared to accept him as an ordination candidate, while leaving the way open for John 'to change his mind later on while he is at the University'. Bishop Haigh continued:

> He also understands that as the Government regulations stand at present the acceptance of him by me as an ordination candidate does not carry exemption with it from military service, and he is more than ready to leave that question until it has to be faced later on. I assume, also, that if and when he is able to finish his two parts of the Tripos at Cambridge, it would be possible for him to go for, say, at least a year to a Theological College in order that he might pass the General Ordination Examination and have some post-graduate study.
>
> Before writing to him formally in this sense, I naturally should wish to know that I have your good-will and concurrence in so doing? He assured me that I should have, but I ought to have it from you personally as his mother; and I should be grateful if you could tell me that you can safely speak on behalf of his father. I should be writing to his father but I know that he is in France. I understand from the boy himself that his father is, not unnaturally, a little uncertain and possibly rather disappointed about the way his inclination is tending, but I gather he would take no exception to my doing what I propose to do?[7]

Such a letter must have brought into very sharp focus a family tension which was to remain with John and to become more and more distressing for some years to come. His father was not at all in favour of John's hopes to be ordained. It would bring to nothing, in his eyes, the high hopes he cherished for his son. John was already distinguishing himself as head boy of Rugby; and showing a gift for modern languages that augured well for a successful and worthwhile career in the diplomatic or foreign service. One of Dr. Arnold Stott's housemen was a guest at the customary House Physicians' dinner party in Harley Street a few months before the war and in the course of conversation asked Dr. Stott what his son planned to do in life when he left school. 'I have never forgotten his reply to a point which obviously affected him very deeply'; Arnold Stott made uncomfortably clear his sense of disappointment and resentment 'that John should want to go into the *church*' – with an indescribable emphasis on the final word.[8] No doubt in his heart of hearts he hoped that this offering for ordination would prove to be 'a phase', something John would 'grow out of'. The thought of John accepted by a bishop and in touch with a theological college was a cause of frustration and resentment, just at a time when it was seldom possible for father and son to talk together.

But more serious, because more immediate, was the question of exemption from military service. Arnold had served with distinction in the First World War, and was even now in France, rising through the senior ranks of the RAMC. Joanna, John's elder sister, was doing war-work as an Inspector of Factories; Joy was in uniform in the ATS.[9] To a patriotic soldier of that generation there was something deeply shaming in the thought of a son, already older than some of the wounded soldiers passing through Arnold's field hospitals, who was seeking to evade the plain duty of defending his country in her hour of peril. Memories of the treatment of conscientious objectors in the first war, the white feathers, the terms of imprisonment, the ostracism and misunderstanding, must have made such a course unthinkable to a father already disturbed and disappointed by John's new commitment to the Prince of Peace.

Lily replied to the bishop's letter, saying that she was forwarding it to her husband who was 'on the eve of starting on a tour visiting base hospitals, and letters may therefore be delayed'. She went on to say:

... My husband and I both feel (and John agrees to this) that the boy should keep an open mind as to his career until he has taken his tripos at Cambridge.

We should prefer that he should not be committed in any way until then – not even the moral commitment of which you speak.

SERVICE is the greatest urge within him and his standard of Christian duties is very high – but he is young, very impressionable and sensitive above the average. We feel that he should be free for some time yet.

You may have heard that we had planned a diplomatic career for him. He has a flair for modern languages and other qualities which we thought suitable. There seemed also great scope for the 'urge' which I have mentioned.

Parents, I realize, must always be ready to adjust themselves to the developing child. We are keeping an open mind and wish John to do the same for the present. Later – we know that his mature choice will be the correct one.

As regards military service and the oath about which he was worried – thank you for clearing this up for him. It is as I thought

– the study for ordination compares with the study for the medical profession. It has to be well advanced for it to rank as reserved occupation for the candidate. I feel that I *can* voice my husband's opinion now in saying that we are extremely grateful for your very kind interest in John. I remember his confirmation vividly – also your talk to unworthy parents – Believe me – he is very worthwhile![10]

Meanwhile, John was writing to his old school chaplain, O. R. Fulljames, then serving as a naval chaplain in Liverpool, to ask him to act as one of the referees required for acceptance as an ordinand. Fulljames was 'only too glad to accept such a responsibility', adding 'I believe a great many should feel the call quite early.'[11]

Towards the end of February, Mervyn Haigh wrote twice further to John to tell him the results of his enquiries. It began at first to look as if the exemption John was seeking would fall within the government regulations. The bishop wrote:

More quickly than I expected I have now heard that the Government is prepared to regard as persons in Reserved Occupations Ordination candidates who had matriculated – or passed an examination exempting them from matriculation – at the time war broke out. Might I know whether, as I imagine, you had passed such an examination before war broke out, and if so in what form?

I have still not heard further from your mother telling me that your father concurs in what she said to me.[12]

But even as this letter was written, Arnold in France was receiving Mervyn Haigh's earlier letter, sent on by Lily. He replied in categorical terms both to his son and to the bishop. On hearing from him, Mervyn Haigh wrote again to John at Rugby:

Just when I thought your case had been satisfactorily settled, I have received a letter from your father, in which he says – 'I am in entire agreement with my wife's letter to you, and my wish is that you do not accept my son provisionally as a candidate for Holy Orders at the present time. I am most anxious that he should take no step with regard to his future career until he has taken his degree at Cambridge.' In these circumstances I do not see how I can take any definite action …

As I told you, the Bishop of Manchester would have been prepared to send in your name for consideration for exemption from service, but in the circumstances I shall have later to tell him that I cannot go further in the matter.

I will not reply to your father's letter until I have heard from you again.[13]

John too had received a letter from his father. In the painful story of the differences between father and son, which unfolds over a period of years both at Rugby and at Cambridge, it is possible that something of this sadness, anxiety and estrangement could have been avoided had they been able to meet more often, and talk face to face. Arnold's letters at this early stage are full of affection ('My dearest Johnnie' ... 'I love getting letters from you' ... 'your loving Daddie'). One such consists of four closely written pages in a minute hand, addressed from the Headquarters, Dieppe Sub-Area, of the British Expeditionary Force. Following affectionate greetings, the letter continues:

> The Bishop of Coventry wrote to Mummy, as I expect you know, and she sent on his letter and her reply with which I entirely agree, and I am writing him in the same sense. I feel very strongly that it would be a mistake to be accepted *now* as a candidate for ordination. As the Bish. says, altho' this would not really commit you, it does commit you morally not to change your mind 'except for obviously good reasons'. That practically means that you are deciding on your future before you are 19 and while you are still a licky ['little'] school boy! Surely we decided some longish time ago now that no decision would be taken until you've done your 3 years at Cambridge? Why all this hurry? There's no *need* for any decision now. The question of oaths and military service doesn't arise for, as I think you know by now, theolog. students like medical and many other students have to be well advanced in their studies to get exemption. The idea of *wanting* to avoid milit. service hasn't and couldn't enter my mind. In any case you won't have to register till you are 20, when you would be in your first year at Cambridge and I think they let you finish your first year. I doubt very much if the war will last as long as that.
>
> You said in your first letter 'I want to make the most of my education and talents and live the best and most useful life I can.' That sums up very well my wishes and hopes for you. I have long realised you have grand talents, character and wonderful possibilities of being useful for your fellow-man. I feel I have a great responsibility in helping you to do what is best, and I intend to do all I can. That is why I have been so anxious that no decision is made until you are older and more experienced. Will you in the next months be

thinking over, and discuss with Mr. Slater and the H.M. and others, what you should do at Cambridge. I suppose the Modern Languages tripos is in 2 parts. Should you take both, or only part I and then some other tripos – if so, which? In that connection I want to say this. Even if I was more wholeheartedly in favour of your entering the church, I should be very much against your beginning theology, in your second year. I feel v. strongly that you'd make a better clergyman, or schoolmaster, or both, with the longest possible general education first, giving yourself an oppor-tunity of developing a broad outlook and knowledge of the world.[14]

The letter concludes with a further page of fatherly advice: John should keep an open mind, consider doing something quite different before ordination, perhaps aim eventually at a headmastership. 'Don't worry,' his father says to him: 'All will be well in the end ... do all you can to widen your outlook and attain wisdom!'

A further exchange of letters with Bishop Mervyn Haigh made it clear that in the light of Arnold's refusal to agree, he could not consent to register John (still a schoolboy, and a minor) as a candidate for Holy Orders. John digested his father's letter, and on Easter Sunday 1940, writing from Rugby, he set himself to reply to it with (he told his father) 'some trepidation'. The heart of the letter is a plea that his parents should not 'stand in his way'. He writes:

I see the need of the world and it's my very great ambition to serve the world in some way and to meet that need. I feel daily more convinced that it is by ordination that I can best fulfil God's purpose for my life. I'm writing to ask if you will trust me and my judgment sufficiently to ... allow me to have my name put on a list of provisional ordination candidates now.

The letter as we have it is a draft, and there is now no way of knowing how close a relationship it bears to the final letter actually sent. But in the draft John bares his soul:

I want to put before you as never before in my life (and I hope never again) my really sincere and rational appeal: ... *please* do let me go ahead with my desire which is so like the desire you had at my age to be a doctor! I *am* unhappy because you treat me as a child ... and I feel dreadfully thwarted ...[15]

So the issue continued unresolved into the summer and John's last term at Rugby. Correspondence with Patrick Duff of Trinity, who would be his tutor, appeared to confirm that when the time came exemption from military service was unlikely. On a more domestic note, and presumably at his father's suggestion, John asked about rooms out of college, perhaps prompted to do so by Arnold's recollection of being ill in Trinity thirty years before. Duff replied:

> The Junior Bursar tells me you have asked for rooms out of College. This he would be quite willing to arrange, since the great majority prefer to be in College, and he is always glad of extra rooms. On the other hand, as your Tutor, I should like you and your father to reconsider the question. If you live out of College, you miss a good deal, and cannot make the contribution you ought to make to the life of the community. If your father is influenced by the horrors of being ill in College in his day, you can assure him that things are very different now. There is an excellent nursing-home [in Cambridge], a sick-room in College to which men less seriously ill can be moved, a W.C. on almost every staircase, and a trained nurse who visits three times a day anybody who is ill in his rooms. The decision rests with you and your father, but I should like you to consider these points before definitely settling the matter.[16]

Before leaving Rugby, John committed to paper his thoughts, as far as he could collect them, on the issue of 'Why I am unable to believe that I, as a Christian, am at liberty to fight'. It seems to have been the culmination of various pencil jottings over the previous few months, and survives attached to yellowing newspaper cuttings from *The Times* and the *Daily Mail*: 'Hate is indispensable to victory' – the words of Mussolini – are underlined in ink; and the cuttings record a broadcast by Moscow Radio: 'Your duty is to hate the Germans with all the power of your souls ... let the flame of your hatred burn the enemy to cinders ... Do not forget Comrade Stalin's order to you: You must hate the enemy with all the power of your being.'[17] For a schoolboy, even a boy of nineteen, this personal memorandum indicates the seriousness with which John considered the question. Eight reasons are listed, supported by biblical proof-texts from a dozen books of the New Testament. They touch on commandments such as 'resist not evil'; questions such as 'Is it to the glory of God?'; and the example of Jesus: 'Can you imagine JESUS fighting?' he asks himself. 'Yes,' he replies, 'did He not drive out the merchants from the temple? He would be righteously indignant and angry – as He was then.' And he continues:

> I can see Him standing up openly, defying the wickedness of the Nazis and condemning their unbelief, to show men His holy hatred

of sin. But I cannot see Him thirsty for their blood, crouching behind some bit of cover, shooting them down as they approach. I can see Him bringing all Germany to an end for their sin. But I can see Him doing the same to England ('for there is no difference …').

The final phrase is a reference to Romans 3:22–23: '… for there is no difference: For all have sinned and come short of the glory of God …'

There it seems the matter rested through the summer holidays, busy with camp; and through John Stott's first term in Cambridge. But as that term came to an end, the correspondence is renewed. It is clear that John Stott had sought a further interview with the Principal of Ridley Hall, Paul Gibson, who had asked him to furnish evidence which the Bishop of Manchester as Chairman of CACTM could use in seeking exemption for him. John Stott wrote to Hugh Lyon, his former headmaster, asking for a letter which could be sent to the Bishop of Manchester; and also to Mervyn Haigh, the Bishop of Coventry. Haigh had last written to him (according to the surviving correspondence) in April six months before, a kind and pastoral note:

Dear Stott,
I am sorry that you are passing through such a difficult time, but if I were you I should not try to press your father unduly at the present stage of things, but go foward believing that somehow it will work out all right.

Yours sincerely,
Mervyn Coventry[18]

Eight months later, a fortnight before Christmas, John Stott wrote to the bishop from the family home near Guildford to say that he was finally in a position to apply for exemption from military service as a committed ordinand:

Woodlands Farm House
12. xii. 40
My Lord,
You will, I expect, remember that you saw me in Rugby on February 7th 1940, preparatory to accepting me provisionally as an ordination candidate and sending my name through to the Bishop of Manchester. You will also, I expect, remember that you did not feel able to do this in the end because my father then wished me to

take no step with regard to my future career until I had taken my degree at Cambridge.

Since then, after much thought and discussion, I have decided to apply for exemption from military service, being honestly convinced that I can, in the long run serve my country better in this way – that is, by continuing uninterrupted my Cambridge course in preparation for ordination. My father has consented to this. By that I mean that he is willing now, although he does not altogether agree with my decision, to give me a free hand.

Not wishing to trouble you in what must be terribly distressing times for you I have seen the Principal of Ridley Hall, who has kindly offered to send my name through to the Bishop of Manchester. Before doing so however, he would like me to furnish him with evidence of my sincerity.

I am therefore taking the liberty of asking you if you will be good enough to send me a formal letter (which the Principal of Ridley Hall can then send through to the Bishop of Manchester) stating (1) that I informed you in January 1940 of my intention to take Holy Orders and (2) any other information you may feel able to give as evidence of my sincerity.

I remain, my Lord, your obedient servant.

John R. W. Stott[19]

The Bishop of Coventry wrote without delay to the Bishop of Manchester, asking whether John Stott could now be brought within the amended regulations of the Government, and enclosing evidence from Hugh Lyon, the Headmaster of Rugby; Paul Gibson, the Principal of Ridley Hall; O. R. Fulljames, his former school chaplain; Patrick Duff, his tutor; John Burnaby, senior tutor of Trinity; and from Bash, confirming his suitability for ordination, and (where known to them) the fact that he had expressed this intention before war broke out.

2

Because John Stott seems to have come finally to the decision to apply for exemption while he was at home during the Christmas vacation, no correspondence exists conveying this decision to his family. No doubt Lily was aware of it, and probably unhappy about what her husband would make of it; but aware, too, that in response to their son's plea to be allowed to decide for himself it would not come as news entirely unexpected, however unwelcome, to Arnold in France. But if John Stott allowed himself to feel that now the die was cast he would be able to put the matter behind him, he was sorely mistaken; one of the most trying periods of his life was only just beginning. Indeed, it was many years before John Stott felt able to refer publicly to the breach with his father that this decision precipitated. There is a brief allusion to it in an interview he gave in 1974[20]; and again some ten years later in his tribute to Bash as part of John Eddison's symposium:

> ... I mention my own pacifism only because of its effect on my relations with my family and therefore with Bash. My father became a Major-General in the Army Medical Service, and understandably could not come to terms with having a son who was a conscientious objector (although as an ordinand I was given exemption from military service and never needed to go before a tribunal). For about two years he found it virtually impossible to speak to me, and could not make up his mind whether he could continue to support me at Cambridge. Since we were a very united and affectionate family, we all found those years extremely painful. It was because of this alienation from my father that Bash became almost a surrogate father to me.[21]

John Stott seems generally to have found it easier to include personal references both as he grew older, and when speaking to overseas audiences (they are seldom found in his preaching). Nearly ten years after his tribute to Bash he was interviewed for the *Christian Bookseller* and spoke of his father's attitude at this time:

> He really couldn't take having a pacifist son, so he didn't actually speak to me for two years. My mother was very torn, because we were an affectionate family.
>
> When in the holidays I would turn to embrace my father, he would turn away from me. My mother wanted to be loyal to my father while at the same time wanting to be understanding towards me.
>
> She wrote several long letters begging me to join up.[22]

It is not hard to see how such an experience would leave its mark upon a man. Although after the war a better relationship with his father was gradually restored, it was never on quite the same footing of mutual affection and confidence. Looking back, John felt in later life that he had been 'very insensitive in the way I handled it with my parents';[23] and certainly it is not difficult, reading the correspondence that remains, to feel deeply for Arnold Stott, faced with intransigence and what must have seemed perilously like blind wilful obstinacy and self-delusion in his son.

BEGINNINGS

1. Dr Arnold W. Stott, St Bartholomew's Hospital before World War 1

2. John Stott's parents, Arnold and Lily Stott, in the early 1950s

THE
1920s

3. Dr Arnold W. Stott, World War 1

4. On holiday: Nanny Golden with John and Joy

5. Joy and John in Park Square Gardens, 1924

6. *John, Joanna and Joy*

7. *John and Joy: cricket on the cliffs*

8. *John Stott's fourth birthday: a picnic at North Mimms, 1925*

9. *Sports day at Oakley Hall, 1929*

10. At Oakley Hall, 1931

11. Birdwatching with Alfred Stansfeld near Southwold, Suffolk.
John Stott on right with binoculars

12. *Robbie Bickersteth*

13. *Joy, Joanna and John*

14. *Oakley Hall Football XI, 1934. John Stott is on the captain's left*

15. *Summer holiday,*
Germany, 1936

16. *In the quad at Old Kilbracken,*
John Stott's house at Rugby School

17. *Work camp at Whitehaven, 1936. John Stott is on the left of the picture*

*18. As King Richard II, Rugby School play,
June 1939*

19. John Stott's father with pipe and brandy glass in the housemaster's study, Kilbracken

*20. Rugby School: the Close, with the tower of the chapel.
The Memorial Chapel is on the left of the picture*

21. Rugby School: the Memorial Chapel, consecrated in 1922 (Photographs 20, 21 © English Life Publications Ltd)

In these more liberal days, it is easy to overlook the climate of revulsion felt by many ordinary people for the 'conscientious objection' that kept young men – for what seemed high-flown, academic, and sometimes (at bottom) self-centred reasons – from military service. One can picture Arnold Stott's agony of mind: for the good name of the family among his friends and colleagues, for its own internal bonds at a time of his prolonged absence at the call of duty, and for the wrong turning he was sure his son was taking which he might later bitterly regret. No doubt, too, it was all of a piece in his own mind with his son's idealistic and comparatively recent plan to throw up the career for which he had been lovingly educated, and become a minister of religion: 'My father of course didn't draw any distinction between being an ordinand, a pacifist and a conscientious objector and to him, I was a conscientious objector.'[24]

It must, therefore, have been with much unease that John Stott open-ed his mother's Sunday letter soon after the start of term, January 1941. His father had come home unexpectedly on twenty-four hours leave:

> You know I expect by now that Daddy came to us for one night –
> Thursday. It was delightful to have this unexpected visit – however
> short. He seemed in great form ... Daddy and I sat up till past
> midnight talking about you. – I was very distressed to hear that he
> has decided not to pay your university expenses after your first year
> – during the war. – He should have told you this of course when
> you discussed with him the scheme of taking 2 years over the first
> part of your tripos. You seem to be in the soup now Johnnie and it
> worries me thinking of what you may be planning to do. – I'm
> afraid that I do agree with Daddy that you should give service to
> your country when you are called up – if you don't hold with actual
> fighting – the government has many other plans and very few
> young fit men are going to get exemption.[25]

Lily goes on to urge John not to seek funding elsewhere, but to complete Part I of his tripos in a single year, giving up the camp secretarial work to do so. Though the letter is loving and full of sympathy, his mother's views are firm: 'I am convinced that national service for all is right and *every* career must be interrupted for the time being.' The letter is annotated in John Stott's minute hand: 'The order is not State 1st, JESUS 2nd, but JESUS 1st, State 2nd ... I must "obey God rather than men" (Acts 5:29).' He sent a brief affectionate note almost by return of post:

> Thank you very much indeed for your understanding letter,
> Mummy dear. I am only writing a p.c. because I cannot as yet

answer you fully. I want to see Daddy again first, and I also want
another day or two to think my whole position out fully.
Meanwhile please remember that whatever I ultimately decide to do
in a day or so, – will be in answer to a call of duty and not in
answer to personal whim or stubbornness. *Always* your loving son.

John[26]

Lily replied to this with two further letters, written on consecutive
days, indicative of her extreme concern that events were rapidly passing
beyond the control of herself or her husband, now back in France:

Woodlands Farm House
Jan. 25. 1941

Dearest Johnnie,
Thank you for sending me a postcard. It was something to be going
on with but I don't mind admitting that I am horribly anxious
about the decision you are going to make. My prevailing fear is that
should you be given exemption from national service – you may
accept training for ordination from some fund or charity, remain
beholden to them for the rest of your life and never really fulfill
your highest talents. Dear Jonathan perhaps you realize a little bit
that you are gifted a lot above the average – in fact rather
exceptional and it would be a thousand pities that you should enter
through a back door – whereas if you only wait for the duration –
your training will be grand, open, independent and happy. – We
can none of us understand that this haste should have such a prior
claim and all feel that more and more everyone should give prior
claim to service to the country to which after all you owe so many
benefits and which is worth defending – to say nothing about the
truly devilish things we are trying to put down. As I said in my last
letter – you will have so many chances for work nearest your own
heart in whatever work you do for the country – I cannot see that
the 2 or 3 years gained in being ordained earlier by whatever means
has anything to offer in any way advantageous. I think we are all
reconciled to your doing no active fighting as your conscience
dictates otherwise. Please think and weigh well the issues and take
the long view with vision. You are young and very uneducated yet
in many ways – dear Jonathan. – I seem to be praying for little else
these days but that help and vision may be sent you.[27]

Lily's letter the following day speaks of her concern about how difficult it will be for John to talk this over with his father – 'Oh dear, I feel it is such a crisis in your life.' She begins her letter:

> You will say 'there is that blessed Mother of mine again!' Last night before bed; after much rather worrying thought about you. I opened my evening Scripture portion … on Feb. 8th and read immediately a portion of what might possibly help you. – It is on the question of service to one's country. Please read it. I am sending it to you in case the small Scripture Union portion has not the same.[28]

A few days later, with no immediate prospect of being able to talk with his father face to face, John Stott wrote a long personal letter (nine sides in the draft which survives) to his father to say 'I have made up my mind'. Before going into his reasons the letter is at pains to express family love and affection, sorrow for the pain this is causing, and a wish that 'the easy course' of following his parents' wishes was possible for him. He continues:

> The reasons for my decision are as follows:
>
> 1. *Obedience to my call.* Whatever you may think of it, I have had a definite and irresistible call from God to serve Him in the Church. During the last three years I have become increasingly conscious of this call, and my life now could be summed up in the words 'separated unto the gospel of God'. There is no higher service; I ask no other.
>
> Mummy said recently in one of her letters: 'At present other things come first'. This to me is where her argument breaks down. In my life other things do not and cannot come first. I am not at liberty to put other things first, for I am 'separated unto the gospel of God'.
>
> As for the family's idea that a matter of 2 or 3 years 'cannot make all that difference' – do you think that 2 or 3 years during which I reject my most sacred calling really 'makes no difference'? It is largely a matter of principle. Were I to do any service, good or bad, which is not directed towards the one object of 'preaching the gospel' in days to come I should be laying aside the authority of God.
>
> 2. *Service to my country.* This may sound paradoxical at first, but let me explain: Mummy said in another letter: 'give prior claim to service to the country'. Do you then think that I would not be serving my country by going on with my course for ordination? The Government have said the contrary, and it seems self-evident to me that I should be serving my country for the following reasons:

(1) Post-war reconstruction. We hear a lot about this nowadays, and surely you don't deny its importance? You would all agree that in the end it is 'spiritual values' (I purposely use a vague expression) which matter. If medicos are exempt for their services in dealing with disease after the war, how much more should ordinands for their services in dealing with the diseases of the spirit? Churchill himself said the other day that after the war we should need new hearts to bring peace to a distraught world (or words to that effect). The *Times* said on 16.1.41: 'A recent letter ... reaffirmed the truth that no scheme of national reconstruction can be adequate which does not include such changes in our system of national education as will make it ... definitely Christian in purpose.' Who is to effect this if it isn't men trained for the purpose? ... Wavell said in December: 'After final victory will come the real struggle to build up a world worthy of the principles we are fighting for – freedom and truth and peace and goodwill.' Who is to set forth these principles if it isn't men who have clung to them and are trained and willing to preach them whatever the cost?

(2) The country is best served if its citizens are obeying God. The country's best place is in the centre of God's will, and it will not attain that place unless its individual citizens are fulfilling God's will in their own lives: I have already told you how this affects me.

(3) You are fighting a physical war against 'flesh and blood' in order that man may have peace with man. I am fighting a spiritual war against 'principalities and powers' in order that man may have peace with God. If man is in a state of 'peace with God', it follows inevitably and at once that he is in a state of peace with his fellow-men, because 'the fruit of the Spirit is love'. But even if men were in a state of peace with each other it would not necessarily follow that they would be in a state of peace with God, except in so far as men cannot live in peace with each other unless they are right with God, which is of course the fundamental cause of the chaos in Europe today. I have been called to the one war, you no doubt to the other. Both are service to our country. I respect you for your service; will you respect me for mine?

These, then, were his conclusions 'arrived at in spite of myself'. He goes on to ask:

How does it all affect my relations with home? I want you to do what you think best from the point of view of the whole family and not of me. Have you definitely decided not to support me up here after my first year? I cannot believe that you have, since surely you

see that I am doing my duty in the light of obedience to my call
and service to my country?

Even if we disagree, Daddy, remember that I for my part love
you still and remain your deeply grateful son

John.

P. S. As this explains my position, you will no doubt be passing
it on, in due course to Mummy?[29]

Not unnaturally, further letters from home continued to arrive – Lily
Stott was now writing every few days, and dreading what an envelope in
her son's handwriting might bring as he proved deaf to all appeals:

Your letter arrived by the afternoon post on Saturday. It lay on the
dining room table for a couple of hours before I could pull myself
together. – Then when I opened it and started reading – it felt as
tho' my inside dropped down to my shoes. – There is no doubt and
no opposition from us for the choice of your calling – dear
Jonathan but we cannot see or understand that you should feel, that
you can calmly and quietly continue your studies to this end (even
tho' the calling is a sacred one) as tho' ... peace was ruling the
world and that the greatest and most crucial and important war for
civilization was not convulsing the world ...

Daddy definitely feels he should not pay for your education at
Cambridge after this year (he told me so) as though there was no
war on ...[30]

Supportive and affectionate as Lily Stott undoubtedly sought to be
through this difficult time, she could not avoid feeling that even her
'Johnnie' was proving remarkably blind to what was obvious to almost
everybody else. She writes again a week later:

I am sorry that you have not heard from Daddy either – the
uncertainty about things must make things difficult and awkward
for you – I have not heard from him since last Saturday fortnight. I
expect he is very worried about your affairs and trying to make up
his mind as to the best thing to do ... Dear Jonathan – I almost get
cross sometimes – your view seems soft and swollen headed
sometimes (as to your idea of being so very important as to speed in
ordination) ...

and the letter goes on to ask if John had news of a tribunal, or any letter
from the Bishop of Manchester.[31]

In fact the Bishop of Manchester had written some days earlier to the Principal of Ridley Hall; and a copy of that letter was even then on its way to John Stott at Trinity. It was inconclusive, but not hopeful:

> The Ministry of National Service a good many months ago decided that it did not feel able to ask the War Office any longer to release attested men, and I am not quite sure, therefore, whether there is much hope of being able to secure Stott's inclusion within the Schedule of Reserved Occupations. I am making the effort.[32]

Though in a tiny minority, John Stott was not quite alone in the difficult position here described. Philip Tompson, his friend from Rugby was at Emmanuel, and his tutor was wrestling with very similar difficulties on his behalf. The tutor's letter of March, 1941 to Philip Tompson's father summarizes their position:

> I am afraid that I see no way out of the difficulty in which your son's conscience places him. Had he not attested at school he should have appeared before a Tribunal which would probably have given him non-combatant duties. Had the age of conscription remained at twenty I do not think the War Office would have called him to service until he were of the same age as those who wait for conscription, and in the period of time he might to some extent have changed his mind. With the lowered age of conscription it is sure that he will be called to service by the War Office unless someone there takes notice of letters written to the Secretary for War. With my advice your son wrote to the Secretary for War asking whether some notice could be taken of the change of his mind. The most fortunate decision would be that the War Office should release him from attestation, allow him to register in which case he could plead before a Tribunal. I have, however, next to no hopes that anything will be done and feel that there is no real choice except between two alternatives, on the one hand to abandon his conscientious objections which seems to me unlikely, and on the other hand to allow himself to be arrested as a deserter and to continue to be subjected to army punishment for refusing duty until for mere administrative convenience someone decides to allow him the benefit of his conscience. I have advised him in this sense but do not feel quite sure that he has understood his position. I have myself no doubt of the sincerity of his conscience and his desire for ordination. Desire for ordination has no particular relevance for the system of reservation of ordination candidates is fast being abandoned and in any case candidates may waive it by

enlistment which is technically what your son has done. The whole difficulty obviously arose when he voluntarily enlisted at school and I am afraid in the haste of War a mechanism for the release from service of young men capable of altering their minds has not yet been created.[33]

It seems likely that about this time Arnold Stott was able to visit Cambridge, and to talk with John and with Patrick Duff, his tutor. It may have been as a result of this visit that John Stott was asked to seek advice from those who might help him come to a better understanding of the issues. He later recalled:

I was sent to at least three clergymen to be sorted out, and looking back I am really horrified at how badly they dealt with me. Not one of them introduced my mind to the concept of the just war. I had never even heard of the just war theory.[34]

Two of the clergymen were chosen as likely to try to persuade John Stott that his views were misconceived and that, in the words of Article XXXVII, 'It is lawful for Christian men ... to wear weapons, and to serve in the wars'. It seems that neither helped him in any way.

The third was resident in Cambridge, Canon C. E. Raven, Regius Professor of Divinity and Master of Christ's College. Raven's views were well known. He had served in the trenches as an Army chaplain in the First World War, before finally committing himself to a Christian pacifist position:

... He came to it by no easy path, for he had struggled in 1914 already with a call to war and a call to peace; and it was not until the 1920s that he finally made up his mind. It was partly the mode of the twenties – the Great War must have ended all wars in right-thinking folk's minds; like so many of his generation, he had no presentiment of Hitler before he came to power. But he also had a deeper and more penetrating insight into the nature and the horror of war, and into what must now be recognised as a tragic dilemma facing all serious Christians ...[35]

He was an early sponsor of Dick Sheppard's Peace Pledge Union; and if Sheppard was the popularist of the peace movement between the wars, Raven was its leading intellectual.[36] A man of immense enthusiasms, he was as fervent and outspoken in this, despite its unpopularity, as in so much else. Moreover, his sympathies were the more easily enlisted because in spite of high academic office he himself suffered under a persistent sense of rejection: 'banned from the BBC and dropped by almost all the leaders of the churches.'[37]

Charles Raven had been an undergraduate at Caius forty years before. He shared with John Stott, the Trinity undergraduate, not only this convinced pacifism but a deep and informed love of birds and of the natural world. As a lecturer, he was

> ... dramatic, electrifying, unforgettable. The eyes of a visionary, the voice of a prophet, the gestures of one totally absorbed, the seemingly effortless flow of language, the mastery of his subject which enabled him to deliver a major lecture or sermon without a note, these were the outward features which made him a legend in post-war Cambridge.[38]

Raven loved to lecture on the famous confrontation between the Bishop of Oxford and Thomas Huxley at the 1860 meeting of the British Association in Oxford. He would stride up and down the largest lecture room of the Divinity School, tall, distinguished and ascetic in his doctor's gown, describing in vivid detail Huxley's crushing retort to Bishop Wilberforce about an ape for a grandfather. It was easy to see that his sympathies were with the scientist. Certainly they were not with the CICCU. In his early autobiography he recalled his own undergraduate impressions before the First World War:

> ... The university has always had a strong evangelical tradition, and at the beginning of the century almost the only religious society that affected the students was the C.I.C.C.U., whose tenets have always included a belief in the verbal inspiration of scripture. For their zeal, courage, and devotion no praise can be too high: they were, I think, respected even if left severely alone. But for most of us their intellectual position was simply a mockery. It seemed incredible that anyone with sufficient education to pass the Little-Go should still believe in the talking serpent or Jonah's whale or Balaam's ass or Joshua's sun or the cryptograms that foretold the Second Advent. Yet such men not only existed but were enthusiastic in the search for proselytes; and they were the only Christians that I met during my first two years. Jesus, but for them, might almost never have been: and they made Him peculiarly unattractive.[39]

Perhaps the years had mellowed this harsh view of the members of CICCU. Perhaps indeed John Stott presented a different picture of the CICCU member from the stereotype in Raven's mind, loosely based on his recollections of thirty years before.[40] To his great credit he fully recognised John Stott's sincerity and determination, and set himself at once to give what assistance he could. Here at last was a man of unquestioned stature and authority who could sympathize with the moral struggles of the undergraduate John Stott, and respect his uncompromising pacifist convictions. Not only did Raven offer counsel and advice but he also wrote himself to the long-suffering Bishop of Manchester. This time the reply was more hopeful though only some three weeks had passed since the bishop's pessimistic letter to Paul Gibson. He wrote:

> My dear Master,
> Thank you for your letter about J. R. W. Stott. I have had, as you expected, some correspondence with Gibson about him and although there was a difficulty, due to the fact that he had attested, I sent his name to the Ministry at the end of January and got the usual acknowledgement without any demur on their part. I presume, therefore, that Stott's name is entered amongst the reserved, but if any difficulty arises your letter will help me in any action that needs to be taken.
>
> > I hope you are well and flourishing.
> > Yours very sincerely,
> > Guy Manchester[41]

3

Meanwhile the date set for the registration of John Stott's age-group was drawing uncomfortably close. He had evidently been trying to discover what the future would hold for him if exemption was not given: and what he had to share with Lily made uncomfortable reading. She wrote to him, saying how miserable his letters had made her feel:

> … However enough about my reactions which really do not come into the picture at all. I certainly had not grasped that your tribunal would be a military one nor had I considered the grim alternative of prison. I cannot follow the line of thought that prefers becoming a burden to the state and leading an entirely useless confined existence when all the opportunities to being a helpful, useful and resourceful citizen are open to you. – There are many civil services calling out for volunteers. Your decision seems so stuffy and crooked to me as tho' you had a complex of sorts. I am almost tempted to believe that Bash's influence is not all to the good. – I

hope indeed that Daddy will be magnanimous and that you will get exemption. I look forward to hearing from you your reasons for no service of any kind. – Please, Johntie, never again talk about not being able to come home unless you want to break our hearts altogether. Should the worst happen (and I can't believe it will) you must rise above awkward feelings – there will always always *always* be a welcome.[42]

The long-drawn-out saga continued through the Easter Vacation. A letter from the University Board of Military Studies spoke hopefully of the War Office: 'I think they will agree to releasing you from your attestation now that I have sent them the necessary further evidence'.[43] But the hope-deferred continued: 'It is clear that you have not actually been released yet', wrote Patrick Duff ten days later.[44] The Board of Military Studies confirmed in mid-April that 'we have got some distance with the War Office about your release'.[45] But even while the news of his exemption eluded him, his father was still unrelenting over the question of further financial support. Lily sent him a pencilled letter the following week:

on Nottingham Station
April 22, 1941

My dearest Johntie,
The loud speaker has just announced that my return train will be 13 minutes late so as I intended writing to you anyway on the train I thought the letter might be more legible if I wrote while still stationary.

Daddy and I had a long and serious talk about you on the car journey back from Deganwy. So serious and absorbing was it that we several times took the wrong turning. – (we have just started in the train so forgive me if the writing deteriorates). Daddy is writing to you within the next two or 3 days and is sending the consignment of money for this term. Johntie, he feels that his conscience will not allow him to continue paying for your education at Cambridge after this term. I'm afraid, dear one, that the whole family thinks that you *should* do some form of definitely *national* service in the country's emergency. A capable, fit, and talented man like you should not continue your life as it is when so many others are having to give up everything for the time being. I still hope that you may come round to this point of view – the war has touched you not at all yet – it is so full of tragedy for so many people – there is much that you could do to help. *After* the war Daddy is prepared, he says – if you are still of the same mind – to help you all that he can. Duff has shown him letters from Gibson, the head of the theological college and from the Bishop of Manchester in which they both say that undergraduates should be encouraged to do national service. The church advocates it – *vide* letters from both archbishops. As I have said before – the work nearest your heart can be continued alongside the national work – I can't help feeling that later you will regret it very much if now you detach and shut yourself away from any participation in the world's crisis – that is if you *can* by hook or crook obtain the funds. – I trust dear Jonathan for your sake that you will not be able to do this ... I feel anyway dear Jonathan that you have your wits about you and are sensible and capable and that you will do nothing foolish in this difficult time of your life. I think that Daddy means to continue your clothes allowance – he will tell you about all this in his letter.[46]

April 27th was John Stott's twentieth birthday. His mother sent a cake made with five eggs – they kept their own hens at Woodlands Farm House – 'and Bash's ½ lb. of margerine'. John Stott wrote to his father to thank him for a cheque for £71 to meet his college bills, and continued (his anxiety to be understood betraying him into occasional and uncharacteristic pomposities):

I've spent a very happy, if uneventful birthday. It's bitterly cold, so I've been sitting indoors by the fire, – apart from a stroll this morning. It's just after tea now, and I've been enjoying Mummy's rich cake, – most sumptuous for these days!

I'm all settled in for another term, and feel fairly well prepared for my exam which begins on June 2nd. I'm managing to put in 7–8 hours' work a day; so the weeks will pass quickly.

I played a good game of tennis the other day. By 'good' I don't mean that I played well, because I didn't! In fact I was shamefully out of practice. Still, it was great fun, and I'm looking forward to getting regular games this term.

I was sorry to read the last sentence in your letter about 'a less pleasant subject'. I imagine that you were referring to the question of national service. May I put the whole business before you again as plainly as I can? I want to be frank and we haven't had an opportunity recently of talking about it all, so I'd like to bring you right up to date.

The latest news only reached me a day or two ago. It was in the form of a letter from Col. Murray to Mr. Duff (which the latter showed me), and it seems definite now that I have been granted exemption. The War Office have put me in a reserved category on the ground that I am an ordination candidate. Mr. Duff says that this is the War Office's last word and means in effect that I won't be called up.

I mention this first, because I should like it to act as a basis for what I want to explain now. You are very anxious, I know, along with the rest of the family, that I should do some sort of national service, and I have sought to show you all from the beginning that I do not feel able to do this. My reasons are three, two of which you know already from my letter of last term:

1. *The Basis of Exemption.* It is absolutely clear from the War Office's decision, as revealed in Col. Murray's letter, that I am only reserved on one condition. That condition is that I should continue my preparation for ordination up at Cambridge by getting my degree first, and then going to a theological college. Were I to go down from Cambridge in order to do some Nat. Serv., I would not be fulfilling the condition on which I have been granted exemption. This means that I should be called up, brought before a military tribunal as a conscientious objector, and would be ordered to do one of three things:

(a) fight

(b) do non-combatant service

(c) return to Cambridge.

I would agree to the third, but would refuse to do (a) and (b), and that, unpleasant as it may be to all of us, would mean prison. Therefore the alternative before me is not

National Service or Cambridge

but   Cambridge or Prison.

2. *Service to the Country.* Here let me answer a point Mummy raised in a recent letter. She said that the Church and both archbishops advocated the doing of national service. This however only states half the truth. The Church and the Government are agreed about the position of ordinands, that they should continue uninterrupted their ordination course so that the country may not be destitute of such men in years to come. This fact is made self-evident by the existence of the council over which the Bishop of Manchester presides, which acts as advocate for ordinands who consider it their duty to apply for exemption. Both Mr. Duff and Mr. Gibson have advised me to bide by this council's decision:– to take exemption if it is given, and to do National Service if it is refused. As exemption has been granted, I am following the advice of both Mr. Duff and Mr. Gibson in accepting it on the condition, you will remember, that I continue my work at Cambridge.

3. *Obedience to my call.* I don't wish to resurrect the old story, but this point largely accounts for my policy. I simply cannot lay my call on one side. I don't want to appeal to you, Daddy, but you are such a shrewd judge of character and have such a deep knowledge of human nature, that surely you must see that I am not shirking national service? Far from it. The easier way for me would be to give in to your wish and do some sort of service, for I hate this family rupture. – But Daddy I want you to realise that I *must* follow my call. Men down the ages have had to face similar problems, and those who've yielded to the will of the majority have often gone under and never come to the surface again. And I know enough history to know that it's the men who have stood up for their ideals and championed their cause, come weal come woe, that have left the world a better place. I would not presume to claim equality with the mighty, but I am seeking to follow their example in my own sincere and humble way. I can do no more, and I ask to be respected.

Think not that I am going to live a normal, peaceful, comfortable, secluded life. I'm going to throw myself body and soul into the struggle for right. My desire is to see the world a better place, and I will not spare myself in this endeavour …

As for finance – you may not feel able to go on supporting me. But were you to be tolerant and magnanimous enough to do it, there will never lack gratitude in your

Ever loving son
John[47]

Whether because his movements meant that this letter was delayed in reaching him, or whether Arnold Stott was unable to come to any decision, it was three weeks before John Stott received his father's reply. In the meantime he had continued to exchange letters with his mother: and, faced with the facts of the situation, she was at last not only ready herself to accept them, but to urge Arnold to do the same. She wrote on May 7th:

Bash called in this evening for the things he had left behind. I was sowing beetroot at the time but laid down my trowel and asked him to come in for a talk. I hoped to get out of him the details of your present position which you have written Daddy. – As a result I understand the position thoroughly at last and have written Daddy to-night asking him that as the Gov. and the War Office have both decided that you can best serve your country by continuing with your work and so have given you exemption – whether he will be

generous and tolerant, face facts and pay your fees. – There seems
no alternative now and I feel sure that he will regret it if he does
not.[48]

Finally, on 19 May, John Stott received by priority telegram the long-
awaited answer as to his father's continuing support:

AM CONSENTING BUT WITH GREAT RELUCTANCE
AND UNHAPPINESS. STOTT.

It was not the end of the story, but at least it was the begining of the end.
A month later Patrick Duff was able to write to John Stott:
'Congratulations on your First'.[49] Considering the circumstances,
anxieties and tensions, it was a remarkable achievement.

Looking back, these 'old, unhappy, far-off things', still have power to
engender a feeling of profound sympathy for a family circle so divided
and so distressed. For the father, moving every day among the casualties
of war, and with both his daughters active in the service of their country,
it is not surprising that grief and frustration at his son's continuing
obstinacy should be a cause of bitterness and alienation. Granted that
they had few opportunities of seeing each other, John Stott's recollections
of how his father would not speak to him for two years, and would even
reject the natural advances of affection to which father and son had been
accustomed, still make painful reading fifty years later. To an
undergraduate inevitably insecure, isolated in what seemed to him a stand
for conscience's sake (and perhaps tempted to dramatize his situation),
caught unwittingly in the toils of the Government war-machine, living
week by week with hope deferred, it must have been a searing experience.
If his mother was right in describing him as 'sensitive', it would have
provided an early bench-mark of Christian fortitude which few later
experiences would have to match. At the same time, given his life-long
singleness, and what some women in his younger days felt to be an
almost monastic concern to maintain his reserve and keep his distance,
there will always be those who draw a connection between this side of his
life and the pain of misunderstanding and rejection by his father at a time
of peculiar stress. Looking back, John Stott would sometimes say that
because of these difficulties at home, there was a sense in which he found
in the CICCU 'a surrogate family, a substitute family'[50] and so learned by
experience the significant part that Christian fellowship can play in the
life of discipleship.

Through most of the period covered by this correspondence the events
of the war gave little encouragement. Arnold Stott had been on the last
ship back to England from St. Nazaire at the fall of France in 1940. May

and June 1941 were 'the most dire months of the war'.[51] Hitler had not yet invaded Russia; Pearl Harbour was still six months away. Lily and Arnold (and Joy also, who wrote at least one long letter urging her brother to join up with the rest[52]) clearly felt deeply that these were days when any young man of any character should be ready to sink his own concerns in his country's need.

And there were other pressures and other correspondents. Among them was Robbie Bickersteth, writing from the Company Commanders' School in Bangor Castle, Co. Down. John Stott had heard from him only spasmodically, because of the exigencies of active service. Robbie had written towards the end of 1939 on the letterhead of the 6th Battalion, The Seaforth Highlanders:

> … Life is full of surprises but this is one of the worst! Who would ever have thought that I, with what you once so fondly called my 'motherly' instincts would end up as a soldier!
>
> However a mere uniform (even a kilt and sporran Johnnie which I must say I rather enjoy wearing!), haven't changed the *old man* very much.
>
> I was called up the day before war was declared and have been gradually acquiring a military veneer ever since.[53]

Robbie was still a particular friend, and had been an early boyhood hero. Opposition from him, however gently phrased, must have been specially painful. He argues passionately the need of the men he meets daily in the ranks for 'the Word of God'; and that 'a man who has lived some years as a soldier will make a far better parson afterwards'. He urges John, should he be refused exemption, 'not to fight blindly against the civil power'. And he too adds unequivocally, 'I declare to you that you are wrong.'[54]

If sympathy is inescapable, so equally is a sense of irony. It was during this period that (as part of the process of nailing his colours to the mast) John Stott became a member of the Anglican Pacifist Fellowship. But the day would come when his own study of the Scriptures would carry him beyond any simplistic viewpoint and he would resign his membership because he no longer believed that the pacifist position was the only possible one for a Christian. The issue was sharpened for him by the thermo-nuclear debate of the 1960s; and in wrestling with these issues he came to believe that 'we cannot say that war is wrong in itself. War has sometimes been, and may again be, the weapon of God's wrath and righteous judgment.'[55] Twenty years later, because of the indiscriminate nature of nuclear weapons, he wrote and spoke unequivocally as a 'nuclear pacifist', though admitting the moral and political anomalies of such a position.[56] Had a biblical theologian been able to unfold to him in his days at Trinity the apostolic teaching on the authority of the State, and the Christian theory of the 'Just War', then perhaps all this estrangement, loneliness and heart-ache might have been avoided. But history is shaped, not by what might have been but by what was. And in the over-ruling providence of God, it is hardly fanciful to see in these fiery trials the forging of a character fitted to meet a lifetime of challenges ahead.

EIGHT

Reading Theology: Ridley Hall

1

With the publication of the Tripos class-lists in the summer of 1942, John Stott was able to put behind him the French and German which had been at the centre of his studies since School Certificate at Rugby, and begin to read theology. Though 'very upset' that he secured a First only in French and not in German, he did not regret these two years of his Cambridge course. Fifty years later he recalled:

> The greatest help in learning to use words with care and accuracy was writing essays in French and German. There is a precise word which fits every situation, and the sort of education I had has been a great help to me in my preaching and writing ministry.[1]

His father, now a Major-General, continued to make no secret of his opposition to John Stott's further residence in Cambridge; and he distrusted the influence that the teachers of academic theology might have upon his son. He wrote to Patrick Duff to ask whether they would be likely to broaden John's outlook – which he clearly felt to be unreasonably 'narrow'. Duff told John Stott: 'I have painted him a pen picture of Mr. Burnaby from my 25 years' knowledge of him which ought, I hope, to do the trick.'[2] This was a private joke between John Stott and his tutor. John Burnaby, at that time senior tutor and college lecturer in theology, was not a man to encourage 'enthusiasm' or extremism. The impression he gave was of 'a melancholy-looking person' and one 'who always saw difficulties ahead'.[3] Though his friends knew him as an accomplished actor, musician and folk-singer, this was a side of his character which came as a surprise to those who saw him only on formal occasions. At the time when John Stott began to read theology under his supervision he had recently been ordained: in 1952 he succeeded Michael Ramsey as Regius Professor of Divinity, and on his death in 1978 *The Times* published in his obituary a striking pen-portrait:

> His pungent humour was terse and penetrating, and this, combined with his outwardly melancholy expression, to give [sic] him something of a Grock-like quality. To work on easy-going terms with other people was not always easy for him; and his characteristically abrupt, jerky sentences could make him appear austerely remote and sometimes, if he felt deeply about a point, even alarming ...[4]

A more rounded account of this versatile man appeared in the *Trinity Review* on his retirement as Regius Professor in 1958. It recalled his service in the First World War, and added to an astonishing list of his range of unexpected accomplishments a tribute to his love of family exhibited in a picture of him with his grandchildren:

> It is a charming sight to see a Regius Professor of Divinity, and an Augustinian scholar to boot, amusedly observing unregenerate human nature in small children as it exhibits itself in the Fellows' Garden.[5]

Instead of the customary tutorial group of three or four, John Stott received individual supervisions from Burnaby in his small dark study, filled with tobacco smoke from his pipe. Sometimes Burnaby would lapse into long silences when he did not know what to say next, and his pupil felt no responsibility to initiate conversation. Their views frequently diverged: John Stott recalls a brief correspondence after he had gone down from Trinity in which Burnaby maintained that Jesus was contradicting Moses in Matthew 5, whereas John Stott maintained that the six antitheses ('you have heard that it was said ... but I say ...') expressed Jesus's disagreement with tradition rather than with Scripture, the teaching of the scribes but not of Moses.[6]

Most of John Stott's work was done in his own rooms or in the great reading room of the University Library. Sometimes in the summer term he would work out of doors in the Trinity Fellows' Garden, 'a little distracted by the musical strains of the Blackcaps and Garden Warblers and by a Lesser Spotted Woodpecker.' In his final year he did not attend a single lecture in the University:

> Little that we were given by lecturers appeared to be original. One soon learned that most of it was culled from their own or others' books, so it saved lots of time to go straight to their sources. I bumped into Henry Hart one day in King's Parade: 'Let me see, you attended one of my lectures once ...!'[7]

Two years were needed to read Part 1 of the Theological Tripos. This would mean that though John Stott would graduate as BA after the first year, he would remain in Trinity as a post-graduate student until the summer of 1944, and then move across Cambridge to Ridley Hall, his chosen theological college, with a view to ordination in December 1945. Academic theology in Cambridge before the war had been something of a graveyard for evangelical religion:

> Liberalism was becoming more and more aridly negative. Theological study did not even pretend to be much of a preparation for the ministry. It was more of an academic philosophical exercise for the solving of intellectual problems. To study theology was to enter a spiritual wilderness ...[8]

By the 1940s the scene was slowly beginning to show some signs of change, though a fully conservative approach to the authority of Scripture would have found no place within the Divinity Faculty. Patrick Duff could be reasonably confident that (whether or not they could be relied on to 'broaden his outlook' in the way his father hoped) the members of the Faculty would present John Stott with a series of challenges to the biblical foundations of his faith. C. F. D. Moule,[9] then Vice-Principal of Ridley Hall, was almost alone in beginning his course of lectures with prayer; apart from this, the 'Queen of the Sciences' (as theology had been known to an earlier generation) might have been any branch of secular knowledge. The flavour of John Stott's impressions of the Divinity Faculty can be judged by his recollections of B. T. D. Smith in his *Response* to David Edwards on the question of biblical authority:

> I also wonder why you seem so anxious to persuade me that inerrancy is untenable? Is it entirely your concern for intellectual

integrity? But I am committed to this also. Your assault has reminded me a little of Dr. B. T. D. Smith, who taught the synoptic gospels at Cambridge in the 1940s when I was a theological student. It was said that as a young man he had been an ardent Anglo-Catholic, but that now he had entirely lost his Christian faith. He seemed to take what Oscar Cullmann called (in *The Christology of the New Testament*, 1959) 'an almost sadistic pleasure' in finding discrepancies! I shall always remember the beginning of his lecture on Luke 3:1ff. Rubbing his hands and licking his lips with evident glee, he said with his famous lisp: 'Thith pathage thimply brithleth with difficultieth!' Now, please, I'm not likening you to him! But I still ask 'Why?' I wonder whether it has anything to do with a fear of what C. S. Lewis in *Surprised by Joy* (1955) styled 'the tyrannous noon of revelation' (p. 63)? Could it be that you think submission to biblical authority is incompatible with intellectual freedom?[10]

Perhaps the most famous figure in the Divinity Faculty, alongside Charles Raven, the Regius Professor, was C. H. Dodd, a Congregational minister, then at the peak of his career. He had been appointed Norris-Hulse Professor some seven years before, the first Free Churchman to be a Professor of Theology at Cambridge.[11] His was a name to conjure with:

> ... He was a good talker and a supremely good listener; a tiny bird-like person, sharp and quick, precise and enchanting, warm and kind. He spoke with authority and assurance, qualities which maddened some of those who thought his approach to the gospels fundamentally wrong ...[12]

Dodd is regarded today as providing 'a good deal of the biblical arm for the wider return to orthodoxy' and as one who 'did most to convince the common Christian, and scholars too, that first-class modern biblical scholarship could really be reconciled with, and indeed support, a traditional belief in Christ'.[13] By the standards of academic theology, Dodd therefore was both more pastoral and more orthodox than most; but John Stott did not find his brisk self-assurance made him attractive to listen to. Nevertheless, week by week, he attended Dodd's supremely articulate and eloquently confident lectures, while weighing but steadily resisting his more liberal arguments:

> He lectured on St John's Gospel particularly, and the Hellenistic background of the Gospel. It was very well attended; there must have been a couple of hundred students there and one of my difficulties in reading theology was not so much the individual

liberal arguments but just looking round that room of 200 students drinking in every word of the great Professor C. H. Dodd and saying to myself, 'I'm the only person who doesn't agree with him.'[14]

Some fifty years later Lord Runcie was cruising on the *Queen Elizabeth II* and fell into conversation with David Spence of North Carolina, who asked him about John Stott – to whom Robert Runcie, as Archbishop, had recently awarded a Lambeth DD. Lord Runcie's comment was that John Stott had a brilliant mind, had been taught in the best Cambridge tradition of liberal theology, and had secured a first-class degree. But then Runcie added: 'The trouble was, he didn't believe it!'[15] It would be a mistake to assume from this light-hearted comment, which expresses the literal truth, that John Stott was somehow able easily to dismiss or to refute the liberal position. On the contrary, it was always a costly business. 'What was difficult to cope with', in Oliver Barclay's description of this time, 'was the extraordinary confidence' with which speculative and indeed transitory theological assumptions were offered as the obvious truth.[16] It was an early introduction to that 'pain in the mind' which was to accompany much of John Stott's later writing, fighting his way to fair assessments of unwelcome arguments, maintaining with intellectual rigour his evangelical position only because he found it to be true.

Faced with emotional isolation from his home and intellectual isolation in his studies, there were few people in Cambridge to whom John Stott could turn with confidence in his desire to combine intellectual integrity with faithfulness to revelation. Whatever God had said, that he was determined to believe; but (as every Bible student knows) this left many questions unanswered. Thirty years later he chose a simple – almost simplistic – example by way of illustration:

When I was a Cambridge undergraduate, I can remember being rather perplexed by the verse which says that the ten commandments were written on stone tablets by the finger of God (Exod. 31:18; Deut. 9:10). Was I required to believe this literally? Did a divine finger really appear and somehow inscribe Hebrew letters on stone? Certainly it is not impossible, for 'the fingers of a human hand appeared and wrote on the plaster of the wall, near the lampstand in the royal palace' in the case of King Belshazzar, announcing his imminent doom (Dan. 5:5, 24–28). But today I am not so sure that we were ever meant to take literally the statement about the finger of God writing the law. For now I have read the Bible more thoroughly, and I have come across other references to God's fingers, all of which are symbolical.[17]

Among the few senior members of the University able and ready to lend support in these academic struggles was Dr. B. F. C. Atkinson, a double First and a distinguished if idiosyncratic scholar in his own field. Keeper of Western MSS and then Senior Under-Librarian at the University Library, 'Basil', as he was universally known, was a strong supporter of the CICCU,

> ... a stalwart friend to all its members and a great resource of wisdom both to them and to the movement as a whole. He was one of the university's two experts on ancient languages but, more important in this context, he was a deeply prayerful Christian.
>
> Eccentric to a degree few other dons achieved, he used to ride through Cambridge on an old upright bicycle, dressed in a blue pinstriped suit and a green pork-pie hat, and his voice, strong and with extraordinary emphasis placed upon almost every word, was often mimicked by his many friends. He used to read the lessons at St Paul's Church on Sunday mornings, and when it was known that on a particular Sunday he was to read Daniel chapter 3, the attendance was greatly increased. Stories about him abound to this day among his old friends ...
>
> They used to say that you could tell the state of the CICCU by its appreciation of Basil: when the CICCU was strong and healthy and full of zeal for evangelism, its leaders had a great respect for Basil and valued his advice; but when it was struggling with dissension and lacking evangelistic zeal, Basil was probably being ignored or treated only as an elderly outsider.[18]

He never married; and lived first with his old mother and latterly with his sister, entertaining members of the CICCU with never-failing hospitality and ever ready to advise, to counsel and to warn. He was well aware that there was about him a touch of that eccentricity which marked a passing generation in the university. He enjoyed telling against himself a story of a visit he paid to London to speak for the LIFCU, the London counterpart of the CICCU:

> I had been asked to address a weekday evening evangelistic meeting, and I turned up and did so. There was an undergraduate in the chair and, when I had finished, he got up and announced, 'We thank Dr. Atkinson very much for coming to speak to us this evening. Tomorrow we are to have two undergraduates from Oxford, perfectly normal human beings.'[19]

Those who heard him recount this (it was one of his favourite stories) will find their lips framing the last four words in irresistible mimicry of Basil's emphatic and distinctive intonation!

A characteristic story is told of him preaching at an open-air evangelistic service in Cambridge and mentioning heaven. 'A student shouted out "What do you know about heaven?" With that seraphic smile Basil replied, "I live there".'[20]

Basil Atkinson was the better placed to sympathize with John Stott since he himself had been imprisoned as a conscientious objector in the First World War. He had published in April 1939 a pamphlet *The Christian's Duty in War* which warned that to follow Christ faithfully 'may entail far greater sacrifices than the twentieth-century Christian has been accustomed to'.[21] This is probably to be taken less as a reference to the hardship he himself had experienced as a pacifist (and the mild ridicule he excited among, for example, some Deans and Chaplains) than to the sufferings of the early church in times of persecution, and of the Reformation martyrs, which he had described in one of the earliest IVF publications, *Valiant in Fight*.[22] But Basil's mind was too eccentric and his undoubted linguistic scholarship too far removed from current issues for him to be much more than an encourager, a stalwart sympathiser, in John Stott's theological struggles. Bash was not equipped to help him here. Others who could do so were sorely needed. Douglas Johnson was one such. It was through his friendship with Oliver Barclay that John Stott had come to know and be known by Dr. Douglas Johnson, for thirty-seven years the dynamic and self-effacing Secretary of the IVF. Douglas Johnson, or 'DJ' as he was affectionately known, was an achiever, with a far-reaching vision. As a young doctor he had intended to be a medical missionary, but was asked instead to remain in the UK and accept the post of part-time general secretary of the embryo IVF, 'at the rate of £150 per annum, subject to the money's being in hand'. Unconvinced, he turned for advice to Professor Rendle Short of the Bristol Royal Infirmary:

> When he consulted Rendle Short – a renowned recruiter of medical missionaries – the latter urged him to stay at home and build up a movement that would send many more labourers. (On leaving, Douglas Johnson asked, 'Well, what shall I say at the Judgment Seat if I am asked why I did not go to the mission field?' 'Oh,' replied Rendle Short, 'you just leave that to me!').[23]

It was said that DJ's favourite quotation was by a last-century author of a book on naval strategy: 'When you are trying to accomplish something you should first decide what is the *final objective* you are seeking to attain, and then *never lose sight of it*.'[24] It was in single-minded pursuit of his vision that he turned to the study of theology, in which he read seriously for the rest of his life. He had a great admiration for the famous trio of Cambridge New Testament scholars who held sway towards the end of the nineteenth century: J. B. Lightfoot, B. F. Westcott and F. J. A. Hort. Westcott was the senior, and as Fellow of Trinity had numbered both Hort and Lightfoot among his pupils. These three 'were the natural leaders of the enterprise which produced the Revised Version of the Bible in 1881'.[25]

On DJ's death in 1991 at the age of 86 *The Times* obituary rightly recognized the nature of his achievement: 'In many of Britain's universities today, the largest voluntary society is the Christian Union. If any one man was responsible for their present size and strength, it was Douglas Johnson.'[26] But Douglas Johnson's vision was not limited to the universities:

> ... He wanted to put the Evangelical wing of the Churches back in the mainstream of public debate. To do that, he had to found a movement in the universities which was prepared to go back to the doctrines of the Reformation, to rescue biblical scholarship from the domination of liberals, and to bring Evangelicals back from decades of pietism and to have a firm position from which to challenge the rise of secularism.[27]

Geraint Fielder, writing in the 1980s the story of the UCCF,[28] saw in the friendship between Oliver Barclay and John Stott a valuable means of bringing Douglas Johnson and Bash to a more positive assessment of each other's distinctive work for the gospel. Oliver Barclay looked to DJ much as John Stott looked to Bash:

> A friendship so congenial and formative helped to gel some of the best in parallel evangelical strengths and to be constructively critical of some of its weaknesses. It was becoming clear that Oliver was Douglas Johnson's heir-apparent, and John Stott seemed set to follow Bash. 'DJ and Bash did not see eye to eye with one another, Bash regarding DJ and the IVF as too intellectual, so that he did not want his officers to attend IVF conferences; while DJ, though admiring Bash's evangelistic zeal, felt he was unbalanced in some of his emphases ...'[29]

It is arguable that through this undergraduate friendship, DJ and Bash were able to increase their respect and understanding for each other, while continuing to work each in his own field with unabated conviction and singleness of mind.

Though not resident in Cambridge, DJ was a regular visitor. Unlike

Bash, he had a clear conviction that pietism was not enough, but that an evangelical faith, if it was to be a vital force in the modern world, must be equipped to win the intellectual battles with liberal and unbiblical theologies. He befriended John Stott and encouraged him in this vision. Two years before his death, DJ recalled meeting the young John Stott in King's Parade 'looking very unhappy';[30] he was at the height of his troubles with his father and had just received a painfully unwelcome letter. DJ took him off for coffee and was shown the letter – and no doubt offered both comfort and advice, and the backing of his prayers. It was DJ's initiative which a few years before had led to the formation of the IVF Biblical Research Committee: and from this Committee sprang the Tyndale Fellowship for Biblical Research and the foundation of Tyndale House, Cambridge as a centre of research and study for evangelical biblical scholarship. John Stott spoke on behalf of Tyndale House in 1992 at the launch of a further building appeal, soon after DJ's death:

> I find it poignant that this meeting should take place three months after the death of Dr. Douglas Johnson. For 'DJ' is one of the unsung heroes of the Christian Church in this country. He saw the priority need to recover evangelical biblical scholarship. It is probably to him more than to anybody else that the original vision for Tyndale House was given.
>
> When I was myself an undergraduate at Cambridge during World War II, the Divinity School was entirely liberal in its orientation. I believe there were no evangelical believers in any British university post related to Theology (even F. F. Bruce's influential career had scarcely begun) ... If anybody was rash enough to read for the Theology Tripos, and managed to survive, it was regarded as a miracle or certainly (depending on one's theological position) a conspicuous example of divine providence.
>
> But now the situation has radically changed ... There are, I believe, about 50 evangelical academics in university posts related to antiquities, Old Testament, New Testament, Theology, Ethics and Church History. And Tyndale House, its Fellowship, and its outstanding biblical library, constitute a unique resource for evangelical scholarship.
>
> So DJ's vision was right, and must be further expanded. We shall never capture the church for the truth of the gospel unless and until we can re-establish biblical scholarship, hold (and not lose) the best theological minds of every generation, and overthrow the enemies of the gospel by confronting them at their own level of scholarship.[31]

And it was DJ who introduced John Stott to the life and work of Charles Simeon, the celebrated vicar of Holy Trinity, Cambridge, 150 years before. John Stott paid tribute both to DJ for his vision for the recovery of evangelical biblical scholarship, and to Simeon's inspiration, in his introduction to a collection of Simeon's addresses published in 1986, to mark the 150th anniversary of his death:

> It was during my undergraduate days at Cambridge University that I was introduced to Charles Simeon. I owe the introduction to Dr. Douglas Johnson ... whose vision for the recovery of biblical scholarship (and in particular for the Tyndale Fellowship for Biblical Research) has never been adequately acknowledged by the church. Simeon's uncompromising commitment to Scripture, as the Word of God to be obeyed and expounded, captured my admiration and has held it ever since. On many occasions I have had the privilege of preaching from his pulpit in Holy Trinity Church, Cambridge, and standing where he stood, have prayed for a measure of his outstanding faithfulness.[32]

2

Life in Cambridge continued, diminished and greatly altered, but making the best of war-time conditions. In the winter of 1942 Gow counted 'close on a hundred and fifty people assigned to one College ARP duty or another' in Trinity.[33] For John Stott, the priorities were still academic work (for which his country had granted him exemption from active service), the task of Camp secretary, and the ever-present pastoral and teaching role for which the CICCU did not hesitate to use his gifts. He continued, too, what he had learned from Bash, in the role of pastor and counsellor by correspondence to friends away on active service. They wrote to him, looking for friendship, guidance and spiritual encouragement from army depots and barracks, from RAF stations and the Air Ministry, and from a variety of temporary billets. Some of the letters have survived longer than their writers: one is annotated 'Killed in action, NW Europe, March 1945'. A correspondent writes, not untypically, 'A few words you said when we met click in my mind – "one's personal relationship to Christ, that is the all-important thing".[34] It was not always easy to do justice to these competing claims. An undergraduate from one of the women's colleges remembers finding her way through the black-out to John Stott's rooms in Whewell's Court – one of the comparatively few buildings of the university to suffer damage from enemy action:

My first real encounter (if that is what it can be called) was when I had been deputed to invite him to lead one of our college Bible studies. I crept up the dark staircase ... and was about to knock on the big oak door of his rooms when I spied a neat, typewritten notice 'Working 8 a.m. – 8 p.m. Please do not disturb unless absolutely necessary'. What sort of a man is this? I thought, as I melted down the stairs into oblivion. Leading Bible studies seemed too much like a disturbance! He never was invited again.

I saw John on many other occasions when I was in the University Library, and began to observe how he worked, with iron self-discipline. He would enter silently, go to his accustomed corner, reach for the books in the same area and settle down immediately with total concentration, apparently oblivious of whatever else was happening around him.[35]

June 1943 saw the fruits of this application in a First in Part 1 of the Tripos and a Senior Scholarship from Trinity. John Stott graduated as BA on 22 June, and after a long summer vacation, much of it given to the work of Camp, prepared to tackle his final year at Trinity. However, a month before the start of term, and in the knowledge that his son had now secured his degree, Arnold Stott renewed the disturbing correspondence about continued exemption from military service. Writing from York, he added below the date: 'The 4th anniversary of the outbreak of the war'. The letter begins with thanks for John's birthday letter, and the present of a Wardonia razor ('Actually I had already 2 Wardonia razors but a third, and the latest pattern I expect, was a useful addition'). Arnold Stott continued:

I expect I shall be hearing about your plans for the next year. One of the things I admire Mr Churchill for most is his caution and refusal to prophesy the future of the war. But it does seem as if there is a good chance of its finishing within the next 12 months. For the rest of my life it will be an abiding sorrow to me that you have chosen to stand aloof; if sufficient of your friends and countrymen had taken the same course, disaster too horrible to contemplate, would have overtaken your country and the world. I believe you will later regret it, and, tho' memories are short, I believe it will diminish your power to be of help to others in the future.

The other thing that worries me about you is this camp business. I told you a few years ago that it was taking too much of your time but you denied it. It has been increasingly obvious ever since that I was right. I believe your close association with it has prevented your discovering other interests and hobbies; it has clearly associated you with only one aspect of life and I believe is mainly responsible for your narrow outlook and failure to face realities. I was very disturbed to learn from Mrs. Slater recently that you have visited Rugby on more than one occasion and failed to call on them – in fact have, as I understand it, tried to hide from them the fact that you had been in Rugby. If true, I could not have believed you capable of it.

Your loving
Father[36]

John Stott replied; term duly began; it must have seemed that his father had accepted the position. November, however, brought a further letter from York:

I think it was in May 1941 that I consented, with the greatest reluctance, to continue to give you financial support at Cambridge. Some time previously a provisional amount of £70 a term was decided. Since you went to Trinity I have had no word from you about your finances, but I presume the above amount has at any rate been sufficient. When I said I would give you financial support I had no definite term in view, but I certainly had in my mind a hope that your outlook would change and that you would come to realise the extraordinary anomaly of your remaining at Cambridge in war time. No such change has taken place and, as I understand it, you have now made arrangements to remain at Cambridge for a further period of two years. Being of age, you are of course entitled to make any arrangements you wish without consulting me but I find it hard to believe that you expect me in such circumstances indefinitely to finance you.

In my view the time has come for you to pay your own way – by selling such amounts as are necessary of the Birmingham Stock which I presume is still in your possession. Coutts will of course do this for you. In the meantime I enclose cheque for £70 to pay off any sums outstanding up to the time you took your degree. If this amount is insufficient, please let me know. If it is more than is necessary, no doubt you will return the balance.[37]

On receiving this letter John not unnaturally consulted his tutor. It would still be a full two years before he could be ordained. Possibly the Birmingham Stock (a legacy from his grandmother) would not be enough to support him for that long. At any rate Patrick Duff felt it might be necessary to look for further grants or bursaries. He therefore wrote – perhaps unwisely – to Mrs. Stott within a day or two of the arrival of Arnold Stott's letter:

> John came to me this morning in some distress and showed me a letter he had received from his father about financial affairs. General Stott said that as John was staying up for more than the three years needed for his degree, he did not think he should be expected to support him any longer, and suggested that he should pay his way by selling the Birmingham Stock inherited from his grandmother. I write now to ask whether you think this should be taken as a final decision or is open to re-consideration. As you know, John has been given deferment of service by the War Office with the express object of being ordained, and he will in fact, by carrying out his present programme, be ordained at the earliest possible moment or within a few months afterwards. If his father considers that he ought to use up his capital to keep himself during these two years of preparation for the Ministry I cannot call it unreasonable, but I should have thought it ought to have been made clear before now. General Stott has no doubt hoped throughout that John would change his mind and either join the army or do National Service of some other kind; but John has in fact been perfectly consistent and is only doing what he always said he intended to do. I have myself been sorry that he could not make any concession, but I am sure he has felt himself bound in conscience to go steadily on with his preparation for Orders and has always been as conciliatory as was consistent with this.
>
> If John is not to receive any more money from his father, we shall have to consider whether more can be obtained from other sources. But before making any applications I should like to know your view of the situation.
>
> John may not have told you that he did extremely well in his theological examination last term, and his election to a Senior Scholarship is a real and well-earned distinction.[38]

Lily no doubt sent the substance of this letter on to her husband in York. Ten days later he wrote again to John, a firm but fair-minded letter:

> If in future you do not agree with, or wish to discuss, anything contained in a letter of mine, kindly communicate with me direct, and not indirectly through Mummy via your tutor or anybody else.
>
> My last letter to you was not intended to close the door to discussion. I gave you my view and I have not changed it. My

suggestion about your Birmingham Stock seemed to me a proper way of solving my difficulties. Altho' it has aroused such opposition, I have not yet heard any argument against it.

Nevertheless, I confess that I had forgotten that Mr. Duff wrote to me in March last and told me of your intentions, and I feel that he is right in feeling that, altho' no reply from me was required, my silence meant consent.

I have therefore decided that I shall have to continue to finance you, though my reluctance has in no way diminished.

I do not wish to see your accounts, but I shall expect you to let me know each term what sum you require from me to meet your obligations after exercising all reasonable economy.[39]

John wrote an affectionate reply, with explanations, apology and gratitude; and from about this time the correspondence begins to mend, and relations between father and son to become less strained. But in writing (as he had in September) of how his son's decision would be 'for the rest of my life ... an abiding sorrow' Arnold was expressing a sad and literal truth. Although their relationship was to a considerable extent restored, and Arnold later took a lively interest in his son's doings as a curate, the buried scars of their wartime differences remained. The bright, confident morning of their early years together was never to be quite recaptured.

3

By the summer of 1944 the tide of war had decisively turned.

... In June 1944 came the long-awaited Allied invasion of France. In August Paris was liberated. By September the Rhine was reached. Despite still powerful German resistance throughout the winter and the launching of rocket attacks upon London, the end was now in sight. The fate of the world was settled when Roosevelt, Stalin and Churchill met at Yalta in February 1945. The frontiers of Europe were to be redrawn.[40]

In all this, Cambridge had had its own part to play:

On the national scale – aside perhaps from the Bletchley Park code-breakers – Cambridge's enduring claim to fame is that the D-Day invasion of northern France was planned on the banks of the Cam. For four nights (28–31 March 1944), with military pickets on the gates, Trinity was thick with officers from all three services being coached for their parts in Operation Overlord. Great Court provided accommodation and the Master, historian G. M. Trevelyan, gave over the Lodge for use as headquarters. Activity was so intense that it even spilled over to St John's, where the Combination Room was turned into a beautifully constructed model of the Normandy beaches, complete with cliffs and relief.[41]

With less than a year between D Day and VE Day, talk of post-war reconstruction was in the air; but the death of William Temple in October 1944 seemed a crippling blow to a church which, having devoted so many of its resources to a nation at war, was now beginning to face the challenges of peace. Temple had been Archbishop of Canterbury for only two years and while Winston Churchill's reported description of him on the bench of bishops ('a sixpenny article in a penny bazaar'[42]) may have been unkind, yet his commanding powers and intellect were going to be sorely missed.

A year before he died, Temple had asked Christopher Chavasse, Bishop of Rochester, to chair a new and large Commission on Evangelism, which was to prepare the post-war church to carry the gospel to a nation scarred by war, with high aspirations for the new world beyond the peace. The report *Towards the Conversion of England*, published in June 1945, attracted enormous comment in the secular press. The first printing was sold out within twenty-four hours and the Report was reprinted six times in the next six months. It seemed as if evangelism might at last find a worthy place high on the agenda of the national church. The famous definition of evangelism (often attributed to William Temple, and dating back to a previous 'Committee of Inquiry' on evangelism at the close of the First World War) which appeared on the first page of the Report is still, though not without its critics, in current use:

> To evangelise is so to present Christ Jesus in the power of the Holy Spirit, that men shall come to put their trust in God through Him, to accept Him as their Saviour, and serve Him as their King in the fellowship of His Church.[43]

In the event, little came of the Report. Bishop Chavasse was said to be 'deeply disappointed'.[44] The Church Assembly – which had asked the two Archbishops to set up such a Commission – lost its nerve:

> The Church Assembly refused to accept the most important recommendation of the Commission to set up a Council on Evangelism, asserting its inability to provide the money for such a

venture and maintaining that the responsibility for follow-up rested with the dioceses. Archbishop Fisher is on record as saying that he refused to set up the Commission 'because there did not seem to be any desire for one. Because everyone seemed to distrust schemes or organisations for the promotion of evangelism – and I share that distrust.'[45]

It was not a climate to give much encouragement to a young man on the threshold of ordination, and sure of God's call to make the gospel known.

As John Stott's four years at Trinity were coming to an end, Robbie Bickersteth was killed, in June 1944. In spite of the difference of age, John Stott's influence on him, mainly by friendship, correspondence, and by introducing him as a visitor to camp, had played a real part in turning his mind towards ordination, once the war was over: but that was not to be. John Stott himself, after a further First in Part 1 of the Theological Tripos (he had used the lunch-break between the papers to teach a friend to distinguish between Swallows, Swifts and House Martins on the Backs![46]) was invited to remain in Cambridge and to read for a doctorate.[47] (Professor Raven was one of those who encouraged him to do this. Years later Raven was sitting next to one of John Stott's curates at lunch in the Rectory, and confided to him that John Stott 'had the record for accurately quoted verses from the Bible in the Tripos Examination'.[48]) An academic career, and in time a College Fellowship, seemed assured. But the call of the pastoral ministry was paramount; he had been in no doubt since Rugby days soon after his conversion that this was his true calling. After a brief holiday he was admitted to Ridley Hall, Cambridge, in the Long Vacation term, 1944, to prepare for ordination.

4

Ridley Hall had been opened in 1881, 'the practical answer on the one hand to Ritualistic, and on the other to Rationalistic, propaganda.'[49] From the first it was committed by its trust deed to an evangelical position, so that those of a different outlook felt almost at once that a less distinctive college was essential:

> Ridley Hall opened its doors in 1881. Lightfoot and Westcott had been warm supporters of this scheme until they discovered that one of the founders, Bishop Perry, had written some theological stipulations of an evangelical character into the trust deed for Ridley Hall; and so ... they founded the Clergy Training School in the

same year, 1881, to represent the Anglican church, as they saw it, in a fuller sense. The Clergy Training School was renamed Westcott House after its chief founder's death.[50]

In fact the trust deed for Ridley Hall (as for Wycliffe Hall in Oxford, a sister foundation) provided simply that the theological instruction shall be 'in conformity with the principles of and in close connection with the Protestant Reformed Church of England';[51] but the meaning of these phrases is amplified by a statement emphasizing the plain meaning of certain of the Thirty-nine Articles 'in their literal sense'. It was presumably to this elaboration that Professors Lightfoot and Westcott demurred. Lightfoot indeed, writing in *The Guardian*[52] made it clear that his stated objection was to the principle rather than the content of the trust deed.

It says much for the courage and determination of Handley Moule, the first Principal of Ridley Hall, that he was not deterred from accepting the appointment. His theological position, which he maintained equally firmly as Bishop of Durham, was such that the content of the trust deed would not cause him difficulty; but the names of Lightfoot and Westcott were so respected in the university (and beyond) that the withdrawal of their support could only have been seen as shedding doubt, if not odium, on the foundation of the new Hall.

In the first sixty years of Ridley Hall's history, up to the 1940s, there were only four Principals including Handley Moule. The first two had become diocesan bishops;[53] A. J. Tait, the third Principal, was appointed a Residentiary Canon of Peterborough in 1924 (combining it with the Principalship until 1927 when he left Cambridge). His successor, under whom John Stott was to train, was the Revd. J. P. S. R. Gibson, known disrespectfully as 'Gibbie'; by 1944 he had already been Principal for seventeen years. It was during his time, at a debate in the Union, that the geneticist, J. B. S. Haldane 'argued that organized religion made its appeal only through fear and shame and was only necessary for emotional and defective people. He claimed that the theological colleges were filled with what he called the dregs of the universities.'[54]

Born in Paris in 1880, Paul Gibson was the son of a Methodist minister, and his decision to join the Church of England was largely due to his wife. He himself recalled how he had tried to run away on the morning of his ordination, 'thoroughly upset by the ecclesiastical atmosphere of the Retreat'.[55] In Cambridge he was usually seen with a flower in his buttonhole; seldom in a clerical collar. It seems likely that the original founders of the Hall and drafters of its trust deed would have been surprised at his appointment. Professor C. E. Raven, writing in 1945, described the change that came over Ridley Hall during Gibson's time:

Ridley had previously stood for Evangelical orthodoxy, for a great doctrinal tradition which was at once conservative and judiciously scholarly. Now it showed less concern for the learning of the past than for the problems of the future, for the precision of exact exegesis than for the quality of general outlook, for the discussion of controversial issues than for action in the cause of reform. The Principal's interest in science and the humanities, his indifference to matters of ecclesiastical and institutional importance, his open advocacy of intercommunion – these created a reputation in certain quarters for innovations, and in others for recklessness.[56]

It is not difficult to see that John Stott with his deep concern 'for the precision of exact exegesis' would feel a sense of isolation from the tenor of some of the teaching at Ridley Hall, and its apparent priorities in ministerial training. Donald English wrote of him at this period:

... He went to Ridley Hall towards the end of the war, when it was at a low ebb, with few students. University lectures in theology were highly critical, but he was unimpressed because the criticism seemed not to be coming from a specifically Christian point of view. The challenge of the lectures was not in their academic or spiritual power. The challenge was rather in the loneliness he felt in seeming to be one of the few who didn't see things that way. The effect of both the University teaching and the situation at Ridley Hall was to send him even more deeply into detailed Bible study, both searching for and increasingly discovering the inner logic which it contained.[57]

The 'few students' were little more than a handful. Only three staircases were in use to accommodate thirteen men (by Easter 1945, only eleven), and the new Vice-Principal, the Revd. C. W. J. Bowles. John Stott was on 'E' staircase, together with John Sheldon from Trinity, and John Bridger and Philip Tompson from Rugby days. All four were still closely involved with the CICCU and with the work of camp.

A novel feature of wartime life at Ridley was the presence of women students. This would have been a delight to the Principal and his wife, early pioneers in the cause of women's ministry (and indeed ordination). But these women were not primarily his students, only his guests. They had arrived from Foxbury, the CMS women's training college in Chislehurst, Kent (then a defence area) as evacuees early in 1941. The Principal wrote of them:

They appreciate the use of 'G' and 'H' [staircases], and their presence not only adds richness to the life of the Hall, but assists us in meeting overhead charges ... They have their own exits and their entrances. They attend Hall and they have their table. They come to some chapels and lectures. Otherwise they work under their own Principal and staff.[58]

With his degree behind him, and using his time at Ridley more for private study than for lectures and supervisions, John Stott was free to continue both his work for camp and his support for the CICCU as a graduate friend and elder statesman. He was still not formally a member of CICCU because of the promise to his father: but in the column headed 'Donations' in the Treasurer's account book, though the entries were few, his name appeared with a regular gift in lieu of subscription.[59] At that time the CICCU group in almost every college met weekly during term for a College Bible Reading. Sometimes these would be led by their own members: more often by clergy or lay people from local churches. Basil Atkinson was in constant demand, as were those CICCU members who had moved on to Ridley Hall. From Ridley it was not uncommon for John Stott to be taking weekly Bible-readings for the CICCU groups in four different colleges; and he was assiduous in supporting the weekly evangelistic sermons in Holy Trinity Church. Myra Chave-Jones's views would have been shared by many from Newnham and Girton in particular:

> I first encountered John in the 1940s when he used to be one of the stewards at the CICCU sermons. He looked handsome and impressively dignified in his sweeping graduate gown. It was always nice to be shown into a seat by him.[60]

She was not alone in thinking this:

> The Sunday night CICCU sermons were now attended by students from evacuated London colleges. Barclay and Stott were ushers at these events. Early on in her first term Shirley Johnson of Queen Mary College, London (later Mrs Bill Lees of OMF), had been invited to the sermons. She soon noticed how graciously the two ushers smiled at all the men, 'but when the girls came in, they showed us to our places with their eyes to the ground. I tried to get one of them to smile at me, but I did not succeed; and when Bill told John this some years after we were married, his comment was, "Oh, Bill, aren't you glad I didn't?" '[61]

A characteristic initiative at this time was the reconstituting by John Stott 'on a more popular basis' of the CICCU's 'Theological Problems

Study Circle'. He was careful to gain the Executive Committee's approval, and in his final term at Ridley circulated an invitation to a weekly meeting to study Colossians 'more thoroughly than is possible at the Sunday afternoon Bible Reading'. This 'Senior Bible Reading', as he called it, was a prototype of many ad hoc groups for Bible study, and later for the discussion of various contemporary issues in the light of Scripture. Perhaps Bash's influence can still be detected in the phrase 'Some of us have felt it laid upon us …' but the 'Conditions of Membership', in one form or another, were to become a familiar feature of the groups that John Stott convened over the next forty years:

> *The Conditions of Membership*, (a gentlemen's agreement, as rigorous as one's conscience dictates):–
>
> (i) To come regularly, having previously studied the relevant passage, with or without commentary,
>
> (ii) To regard our meeting as an addition to, and not a substitute for, the Sunday afternoon Bible Reading.[62]

The 'Plan of Action' listed seven weekly dates, with the verses to be studied on each; and on the reverse of the letter no less than twenty-four commentaries are suggested ('all in the University Library, and I have the Class Marks') from Chrysostom to Westcott, half a dozen of them on the Greek text.

During their first Long-Vac term together at Ridley, John Sheldon kept a diary. It tells how 'When I was ill in bed at Ridley John came and read keen books to me in the evening. The next day he came and read "Torrey on Moody"[63] to me.' A fortnight later Sheldon had 'a time of encouragement with John Stott' and the following week 'JS and I went to the hospital [Addenbrooke's Hospital, then in Trumpington Street] together and it was an unforgettable time. John spoke in his own inimitable style on "Forgiveness, Friendship, Freedom". He sang a solo – "Jesus satisfies" – in one ward. Simply terrific!' Life at Ridley allowed John Stott, in his last year in Cambridge, to spend time freely with individuals, and to befriend and pastor the trickle of men already returning from the war as well as younger undergraduates. One such remembers:

> I shall never forget bumping into him during my first week in Cambridge as a freshman in October 1944. I had met him before, but hardly expected to be recognized, let alone remembered. We were outside my college, Pembroke, and John was on his bike. He stopped when he saw me, chatted for a moment, and then asked me if I planned to go to the pre-terminal meetings of the CICCU (the Cambridge Inter-Collegiate Christian Union). I told him I knew

nothing about them. He explained, and said the first meeting would be that evening in Trinity OCR – the Old Combination Room above Great Court. Perhaps he saw irresolution in my eye: 'Do you know where that is?' he asked. I shook my head. He glanced at his watch, and leaned his bicycle against the wall, saying, 'I'll take you there. It takes just seven and a half minutes.' So we walked together along King's Parade to Trinity, across the Court, up the famous steps, and so to the OCR. John opened the door to show me the gracious high-windowed empty room. Then we walked back (I'm sure it will have taken fifteen minutes precisely) and John retrieved his bike, said, 'See you tonight, then,' and rode off to Ridley Hall. That was forty-five years ago, and a turning-point in my life.[64]

John Sheldon was not the only friend to whom John Stott ministered through 'keen books' – a phrase which might mean devotional books like S. D. Gordon's *Quiet Talks* series, something more fiery and stimulating like R. A. Torrey's *Revival Addresses*, Anglican Protestant teaching from J. C. Ryle, or Christian biography such as Handley Moule's *Charles Simeon* or G. F. Dempster's tales of London's docklands, *Finding Men for Christ*. These – as well as more weighty works – were often missing from his shelves, on loan to students. He was busy, too, committing to paper suggestions and instructions which up till then had depended on word of mouth – a kind of oral tradition. Papers were circulated to the CICCU College Representatives on the best way to manage a 'Freshers' Squash' – a start-of-year meeting to introduce freshers to the CICCU and (perhaps) to the gospel. One such, on how to win a friend for Christ, circulated in draft under the title *Personal Evangelism* and was later published.[65] In his last month at Ridley, before leaving Cambridge for good, he prepared for the President of the CICCU a draft which for some years formed the basis of the letter of invitation sent to the CICCU weekend speakers. It was intended both to give some idea of the nature of the ministry expected from them, and also tactfully to offer suggestions of what was unacceptable. Basil Atkinson had noted many years before that it was important to offer guidance to those coming to speak; since, left to themselves, 'we had rather a lot of sermons based on the rich young ruler'.[66] So, with regard to the Saturday night Bible-reading, speakers were told:

We are anxious to avoid on the one hand a devotional talk which hangs loosely upon a passage or upon one or two texts, and on the other a string of texts so numerous that in referring to them the speaker is unable to pause on each and elucidate its meaning.

At the end of the letter, speakers were given an indication of the themes taken on Sunday nights up to that point in the term:

> With regard to the Sunday evangelistic sermon, in view of the fact that a number of unconverted men come regularly Sunday by Sunday, we are anxious that as wide a range as possible of Christian teaching should be attempted each term. Sometimes at the end of a term we have surveyed the course of sermons preached and found that integral parts of the Gospel have been omitted. A list is given below of the principal topics of sermons preached so far this term. Perhaps in seeking God's guidance for your message, you would feel able to take into consideration vital Christian truths not yet expounded.
>
> We hope that these suggestions will not be rejected out of hand as the aberrations of the young and attributed to the possession of zeal without knowledge. We have been encouraged to put pen to paper partly by a desire to avoid the mistakes of the past and partly by the request of some speakers for this information.[67]

To these terms at Ridley belongs also John Stott's first published article (apart from editorials in *The Meteor*, the Rugby School journal), 'Child Conversion'; for the magazine of the Scripture Union. Originally an address given at a conference for CSSM helpers, based on his experiences at Borth and on other evangelistic forays in company with Bash, it offers four suggestions 'on the subject of the winning for the Lord Jesus of children between the ages of six and sixteen'. He suggests that such work is possible – children are not too young to respond to Christ; that it is important – 'we must tackle the disease of sin in its early stage'; that it is advantageous – 'a lifetime of service lies before the child'; and that it is dangerous – he cites the dangers of shallowness and staleness.[68] Perhaps it owes something to a famous article by Josiah Spiers, founder of the CSSM, entitled 'The Value of a Child's Soul'; but the article is based on practical experience interpreted by biblical principle, with quotations from Jeremiah, the gospels and the New Testament letters. It was soon to be exemplified in his own work with the children of the All Souls Church School and young people's organizations in his London curacy.

It was largely due to the Vice-Principal, Cyril Bowles (later Principal, and from 1969–87 Bishop of Derby) that John Stott's experience of Ridley was not as negative as David Watson's some twelve years later. In his autobiography David Watson described his time there:

> I disliked the formality of Ridley chapel services every day; I rejected

any teaching that I considered remotely 'liberal'; I found the staff giving theoretical answers to questions I was not yet asking; and my foremost priority was still my evangelistic work in the university, often at the expense of activities at Ridley Hall, most of which I regarded as interfering with the real work I felt called to do. The staff were patient with my spiritual arrogance and critical attitudes, and I am sure now that I would have grown in my knowledge of God far more had I been a little more humble and positive in my approach.[69]

As far as the Principal's lectures went, John Stott (with the theological Tripos fresh in his mind) felt something of the same:

His patron saints were John Oman and Charles Raven ... he was a kind man, a dear man, and seeking to be conscientious when I expect he was well beyond retirement age, but his lectures, I'm afraid, were rather pathetic. They were a patchwork, summaries of different books that he'd read, but they weren't woven into a coherent tapestry. He was also very slow of speech so I'm a bit ashamed to say that we used to write letters during his lectures because we just didn't get anything out of them.[70]

Things were better when C. F. D. ('Charlie') Moule was lecturing. He had been Vice-Principal of Ridley until 1944 when he left to become Dean of Clare. He combined immense brilliance as a New Testament scholar with personal humility, friendliness and charm. He was a great-nephew of the first Principal of Ridley, Handley Moule, Bishop of Durham; though Charlie Moule's evangelical scholarship was rather more liberal in its approach than Handley Moule's traditional orthodoxy. Ridley students would wait for signs of this divergence: 'When he said something we regarded as outrageous we would wag our fingers at him and say "Charlie, what would Uncle Handley have said?"'[71]

Cyril Bowles, the Vice-Principal, was wise enough to offer John Stott suggestions for guided reading, rather than the Ridley lecture course which would cover ground already familiar. John Stott read every day in the great reading room of the University Library such works as Augustine's *Confessions*, the *Stromateis* (or 'Miscellaneous Studies') of Clement of Alexandria, and Origen's *De Principiis*. In addition, perhaps in response to Arnold Stott's requirement of broader fields of study, Cyril Bowles suggested that he should read some Freud; and he was much struck by Freud's exposition of the characteristics of infantile regression, since these exactly described the younger of his mother's two sisters, Louise Hutchesson, known to the family as 'Auntie Babe'. When next the opportunity presented, John Stott plied his Aunt with leading questions:

> 'Auntie, do you sleep with your knees tucked up to your chin?'
> 'Yes, always.'
> 'Do you like the rhythmic movements of a ship at sea?'
> 'Oh, I love it.'

John Stott went carefully through Freud's distinguishing symptoms and she agreed with them all: 'Auntie Babe' seems to have been peculiarly perceptive as a family name for her.[72] As she grew older, her life became increasingly secluded and withdrawn.

In place of the General Ordination Examination, graduates at Ridley Hall sat for the 'Cambridge Ordination Course' examinations, officially known as the Cambridge Scheme for the Training of Graduates for Holy Orders. The examiners in June 1945 included Charles Raven, C. F. D. Moule, and Ian Ramsey, later Bishop of Durham. John Stott took parts 1 and 2 combined, 'satisfied the examiners' (there were no classes) and was the only graduate to achieve a starred Distinction in any paper: in his case, in both papers on Doctrine.[73] Though he was to retain a certain wry affection for Ridley, he could not feel that he had received much from his time there:

> I derived greater benefit indirectly from meetings at the newly-established Tyndale House in Selwyn Gardens, home of the Tyndale Fellowship for Biblical Research, and from the privilege of preaching in local churches on Sundays, or giving Bible readings to CICCU college groups on weekday evenings.[74]

In the summer of 1945 the war finally ended. VE Day, 8 May, was celebrated with a great bonfire on Midsummer Common. VJ Day, 15 August, marked the final surrender of Japan, nine days after the bombing of Hiroshima and less than a week after Nagasaki. These two bombs between them killed nearly two hundred thousand people: 'The war was thus quickly over, avoiding a lot of hard fighting, but at the price of a cheque which all future humanity would have to honour: the price of living in the shadow of atomic war.'[75] Yet the victims of Hiroshima and Nagasaki were themselves only a tiny proportion of the 50 million deaths of the Second World War. Looking back from a distance of more than thirty years John Stott himself spoke of the 'ghastly nightmare' of a world at war; and discerned in the hunger for post-war reconstruction an 'innocent idealism' – whose twin sister would be disillusion.[76] Certainly the country, and not least those serving in the forces at home and overseas, was in a mood for change. The general election of July 1945 (two months after victory in Europe but before Japan's surrender) which took Churchill from office was an expression of a determined desire for a new social order, and the taking of an opportunity which, thirty years before at the end of the First World War, had somehow slipped through the nation's fingers and come to nothing.

5

John Stott was now within reach of the goal to which his studies had been directed, not without some personal cost, while so many of his contemporaries had been away at the war. With the coming of peace a new Principal was appointed to Ridley Hall, Falkner Allison, the eldest of the four Allison brothers, all of whom had trained there for ordination; his greatest contribution lay in his own solid experience of parochial work. Perhaps it was partly his appointment that lay behind John Stott's decision to spend a further term at Ridley Hall, postponing his ordination until Advent. In May he suggested this to his father and received a characteristic reply. Leaving aside John Stott's somewhat surprising consideration, that by staying on, in the role of 'Archdeacon' or Senior Student, he could be of use to the new Principal, his father, not for the first time, made it clear that he hardly counted the study of theology as contributing much to an education:

> Your second 'advantage' was that you would 'value a term's work
> on your own without … considerations of exams.' But what sort of
> work? If it is the further reading of theology, I could not agree. But
> if you are ready to spend several hours a day – mainly reading – in
> an attempt to widen your outlook and to fill in some of the gaps in
> your education which I have been [un-?] able to prevent – then I
> will gladly consent, for I still feel myself morally responsible for
> providing a proper education until you begin work on your own.[77]

In writing to thank his father for his readiness to finance a further term, John Stott was quick to assure him that he had not been intending to concentrate solely on theological reading: 'I imagine you would be agreeable to a diet including a mixed grill of history, psychology, science etc.'[78] Such a course will have helped to whet his appetite for the wide variety of books and the range of contemporary thinking which marked his later 'reading groups' and private study.

Camp, meanwhile, was preparing for a peacetime role. In the December 1944 vacation John Stott, with Bash and John Eddison, had explored the possibility of a new base, more accessible to the sea than

Clayesmore. They visited Allhallows, Rousdon, with its attractive cliffs and coastline, and made one or two other tentative explorations, but in the event decided to stay at Iwerne Minster for the foreseeable future. Fifty years later camp is still based there at Clayesmore School. Bash had hoped that John Stott might feel called to give his whole time to camp work, perhaps as an ordained schoolmaster or in some leadership role on the staff of the Scripture Union; but it was always unlikely that camp could offer the scope his gifts and energies would need. The three camps of summer 1945 were his last as Secretary; and though he occasionally visited Iwerne after his ordination it was the end of an era. Sad though it was to leave a work to which he had given so much, and where he had so many friends, John Stott himself was ready for a new challenge. John Eddison writes:

I think as his time at Cambridge drew to a close, John began to realize that his future did not lie with the work of camp, much as he loved and valued it, and much as he owed to it. I remember one incident late at night when we were down at Iwerne Minster. It was near the end of the summer camp of 1945 (John's last as Secretary), and several of us were gathered in the kitchen where we used to meet, with the grudging approval of Bash, to drink tea and gossip. Somewhat exceptionally John joined us. He was in a hilarious mood, started throwing eggs about, and would not go to bed just because 'Nanny' (Bash) told him to do so. It was all in fun, of course, but I sensed a feeling of emancipation which I hadn't noticed before.[79]

By this time, too, his immediate future was settled. He would take a title at All Souls, Langham Place, where he and his parents had worshipped before the war. Harold Earnshaw-Smith, the Rector of All Souls, was a regular visitor to the CICCU and had preached at their broadcast service in John Stott's second year at Trinity. In 1945 he came on a similar visit to preach for the sixtieth anniversary of the CICCU. John Stott read the lesson from John 3, and Earnshaw-Smith came up to him after the service to enquire if he had yet settled where he would serve his first curacy. On learning that he was still uncommitted, he invited him to All Souls. John Stott had long admired Harold Earnshaw-Smith and it was provisionally arranged that he would join the staff of All Souls in December, at a stipend of £230 a year. Here too his father was consulted, and expressed his opinion with his usual astringency: 'Human nature varies but little – in class or country. So that I should think it matters little where you start. I think you will find you have a great deal to learn after all these years of sheltered and academic life.'[80] John Stott replied eirenically, confirming his feeling that All Souls would be 'a good place in which to begin'. It was to be a 'beginning' that remained constant for well over half a century.

There was no curate's house, but John Stott had known at Kilbracken and Trinity (and also at camp) Marcus Dukes, the son of two distinguished doctors who lived at No. 1, Queen Anne Street, within a stone's throw of the church. Through Marcus, John Stott had come to meet his parents; and it was now arranged that they should put him up 'for a week or two', assuming their house would be repaired and habitable in time. In the event John Stott remained with them, living in their home, for the best part of seven years. The Dukes were Quakers, and not therefore members of All Souls.[81] Cuthbert Dukes was a distinguished pathologist engaged in cancer research; his wife Ethel, daughter of a Methodist minister, was one of the founders of the National Marriage Guidance Council,[82] a robust and autocratic lady known to her husband as 'Her Majesty'. Marcus, an engineer, was away from home doing relief work in France.[83] Dr. Ethel Dukes wrote six months before the ordination:

> Things have been very difficult in the house during the war. However, some of our maids hope to come back to us, but we cannot have them until the repairs are done and the furniture back.
>
> We hope all these things will be accomplished before Xmas (at any rate enough repairs to have the furniture and the maids) and then we might be able to take you in. We should very much like to have you ...[84]

A month later Earnshaw-Smith wrote asking for confirmation of his plans since he had heard rumours that John Stott might be staying on in Cambridge. A reply soon reached him from Ridley Hall:

> I have also been waiting until our new Principal has happily settled in before consulting him and seeking his approval.
>
> My plans are straightening out. I have definitely rejected the possibility of reading for a fellowship; and hope to be ordained at Advent ... If I may say so, I am very much looking forward to coming to you... I know what a very great deal you have to teach me, and I do hope you will never hesitate to 'reprove, rebuke, exhort'. I am deeply anxious to learn ...[85]

In November all candidates for Deacon's Orders in the London Diocese were required to sit the Ordination Examination on the Christian faith, the Holy Scriptures, the Prayer Book and the Pastoral

Office. It was a good start to his life as a curate in the diocese that John Stott should learn a few days after Christmas that he had been awarded the Pilkington Prize for his papers in this examination, to a value of £1.10s! In addition candidates were required to submit an original sermon ('such as would take about twenty minutes to deliver') on the text 'Thy kingdom come'. With this was required a wealth of further documentation: certificates of birth and baptism, college testimonials and proof of graduation, letters of testimonial from three incumbents (countersigned by their own bishops if they were not beneficed in the London diocese), a form of Nomination to a Curacy, with the joint Declaration of the Incumbent and Candidate appended, and the *Si Quis*, the public notice read in the candidate's church, inviting any objectors to come forward. There does not seem to be any record that the Bishop of Coventry (no longer Mervyn Haigh, now Bishop of Winchester) had to agree to release his candidate to be ordained in another diocese.

At last it was all done. John Stott left Ridley Hall and Cambridge for good to become again a Londoner. After a few days at home in Surrey he joined the other candidates at a Retreat House in Hampstead a week before Christmas in time for supper and Compline. He was conspicuous among them, if only for the suit of plus-fours he chose to wear for the retreat, made from Scottish tweed bought in the Hebrides on his visit with Robbie Bickersteth; it was his personal statement, distancing himself from the formal and ecclesiastical atmosphere beginning to close around him.

Before leaving Ridley he had sent out the usual prayer card to a wide circle of friends:[86]

> Your prayers are asked for John R. W. Stott who is to be ordained deacon by the Bishop of London in St. Paul's Cathedral at 9.30 a.m. on St. Thomas's Day, Friday, 21st December 1945, to serve in the parish of All Souls', Langham Place, and St. Peter's, Vere Street, London, W. 1.

> 1, Queen Anne Street,   Ridley Hall,
> London, W. 1.   Cambridge

It went to Aunt Babe and to Nanny Golden, to Major and Mrs. Letts of Oakley Hall, to F. C. Slater his Rugby housemaster, and to many friends from Cambridge. Basil Atkinson, Oliver Barclay, John Burnaby, John Sheldon, Henry Chadwick – there were about 150 names in all, many of them friends from camp. Of the letters he received in return a few survive. Hugh Lyon had written from Rugby:

I am more than interested in your prospective ordination. You may be sure of my thoughts and prayers and I much hope that the strong feeling of vocation and exhilaration which you feel at the prospect will stand you in good stead through the months and years ahead, which are not likely to be easy ones.

As you probably know, Earnshaw Smith's boy has just come to Rugby, and I have just promised to go to speak at one of his weekly Services at St. Peter's in the spring.

Forgive a brief and rather formal letter. I think you know what I wish for you and how happy I am about your decision.[87]

Robbie Bickersteth's widow Penelope wrote: 'How Robbie would have loved to be with you in body'.[88] Cyril Bowles, Vice-Principal of Ridley Hall, sent a pastoral letter: 'I want to express my strong personal regard for you ... I hope to give you on Friday whatever support my presence can give.'[89] Gladys Beale, who had taught him music at Oakley Hall, had written from Gloucestershire where she was running a pre-prep school to promise him her prayers and to add: 'You have two great gifts, lack of which hampers many parsons, a clear speaking voice and being able to sing!'[90] Florence Myers, who had cooked for camp on a number of occasions, remembered that he had once had thoughts of the diplomatic service, and reminded him that he would be instead 'an ambassador in bonds' – going on to hope that he had been able to make 'some arrangement about an honest mid-day meal (NOT bread-and-cheese!).'[91] And his sister Joanna, newly married, wrote from Manchester:

It's strange to think that the time has really come after all these years. As you know I haven't been able to understand your point of view all the time about it – but I can see quite clearly that it is what you want, and that it is what you have been working and aiming for, for years, and it *has* dawned on me that you are 'just the type of person needed' ...[92]

From St. Andrew's Hospital, Northampton, Aunt Ella wrote affectionately with a cheque to buy a present: 'I believe Church vestments are very expensive,'[93] while Great-Aunt Emily told him 'You *daily* have my prayers' and enclosed a few 'pearls of great price'; which were seven verses of Scripture, carefully chosen and copied out with emphatic underlinings, in her elderly spidery hand: 'I send an angel before thee ... *shine* as *lights* in the world ... *ye know* that your labour is not in vain ... I will never *leave* thee nor forsake *thee*.'[94] Nearly fifty years later in a sermon around the time of his seventieth birthday, John Stott told an All Souls congregation of another verse of Scripture that he met in the course of his daily Bible reading, just before his ordination, which became to him

> ... a crucial clarification of the ultimate goal or objective of the ordained ministry. Indeed, I know no better motto for anybody in full-time Christian or pastoral service than this, to 'lay it to heart to give glory to God's name'. It became in a sense my motto, that in all forms of Christian leadership and ministry what we are concerned about is not the glory of our own silly little name, but the glory of the name of God.[95]

The ordination by William Wand, the new Bishop of London, was in the crypt of St. Paul's Cathedral on the morning of St. Thomas' day, December 21st. John Stott's family, including both his parents, were there to see him made deacon. It fell to him to read the Gospel ('I just felt I wanted all the world to hear you' wrote Nanny Golden afterwards):[96]

> Let your loins be girded about, and your lights burning; and ye yourselves like unto men that wait for their lord ...[97]

Bishop Wand laid hands on him and delivered to him a copy of the New Testament with the traditional charge: 'Take thou authority to read the Gospel in the Church of God, and to preach the same ...' Outside after the service the bells were ringing for London's first peacetime Christmas for seven years. A new beginning was in the air.

NINE

Assistant Curate: All Souls and St Peter's

1

Following the end of the war, and shortly after John Stott was embarking on his curacy, Mass-Observation conducted a survey of what Londoners in an unspecified London borough thought about religion. The survey concluded:

> Not more than one person in ten ... is at all closely associated with any of the churches, and about two-thirds never or practically never go to Church. The majority, however – four out of five women and two out of three men – give at least verbal assent to the possibility of there being a God, and most of the rest express doubt rather than disbelief. Uncompromising disbelievers in a Deity amount to about one in twenty.[1]

The picture is not unfamiliar, but the challenge presented by such statistics to the pastor of a parish, and a minister of the gospel of Christ, was unmistakable.

Harold Earnshaw-Smith, the Rector of All Souls, whose assistant curate John Stott now became, was a man of much individuality, faith, courage and charm. He was a native of Cambridge, where his father owned the Deighton Bell bookshop. There were tragic and painful difficulties in his early family life and upbringing which left their mark on him in a certain natural shyness and self-deprecating humour which helped to hide his real feelings even from those who knew him best. He came to a living faith in Christ as an undergraduate through the CICCU: 'his conversion was for him a deliverance from what he experienced in the home of grief and pain ... the gripping power of evil and loss of control.'[2] From this strong sense of deliverance and freedom sprang his love for all kinds of people; and for the gospel of grace, which was the lifelong theme of all his ministry.

His own curacy had been in the very different surroundings of St. James's, 'the grandest church in Bermondsey'[3] set between the Southern Railway embankment and Jamaica Road. The London County Council housing estates had hardly begun, and the area was a mass of small terraced streets and cramped courts and tenements characteristic of 'East End' south London. It was the start of the First World War, 1914; and Earnshaw-Smith soon added to his parish responsibilities the chaplaincy of the Cambridge Medical Mission, a club, dispensary, sanatorium and settlement, linked with and much supported by the CICCU, from which the name 'Cambridge' was derived.[4]

Following this curacy, Earnshaw-Smith did pioneer work with the Church Missionary Society in northern Nigeria (overseas missionary work was to remain a lifelong interest); and then returned to south London to take charge of the Bermondsey Mission on Harold Salmon's retirement. Next came two years as a college chaplain at Gonville and Caius, Cambridge (he himself had been a classical scholar of Christ's); followed by a return to south London as Vicar of Christ Church, North Brixton in 1927. After a brief but influential period as Vicar of Watford, he was appointed Rector of All Souls in 1936 on the resignation of Arthur Buxton. By the time that John Stott joined him he had been Rector for nine years, six of them in the exigencies of war-time central London, and had seen his church so severely damaged by enemy action that it could not be re-opened until well after the war: it remained closed from 1940 to 1951. Through the blitz he and his staff (including a Church Army Sister, Sister Jordan, who had come with him from Watford) had exercised a remarkable and courageous ministry night after night in the air-raid shelters deep underground, packed with humanity, many dog-tired and frightened, some homeless or bereaved. Services were held regularly on all four platforms of Oxford Circus tube station.

It had not been an easy decision for Earnshaw-Smith to leave Watford at a moment when God was using his ministry in a remarkable way. He wrote in a private prayer-letter to a few friends about his new church and parish:

> The traditions of the church are not so definitely Evangelical as in Prebendary Webster's time, and I shall need much grace, tact and firmness to deal with the present situation and win the confidence of the people. The Parish contains opposite extremes of wealth and poverty and it is not easy to make the Church a spiritual home for both. Financially we have to face heavy deficits on both capital and revenue accounts. Such are some of the difficulties!
>
> But in spite of everything All Souls stands in a wonderfully strategic position for the Gospel and there are no limits to what God can do, save those set by our little-faith. Next door to us is Broadcasting House with its hundreds of employees; across the road is the Langham Hotel with visitors from all parts of the world, and near by is the Regent Street Polytechnic. In the Parish are a number of great business houses, and the Middlesex Hospital affords opportunities for work amongst students and doctors. It should be possible to arrange lunch-hour or after-business services for many of the young people who work in the West End. We have our own Church School with six hundred children and hope to restart a Sunday School... And surely Oxford Circus should be a great place for 'Fishing'!
>
> Please pray that we may know just how to enter these many doors for the gospel.
>
> I am taking with me from Watford Sister Jordan of the Church Army who has been with me all my time there, and in December Mr Kenneth Hooker is coming as colleague; they will both value your prayers.[5]

On his first Sunday, the day following his institution, Earnshaw-Smith found the Holy Table prepared as usual for the celebrant to take an eastward position with his back to the people, one of the 'ritualistic' changes that Arthur Buxton had brought to All Souls. Beginning as he meant to go on, he quietly took his place, in loyalty to the Book of Common Prayer, 'standing at the north side of the Table'.[6] Links with Broadcasting House were quickly established, Earnshaw-Smith himself taking a regular broadcast Children's Service; and Kenneth Hooker, his new curate, giving a fifteen-minute talk on Thursday mornings in the series 'Lift Up Your Hearts'.[7]

One of Harold Earnshaw-Smith's early curates was John V. Taylor, later General Secretary of CMS and then Bishop of Winchester, who recalled him with affection:

During my student days his was a revered name in Evangelical circles as a Keswick speaker and as a Vicar of Watford who drew very large numbers to his Church and brought many to Christ, especially among the younger generation. He moved to All Souls Langham Place some years before I was ordained. I had met him as a visiting speaker at CSSMs and was immensely proud to be invited by him to serve my title at All Souls. Kenneth Hooker was then still with him as Senior Curate ...

The word that first comes to mind when thinking of Earnshaw Smith is 'grace'. It includes its full theological sense but also includes graciousness. He was a gentleman, with a strong measure of instinctive good taste and natural, but never studied, social graces. He was essentially at ease in Harley Street and Queen Anne Street ... – what I learnt most from him was gracious simplicity in the conduct of worship and the preaching of the Word. He preached the Word faithfully, including its sharpness, but on his lips it was always Gospel, always an appeal ... My own most lasting inheritance from Annie [Earnshaw-Smith's affectionate nickname], I like to think, was the sense of prayer which he managed to instil into his services, especially the Holy Communion. I learnt from him the Anglican joy of things done decently and in order, the careful choice of hymns, the rejection of anything shoddy ...

Two months after I arrived as a deacon he set me to preach six mid-week Lent addresses. I chose to do a course on the Life of St. Peter. The first of them went on far too long. As we got back into the vestry he clapped a hand to his forehead, exclaiming, 'My dear boy, I asked you to give us six addresses, not pile them all into one!'[8]

2

From 1936 to 1939 the work at All Souls was steadily gaining ground, only to face for a second time the set-backs of a capital city at war. Late in the evening of 8 December 1940 the Defence Officer fire-watching on the roof of Broadcasting House was horrified to see a huge land mine, attached to a vast dark parachute, floating silently down into Portland Place. The parachute seemed to extend the whole width of the street. He was able to report the presence of the bomb before it exploded at 10.55 p.m., a few minutes later. All the offices on the west side of Broadcasting House were wrecked:

There was widespread and extensive damage with the BBC and Langham Hotel suffering very badly. All houses on the west side between Portland Place and Duchess Street were damaged as were the properties at Seymour Place and Harrowby Street. Water and gas mains were destroyed and there was serious flooding for several days from the BBC; thankfully the gas mains did not explode. There were two fatalities from the BBC, one a policeman, and large number of other casualties; a substantial number needed hospital treatment. The incident file for the survey of the church carried out the next day states that '... *the ceiling is down – all doors and windows broken – centre filled with rubbish – walls standing apparently undamaged but not surveyed yet.*'[9]

The blast so damaged All Souls' famous steeple that thirty feet of it had to be taken down. The whole roof of the church had lifted and then dropped, bringing with it the ceiling and some of the main beams. Tons of fallen plaster did much damage to pews and choirstalls. Earnshaw-Smith was photographed in the rain by the local newspaper the following morning digging the carpets out from under the debris. Sister Jordan had been on night-duty in a nearby air-raid shelter:

At dawn I left for home, only to find every door in the Church House blown off, the window frames hanging down, and everything in disorder. It was a great sadness to see the Church we loved so much bruised and broken. As soon as it was sufficiently light, we began to dismantle the Church, collecting books, hassocks, curtains and carpets as best we could. In the middle of it, the Surveyor came and refused to allow us to carry on, because pieces were continually falling, unless we wore our tin hats ...

It was amusing to see the Rector, who was always so spick and span, looking more like a sweep than anything, with his flannels tucked into his gum boots and his face and hair as black as coal. I hardly liked to tell him – and then found later that my face was just as bad!

The following Sunday I waited by the wounded Church to meet members of the congregation who had not heard of the damage and came for Morning Prayer as usual. We walked together to St Peter's ...[10]

Harold Earnshaw-Smith was already acting as Priest-in-Charge of St. Peter's, Vere Street, where the Reverend R. S. Lound was a sick man. He is said to have suffered from shell-shock as an army chaplain during the First World War, and had been invalided away from London during the blitz; he never returned to St. Peter's. During the remaining wartime winters the evening services were held in a hall in the Regent Street Polytechnic since St. Peter's could not be blacked-out.[11]

So St. Peter's, Vere Street, the former 'Oxford Chapel' of the Cavendish Estate, became the new home of the All Souls congregation. It is a charming early eighteenth-century building by James Gibbs, the architect of St. Martin-in-the-Fields, as well as of the Senate House, Cambridge, and the Radcliffe Camera in Oxford. It had been re-named 'St. Peter's' after restoration in 1832. In the 1860s it was famous for the ministry of the controversial F. D. Maurice, leading Christian Socialist and sometimes reckoned 'the greatest moral and social prophet to arise within the Victorian Churches'.[12] When Charles Dodgson ('Lewis Carroll', author of *Alice*) was in London he could sometimes be found in the congregation. He wrote in his diary: '... as usual to Vere Street Chapel ... As a great many stayed for the Communion I offered my help ...'[13] A century after its restoration it ceased to be a proprietary chapel and became the parish church of St. Peter with St. Thomas. It was to this church, seating hardly more than 500, that All Souls transferred their services in December 1940. Under later pastoral reorganization it became a daughter church of All Souls, and the regular home of the Family Service in the 1960s and early 70s.[14] It was therefore in St. Peter's, not in All Souls, that John Stott ministered throughout his time as curate and for his first six months as Rector.

John Stott was fortunate in the man to whom he could now look for practical training in the day-to-day work of parish ministry. He found him 'an outstandingly good role model' and added 'I would willingly have blacked his boots'.[15] Earnshaw-Smith loved Christ, and loved his people. He had a very affectionate way, pastorally. He would wander around the church for twenty minutes before the service, probably even right up to eleven o'clock, going up to a pew and holding out his hands and welcoming people: they loved him and he loved them, especially the faithful elderly ladies and the families from the poorer end of the parish. Newcomers were made to feel particularly welcome. A young medical student, fresh from Cambridge and a stranger to London, always remembered the kindness and warmth with which Earnshaw-Smith would greet him at the door of St. Peter's after a Sunday Service, putting his surpliced arm round the young man's shoulders 'like the wing of a seagull: I felt very welcomed and touched.'[16] His gifts were pastoral rather than administrative. He had no secretary; there was no congregational register. John Stott still recalls finding him one day sitting on the floor of his tiny study sending out a circular, stuffing the envelopes and licking the stamps himself.[17]

Sister Jordan and Earnshaw-Smith had a high regard for each other, having worked together through all his time at Watford. 'Rector dear', she would say: 'Sister dear', he would reply. 'That was very naughty of you, Rector dear' would be her characteristic response when she discovered (sometimes rather late in the day) that he had been pulling her leg. She would invite the Rector to come and speak at one of her meetings for women; he would sing to them and was always ready to join in their parties. John Stott, too, found he could keep in her good books by attending the Thursday afternoon women's meeting 'or at least coming in for tea when the meeting itself was over'.

In church, Earnshaw-Smith had the gift of conveying a profound sense of worship, leading the service with simplicity and reverence, a feel for liturgy and a fine command of the English language. Curates were always welcome at the Rectory where he and his wife Dorothy ('Doro', he called her) would entertain them, and where they would meet the Earnshaw-Smith children and play family games in the big first-floor drawing room. He combined warmth and friendliness with a natural dignity and a total lack of pomposity. He was full of mischief with an undergraduate sense of the absurd. John Taylor remembers him in the vestry, just about to join the choir before a service, struggling into his surplice and singing out suddenly 'O, for a shirt that will not shrink!';[18] and John Stott recalls an experience probably shared by many of 'Annie's' curates:

> He had this outrageous sense of humour. In the middle of the service he would come up to one of his curates and say 'Let me see now, you're preaching this morning aren't you?' He did it to Geoffrey Lester [senior curate] and he did it to me, just to put the wind up us![19]

Harold Earnshaw-Smith's preaching was thoughtful, Christ-centred, often evangelistic, and in essence biblical and expository at a time when the art of expository preaching had not yet been fully re-discovered by Anglicans. He was in no doubt that 'the true Evangelical ... is especially to be marked by his emphasis on evangelism and his use of the Bible.'[20] From his earliest days he had stood firmly in an evangelical tradition. As a college chaplain in Cambridge he was a valued senior friend and advisor to the CICCU, organizing and leading evangelistic services on Sunday evenings in the Victoria Cinema on Market Hill or, during the summer term, in the Market Place itself.[21] He managed to combine his chaplaincy work with the part-time role of the first 'travelling secretary' of the IVF and made frequent visits to the other universities from Cambridge in the early 1920s.[22] By the 1930s he was among the distinguished group of IVF Vice-Presidents, and a member of the Advisory Body, well-known and trusted as an evangelical leader.[23]

In July 1939, when John Stott had not yet come up to Cambridge, Harold Earnshaw-Smith preached in Great St. Mary's a broadcast sermon during the Fourth International Conference of Evangelical Students (with over 1,000 delegates from thirty-three nations) on the theme of 'Christ our Freedom', which well exemplifies his message, whether in Cambridge or Bermondsey, All Souls or Africa:

> To us Christianity is Christ. To close the mind to Him is to make nonsense of history and to mock at the whole of human experience; to know Him is to have the answer to the greatest riddle of all and to find the winds of God flowing freely through every avenue of the mind ... Christ is our freedom from the dogging sense of sin and condemnation ... there is no freedom in the world to be compared with the sense of release that comes with a realisation of the forgiveness of God; when, in one liberating moment, I see the Cross as the saving act of God, and know that He loves me in spite of my sin.[24]

3

The first half of the twentieth century was not an easy time for those who called themselves evangelicals. A hundred years before John Stott began his ministry at All Souls *The Times* had conducted (with some difficulty over exact shades of opinion) a survey of the principal clergy of the London diocese. Of the ninety-eight listed, over half were seen as Evangelicals.[25] Yet only thirty years later the same paper compared the ebbing fortunes and diminished influence of the evangelicals to a deserted harbour on a silted estuary: 'Over the years the sea has ebbed away from it. Now only the mouldering buildings and forsaken quays remain as a witness to vanished life, prosperity and influence.'[26] Matthew Arnold, the leading critic of his day, noticed and described the same decline among the evangelical party in the church:

> The power is passing from it to others who will make good some of the aspects of religion which the Evangelicals neglected ... The Evangelical clergy no longer recruits itself with success, no longer lays hold on such promising subjects as formerly; it is losing the future, and feels that it is losing it. Its signs of a vigorous life, its gaiety and audacity, are confined to its older members, too powerful to lose their own vigour, but without successors to whom to transmit it.[27]

It was this same dependence upon an 'old guard' that lay behind Hensley Henson's typically caustic quip when, during the days of the 1928 Prayer Book controversy, he described the evangelical party as 'an army of illiterates generalled by octogenarians, a description more unkind than untrue'.[28] The ranks of the Evangelicals no doubt contained many simple believers whose Protestantism was instinctive rather than articulated, but they were not as illiterate as Hensley Henson professed to believe. And on the particular issue of the 1928 Deposited Prayer Book, history has vindicated them: 'Parliament seems to have judged more correctly than the Church'.[29]

In 1939 Geoffrey Fisher moved from Chester to be Bishop of London. His private assessment of the evangelicals in his new diocese was less pungently expressed than Hensley Henson's, but hardly more encouraging. His biographer wrote:

At the other end of the ecclesiastical spectrum [from the Anglo-Catholics] were 'the real Evangelicals' – the description is the Bishop's – with whom by early upbringing, temperament and conviction he had more in common and greater sympathy. Most prominent amongst these was Archdeacon Sharpe whom Geoffrey Fisher greatly respected as a person but did not regard as a churchman of real significance. If the Anglo-Catholics were an influential, dominant and well organised party, the Bishop regarded the Evangelicals as a 'cowed, beaten, depressed group' needing encouragement. 'They knew that they were kept out of everything by the Anglo-Catholics,' he affirmed 'so they just kept to themselves and ran their own parishes, knowing that they were disapproved of by the Bishops as a whole.'[30]

This was the situation as John Stott himself found it and described it when he began his ministry at All Souls:

When I was ordained in 1945, soon after the end of World War II, there were few evangelicals in the Church of England. For over a century Anglo-Catholic thought had predominated, though weakened by liberal theology ... There were no evangelical bishops and no evangelical theological teachers in any university. The few evangelical clergy there were fought bravely, but had their backs to the wall. The evangelical movement was despised and rejected.

This was a tragic situation, because we evangelicals claim that the constitution of the Church of England is itself thoroughly evangelical and reformed. It is true that since the Reformation there have been three strands or parties within Anglicanism – Evangelical,

Catholic and Liberal – which are sometimes amusingly described as 'low and lazy', 'high and crazy', 'broad and hazy'. Yet the 1662 Prayer Book and the Thirty-Nine Articles (which remain the official doctrinal standards of the Church of England) are definitely evangelical. They bear witness with clarity to the supreme authority of Scripture and its sufficiency for salvation, and to the salvation of lost human beings on the sole ground of the atoning sacrifice of Christ embraced by faith alone and through the regenerating work of the Holy Spirit. But for years these fundamental gospel truths had become obscured.[31]

Part of the problem, as so often in the past, lay in evangelical disunity; or rather the inclusion within the description 'evangelical' of those who might hold certain convictions in common but differ widely upon others, hardly less important. Until the Second World War a more 'liberal evangelicalism' laid claim, with almost total success in the eyes of the establishment, to be the true or dominant evangelicalism, the successors to the great days of Simeon and Wilberforce. It is in fact never difficult to arrive at the conviction that heroes of the past, if they had been one's own contemporaries, would think much as one does oneself. Liberal evangelicalism, as a modern movement, can be traced back to the formation of the 'Group Brotherhood' in 1906, which 'remained for more than eighteen years a private, almost a secret organization'.[32] But in 1927 the leaders of the movement published a symposium to explain their position under the title *Liberal Evangelicalism*.[33] Though the intention was eirenical, it was clear that on a number of crucial touchstones, including the inspiration of Scripture and the understanding of the atonement, they had parted company with what had generally been a clear and distinctive consensus among evangelicals. Those who felt that the publication of such a book marked a growing divergence which time would be likely to exacerbate had history on their side. The final essay in the book, 'The Future of the Evangelical Movement' was contributed by E. W. Barnes, Master of the Temple. Twenty years later, as Bishop of Birmingham, his convictions developed in *The Rise of Christianity*[34] were such as to give pause, not merely to evangelicals, but to the whole House of Bishops. Archbishop Fisher in a Presidential Address to Convocation felt obliged to say: 'If his views were mine I should not feel that I could still hold episcopal office in the Church.'[35]

But it is easy to be wise after the event. In the 1920s and 30s it was the liberal evangelicals who appeared to have something of relevance to say to a post-war generation: while the conservative evangelicals were engaged in fighting rear-guard actions, forced continually onto the defensive. And because they were concerned to conserve and uphold a 'faith once delivered' they were easily represented as more concerned with the past than with the future. So for a time, liberal evangelicalism appeared to breathe new life into an understanding of the Christian faith which was, since the rise of Anglo-Catholicism, sorely out of fashion.

It was against such a background of evangelical division and doctrinal uncertainty that Harold Earnshaw-Smith had maintained his personal stand as a conservative evangelical, both in the service of the IVF and in missionary and parochial work. Warm-hearted and tolerant, he was yet one of those faithful few whom John Stott would have had in mind when describing for a continental readership the decline in evangelical influence 'for about a century until the Second World War':

> Even while in eclipse, however, Evangelicals have dared to maintain that they *are* the Church of England in its purest form; that they are the loyalists, remaining faithful to the reformed constitution of the Church as set forth in its Prayer Book and 39 Articles; and that the Catholic and Liberal traditions are regrettable deviations from the norm.[36]

Two years after John Stott had joined his staff, Harold Earnshaw-Smith was one of the speakers at a Congress held under the title *Evangelicals Affirm* in preparation for the Lambeth Conference of 1948. The speakers were said to be 'generally representative of the varying shades of Evangelical tradition within the Church of England',[37] though of the twenty contributors most were representative of a distinctly liberal evangelicalism. A copy of the Report was sent to every bishop attending the Lambeth Conference. Earnshaw-Smith's contribution was on 'The Bible in Evangelism' and within the limits of a brief address (one of eighteen delivered in a two-day conference) it upheld the evangelical reliance upon Holy Scripture. But there was no paper upon scriptural authority as the keystone of evangelicalism, nor on the uniqueness of Christ, nor upon the centrality of the Cross. No wonder that thirty years later, preparing for the first National Evangelical Anglican Congress, John Stott should go on record as declaring the need for any such Congress faithfully to make clear the doctrinal foundation of an evangelical faith:

> At Keele we hope, both in the book and in the statement, to restate some salient parts of the evangelical faith. To be candid, it is vital that 'evangelicals affirm' at Keele in 1967 a good deal better than they did in London in 1948. It would be disastrous if this part of our duty were dismissed as platitudinous or irrelevant. There can be no evangelical policy without evangelical belief. Besides, it is not true to say that the generality of Church of England members know

what evangelicals believe. I am frequently astounded by the ignorance and misunderstanding of evangelical belief displayed even by church leaders who ought to know better.[38]

It was for the re-establishment of a historic and uncompromised evangelicalism, able to meet with integrity the new intellectual challenges both theological and secular, that All Souls was now to stand under John Stott's leadership. Perhaps it is no coincidence that 1967 which saw the 'official closing'[39] of the Anglican Evangelical Group Movement should have been the year of the first of the two National Evangelical Anglican Congresses[40] which, under John Stott's inspiration and direction were to mark a turning point in the recognition of a revitalized classic and conservative evangelicalism.[41] Paul Welsby, recounting the history of the period, saw this from the viewpoint of an observer rather than a participant. He writes of the 'new-found self-confidence of the evangelicals', describing them as 'more powerful, articulate, and intelligent than they had been for many years':

In the pre-war and immediate post-war years many evangelicals had been more concerned with preserving their own purity of doctrine than with attempting to co-operate with others in evangelism and the ecumenical movement and were too parochially orientated to take any influential part in the higher councils of the Church. It was the attitude of a depressed minority which regarded themselves as a group apart, as almost a Church within the Church. As long as this attitude persisted there was little chance of evangelicals becoming an effective force in the Church of England. During the nineteen-fifties, however, a gradual change took place and this was largely due to the status and influence of one man. John Stott was a person of wide vision and deep understanding, and very persuasive. A gifted expositor of the Bible, a prolific writer and an evangelist, he was also a statesman who possessed the ability to understand other points of view. He was vicar of All Souls, Langham Place in London from 1950 to 1977 and under his leadership that church became the heart of evangelical Anglicanism.[42]

4

For the youthful John Stott of 1945, the new curate busy settling into his bed-sitting room at the top of 1, Queen Anne Street, a round of Christmas services followed hard on the heels of the Advent ordination. Besides the Rector and Sister Jordan there was a senior curate already on the staff, Geoffrey Lester, who had graduated from Trinity College, Cambridge, the year before John Stott went up. He had served in the Irish Guards and been invalided out through polio which had left him with a slight limp. John Stott remembers him with 'a silver-topped swagger stick dragging one foot as he walked. He had black hair and was very handsome and a great singer. He broke a lot of female hearts.'[43] He and John Stott worked together for rather less than a year (though Geoffrey Lester assisted from time to time during Harold Earnshaw-Smith's continuing illness) but the memory of his romantic figure remained green in the parish. The Verger at the time was George Denham, a little cockney who began every sentence with the words 'Me and Mrs. Denham, we says ...'. He used to clean the church, with the stub of a cigarette in his mouth; and when John Stott (or, presumably, any of the clergy) appeared would drop it hastily under a convenient pew. One day he came up to John Stott in a confidential way, clearly with something to impart. It went like this: 'Me and Mrs. Denham, we says, that there Mr. Lester, 'e were a lady's man, 'e were; but me and Mrs. Denham, we says, *you ain't!*'[44]

No sooner was Christmas behind him than it was time to begin one of the major tasks of any curate, parish visiting. Behind Harold Earnshaw-Smith's diverse interests and easy ways 'was a very old-fashioned clergyman',[45] in the sense that he liked his curates to visit in the parish from house to house and to keep visiting records and make regular reports. It could be an educative experience. Geoffrey Lester was once visiting in Great Titchfield Street; he rang the bell of an upstairs flat to find the door opened by a young lady in her dressing gown. Looking at the curate on the doorstep she said 'Well, I've got a gentleman with me just now: can you wait?' He was left to guess at what she thought her second visitor had come for!

Only a few pages now remain of John Stott's first visiting diary, started in the very early days of 'the new curate':

Monday, Dec. 31st 1945

First full afternoon's visiting. Supplied by Mrs. Denham, verger's wife, with list of mothers together with staccato comments ('old', 'deaf', 'widow', 'nice'), sallied forth. Mrs. Todd was evidently out. Three rings at her door failed to make her appear. Disappointing start! Meanwhile, watched street Arabs playing football. Strange how cherubic boys in white surplices on Sunday can shout and punch like pagan toughs on Monday. Moved down dirty Hanson Street to Chinese Mrs. Yow. Looked like death, with sunken pallid cheeks, whilst Mr. Yow reclined beaming in bed, hugging baby

Barry. A look of furtive horror flitted across her face when I suggested a prayer as we advanced into the New Year. But they meekly submitted and seemed grateful afterwards.

Mrs. Hollidge I knew to be a very deaf widow. I found the house, but it had about 20 flats in it and there was no indication outside as to who occupied which. I barged in. There was a light under the door immediately on the left on the ground floor, and the door was ajar. I knocked, but no-one came. I knocked again and called 'Is anyone in?' – No response, although I heard rustlings within. My mind teemed with visions of secret liquor being stowed away, or the corpse being quickly hidden; or might it be deaf Mrs. Hollidge herself? – I peeped through the crack and saw an old, wrinkled woman, apparently oblivious to my knocks and calls. – Just then a man entered, and he confirmed that she lived there so I marched boldly in. Within a few moments my mouth was within two inches of her right ear, while strands of her grey hair found their way into my mouth. She clasped my right hand in both hers and stroked it, quivering with emotion. I bawled out how one couldn't feel lonely if one knew Jesus as Friend and Saviour, and all the street must have heard.

My next visit was to Irish Mrs. Evans. Her two daughters Marie and Dorothy were dressed up as angels (shades of the school Nativity play). Screams of delight greeted my attempt to dress up in similar guise, and one by one they came onto my lap for Ride-a-cock-horse and onto my back for a pickaback, until baby Desmond hit his head against the gas lamp, and we all got a bit scared. Mr. Evans soon came back from work, and we all knelt for prayer, Mr., Mrs. and the three kids. It was lovely.

The popular image of All Souls as a West-end parish – or perhaps simply as a fashionable church with an eclectic and upper-crust congregation – is far from the truth. The parish reaches from Marylebone High Street to Tottenham Court Road, including an area which is a kind of Soho overspill on the north side of Oxford Street. It is a centre of the garment industry, the 'rag trade'; a place (in the 1940s and 50s) of small apartments and family businesses with much over-crowding, Greek-Cypriot restaurants, Spaniards and Italians, with some Indian and (later) Bangladeshi families. It was back-street cosmopolitan London, with a population not far short of 10,000. A stone's throw from the church, in Hanson Street, there stood Latimer House, a hostel for working boys in London administered by a Christian foundation, the Kingham Hill Trust.[46] All Souls had good links with the management, and one or other of the staff of the parish used to visit regularly, and often take evening prayers. A later entry in the visiting-diary records one such evening. The 'Tony Waterson' mentioned was a camp and Cambridge friend (later Professor A. P. Waterson) doing clinical medicine at the London Hospital.

One day in March 1946 I went to Latimer House to take prayers as usual, and, entering the table tennis room at once spotted a cripple boy, a newcomer. Quickly got into conversation. He had been in the London Hospital so I at once asked if he knew Tony Waterson. And he did! – knew him well, for Tony had befriended him. – How wonderful is the providence of God!

Soon came to know him well. Came to several meals. – Orphan, infantile paralysis, and 'grandpa''s second marriage had all led him into extreme depression and bitterness against God ... 'Why should God send me all this suffering?' I seemed to make very little progress in preaching the gospel. He would not hear of it. – He tried to compensate for reality's problems by a life of phantasy amongst ideal characters of fiction (*e.g.* Catherine) and by imagining self as great actor. – Then he divulged that he had resolved to end his life. He had fixed the day for three weeks' thence, Good Friday, writing in his diary against that day 'For better or for worse I drink this bitter cup if providence so wills.' He had chosen Good Friday partly because it allowed time in which to acquire poison and partly because it was day of Jesus' death; 'I liked Jesus very much, although I pretended not to.' I pleaded. Warned him of God's judgment, offered him my friendship throughout life, but all of no avail. – On April 5th I left for Easter camp at Clayesmore, having got him to promise that he would do nothing until I returned, and that he'd read John's gospel on lines of John 7:17.

During camp he wrote twice – letters revealing his bitter opposition. How far away he seemed still!

On Friday evening before lantern service met him on steps of St. Peter's. 'Are you busy?' 'Moderately; why?' – He came nearer, looked down his nose and shivering with emotion, began feverishly to finger my coat buttons. 'I've decided on this day which I'd fixed for ending my life, to become a Christian instead.' Overjoyed, I asked what had led to his decision, and he said it wasn't fair that Jesus was crucified like that.

After the lantern service he came back to Queen Anne Street and we chatted. I went through ABC, which he clearly understood, and was quite certain he *had* taken the step at 4 p.m. that afternoon.

'ABC' in this account refers to the three headings often used by Bash[47] and then by John Stott and many others to make clear the way of salvation. It is used in his own booklet (written four years after this account) *Becoming a Christian*. The letters stand for

> *Admit* (or *Acknowledge*) your need of Christ
> *Believe* that Christ died for you
> *Come* to him.

John Stott went on to explain how to 'come' to Christ in the picture drawn from Revelation 3:20 of Jesus Christ knocking at the door of the human heart, with the promise, 'Behold, I stand at the door and knock; if any one hears my voice and opens the door, I will come in to him and eat with him and he with me.'[48] The diary continues:

> 'Do you know Jesus has come in?' He wasn't sure, but during the lantern service he had covered his eyes with his hands and had felt as if Someone had put His arm round him and said 'At last you have come to Me'! – I explained the promise, and went on to outline the cost. It meant repentance: Yes, he was ready for that. And this would include turning his back on any idea of taking his own life. He looked solemn and closed his eyes. In a few moments he said 'Yes, I accept that' – and would mean letting others know. Yes, he could take that too.

The fresh-faced curate in a gleaming dog-collar must have seemed an easy touch to the tramps and vagrants on the London streets. Most clergy found that it was a necessary rule not to give money, though the variety of plausible excuses and ingenious 'special circumstances' were never-ending. The diary records a first encounter with a man called Harry Mossop whom John Stott befriended fairly continuously over a period of years.

Sunday May 5th.

Took service at Latimer House at 11, but 'chanced' to return to St. Peter's at about 12.15. People were dispersing. Nearly all gone … a down-and-out in frayed coat and slouch hat accosted me and asked for a chat. – Wanted cash. Said I had rule and couldn't; but offered him an egg. Said he'd nowhere to cook it and couldn't I break my rule. No, I couldn't, but if he came to Queen Anne Street at 1p.m. I'd see what I could do with food. He said he'd come, and departed. I didn't expect to see him again … And at 1p.m. the bell rang, and there he was! We had a friendly lunch. He'd held commissioned rank in Indian army, but drink had sunk him. Very well spoken man, wide vocabulary, well educated. Now destitute ... We chatted, and I went through ABC. – He sat looking down his nose. Said he probably would 'make the effort'. But I tried to show him this was different from taking the step. – He began to understand, especially liking Rev. 3:20 and the story about the latch on the inside. – Was he willing to face the cost, not touch drink again, etc. ? He wanted time to think it over. – It was risky but I let him go, and he promised to come to 6.30 service at St. Peter's. – I wondered if he'd come, but there he was in the back pew! ... He and I went back to supper ... and he said he'd decided to 'do my utmost to go the way you've outlined'. This didn't sound too promising. Did he really understand the step? Had he really faced the cost? Further questioning revealed that he had, so we knelt and he prayed. 'Dear Lord, I am asking Thee to come into my heart ...' He'd never prayed aloud before, he said, in his life but he'd never been more earnest either. – So he went, grateful and apparently meaning business.

Parish visiting in the Harley Street neighbourhood was somehow much more difficult. Many remembered Dr. Arnold and Mrs. Stott – and indeed John himself – from their years as residents. It was not easy in a West-end drawing room to suggest to a busy consultant and his family that they should join him in a prayer, or a reading from the Bible, as part of a pastoral visit. John Stott was determined to do this, whenever possible: but had always at the back of his mind a sense of the acute embarrassment he and his family would have felt had Earnshaw-Smith (or, worse, some young curate from All Souls) come to visit, and then asked to read the Bible and pray with them, during one of the evenings when he and Joy were dancing to the gramophone in the big first-floor drawing room at 65 Harley Street before the war. Some years later he found that, without being aware of it, he had come to follow Billy Graham's practice, and to carry his Bible openly when paying pastoral visits:

Billy always seems to carry his Bible with him as a kind of badge of his Christian commitment: and I used to find it helpful to have the Bible under my arm when I entered into the house, or the room, because people of course saw it and realised that I had come on spiritual business. I found it easier then to take the Bible out from under my arm, and say 'I wonder if you would allow me to read a few verses to you and pray with you before I leave?'[49]

A year or two earlier Geoffrey Lester had started a mid-week evening meeting known as the Wednesday Club. Young people from the age of about seventeen and on into their twenties would gather either in an old school building off Oxford Street, or in Church House behind All Souls (though the church was bombed, Church House was still in use) using meeting-rooms both upstairs and downstairs, but unable to grow in numbers for lack of space. A similar problem over accommodation was being felt by the neighbouring evangelical church of St. Paul's, Portman Square, where John Bridger was curate to Prebendary Colin Kerr.

Before long, Earnshaw-Smith asked John Stott to take on the leadership of the Wednesday Club, and he began to search for more suitable premises in which to meet. He investigated the bombed site of St. John's, Fitzroy Square, auction rooms in Mortimer Street and a gymnasium in Great Portland Street. None of them seemed suitable.[50] Then in Duke Street, just south of Wigmore Street and almost on the boundary between the parishes of All Souls, Langham Place and St. Paul's, Portman Square, he found the very dilapidated buildings of the Grays Yard Mission, which had been established as a Ragged Church and School more than a hundred years before. Following the Forster Education Act of 1870 it became a night-shelter, a hostel and soup-kitchen for some of the many homeless men in London, as a practical expression of the Gospel.[51] The main hall, added later, dated from 1888, and had been used as an army drill hall during the Second World War.

Between the wars the Grays Yard Mission had been the special concern of the Hon. Constance Waldegrave, a member of All Souls; but by 1938, following her death, the work had ceased. Paul Broomhall, one of the Trustees, was known to John Stott and it was arranged that the two churches, All Souls and St. Paul's, should put money into restoring the premises and then should share the use of them. There was of course a good deal to be done first. John Stott wrote to his mother about a month after his arrival in the parish, asking her on her next visit to bring some old clothes from home:

> There's a prospect of manual work in getting a hall ready for our youth club and I've nothing suitable to wear! Wish I had some dungarees! … my correspondence is hopelessly behindhand. Things will ease off soon, but I'm busy launching a boys' club and largely reconstituting the youth club. I meet the PCC this evening with a formal proposition about taking over another hall![52]

Here in the re-named and refurbished 'Waldegrave Hall'[53] the Wednesday Club grew to about 150 members, and formed a valuable focus of friendship, and a meeting place for younger members of the church and their friends. Many newcomers to London were introduced to All Souls, and often to active participation and committed discipleship, through its weekly fellowship.

On Sunday morning it was the curate's job to lead the Children's Church, held in St. Peter's for half-an-hour from 10.00 to 10.30, before the main morning service at 11.00. He was helped with a strong team of young women, including Elisabeth Earnshaw-Smith, daughter of the Rector. He is remembered as 'excellent with the children *and* with his team of young women'.[54] The children were mostly from the professional families in the 'West-end' area of the parish; and sometimes their attendance at Children's Church provided an opening to visit homes where the parents had little or no previous church connection. Every year in April, about the time of John Stott's birthday, there would be a visit to the zoo; and at Christmas there was a party: 'I can remember John playing his piano-accordian to the tune of 'The more we are together, the merrier we shall be'.[55]

To reach the unchurched boys of the parish something else was needed. At the Rector's request, John Stott explored what a number of Christian youth organizations could offer, and decided (following a suggestion by Sister Jordan) that for his purpose the best would be 'Covenanters', founded about fifteen years before as an interdenominational non-uniformed Bible-based organization for children and young people linked with a local church. The All Souls group of that generation is still a living memory at Covenanter headquarters:

> The type of boys John Stott has a deep concern for were those who lived around the Langham Place area, who left school at 14 and found employment as newspaper lads, market traders in Great Titchfield Street or in menial jobs in West End stores. Many were from Greek or Turkish families and were socially estranged from the more eclectic congregation of All Souls.
>
> These lads were by no means the easiest to handle and their presence at Covenanter Camps was often a source of embarrassment and anxiety for the Officers of the camps concerned. At times, I recall, applications from Langham Place boys for camp places were often received with unease and John Stott would plead to have the boys accepted and would make them a matter of earnest prayer. With the result a small number were converted and some later would be found attending church. The boys would have a strong group mentality and were rarely seen in single company. Many are the stories that surround their behaviour such as when a group of them chose to turn up for the evening club meeting in a taxi![56]

There was also a section for younger members, known as 'Junior Covenanters' or 'Jucos' which served largely the boys attending All Souls Church School. John Stott was already a familiar figure in the school, 'going to play football with the boys. He looked so young and full of fun that he seemed to be one of them.'[57] The All Souls team were formidable challengers under the curate's coaching, ending one season as an unbeaten side, 'played 12, won 12'. They played mostly in Regent's Park, where John Stott would occasionally referee as well as coach. He likes to recall how one day he yielded to persuasion, and against his better judgment, allowed Arthur Chard, a fourteen-year-old from All Souls School, to referee the game. Arthur stood no nonsense: if a member of his team was complaining and making too much noise, he would stand in the middle of the pitch, arms akimbo, and shout 'Shut yer moanin' 'ole up!'[58] Fifty years later John Stott is still able to recapture the authentic tones of his London Jucos of the 1940s, and to remember many of them by name. They used to meet on Monday evenings in the Waldegrave Hall – an 'unpredictable event'! Students were often roped in to help run the club, including medical students from the nearby Middlesex Hospital:

> One evening my stethoscope aroused interest and had to be tried out. With its ear-pieces securely stuck in Arthur Chard's ears and the other end firmly placed on a volunteer's chest, Arthur remarked after a moment's listening, 'Cor, ee ain't got no 'art'.[59]

After club John Stott would take the students in his 'jalopy' (a kind of jeep with flapping canvas sides, thought to have been a Dutch ex-army truck, which he had bought for £100), to the Glory Café, opposite the Middlesex Hospital. Memories are mostly of egg-and-chips – if there was lamb on the menu it would often be spelt without the final letter – and of his mischievous repartee with the Greek-Cypriot proprietor and his staff.

Among the high spots of the year, looked forward to by curate and boys alike, were the camps together; at Whitsun in a farm on the banks of the river Wey (where Lily Stott would come and visit them), and in summer further afield:

> They would set off on bicycles, or in his ex-army pick-up truck known to the parish as his 'old jalopy', crammed with tents, blankets, cooking pots and camping gear. Camp fires, rain and mud, brilliant sun – all the usual ingredients of a camping holiday – would be there in full. But there would be more. Round the camp fire each night there would be an opportunity for these back-street

London youngsters to think together, Bible in hand, under John's gentle leadership, of life's serious issues.[60]

In many respects it would be difficult to find 'camps' more unlike the public-school houseparties at Iwerne Minster, to which John Stott had devoted so much of his energies before his ordination, than these down-to-earth rough-and-tumble camps, close to nature and under canvas, with the young cockneys of Soho-north-of-Oxford Street. But the aims were identical, the spiritual battles all too familiar, and lessons learned at Iwerne in communicating the gospel to young people proved their value. It was not only at Iwerne Minster camp that lives were changed; there are All Souls Covenanters and Jucos in Christian ministry today who look back on what such camps meant to them in their formative years:

> I first met John when I was about 13 years of age ... I was already a Christian. It was at a Boy Covenanter Camp at Cromer. He was my tent officer as well as Padre of the camp. He had brought along a rowdy group of his 'boys' from Langham Place, including a boxer, Tony Mancini, and a barrow boy called Arthur, who thought that the initials JRWS stood for 'John Rochester Winchester Stott'.
>
> John would wake the camp up parading round the tents playing his accordion. His favourite (easy to play) was 'Come and serve the Master'. He showed great interest in us. We could go to the Quiet Time tent. John had his own devotions beforehand, praying upright on his knees in order to keep himself awake (so I heard from the camp Commandant). He shaved with a cut-throat razor without drawing much blood – it was a symbol of his excellence at everything! Like many of his boys, I had my first taste of bird watching, lying on my stomach in a field with John.
>
> It is an experience common to so many that he could remember us by name years later. Even when I returned home from Peru on my first furlough he greeted me by name at the door of All Souls![61]

John Stott was only too well aware that many of his boys were returning home from camp to family and friends indifferent or openly hostile to any Christian profession; and to homes with few opportunities of privacy for private prayer. He knew, too, how difficult it would be for some of them to begin to identify with the All Souls congregation, and how easily a raised eyebrow or a hint of condescension could penetrate their defences. He wrote a note to the Church congregation:

> It was a good camp. Despite friendly but determined opposition, the message brought to the boys at Prayers each day bore fruit. Few

of us have any idea of the struggle our boys have to undergo if they really give their allegiance to Jesus Christ. It takes a real man to stand up for decency and honesty, let alone for real Christianity, in the surroundings in which some of them live and work. Yet a few have boldly taken their stand. Will you pray for them? And when they come to Church on Sunday nights – give them a welcoming smile!

J. R. W. S.[62]

There were soon classes for All Souls Girl Covenanters also, under committed lay leadership; though they would sometimes look to the parish clergy – John Stott included – to give talks and Bible Studies or to act as Chaplain. Indeed, it was one of the Girl Covenanters who delivered a long-remembered tribute to their new curate: 'Cor, you ain't half a lovely priest'.[63]

Half way through John Stott's first year in the parish his Rector fell ill: 'for the first time in living memory (at any rate at All Souls and St. Peter's)' Earnshaw-Smith wrote in the parish magazine, 'I have a Sunday to myself through illness.'[64] In July he suffered his first coronary, and was clearly going to be away from the parish for some time. John Stott was still only in deacon's orders. Geoffrey Lester was deeply involved in mission work[65] but continued to do what he could, and retired clergy (among them the veteran G. R. Harding Wood who had been curate there before John Stott was born, and Charles Strong from the Cambridge University Mission) helped with the preaching and the Communion Services. It was some weeks before the Rector returned, but still convalescent and able to do very little, so that the weight of the parish rested more and more on his curate's young shoulders, with the help of Sister Jordan.

It was not until the end of 1948 that a second curate arrived, Gordon Mayo, straight from five years as an RAF chaplain, mostly overseas. Alan Stibbs, Vice-Principal of Oak Hill College where Gordon Mayo had trained, had referred him to Earnshaw-Smith to take the place of John Stott who (it was assumed) would soon be due to move on. In the event he and Gordon Mayo worked together there throughout the period of their Rector's illness and death: they were fellow curates at the time of John Stott's appointment as Rector. Gordon Mayo had already arranged to take up a post in Africa after this brief second curacy in England, and it had been agreed with Earnshaw-Smith that he should stay two years and then go abroad. Any awkwardness there might have been at John Stott's appointment (he was the younger man by three years, ordained three years later, unmarried, and without service experience) was therefore mitigated by the knowledge that Gordon Mayo's future plans were firmly settled before he came.

The two men were very different. Gordon Mayo was feeling his way, and finding a West-end parish foreign soil after his work in the RAF. John Stott seemed to him perhaps a little too urbane and organized, his large Filofax diary and notebook never out of his hand: 'You really did have to book weeks in advance'[66] to spend time with him. And John Stott evinced a capacity for concentrated work which at times made him an uncomfortable partner for a married colleague to try to work with – a situation that was made, if anything, more acute when he was asked to assume the mantle of priest-in-charge and then of Rector. One of the team of lay people deeply involved in the work of All Souls felt strongly enough to send a note of protest:

> I know the temptation to 'do it yourself' and save time and temper,
> but it is not the most unselfish way. You're not 'pig-headed' but
> your sweet-reasonableness has a good deal of iron purpose in it and,
> to mix my metaphors, it is much easier to be a one-man-band than
> to try to harmonize with anyone else!'[67]

Given John Stott's temperament, his style of teutonic thoroughness, and his comparative youthfulness and lack of experience, it is not surprising that he found he could manage best by giving personal attention to detail and by what seemed to some to be an obsessively careful management of his time and diary. It was important to him to lead and teach with confidence and the assurance that comes from study and preparation. Perhaps at times it may have seemed a little super-human. Gordon Mayo still recalls the appreciation he received after a sermon in St. Peter's when he confessed that he was out of his depth on some theological issue, and 'hadn't a clue'. The congregation, used to a style of confident affirmation and to preachers not given to sharing their doubts from the pulpit, found it (they told him) a refreshing experience.[68]

Amid the pressures of the work at All Souls, John Stott found time to respond to a limited number of invitations to preach and teach beyond the parish, usually in connection with Christian student work. With Dr. Oliver Barclay (by then assistant secretary of the IVF) he had visited the Groupes Bibliques des Ecoles et Universités in August 1946 at Morges, a small town on the north shore of Lake Geneva; and paid a second visit to them in 1948. He was in both Oxford and Cambridge most Octobers for 'Freshers' Squashes' and preached the Freshers' Sermon for the Oxford Inter-Collegiate Christian Union (OICCU) in 1948. He broke new ground, too, with a visit to the South West Inter-Faculty Christian Union (SWIFCU), where he conducted a kind of mini-mission in what a few years later would become the University of Exeter. In London he was regularly on his bicycle to one of the teaching hospitals to speak at the Christian Union; or to Bedford College in Regent's Park; or to take a Bible-reading at one of the many scattered London colleges affiliated to the London Inter-Faculty Christian Union (LIFCU).

Thanks to the training Bash had given him, John Stott was a seasoned speaker long before he came to All Souls. When he came to write his book on preaching[69] he paid him special tribute among 'some of the many people who have helped me in the writing of this book':

> I begin with the Rev. E. J. H. Nash, who showed me the way to Christ when I was almost seventeen, nurtured me and prayed for me with astonishing faithfulness, developed my appetite for the Word of God, and gave me my first taste of the joys of expounding it.[70]

But to preach regularly in West End London was a demanding assignment. Preaching by well-known names from London's famous pulpits was still a significant part of the city's life:

> Even the Second World War, although it accelerated the process of secularization in Europe, did not quench preaching. During and after it three distinguished Methodist ministers occupied London pulpits and drew large crowds – Leslie Weatherhead at the City Temple, Donald Soper at Kingsway Hall (and also in the open air at Marble Arch and on Tower Hill), and Will Sangster at Westminster Central Hall. A wit once remarked that they could best be distinguished from one another by their three loves, since 'Sangster loved the Lord, Weatherhead loved his people, while Soper loved an argument.'[71]

More significantly still, Westminster Chapel continued to maintain a tradition of expository preaching, 'a sustained exposition of the sacred scriptures':

> Its aim is to awaken and confirm faith. It requires of the preacher a disciplined subjection to the authority of revelation so that he may declare the mighty acts of God for the liberation of the human race from its slavery to egotism, anxiety, futility, frustration, suffering, and the fear of death. Through a large part of the present century this type of preaching fell into abeyance, partly because it was associated with an older view of Biblical inspiration, and partly because liberal accommodations of the faith found it more convenient to take a text as a pretext, than to pretend to expound a

passage of Scripture. Apologetical, ethical, or topical sermons were the rage. Hence the expository sermon was, for the most part, considered *passé*.

The great exception to the rule was George Campbell Morgan, an autodidact, whose Biblical sermons and lectures were extraordinarily popular on both sides of the Atlantic ... Campbell preached to crowded morning and evening services, and at his Friday Night Bible School he lectured to between 1,500 and 2,000 eager students of the Scriptures. His conviction was that 'the preacher is not merely asking a congregation to discuss a situation, and consider a proposition, or give attention to a theory. We are out to storm the citadel of the will and to capture it for Jesus Christ.'[72]

Campbell Morgan died in 1945, the year that John Stott came to All Souls as curate. But Dr. Martyn Lloyd-Jones, aged forty-five and at the height of his powers, had been preaching regularly at Westminster Chapel through the war years and (though this was not clear to him at the time) would continue to do so, with marked effectiveness, for the rest of his ministry. Professor Horton Davies (quoted above on Campbell Morgan) writing in the early 1960s, gave it as his impression that

What is of special interest is the general return to expository preaching in the last two decades of the period as a result of the Biblical and theological revival. There is no question that this is not only deeply necessary but also that it is widely appreciated. At the present time the two largest congregations in London have been gathered by expository preachers. One is the congregation of Westminster Congregational Chapel under the ministry of a former Harley Street physician, Dr. Martyn Lloyd-Jones, and the other is All Souls, Langham Place, where the Rector is the Rev. John R. W. Stott.[73]

John Stott was to find in Dr. Lloyd-Jones (twenty years his senior) a colleague and partner in the work of the IVF and student evangelism for many years to come; though the two men were to differ widely and publicly in their views on evangelical unity while maintaining a warm personal respect and friendship. One London student never forgot a brief conversation one Sunday evening with John Stott on the steps of All Souls as the congregation were departing.

'Hello,' said John Stott. 'I thought you went to Westminster Chapel.'

Shy and embarassed in the presence of the great man, I stuttered out: 'No, I'm not a follower of the great Doctor.'

'Aren't you?' he said. 'I am!'[74]

5

John Stott's first sermon in the parish was preached in St. Peter's Vere Street about a fortnight after his ordination; wisely, he chose from his files (which even then were being kept on the tiny 5" x 3" index cards which he would use all his life and which in his seventies would prove difficult for him to read) a sermon he had preached from Ridley Hall at Six Mile Bottom, just outside Cambridge, six months before. It was on Romans 3:22–23 on the theme of 'No difference', of how 'all have sinned and come short of the glory of God', moving on to Romans 10:12–13, where Paul tells the Romans that 'There is no difference ... for whoever shall call upon the name of the Lord shall be saved.' His notes remind him *'Important face sin, as then appreciate remedy.'*

From the middle of 1946 the magazine *All Souls* began to carry regularly the summary of one of his sermons, usually preached a month or two before; and in the autumn of 1948 under the title 'God's truth through man's temperament' he preached a series on the writers of the New Testament, which would in time become the basis of the first of his many books.[75] Some preachers do not feel the need for any feedback or criticism. Some, if they happen to be married, look to their wives. John Stott arranged for a member of his congregation whose judgment he trusted to provide comment and criticism. In the 1940s this was A. P. Waterson, at first a medical student and then a young doctor at the London Hospital. One Sunday evening, 17 March 1946, for example, John Stott preached on 'Abiding in Christ' from John 15. Tony Waterson sent in response a diagrammatic analysis of the sermon's structure and a detailed explanation of the difference between sap in a plant, and blood circulating in a body! Sometimes such comments generated a correspondence. John Stott wrote to Waterson the following month:

I rather feel that, now I've settled in a bit, it is too much to ask you to write a full critique each time. Could we have the arrangement that you send a line *only* if you've a special word of criticism or commendation? Could you be specially sensitive to these 2 broad questions about each sermon:

(1) Is it worth saying?

(2) Is it well said?

i.e. (1) Is there a real message here, something vital, relevant,
  gripping?
  (2) Has it gone across – or was it too heavy, too complicated, too
  boring, etc. ?
  I'd be awfully grateful if you could do this. It's really especially
adverse criticism I want to hear – such as you might overhear while
leaving church![76]

The letters continue well into 1948. John Stott's replies indicate
something of the struggles he had through Earnshaw-Smith's illnesses,
when much of the burden of the parish rested on his shoulders. 'Don't be
too hard on me during these weeks! I am fighting against time, and am
preaching myself dry, as I simply have not time to read and think!'[77]

The following summer the pressures of work as a junior hospital
doctor made Tony Waterson relinquish this task. Writing to thank him,
John Stott offered his own self-analysis:

My own greatest criticism of myself (which you've never
mentioned!) ... is that I'm too heavy, and try and put over too
much and too 'theological' stuff for the background of the average
listener. But I find it hard to control myself! I'm still rather puzzled
about the harsh or forced delivery. I think you mean intensity (do I
frown a lot?!), but I'm not sure it really is something to eliminate,
or something which really is myself and which it would be
unnatural to cut out.[78]

John Stott found another medical student, David Trapnell from the
Middlesex Hospital, to continue with regular assessments. The choice of
medical students was deliberate: they represented the younger element in
the congregation, and by training they were equipped to observe, dissect
and analyse.

Perhaps because of the subjects chosen for his sermons, and perhaps
because of the nature of his preparation, John Stott was beginning to gain
a reputation for sermons longer than those to which the people of All
Souls were accustomed. His Rector used to try to tease him out of this
habit since it was not wholly popular with the congregation. On one
occasion Earnshaw-Smith had been invited to preach at the neighbouring
church of All Saints, Margaret Street, noted for high-church practice and
elaborate ritual. At the end of the service, having said good-bye to the
congregation at the church door, disrobed in the vestry and taken leave of
the vicar, Earnshaw-Smith strolled home past All Souls, to see if there
might be any lingering members of his own congregation whom he
should greet. Instead, he found the service still in progress, his curate

well-settled in the pulpit expounding in some detail Pilate's question 'What is truth?'. It was an occasion he was not allowed to forget for some time to come.[79]

It is no great step from preacher to writer, and not surprisingly John Stott was becoming increasingly aware of the powerful ministry of the printed word. In March 1947 he took advantage of the fact that Lord Kemsley, Chairman of Kemsley Newspapers, was a neighbour and a parishioner, known to Cuthbert and Ethel Dukes since his home, Chandos House, was just across the road on the corner of Queen Anne Street and Chandos Street. Kemsley Newspapers at that time owned the *Daily Sketch*, the *Sunday Graphic* and the *Sunday Times,* as well as local newspapers: by 1947 Lord Kemsley was selling 26 million newspapers a week.[80] John Stott wrote to him; and the letter survives as a hand-written draft:

10 March 1947

My Lord,

I write with considerable diffidence because I do not doubt that I am infringing some of the elementary rules of Press courtesies and conventions. I can only ask you to believe that I am not conversant with the etiquette.

My purpose in writing, in a few words, is to enquire whether, in view of the approach of Easter, you would consider publishing in one of your papers a series of popular articles on the great theme of Christ's Resurrection? I have in mind a piece of serious Christian apologetics to a now alas! largely non-Christian public, but couched of course in direct, man-to-man language.

I sincerely apologise if it is unorthodox to approach you personally in this way, but I at least have the pretext that you have some connections with our church, and also that I have the honour to live almost opposite Chandos House, with Dr. Dukes who attends Lady Kemsley. But I should like especially to add that I believe this subject of Christ's Resurrection and consequent Living Impact on men today is of vital significance. You will appreciate, my Lord, that I am seeking neither money nor publicity for myself. I should be more than happy to be unrewarded and anonymous. But I am deeply moved by the Easter message of Christ Risen, Living, Active, Challenging, – and I wondered if you would consider helping further to jolt our contemporaries out of their materialism and indifference to God? If only our generation could recapture the sense of God which a generation or two ago moulded politics and preserved ethics. Is there any other hope ultimately?

My Lord, would you give me a trial in putting this imperishable message before your public? I believe I could make it readable.[81]

The response was by no means wholly discouraging:

Kemsley House, London, W. C. 1

13 March 1947

Dear Mr. Stott,

I have given a lot of thought to your suggestion about a series of popular articles at Easter time, and I am afraid it is rather impossible this year.

If we had the increase of paper which we so badly need I would probably welcome the opportunity of doing as you describe, and in addition, the Sunday Times, the Sunday Graphic, the Daily Graphic and all the morning and evening papers of this Group are already committed to articles on this subject by our regular contributors.

I am naturally very interested in all you say, and just lately have been hearing about the Christian Commando Campaign for Greater London, which shares your concern at the present growth of materialism.

I was very pleased that you wrote to me direct, and I feel genuinely sorry that your idea cannot be adopted at the moment.

Yours sincerely,
Kemsley[82]

John Stott put this dream behind him, and turned instead to opportunities nearer home. His first contribution to the *Life of Faith*, the old-established weekly of the Keswick Movement, dates from 1949, as does his first article for *Inter-Varsity*, the journal of the IVF.[83] For them also he wrote two small booklets, *Personal Evangelism*, based on a talk he had given more than once since Ridley days, and *Becoming a Christian*, an evangelistic booklet owing something to *Life at its Best*, but more adult and reasoned in its approach. This was to be a major evangelistic tool in Guest Services at All Souls, and in countless university missions over the coming decades. It appeared first in 1950 and has never been out of print.[84]

On his days off, John Stott would often take the chance to go home to see his parents, now living at Worplesdon, near Guildford. His father no longer called himself 'Major General', but for his distinguished service career (he had played an important part in the wartime organization of the medical services) he was created a KBE in 1946; and on leaving the army was made honorary consulting physician. Two years later, in 1948, he was appointed Extra Physician to the Royal Household. In 1950, the year his son became Rector, he retired from the staff of the Westminster Hospital where he had been Senior Physician.

On Christmas Day it was John Stott's custom to stay in the parish after the morning service was over, and to go visiting. Some of the house-bound pensioners on his list might have no other visitor at all that day. On Christmas Eve, and on Christmas Day, he used to deliver about eighty parcels as gifts from the church to the needier homes of the parish. Harry Mossop, the tramp referred to in his early parish diary, came to lunch at least once on Christmas Day, and John Stott cooked eggs and bacon for both of them in the basement kitchen at 1 Queen Anne Street.[85] It was the memory of such visits that later prompted him to start a system of Old People's Welfare Visitors, perhaps fifty or sixty of them at one time, regularly caring for the old and house-bound of the parish.

Such contacts with Harry Mossop and others like him inspired John Stott, comparatively early in his time as curate, to experience for himself a glimpse of the life lived by the vagrants and homeless on the streets of London. Perhaps too it owed something to George Dempster's accounts of his adventures in East End dockland, the first of which had been published when John Stott was still a schoolboy. The books were on his shelves: and he liked to lend them to young Christians by way of challenge and inspiration.[86] He decided therefore that for a couple of days he would 'disappear' from home, friends and parish, and tramp the streets, to discover for himself at least a little of what it meant to be one of London's underclass:

I wanted to feel what it was like to be rejected by society. So I put on some very old clothes; I let my stubble grow for several days. We had identity cards in those days, so I put mine in my shoe, and then I started wandering about near the river and the Embankment, where the tramps were. My first night was spent under the arches of Charing Cross Bridge, surrounded by tramps, men and women whose only covering apart from their clothes was newspapers. I didn't sleep very much, it was very hard on the pavement, the tramps were all coming and going; some of them were drunk and made a lot of noise, and it was very cold; I don't remember what month it was but I have an idea it was October or November, the beginning of winter. So I was very thankful when the sun came up, and it was a lovely day. I remember I walked through the East End of London, and because I'd had very little sleep, I lay down in the sunshine on a bombed site, amongst the Rose-bay Willow-herb, and fell asleep. However, before that, at dawn when shops were beginning to open, I went to a number of ABC tea shops – I had deliberately taken no money with me – where one of the employees would be cleaning the steps outside. I asked if they could give me a job, for a cup of tea, or for a breakfast, but none of them would. I began to feel very rejected.

That night I went to the Whitechapel Salvation Army doss house and queued up for a bed. I remember that the Salvation Army officer who was at the window where you booked in was rather brusque or impatient, not to me, but to somebody else. So, forgetting who I was meant to be, forgetting my role, I said to him 'As a Salvation Army officer, you ought to be trying to win that man for Christ – and not talking to him like that' and he looked at me very sharply, wondering who on earth this was; I think I tried to do it in a Cockney accent! But anyway I got a bed; it was in a dormitory, with no cubicles and no privacy. It was a dreadful night: many men were coming in during the night drunk and shouting, and one or two of them were obviously mentally disturbed. So I again got very little sleep, and by the morning after this, I'd had enough. I really had begun to feel like an outsider, a castaway. So I then went to Toynbee Hall, and I dropped in there, I think, and asked for breakfast. The man who interviewed me was immediately suspicious – probably my accent wasn't good enough – and I think he said something like 'the show's up; you'd better tell us who you are'. By then I was quite glad to do so. I didn't tell them I was a clergyman, but I got out my identity card, and showed it to them. So they gave me breakfast, and I went back to 1 Queen Anne Street and found the Dukes. They had a strong social conscience and were very interested in my experiment, for what was really only forty-eight hours.[87]

6

Early in 1947 Earnshaw-Smith was again ill and off work. By this time requests were beginning to come from a variety of quarters, seeking the help of the promising curate of All Souls. Ernest Kevan, Principal of the London Bible College (then in Marylebone Road, and so on the boundary of the parish) wrote asking whether he might act as their New Testament Tutor – 'the work here has grown to such large dimensions and has grown so rapidly.'[88] It was a task John Stott would have relished, but he replied saying that for at least a further year he could not consider it, since his Rector was still far from well. In the following year things were no better: the Rector was ordered by his doctors to take 'several months rest'. The coming of Gordon Mayo in October did something to ease the burden; but by 1949 it was clear that in the normal course of events John Stott had more than served his full curacy and should be moving on. On 14 March Harold Earnshaw-Smith was writing to John Lefroy at Ridley Hall to see whether he might come to All Souls as John Stott's successor. A fortnight later he wrote again: 'After a tempestuous week of uncertainty John Stott has now decided to stay on here. He is going to do a good deal of reading ...'[89]

Approaches had been made to him for some time past, most of which he had no difficulty in deciding to take no further. Earnshaw-Smith himself, writing from Worthing in October 1948 apologises for one of them:

> I am not responsible for the ridiculous offer of-----, which is a paralytic parish. I was not at the Trustees' Meeting.[90]

One possibility seriously considered was to join the chaplaincy staff at Eton; but though he was attracted at the thought of the renewed link with camp, a day spent there failed to convince him that this was God's plan.[91] Nearer his heart, though in a different way, was an invitation to be Chaplain of the Docklands Settlement in Canning Town (which, ten years later under David Sheppard, would become the 'Mayflower'). He paid a lengthy visit to them, and continued to dream of 'a slum parish and an experiment in real Christian democracy',[92] but the time was not right. It must have been with a sense of relief that Earnshaw-Smith was able to write of John Stott in *All Souls* in May 1949: 'You will be glad to know that after a period of indecision and the offer of many other posts he has decided to stay on at St. Peter's for the present' – and to add that the Bishop of London hoped that he would find time to read and study. It was either a peculiarly fond hope or (more likely) Wand knew his man.

At Christmas Earnshaw-Smith was in bed and unable to take part in the Christmas Services; and so he continued through January and into February. A brief but affectionate letter of thanks to Gordon Mayo written at this time is subscribed 'from your inadequate and practically useless Rector.'[93] Early in 1950 John Stott was asked (probably at the instigation of Archdeacon Sharpe) to consider an incumbency in the London diocese, St. James-the-Less, Bethnal Green, in the patronage of the Church Pastoral-Aid Society. He consulted Bishop Wand, whose reply confirmed his own inclination that it was not the moment when he could leave All Souls:

My dear Stott,

I had heard of the Archdeacon's endeavour to entice you to the East End and, as I knew that you had long wished to work in those surroundings, I was awaiting with a good deal of interest your reply.

Now that I find the question coming up to me I feel that I can only say that it is, generally speaking, one's duty to remain where one is unless one is quite sure that the Divine call is to work elsewhere. That is a piece of general advice which you can apply to your own case.

But I am bound to say that looking at the question as you put it to me, from a purely commonsense point of view, it does not seem to me that you are sure enough of the desirability of the move to warrant you making it.

I think that is all I can profitably say about it. We, as you know, should have been perfectly happy for you to go to the East End, but I think that if I were you I should want to feel that it was quite definitely the right thing and God's will for me before I ventured to take it on.

> With all good wishes.
> Yours sincerely,
> + Wm. London[94]

Early in March, Harold Earnshaw-Smith left home to convalesce at Worthing on the south coast. In a long letter to him John Stott wrote:

My very dear Rector,

I was very sorry that in the rush of many things we were not able to talk and pray unhurriedly before you left. I hope when you return we shall have an opportunity to think quietly about how the new arrangement will work out. I'm glad of a chance to write to you, as there are one or two matters on my heart and conscience to say to you.

The first is how deeply delighted and grateful to the dear Lord I am to be given the privilege of 2 or so more years with you. This isn't idle talk. Please don't talk any more about my 'sacrificing my career' etc.! I don't feel this in the slightest. Besides, it can't be true if it is *His* will that I should stay, and this we believe it to be. So please believe me when I say how much I am at peace about it all, and how much I am looking forward to the enjoyment of more fellowship with you in the gospel.

Secondly, I do want to say, if I may clear the air here too, that I hope you will bring yourself to regard me as much as possible as your trusted assistant! I have no desire to be 'Assistant Rector' for the glory of the thing, but I have a deep desire to assume this office for the work's sake and for your sake. Now you and the Big Four have agreed to letting me have a secretary, I hope you'll allow me to take off your shoulders just as much as possible. We'll need of course to work out the details, and I'd like guidance as to how much you'd like to be consulted and how far in day-to-day decisions you'd like me to carry on without worrying you; but it gives me great joy to think that I may have some share in helping to prolong your ministry here.[95]

A week later Earnshaw-Smith died in his sleep following an attack of cardiac asthma. 'We are an orphaned church', John Stott wrote in the special April issue of *All Souls*, beneath a notice from the churchwardens that the Bishop of Willesden, acting on behalf of the Bishop of London, had asked him to be priest-in-charge of All Souls and St. Peter's until a new incumbent could be appointed.

All Souls is a Crown living: the Rector is appointed by the Crown on the advice of the Prime Minister, who in turn is advised by his Patronage Secretary, generally after consultation with the parish and with the Bishop of the diocese. Clement Attlee was Prime Minister, regarded by many as a 'prototypical Anglican', but in fact not a believer. He had abandoned at Haileybury his belief in God, while continuing to hold high moral and social principles.[96] He took a keen interest in ecclesiastical appointments: 'one friend remarked that it was very difficult to have a relaxed discussion with him on any subject except bishops and cricket.'[97] As a young man he had fallen under the spell of John Stansfeld, 'the Doctor' of the Oxford Medical Mission in Bermondsey. Attlee had been head of his own school mission, Haileybury House in Stepney, and long afterwards would declare that 'work in a boys' club had been the best preparation of all for the high office of Prime Minister'.[98] Sir Anthony Bevir, an Old Etonian from Co. Mayo, was the Prime Minister's Secretary for Appointments:

He had joined the team at No. 10 in 1940, beginning as one of Chamberlain's private secretaries and continuing in that capacity under Churchill and Attlee. In the early days there was no clear allocation of duties, but over the years Bevir found himself concentrating more and more on ecclesiastical work. In 1947 it was thought desirable that a single secretary should advise on all appointments which lay within the prime minister's prerogative; and Bevir was given this particular portfolio. Part of his duties consisted in going round the country to see people and collect opinions – and in the process to compile a useful dossier of men deserving consideration for appointment as bishops. He became a storehouse of facts, figures and judgements about the clergy (Attlee called him a 'walking *Crockford*').[99]

Thanks to Bevir's efficiency, it was not long before the Churchwardens received a questionnaire from the Prime Minister's office. Geoffrey Bles (remembered as the publisher of J. B. Phillips and C. S. Lewis) presided as senior churchwarden at a meeting of the PCC on 21st March. It was agreed that in reply to the question: 'What are the church's views now obtaining?' they should reply 'Evangelical with conservative emphasis, combining a biblical preaching ministry with a dignified worship'. They went on to consider the qualities they were looking for in a new incumbent:

(1) He should be a fine preacher to continue the tradition of F. D. Maurice, Webster, Mowll, Page-Roberts and our late Rector.

(2) In view of the work involved in the restoration of All Souls, he should be a capable man of affairs, able to deal carefully and expeditiously with various kinds of business.

(3) In view of the very many poor families in our parishes, he should be one who loves the poor and loves to work among them.

(4) Perhaps most important of all, in view of the prevailing drift away from Christianity among young people, he should be a young man, who has the affections and confidence of young people, with a special interest in Clubs for boys and girls.[100]

George Cansdale, later churchwarden, was a member of the PCC. An enthusiastic bird-lover, he had been a Forest Officer with the Colonial Service, acquiring an ever-increasing interest in the animals and reptiles of Africa:

... I had no thought of turning my life-long hobby into a career, but God was gradually leading me in that direction, as I organized regular shipments of animals – mostly rescued from the cooking pots of farmers and hunters around my station – to fill some of the many zoo cages left empty by years of war.[101]

It was on leave during 1947 that he was unexpectedly invited to resign from the Colonial Service and become Superintendent of the London Zoo. Later he was to become nationally and affectionately known as 'the

Zoo Man' in his own television programme. He was a member of a small delegation from the PCC which went with the churchwardens to make their views known to Anthony Bevir: 'We had to tell the Crown we were only interested in one name.'[102] This can be seen clearly enough in the four criteria which were minuted by the PCC. They did not (unusually) ask for a married man; John Stott was already widely known as a fine preacher and remarkably efficient administrator throughout his Rector's recurring illnesses; he had always taken a special interest in the poorer families of the parish; and was a young man (still only twenty-nine) known to have a particular concern in the church's clubs for children and young people.

When the churchwardens met the Bishop of London on 30 March they made it clear that they wished to press for John Stott's appointment. With Anthony Bevir, too (in spite of the fact that since the Crown was Patron, the legal rights of the PCC were minimal) they had no difficulty in conveying their real feelings. George Cansdale, not a man to beat about the bush, remembered it being made plain 'that if an attempt was made to give us anyone we felt unsuitable, we could not guarantee any co-operation'.[103] Others, too, who had the ear of Anthony Bevir, were pressing John Stott's name; partly influenced by a sense that evangelicals were not getting their fair share of Crown appointments.[104] But to appoint a young curate to be Rector of the parish where he has served his title, while by no means unprecedented, was sufficiently unusual to give Bevir pause. No doubt he consulted Wand, Bishop of London, who knew the views of the churchwardens, and himself thought well of John Stott. Indeed, it is not impossible that Wand foresaw some such eventuality as this in writing as he did on 22 February suggesting that it is 'generally speaking one's duty to remain where one is unless one is quite sure' of a call elsewhere.

The Bishop of Willesden, on the other hand, the suffragan bishop in charge of the day-to-day work in that part of the diocese, was a good deal less convinced, though there was only one reason for his misgivings: 'We didn't think he'd stay'.[105] It was not unreasonable. John Stott had already served a curacy considerably longer than the current average; he had been priest-in-charge since the Rector's death; it was known that he had refused a variety of invitations, and thought that his heart was probably given to work in the East End. But time would show that fifty years later John Stott was still at All Souls, having been parishioner, curate, Rector and Rector-Emeritus; and that throughout his life (with a brief exception during wartime) his home has been within a few hundred yards of All Souls church.

On 3 May John Stott received a formal note from Bevir:

10 Downing Street
Whitehall.
3 May, 1950

Dear Sir,

Your name has been brought to the notice of the Prime Minister in connexion with the vacancy at All Souls, Langham Place.

If you wish to be considered, with others, in connexion with this benefice, I should be glad if you would complete the enclosed form and return it to me.

Yours very truly,
Anthony Bevir

Five days later the form was duly returned on 8 May. On 8 June Bevir wrote again:

10 Downing Street
Whitehall.
Confidential   8th June, 1950

Dear Sir,

I am desired by the First Lord of the Treasury to say that he will be happy to submit your name to the Crown for appointment to the benefice of All Souls, Langham Place, Marylebone, with which St. Peter, Vere Street, is shortly to be amalgamated. Mr. Attlee makes this communication to you in the belief that, subject to the provisions of Parliamentary Enactment, you are prepared to give due obedience to the Bishop of the diocese in matters of discipline and ceremonial.

As His Majesty's approval must be obtained before any announcement can be made, I have to ask that you will treat this offer as confidential: and I shall be glad to hear at your early convenience whether it is agreeable to you.

Yours very truly,
Anthony Bevir[106]

This time matters moved speedily. By 12 June Bevir was able to write 'the king has been graciously pleased to approve your appointment.' The PCC, meeting at the end of June with John Stott (as Priest-in-Charge) in the chair and no doubt to his embarrassment, expressed their pleasure:

Amid unanimous approval, Mr. Bles remarked that the appointment strengthened faith in regal infallibility, and we trust that Mr. Stott will remain with us for many years to come.[107]

The July issue of *All Souls* began with the simple announcement:

Our New Rector

His Majesty the King has been graciously pleased to appoint the Reverend J. R. W. STOTT, M. A., to the living of All Souls, Langham Place.

The news of this appointment has been received with joy and thankfulness by the whole Parish.

The Churchwardens

It was the call for which he had been waiting; and for which God had long been preparing him.

The 1950s

TEN

Rector of All Souls:
A Strategy for Evangelism

1

The first twelve months of the new decade were for John Stott a time not only of extreme busyness (that was nothing new) but also of constant change. At the start of 1950 he was assistant curate, carrying much of the day-to-day work of the parish during the Rector's continuing illness and absence. Early in March the Rector died, leaving him as curate during a vacancy. A few weeks later he was appointed priest-in-charge until a new incumbent should be instituted. By June he was Rector-designate; and at the end of September he had become Rector. To some members of the congregation the announcement brought a sense of shock. However much they liked their 'young curate' he seemed absurdly inexperienced, dogmatic and uncompromising in his views, in contrast to the mature, benign and well-loved Rector they had known. Elisabeth Earnshaw-Smith, not surprisingly, found it difficult to accept, 'amazed that this young upstart should take over from my father ... so unlike the vicars I knew who were my father's friends.'[1]

For John Stott himself it was a major turning point for his whole life, in the midst of an exceedingly busy and testing time. In an intimate letter to Mrs. Harding Wood (wife of 'Uncle Harding', the G. R. Harding

Wood who had been curate at All Souls before the First World War) he opened his heart:

> I never dared pray for this. I kept praying that His will might be done, and I kept disbelieving that I might be His will! Often I humbled myself before Him and assured Him I had no personal, ambitious wish for the post, and would not be personally disappointed if He passed me by in favour of someone else. But I did earnestly ask that our beloved church might be spared the ordeal of a false apostle. Then came His answer. Emotions of all kinds overwhelmed me. I was honoured and humbled, reassured and frightened, grateful and fearful. Looking back, I can only conclude that the long periods of uncertainty and perplexity through which I passed were allowed for this purpose. I was constantly restrained from leaving dear H. E. S., and surely it was for this. I wondered why He kept me so long in doubt. In my short Christian experience I had grown accustomed to His gracious clarity of guidance. But now I was in darkness! Yet I held on in blind, and sometimes impatient and wavering faith, obeying His 'Be thou there until I bring thee word'. Then the light broke ...
>
> Again and again in these last days 'My grace is sufficient for thee' have been ringing in my ears. Were it not for this, and for the lovely letters I've received I think I should be overwhelmed by the responsibility: as it is, I'm wonderfully at peace. But I do need your prayers. I know you will give them to me ... Deliverance from pride in success, and from depression in setback; patience and love, wisdom and vision, humility and moral courage. These and many other graces do I need ...[2]

In fact his immediate need was not only prayer for himself but curates for the parish: and these were in short supply. Over the previous ten or twelve years the number of curates at work in the Church of England had fallen by more than half.[3] When Gordon Mayo sailed for Africa within weeks of John Stott's institution, he left the new Rector and the faithful Sister Jordan to carry the parish between them. The appointment of a successor was clearly a priority: John Stott arranged that F. D. B. Eddison, curate of St. Matthew, Fulham, and so already in the diocese, should come to join him early the following year. They were friends from camp and had both been at Trinity, Cambridge. Donald Eddison was a little older than his new Rector, but had been only two years in Orders, following active service during the war. By an imaginative arrangement, he also became Chaplain of the Regent Street Polytechnic, almost opposite the church. This was Quintin Hogg's foundation, established originally to meet the needs of young men not only educationally, but socially and spiritually as well: its motto 'The Lord is our strength' can still be seen in a large mosaic on the floor of the main entrance hall of what is now the University of Westminster. At the turn of the century, fifty years before, over 1,000 young men would attend its Sunday Bible-classes. In the 1950s the educational provision it offered could be summed up as 'anything for anybody at any level at any time' – which included day and evening courses, full and part-time. It was a very considerable area of ministry on the doorstep of the church.[4]

In the July 1950 issue of *All Souls,* which carried the announcement of his appointment, John Stott wrote of feeling 'more humbled than honoured' and asked for the prayers of the congregation. In addition, the magazine carried two significant articles from his pen, a 'Call to Prayer' and 'A Five-Point Manifesto'. The first was a plea to his readers that they should make the weekly prayer meeting central to the life of the congregation: 'About 450 come to church on Sundays to worship: about 25 come to the Church House on Thursday to pray. We have begun a new chapter in our Church's history ... so we must pray if we are to succeed.'[5]

The manifesto was a summary of the first sermon he had preached as Rector-designate, only days after the announcement. Taking as his text Acts 2:42, he set out 'the model we must imitate ... as we peer into the unknown'. Study, fellowship, worship and prayer were to mark a church who were also 'together in Evangelism'. Each point of the model was firmly applied to the immediate situation:

> ... All Souls with St. Peter's is a Parish Church. Our first duty is local, and yet our impact on the neighbourhood is small and the percentage of Christians in the population negligible. The multitudes are outside. Are we too respectable to go out and bring them in? Too afraid of public opinion to employ well tried methods? Too sensitive to convention to devise new means of reaching the unbeliever? The task is beyond the power of the clergy. A staff of 10 curates could not do it. There are only two alternatives. Either the task will not be done, or we must do it together, a task force of Ministers and people thoroughly trained and harnessed as a team for evangelism.[6]

John Stott at this stage of his life knew himself to be 'a product of Iwerne and the CICCU, having learned from them whatever I knew of evangelistic and pastoral work.'[7] Faced with this awesome opportunity, he was itching to apply their well-tried principles, which he had seen God use and honour, to the realities of a Church of England parish. In his own mind he enumerated five criteria which he hoped to bring to bear on the life of his new charge: the priority of prayer, expository preaching, regular evangelism, careful follow-up of enquirers and converts, and the systematic training of helpers and leaders. It was now a question of being able to adapt them from work among students to a parochial situation, and then to devise means and structures to put them into practice.

Those who had heard his first sermon as Rector, his manifesto (or had later read it in *All Souls*), would have sensed that their Rector would soon be returning to this theme. They did not have very long to wait.

In August John Stott set off on holiday with a couple of friends. One of them was the John Lefroy who might have succeeded him as curate had Earnshaw-Smith lived and who was later to join his staff:

> We set off not knowing where we were going in John Stott's Austin van with a tent apiece. John's aim was to drive as fast as he could and as far as he could to an extremity of Britain. I have photos of him finishing the parish magazine, *All Souls*, on the pier at Stranraer and of our three tents pitched in a bog in Ardwell bay. I have always thought it was an expedition like this that led him to stumble on Hookses, at the end of another British peninsular.[8]

Now that his future was settled, John Stott's mind was teeming with future plans for his church, even on his Scottish holiday: 'I have not been able to get you all out of my thoughts' he wrote; 'My mind has turned constantly to St. Peter's.' In his editorial letter he describes himself as

> ... perched precariously at the end of Stranraer pier, looking out across the splendid harbour, encircled by graceful Herring Gulls and listening to the plaintive pipings of Oyster Catchers. A little Scottish lad of about 10, seeing me writing, has just sidled timorously up and said: 'Och, are ye a poet, mon?'[9]

Following a few domestic announcements and expressions of appreciation, the letter from Stranraer goes on to give details of his Institution as Rector, and a provisional date the following year for the re-opening of All Souls. But these are clearly not the central issues:

> The question which rests most heavily on my heart at present is how to reach the hungry multitudes who are without Christ. We are not unmindful of the fact that many come to St. Peter's who do not live in the parish. Nevertheless, God has entrusted to us the care of some 10,000 souls living within the parochial bound-aries. As Christians living near or worshipping in St. Peter's we have

an unmistakable, inescapable responsibility towards our neighbours who are strangers to Christ and his gospel of grace ... I visualise (and hope before next month to be able to explain in detail) the training of a considerable number of Church members for the task of bringing the Gospel of our Saviour Jesus Christ to every house in the parish. We cannot play at this. It will mean real sacrifice in our busy lives to commit ourselves to thorough training once a fortnight for six months, and then to go out two by two to visit from house to house. The course of training will need to cover the theology of the Gospel, the personal life of the Christian worker and the technique of evangelism. Can we hear this call of Christ to discharge our duty to the mass of non-churchgoers?[10]

The establishing of structures to accomplish this was to be a major theme of the decade; and, more than any other single factor, to establish the unique position of All Souls as trail-blazer in parochial evangelism.

On Tuesday, 26 September, John Stott was instituted to his new charge. All Souls would not be finally restored until the Spring, so that the service took place in St. Peter's, with William Wand, the Bishop of London, both instituting and preaching. With remarkable prescience, perhaps based on the high standards of the essays that John Stott had been required to submit before ordination, Wand used the occasion to remind the new incumbent to keep up his reading amid the pressures of a busy parish; and charged the churchwardens to make sure that he had time to do so. John Stott's parents were both present, as was Bash, who in a letter to him afterwards about possible curates went on to recount his conversation with Sir Arnold Stott after the Service. The reception was held at the Royal Institute of British Architects in Portland Place: Bash described how he found John Stott's father

... standing smoking a cigarette and looking very proud of you and yet out of his depth by turns, and this is how the conversation went –

Me: 'Good evening, Sir Arnold'

Slowly turning his head – after a long pause – a growl: 'Who are you?'

Me: 'I'm Nash, John's friend. We met in 1940. Do you recall me?'

Long pause – a grunt. 'Yes, I do. What are you doing?' (in a muffled grunt)

Me: 'Oh, youth work. You must be a proud man tonight. Wasn't it to be the Foreign Office or the Church, Sir Arnold, in those pre-war days?'

(a sour look – almost startled – another puff): 'I was never against this – I only wanted no hasty decisions.'

Me: 'You've hardly a grey hair; you wear very well!'

'I'm thin, you see' (with no smile at all until just one at the end after a pause).

By contrast, Lady Stott, he wrote, had come up to him, beaming all over, butted into his conversation with someone else, and said 'I must shake hands with dear Bash again!'[11]

On the Sunday following his institution, every new incumbent was still obliged by law 'openly and publicly in the presence of the congregation there assembled' to read the Thirty-nine Articles and to make a solemn Declaration of Assent:

> I assent to the Thirty-nine Articles of Religion, which I have now read before you, and to the Book of Common Prayer and of the Ordering of Bishops, Priests and Deacons. I believe the Doctrine of the Church of England as therein set forth to be agreeable to the Word of God; and in public prayer and administration of the Sacraments I will use the form in the said Book prescribed, and none other, except so far as shall be ordered by lawful authority.

To many clergy even in 1950 such a requirement to 'read themselves in' seemed no more than a tiresome formality. A few went so far as to indicate that the declaration was made under duress; and should not be taken as conveying their real mind. Thirty years later, shortly before the Form of Assent was changed to the present form (which is simply an affirmation of loyalty to 'this inheritance of faith as your inspiration and guidance under God ...'), Bishop Mervyn Stockwood of Southwark used to advise his clergy to add the words 'In so far as the mind of Christ permits' at the end of their Declaration, and assure them that he would not enquire whether they 'read themselves in' on their first Sunday – and indeed hoped they would not do so.[12]

To John Stott, however, this 'reading in' afforded an opportunity, which he was to take annually for many years to come, to remind his congregation of their Protestant heritage, and to expound the Articles as 'agreeable to the Word of God' in Scripture. When in 1963 *The Times* had a correspondence on the subject of the Articles, he felt that his experience justified a letter:

> Sir, – 'as for clergymen', wrote the good Bishop J. C. Ryle of Liverpool, 'if I had my own way, I would require them to read the Articles publicly in church once every year.' Lest it should be

thought that all Church of England clergy conscientiously object to the Thirty-Nine Articles, I am happy to say that in my case Bishop Ryle has his way. For the past 12 years, on the Sunday nearest the anniversary of my institution, it has been my practice to read the Articles publicly, half at Morning Prayer and half at Evening Prayer. The reading takes a quarter of an hour; I then spend a further quarter of an hour commenting on one of them. I do this for two reasons. First, I am glad every year before the congregation to renew my assent to the Articles. Secondly, I am convinced that the widespread ignorance of the reformed doctrines of the Church of England is one of the major causes of its weakness today.

The articles are not perfect. I myself have hesitations about some comparatively minor points in them. Archbishop Lord Fisher is no doubt right that they could do with some revision and improvement. But as a general statement of reformed doctrine concerning God, man, salvation, and the Church, they are excellent. The only proper reason for objecting to the Articles would be a demonstration that they are unbiblical; for what they teach, they claim to teach 'by most certain warrants of holy Scripture'. It is precisely because they are so thoroughly scriptural that an assault upon them should alarm all loyal churchmen. Dr. Hughes is right that such an assault is not upon the Articles themselves, but upon the true and wholesome biblical doctrine which they express.

Yours faithfully,
John R. W. Stott,

Rector of All Souls, Langham Place.
12 Weymouth Street, W. 1, May 30.[13]

Perhaps there can be no better justification of his practice than the inscription in John Stott's presentation copy of the book, *On the Thirty-Nine Articles: A Conversation with Tudor Christianity*.[14] The author, Oliver O'Donovan, had been a boy at University College School in the 1950s, singing treble in the All Souls choir. There he had made a response to the gospel at the age of ten or eleven; and well remembers a few years later being prepared for confirmation by Julian Charley, 'following JRWS's scheme, of course, suitably modified for those of tender years.'[15] When, thirty years on, as Regius Professor of Pastoral and Moral Theology at Oxford, he came to write the book, he added the inscription: *JRWS, with affection and regard: who first taught me to appreciate the Articles and to love Christ. O. M. T. O'D. 15. i. 87.*

2

Throughout John Stott's first winter as Rector plans continued for the re-opening of All Souls. The pages of the parish magazine speak of the need for 'an army of cleaners and polishers', and of the re-equipping of the church ('I wish someone would send us another £1,000'[16]) with 'hassocks, hymn books, prayer books, psalters, robes, linoleum, carpets ...'[17] But beyond these practical matters the eyes of the congregation are continually directed to their real task 'of building up the church's life. For ten years many hundreds of people east of Portland Place have been virtually unchurched. We must resolve to extend to them a warm, unselfish welcome, as they begin to come back ...'[18] To this end, the PCC had agreed at the start of the year that all sittings should be free and that in the interests of offering newcomers a welcome, they should forego the £60 a year in pew rents which the church had enjoyed before it was bombed.[19] By Easter the structural repairs were finished and the redecoration almost complete:

> The partial destruction of the building had made it possible for the architect to approach the task with greater freedom. A much lighter green colouring now was adopted than in his 1924 scheme, in order to counter the inevitable grime which would accumulate over the years; gilding was to be the main decorative feature, and the windows were to have ground glass, bordered with yellow. In all, Mr Goodhart Rendel was confident that Nash would have approved of these changes. There remained only to construct the new choir stalls, designed with a Regency flavour of black and gold, and to install the organ in the west gallery.[20]

In the event, Sunday morning, 29 April, brought 'a crowded church and the sense of God's presence'[21] for the Service of Rededication. On the front of the Order of Service three dates reminded parishioners of their history:

> *Consecrated on 25th November, 1824*
> *Damaged on 8th December, 1940*
> *Reopened on 29th April, 1951*

The lessons were read by Arthur Buxton, former Rector, and by G. R. Harding Wood, former curate; the Bishop of London preached and the prayers included three which had been used at the consecration of the church 126 years before. Finally, the congregation streamed out into Langham Place to the triumphant strains of Jeremiah Clarke's

Trumpet Voluntary: All Souls Church was back in business.

The challenge now was to build up the congregation. St. Peter's had been able to seat at most some five or six hundred; it had been packed in the years after the war, so much so as to form a disincentive, since one had to arrive early to be sure of a seat: the restored All Souls seated nine hundred with comfort. For this reason alone Tom Rees had prophesied that on moving out of St. Peter's the congregation would begin to grow, and he was quickly proved to be right.[22] In September, six months after the re-opening, the BBC broadcast an Evening Service from the new church for the first time; the *Radio Times* included a current photograph of Upper Regent Street, the familiar portico, at last free of scaffolding and builders' materials, towering above a throng of old-fashioned London taxis, but with a sadly truncated steeple still short of the last thirty feet or so. Not until November would it begin once again 'to stretch its pointed finger to the skies' in the 'pristine elegance' of Bath Stone and bronze.[23] By then a new deacon, J. T. C. B. Collins, had joined the staff.

Like his Rector, John Collins was still unmarried. They had overlapped briefly at Cambridge, but had got to know one another at camp where for some years after his ordination John Stott was still in the habit of calling in to see old friends; and later to look for suitable curates. John Collins had returned to Cambridge after national service, had been President of the CICCU, and had therefore acted as host to John Stott when he came to Cambridge to preach the CICCU sermon. At first, accommodation presented problems; though Mrs. Earnshaw-Smith and her family had vacated the Rectory within a very few weeks of her husband's death, the house was not yet ready for occupation and question marks hung for some time over its suitability for its purpose. John Stott looked forward to the day when he might move in, and be able also to offer lodgings (always a problem in central London) to some of his unmarried curates and to two or three students or bachelor members of the church. But in the meantime John Collins made his home 'in a decayed hotel in Manchester Square, full of alcoholics. I could hear them going upstairs every night with their hold-alls of bottles.'[24]

With two curates and Sister Jordan in post an approach by a promising ordinand at Wycliffe Hall, Oxford, James Packer, could not be pursued. Packer himself was uncertain when he would be free to come, since he had applied for a Commonwealth Fund Scholarship for study in America.[25] In years to come, he and John Stott were to work together on a variety of projects and share the same platform at many conferences and congresses.

All Souls had long had a reputation as a home of good preaching, and in his time as curate John Stott had helped to maintain this tradition.

Unusually for a curate, he had been invited to preach in St. Paul's Cathedral, probably at the instigation of Archdeacon Sharpe, one of the residentiary canons. His name was becoming known as a thoughtful biblical preacher with a powerful message and an impelling delivery. Since his Cambridge days, Charles Simeon had been one of his heroes (he was later to write the introduction for an anthology of Simeon's sermons, describing him as 'one of the greatest and most persuasive preachers the Church of England has ever known'[26]). From Simeon, among others, he had begun even before his ordination to recognize the difference between the 'camp talks' tradition of which he had made himself a master under Bash's influence and early training, and the opening of the Scriptures in a full-orbed pulpit ministry, to bring the word of the Lord to the congregation in the power of the Spirit. From the start he had gone out of his way to seek informed criticism which might help him improve his preaching.[27] Then in 1958 he founded a private study-group, 'Christian Debate', to help explore some of the issues about which he would want to write and preach, especially on matters of social concern – 'pressing problems which even five years ago we might have ignored.'[28]

The group met first on 5 December in the Rectory, though as time went on it moved to other locations. Members were originally asked to bring sandwiches; later a meal began to be provided and for a short period it could almost be called a dining club. Papers would be read by the members, or by an invited speaker, followed by discussion and debate. What was valued would be garnered and put in order during the chairman's summing up towards the end. It was the prototype of various study and reading groups, for different purposes, which John Stott would convene at different times in his ministry. Though it met only three or four times a year, in the course of some thirty-five years a very wide range of issues were discussed. 'Christian Debate' was part of the long-term preparation for preaching. Something of the struggles involved in short-term preparation is revealed in an entry in his personal pocket diary dated 15 April 1959 under the heading 'Special subjects for prayer':

Resolved always

   a. to *begin* Sunday sermon on previous Monday

   b. to *finish* at least all but writing out before Sunday begins

   c. to reach Vestry at least ¼ hour, and preferably longer, before each service begins.[29]

It had long been a tradition at All Souls that preachers had to earn their congregation. John Stott worked hard at this and encouraged his curates to do the same. Stories began to gather round him. How, noting a certain restiveness in part of the congregation at a more-than-usually lengthy sermon, he urged them to be patient – 'I too have a Sunday lunch in the oven.' Or how, preaching in St. Peter's one Easter Day, he spoke eloquently of the change that came over the disciples in the days following the resurrection, with the Apostle Peter transformed 'from a rabbit into a lion'. A literally-minded lady in the congregation wrote to protest at this expression as suggesting the transmigration of souls between the human and the animal kingdoms. Some of John Stott's friends, when they heard of this, asked him how he replied. 'Oh,' he said, 'I sent her a postcard with the words "you cuckoo!".'[30]

His curates also enjoyed telling how at a wedding he began inadvertently with the opening exhortation from Morning Prayer: 'Dearly beloved brethren, the Scripture moveth us in sundry places ...'. Calmly and without hesitation he then changed gear so smoothly that only those listening to the sense rather than the sound of his words realised there was anything amiss: ' ... in sundry places ... to join together this man and this woman in Holy Matrimony.'[31]

Wilbur Smith, a noted American preacher, visited All Souls in the mid-fifties and described his impressions for an American readership. John Stott was then not yet thirty-five and not a 'wrangler at Cambridge'[32]; nevertheless, what follows is the contemporary impression of an experienced observer:

> At All Souls', Langham Place, I went to worship on the first Sunday of July. Here the rector is the Rev. J. W. R. Stott, a man in his early forties, who was, I understand, a wrangler at Cambridge. The beautiful auditorium was crowded with a very notable group of people. I believe apart from Westminster Abbey, and perhaps even including that, Mr. Stott regularly preaches to the largest congregation in any Anglican church in London. The church is filled morning and evening, even when it rains, and the evening audience is made up for the most part of young people, many of them students of the universities. The church carries on a tremendous program throughout the week.
>
> Mr. Stott is an evangelical preacher from beginning to end. The service was Anglican, but not over-ritualistic, and the preaching was the preaching of an unadulterated gospel. He took for his text the healing of Naaman. A sermon on the subject *could* be quite ordinary – I mean nothing but a sequence of axioms, and a little uninteresting to folks who know the story by heart. But not the way he developed it ...
>
> In a gracious but clear way, in the power of the Holy Spirit, he told that audience, many saturated with culture and learning, that there was only one cure for this disease of sin, and that was in

Christ, the Lamb of God, and only one place where we could find that healing, and that was in the shed blood of Calvary. That morning my soul was bathed in the dew of heaven, and, may I add, that it has been a long, long time in my own beloved land that I have felt the whole service one of true *worship* offered to God as in that morning at All Souls' Church.[33]

Amid the pressures, John Stott devised a number of expedients to support him in his ministry. The first was simple but far-reaching: the regular setting-aside of time, away from colleagues, desk and telephone, to think and plan ahead; and in an unhurried atmosphere of prayer to devise strategies, to prepare courses of addresses, to plan his diary, and by this means to remain in control of a fast-moving future programme. So crucial was this simple stratagem that, looking back over his ministry at the age of seventy, he listed L. F. E. Wilkinson (a close personal friend of Harold Earnshaw-Smith's) among a list of seven 'people who have influenced me', alongside his parents, Robbie Bickersteth, Bash and Dr. Martyn Lloyd-Jones. He had heard Wilkinson speaking at a conference:

At what used to be called the annual one-day Islington Clerical Conference one of the speakers one year was the Rev. L. F. E. Wilkinson, or 'Wilkie', Principal of Oak Hill Theological College. I have now forgotten what he said, except for one thing. He told us that in his view every clergyman ought to keep a quiet day once a month, in which to look ahead and seek to be drawn up into the mind and perspective of God regarding his ministry. It was a heaven-sent message for me. Having become Rector of All Souls in 1950, at the rather tender age of 29, it was not long before everything got on top of me. I started having the traditional clerical nightmare, finding myself half way up the pulpit steps and suddenly remembering that I had not prepared my sermon! But 'Wilkie' saved me, though I don't think he ever knew it. I went home from the Islington Conference that January, and immediately marked one day a month in my engagement book with the mystic letter 'Q' for QUIET. That monthly day (when I went out of London to a friend's home) became a life-line.[34]

The 'friend's home' was in fact a family home near Pinner on the western outskirts of London where Mrs. Phyllis Parsons, a former member of the congregation, lived with her husband and two daughters. This became John Stott's retreat:

I would arrive mostly quite early in the morning, about 8.00 or
9.00, and she would put a room at my disposal, and leave me alone.
She would kindly bring me a cold lunch, but not disturb me, and I
would have twelve hours in which to be quiet. I used to keep for the
monthly quiet day all those things that needed time, time to think,
time to prepare, time to plan, time to write my editorial in the magazine, a difficult letter that needed time to think before answering it.
All these things that needed time I would keep for the quiet day –
think them through and pray them over. It immediately lifted the
burden from me, and I've hardly ever had a 'clerical nightmare'
again. In fact that monthly quiet day became so important to me
that for quite a long period it became a weekly one, and I preferred
to have a quiet day a week than to have a day off a week.[35]

Later, when Mrs. Parsons moved to Cambridge, John Stott found new
friends on the edge of Hampstead who would do the same for him.[36]

A further help to the new Rector in long-term preparation for the
continual demands of preaching and speaking was the early-morning
Friday Bible study group which he had started as a curate for a few
friends; and which continued, with changes in membership as those
attending moved into or out of London, over many years. They met in
the old vestry at the back of the church, which had remained in use even
when the church itself was closed following the Portland Place bomb.
Sister Jordan lived in a tiny flat on the top floor of this block (now All
Souls Church House) and it was her task on a Friday morning to see that
the outer door was unlocked before 7.00 so that John Stott and his
friends could use the building. One morning they gathered on the steps,
non-plussed because the door remained firmly locked against them. John
Stott moved into the middle of the street, deserted at that hour, and
called with all the power of his lungs to the curtained windows of the top
flat: 'Sister Phoebe ... Sister Phooeebee!'. Sister Jordan had perhaps been
known to the late Rector by her Christian name, but to no-one else on
the staff. So it was a startled face that appeared at the window, before the
door was unlocked, and the Bible study could begin.[37] Many of those who
took part retained vivid memories of these Friday mornings. Ian Lodge-
Patch, for example:

About 1950 I was living off Baker Street – John Collins was for a
short time in the same decaying lodgings. Perhaps it was through
him that I joined a group of five or ten who met in All Souls' vestry
every Friday morning from 7.00 to 8.00 ... when I started going we
were reading Hebrews together. John's method was to get the group
to read a chapter through and then to discuss it verse by verse – or a

few verses together – bringing out the meaning, comparing Scripture with Scripture to illuminate what lay before us, teaching us principles, or common errors like arguing from analogy, or bringing into a discussion things that were quite irrelevant. I recall doing just this – with, no doubt, a pious earnestness – and receiving, after a short silence, John's comment, 'Ian, it has nothing whatever to do with it ...'

These early mornings, which continued for me into 1954 or 1955 revolutionised my Bible-reading and showed me not only how it should be done, but taught me how to do it. Although John could have given us an edifying account of the passage or the book before us, he took a line that not only taught us, but taught us *how*.[38]

There was usually a strong medical contingent at these early mornings, on their way to their respective hospitals. Ian Lodge-Patch was to become a consultant psychiatrist; but there were also future surgeons, GPs and medical missionaries. Michael Alison, later MP, was among the group; and of course the All Souls' curates were regular attenders – even if Donald Eddison used occasionally to earn a black mark by arriving only in time for breakfast; this seems to have been sometimes at Lyons' tea shop and sometimes at the ABC café. By contrast, John Stott is remembered as arriving to lead the group at 7.00, having already dictated twenty letters.[39]

3

In the high summer of 1952 the Rectory at No. 12, Weymouth Street was finally ready. It is marvellously convenient for the church and parish, since Weymouth Street is only five minutes easy walk from All Souls. No. 12 is a high narrow building, typical of many West-end terraces, not unlike a doll's house to look at, wedged between a block of flats on the east, and the imposing premises of the Royal Institute of British Architects on the west. The Institute had approached Earnshaw-Smith, and now wrote to John Stott, seeking to buy the house in order to extend their premises. 'The answer on each occasion has been the same, that the church was willing, on condition that they found us an equivalent building in or near the parish, at no cost to ourselves. End of correspondence!'[40]

The house has thirteen rooms, and must have been a nightmare to servants; to get from the basement kitchen to the fourth-floor attic is to climb ninety-three stairs. What was a bachelor clergyman, who for five years had been living in two rooms or a bed-sitting room, to do with such a house? The answer, to which the PCC readily agreed, was to turn it into a hostel, providing seven bed-sitting rooms for curates and others connected with All Souls, as well as living accommodation for the Rector and a housekeeper and cook. A Rectory Management Committee was brought into being. The basement housed the kitchen and a large communal dining-room. John Stott took over the study just inside the front door, formerly the dining-room, a gracious room with plenty of space for books, and one of the upstairs bedrooms. Harold Earnshaw-Smith's study became the cook's bed-sitting room. On the first floor the elegant drawing-room, with its Adam ceiling and fireplace, was in constant use for meetings of many kinds, while the secretary later had her desk in one corner; and the remaining rooms became 'bed-sits' for a house-mother, and for one or two single curates and a handful of post-graduates, often medical students at London hospitals, or ordinands. They knew their temporary home as 'The Wreckage' – a cross between a Rectory and a Vicarage – or, even more disrespectfully, as 'The Stottery'. In time these former residents became a distinguished but far-flung community of academics, clergy, doctors and Christian workers scattered across the world.

The first to move with John Stott into No. 12 were the two curates, Donald Eddison and John Collins, together with four students. It was a long-awaited moment when, according to the Rector's letter in the August issue of *All Souls* (using a different combination of Vicarage and Rectory) 'the Wreckage will have become a Victory'.

The longest-serving house-mother was Miss G. J. E. Packer, Gwen, known to everyone as 'Packie' (or, in her absence, as the Mother Superior) who moved in during the autumn of 1953. She is remembered as a tall, elegant lady, loved by generations of missionaries' children for whom she had opened a small home in the 1920s, which she maintained for some twenty-five years. During the First World War the man whom she hoped to marry was killed in action; and, like many others who suffered similar tragedies, she declined all subsequent suitors. But she took it for granted that this treasured relationship qualified her to give expert advice in all affairs of the heart; and many residents of the Rectory found they could unburden themselves to her and seek her counsel and a place in her prayers. It was widely believed – indeed, John Lefroy remembers her saying so to some of the residents – that had she been younger, it would have been her intention to secure John Stott as the husband she never had.[41]

The house had no common room apart from the basement dining-room, so there was little social life beyond coffee-drinking and conversation in the bed-sitting rooms or over meals. The residents met at breakfast round the big table in the basement, and might not see each other again until the evening meal; on Sundays they would lunch together and then meet for a relaxed late supper with the pressures of the day behind them. It was by no means simply a clergy-house, and is remembered as a cheerful community, rubbing shoulders easily enough with one another most of the time. Even so, the ideal of community life was sometimes elusive. There were few late-night parties: then, as now, John Stott was an early riser. The well-publicized but optimistic suggestion that one of the benefits of their clergy-commune at the Rectory was that the staff could shut themselves in every day until lunch time, 'to pray, read and think without interruption' gave rise to some amusement in both local and national press.[42]

'We were a very young team,' John Collins recalls,

> and there was a pleasantly schoolboyish quality in our lives. We had a succession of housekeepers at 12, Weymouth Street, one of whom did not get on well with John Stott. John Lefroy saw his opportunity, and managed to persuade her that John might well be a secret drinker (in those days we were all teetotallers – 'not one drop', at least in the parish, and even when John's parents came up on great occasions, they were only offered soft drinks, much to Sir Arnold's distaste). The housekeeper took John Lefroy seriously, and from then on was always expecting to come upon hidden hoards of empty bottles.[43]

Other residents have their own cherished recollections. Julian Charley recalls John Stott being taunted by a Canadian resident over communal breakfast in the Rectory, because he always read *The Times*. 'You should read *The Guardian*,' the resident suggested. 'It's a much better paper – look, it's even got a picture of a black-headed gull flying past a lighthouse.' John Stott took the paper and looked at the picture. 'Actually,' he said mildly, 'it's an immature Kittiwake.'[44]

Sometimes the visitors would be younger clergy, friends from camp days perhaps, spending a Sunday off in London. Richard Gorrie was one of these, then in his first curacy at St. Clement's, Oxford, and never forgot a challenging example of the Rector's practical Christianity:

> I was looking forward to hearing John preach twice, in fact three times as he went on to an informal outreach service at St. Peter's Vere Street around 8.30 p.m. One of the passers by who was fished into St. Peter's was a homeless man. John took him home for a meal, gave him the use of his own bedroom, and fixed up a camp bed for himself in his study. His housekeeper told me that he did this quite often for needy folk.[45]

Visitors from overseas were sure of a special welcome. In 1953 an American gospel singer, Frank Boggs, came to London to sing and direct the choirs for Tom Rees in his Albert Hall rallies. It was arranged that he should sing at All Souls on the Sunday morning, and John Stott invited him to the Rectory for supper on the Saturday evening. He recalls:

> I met his curates. They all accepted this tall, thin Texan in a cowboy Stetson hat with warmth. After the meal, John was fascinated in hearing of the spiritual awakening during my college days at Baylor University, Waco, Texas. God had rocked our Baptist universities and churches, calling many thousands to the ministry. As I told him, he would say 'hallelujah' over some particular spiritual victory.
>
> Next morning I experienced the special warmth of All Souls for the first time. Having been raised in the First Baptist, Dallas, under Dr. Geo. Truett I had never heard a 'hallelujah' – much less from an Anglican rector. As I wrote my mother, 'John is an amazing blend of high church/low church, of dignity and warmth, of amazing scholarship and the human touch.'[46]

The summer of 1953 saw Donald Eddison's departure from the staff. 'It is not what I have done at All Souls, but what I have learned,' he wrote in reply to the Rector's letter of thanks, 'that has been of most value'.[47] He had been responsible for the Chaplaincy of the Regent Street polytechnic: the next curate, R. E. H. Bowdler, was to assume the innovative role of Chaplain to the big Oxford Street stores, most of which lay within the parish. Then at the start of 1954 C. J. E. Lefroy came as an additional curate, combining this with work among students.

About this time John Dugan was appointed as 'Church Bursar' (originally 'personal assistant' to the Rector, but the title was felt to sound too feminine), and he too, as a bachelor, joined the growing community at the 'Wreckage'. He was known (rather to his regret) as 'Desmond' to avoid confusion with the other Johns, and with his relaxed and easy-going manner, and his total resistance to being interested in birds, provided a valued counterpart to the Rector's incisive mind and energetic enthusiasms. Further appointments in the second half of the decade saw the arrival of Frances Whitehead as Church Secretary in place of Miss Warden; Vera Williams to follow Sister Jordan; and Geoffrey Rawlins, Julian Charley, Michael Harper, Tom Robinson and Martin Peppiatt to the growing list of All Souls' curates.

Organists, too, were important members of a church with a strong musical tradition in the heart of London. Sometimes the young Rector allowed himself to think it part of his duties to see that they did not take themselves or their music too seriously. On one occasion, very soon after a new organist, Magnus Black, had been appointed, there happened to be five weddings one Saturday, and, for some reason, all were taken by John Stott. In those days, there was a 7–10 minute address. That evening John Collins saw Magnus and asked him how he had got on:

> He told me, in an awed whisper, that John had given five entirely different addresses. Later, I mentioned this to John. He roared with laughter, and said that he had more or less run through all his wedding addresses in order to impress Magnus![48]

Another organist, Freddie Geoghegan, a brilliant musician, son of a Russian mother and an Irish father, liked to practice in All Souls at night. In the dark church, with only the reading-light above the console, he could play undisturbed. John Collins again:

> On at least one occasion (I know because I was present, and I suspect that there were others) John crept in quietly while he was playing, came up behind him, waited until there were plenty of stops out, and then placed both his hands down flat on the keyboard, making the most dreadful noise. I don't think Freddie enjoyed the joke nearly as much as John did. He leapt six inches off his seat, put his head in his hands, and took some time to recover. John was quite unrepentant ...[49]

It was a time not only of great activity but of much innovation in the parish. At the heart of it lay a new emphasis on expository preaching, and the training of a succession of curates in the preacher's task – so much so, that from each in turn until he had found his personal style, the congregation professed to recognize 'his master's voice'. Second only to this, and very much part of it, was a strategy of parochial evangelism which was the biggest single factor making for growth and enrichment in the life of the church. Such evangelism was not, however, confined to a single 'strategy' but steadily built into every aspect of the church's life. With All Souls once again commanding the top of Regent Street, the fluted spire newly rebuilt, the doors of the circular portico open in welcome, visitors came in increasing numbers. Many came to attend the weekday or Sunday Services; more, probably, to view the church as part of London's 'tourist trail'. For these, as much as for the regular congregation, a new illustrated guide was published in 1954, to offer a brief introduction to the church building, its history, its work and its message. John Stott contributed brief summaries of the last two: besides reference to the Church Day School, to the regular services, and to the special activities, he emphasized the church's missionary interest ('twenty-six on the foreign field who once belonged to All Souls') and the Hour of Prayer ('the church's central meeting during the week'). The final section of the *Guide*, 'The Church's Message', began with the spire and Westall's famous picture on the east wall, to show that 'ours is in fact a sign-post ministry ...

> ... Our great desire is to direct men and women not to ourselves, nor to our church, but to Jesus Christ. He is the centre of our vision. He is the object of our witness. We have three unshakable convictions about Him. The first concerns who He is, the second what He came to do, and the third what He is asking of us.[50]

The visitor was left not only with historical and architectural information but with a direct evangelistic challenge. The location, as well as the reputation of the church, meant that a substantial part of the congregation would either be visitors to London, for shorter or longer stays, or else 'eclectics', in the sense of drawing on members from beyond the parish boundaries. From time to time the Rector would remonstrate with the congregation, telling them that no one should be attending All Souls if they were passing another evangelical church en route. There is an authentic story of a literally-minded student faced with this challenge who satisfied her conscience by making a considerable detour on her bicycle, Sunday by Sunday, from the flat she shared in north London, so that she could look the Rector in the face as one honestly entitled to be there![51]

Another early initiative was an annual 'Doctors' Service' every St. Luke's tide. This was introduced as a way of building bridges with the Harley Street residents, and the various professional medical bodies within the parish. Both All Souls and St. Peter's had at different times been styled 'The Doctors' Church' and the Rector was well-known as the son of a distinguished medical family. At the first of these the lessons were read by the respective Presidents of the Royal College of Physicians and the Royal College of Surgeons; and every year John Stott preached on a theme particularly relevant to such a congregation: 'True Health' (from 1 Thessalonians 5); or 'The Human Body' (from 1 Corinthians 6); 'The Nature of Man', 'Attitudes to Suffering', 'Luke the Physician', 'The Scientific Method', 'The Doctor as a Person' – and, towards the end of the 1960s, in a time when pro-life issues were to the fore, on 'A Christian Philosophy of Life and Death'. Following the Service, a lunch was held for those taking part, often at the Royal Society of Medicine, opposite St. Peter's, Vere Street, or at the Royal College of Physicians in Regent's Park. Eventually, after some twenty years, it broadened into a Medical Service, to include nurses, paramedical staff, and all involved in the work of medicine.

Much less well-known were the monthly healing services, which grew from John Stott's understanding of the ministry of Jesus. Although comparatively small numbers were involved, the Services were planned and arranged with meticulous care and were in advance of most current practice. Something of John Stott's own attitude to this ministry appears in a reply written in 1955 to a young and highly-perceptive Christian doctor in his congregation: like the Rector himself, he would have been very aware of the pastoral sensitivities, the cruelty of arousing false hopes, and the dangers of appearing to effect 'miraculous cures'. John Stott's letter makes it clear that he saw this as part of the spiritual ministry of the church, a decisive committing of the sufferer into the hands of God:

> Thank you for your letter. It is difficult to answer your questions with any accuracy. I never enquire from people seeking help at a Healing Service exactly what their illness is. I feel myself to be quite unqualified to do so, and I do not think it is really relevant. We therefore welcome at a Healing Service anybody who cares to come, whatever their complaint, provided we consider them spiritually ready. As for results, I do know of one or two cases where definite healing appears to have resulted. I have not investigated the claims, obviously. I know of other cases where there has been relief of pain but a continuance of the illness. Others do not seem to have had any physical result, but all say that it has been a real spiritual blessing.[52]

The name was later changed to 'a service of prayer for the sick'.

On a normal Sunday at All Souls the morning service was at 11.00. Before that, however, there was a 'Children's Church', for about twenty boys and girls and their parents, comfortably filling the south aisle. As curate, John Stott had been responsible for this. The move into All Souls, and the subsequent renovation of St. Peter's, made it possible to re-think this pattern, and to transform the 'Children's Church' into the 'Family Service' which continued in St. Peter's under John Collins until he was appointed to St. Mark's Gillingham in the Medway Towns. The Family Service then passed to Geoffrey Rawlins, who was to remain an All Souls curate for nearly ten years. Among the projects he introduced was a 'Barrow Bookstall' in the local market, selling Christian literature, and a quarterly *Parish Paper,* well-illustrated and popular in style, distributed from house to house.

An unusual opportunity open to few churches was the appointment in the summer of 1953 of the Revd. R. E. H. Bowdler to be curate of All

Souls and Chaplain to a group of Oxford Street stores – as one of the papers put it 'His pulpit among the nylons'.[53] The idea of such an industrial chaplaincy was not a new one: and under Earnshaw-Smith All Souls had long sought to extend its ministry by holding lunch-hour services for the thousands of non-resident 'parishioners' who had homes elsewhere but spent their working lives in that part of central London. In the five stores which came to share the Chaplaincy (and contribute to the stipend) there were some 7,000 employees, as many as in a medium-sized parish.

John Stott went himself to see the Chairmen or Managing Directors of the five major stores in the parish, Debenhams, D. H. Evans, John Lewis, Marshall and Snellgrove and Peter Robinson. Selfridges was in Colin Kerr's parish, and so his church was responsible for their chaplaincy arrangements. The man in charge at Peter Robinson happened to be a lay Reader in his local church, and welcomed the idea. Less immediately receptive was John Spedan Lewis, son of the founder, 'an emotional, combative and outspoken man, often appearing arbitrary and domineering'.[54] To him John Stott outlined the scheme:

His retort to me was 'Well, I shall have to consult the Partners, and if they want a Buddhist Chaplaincy as well as a Christian Chaplaincy, we would have to agree.' And I said, 'Well, if there were enough Buddhists in the Partnership to warrant it, I would see no difficulty …' My line was to say that all enlightened institutions had their chaplain these days, the Army, schools, colleges, prisons. In the event they all agreed and arranged to contribute to his support, and to put an office at his disposal.[55]

The Chaplain to the Stores had very little opportunity of ministering to his flock on Sundays – they mostly lived in distant suburbs. New ways had to be found of reaching such a diverse 'parish'. So it was largely by the lunch-hour services (and by special 'Stores' services three times a year), by the encouragement of a Christian Fellowship within each store, by evangelistic films, discussions and weekends, and (not least) through the Billy Graham Harringay Crusade of 1954 that the gospel was brought continually before these non-resident parishioners. Much of the value of the work done, as with most pastoral work, was quite unquantifiable. It was seldom easy, in the working day and amid the pressures of a busy store, to find time to know people well enough to talk of spiritual things:

Lunch-hours are short (and there are only a limited number each week); for many there is a long journey at the end of the day; and although I have complete freedom to approach people during work hours, customers and business naturally must come first.[56]

When Richard Bowdler left in 1958 to join the staff of Church Society as Secretary of 'Pathfinders', a national Church youth organization,[57] he was succeeded as Stores Chaplain by Michael Harper, then for a brief period by Peter Bagnall and later still by Barry Dawson.

With so much evangelism, teaching and nurture taking place, it was inevitable that a proportion of those who came into touch with All Souls would feel called to some form of full-time Christian service or ministry. John Lefroy and John Collins' wife, Diana, had both been running informal Vocation Study Groups to help such people discover God's purpose for their lives. In 1956 the PCC approved a more formal scheme, with some sort of committed membership:

> The proposal was that those who, after careful consideration and definite prayer, believed that God may be calling them, would be invited to sign a card by which they would commit themselves to seek God's will for their lives, to pray regularly that God will disclose it, to prepare themselves for the possibility of full-time Christian service and to be ready to go anywhere that God may call.[58]

This card would be counter-signed by the Rector, as an indication that the church fellowship recognized and welcomed this sense of call and readiness to respond. After some searching for a name ('Christian Volunteers' was considered and rejected) the group was called 'The Philadelphia Fellowship' following the 'open door' of Revelation 3:7–8: it was so called because its members were investigating open doors of opportunity. Introducing it to the congregation John Stott was able to write of four members leaving for, or returning to, the overseas mission field, while eleven others were beginning training at Bible or Missionary College.[59]

A further long-awaited development of the work of the parish came towards the end of the decade with the opening of the All Souls Clubhouse in Cleveland Street, some 500 yards from the church. The concept of a church centre in the east end of the parish had been dear to Earnshaw-Smith's heart, as it was to his successor's, but little or no progress had been made until, three years after his institution as Rector, John Stott reminded the PCC that when he first came to the parish as curate in 1945 Earnshaw-Smith had been talking of the need for something of this kind. His vision was for a church presence in the form of a Community and Christian Centre amid the crowded homes and tenements of the eastern part of the parish: a place 'for homely mission services and for youth clubs'.[60] It was not easy to find a suitable property in the heart of central London, but eventually the 'Trinity Clubhouse' began to seem a possibility. It consisted mainly of a former school, later used for church youth work; but in a very poor condition, still with gas brackets hanging from the ceilings. It took its name from Holy Trinity, Marylebone, the church which became the headquarters of the SPCK. Negotiations were tortuous and protracted – four properties had to be acquired, involving not only the Charity Commissioners, the Ministry of Education and the London Church Fund, but also the Howard de Walden Estates. In addition, the Clubhouse lay just outside the parish, and a boundary alteration had to be agreed with their neighbours, with the diocese, and with the Church Commissioners. The construction work to be done seemed daunting, but at least there was space for a variety of club activities, and the location was right. Eventually, thanks to a generous and timely gift,[61] the ramshackle structure became a major youth and community centre for that part of London, with recreation rooms, gymnasium, and various hobbies and club facilities, so forming a logical development from the Covenanter and Juco clubs held in the old Waldegrave Hall in Duke Street. It was staffed by volunteers under two full-time residents, a Warden and an assistant.

The Clubhouse finally opened in November 1958 with the Rev. Tom R. Robinson, a young Canadian already on the church staff, as the first Warden.[62] Tom Robinson had been student chairman of the mission committee when John Stott had visited the University of Toronto in October 1956. A year later, newly married, he and Mary accepted an invitation to spend a few months on the staff of All Souls, to experience something of English evangelicalism before settling down to ministry in Canada. He had been there barely three months before John Stott asked him to stay on as the first warden of the Clubhouse. He recalls:

> The Clubhouse was really a very daring experiment. Of the three hundred and ninety-two children and young people who came on the first day, I think only a few of them had ever been inside the church, though many of them went to All Souls School. In spite of that, many of them knew John and he knew most of them. There were approximately sixty part-time volunteers who helped in the club, in the kitchen or in the clubs. Many of those were drawn from the Wednesday Club, and many romances found a beginning there. I have three particular memories of those days that say a lot about what was going on. The first was a young man of about fifteen who stayed around after club one night. He wanted to know if this Jesus we were always talking about lived before the war or after. There

was an elderly man who lived around the corner from the Clubhouse who shuffled each Sunday night to the evening service at the club in his slippers and cloth cap, but who each Sunday morning went to All Souls in his black suit, black coat with velvet collar and black bowler. He was not unlike the two boys who sang in the choir for a time at All Souls but also came to the club. At church I was always 'Sir', at the club I was always 'Tom' without any deliberation. We worked hard at our job but were always aware that John knew better than we did the people we were working with, and what was going on at the Clubhouse.[63]

Throughout John Stott's time as Rector the Clubhouse retained a particular place in his affection, catering as it did for the poorer families and youngsters of the parish who found it difficult to see All Souls as in any real sense 'their' church. He liked to visit it, and would often be found at the Clubhouse Christmas dinner, when about fifty parishioners living on their own, who would otherwise spend Christmas Day alone, would sit down together as guests of the church.

4

Month by month, it seemed, the range and scope of the church's activities continued to expand. There was always some new development on the way. People began to speak of All Souls as 'not so much a church as a denomination!'[64] For all this there was a price to be paid. John Stott's diary and timetable were seriously overloaded, and it was becoming increasingly difficult for him to make himself as available as some would have wished, even to his own staff, let alone the congregation. Yet even this demanding lifestyle left room for the personal touch: a name remembered, an enquiry after a sick child, a gesture of support and fellowship. One young All Souls missionary, catching a train from London to Liverpool in order to sail to Pakistan, never forgot how she found the Rector at the station to say goodbye, and to present her with a Bible as a gift from the church.[65]

One or two curates, reflecting on this time, felt that though they had been part of a great team, they had not always been able to count on much personal pastoral care. They were expected to be mature enough to sort out their own problems and manage their own affairs, the more experienced lending a hand to the newly-ordained. But however hard-pressed he might be, John Stott took seriously the task of training curates in skills essential to their future ministry. Sometimes it was simply practical details of how things should be done 'decently and in order' in a church like All Souls. Tom Robinson writes,

One of my early memories of services at All Souls was being instructed both in the art of turning precise corners while in procession, and of spending time in the church with Robin Sheldon, being trained in the art of reading the lessons and taking part in the services with a proper accent. It all seemed perfectly natural to me at the time.[66]

More significant was the task of learning to preach. John Collins recalls how,

for the first two or three years, John always offered me a (voluntary, but with strong encouragement!) supervision, after the event. In fact I found this so valuable that he generously continued it, off and on, to the end of my 6 years. He was very kind, always including praise, but questioning weaknesses, down to small details. For instance, after a year, having a light voice and with no knowledge of voice production, I always ended Sunday with a sore throat. He therefore arranged for me to have half a dozen sessions with a voice trainer, for which, I suspect, he paid himself, and this certainly helped. Occasionally he became irritated and even angry with me over sermons. Once was because he thought that the material was too thin, and that the only good thing about the sermon was some material I had pinched from one of his! (Bertie Harland, a sidesman and later a missionary in South America, used to base some of his talks in surrounding parishes on John Stott's 'three pointers'. John described this as RIP preaching – Reproduced in the Provinces.) On another occasion, I had implied that anybody who was truly consecrated would end up ordained. He felt quite rightly, that this was tough on all the devout doctors, lawyers, business men etc. in the congregation. So his rebuke was richly deserved, and I learned an important lesson ...

Looking back over his ministry, John Collins came to feel that the most valuable training he received from his Rector was how to preach expositionally:

He did this mostly, but not entirely, by example. His own sermons were nearly always expositions, and arose directly out of his study of the Bible. In addition to his own private reading, he would share this study with us at least twice each week. The staff meeting was on Monday, and began with 45 minutes of Bible study. The whole staff was present, and we were expected to contribute our thoughts from the passage. These were subjected to kindly appraisal and comment from the chair, and only rejected if, after examination, the thought was considered not to be found in the text. Mr. Highland, the verger at All Souls, who was an ardent dispensationalist, found these sessions perplexing. He believed that 'rightly dividing the word of truth' meant dividing it into dispensations, and this greatly amused John; and their debates always ended in laughter.[67]

Since his days as head of school at Rugby, and again as camp secretary, John Stott had been concerned to master the art of delegation. One reason why so much was committed to paper in terms of briefings, instructions and memoranda, was to make it possible for his curates to learn and become responsible for the different aspects of All Souls' ministry, and to set such boundaries to their freedom of action as would ensure a proper continuity. When John Collins had been curate for a year, soon after his priesting, he found himself responsible for the parish in the Rector's absence:

Another aspect of training for which I was very grateful was that, as soon as possible, John would pass on responsibility. In November 1952, about a year after my arrival, he went up to Cambridge to conduct the CICCU mission. The first Sunday of the mission coincided with the monthly Guest Service, which was the most important evangelistic event of the parish. He asked me to preach, and I well remember how thrilled he was when I went up to Cambridge the next day, and was able to report that there had been a number of professions of conversion. From then on, he asked me to take these Services several times a year, usually when he was absent. In this way, my faith grew stronger, and inevitably I took a deep interest in parochial evangelism of all sorts. The same happened with the Training School. He took it for two years; he then invited me to conduct it for a number of years. I used his notes, but had to clothe and illustrate them myself. This meant, of course, that I had to study and master all the basic doctrines of the Christian faith. In my last three years, John began his travels abroad, and I was left in charge of the day by day running of the parish. This meant that I was briefed on chairing the standing committee, and generally had to make myself familiar with the administration of the parish. I would watch and take notes, but John would often talk over problems with me, or ones I wanted to raise with him. On the details of administration, it was all example. I don't remember explicit instruction except for the importance of making careful entries in one's diary. If we didn't make a note when asked to do something, he would repeatedly draw attention to it – 'You have made a note, haven't you?'

Another lesson John Stott was careful to pass on to his curates – again, as much by his own example as by precept – was never to take anyone's spiritual condition for granted:

> He would stand in the porch after each service, and would be very quick to button-hole strangers. He would then invite them to the Rectory to get to know them better, and every week he had many such interviews. He would ask them about their spiritual pilgrim-age, and then came the key question. 'Have you actually asked Christ into your life, or are you still feeling your way?' If there was uncertainty or hesitation, he would explain the steps to faith in Christ. In this way there were many conversions ... For example, one Sunday evening a family turned up and sat in the front row. There was the father, the mother, an elder sister who got them there, and two attractive teenagers – a boy and a girl. After this had occurred a number of Sundays, John said to me, 'Let's ask the two younger ones to tea, and after we have had tea together, I will talk to the boy and perhaps you would talk to the girl'.[68]

The family themselves were wealthy, with a characteristic and highly individual lifestyle. The two younger children never went to school but had tutors at home. 'Home' included a private golf course 'into which we turned the horses: they used to roll in the bunkers'. The eldest – ten years older than her sister – had become a Christian while in France, and was given the name of All Souls as a good church to join on her return to London. Her younger sister takes up the story:

> We all went to All Souls one Sunday evening. When we reached the door at the back of the church where John Stott was standing greeting people, he beamed at us, my brother and me: 'So these are your brother and sister,' he said to our sister. He asked us if we would like to have tea with him, and I noticed he had in his hand a black book and a pen. He referred to it and wrote things down as he spoke to people.
> The four of us had tea in John Stott's study – John Collins, John Stott, my brother and me. It was a happy tea, we laughed and joked and talked, we drank tea and ate cakes. Then John Stott grew serious: 'We need to talk further about spiritual things,' he said. John Collins and my brother went upstairs to John Collins'

room, and John Stott and I stayed where we were. He told me
about Jesus Christ. He told me what Jesus Christ had done for me,
he spoke of his death upon the Cross for the sins of mankind, he
told me how Jesus had risen from the dead and was sitting now on
God's right hand. He spoke of grace, of love, of the triumph of
goodness over evil by the power of Jesus Christ. He spoke of how
Jesus longed for me to worship him, to follow him all the days of
my life.

How old was I?

'Fourteen,' I replied.

'And what do you want to do?' he asked.

'Medicine.'

He opened his Bible to show me John's Gospel, chapter 3, verse
16: 'God so loved the world that he gave his only Son, that whoever
believes in him should not perish but have eternal life.' He prayed
for me; and as I listened, I found such a well of joy, of
understanding, of what I was, and why, and of questions vaguely
disturbing one's mind now beginning to be answered.

The service that evening saw a packed church full of young
people and families. John Stott, preaching from the pulpit, held
aloft a large framed picture of an overgrown wooden door outside of
which a man was standing, Jesus Christ himself, holding a lamp in
one hand, and with his other hand raised, knocking on the door. I
remember John Stott quoting the words of Jesus from Revelation,
chapter 3, verse 20: 'Behold, I stand at the door and knock; if
anyone hears my voice and opens the door, I will come in to him
and eat with him, and he with me.'

I remember too John Stott's words at the conclusion of the
service: 'If there is anyone here who feels they would like to ask
Jesus Christ into their hearts tonight, or would like to enquire
further, please stand up and come forward to the communion rails.'
I rose to my feet at once, in a single movement. In a moment, I was
up and moving forward, and by my side was my brother, who had
risen in the same second. Together we went forward and accepted
the Lord Jesus Christ into our hearts and lives.[69]

It was long afterwards when the younger sister provided the account
given above. But as a fourteen-year-old she wrote to John Stott soon after
that eventful Sunday evening:

> Wasn't it wizard that the parents came to your last 'Guest Service',
> it was a terrific fight but they came eventually!! Mr Eddison [the
> curate] said on the previous Sunday, that everybody should bring a

person with them, so I got Mummy, [my brother] got Granny, and Daddy just came! They enjoyed it very much; and Mummy now says that church-going becomes a habit!!

When are you coming over, because the parents want to talk with you, and if you come for an afternoon and evening you can do some bird-watching!!!!

Lots of love,[70]

Among the hundreds of parishioners, families, students and occasional visitors to All Souls, there were always a number who felt they enjoyed a 'special relationship' with the Rector beyond what was actually the case. His pastoral care for individuals, coupled with his astonishing memory for names and circumstances, meant that this was an easy mistake to make. Some of these, of course, were ladies in the congregation who had convinced themselves that they were called to an altogether warmer and more exclusive relationship with their highly eligible unmarried Rector than he seemed willing to recognize. Some were clearly unbalanced: others deluded by wish-fulfilment. One used to attend service after service, seated conspicuously in the very front of the church. Churchwardens and Rector shared a sense of some anxiety about her intentions, as did the curates:

She started writing to John Stott every day and he, with teutonic conscientiousness, filed all her letters in case legal action ever became necessary. She then moved her seat from the front row of the nave to the gallery, close above the pulpit. John feared (and we all agreed that it was a very serious possibility!) that one day she would jump in, and then what would he do ... ?[71]

When Robert Howarth was on the staff of All Souls in the early 60s the problem was unchanged. Howarth was Counsellor to Overseas Visitors, whose numbers had always been significant because of the church's location and international reputation, but had increased steadily with the Rector's travels. One of his tasks was to stand beside the Rector after each service as the crowd poured out into the portico. There would almost always be visitors to London, often from overseas, who would have heard him preach – perhaps many years before – in some mission or convention, or had been helped by his books, and wanted an opportunity to meet him personally:

He would engage them briefly and then pass them on to me so that I might invite them to one of our bi-monthly Visitors' Buffet

Lunches, or to some other All Souls International Fellowship activity. But this was also a device to protect him from those who would monopolise him; and from the attentions of our resident eccentrics ... Unfortunately some of these were not easily deflected: I well remember George Cansdale, as churchwarden, being set upon by a bicycle-pump-wielding woman whose intentions towards John required his intervention. [72]

Ladies of the church who came for personal interviews might well find they were greeted by the Rector in his cassock. When, for example, Frances Whitehead arrived for a talk with 'Mr. Stott' soon after her conversion (Christian names were still more than a decade away), she found him so dressed, seated formally in the vestry.[73] In this instance, as no doubt in others, it was because interviews were often fitted in between services with no time to change; but it also served as a useful reminder to some of the women of the congregation that they came to visit him as their pastor.

It might have been expected that the bachelor curates would have experienced the same difficulties; but that does not seem to be their recollection. Ted Schroder lived in the Rectory towards the end of the 1960s and looks back on what in some ways was a different world:

> Living in the Rectory was quite unique – reminiscent of the days when all curates were single under a bachelor Rector, with a housekeeper. Margaret Shinn provided for us at the meal table. She was a sweet lady whom we all adored. Her Salvation Army background kept us all in line. When she eventually retired John Stott continued to look after her, and care for her well-being until her death. In these more sexually aware times, it is amusing to contemplate the environment of trust in which we exercised our ministry. The curates worked out of their bed-sitting rooms. In our innocence we saw no problem about entertaining ladies, leading Bible studies, counselling people in distress in these intimate surroundings. After a while, I decided I needed some privacy of my own and managed to acquire another room for my bedroom.[74]

It was Ted Schroder, too, when in charge of the Wednesday Club, who made what at that time was seen as a serious error of judgment. He invited a Christian drama group, barely recognizing that this might raise issues of principle:

> When I reported on our week's activities at the staff meeting, John was anxious. He was unsure in those days about the theatre, and

wanted to be consulted before we brought in such innovative programs. I was not aware that this would be a problem and stated that I had not felt the need to ask for his permission. John said before the staff, 'I shall have to publicly rebuke you for this.' Of course, this occasioned some tension in our relationship, which was rather uncomfortable. Later that night I heard a knock on my bedroom door. John sheepishly came in and asked for my forgiveness for his behavior. This was a sign to me of his humility, that he was willing to come and ask a subordinate for forgiveness. It served as a model to me the rest of my life.[75]

In all its varied activities All Souls exemplified the manifold life of many a busy London church. At the same time John Stott was becoming increasingly in demand for a wider ministry at home and overseas, and carried with him the ever-present consciousness that he was pledged to read and write and must somehow contrive the opportunity to do so. But the single major evangelistic thrust, the controlling strategy of those years, has yet to be recounted. It was a many-sided vision, at that time unparalleled elsewhere, though later adopted eagerly by many churches.

5

Adrian Hastings' verdict on the Church of England in the 1950s is that 'it was not a disturbing phenomenon'.[76] The climate of the times favoured a steady post-war growth; confirmation, communion and ordination figures were rising; and even though baptisms were beginning to decline,[77] there was a certain complacency abroad. But it was perfectly clear to the new Rector that the people of his parish, let alone the many visitors and the transient population of students who looked to All Souls, would never be evangelized by the efforts of the clergy alone: 'a staff of ten curates could not do it.'[78] It was a task for the whole church; and if the church was to tackle it, then the church must be equipped and trained. So much was, in theory at least, common ground. Evangelism by the laity was clearly biblical, and the only realistic policy commensurate with the need. As often happened when he wished to commend biblical principles to the church at large, John Stott was able to do so in the words of William Temple:

> Lay evangelism is already a generally accepted idea in this country. Archbishop William Temple expressed his conviction in the words: 'There can be no widespread evangelism of this country unless this

work is undertaken by the laity.' The report *Towards the Conversion of England*, which stirred thousands of readers, popularized the idea and was widely discussed. But the idea has remained largely a theory. Much has been said. Little has been done.[79]

From the moment he became Rector-designate John Stott had been determined that All Souls should take up this challenge. He bent his mind to find ways in which this vision of lay evangelism might become a reality: and so devised a detailed initiative combining evangelism, nurture and training. The spearhead would be the 'Guest Service', a careful presentation of the gospel, intended for newcomers, with an invitation to respond. These came to be held once a month in the evening and once a quarter in the morning. But their success depended on the readiness of Christians to catch the vision, and to pray for, and then bring to the Guest Service their unconverted friends. More than this, 'Counsellors' would be needed to get alongside those who were ready to make a commitment to Christ, so as to guide them towards a step of faith. To achieve this, these Counsellors would have to be selected and trained: and this was clearly the place to begin.

The other parts of this evangelistic initiative, the 'At Homes' and the 'Nursery Classes' were to do with following-up and nurturing those who made a Christian profession. All this was to grow, as God blessed and used such a pattern of ministry, into a detailed system of evangelistic strategy: but for the moment there was no time to be lost in making a start. Exactly a week before his institution the Rector-designate outlined to the thirty members of the PCC his plan for a Training School, leading to a team of trained and commissioned workers such as would be needed once the Guest Service pattern began in earnest. It was therefore proposed to start next month

> … a Training School giving a six months' course in the Theory and Practice of Evangelism. Twelve lectures would be given on alternate Mondays at 6.15p.m. in Church, ending with a Commissioning Service in Church on Palm Sunday by the Bishop of Willesden for those who had completed the course. The syllabus would consist of the Theology of the Gospel, the Personal Life of the Evangelist, and the Practical Technique of Evangelism. The intervening Monday evenings would be spent in practical work in the parish, and the Training School would be for people of any age. It was probable that the course would be repeated every autumn and winter, with a Bible School in the summer.
>
> This proposal was received with enthusiasm by members of the Council who promised their support.[80]

Although the policy was one of continual and evolving improvement, once the Training School had settled into its annual pattern it continued to run like clockwork. A duplicated summary of the lectures (which later became a printed booklet) meant that successive curates could be trained to take charge of the lecture-course, with the content remaining consistent from year to year. Later still, the lectures were offered on tape or cassette, which helped to carry the 'All Souls Training School' to many other churches, including a number overseas, who wanted to follow the same pattern. John Stott prepared a slide-presentation 'Mobilizing the Church for Evangelism' which was used to help his fellow-ministers understand the vision, and begin to see how they might put it into practice locally.

Today such a 'Training School' is part of the life of many churches – but in 1950 it was radically new. In June 1952, when the School was still in its infancy, John Stott agreed to speak at the London Diocesan Conference on the subject of 'Parochial Evangelism by the Laity'. At the request of the standing committee he later expanded his address into an eight-page leaflet which went rapidly through a number of editions.[81]

In 1955 Chad Varah, later to achieve fame as the founder of the 'Samaritans', paid a visit to an All Souls' Guest Service in order to write about it for the new magazine *Church Illustrated*, in a series 'Powerhouses of Faith'. He described 'genial, burly George Cansdale, of zoo and TV fame', welcoming the congregation to a church already pretty full. After shortened Evening Prayer the congregation settled down for the sermon with 'a marked feeling of expectancy':

> From my place in the gallery I could see almost as many faces as the Rector in the pulpit: the faithful, devoutly 'willing' power to the preacher or comfortably sure he has it; and the guests, hopeful or apprehensive, hungry or sceptical, according to temperament ...
>
> The defensiveness faded from many guests' faces during his simple and masterly exposition of the parable, and then he was able to get good-humouredly under their guard. 'Christianity like a banquet? I can see from your faces that you think of it as more like a funeral!' Then the skilful probing for each one's trouble – anxiety, fear, loneliness, guilt, dissatisfaction, doubt, lack of purpose – and the flicker of a response here and there as the diagnosis fitted. 'Come, for all things are now ready.' 'Christ has done all – the banquet is spread – He Himself is the banquet – you are invited.' And always the persistent re-iteration of 'Come ...'.
>
> Mr Stott has a quietly persuasive style, with no mannerisms, tricks, or fireworks – earnest, urgent, without unction or senti-

mentality ... why should *this* parish find 'the Lord adding to the Church daily such as were being saved'?

I hoped to find the answer at the 'Continuation service,' when those who stayed behind for a rather elastic ten minutes (enough of them to fill the nave) were promised instruction in *how* to come to Christ. The Rector, now in cassock and bands, repeated his main theme even more simply, inserted an appeal to any who found it too unsophisticated, and invited his hearers to make their decision. He led them in a prayer similar to the one he had used in making his own decision 'sixteen and three-quarter years ago,' and then told those who were willing to give themselves to Christ that they must 'come forward and tell me so.'

For a long minute no one moved, not even the three I had tagged in my own mind whilst studying the congregation during the main sermon. I began to worry as the Rector stood waiting, not looking round anxiously, but with the detached patience you see in an experienced Confessor who knows what's coming. I knew the appeal to the sophisticated would have missed its mark even if any such had stayed behind, for there are genuine doubts which hadn't been dealt with and the whole effort had been (rightly) directed at a different and far more numerous type, but surely ... Perhaps if one starts, others will follow ...

The first three were the ones I had noted – an elderly man, a young man, a girl. They were followed by eleven others. Ten of the fourteen, I later learnt, were new converts, and this was well below the average 'score' (in both senses). The Rector spoke briefly to each, handed over a booklet, and introduced the convert to a 'counsellor' from the waiting row of lay evangelists.

I discovered the following evening, when the Rector spared me an hour at his pleasant Clergy House near Regent's Park, where these counsellors came from and what happened to the newly converted. Forgetting to munch the sandwiches which were all the dinner he had time for, Mr Stott showed me the scrap book he takes with him when asked to speak at conferences about his method of evangelism. Nothing is left to chance. Here are copies of all the carefully-prepared leaflets, booklets, study courses, examination papers, letters of welcome, 'fishing' cards, report cards, record cards, and other printed matter which steer the lay evangelist and his charges along a tried and tested course.[82]

The carefully-kept statistics of the Training School and Commissioned Workers show that about half of those trained and commissioned were still engaged in this form of lay ministry seven years later.[83] By that time one in five had left London: and in some cases at least had carried the vision of a trained and witnessing laity to their new church.

The principle of the 'Guest Service' as a method of parochial evangelism had also travelled. 'Evangelistic Services' had of course been used in many places over many years; what All Souls demonstrated was a way of combining regular parochial evangelism with Anglican Evening (sometimes Morning) Prayer. Lance Shilton, at that time Rector of Holy Trinity, Adelaide, was quick to see the importance of this principle, and to carry it back with him to Australia. He had been at All Souls for a Guest Service on a visit to London in 1956: and though he had often attended evangelistic meetings in Australia which gave an opportunity to respond to the gospel, he sensed that this integration of evangelism into parish life was something new:

> Since my great passion was evangelism, within three months Guest Services were introduced at Holy Trinity and held regularly through the whole sixteen years that I was Rector.[84]

Over these sixteen years, Lance Shilton calculated, more than 1,000 people remained behind after the Service to enquire further:

> Actually, everyone in the congregation at the Guest Services made a decision. Some decided they were already Christians. Some decided to become Christians and some decided to do nothing about it at that time. Others decided to rededicate their lives to Christ at the service. All decided whether or not they would remain for the Continuation Service. The address emphasised the need for decision about Christ.[85]

When in 1973 Lance Shilton moved to Sydney to become Dean of St. Andrew's Cathedral, he continued to use Guest Services as a regular part of the Cathedral's outreach to the city.

Although John Stott was a leader in this field, he was not alone. Six months after his address to the London Diocesan Conference he was speaking at the Islington Clerical Conference organized and chaired by the Vicar of Islington, Maurice A. P. Wood,[86] on the same theme: 'The Training of the Laity in Evangelism'. *The Times* gave a nine-inch column to their report of the Conference:

> Mr. Stott said that until every Christian became as enthusiastic for his church work as every Communist was for his party's propaganda they would not see this country evangelised. He said that the scheme which he visualised had the advantages of being biblical,

natural and healthy, and practical. The bare bones of a plan for nation-wide evangelism already existed. The man-power was there – 'slumbering drowsily in the pews.'[87]

Maurice Wood, meanwhile, was himself engaged in a scheme of lay training in his own (very different) parish of St Mary's.[88]

There were those who, listening to the persuasive exposition of these methods by the privileged Rector of a West-end church, felt moved to enter a protest. One North London Rector wrote,

> I've read a report of your speech to the Islington Conference and I write to suggest that you resign your comfortable living at All Souls and that you ask the Bishop to appoint you to some tough parish in the diocese where you can attempt to practise what you have preached ...[89]

It was an understandable reaction, particularly in the case of those who worked long and faithfully in unrewarding surroundings for little visible result. 'All Souls is a special case,' they would say. 'Our numbers are too few, our people lacking in education and in confidence, our church building cold and unattractive, our parishioners uninterested.' And looking at the great wastes of East and South London and the struggling church life of so many run-down parishes there is little doubt that, in their own terms, they were right. John Stott's methods, wonderfully suited to his own situation and to many like it, could not easily be transplanted as a panacea into the different conditions of many a run-down church. Even in Islington, for many generations an evangelical stronghold, and even under the inspiring leadership of a Maurice Wood, the fruits were markedly more limited than at All Souls – as indeed might be expected. It is difficult not to feel some sympathy with faithful (and sometimes desperate) clergy with tiny congregations in huge back-street churches, who resented the apparent implication that this scriptural strategy was equally applicable to every situation. Perhaps in John Stott's own mind it was. David Sheppard, as an ordinand at Ridley Hall, remembers a particular occasion:

> I recall John Stott coming to a meeting: I forget if it was for ordinands, but it was of that character. He had been talking about his parish strategy and about the strong lay leadership which was developing. One very unfriendly questioner asked, 'What would you do if you had no Sunday School teachers in your parish?' John's reply was, 'I would close the Sunday School and pray and work for the teachers.'[90]

The irony of all this, unappreciated by his critics, lies in the probability that had he himself been in their position, John Stott's gifts and energies might well have begun to make progress in lay training possible. It was not only All Souls that was different, but its Rector – and this, for obvious reasons, he was unwilling to recognize. Nevertheless, the Guest Service was more than a 'technique' which could only be made to work in the exceptional circumstances of All Souls.

Records kept at the time show an average of a little over a dozen people responding to the preacher's invitation at every Guest Service. It was crucial that they should be speedily followed up, and their feet set firmly on the road of Christian discipleship. John Stott devised two strings to this bow:

> Those who profess faith in Christ at a guest service are invited to an 'At Home' about a week later, at which a talk is given on Christian life and growth. They are also told about our so-called 'nursery classes'. This strange and rather daunting expression describes special classes for new Christians. Being new-born babes in Christ, their place is after all in the spiritual nursery! Nursery class leaders are mostly lay people (commissioned workers again), to whom is entrusted the privileged task of nurturing the lambs of Christ's flock. In these classes the new Christians learn how to read the Bible and pray, and are gradually drawn into the fellowship of the congregation.[91]

Even before the 'At Home' the Counsellor who had talked with the enquirer at the end of the Continuation Service would have been at work. There was a private handbook, *The Follow-Up of Converts*, giving precise instruction of the 'four main stages in counselling, A, B, C & D'. These initials stood for Assurance, Bible Reading and Prayer, Church membership and 'Details' – name and address and so on. It was the Counsellor's task to see that these 'details' reached the Rectory the same evening so that the Rector could write to each one personally on the Monday with an invitation to an 'At Home' a week later. There they would meet the Rector and some of the staff: and since the guests included all those who had made a profession of faith in the previous month, not only at the Guest Services but through mid-week services, personal counselling and the like, the big first-floor drawing-room at the Rectory was often filled with thirty or forty people. John Stott would end the evening with one of three or four talks: 'Know, show, grow' was a favourite;[92] it was used so often that his colleagues used to tease him about it. Other workers called 'Nursery Class leaders' were also invited to these At Homes so that they could meet those who would be joining their class. It would not have been difficult to devise a less embarrassing name for these groups: but the use of 'Nursery Class' underlined the position of new converts as beginners in the school of Christ, and offered a tiny challenge to their natural pride. (Later, however, they were renamed 'Beginners Groups'.) An important element of the class was the introduction to Bible reading and prayer, both as a group and in a personal Quiet Time. Baptism, Church membership, perhaps links with a Christian Union, were all dealt with, together with a first introduction to the idea of Christian witness and service, and to the use of Christian books as a means of grace and growth in Christ.

Such a thorough and systematized pattern of evangelism and nurture was ideally suited to the large opportunities confronting such a church as All Souls. But system and attention to detail were always subservient to the personal needs of the individuals that were being offered nurture and pastoral care. There is plenty of evidence that those who did not somehow fit the system were still cared for. Geoffrey Turner, later to be ordained, described his own experience:

> The dawn of my faith in Christ happened when Gill (now my wife) took me to a Guest Service at All Souls. Although I made no response on the evening, that did follow a fortnight later just before my departure to the Trucial States where I served with the Scouts for two years. Gill told John of my conversion and my strange situation (among a small number of British Officers commanding an Arab Regiment) and he kindly wrote a series of letters encouraging me to read the Scriptures and pray ... a tremendous encouragement ... to someone new-born and far from any natal clinic.[93]

But for most of those who came to faith in Christ through the Guest Services, and the other evangelistic ministries of All Souls, the Nursery Classes were the foundation of their Christian nurture. A steady stream of testimony showed that through this painstaking and careful strategy, God's Holy Spirit was at work. Some told their story in the church magazine. 'A Hospital Matron' described her 'forty-eight years of search for the truth'. In her early days she sought for meaning in religion, both through the Church of England and as a convert to Roman Catholicism, but with the reality of personal faith eluding her: 'There followed 33 years in which I was firmly agnostic.' Then at a local clinic treating her arthritis she became friendly with her physiotherapist:

> One day I was rather ill and she was very kind to me, and she said something about the Lord – I do not remember what. I replied,

'Oh, I have no faith.' I started something then! But here was a sincerity and faith I had never met before. She persuaded me to come to an evening Guest Service. I knew what it meant, but I was not going to do anything like that! But I had never been in a church like this before. There was warmth and friendliness instead of stiffness. As the service went on and the sermon came, I felt as if I was being torn in two. I stayed on afterwards and had an almost overwhelming desire to go up to the front, but feared it might be only emotionalism.

I was furious with myself for getting so 'rattled'. A sleepless night and next day I felt I *must* reason the thing out. I could not give it all up – it had made too deep an impression. Feeling very brain-weary, I did what I had often done as a matron, when faced with a difficult situation. I got out a 'thriller' and read it through. When I had finished I was feeling quite happy and matter-of-fact again, and I was going to get up to do something, but I could not. Quite suddenly I had a deep sensation of peace, something I cannot adequately describe, but I was completely wrapped round in it and lost to everything. It gradually came to me that the long, weary journey was over at last, that I was home, with a peace which passeth understanding and a living faith in Christ such as I had never known before.[94]

Again, a young businessman described how, having refused two or three invitations to the annual Doctors' Service, he went to All Souls in the week following his father's death: 'I had enjoyed a lifetime of love and intimacy with him ... now I felt absolutely lost.' He went again in the evening to the Guest Service:

I felt a compulsion to stay on to the continuation service and, when it was over, I knew that this was my chance. It was now or never, and I went forward to meet the preacher – and by God's grace to start life again. I hoped that He would do something better with my life than I had in the past. He has. I know that the past is forgiven, and now I try to forget it and strain forward to what lies ahead.[95]

Others have written to John Stott personally, often on an anniversary, sometimes after many years, to say that a Guest Service was for them a turning point.

In February 1968 John Stott gave the Pastoral Theology lectures in Durham University. He offered some account of the lay training and commissioned workers' programme at All Souls, with a brief evaluation in the light of seventeen years' experience. He noted two weaknesses: the first in the realm of inadequate supervision:

> I myself have only recently learned that the true art of delegation is not to hand over work to somebody else and then forget about it, but to commit work to a deputy who knows that he is responsible to you and can at times report back and seek advice.[96]

The second weakness was one later picked up by some within the congregation who felt that the Commissioned Workers policy was being used as a means to control too closely those who were, and were not, active at the centre of the church's witness. John Stott showed himself aware of this danger:

> It actually inhibits the free enterprise of those not commissioned, because they may feel they have no liberty to work for Christ if they are not commissioned. In this situation we need to insist strongly that Christian people are perfectly free to fulfil their duties to witness and engage in other forms of Christian activity without waiting to be organised into it by the local church or needing official permission to begin it! The purposes of training and commissioning are to encourage, improve and co-ordinate the service of the laity in the local church and parish, not to frustrate it or quench the Spirit.[97]

But these two potential weaknesses were contrasted with three particular advantages. First, the principle of teamwork; second, the opportunity, rightly used, of a proper share by the church leaders over who should do what, in the church's name. The third value he notes is that of affirming the role of Commissioned Workers both in their own eyes, and among those they seek to serve. 'It gives me confidence,' one has written 'to know that I go as a representative, and with the support, of the Church.'[98]

Nor were practical gifts forgotten. The 'Guild of Help', started in 1954, not only met some of the most practical needs of a busy church, but also demonstrated that there was no intellectual élitism limiting the use of much-needed gifts. There were from the outset thirteen distinct groups within the Guild, each under its own leader, responsible for housekeeping (such as catering and cleaning), for the crèche, for hospitality, for 'fishing' in Oxford Street (that is, inviting passers-by to join the church service about to take place), clerical assistance and so on. All Souls was a church that encouraged all its members to be partners rather than passengers.

What seems most remarkable in retrospect about this fourfold pattern of Training School and commissioned workers, guest services, At Homes and Nursery Classes is the way in which the entire interlocking pattern was devised and put in place as a single whole, without the need for pilot schemes or trial runs. Add to that the steady growth experienced under the Spirit of God, as curates and helpers came and left; and the fact that twenty years later the same pattern was still in place, still effective, still bearing fruit. Moreover, it formed a pattern which was readily adopted both in England and in other parts of the Anglican Communion. The Diocesan Missioner of Sydney, Australia, was able to tell John Stott after his visit there in 1958 that some 250 parishes were using his filmstrip with recorded commentary, 'Mobilizing the Church for Evangelism', which explained the principles in considerable detail.[99] Looking back, John Stott's original claim seems to have been amply justified. Speaking in 1952 as a very junior incumbent, he had told his fellow-clergy of the London diocese that, in the field of lay evangelism, 'much has been said. Little has been done. It is my purpose to outline a scheme whereby the average parish can convert theory into practice.'[100] Critics might protest that All Souls was hardly 'an average parish'; but plenty of other parishes, some unquestionably 'average', have been ready to learn from this example.

ELEVEN

A Wider Vision:
Evangelical Initiatives

1

In 1951, John Stott's first full year as Rector of his new parish, the country was still struggling with the after-effects of war. On London's South Bank the 'Skylon', symbol of the Festival of Britain, floated floodlit in the night sky, a gesture of faith in a brighter future. But it was a very different world from that of the Great Exhibition of 1851, just a century before, which proclaimed the everlasting security and increasing prosperity of Empire. Petrol rationing was over, but the meat ration was lower than in the days of the war – thirteen ration books were needed to buy a leg of lamb. The Korean war rumbled on, with British troops among the multi-national presence of the United Nations. More sinister still, the US war department claimed that the first test of a hydrogen bomb on an atoll in the mid-Pacific, 'exceeded expectations', and proved to be hundreds of times more powerful than the bombs dropped on Hiroshima and Nagasaki six years before. The following year brought the death of King George VI and the start of a new Elizabethan age. Stalin died; Winston Churchill was slowly fading from the political scene. The mid 1950s saw the Suez crisis, the crushing of the Hungarian rising, the Warsaw pact, the Treaty of Rome. By the end of the decade the first

Russian rocket had reached the moon, while the terrestrial traveller began to discover the hovercraft, the Mini, parking meters and the first motorway, with CND marchers on the road from Aldermaston. After years of post-war austerity, incomes began to rise dramatically:

> ... those who before had been obliged to be thrifty now found within their means consumer goods and domestic appliances they had never dreamed of possessing. Between 1956 and 1960 the country's hire purchase debt rose faster than at any other time before or since. The possession of cars, washing machines, refrigerators, and television sets became the rule rather than the exception in working-class homes and large sums of money were spent on alcohol, tobacco, entertainment, and holidays. Young people used their new-found wealth to purchase long-playing records and transistor radios ... Materialism, never far below the surface, came to be regarded as an appropriate way of life.[1]

Clearly, for a minister of the gospel on the threshold of the 1950s, challenging years lay ahead.

Already, even in his curacy, invitations had begun to come to John Stott to join the committee of this society or that; and among the few he had accepted was the Council of the World's Evangelical Alliance,[2] established in the 1840s as a forum for thought and action among evangelicals across denominational boundaries. It was one of the pioneers of later ecumenism, the more successful because of a shared commitment by its members to the authority of the Bible and the spread of the gospel. Now that international travel was again possible, the World's Evangelical Alliance (WEA), with its counterparts in other countries, determined to hold 'an International Convention of Evangelicals (of lands round the world)' to meet at Woudschoten, a few miles east of Utrecht in the Netherlands. Ninety-one delegates gathered from twenty-one countries, meeting in a student retreat centre for six days in August 1951. John Stott addressed them on the first day, a Sunday, with an exposition of 1 Corinthians 12 on 'The Holy Spirit and the Church'. During the week the World Evangelical Fellowship was constituted with three aims taken from Philippians 1, the furtherance of the gospel, the defence and confirmation of the gospel, and fellowship in the gospel. According to Jack Dain, one of the British representatives, he and John Stott were sitting together on a sofa in between the sessions. John Stott took from his pocket a Bible, and Jack Dain pencil and paper: 'John Stott dictated them; I wrote them down.' They were unanimously accepted by the Conference.[3] It was his first taste of work for and within the structures of worldwide evangelicalism, which would later bear fruit in, for example, his vision for the Evangelical Fellowship in the Anglican Communion, and his work for the Lausanne Congress on World Evangelization.

It was primarily in evangelism, something of a Cinderella in Church of England thinking, that John Stott sought to engage such energies as he could spare from the immediate pastoral work of All Souls. Even while he was establishing the pattern of Commissioned Workers, Guest Services and Nursery Classes for his own people, he was looking beyond his parish boundaries to a wider field. This began, so to say, apparently by accident. In March 1950 Maurice Wood as Vicar and Rural Dean of Islington was leading a mission at St. Peter's, Harold Wood in suburban Essex, not far from Romford. His wife Margery, already unwell, became seriously ill in the course of the week's mission. Maurice Wood asked John Stott as an old friend to come to his rescue and take the final weekend. John Stott dropped everything and did so: in the history of St. Peter's, Harold Wood, it proved to be a turning point. There was already a biblical ministry but with this mission the gospel began to take root among church members in a very significant way – 'it began to be an evangelical church'.[4] Key members of the congregation were converted to Christ: and the mission, coupled with the Billy Graham crusade at Harringay a few years later, provided the backbone of the church membership through the growth of the next decades.[5]

Following this experience, John Stott arranged that in November of the following year All Souls should undertake what was described as 'a congregational mission by one parish to another in the same (London) diocese'.[6] He was himself the missioner, assisted by members of his staff and by twenty assistant missioners chosen from among the earliest Commissioned Workers. Paired off with members of St. Martin's Gospel Oak (the receiving church) they engaged in systematic visiting in preparation for the week of mission. In the event, something like 100 people attended every night, rising to about 300 on the final evening. This was less than had been hoped for; but they were able to report moving occasions towards the close of the mission when first the wife of a churchwarden, and then the organist of the church, bravely told the congregation how they had found Christ as Saviour during the last few days. John Stott and his helpers returned to All Souls with 'a strong impression in our minds that our association with St. Martin's cannot be abruptly severed. God is beckoning us on to something more.' Perhaps it might be possible for some of the All Souls church members to become more permanently attached to St. Martin's? – 'a kind of spiritual blood transfusion'.[7] It was the same vision of the call to 'Christian relocation' that John Stott was to urge many times in the future as the means to tackle the missionary needs of inner-city parishes. In the case of Gospel

Oak, it was simply a 're-location' of church membership; but as his thinking developed, that was to become the call for 'authentic incarnational mission' which formed the continuing theme of many addresses and articles, and was to find a place in more than one of his books.[8]

There was little to suggest, in spite of the dedicated attempts of some of the All Souls team, that the link between the parishes could be effectively maintained once the impetus of the mission began to fade. Nevertheless, they saw real conversions; and it served to challenge any inward-looking attitude on the part of All Souls, equipped as it was far above the average with mature Christian leadership.[9] Though this was not an experiment much repeated, it was not entirely an isolated example as John Stott searched for the right medium through which to extend his burden for evangelism beyond the parish boundaries. The following year he was co-leader of a mission in Highgate School,[10] and All Souls members were part of a Youth Mission at St. Paul's Canonbury. A further major aspect of John Stott's ministry of evangelism began with the invitation to lead the CICCU Mission in 1952. This and other university missions of the 1950s and 1960s became a highly significant part of his extended ministry as later chapters will show.

Meanwhile, the Council of the WEA at their offices in Bloomsbury had begun to consider a new and more dramatic enterprise. Following his Los Angeles Campaign (the word 'Crusade' was not used until Columbia a year later) the name 'Billy Graham' was already a household word in America. From the summer of 1945 Dr. Graham had been travelling on behalf of 'Youth for Christ International' which he had helped to found. This was the period in which he 'visited forty-seven states, logging at least 135,000 miles and receiving United Airlines' designation as its top civilian passenger'.[11] He visited England twice in 1946, first in the Spring and again that Autumn, initially under the auspices of Tom Rees, and then for a six-month tour which included no fewer than 360 meetings:

> The winter was bitterly cold, the worst in decades ... To save money, the group frequently boarded in homes rather than in hotels, and Graham and George Wilson often slept in the same bed fully dressed and wearing shawls over their heads to keep warm. On occasion they spoke in stone churches so cold and dank that fog obscured part of the congregation from their view.[12]

John Stott had first met Billy Graham when, at the invitation of Prebendary Colin Kerr, they shared an open-air meeting at Speakers' Corner in Hyde Park. Apart from the character of the man himself, his 'machine-gun delivery' left a strong impression: 'the English people wanted to take breaths for him ... he bashed the Bible into them.'[13]

These visits had left their mark, and suggestions and reports kept coming to the WEA that this young American evangelist might be God's man for the hour. In March 1952 Billy Graham let it be known that he would be paying a private visit to London, and would be willing to address a meeting of ministers and other Christian leaders on the theme of evangelism. The meeting took place for some 750 Christian leaders in Church House, London, on 20 March; it was immediately followed by a private conference in one of the committee rooms, to consider how best to extend an invitation to Billy Graham and his team to conduct a major crusade in England. An approach to the Archbishop of Canterbury, Geoffrey Fisher (since Billy Graham had made it clear that he would want such a visit to be sponsored by the churches themselves) resulted only in a reference to the British Council of Churches, who put forward a plan for a 'pilot' crusade on a more local scale in some provincial city. Billy Graham was unable to accept this, and on 24 July a cable was finally sent to America by Roy Cattell, WEA General Secretary:

> Tentative invitation to visit London given you in March now unanimously confirmed by World's Evangelical Alliance Council, who will immediately form special executive committee.[14]

The crusade was to be based in London, and after some difficulty in finding an auditorium, the committee booked Harringay Arena in North London – thus adding the word 'Harringay' to the vocabulary of a Christian generation. Members and ministers of many churches still testify, forty years on, that 'Harringay' was the place where God spoke to them. The Arena, seating almost 12,000, belonged to the Greyhound Racing Association. When the contract was signed, the managing director was confidently expecting that it would be broken within a fortnight, since no speaker had ever filled it for more than a single night.[15] In the event, the crusade ran for the whole of March and April, and for most of May. On Saturday, 22 May, 120,000 people filled Wembley Stadium for the final meeting. Harringay demonstrated that Billy Graham had a message that this country was more than willing to receive from him; and even before the crusade was over, plans were being prepared for a return.

2

All Souls as a church was deeply involved in Harringay. John Stott himself was there 'most nights'.[16] In an interview with Dr. Robert Ferm almost twenty years afterwards he recalled something of those times:

Nine years after the war (which it was in 1954) we had got into what you might call the post-war stage of disillusionment. For five years or so after the war, people were still talking in positive terms of reconstruction and were expecting to be able to construct a new and a better society. But disillusionment set in after 1950 and I think was fairly strong by 1954 ... There was a spiritual vacuum in the hearts and minds of people who were looking for something in that period of disillusionment.

Asked further about how far All Souls was involved, he continued:

We had buses every night from All Souls, and took many, many hundreds ... And we had a very large number of referrals. During the three months of the crusade, I think we had 500 names altogether. If I remember rightly, 200 of them had given the name of All Souls and 300 were assigned to us. Many of the latter we were unable to get in touch with because they had given hotel addresses and were evidently 'birds of passage'. But quite a few were definitely drawn into the fellowship of the church.

Perhaps I could add one thing while it comes to my mind, trying to assess the effect of the crusade in our own church. We had already held every year what we called an Annual Training School to train church members for active evangelism in the church. We started this in 1950, and have had them ever since for twenty years. An average of forty or forty-five successfully completed the course and were commissioned each year. But the year after Harringay, ninety people were trained and commissioned. The number almost exactly doubled. Then our annual enrolment dropped again to about forty-five or fifty. This is a very interesting objective bit of evidence. For me, one of the great effects of the crusade was not just in winning people to Christ, but in giving Christians ... church members ... a taste through counselling of the joys of witness and service.[17]

Throughout the twelve weeks of the crusade, John Stott himself was a regular attender, often accompanied by friends for whom this might be a unique opportunity to hear the gospel. People were not only willing but delighted to hear for themselves the American preacher whose name was in every newspaper.

John Stott, as a member of the Council of the Evangelical Alliance, had helped to set up the Executive Committee which took responsibility for the crusade. About half were drawn from the EA Council and half were co-opted for their specialized knowledge or experience. John Stott himself did not serve on the crusade Executive Committee, but undertook to arrange for Billy Graham and his team to stay at the Stratford Court Hotel near Oxford Circus, which made them temporary parishioners of All Souls. In his autobiography Billy Graham describes it as 'probably the smallest and cheapest hotel in London'[18] – chosen to avoid any appearance of extravagance. The description reveals how little he knew of London at that time beyond the West End; but by the standards of most visiting Americans it was small and modest, with the great advantage of being central.

John Stott quickly became friend and informal pastor to the team. On Good Friday, about a month into the crusade, he presided at a service of Holy Communion for the team in St. Peter's, Vere Street (which he later noted as 'perhaps their first exposure to Anglicanism!'). A warm friendship was growing fast between John Stott and Billy Graham. They were much of an age (Graham the older by some three years) and in their commitment to evangelism, to the evangelical gospel and the faith of the Scriptures, found common ground. John Stott, writing when Harringay was over, was concerned to defend Dr. Graham's ministry:

One of the commonest criticisms levelled against Billy Graham is that his converts don't last. It is a largely unfair criticism, for two reasons. First, no evangelist the world has ever known has kept all his converts. Some seed always fails to take root, or its growth is choked. It is even written of our Lord himself that 'many of his disciples drew back and no longer went about with him'. More-over, I ask myself about my own confirmation candidates of former years. How many have stood the test of time? I wonder if the proportion of those who have remained loyal and active churchmen is any higher than that of enquirers at Billy Graham crusades.

Secondly, without any doubt, many *do* last. I know this from my own experience. We have had in our congregation, and still have, a number of people who owe their Christian faith and life, under God, to Billy Graham. Let me tell you about two of them.

The first was a girl of seventeen when Billy Graham came to London in 1954. She had just left school, was doing the debutante season and studying at the same time for University entrance. She is now married to an MP and has three children. She is still an active Christian. Two things struck her about the crusade. The first was Billy Graham's forthright message. 'Billy Graham didn't digress,' she told me. 'He preached Christ crucified and him only.' Secondly, she was immensely impressed by the love which the Billy Graham team members had for each other and for everyone else.

Another Harringay convert was a student in London at the time. Since then he has been a missionary in Kenya, working among Mau Mau detainees. He is now a member of our full-time staff at All Souls. I asked him what helped him most in the crusade. This was his answer: 'that it was for me personally to appropriate what Jesus Christ had done for all men. So far as I know, I had never heard this, although I was a baptised and confirmed Anglican.'[19]

Billy Graham, for his part, wrote to John Stott (interestingly, and perhaps as a sign of the respect in which he was held by the team, to 'Dear Mr. Stott' – though this was less unusual in the 1950s) within twenty-four hours of the closing meetings of the crusade:

I want to take this opportunity to thank you in person for lending your name in support to this crusade. Many of us had fears, doubts and reservations prior to March 1st, so much so that some declined lending their names. You were ready to launch out by faith and stand with us! We are deeply grateful. This has been the Lord's doing, and it is marvelous in our eyes. As we have sung night after night at Harringay, 'To God be the glory, Great things He hath done.' We thank God upon every remembrance of you.

I am going to take a few days of rest before going to Cliff College on June 7th, and then spending three days in Glasgow, which will be followed by our Continental tour; and then home by July 6th. We would appreciate your prayers for our next two campaigns that begin August 22nd in Nashville, Tennessee; and October 3rd in New Orleans, Louisiana.

We must continue to pray that the churches will feel the impact of what the Lord has done these past three months.

Gratefully yours,
Billy[20]

It had been a remarkable time. Billy Graham had preached to 'the greatest religious congregation, 120,000, ever seen until then in the British Isles';[21] he had spoken at both Oxford and Cambridge to crowded congregations of students and dons; Winston Churchill had invited him to Downing Street and talked with him for forty minutes. On his return a year later he paid a private visit to the Queen Mother at Clarence House, and preached the following Sunday before the Queen and members of her family at Windsor. It could be said of him in Britain at that time, as it was said of his Master, that 'the common people heard him gladly'. Why should it be, John Stott was asking himself, that our churches are half-empty and yet night after night thousands come to hear Billy Graham, 'and the answer I gave myself was this: "I believe Billy was the first transparently sincere preacher these people have ever heard".'[22] At a final meeting for pastors after the London crusades John Stott was asked to speak, and gave three or four reasons why he believed God was using Billy Graham. They bore some similarity to Torrey's seven reasons why God used D. L. Moody;[23] and John Stott developed them further at some length in his Foreword to a biography of John Sung, 'the greatest evangelist China has ever known', published about that time.[24] He identified four key characteristics: that John Sung was a dedicated man; that he knew the place of power; that he was real; and that he worked through the churches. And John Stott commented, 'It is particularly interesting to notice four outstanding features of Dr. John Sung's character and ministry which are also to be found in those of Dr. Billy Graham.'[25] Even Archbishop Fisher, notably cool and non-committal at the outset, appeared with Billy Graham on the platform at the final meeting of the Harringay crusade, held at the Empire Stadium, Wembley. Visibly moved, after offering a closing prayer, at the sight of so many moving across the turf in response to the appeal, he turned to Grady Wilson sitting next to him on the platform, saying 'We'll never see such a sight again until we get to heaven'. Wilson put his arm round Fisher's shoulder in the emotion of the moment and replied 'That's right, Brother Archbishop, that's right!'[26]

Following such events, it was not surprising that in many circles, secular as well as religious, talk of spiritual revival was in the air. Indeed, so great appeared to be Britain's readiness to hear the gospel that had it not been for commitments already made, Billy Graham might have returned in the late summer of 1954 for as long as he was needed. It was discussed by him as a serious possibility to be given careful thought and prayer. John Pollock wrote later in the authorized biography:

> By the time of these discussions Billy Graham was tired beyond measure. He believes this affected his judgment. Looking back, with the hindsight of more than a decade, Billy Graham is certain he should have stayed.[27]

But in the event, it was agreed that he should wait a year, and return then for a further week's crusade in London, using Wembley Stadium. This would immediately follow the 1955 Glasgow crusade which was already planned and promised.

The conclusion of Harringay and the prospect of this crusade on a larger scale though for a shorter period, at Wembley Stadium in the summer of 1955 had been exercising the mind of the Evangelical Alliance

Committee. The size of the statistics at the close of the Harringay crusade presented both a challenge and an opportunity:

> When relay services and meetings held by associate evangelists were added to those at which Graham preached, the total attendance for the twelve-week crusade topped two million. Of that number, 36,431 filled out decision cards and received counselling. According to BGEA figures, 90 per cent of those reported some kind of church connection, but 75 per cent regarded themselves as making a first-time decision, suggesting the connection was quite nominal. Approximately half of all inquirers described themselves as essentially 'unchurched'.[28]

Not all 'inquirers' were converts: some never reached a point of decision, some came forward in unresolved confusion of mind, some were wayward Christians looking for a fresh start. Plenty of critics believed that almost none would stand: J. B. Priestley called them 'victims of emotion' and was sure that only 'a tiny minority are genuinely converted'.[29] But Stanley High, a senior editor of the *Reader's Digest*, investigated the facts ten months on from Harringay for his book *Billy Graham*. He talked to many ministers (John Stott among them), listened to many testimonies, and convinced himself that a high proportion of professed conversions were both new and real. As against pessimistic and subjective prophecies like Priestley's, he tells how

> ... in February, 1955, the influential *British Weekly*, non-denominational church paper notably neutralist on Billy Graham, undertook to find a more conclusive answer. It polled a cross section of British clergy of all denominations on 'What's Left of Harringay?' At the end of nearly a year it found that, of outsiders, neither church members nor churchgoers, converted at Harringay, 64.03 per cent – after nearly a year – 'are still attending church and taking part in church life regularly.'[30]

Though later surveys and further analysis were to suggest that more enquirers already had some church connection than early figures indicated, nevertheless this was the best information available at the time. With the Wembley crusade of the following year sure to add to them, if not double them, it was clear that there was a huge constituency of new Christians with little or no church background who would need to be built up in the faith. John Stott was chairman of the Evangelical Alliance Literature Committee, who saw that some of this task of follow-up and nurture could be helped by Christian publications and in particular by a regular journal. There were of course a number of weekly and monthly papers already published for a Christian readership, ranging from denominational weeklies to learned quarterlies; but there was next to nothing with a popular and contemporary approach – a Christian 'glossy', with colour art-work and photography, of a kind that could sit comfortably on the same coffee-table as the illustrated weeklies to be found in so many homes. In America there was quite a range of possible models; in Britain, after wartime austerity, paper controls, and shortages of many kinds, there did not seem to be anything comparable with, for example, *Moody Monthly* or *His*.

So the idea of such a magazine, arising directly out of Billy Graham's visit, began to be considered by the Committee. They saw it as designed to offer Christian teaching and pastoral follow-up in an acceptable and contemporary way to the thousands beginning a new life with Jesus Christ. Frank Colquhoun, editorial secretary of the Evangelical Alliance, was about to take on a new parish; the time he himself could give to such a project would therefore be limited to general editorial oversight. A new editorial secretary, who would devise, edit and produce such a magazine was needed. In the autumn of 1954, with Wembley still eight or nine months away, John Stott approached Timothy Dudley-Smith (the writer of this book), at that time in charge of the Cambridge University Mission in Bermondsey, and known to have a special interest and concern for the Christian ministry of the printed word. His first response was one of cautious enthusiasm to which John Stott replied persuasively:

My convictions are: –

1. Literature is tremendously important. Its power down history has been immense. There is no respectable keen evangelical body doing literature except Inter-Varsity Fellowship and that is specialized. The Council will back anything likely to serve the gospel. Money no object! The aim of the magazine is to provide sound and constructive devotional, doctrinal and training reading matter for the vast population of Christians who now read nothing at all, – or only the *Life of Faith*.

2. We need a parson because (a) he has the theological training and education to control editorial policy and write good articles himself; (b) he will have contacts with many other ministers through it; (c) he will be reaching a congregation far, far bigger and more influential than any church could hold – young Christians, Sunday School teachers, workers and other ministers.

The thing is that EA now has the ball at its feet. It is sponsoring the next Billy Graham crusade beginning on May 9 at Wembley, and has the confidence of the Christian public. It is on the crest of the wave, and *you've* got to do the surf-riding!³¹

The magazine, under the title *Crusade*, published its first issue in June 1955, reporting on the Wembley crusade the previous month, and with a cover picture of Billy Graham and the Archbishop of Canterbury together. The first editorial set out the aims which John Stott's Committee and the editors had for it:

We believe CRUSADE will be valued not least by the great company of people in almost every part of Britain who have been helped by the Graham Crusades in London and Glasgow. There are today literally thousands of such people who have been brought into a new and transforming experience of the power of Christ as a direct result of Billy Graham's ministry. They stand on the threshold of the Christian life. They have taken the first vital steps with Christ, but they want to know how to go on with the Lord ... to learn more about the Bible and the great doctrines of the faith ... to have a stronger hold upon the principles of Christian worship and discipleship ... to be equipped for the service of the gospel in the world.³²

In fact John Stott, and the rest of the Council of EA, were mistaken over the financial position of the Alliance. His cheerful 'Money no object!' of November 1954 was to become a financial crisis within a year. The strength of his personal support in those difficult times remains a vivid memory, not least kneeling in prayer with him in his study at the Rectory, claiming the promises of Jeremiah 29:11.³³ Thanks to the personal generosity of Lieutenant-General Sir Arthur Smith, Chairman of EA, and other individual donors (some of them approached by John Stott) the magazine survived and flourished. In 1982 the name was changed from *Crusade* to *Today*, and to *Leadership Today* five years later. In its early days John Stott was a regular contributor, from the first issue³⁴ onwards: and in the Christmas issues of 1955 and 1956 'John Stott's Christmas Quiz' was a light-hearted challenge as to how well (or otherwise) readers knew their Bibles. *Crusade* was also to carry his first significant contribution on an issue of current theological controversy, the debate on 'Fundamentalism',³⁵ to be considered in a later chapter.

The Wembley crusade again attracted huge numbers, undeterred for the most part by the unceasing rain which made the Empire Stadium a sea of umbrellas night after night during the week. 'It is hard to see that the old charge of emotionalism can ever be brought again as the reason for the many who have responded to Graham's appeals,' wrote Roy Cattell:

> The weather was cold, and intermittent showers continued all through the evening. Nevertheless at 7.30 when Dr. Graham, the Bishop of Barking, Chairman of the Executive Committee and the Rev. F. P. Copland Simmonds, Moderator of the Free Church Federal Council, emerged to face the cameras, the stadium was well filled. The whole service was recorded by the B.B.C. for use on the Overseas programmes, and the questions that had been in the minds of many were quickly answered. Could the people hear? Could Dr. Graham hold their attention in spite of the cold, the many standing, the rain? Would people respond, crossing their bridges and standing on the turf to be counselled and helped? Rain, which had fallen during the preliminaries, ceased as Dr. Graham began his address ... The setting sun appeared from behind the clouds at the Western end of the stadium, giving a radiance to the scene. At the conclusion of the address, when the invitation was given, the sight of thousands streaming across the turf was one that none who saw it will ever forget.[36]

During the week, 23,000 came forward as enquirers and were counselled, on the 'sacred turf', squelching through the pools to register their decision. Understandably, the statistics did not compare with the thirteen weeks of Harringay: probably far fewer non-churchgoers made up the Wembley crowds. John Stott's considered assessment was that Wembley hardly fulfilled its promise, when compared with Harringay. There, in his view,

> ... the influence and the impact built up over the weeks and the months in a very striking way, whereas the one week at Wembley in 1955 did not have an opportunity to build up in the same way. The weather was also extremely bad ... it rained almost every night. There were large numbers who responded, but the Wembley stadium is so huge, that it tends to be very impersonal. You can't see Billy across the turf at Wembley. I didn't like it so much.[37]

Against that must be set Hugh Gough's comment, nine years later, when as Archbishop of Sydney he was asked to look back on the Wembley crusade: 'There are thousands of men and women in the Kingdom today because of it. Therefore can we say it was a mistake?'[38]

Billy Graham's British crusades (he was at Glasgow's Kelvin Hall for a Scottish crusade in the weeks before Wembley) played a significant part in that revival of Evangelicalism which contemporary historians trace to the post-war period. To D. W. Bebbington, the impact of Billy Graham was 'probably the most important factor' in the resurgent vitality of the conservative evangelical tradition.[39] Adrian Hastings looked beyond the limelight that was focused on Billy Graham, to those 'local representatives' whose home-grown work and ministry lay in this country, and continued here year by year:

> One mission – even conducted by Billy Graham – does not make a revival and, important as American preachers have always been for fully fledged Evangelicalism, the revival really depended even more on its local representatives, and more than anyone else on John Stott. If we take the triennial missions to Oxford and Cambridge of the Christian Union in the fifties – a very crucial part of the whole strategy – while Graham preached the 1955 Cambridge mission, Stott preached those of 1952 and 1958 and the Oxford missions of 1954 and 1957. He had become Rector of All Souls, Langham Place in 1950, the church in which the BBC records its daily service. From then on Stott must be accounted one of the most influential figures in the Christian world, standing as he did at the point of intersection of the Evangelical movement and the Church of England.[40]

3

Before the first issue of *Crusade* magazine was off the press, there were the low-key beginnings of an enterprise of quite a different kind, the revival of an informal fellowship of younger clergy, under the name of the 'Eclectic Society', a title suggested by John Lefroy when the idea was first discussed at an All Souls staff meeting one Monday morning in his Queen Anne Street flat.[41] The original Eclectic Society was founded in January 1783, with only four members: John Newton, Richard Cecil, Henry Foster and the layman, Eli Bates. Charles Simeon later became a 'country member'. They met once a fortnight in Richard Cecil's vestry at St. John's Chapel, Bedford Row, now demolished; the silver teapot, sugar-tongs and spoons they used are still in the possession of the Church Missionary Society. They read papers discussing such questions as what constitutes Christian unity, how best to prepare sermons or visit the sick, how to comfort afflicted consciences, and 'the best method of planting the gospel in Botany Bay'. But they were also innovative in the church, as evidenced by the founding of CMS.[42]

Presupposing, perhaps, among his contemporaries a closer acquaintance with church history than all of them could boast, John Stott wrote a few days after Easter 1955 to twenty-two friends, many of them former Iwerne campers or known from Cambridge. Most were curates in or around the London area, including the three on his own staff, but there were five or six young incumbents like himself:

12 Weymouth Street,
London, W. 1
4th April 1955

'The Eclectics'

I expect you remember how John Newton and Richard Cecil in the year 1783 founded 'the Eclectic Society' 'for mutual intercourse and the investigation of spiritual truth'. They gathered a few like-minded ministers (and laymen) together regularly for fellowship.

We here have for some time had it in our minds and on our hearts to do, on a tiny scale, the same kind of thing. We'd love you to join us perhaps twice a year so that we can spend a day off together.

The main purpose is fellowship, but we mean to take the opportunity to pray together, and spend a bit of time discussing some matter of common interest and concern. But the time will be free and informal, and not too organised. There is a list below of those who are being invited to the first meeting. It's private!

This first meeting is arranged for Tuesday June 21. We have booked a room in the Crown Hotel, Amersham, from 11a.m. to 6p.m. Lunch and tea are laid on and those who are free can of course stay to supper.

I will send you travelling details if you let me know you plan to come. When you write, will you tell me if you have a car?

Do join us.[43]

The inaugural meeting was full of friendship, but hardly historic. It was agreed at that time that 'membership' should be limited to Anglican evangelical clergy under forty and that meetings should be held twice a year. The programme would include a Bible exposition, probably a paper on some prepared subject given by one of the members, and a free period for 'informal sleep'!

It sounds obvious and anodyne as an idea: some flavour of the eighteenth century still clings to the picture of a group of clergy meeting together as friends on a regular basis to discuss their professional interests, to encourage one another, and to put the world to rights over a meal together. In fact, the almost universal testimony is that young clergy found in the Eclectic Society a value which went far beyond a mere sense of belonging, or a chance to refresh a weary spirit. In greater or lesser ways, membership left its mark on life and ministry, and was recalled years later as a formative experience of those early years after ordination. Gavin Reid summed up two of the factors that contributed to the significance of the Eclectic Society:

> With John Stott's astonishing leap from serving a curacy in All Souls Langham Place to becoming its Rector, Anglican Evangelicalism suddenly found itself with a new leadership figure of a much younger generation. In addition to his youth there was also a readiness to take theology seriously. These two factors gave John a different perspective from the other more patriarchal and isolationist elder statesmen of the Evangelical movement in the English national church.[44]

It was true that evangelicals, even in the post-war years, did not always find it easy to fit in to diocesan structures or deanery chapters: too often, not by their own choosing, they felt the odd man out. Here they could feel at home and among friends, with a contribution to make that would be valued and understood. The private nature of the meetings provided an opportunity to be entirely free in debate, even in questioning the received orthodoxies of the time, without feeling that unguarded comments might be held against one. To many, this combination of fellowship and freedom was of unexpected value. Geoffrey Hart, a curate in Islington, was one such:

> Eclectics meant a good deal to me as a really rather lonely and deeply convinced Evangelical curate in the London Diocese, where the Bishop had at first refused to ordain me and only agreed reluctantly after a year's delay. Rightly or wrongly I felt somewhat embattled, and it was an enormous strength and encouragement to know that there were other like-minded younger clergy and to meet with them from time to time for real fellowship where there was no need either to tone down my Evangelicalism or to be apologetic about it.[45]

The original limit of forty members was very quickly reached. The Constitution was changed in order to retain older members a little longer, so that in place of 'under 40' it now read 'under 40 or so'! Within three years, though still very much a private fellowship 'by invitation', there was a waiting list for membership. The main purpose of the Eclectic Society (John Stott discouraged the term 'Eclectics') was still to be a meeting of friends, able to discuss together in complete freedom – 'to let their hair down'; but in more formal terms, as the Society developed, it provided 'a forum in which younger evangelicals could debate and explore outside the boundaries set by their elders.'[46]

Some of the attraction, therefore, was still to keep in touch with old friends. A good part of it, at least in the beginning before groups began to multiply, was to meet with John Stott himself. 'I think I first met him personally at one of the very early eclectics,' a friend wrote later. 'He chatted to me, was interested in what I was doing and gave one his whole attention; and when one next met him he seemed to have remembered it all.'[47] This was a time of growing ferment in evangelicalism, when there seemed an endless variety of new ideas to be explored. Some of those curates who formed the first members of the Society were serving under vicars who had fought the battles of evangelical truth in the days before the war. Such men could not easily enter, even when they wished to do so, into the opportunities that now confronted an evangelicalism emerging from a long period of neglect – or worse – by the church at large, resulting in a climate of defensiveness and resistance to new ideas. To the younger clergy the Eclectic Society was both a safety-valve and a life-line: but it was something more. Besides acting as a support-group through what was often a difficult time (curacies are by no means uniformly happy) it developed the power of the Christian mind, and opened the Bible in a new way: as guide to the realities of practical life, including ethical and moral choices, as well as nourishment to the spirit.

Like the proverbial amoeba, the Society grew by division. In 1958 the group split into two branches, north and south of the Thames. An Eastern group chaired by David Sheppard, then at the Mayflower, followed a year later, and then the South-Thames group itself divided. A West of England branch was formed in 1961, and then a Northern branch. By the mid 1960s a group of younger evangelical clergy in Northern Ireland was affiliated, and a total of seventeen groups combined to give a membership of over a thousand.[48] They kept in touch by an annual residential conference and by the exchange of membership lists and papers.

Quite the most important effect of the revival of the Eclectic Society in this century was the self-education and mutual support it offered to its members. It raised the sights, and the morale, of a generation of evangelical clergy. It offered a new perception of what might be achieved for the Church of England, of the role of expository preaching, and of the handling of Scripture. Much that was innovative in that fertile period drew at least some of its inspiration from the Eclectic fellowship: the

Family Service movement; the *Youth Praise* songbooks (selling more than a million) and *Psalm Praise*; David Sheppard's concern for the inner-city; the Frontier Youth Trust and George Hoffman's one-world vision which became Tear Fund. Michael Baughen, writing in 1990 as Bishop of Chester, recalled how membership of the Eclectic Society in its earlier days was

> ... a revelation, a release, a dynamic experience. Evangelicals at the time were so often controlled by 'evangelical tradition' in how to act and behave in life. There, in Eclectics, the one condition was the acceptance of the Scripture as Authority – but then everything else was to be tested in the light of Scripture. It was liberating! It was the key to evangelical revival in the Church of England. It was going back to the roots.[49]

Nor was this all. Looking back over almost twenty years, John Stott described the Society as 'the driving force behind the National Evangelical Anglican Congress ...'[50] of 1967, as indeed of 1977. NEAC 1967 may well prove the single most identifiable result of the Society, not only because of the part its members played in the creation of the Congress (which will be considered in detail in volume two), but because without the self-confidence and biblical maturity that it had helped to foster in so many evangelical clergy, the successful mounting of such a National Congress would hardly have been possible. Moreover, the various study groups which had been set up through the Eclectic Society paved the way for the study which was an integral part of the preparation for the Congress and for the elaborate network of study groups which followed it. Even in the 1950s the Society was sponsoring study groups on Baptism (led by John Collins, who had moved from All Souls to be Vicar of St. Mark's, Gillingham), on Marriage and Divorce, on the Associate Ministry (the early dawn of what became the non-Stipendiary Ministry), and on the Services of Holy Communion and Morning and Evening Prayer.

4

The second half of the 1950s was a time of immense activity among evangelical Proctors and members of the Church Assembly as Archbishop Geoffrey Fisher drove forward his programme of Canon Law Revision. Maurice Wood, Vicar and Rural Dean of Islington, and therefore Chairman of the Islington Clerical Conference, worked assiduously with like-minded clergy and laity (Canon T. L. Livermore, Prebendary R. P. Johnston, Malcolm McQueen, Hugh Craig and many others) to preserve the reformed nature of the Church of England, and its biblical basis. To read even a small part of the papers, memoranda, minutes and letters on this subject is to wonder that the leaders in every part of the church found time to do anything else.[51]

Though John Stott was urged to stand for election to Convocation – and later to the General Synod – this was not his calling, though he encouraged others to play a full part in the decision-making structures of the church. His heart was chiefly given to pastoring his congregation and to evangelism. It was this concern that led him to accept Kenneth Slack's invitation to serve, with Martyn Lloyd-Jones and Leith Samuel, on a group set up by the British Council of Churches in the aftermath of the Billy Graham Crusades of 1954 and 1955. The Council hoped to explore the differences between their member churches and the conservative evangelicals, and expected to be concerned mainly with differing biblical presuppositions. Their hope was to find sufficient common ground for united evangelism, in which the evangelicals had demonstrated their leadership. However it soon became clear,

> as Lloyd-Jones had in fact predicted, that they were in disagreement over almost every aspect of doctrine – the atonement, the new birth (was it at baptism?), the doctrine of humanity, the fall, who is a Christian, the church, the sacraments, the person and authority of Christ, and much more. Stott withdrew early on. Lloyd-Jones attended patiently, until finally in 1961 the BCC stopped the talks, partly because they were not producing the desired unity and partly because very few of their representatives now attended. The exchanges had served only to underline the fact that the disagreements were fundamental to the nature of the gospel that was to be preached.[52]

Though there was a limit to John Stott's patience with ecumenical discussions of this kind, he was ready enough to come to the defence of the gospel, the Scriptures, and evangelical truth when these were under threat. In 1957 he was among a small party of evangelical leaders who went to Lambeth Palace to make known to Archbishop Geoffrey Fisher their concerns over Canon Law revision, at that time dragging its slow length along on the floor of the Church Assembly. By then the process was into its eleventh year.

Evangelicals had little to hope from Canon Law revision in terms of securing a church more deeply committed to personal holiness, effective worship, and the spread of the gospel. But they had cause for apprehension, since Fisher, notable as a headmaster, and retaining all his life a headmasterly style, was clear that the revised Canons would represent the law of the church, and should command obedience. He stated his view that 'the clergy ought to be bound by canons; that was what canonical obedience means. Consistory courts ought to be able to impose penalties, even deprivation, for breaches of the canons.'[53] For very many years clergy had been able to sit increasingly lightly to Canon Law. Much of it was hopelessly out of date. It had been publicly flouted, to the point of destroying its credibility, during the battles over ritualism. Moreover, William Temple had taken a different view of its authority from that towards which Fisher was now urging the Church Assembly. Temple had stated that a canon or church rule

> is not in its essential nature something to be obeyed with mechanical uniformity ... It is to be observed with reverent regard, and followed with that freedom of spontaneity which belongs to the spiritual life for the regulation of which it is drawn up. Nothing could more conduce to the true welfare of our Church than a recovery of the original sense of canonical authority as something which claims not detailed conformity, but reverent loyalty.[54]

'Loyalty' can make provision for some differences of interpretation, some freedom of conscience, some appeal to a higher principle, where legalism cannot.

Among the particular points of concern to evangelicals were the fears that a revised Canon Law might on the one hand impose the wearing of ecclesiastical vestments, whose Roman symbolism and association with the Mass was inconsistent with a reformed view of the Lord's Supper; and on the other might remove the traditional and much-valued Anglican freedom of the 'Open Table', whereby (unlike the Church of Rome) Anglicans were able to offer hospitality at Holy Communion to those who were communicant members in good standing of other denominations.

The practice, therefore, was important not only from Christian values of courtesy and hospitality, but because it implied a positive affirmation of the 'validity' of non-episcopal ministry and sacraments, and therefore churches. It was John Stott's custom at All Souls to invite to receive Holy Communion 'any baptized and communicant member of another church who loves and trusts the Lord Jesus', a matter of traditional Anglican hospitality in a congregation which at any given service was likely to include Christians from a wide range of churches overseas. In the early 1960s he was called to account for this. He and Peter Johnston, Vicar of Islington and a Proctor in Convocation, were summoned by Mervyn Stockwood, Bishop of Southwark, and Robert Stopford, recently appointed Bishop of London, to be told the practice must cease. 'We listened respectfully and said we were very sorry, but it was a matter of conscientious conviction to us that the table was the Lord's, and not the church's or ours … they huffed and puffed a bit, and let us go.'[55] At about this time, writing for the church press, John Stott lifted the significance of the Open Table debate to the highest plane of all:

> The real basis on which this practice of inter-communion is grounded is not tradition but theology. It has a clear Biblical warrant. If the practice of an open table is denied, it is not custom only which is violated, but the truth of the gospel. To deny a fellow Christian, a believing, baptized communicant member of his own church, occasional access to the Lord's table in the Church of England simply because he has not been episcopally confirmed, is an offence to the God who has justified him, and an insult to a brother for whom Christ died. Am I to regard a justified fellow-believer as unclean that I withdraw from him? I seem to hear again the heavenly voice which spoke to Peter, 'what God has cleansed, you must not call common.'[56]

Intercommunion was not the only cause of anxiety to evangelicals in the 1950s and 1960s. Church Assembly was committed to the revision of the Prayer Book: John Stott spoke for many who feared, not without reason, that this might move the church's worship to a position inconsistent with her formularies, and so confront evangelical churchmen with issues of conscience. Towards the end of 1959 he wrote in the *Church Times* under the title 'Order or Chaos in the Church's Liturgy', setting out four guiding principles for any change: that it should be moderate; that it should make for clearer understanding; that it should be prepared to learn from others treading the same path (for example, the Church of South India); and finally 'that any change should be agreeable to the Word of God'.[57]

Such attempts to ensure that the revision of Canon Law, and other proposed measures from the Convocations and the General Synod, did not compromise the biblical and reformed nature of the Church of England continued to be one of John Stott's concerns through the years that followed. As was his nature, he generally tried to secure his objects, not by a lone voice of protest, but by setting up institutions designed to achieve desired ends. Through much of the 1960s (and on into the 70s and later decades) the Church of England Evangelical Council, often under his chairmanship, sought to inform evangelical opinion, and strengthen the hand of evangelicals in Convocation, Church Assembly or Synod. Equally, the 'Christian Foundation' series, published under his chairmanship during the 1960s was an attempt to address such issues.[58]

Each of these twenty-two small volumes appeared 'under the auspices of the Evangelical Fellowship in the Anglican Communion' (EFAC). This Fellowship was largely John Stott's creation, and a significant and enduring witness to his strategic vision, and to his patient determination to turn a dream into a reality.

Most of this story belongs to the next decade: but its early beginnings were in 1958 and 1959. Indeed, Oliver Barclay, Assistant Secretary under Douglas Johnson at the IVF, had begun soon after the war to convene a private 'Church of England group' to consult about matters of concern to Anglican evangelicals. It was private, partly because it had no official standing and partly because there was something slightly anomalous in a distinctively denominational group within an inter-denominational Fellowship. It met some four times a year under the chairmanship of the Rev. A. T. Houghton, General Secretary of the Bible Churchmen's Missionary Society, primarily for consultation. No minutes were kept, it co-opted its own members, and membership varied from year to year. After some ten or twelve years of this informal group a proposal was made for something altogether more structured:

> In 1959 the need for a central Evangelical Council was discussed and it was agreed to ask the Rev. J. R. W. Stott if he would convene such a body. He did not feel able to do so, but after discussion the proposal was altered to the creation of an international fellowship. Taking advantage of the presence of Archbishop Gough in the country a slightly augmented meeting was held at the Royal Commonwealth Society on January 12th, 1960 with Mr. Stott in the Chair. At this it was unanimously agreed to go ahead with the plan for an Evangelical Fellowship in the Anglican Communion. It was agreed that membership ought, at least mainly, to consist of national or regional Evangelical Fellowships or Councils, rather than individuals and that it would be necessary to create such a council in England. It was agreed that the 'C. of E. Group' might become that council.[59]

The 'international fellowship' here proposed was not a totally novel idea. The need for something of the kind had become evident during the Lambeth Conference of 1958. Over three hundred bishops had assembled from forty-six countries to discuss five main themes. One of these, 'Progress in the Anglican Communion', contained a sub-section on 'The Book of Common Prayer', and it was of this section that Marcus L. Loane, one of the small number of evangelical bishops, found himself a member. Loane was at that time Bishop Coadjutor in the Diocese of Sydney;[60] he was only present at the Conference as the representative of

Archbishop Howard Mowll who was unwell. Loane's sub-group found itself dealing with the revision of the Book of Common Prayer, and especially the Service of Holy Communion. This was a field dominated by the influence of two Anglo-Catholic writers, Dom Gregory Dix, whose *The Shape of the Liturgy* had been published in 1945; and Dr. A. G. Hebert, some of whose views on eucharistic sacrifice were quoted with approval by the Lambeth bishops,[61] views which appeared to call in question the historic uniqueness and finality of Christ's sacrificial death. Marcus Loane sought to resist liturgical interpretations which failed to do justice to Scripture, but received very limited support except from P. J. Brazier, Assistant Bishop of Uganda, who consistently sided with Loane in the vote, but could add little by way of theological argument. Marcus Loane, looking back on the work of the Committee at a distance of thirty-five years, recalled that it was only the very strong requirement of a unanimous report that prevented concessions to theological liberalism and an unbiblical sacramentalism.

> Leslie Brown and Christopher Chavasse of Rochester were moderate Evangelicals, but thought it necessary to make concessions here and there for the sake of over-all harmony ... Discussion centred mainly on the Service of the Holy Communion. Changes were sought in the language of the 1662 Prayer Book which would allow for a more definite 'catholic' doctrine of the Real Presence and a recognition of the continual offering of Christ as a sacrifice for sin. There was also pressure to provide for some form of Reservation. The one other major debate was over the question of Prayers for the Departed.[62]

Although Marcus Loane was receiving little support from within the Committee, he was able fortuitously to secure some of the help he needed elsewhere. In those days the Lambeth Conference was not yet residential; delegates arranged their own accommodation. Marcus Loane stayed for most of the time as a guest of Canon T. G. Mohan,[63] Secretary of the Church Pastoral-Aid Society, at his home in Sevenoaks, Kent, not far from London. Talbot Mohan was even then a veteran evangelical statesman, and he was able to supply Loane with information and memoranda on issues as they arose. On the specific issue of Prayers for the Departed, Mohan suggested that they should enlist the help of James Packer, at that time tutor at Tyndale Hall, for a reasoned statement in support of the traditional evangelical position:

> Mohan offered to contact Packer on Loane's behalf. The following evening, Mohan placed into Loane's hand a single side of paper

which set out the issues at stake in what Loane recalled to be a remarkably lucid manner. Loane took the document to the next committee meeting, and won the argument.[64]

But it was more and more borne in upon Marcus Loane, in his isolated stand in the Committee, how little the evangelical bishops knew one another across the Anglican Communion, and how poorly-prepared they seemed to be for the theological struggles of a changing church. Mohan and Loane were in consultation with John Stott, and it became increasingly clear to all three men that there was an urgent need to stimulate and develop a united evangelical witness across the whole of the Anglican Communion in this and other areas of theological dispute. John Stott adds:

A second factor influenced me, namely that the Church Union [in some respects the Anglo-Catholic counterpart of Church Society but commanding a more united measure of support] was able to assemble the Anglo-Catholic bishops in the Royal Albert Hall, and parade them in their copes and mitres, whereas there was no comparable body in the Anglican Communion to do the same for evangelical bishops (minus their copes and mitres!).[65]

To these two factors, a third must be added. In the summer of 1959 John Stott visited South Africa to undertake two university missions. There he found (as can be found today) two rival Anglican churches, both claiming to be the authentic representative of Anglicanism in South Africa. The Church of the Province, generally liberal-catholic in ethos, was regarded as the 'official' Anglican church, in communion with Lambeth, and with representatives at the Lambeth Conference the previous year. 'Into the Church of the Province of South Africa,' wrote one historian, 'the Church of England had for many years poured different resources, thus redeeming the shameful neglect of its earliest years.'[66] But there was also the evangelical 'Church of England in South Africa' with a strong historical claim to be regarded as the original church. In the main this represented the early evangelical congregations, who (they felt) had remained part of the Church of England when in 1870 the CPSA became a separate church with a provincial organization and its own bishops. In consequence of its provincial status, larger numbers and liberal-catholic stance, much of the Anglican Communion came to recognize only the CPSA and to regard the (earlier) CESA as irrelevant, if not schismatic. It was an attitude that revealed a 'preference by many Anglicans for status and organization rather than doctrinal standards, liturgical orthodoxy and historical pedigree ...'[67]

'My sympathies were naturally with CESA,' John Stott wrote later,

> ... and I was unprepared for the discovery that there were
> committed evangelicals in the CPSA as well, although their
> relationship with CESA was less than cordial, and they felt isolated
> from the wider evangelical Anglican community. Clearly there was
> an urgent need for a world-wide evangelical fellowship which could
> embrace the evangelicals of both CESA and CPSA.[68]

It was not surprising, therefore, that the request from the IVF 'Church
of England Group' fell on receptive soil. The formation of the Evangelical
Fellowship in the Anglican Communion, and of its English branch
member, the Church of England Evangelical Council, was completed
early in the next decade and is recounted in volume two.

5

Every year, it seemed, of John Stott's first decade as Rector saw him more
and more firmly established in a position of evangelical leadership. But
the broadening of his horizons, and the extended calls made upon him in
wider fields, did little to lessen the demands upon him as Rector of All
Souls. It was a period that saw the departure of tried and trusted
colleagues, in John Collins, Richard Bowdler and Sister Jordan, the
longest serving member of the staff. John Lefroy remained, but was the
victim of a serious (and, in the early stages, life-threatening) illness, from
which his recovery was prolonged and finally only partial. He had already
accepted the living of St. Mary's Addiscombe; but was forced to withdraw
his acceptance, and in the event remained on the staff of All Souls for a
further six years, slowly regaining a measure of health and strength.
Before illness struck, he wrote to John Stott who was away on holiday, to
break the news that his future seemed settled:

> I expect you realise that I am the last curate you will have of your
> own generation, and that the others on the staff feel their juniority
> very consciously. I think that this will mean that you will have to
> realise that to achieve real fellowship may become increasingly
> demanding on your part.
>   I believe that this search for fellowship is tremendously
> important, and that it must be at its deepest in the Rectory and the
> staff meeting if it is to permeate the parish. It seems to me that we
> have tended to take it for granted a little, and then when we have
> looked for it, to discover that it really wasn't there, all the time.[69]

Newcomers to the staff included Tom Robinson at the Clubhouse, Geoffrey Rawlins, Julian Charley (who, like the Rector, had a Cambridge First in theology), Vera Williams from St. Michael's House, Oxford, and Michael Harper to take over the Stores Chaplaincy. Martin Peppiatt arrived at the very end of 1959 from Trinity College, Oxford, and Wycliffe Hall. Curates come and go; they are by nature birds of passage. By contrast, one staff appointment made in 1956 was to last for more than forty years – the arrival of Frances Whitehead, originally as Church Secretary, but becoming successively secretary to the Rector and then, on Michael Baughen's arrival as Vicar in 1970, secretary to John Stott personally. Since then her support has been the indispensable background to all his ministry, all his travelling, all his writing.

Frances Whitehead had been at school in Great Malvern during the war, and on leaving began work in the Radar Research and Development Establishment there. On VJ day she was on holiday with her mother in the New Forest, and in the same guest house was the Rector of St. John's Wood; he and Frances used to go out horse-riding together.[70] Through this casual contact, he secured for her a secretarial job in London with an architect friend of his at the Ministry of Works. He tried to get her to become a member of his church – but without much success. Frances also went occasionally to Holy Trinity, Brompton, where Bryan Green was attracting a considerable congregation; but again, before anything came of this, she went with her mother to live abroad, first in Switzerland and then in South Africa. But by 1951 she was back in London and took a temporary job with the BBC as secretary to a Talks Producer in the Overseas Service, working first in their offices at 200 Oxford Street, and then at the Langham Hotel, opposite All Souls. She recalls clearly

> ... the first time I walked past All Souls in company with a fellow secretary. From the pavement we could see the warm glow of lights on in the building, illuminating the large picture of Jesus Christ which dominates the east end of the church. I was immediately attracted and said to her 'Let's go and have a look at that church'. In the porch I saw a notice announcing Friday lunch-time concerts, and being fond of music determined that I would go one Friday. So my first contact ever with All Souls was to go over to a lunch-time recital, but I was disappointed to find only a handful of people there and, so far as I can remember, nobody making us feel welcome. I did not go back again.
>
> Then one day much later, I happened to be walking round by St. Peter's Church Vere Street in my lunch-hour. The bells were ringing, the sun was shining, and on the spur of the moment I went

in. To my great surprise the church was full, and the sermon was gripping (John was preaching although of course I did not know him then). I soon found myself attending that brief mid-week lunch-hour service in St. Peter's regularly, drawn by the powerful preaching, but it must have been some months later that I linked St. Peter's with All Souls and started going there regularly on a Sunday morning. In those days no-one ever spoke to you in church, you just went and came away. Someone might have smiled, I can't remember, but nobody ever spoke to me, and even if they had I would probably have been embarrassed![71]

Then came New Year's Eve, December 31st 1952, with John Stott preaching on the story of Nicodemus from John 3, followed by an appeal to 'open the door to Christ' based on Revelation 3:20. As before, Frances listened and found the message very compelling and personal. There and then she secretly made her response to Christ, but was too shy to respond outwardly to the invitation to have a talk with the preacher. She spoke to no-one but walked home on her own in the early hours of New Year's Day, rejoicing over the step of faith which she had taken. 'I was thankful,' she said later, looking back to that night,

> ... that there was no human pressure on me to make a decision. The experience was very vivid, but it was entirely a matter between God and me, because no one ever spoke to me personally about it, and I know I never discussed the Christian faith with anyone at that time. However, it was about nine months later, I think, that I began to feel that I ought somehow to get myself integrated into the life of the church and not remain on the fringe. I didn't know what to do, how to get known, how to get involved, but I picked up a congregational register form at the church. This had a little box you could tick if you wanted to give help in the church, so I thought that if I ticked the box, someone might contact me and I wouldn't have to make the first move!

Sure enough John Stott himself got in touch and arranged to interview this Miss F. Whitehead, simply because she had indicated a desire to help, although she really had 'no idea what one did in the church'.

> I think he soon realised that I must be a new Christian and, because time was short then, he invited me to come back again for a second talk. This time he took me through 'the way of salvation'. We looked at some Bible verses (I think I had hardly ever opened one before) and he asked me 'What are you trusting in, if you want to

go to heaven?' I replied 'I'm trusting in Jesus'. Incredible! I don't know how I knew that, but somehow I did.

So Frances found herself joining a 'Nursery Class' to learn the basics of the Christian faith; and was soon given a job for the church addressing envelopes. Later she became involved in leading a Nursery Class herself and went through the Annual Training School; and about three years after her conversion began to wonder if God was calling her to go to Bible College, perhaps to train for missionary work. She went to see John Stott to ask his advice, and at one point in the conversation he remarked 'You'd better come and be my secretary', which was so surprising that she did not take it seriously. But about a week later John Stott rang her at the BBC to ask if she had thought any more about it?

'More about what?'
'About coming to be my secretary.'
'No! I didn't think you were serious!'

So, once more, Frances went to see John Stott, and was formally invited to come and work as Church Secretary; the one thing that worried her was that she would not be up to it and her tenure would be short-lived!

In fact she quickly proved herself as a valued member of the All Souls team, becoming an indispensable colleague in every aspect of John Stott's work, dealing with correspondence from all over the world, maintaining the work of his private office during his many absences, typing his books and articles, arranging meetings and interviews. More than that, for many years she has handled most of the day-to-day routine work and finances of the Evangelical Literature Trust and the Langham Trust's Third World Research Scholarship scheme. Frances Whitehead's story is closely interwoven with John Stott's from this time on. In whatever he undertook, she was secretary, administrator, bursar, and occasionally caterer and cook; and in the professional aspects of his ministry, closer to him than anyone else. As the work has changed, so have relationships: 'When I first joined the staff all was exceedingly formal; one stood somewhat in awe of John Stott who called everyone by their Christian name (I was 'Frances' from the day I first met him), but no female church member was ever allowed to use his!'[72] 'Frances' she has remained: but with affectionate additions: 'Frances the omnicompetent' at times; to the early inhabitants of the Rectory, 'Frances – SOAK' (Source Of All Knowledge); to later generations of Langham Scholars, 'Aunty Frances', alongside 'Uncle John'.

6

Through much of his ministry attempts were made to draw John Stott away from his work at All Souls to other parishes, or other spheres of work. Three such significant invitations came to him in 1955, 1956 and 1958.

On 6 April 1955 Sir Anthony Eden succeeded Churchill as Prime Minister. Sir Anthony Bevir was still the Appointments' Secretary. The first bishopric for which Eden had to make recommendations to the Crown was Bradford, vacant after an episcopate of twenty-four years. The retiring bishop was A. W. F. Blunt, nicknamed 'Abdication Blunt', as being the first to break the uncomfortable silence over Mrs. Simpson and the King. Bevir wanted J. A. Ramsbotham, Suffragan Bishop of Jarrow; Garbett, Archbishop of York, urged consideration of Donald Coggan, on the ground that 'It would be an advantage to have a scholarly Evangelical in our Upper House.' In the event Donald Coggan was consecrated Bishop of Bradford in January 1956.[73]

F. D. Coggan (later Lord Coggan) was at that time Principal of the London College of Divinity, then in Ford Manor, Surrey, where its lease was due to expire in two years time. An eleven-acre site had been purchased in Northwood, Middlesex, to which the College planned to move in 1957. Donald Coggan had been Principal for over eleven years, very difficult years in the life of the College: his stipend had remained unaltered since 1944, and the quarters allocated to the Principal and his wife, so the CACTM Inspectors found, were 'almost unbelievably limited to one large bed-sitting room on the first floor ... to admit the maximum possible number of students for the College's benefit.'[74]

In 1952 Dr. Coggan had declined an invitation to become General Secretary of the British and Foreign Bible Society, and early in 1955 had resisted 'a good deal of pressure' to become Principal of Wycliffe Hall, Oxford; in both instances, because his College needed him. At last, on 15 October 1955, the foundation stone of the new buildings was laid at Northwood. Three days later Donald Coggan received the Prime Minister's letter 'asking his agreement that a nomination be sent to Her Majesty for his appointment to the Bishopric of Bradford.'[75] No doubt with anxious hearts the Council met in November 1955 to try to find the right successor. Bishop Ralph Taylor was in the chair, and wrote to John Stott the following day:

> It is a critical time in the history of St John's Hall, and not only because of the erection of the new buildings and the impending transfer of the College to Northwood in 1957. I think you will be aware of other and greater issues at stake.

In regard to yourself – you may well plead that you have had no previous experience on the staff of a Theological College; but you are a born teacher and we have no questions on that score, while your preaching and pastoral experience will be a great asset.

May it not be in the purpose of God that you should have a period of greater opportunity of study and thought, in which to lengthen the ropes and strengthen the stakes, before you are called to a place of even greater responsibility and wider opportunity than you now occupy? ... the fact that the Council have been led to a unanimous decision constitutes for you a challenge that cannot easily be set aside.[76]

This letter was among the pile that awaited John Stott on his return from Cambridge at the end of the 1955 Billy Graham CICCU mission. He had only been Rector of All Souls for five years; and was already engaged to spend four months overseas towards the end of the following year. It was clear to him that he had not yet completed the work to which he believed God had called him at All Souls; and, after taking advice, with thought and prayer, he therefore wrote to decline.

In December the Council of LCD met again, and (perhaps predictably) asked him to reconsider. Along with the President's further letter, Talbot Mohan, Secretary to the Council, sent a personal note, full of characteristic wisdom and persuasiveness. 'I am glad for the sake of the College and the Church that you have been asked to think again,' he wrote,

> for much as I rejoice with all my heart that All Souls is such a 'beacon in a darkening world' yet I would rejoice still more if the Lord led you to LCD ...
>
> From my talk with you before you went away to seek God's will, I felt convinced that your answer would be 'No'. I felt that I had been a failure in my talk, and I nearly wrote to you to try to create a better impression. I felt I had stressed in an unattractive way the need of saving LCD. from a liberal emphasis, rather than stressing the immense influence which you could exert through the College. I hope my crude speech will not lead you to think that the council are narrow in outlook or opposed to dignity and beauty. They are only narrow in the sense that they are zealous for the Biblical Gospel.
>
> One whose tendency is much more liberal than mine said 'John Stott could transform the whole face of England if he went to LCD', much more effectively than at All Souls ...
>
> I do trust therefore John that you will think again. I know the

weight of advice on the other side. I know for example how
Douglas Johnson would be inclined to feel that All Souls was the
more strategic position, but Douglas, with all his great wisdom and
gifts of judgment, is not a member of the C of E and is therefore
not able to see the position from that view point. His survey is
interdenominational.

Having said all this I do repeat that I only want God's will to be
done in this. If it is not His will then I am content ...'[77]

Douglas Johnson was certainly one of those whom John Stott
consulted when faced with this urgent plea to reconsider. Writing to fix a
time to meet and talk, DJ added

I can easily give my first reaction. If I were the Archangel in charge
of 'postings' I should leave that said Rector where he is as long as
possible (the Crown will not necessarily appoint an Evangelical),
shield him from too many committees and organising, and let him
go on being what God obviously meant him to be.

And, looking well into the future ('a good few years more') he added:

I hesitate to say Bishop because an Anglican Bishop has so much
civil service type of duty which gets in the way of the Word.[78]

So, after some exploration and much prayer, the invitation to LCD
was declined: and John Stott settled again into the work to which he had
set his hand. But six months later he again received a letter of invitation
which required a new openness to what might be God's call:

Diocesan Church House
George Street
Sydney
24th July, 1956

From
The Archbishop of Sydney

My dear John Stott,
As you probably know, the Diocese of Sydney, for many years, has
had the help of two Coadjutor Bishops, as well as the Diocesan.
Recently, permission was given for the Diocese to have a third
Bishop, for the Church population in the Diocese continues to
grow rapidly and already we have more than one-third of the total
adherents to the Church of England in Australia within the
boundaries of this Diocese. A very capable young Australian,

formerly Archdeacon R. C. Kerle, was Consecrated on 1st May and will, I am sure, be a very great help in the routine work of the Diocese. Before he had begun to function, the senior Bishop Coadjutor, Bishop C. V. Pilcher, resigned, owing to age and ill-health. As I have now been Archbishop for 23 years, and having reached the age of 66, the appointment of Bishop Pilcher's successor is extremely important, as it is very probable that a new Archbishop may be appointed during the next 5–10 years. The Bishops Coadjutor, in office at the time, will have great responsibility in maintaining the evangelical tradition of this, the only large evangelical Diocese in Australia, and it will be tragic if its character should be changed.

I write to ask whether you would prayerfully consider coming to our help as a Coadjutor Bishop ...

The Archbishop went on to explain something of the strategic importance of the Diocese of Sydney within the Australian Church, its Theological College, its two Universities, Naval, Military and Air Force bases and 'more parishes and clergy than any other Australian diocese'. He continued:

In the midst of your busy and responsible ministry, I hesitate to make this suggestion, but, again and again, as I have prayed over the future of our Church in Australia, your name has come to mind, and I urgently beg you to think and pray about it before you make your decision.

The procedure would be that, if I may put forward your name, I should do so to the Standing Committee of the Diocese. If they approve, it then goes to the Bishops of the Province of New South Wales to ask whether they are satisfied over certain technical matters, and, if then I receive a reply in the affirmative from the majority of them, then announcement is made.

Believe me,
Yours very sincerely,
Howard Sydney[79]

Once more John Stott prayed, considered and consulted: but having acknowledged the letter briefly in early August, he finally wrote to decline. Apart from the reasons which had applied to the invitation to become Principal, he cited his elderly parents (his father's health was failing fast and his mother moving into her late seventies) and the fact that he had set his hand to the Clubhouse project in All Souls parish, and

THE
1940s

22. All Souls Church, Langham Place, 1940

The
1940s

23. *Summer camp at Clayesmore School, Iwerne Minster*

24. *'Bash' as commandant with John Stott as camp secretary, on the Clayesmore School forecourt, early 1940s*

25. *John Stott with his mother at Woodlands Farm House, about 1940*

26. *Cambridge from the tower of Great St Mary's in the 1940s, looking over Trinity College*

27. *Major-General Arnold W. Stott, World War 2*

28. *All Souls 'Jucos' in Regent's Park in the 1940s*

29. *Curate of All Souls, late 1940s*

THE
1950s

30. *Bomb damage at All Souls. The spire was finally restored in November 1951, six months after the church was reopened*

31. *The Revd Harold Earnshaw-Smith, Rector of All Souls, 1936-1950*

32. *All Souls, reopened after the war*

34. *John Stott and John Collins sailing on Milford Haven, 1952*

33. *St Peter's, Vere Street*

35. *Frances Whitehead at her desk: a later photograph*

36. *The young Rector*

37. With Billy Graham and Belshazzar at Montreat, North Carolina, Christmas 1956

38. Her Majesty The Queen Mother at All Souls, Christmas 1955

39. Being welcomed to the University of British Columbia for the student mission, January 1957

40. The Hookses, Dale, Pembrokeshire: John Stott's retreat in West Wales

41. *Billy Graham's mission to Cambridge University, with John Stott (on Billy Graham's left) as Chief Assistant Missioner, November 1955*

felt an obligation to see this established and given permanence. Once again he was asked to reconsider his decision: but this did not present difficulties. His course was clear, and he declined.

The Archbishop's reminder that his own successor would be appointed 'during the next 5–10 years' proved less than accurate. In 1958 the Archbishop, not a well man, suffered a heart attack after a great service in Sydney Cathedral and died in hospital.[80] There was no obvious answer as to who should succeed him.

> The Archbishop and others [had] sought to provide some possible answers by inviting English clergymen to Australia so that they might see and be seen for future reference: Bishop Hugh Gough of Barking, who visited Sydney in 1957 to address a Clergy School, and the Rev. John Stott of All Souls Langham Place, London, who conducted a Mission at Sydney University in 1958, were two such English invitees. But when Archbishop Mowll died of a heart attack in October 1958 at the age of 68, the identity of his successor was no clearer.[81]

In Sydney the Electoral Synod met in late November 1958, a matter of months after John Stott's visit and his name was among the sixteen nominations. Bernard Gook, the Diocesan missioner with whom John Stott had worked closely in meetings for clergy during the summer, wrote to urge him to allow his name to go forward. The letter was sent on to Cambridge where John Stott was in the thick of the CICCU mission. But he replied as soon as he was free to do so, in some detail, dividing his thoughts into three sections. First, he stated his own complete confidence in Marcus Loane, the most likely Australian successor: 'to me he is head and shoulders above me as a candidate'. Then he added a section about himself:

> I am honestly persuaded that I don't possess the necessary qualifications. At 37 I am much too young, especially with coadjutors older than I, and I could scarcely succeed in uniting the diocese. More important still, I have not the spiritual maturity, experience or gifts for such an influential position of leadership. Again, I am not married, and I feel sure you need a married Archbishop. Further, I am not an ecclesiastical statesman. Religious controversy is anathema to me, and although I have been drawn into it against my will, I find it distasteful and difficult. I have refused to stand for Convocation two or three times here because it is not my line. I feel called more to the ministry of the word and to a pastoral ministry. Another point concerns my family respon-

sibilities. As my father has just died, it would not be easy to leave my widowed mother in her old age.

He concluded:

> I honestly don't think you could expect me, therefore, in this very difficult situation to say I would 'consent to serve' if elected. Nor do I think it wise that I should be nominated, though, naturally, if Synod were to invite me, I would give the most serious and earnest consideration to their invitation. But I cannot commit myself at this stage. I am *very* sorry if I am making things more difficult, but I can only write what I feel. Be assured of my prayers. We of course only desire His will and glory.[82]

Before this letter was even written it was overtaken by a cable from a lay member of the Synod, one of the Faculty at the University of Sydney, dated 17 November:

> EIGHT ARCHDEACONS WANT YOU CONSIDERED STOP IMPLORE CONSENT NOMINATION LAWRENCE LYONS

A further cable followed four days later, seeking an unequivocal answer, and prefaced by an appeal to the Pastoral Epistles!

> FIRST TIMOTHY THREE ONE FIRST TIMOTHY FOUR TWELVE TO FIFTEEN STOP ELECTION VACANCY BEGINS TWENTYFOURTH REGARDLESS EARLIER REPLIES KINDLY ADVISE CLEARLY IF WILLING ALLOW NOMINATION BUT IF UNFORTUNATELY NO APPRECIATE YOU NAMING YOUR CHOICE EITHER ENGLISHMAN AUSTRALIAN PLEASE REPLY CABLE ADDRESS RON BAILEY

No record remains of John Stott's reply, except for a note on the cable form in his minutest handwriting which suggests that he responded:

> WILLING NOMINATED BUT UNLIKELY ACCEPT IF ELECTED SUPPORT LOANE[83]

A week later *The Times* made it clear that in spite of his firm resolve not to commit himself to accepting if elected, his name was due to come before the Synod among the final six:

Sydney Archbishopric's
Six Candidates

From our Correspondent, SYDNEY, Nov. 26

Three names from the reduced list of eight candidates for the Anglican Archbishopric of Sydney were considered by the Synod to-night, and that of the Bishop of Barking, the Right Rev. H. R. Gough, was selected for inclusion in the final list.

The others considered to-night were the Bishop of Bradford, Dr. F. D. Coggan, and the Dean of Melbourne, the Very Rev. S. B. Babbage. Those in to-morrow's list are the three coadjutor bishops of Sydney, the Rev. J. R. W. Stott, Rector of All Souls, Langham Place, London, and the Rev. M. A. P. Wood, Vicar of Islington, London. The earlier select list of 16 names included the Bishop of Stepney, the Right Rev. F. E. Lunt, and the Provost of Bradford, the Very Rev. J. G. Tiarks.[84]

No doubt it was a cause of some anxiety among members of the All Souls congregation as they read their newspaper; but it was entirely predictable that those in Australia who wished to press the claims of any other candidate would remind the Synod that to elect John Stott might well prove to be a fruitless exercise as he had given no commitment – indeed had used the word 'unlikely' – to serve even if elected. Lawrence Lyons, who had earlier cabled on behalf of the 'eight archdeacons' wrote to him when it was all over:

Your nomination was very well received and you were placed on the Select list with a higher percentage than Loane but in the voting for the final list 44% of the clergy voted for you and 50% was necessary. In my opinion one of the most influential factors in the minds of the conservatives was the belief that you did not really want to come, a point made strongly by one speaker. Your telegram to Bailey was read just before the vote, or at least just before the nominator (Archdeacon Delbridge) gave his reply, in which he said that you if elected would give the matter the most serious consideration. This however did not entirely remove the above mentioned impression.

The result I accept as coming from a procedure hard to better. There was much prayer from many and a great deal of sober thought and discussion. I hope that you do not regret letting your name go forward. Had Loane received ten fewer votes (out of 600) for the final list he would have been omitted and then the 44% who voted for you would have become very much greater. There was very little in it. Once on the final list you would certainly have received a number of votes from the 'outside-the-diocese' group.[85]

Twelve years were to pass before he was approached a third time to consider an Australian bishopric.

Six months after the matter of the Sydney Archbishopric was settled there came an invitation of quite a different kind, which John Stott was able to accept with thankfulness: it began with a letter from Percy Mark Herbert, Bishop of Norwich:

> The Palace,
> Norwich.
> 8th June 1959
>
> Dear Mr Stott,
> As Clerk of the Closet to the Queen, it falls to me to suggest to Her Majesty men to fill vacancies in the list of Chaplains to The Queen.
> I write to ask whether you would allow me to submit your name in this connection. You must, of course, treat the matter as wholly confidential, until you receive a formal offer of appointment.[86]

A week later the Earl of Scarborough, as Lord Chamberlain, wrote to say 'I have received The Queen's Command to offer you the appointment of a Chaplain to Her Majesty ...'[87]

John Stott had already enquired from the Clerk of the Closet about the duties of a chaplain and had received a reassuring reply: 'It is really an honour without corresponding "duties"!' he was told:

> You will certainly be invited by the Sub-Dean of the Chapels Royal to preach occasionally in the Chapel at St. James's Palace, but as you know the Queen is hardly ever in London on a Sunday and does not have special preachers! You are entitled to wear a scarlet cassock, a badge on your scarf, and (the custom in the past, but I don't think holding now) special buttons on an evening waistcoat![88]

The congregation was naturally delighted. George Cansdale arranged to give a large number of All Souls workers and helpers the opportunity to contribute half-a-crown each, so that they might present the Rector with a cheque for £31.10s. to pay for his scarlet cassock.[89] The appointment was gazetted on 26 June, and he preached his first sermon in St. James's Palace the following January. The appointment was as surprising as it was pleasing. John Lefroy teased his Rector by suggesting that it was a 'consolation prize', indicating that he could expect nothing further from the Church of England by way of honours or advancement. Certainly, among those who watched this kind of appointment, there was a feeling that in a few cases appointment to the College of Chaplains did have something of the consolation prize about it; but this could hardly apply to a man still under forty.

Various rumours circulated as to why John Stott should have been singled out for this honour. It was even confidently suggested that it was at the personal request of Billy Graham;[90] but the true explanation is probably more prosaic. The College of Chaplains numbers thirty-six, and it is the task of the Clerk of the Closet to keep the numbers up to thirty-five (the Queen liking to have the thirty-sixth place in reserve). There were at this time forty-two dioceses in the Provinces of Canterbury and York, so that it was never possible to see that each diocese was represented in the list, and London was bound to be a special case. Usually when a vacancy occurs (because a Chaplain dies, becomes a dean or a bishop, or reaches the age of seventy) the Clerk looks to see if there is any diocese which should be specially considered and consults the diocesan bishop, sometimes asking for the name or names of 'up-and-coming' men. The Bishop of London in 1959 was H. C. Montgomery Campbell, who would have known that William Wand, his predecessor, thought highly of John Stott and would also be aware not only of his work at All Souls but of his growing wider ministry – his long visits to the United States and to Australia (only the previous year) in particular.

Just as it is impossible to be certain what lay behind the original invitation, so there is little that can be said of opportunities to minister to the Royal Family. In general, the office of Chaplain to the Queen does not of itself mean that these occur often. As Bishop Herbert indicated, the Queen herself is seldom if ever at the Chapel Royal in St. James's Palace on the occasion when a particular Chaplain preaches his annual sermon. Chaplains have the opportunity to be presented on appointment and invited to the royal Garden Parties; but apart from this, may only see the Queen when she attends the triennial meeting of the Chaplains from time to time. *Izvori,* a Christian magazine published in Croatia, allowed enthusiasm to outstrip reality when it published an interview with John Stott in 1994, entitled 'Ispovjednik Englieske Kraljice', 'The Confessor to the English Queen'![91]

In the early days, John Stott himself had to circulate a private note to members of EFAC saying that he had learned of some reference during a meeting of the Council to his preparing a member of the Royal Family for confirmation: 'I want to take this opportunity of telling members of the Council that there is no foundation to this rumour; I should be most grateful if they could help to stop it from spreading.'[92] But it was public knowledge that John Stott was among the preachers invited to spend a week-end as the Queen's guest at Sandringham, to lunch with her at Buckingham Palace, and to preach before her and her family at Windsor or in Sandringham Parish Church, an invitation extended to only a select few among her chaplains.[93] Even more significantly, perhaps, on reaching the age of seventy (when Chaplains retire from the College) he was re-appointed as an 'Extra Chaplain', a much sought-after but very limited honour, which the Queen bestows only two or three times in a decade.

John Stott's evangelical convictions were on occasion a source of some amusing embarrassment to the Sub-Deans of the Chapels Royal who usually officiated. Canon J. S. D. Mansel, Sub-Dean from 1965 to 1979, had been brought up as an evangelical with a Brethren background, but had become an Anglican with (by the standards of his upbringing) a distinct tinge of liberalism, and even catholicism. 'He was obviously embarrassed when I came,' John Stott recounts

> because he knew enough about the evangelical constituency to know that I wouldn't altogether approve of his views, and that I knew he had sprung from a Plymouth Brethren background. On one occasion when he was showing me to my car, after drinks, he turned to me and said 'You know, John, I love our Lord', and I replied 'But of course, James; I never doubted it for one moment.' Then he added 'And I love our Lady, too'!'[94]

On another occasion in the chapel of St. James's Palace, Canon G. R. Dunstan was taking the Service as Priest-in-Ordinary to the Queen. He was at that time a Professor of Theology at King's College, London and editor of *Theology.* John Stott's turn on the 'Rota of Waits' (the name given to the list of preachers at the Chapel Royal) fell on St. Andrew's Day, 30 November 1969; but with All Saints Day (November 1) still in mind, he preached again the sermon he had used in All Souls a month before, on death and the life after death:

> I took Revelation 14:13 as my text: 'Blessed are the dead who die in the Lord ...' Among other things I spoke of the assurance which this beatitude gave us regarding the Christian dead. Since they are pronounced 'blessed', it is at least superfluous, and at worst unbelieving and disobedient, for us to pray that they may be what God says they are.

Exactly what was said to provoke Professor Dunstan's disagreement was never clear, but John Stott was made well aware of this in the vestry prayer that followed the Service: 'Lord,' Dunstan prayed, 'grant that what we have heard with our ears we may ponder in our minds and' (with singular emphasis) '*that and that only which we find to be true*, we may believe in our hearts and show forth in our lives.'[95]

7

At the start of 1959 the *Church Times* selected John Stott for inclusion in its regular feature, 'Portraits of Personalities'. The paper was establishment-minded, with a distinct leaning towards the more catholic people and politics of the church. To be so chosen was therefore an honour in itself; and the column (surmounted by a current photograph of the Rector at his desk, unsmiling, but with his roseate cheeks evident even in a black-and-white newsprint reproduction) was distinctly flattering:

> He has accomplished much in the first thirteen years of his ministry
> ... although he writes a good deal, it is never at the expense of his
> parochial duties ... output of work immense ... disciplined life ...
> young man of humility and charm of manner ... acknowledged to
> be one of the outstanding young leaders in the Evangelical tradition
> of the Church today.[96]

One perceptive sentence in the pen-portrait requires a word more. The writer had said, 'Though he is unmarried he has an extraordinary sympathy with tiny children', and indeed this was a trait that many noticed and which had led him to think even in his schooldays that were he ever to become a doctor like his father, he would choose to be a paediatrician.

But that the end of the 1950s should find him still unmarried was something he had not himself expected. Ours is an age when any man – more particularly, perhaps, any Christian worker or minister – who remains unmarried must expect that there will from time to time be dark hints of some latent homosexual inclination to account for this. E. J. H. Nash ('Bash') had met this, being himself not only a bachelor but one who was known to encourage his Iwerne leaders to stay single for the sake of the work. John Stott was at pains to defend Bash's reputation, and to explain the biblical basis of his position, when contributing to the symposium published in his memory:

> Since I worked with him closely for about seven years, both as a
> personal friend and as camp's secretary-treasurer, I am able to say
> with complete confidence that Bash was a perfectly normal
> heterosexual. His own singleness, and his advocacy of the single
> state, were entirely due to his zeal for God's work.[97]

John Stott identified himself with Bash's uncompromising stand for the place of singleness in the purpose of God, and the sanctity of sex and marriage:

> He may sometimes have been too zealous in commending singleness to others, assuming too readily that they also had received this particular gift and calling, but I for one greatly admire his courage and faithfulness in facing issues which many of us shirk. He cultivated a ruthless self-discipline himself in the fight against temptation, and urged upon others the same safeguards and self-control. He was adamant that Christians are at liberty to marry only Christians, and indeed that mature Christians should marry only mature Christians, so that they may help rather than hinder one another in their Christian life and service ... I know no Christian leader who has acted as consistently as Bash in applying the Pauline teaching that those who are chosen for pastoral oversight must have a blameless reputation in sex, marriage and home.[98]

And what John Stott here wrote of Bash could equally be applied to himself. Not surprisingly, the subject arose from time to time in the many interviews he was asked for in his later life. When, more than thirty-five years after his inclusion in 'Portraits of Personalities', the *Church Times* carried an extended interview, this was one of the areas on which the questioner sought to draw him out:

> The most widespread John Stott rumour was that he had sworn off women at an early age in order to devote himself to the ministry. 'I've never taken a vow of celibacy,' he says, ... 'in fact, when I was in my twenties and thirties, I was expecting to marry. There were two particular people who attracted me, although not simultaneously!
>
> 'It's difficult to explain what happened. All I can really say is that when I had to make up my mind whether to go forward to commitment, I lacked assurance that this was God's will for me. So I drew back. Having done it twice, I realised it was probably God calling me to be single. Looking back over my life, I think I know why God has called me to be single – because I could never have travelled or written as I have done if I had had the responsibilities of family. It has been lonely in some ways, but I'm grateful for a very large circle of friends.'[99]

To an American readership he felt able to speak of the regret that he sometimes felt at what he had missed in the area of family life:

I do regret not having had my own family in that I have always loved children and I love home life. I also believe very strongly that marriage is God's will for the generality of human beings, and that marriage, sex and family are all good gifts of the good Creator, and I rejoice in them when I see them in other people.

So, naturally, from time to time, I am envious, and sometimes it is lonely. But it has its advantages in terms of freedom and output, which also I greatly value.

As my ministry developed in the way that it has, with a great deal of travelling all over the world and the writing and with very little free time, I suppose I said to myself that God had called me to be single in order to devote myself to the kind of ministry to which He had called me.[100]

There are those who would want to look behind this, and to ask further questions. When it was said of Archbishop Garbett by his biographer that 'he would have found it extremely difficult to fit a wife in to his time-table',[101] the same page contains a pathetic entry from the Archbishop's private diary wondering 'whether I should have made a better use of life if I had it all over again – but a happy marriage with children would have made all the difference.' Certainly, in John Stott's case, the 1950s saw the consolidation of a lifestyle incompatible with the companionship of marriage. But which was cause, and which effect? Others point to the way in which, at least in the earlier years at All Souls, his very inaccessibility made him a magnet for the sexual attraction of many women (some, indeed, mentally unbalanced: George Cansdale is quoted as saying that he had more problems as Churchwarden of All Souls from the Rector's single state than from any other source).[102] Myra Chave-Jones, who had known him from Cambridge days and worked closely with him in London, summed up her own sense of all this in the phrase 'emotional unavailability':

I think that any truthful book about John should mention the grief that so many women suffered on his account, because it was such a feature of his life and the lives of many who came across him ... women seem to find him irresistible, on the whole. It is probably the combination of his being an 'up-front' person, his innate charm, his ability to make one feel as though one were the only person who matters, but also his personal inaccessibility. All this adoration proved a great trial to him. More than once there was a public outburst during a sermon from some women whose emotional needs were floating loose. He tried hard quite genuinely to be patient and never give any one of them overt cause to suppose that their regard was special to him in any way. But there were many others who became hooked into John's charm, but emotional unavailability, and suffered more quietly.[103]

Speculation aside, the fact is that John Stott began the decade of the 1950s, still in his twenties, confidently expecting that he would be a husband, and probably a father, by the end of it. But ten years later, on the threshold of forty and responding to demands from across the world, this now seemed to him improbable. It was true that (like many another pastor) he had had to learn how to distance himself from the importunities of some of the women in his congregation. Twice in the 1950s he found someone who might have been right for him; twice, in his own words, 'I lacked assurance that this was God's will for me ...' Looking at what the years since then have held for him, it is difficult to quarrel with this assessment.

Two further interviews, dating from the 1970s, offer his own considered view. In the first, he affirmed his agreement with the 'biblical balance' that 'God's general will is for all to marry, but both Jesus, in Matthew 19, and Paul, in 1 Corinthians 7, envisage people being given the "gift" of the single life.'[104] In the second, for an American student journal, the question and answer went like this:

Do you think a person, I suppose you can use yourself as an example, can know at an early age that he or she is called to singleness or is this something you just fall into?

STOTT: I have no doubt there are some people who believe God has called them to be celibate and to commit themselves to celibacy for the rest of their lives. Personally I have real hesitations about the wisdom of that, because I'm not convinced that people know, say in their early twenties, that God has called them to that. If they take a vow of celibacy, I think they may find themselves in grave difficulties later when they may fall deeply in love with somebody and begin to change their mind about their guidance. Then they're in trouble about any vow they may have taken. I'm not in favor of vows of celibacy.

I personally believe more in the second alternative you have given, that people discover it gradually and as the years pass begin to think that God is probably not calling them to marry. They don't meet a person with whom they believe God is calling them to share their life, or they don't fall deeply in love, or their work develops in such a way that it seems right for them to remain single in order to give themselves to their work rather than to a family. And as circumstances build up in this way, they begin to discern that God is calling them to remain single. And that is more the situation with me.[105]

Certainly that was how it was in the 1970s. But back in the 1950s John Stott wrote to congratulate a friend on his engagement, concluding with 'Please tell me how you did it – by numbers!'[106]

8

The decade of the 1950s was not only to see the gradual closing of a door upon John Stott's expectations of marriage and children, but also some major changes in his immediate family circle.

First was his parents' move to Bullens Hill Farm, Stringers Common (again, on the outskirts of Guildford) in 1956. From Woodlands Farm House, which they had rented during the war, they had settled at Cobbetts, Pitch Place, Worplesdon as their retirement home; but it eventually proved too large for them, and after several years there they finally moved to Bullens, a charming cottage, old and low-ceilinged, with a pleasant garden and a barn. Sir Arnold found it cramped and dark after the spaciousness of Cobbetts.[107] His death, not very long after the move, was for his son a further major landmark removed, striking at the roots of earliest childhood. The loss of a father is a significant and sad milestone in any life, but perhaps particularly when the relationship had been as turbulent and elusive as this one. Ever since leaving the Westminster Hospital amid many tributes from colleagues and friends, Sir Arnold had found life increasingly meaningless and frustrating. He died in June 1958; more will be found about this in a later chapter. His wife Lily lived on at Bullens until her death in 1966, valiantly cared for in her later years by their younger daughter Joy (who had come home to help look after her father). On her mother's death, Joy took in 'Auntie Babe' (her mother's younger sister) and made a home for her – it was not an easy relationship – until her death six years later. Joy then lived alone at Bullens, and ran a children's play-group in the house and garden, largely for families on the nearby housing estate, until she moved away in 1973.

While living in London in the 1950s Joy had attended All Souls for a few months; but found herself drawn increasingly towards Roman Catholicism. It was in character with her rebellious nature that, just as she had earlier taken a stand contrary to her parents' opinions and joined the Labour Party, so now she should be attracted to membership of a church outside her family's experience and (as she well knew) at variance with much that her brother believed and stood for. Writing to him in reply (it seems) to a letter asking if she was sure of her reasons, she explained:

I am not strong enough or stern enough to belong to your Evangelicalness – you see, all the things you hate so much, like candles and saints and genuflecting are *Big Aids* to me – and in a Catholic Church one is so sure that *God is there* ... you see, for years I have wandered about spiritually, taking perhaps one little step forward and then 2 large ones back – but, I can't quite explain it, I *cannot* get on with the C of E; so I thought: 'Well, at least I can try to be a Socialist which (for me) is a sort of, perhaps potty, attempt at putting the 2nd commandment into practice; and you know this RC business isn't recent – I've popped in and out of their churches since during the war – and more and more I find a *sweetness* and an *endeavour* towards holiness there, which I have never found anywhere else (this is the 'At Home' feelings). *All* their things which you find so odd, not to say wrong, are, for me, absolutely understandable.[108]

And in a further letter the same year she adds 'My darling, I simply lean and lean towards Rome.'[109] Probably as she wrote this letter she was under instruction, and not long after she was received into the Church of Rome. Joanna, her elder sister and her godmother (married with three young daughters and living in Derbyshire at Chapel-en-le-Frith) was present to support her; and at his own request John Stott met her priest, a well-known Roman Catholic figure in metropolitan circles:

I remember going to see him and he gave me something to read about the Seven Sacraments. I said to him, 'Surely you don't really believe all this, do you?' Joy was terribly shocked that I presumed to say such a thing to a Roman Catholic priest, but he said 'Yes I do; I believe it with all my heart.'[110]

As a brotherly act John Stott offered to be with Joy when she was received. Perhaps it is understandable that both she and her priest declined! In the event, the Church of Rome did not prove to be the permanent spiritual home that Joy had longed for. Her searching and exploring were to continue for much of the rest of her life.

TWELVE

University Missioner: Cambridge, London, Oxford and Durham

1

It is the long-established practice of the CICCU, the student Christian Union at Cambridge, to hold a triennial mission. Three years is a typical student 'generation', and a week-long mission every three years means that every undergraduate can share this particular opportunity to consider the claims of Christ. When John Stott received an invitation from the CICCU to be their missioner for November 1952 he had been Rector for less than a year; but remembering the missions held during his Cambridge years (even allowing for the difficulties of wartime) he had little hesitation in agreeing.

The two preceding missions had both been conducted by Donald Grey Barnhouse, Minister of Tenth Presbyterian Church, Philadelphia, well-known in America as a compelling preacher and expositor. His 1946 mission, 'the CICCU's first great mission after the war'[1] was a historic moment. It 'had about it a thrust of evangelistic power that had not been seen in British Universities since the nineteenth century',[2] an assessment which took as standard of comparison the D. L. Moody mission in Cambridge of 1882. It was that Moody mission which in turn led directly to the astonishing landmark in the call to overseas mission of 'the Cambridge Seven'.[3]

The history of the CICCU shows how the triennial missions have often been a landmark. They provide a new and distinct focus of evangelism towards which the Christian Union members can pray and prepare. The preparation itself is usually found to be of such value that even if the mission were cancelled, the Christian Union would still have benefited. The week's addresses provide an opportunity for a consecutive unfolding of God's purposes in Christ, a plan of redemption set within a Christian world-view, with time for a challenge to the individual to be repeated on succeeding nights, as well as at a host of satellite meetings and less formal occasions. Oliver Barclay supports his view that 'missions have been of enormous importance' in Cambridge by adding to these a further cogent reason:

> In the relatively circumscribed community of the University (Cambridge was not very large ...) a Mission can catch the ear of a large percentage of the University. Publicity, especially personal invitations, creates the situation where a large proportion of the student body can be talking about the theme of the Mission and it becomes easy to invite people to come and hear for themselves.[4]

Three years are a university lifetime for most undergraduates but not for Fellows of Colleges, Lecturers and Professors, the Senior Members of the university. When in 1952 John Stott (himself in residence at Ridley Hall only seven years before) was announced as missioner, many would have looked back to the Barnhouse missions of 1946 and 1949 and wondered if they were in for more of the same. Barnhouse had an immensely powerful personality, a dogmatic style of oratory, 'merciless with other views, including, in CICCU circles, those who did not share his pre-millennial view of the second coming.'[5] In his 1946 mission for example it was arranged that he should speak at a special meeting for members of the Faculty of Divinity. He did so, and the news spread rapidly among the members of the CICCU, received with a mixture of horror and awed respect, that he had chosen to speak from a text in Malachi 2, the prophet's judgment upon the unfaithful priests of Israel: 'I will spread dung upon your faces ...' Three years later, with this precedent vividly in mind, the President of the CICCU, John Sertin, was asked by the committee to sound Barnhouse out beforehand. Sertin was to discover what Barnhouse planned to say at the meeting for the Divinity Faculty, and try to steer him away from such a confrontational approach. Barnhouse listened to Sertin's careful enquiry, and replied 'I thought I would speak on a little text, "I will spread dung upon your faces ..."'[7] Nevertheless, the two Barnhouse missions saw many converted to Christ: including, for example, David Sheppard, later Bishop of Liverpool, and John Habgood, a young scientist from Eton and King's, who was to become Archbishop of York.

Again, as another CICCU mission approached, senior theologians of the Faculty of Divinity would remember only too well the dramatic moment in Great St. Mary's when Barnhouse illustrated God's hand of judgment. The congregation watched mesmerized as Barnhouse pictured the dropping of sinners one by one into hell: 'Poor lost sinner ... (one imaginary soul, held between finger and thumb, picked up and dropped), poor lost sinner, M.A. ... (another), poor lost sinner, Ph.D. ... poor lost sinner, D.D.'[6] 'But' adds Oliver Barclay, 'if he was rough, it was a language which the ex-service undergraduates understood, even if the more smooth seniors thought it bad taste.'[7] John Stott, by contrast, was a slighter, polished and gentlemanly figure, familiar with Cambridge and its ways, Rector of a West-end church, possessor of a First in the Theological Tripos and still remembered as an outstanding and unusual student. 'He was biblical, scholarly though not academic, firm though not caustic, more evidently a man with a love for people than some of the older preachers.'[8] Once again, the mission addresses took place in Great St. Mary's, the University Church. Basil Atkinson recorded how, when the CICCU mission committee asked for the use of the church, they were told it would be refused if 'that same man' were coming again.[9]

Crowds at this first John Stott mission were so great that chairs filled the side-aisles and some stood throughout the service. On the final evening, latecomers had to be turned away. 'I shall never forget,' Basil Atkinson wrote later, 'on the last night of the mission seeing a queue standing four deep up the whole nave of Great St. Mary's waiting to talk to the missioner.'[10] John Pollock, historian of the CICCU (and the CICCU President responsible for inviting Barnhouse in 1946), makes plain what was different. 'It was not so much the numbers attending [Barnhouse had drawn big crowds] which marked the mission as its spirit':

The controversial atmosphere of previous years had gone. From the very first night, when in response to the missioner's invitation over one hundred men and women asked for a copy of St. John's Gospel as a sign of 'sincere search for the truth,' there was a quiet determination in all parts of the University to face up to the issues of personal faith. The main addresses were plain unhurried Biblical expositions, almost unadorned with illustrations and without any attempt to force decision; the closest attention was given throughout; such was the desire for the truth that assistant missioners, as one of them commented, 'marvelled at the ease with which men and women accepted the claims of Christ, counted the cost and received Him.'[11]

No doubt in the sight of heaven 'the ease with which men and women accepted the claims of Christ' was due to the prayer-warriors who fought on their knees the spiritual battles of the week. But in human terms part of the reason must lie in the determination of the missioner 'to use the addresses to teach the central facts about the Christian faith as well as to give direct evangelistic challenge.'[12] The addresses formed a connected series, laying a foundation on which the assent of the mind could prepare for the surrender of the will and heart.

On the first Sunday a crowded church heard a clear and reasoned address answering the question, 'What is Man?' In a continuation service the Chief Missioner asked all those who were prepared to seek the truth honestly and without reservation to accept a copy of St. John's Gospel in the American Revised Standard Version and to promise to read it thoughtfully and carefully. Of the 150 who accepted this booklet, some 45% had decided before the end of the Mission week to follow Jesus Christ.[13]

Among the less familiar features of the mission was a special gathering for Senior Members on the Saturday before the opening Sunday: it seems to have been a plan borrowed from the OICCU, partly at least to avoid an impression of working behind the backs of Senior Members. The meeting was held in Trinity Hall, with the Master of Selwyn in the chair. John Stott, looking to Basil Atkinson 'very young and shy', said in his address that he felt Senior Members 'would like to know exactly what was the message that he would preach to the undergraduates. He then proceeded to tell them clearly the whole Gospel.'[14] The CICCU's official account (written with an eye to those who would be organizing the next mission in three years' time) makes clear that in such a gathering of Senior Members, 'On no account must any receive the impression that this is an attempt to evangelize them' – and in fact John Stott's main theme was an objective account, comprising the history of the CICCU within the university, some reference to past missions, and a careful statement of the theological position of the Union, 'showing that it was based on the Scriptures as the inspired Word of God and the centrality of Christ's death as the Substitute Saviour.' The CICCU Report adds, 'The meeting may be said to have been a success, for it was helpful in breaking down prejudices against the Union and the work of the mission.'[15]

The 1952 CICCU Mission proved to be something of a watershed, both for university evangelism in general, and for John Stott's sense of where his future priorities should lie. Oliver Barclay, writing long afterwards, from the experience of a lifetime in the service of IVF/UCCF (first as Assistant Secretary to Douglas Johnson for some twenty years, and then as General Secretary) believed that as far as IVF was concerned, John Stott's greatest single contribution was made by his university missions. 'He was a new kind of missioner in his thoughtful apologetic/evangelistic approach, and thus did much to create a new respect for evangelicals in the universities, even among the [theological] Liberals ...'[16] When he left Cambridge at the close of the mission, the student committee presented him with a leather-bound RSV preaching Bible which became his companion in the pulpit and in Bible exposition, bearing the honourable marks of constant use. Many who sat under his ministry in those years will remember it. It carried for him the significant associations of this first mission in his own university.

For John Stott himself, this Cambridge mission was to set the pattern for many future student missions, taking him regularly to campuses in the UK and across the world for the next twenty-five years. In Australia in 1986 he was asked by an interviewer how it all came about:

I think God has given me a concern for the student world ever since I was a student myself. I suppose I was a very typical student with the theological, philosophical and moral problems that all students have. It was partly that I felt in my student days in Cambridge that I was not given the pastoral care that I would have wished to have received. It may be that has given me a concern for students, so it was not so very long after I graduated that I was invited in 1952 to lead my first university mission in Cambridge, my own alma mater. For 25 years after that I was on the university mission circuit. The last university mission I felt it right to take was in 1977 exactly 25 years later, back in Cambridge. That was the fourth university mission in Cambridge I had the privilege of leading.[17]

Five years after the 1952 mission John Stott was back in Cambridge for the Freshers' weekend at the start of the academic year, October 1957. It was evident that the blessing of the Holy Spirit on the 1952 mission was still continuing, almost two student-generations later. 'I wish you could have been with me,' he wrote in *All Souls*, 'I shall not easily forget what I experienced':

It must surely be almost without precedent that 450 undergraduates should assemble in church on a Saturday night for the solid study of the Bible?

Then twice that number were crammed into the same church on the Sunday evening for the evangelistic service. They sat on chairs and hassocks in the aisles, sprawled tightly over the chancel and stood at the back when there was no sitting room left. Men outnumbered women by about 10 to 1. The bass unison of a myriad males seemed to rival the choirs of heaven, and one could not fail to be impressed by the thoughtful resolve of those who came forward to say they had committed their lives to Christ. The contemporary movement of the Spirit of God in the student world is one of the most encouraging signs of our generation.[18]

The universal testimony is that in the 1952 mission, preaching came into its own. For many who heard it, Christians and unbelievers alike, it remained a formative and unforgettable experience. An ordinand at Ridley Hall described it in terms of a discovery:

It was there, evening after evening in Great St. Mary's church, that I discovered, really I think for the first time, what expository preaching is. I have striven, very inadequately no doubt, to expound scripture in that kind of way ever since in the very different parishes in which I have served. No doubt scores and maybe hundreds of men will tell you the same sort of thing ...[19]

Nor was it only students who were aware that the preacher seemed anointed by the Holy Spirit in a special way. When, nearly twenty years afterwards, John Stott wrote to congratulate Owen Chadwick on his biography of Michael Ramsey, Chadwick's reply made plain that the impressions of the Cambridge mission of 1952 remained clear in his mind. 'Dear John', he wrote, 'Thanks for the most generous letter about *Michael Ramsey.* In return I can say that the finest Christian preaching I ever heard in all my life was the first sermon which you gave in Great St. Mary's to open a Cambridge mission ...'[20]

A few years later a South African undergraduate, newly converted to Christ, heard John Stott preaching one of the regular CICCU evangelistic sermons, and retained an equally vivid impression:

I remember his very red cheeks which seemed to shine out from the pulpit of Holy Trinity like a pair of setting suns. I remember too the twinkling eyes and the wry smile that accompanied his extraordinarily clear and lucid preaching. I remember thinking after one of those sermons that anybody who refused to respond to Jesus Christ after hearing that, would need their own intelligence questioned and their head read. It had all been so lucid, so clear, so compelling and convincing, that it seemed to me everyone should respond and say 'Yes' to Jesus at that very moment.[21]

The Cambridge mission was followed a year later by a student mission in London, with John Stott giving the main addresses at All Souls on two consecutive Sundays, together with two mid-week meetings in the Great Hall of King's College. There was in addition a team of assistant missioners based throughout the week in the forty or fifty widely dispersed colleges and halls of residence. Compared to Cambridge it was a low-key affair (at least as regards John Stott's personal involvement). Whereas in Cambridge the theme had been 'What think ye of Christ?' in London it was 'That ye might have life' (biblical quotations were commonly to follow the Authorized Version with its 'thee's' and 'ye's' for a few years yet).

Among those who came to the mission addresses was a young student at the University of London School of Pharmacy in Bloomsbury Square, James Parratt. He was a keen soccer player; and a fellow-member of the College team, a year ahead of him, invited him to one of the meetings of the Christian Union. The invitation was reinforced by a girl in his own year whom he had fallen in love with (and whom he later married). Because of this link with Christian Union members, he found himself attending the mission: God spoke to him in a new way and he was converted to Christ. In his diary for 1953, among the College soccer fixtures and the BBC subscription concerts at the Royal Festival Hall, the entry for 17 November 1953 reads: 'Rev. John Stott's address (John 3 v. 14) – have nailed my colours to the mast – became a Christian.' Looking back, more than forty years later, Professor James Parratt recalled that evening:

> On the Tuesday John Stott invited those who wished to 'nail their colours' to go forward at the end to meet him and he gave each one of us a copy of his booklet *Becoming a Christian* – which I still have. What moved me above anything else was the emphasis on the word 'MUST' in that verse [' ... so must the Son of Man be lifted up ...'] and the application in the next with the realisation that the 'whosoever' included me. It was as though it was only me that was being spoken to, although several others went forward.
>
> The background to this conversion experience is as follows. I did not come from a Christian background, had never (or seldom) been to church although there were believers in my year at school ... I remember we gave these Christians a tough time. After my own conversion I contacted them and there was much rejoicing! I am sure their prayers were part of the preparatory work of the Spirit.[22]

2

In the early part of 1954 All Souls and its Rector were deeply committed to Billy Graham's crusade at Harringay: but John Stott was already planning and praying for an Oxford mission later that year. Arrangements had to be made well in advance, and it was in November 1953, just a year after his first CICCU mission that the Vicar of St. Mary's, Oxford, the University Church, wrote to inform John Stott that the OICCU had approached him for the use of his church for the mission. He reported that 'reluctantly and only after taking counsel with the college chaplains' he had felt bound to refuse. The primary reason given was that the Bishop of Durham (Michael Ramsey) had conducted a Mission in the University in February 1953, and that a mission in November 1954, even under quite different auspices, would be too soon. There was also anxiety that such a mission might draw men away from their college chapels.[23] But other information from Oxford seemed to suggest a rather different agenda. The Rector of St. Aldate's wrote to say that Ramsey's mission, excellent in many ways, was inadequately followed up 'and the challenge to conversion was almost completely absent'. He continued:

It strikes me that the OICCU to-day is in the position the CICCU was about twenty years ago, unpopular with the Seniors but making real headway with undergraduates and still trying to establish their policy of separation, which is now the accepted fact in Cambridge. Personally, I think it was a pity they ever applied to the University Church before they have established themselves in this matter; but for that, the issue of the Mission would never have come before the Chaplains.

They have now applied to me to use St. Aldate's, which puts me in an awkward position vis-à-vis the Chaplains.

However, I am quite sure that if evangelism and evangelicalism are to be established in Oxford, this Mission ought to be held, and the OICCU ought to be supported in their policy, and although I shall probably make myself extremely unpopular with the Chaplains by lending the Church, I intend to recommend the PCC to do so ...

If you do come, as I sincerely pray you will, you will find the wicket much stickier than Cambridge, as there is little sympathy with the OICCU in high places, though most admit their effectiveness and numerical strength ... If the College Chaplains provided their needs, men would go, but if the Chaplains had the control of the Mission it would not be worth running. Evangelicalism here, I clearly see, will prove itself eventually by results and not by official sponsorship, and many of us will be behind you and, I hope, helping you in the Mission. The OICCU are a grand group and deserve all the strengthening we can give them. I hope you will recognise that officially it is going to be much more difficult than in Cambridge, but do come nevertheless, and I am quite sure this place is ripe for your message. We shall all be praying.[24]

Julian Charley, President of the OICCU (and later to be John Stott's curate) consulted the Principal of Wycliffe Hall, who encouraged him to proceed with plans for the mission – 'I have felt all along that John Stott as Missioner was most clearly guided by God.'[25]

Geraint Fielder lists as the keynotes of evangelical student life in the early 1950s 'the sinner's faith in the cross of Christ, the believer's love for the Word of God, and a warm recognition of Spirit-given, brotherly unity in those truths'. He continues:

> It was summed up in the title and content of the 1954 mission led by Stott – 'Christianity is Christ' – which was an exposition of basic Christianity. It was at that time that Tom Walker, later a travelling secretary [for IVF], found Christ as Saviour from sin.[26]

Tom Walker's story is not untypical. He went up to Oxford after National Service in the RAF 'an earnest high-church musician', intending to join the respectable and 'establishment' Oxford University Church Union – the OUCU. By mistake he found himself linked up with some members of the OICCU – the Oxford Inter-Collegiate Christian Union – and was invited to attend the first OICCU evangelistic address of term. Looking back, he realized that this had been an essential part of God's dealing with him, on the way to finding Christ for himself. But it was not something he welcomed at the time:

> I had particularly hated the piercing, direct preaching of Maurice Wood, now Bishop of Norwich, in the first sermon of term. I had been invited to what I had been told was THE University Sermon. I thought it would be a very respectable speech, probably in Latin, that any self-respecting church-goer ought to attend. It turned out to be a most penetrating exposition, guaranteed to pierce the armour of a self-righteous sinner. I wanted to leave quickly at the end, but unfortunately my friend who was sitting at the end of the pew wanted to wait for the after-meeting, and I did not have the guts to push past him. Had I done so, I might have walked out on God permanently, but he kept me there to face the pain of self-discovery. I went forward to receive a booklet from Maurice Wood, but I was not yet ready to accept Christ personally.[27]

On the Tuesday of the OICCU mission Tom Walker was reading some small booklets by John Stott that he had been given. He turned to one called *Personal Evangelism,* a guide to helping others find faith; and (though this was not addressed to his condition) it left him in no doubt that he had not yet discovered for himself a living relationship with God. So he turned to the booklet he should have read first, *Becoming a Christian,* which showed him why this was, and what to do about it: 'John put the steps to commitment so clearly in this booklet that I was driven to kneel by my bed in my room at Keble College, and prayed the prayer accepting Christ as Saviour and Lord.'[28]

It was a painful journey of self-knowledge and the humbling of human pride. Tom Walker described it in vivid terms in his book *Renew Us By Your Spirit*:

> But by the Tuesday of the mission week led by John Stott I could say it, and face the pain. 'Lord I realise that I am a sinner. I accept that you died on the cross to forgive my sins.' And then I said: 'and if you are alive from the dead I accept your promise and ask you to come into my heart by your Holy Spirit.' That was a big 'if' for me, since I had real difficulties over the resurrection. But nonetheless I had come to the point of accepting Christ's promise. That for me was the 'whoopee' experience of abounding and overflowing joy – a moment as real in my memory as if it were only yesterday. I remember getting up off my knees and dashing upstairs to a friend's room, shouting at the top of my voice: 'It's real! At last it's real!' I had an experience of God. His Holy Spirit had made Jesus personal to me at last. My friend's reply was cool and calculated: 'Well done,' he said, 'now let's go out and buy you a proper Bible with print large enough to read, and an alarm clock.' The discipline of keeping communion with God in order to grow into his love had begun.[29]

From this beginning, Tom Walker found himself three years later as chairman of the OICCU mission committee preparing for John Stott's second Oxford mission. He went on to be ordained and to be himself a leader of university missions, when the same booklet was used to help scores of students to faith in Christ.

3

The following year saw John Stott back in Cambridge as the guest of the authorities to preach the University Sermon. He took as his text Matthew 18:1–4, and as his theme 'A Child's Humility' – humility in learning, in receiving and in obeying, contrasted with human pride in our mind, our heart, our will: 'This is the criterion of greatness ... this is the meaning of Christian conversion.'[30] Six months later he returned for the triennial CICCU mission not to lead it this time, but as senior assistant missioner to Billy Graham, who had accepted the CICCU's invitation with John Stott's warm encouragement.

On the announcement of Billy Graham's Cambridge mission, a letter appeared in *The Times* over the signature of a Canon H. K. Luce, Headmaster of Durham School:

August 15 1955

Sir, The recent increase of fundamentalism among university students cannot but cause concern to those whose work lies in religious education. No branch of education can make terms with an outlook which ignores the conclusions of modern scholarship in that particular department of knowledge.

In this connexion the proposal that Dr. Graham should conduct a mission to Cambridge University raises an issue which does not seem to have been squarely faced by Christians in this country. Universities exist for the advancement of learning; on what basis, therefore, can fundamentalism claim a hearing at Cambridge? In other spheres, literary and aesthetic as well as scientific, an approach which pays no heed to the work of modern scholarship is unthinkable before a university audience; if it were made, it would be laughed out of court. 'Religion is different,' someone will say; let us not forget that, according to its founder, Christianity lays upon us the duty of loving God with mind as well as with heart and soul.

Is it not time that our religious leaders made it plain that while they respect, or even admire, Dr. Graham's sincerity and personal power, they cannot regard fundamentalism as likely to issue in anything but disillusionment and disaster for educated men and women in this twentieth-century world?

Yours obediently,
H. K. Luce

A spate of letters followed. Mervyn Stockwood, Vicar of Great St. Mary's, the University Church, was quick to point out, 'for the avoidance of misunderstanding', that his permission for Dr. Graham to use his church did not imply any endorsement of his views. Basil Atkinson wrote a careful letter in defence of Graham 'as one who is proud to be taking a small part in the preparation for Dr. Graham's proposed mission to this

University.' A brave letter from Bishop Gresford Jones, then assistant Bishop of Liverpool, provoked an intemperate reply from Michael Ramsey, Bishop of Durham, in support of Luce as one of his senior clergy:

August 20 1955

Sir, Many will be grateful to Canon Luce for raising in your columns the problem created by the revival of fundamentalist evangelism ...

How harmful the new fundamentalist movement has been may be illustrated by the appalling statement in the letter of Bishop Gresford Jones (August 18) that there is an "age-long battle between 'reason' and 'revelation'." Are we to forget the long line of great evangelists, including within living memory William Temple, whose emphasis upon decision and conversion has gone hand in hand with an insistence upon the duty of thought and the rationality of the Christian revelation?

Yours faithfully,
Michael Dunelm

This in turn was followed by F. R. Barry, the influential Bishop of Southwell: 'If I were vicar of St. Mary's, Cambridge, I should have no hesitation in lending the church for Dr. Graham's mission.' John Stott waited for ten days while the correspondence raged, and then sought to add some clarity to the prejudices which were being aired. His letter deserves to be quoted in full:

August 25 1955

Sir, It is surprising that your correspondents on this subject have not paused to define the term 'fundamentalism'. They have assumed that your readers understood the term, that they understood it in the same sense, and that it accurately describes Dr. Graham. Actually, the term clearly has different meanings, and Dr. Graham has publicly denied on more than one occasion that he is a fundamentalist.

That the word had a noble origin has been shown by Dr. Douglas Johnson in the March issue of *The Christian Graduate*. It appears to have been used first in connexion with the (American) Northern Baptist Convention of 1920 to describe the more conservative delegates who desired to 'restate, reaffirm, and re-emphasize the fundamentals of our New Testament faith.' The

Oxford Dictionary defines fundamentalism as 'strict adherence to traditional orthodox tenets held to be fundamental to the Christian faith,' and only adds the doctrine of scripture as an example of these tenets.

More recently, however, the term has become associated with certain extremes and extravagances, so that now 'fundamentalism' is almost a synonym for obscurantism, and it is generally used as a term of opprobrium. It appears to describe the bigoted rejection of all Biblical criticism, a mechanical view of inspiration and an excessively literalist interpretation of scripture. It is doubtless in this sense that your correspondents have employed the term, and in this sense that Dr. Billy Graham and others associated with him have repudiated it.

Clearly a distinction must be drawn between fundamentalism and the traditional, conservative view of scripture. It is neither true or fair to dub every conservative evangelical a 'fundamentalist'. The conservative evangelical desires to lay a truly Biblical emphasis on the necessity of divine revelation, to ascribe to the scriptures no meaner an authority than did our Lord and his apostles, and to accept the Biblical doctrine of scripture as they accept the Biblical doctrine of God and Christ and the Church. The real point at issue in this controversy, revealed by an episcopal disagreement in your columns, seems to be the place of the mind in the perception of divine truth.

All thoughtful Christians would agree with the Bishop of Durham, whose letter you published on August 20, that God's revelation is essentially reasonable, but would have to add that it is often in conflict with the unenlightened reason of sinful men. The Bible is itself aware of this conflict. 'As the heavens are higher than the earth, so are My ... thoughts than your thoughts' (Isaiah, lv, 9). 'Since, in the wisdom of God, the world did not know God through wisdom, it pleased God through the folly of what we preach to save those who believe' (I Cor. i, 21 R.S.V.). Our Lord himself gave thanks that the Father revealed his truth not to the 'wise and prudent' but 'unto babes' (Matthew xi, 25).

There is then in conversion not what the Bishop of Durham calls 'the stifling of the mind' but the humble (and intelligent) submission of the mind to a divine revelation. The proud human intellect still needs to be abased – in England as in Corinth – and the only way to enter the Kingdom of God is still to become like a little child.

Yours faithfully,
John R. W. Stott.

Clearly a nerve had been touched in the church's life. It is difficult to avoid the feeling that along with sincere concerns for intellectual integrity, deep-seated personal insecurities and resentments were coming to the surface. The undoubted success in attracting congregations, media attention, and testimonies to life-changing encounters with Christ were naturally not entirely welcome to men whose ministries seemed challenged by this young American Baptist. No doubt, too, it was annoying to have their tails tweaked in the pages of *The Times* by irreverent and uncommitted onlookers such as the author and barrister, Sir Lawrence Jones:

August 23 1955

Sir, Have your right reverend and reverend correspondents who are opposed to fundamentalism forgotten that at their own ordination they solemnly and publicly declared that they 'unfeignedly believed all the canonical scriptures of the Old and New Testament'?

Your obedient servant,
L. E. Jones

From the correspondence columns the debate moved into the body of the paper. The subject was concluded with a leader (anonymous but in fact written by T. E. Utley, a blind leader-writer who left the staff of the paper that year) by way of summing up. Utley saw 'the contemporary trend of Biblical scholarship' as strongly opposed to the nineteenth-century theological liberalism represented by some of the letter-writers: 'This approach to New Testament scholarship still has its advocates, but it is almost as dead as the earlier fundamentalism.' And at the heart of the matter lay the trustworthiness of revelation:

Dr. GRAHAM is not a fundamentalist in the older sense of the word. He preaches Christianity as a supernatural religion, not as a form of moral philosophy, and, in this respect, he has the support of contemporary Biblical scholarship. It may, indeed, be objected, as CANON LUCE would object, that it would be easier to induce those brought up in a technical civilization to accept personal allegiance to Christ if they were not also obliged to believe that Christ was capable of miracles. No doubt Dr. GRAHAM would reply that it is inconsistent to ask us to accept the evidence of the New Testament as conclusive on one point while treating it as fraudulent on all others.

But the leader concluded by suggesting that the real question was not so much Billy Graham's approach to Scripture but his methods of evangelism:

> Fundamentalism, indeed, is not the issue. What is really concerned in the discussion of Dr. GRAHAM'S methods is whether the mechanism of modern advertising is suitable to the task of religious conversion. Underlying this also is the older problem of whether the appeal of Christianity which is addressed to the whole personality can be addressed primarily to the emotions without the risk of distorting its whole character and making its effect, at the best, ephemeral and, at the worst, dangerous.[31]

In the interests of evangelical integrity, as well as 'the defence and confirmation of the gospel' and the pastoral implications of lingering uncertainties raised by the debate, John Stott contributed to the November issue of *Crusade* an article defining the history and proper meaning of the term 'fundamentalism', tracing it back to 'a series of twelve paper-covered books issued between 1909 and 1912 by the two wealthy Californian laymen, the brothers Lyman and Milton Stewart'. He concluded with four positive points: the absolute necessity of divine revelation; the biblical doctrine of Scripture; our Lord's view of the Old Testament; and the practical purpose of the Bible.[32]

But as *The Times* leader had suggested, the issue of fundamentalism was not the only bone of contention between some members of the ecclesiastical establishment and Billy Graham – a situation exacerbated by what they saw as his effrontery in preaching in a University Church. Michael Ramsey returned to the attack in his journal *The Bishoprick*,[33] and nailed his colours to the mast with the title of his brief article 'The Menace of Fundamentalism'. He had no hesitation in using the word 'heretical':

> I am not certain how far Billy Graham, a man of utter humility and simplicity, is completely at one with our English fundamentalism. He comes from a milieu which is very similar to it, but he has tried to dissociate himself from particular movements and he claims to preach the first steps of Christianity and to say 'now, for the rest, go on to one of the Churches.' There is evidence that he has genuinely done this. There is also evidence (notably from his recent mission in Cambridge) that he has taught the grossest doctrines and flung his formula 'the Bible says' over teaching which is emphatically *not* that of the Bible. He has gone. Our English fundamentalism remains. It is *heretical,* in one of the classic meanings of heresy, in that it

represents a fixation of distorted elements from the Bible without the balanced tradition of scriptural truth as a whole.[34]

Ramsey's article is an illustration of one of the recurring problems in any discussion of 'fundamentalism', namely a tendency to launch into intemperate condemnation and rebuttal before defining terms. The word quickly becomes a mere jibe, an easy way to dismiss uncongenial opinions – opinions which may in fact be founded on something very different from mere obscurantism. Cyril Bowles, the Principal of Ridley Hall, preaching the University Sermon in March 1958, called his hearers' attention to other forms of fundamentalism, adding that

> ... like Biblical fundamentalism, they are to be found chiefly in the Church of England. Since Dr. Ramsey caught sight of what he called the Menace and shouted 'Wolf!', numerous huntsmen have leapt into the chase. Some of these have been distinguished persons in hunting pink, so to say, whose words deserve careful attention, but the utterances of others have been less well advised, and it is remarkable that some of those who have attempted to pursue Biblical fundamentalism to the kill have themselves been fundamentalists of some other kind.
>
> Mostly they have been *ecclesiastical* fundamentalists. In place of the phrase 'The Bible says', they substitute 'The Church teaches'..."[35]

By the time the sermon was preached Dr. Gabriel Hebert had written at length under the title *Fundamentalism and the Church of God*. Possibly he was one of those whom Cyril Bowles would have described as 'distinguished persons in hunting pink'. Hebert was a member of the Anglo-Catholic Society of the Sacred Mission, and at that time tutor at their Theological College in Crafers, South Australia. Cyril Bowles commended his 'attempt to be fair and sympathetic',[36] and Hebert, unlike some who rushed into print, had done his opponents the courtesy of reading some of their publications. Nevertheless, his book pulled no punches in adopting Ramsey's pejorative language and describing fundamentalism '(in the evil sense)' as 'a grave menace to the Church of God'. Moreover he defined with exactitude those whose views he wished to address:

> It is with the conservative evangelicals in the Church of England and other churches, and with the Inter-Varsity Fellowship of Evangelical Unions, that this book is to be specially concerned ..."[37]

With this gauntlet flung down, J. I. Packer published a year later his *Fundamentalism and the Word of God*,[38] in part a reply to Hebert, and one which does not seem ever to have received from its opponents the attention it deserves. It appeared after Cyril Bowles' sermon, but in time to secure a footnote in the pamphlet based upon it and published shortly afterwards. In defending the evangelical from the charge of obscurantism, especially in his communication of the gospel, Dr. Packer concludes:

> J. R. W. Stott well sums up the position: 'In evangelism, then, we shall need to recognize that the men to whom we preach have minds. We shall not ask them to stifle their minds, but to open them, and in particular to open them to receive a divine illumination in order to understand the divine revelation. We shall not seek to murder their intellect (since it was given to them by God), but neither shall we flatter it (since it is finite and fallen). We shall endeavour to reason with them, but only from revelation, the while admitting our need and theirs for the enlightenment of the Holy Spirit.'[39]

Archbishop Ramsey gave little indication of understanding evangelicals nor even of much wishing to do so, though he could of course show great kindness to individuals. In 1961 he and Billy Graham were both at New Delhi for the Third Assembly of the World Council of Churches: they found themselves sitting together one day on the steps of the Assembly Building. Graham recalled the moment in his autobiography:

> 'Now Billy G' – he always called me Billy G or Billy Baptist – 'you know I don't agree with your methods. And I don't always agree with your theology. And in fact, Billy G, you've strengthened the evangelicals too much. That's the thing I'm afraid of.'[40]

Perhaps it was Ramsey's humour, it probably was; but many a true word is spoken in jest. He had no wish to see Anglican evangelicalism strong. Others, too, noticed and regretted this imbalance in his sympathies. When challenged in the House of Lords to say whether he was a Protestant, his answer was, to say the least, ingenuous. He replied to his questioner, Earl Alexander (a Baptist) that he was a Protestant 'precisely in the way in which the Prayer Book and the Anglican formularies use that term ...', the point being that (whether he remembered it or not) 'Protestant' is not a word used by the Prayer Book.[41] Talking with John Betjeman at the Old Palace, Canterbury, a few years after *The Bishoprick* article, his antagonism was unabated: 'He said the chief trouble with the C[hurch] of E[ngland] was the alarming increase of bigoted fundamentalists in it, who ought really to become Strict Baptists or some such extreme nonconformist sect.'[42]

Much later, when John Stott came to review Owen Chadwick's *Michael Ramsey: A Life*, the review was notable for its insistence that Ramsey nevertheless reverenced the Scriptures, defended orthodoxy and was a man of God:

> True, he was a Catholic, as Owen Chadwick makes clear but not, I think, at the expense of essential Evangelical truth. His distaste for the rather crude tactics of Willie Nicholson in his 1926 Cambridge University mission, and his later criticisms of the anti-intellectual emotionalism of some forms of evangelism, were surely reactions to 'fundamentalists', not to authentic Evangelicals. Preaching in West Germany in 1964, he declared that what we learn from Luther is primarily the supremacy of Holy Scripture, salvation by faith not by merit, and the priesthood of all believers. He really believed these evangelical truths ...
>
> This man of theology was also a man of God. It seems to be true that after the archiepiscopate of Geoffrey Fisher, the administrator and canon law reviser, Harold Macmillan diagnosed that the church now needed a Mary to replace a Martha. Bishop Charles Gore had said that 'it was barely possible to combine activities of being a good Christian and a good bishop.' But Ramsey gave the lie to this. The lasting impression which he left on people who met him was one of goodness and godliness. He loved and worshipped Christ.[43]

But as *The Times* leader-writer had shown, the Bible was not the only issue. Along with his vigorous condemnation of fundamentalism as he perceived it, Ramsey coupled an instinctive distaste for the kind of mission address which called for a decision. He would have agreed with the earlier tractarian bishop, Charles Gore, that such methods were unsuited for academic circles. Gore's biographer tells how at Oxford before the First World War

> ... arrangements were being made by college chaplains to hold a mission to the undergraduate members of the University early in the following year. Gore was asked to take it. At first he refused, declaring that he had never been able to attract individuals in such a way as to help them in their practice of religion. Afterwards he was persuaded. A characteristic scene was witnessed at one of the committee meetings. Someone had suggested that senior men should be posted in the University church to 'tackle' individual undergraduates after the services. 'Oh no,' said Gore, 'we will not

"accorst" men in the church. I think the method of public "accorsting" would be fatal. If you put yourself back into your undergraduate days, would you have wished to be "accorsted" publicly in the University church? Oh no. In a world of shadows some things are luminously clear. And one is that undergraduates would dislike to be publicly "accorsted" in the University church.' The proposal fell dead under the repeated strokes of the word "accorst."[44]

Ramsey, though (like Gore) an effective preacher in his own distinctive style, was equally unhappy with an evangelism that sought so specific a commitment. In the final paragraph of *The Bishoprick* article, he returned to this question; with the implication (in the light of what had gone before) that Billy Graham's evangelism was flawed, emotional, and dangerous. The circulation of *The Bishoprick* was small: but the influence of Michael Ramsey and his views considerable. Once again John Stott took up the challenge in the pages of *Crusade*, seeking to answer a series of questions: about the relative places of the mind, the emotions and the will in evangelism; about what doctrines should be included in the gospel presentation; and about seeking an immediate decision, leading to a definite and possibly sudden conversion.[45] This and his earlier article on fundamentalism were expanded and issued as a booklet which played a part in helping evangelicals to keep their nerve, and to offer reasoned answers to popular criticisms, in the face of this semi-official opposition.[46] It was appropriate that when the US edition was published three years later it should be introduced by Billy Graham. In his Foreword he welcomed the treatment of fundamentalism, which had 'lifted the truths behind this great word back to their rightful place in the church'; and commended the explanation of evangelism: 'His analysis of the elements of conversion is about the finest I have ever read.'

With hindsight, it is plain that the word 'Fundamentalism' was the worst possible basis on which to enter into serious debate on the nature of Scripture. To those who knew and respected the origin and history of the word, it denoted a firm adherence to divine revelation and the authority of the Bible as among the 'fundamentals' of the faith. But the term had become (and remains today) so overlaid with misrepresentation, and so associated with negative images of Christian life and understanding, as to have become little more than a means to discredit those who seek to uphold a higher view of inspiration than is acceptable in the current theological climate. Billy Graham himself, writing home from Scotland in the 1950s, told his wife how he was suffering at the hands of 'fundamentalists' who criticized his policies and (sometimes) his message. He wrote:

Some of the things they say are pure fabrications ... I do not intend to get down to their mud-slinging and get into endless arguments and discussions with them ... We are too busy winning souls to Christ and helping build the church ... If this extreme type of fundamentalism was of God, it would have brought revival long ago. Instead, it has brought dissension, division, strife, and has produced dead and lifeless churches.[47]

Although (as *Fundamentalism and Evangelism* makes clear) there was in the debate much confusion about the meaning of words, the essential heart of the issue was the authority of the Bible, and the nature and source of this authority. This was (and remains) a touchstone to the divisions between the liberal and the conservative evangelical. Many who felt in their hearts the reality of biblical inspiration and authority were driven by the assertiveness of contemporary biblical criticism into what seemed to them the only intellectually honest option open to them, a diminished view of Scripture. One such, perhaps more open and articulate than many, was Joe Fison, later Bishop of Salisbury. Before his ordination in 1934, at the age of twenty-eight, he was teaching in a missionary school in Egypt. In one of his later books he described an incident which brought self-knowledge with far-reaching consequences to his life and thought:

I shall never forget an incident in February 1933. I was in the small hall of the English Mission College in Cairo, of which I was then a member of the teaching staff. A Maltese boy named Nestor Cardullo came up to me and asked me the question: 'do you believe the whole Bible is true from Genesis to Revelation?' It was no time for quibbling: it was a genuine question and demanded a genuine answer. I gave it and replied 'Yes' and, as I said it, I knew for the first time that it was a lie and that I did not so believe it. That incident marked the end of eight or ten years of what I believed were fundamentalist convictions. During those years I had worked with the C.S.S.M. and had been one of the refounders of the O.I.C.C.U. ... All that time the basic presuppositions of biblical fundamentalism had underlain what I believed to be my religious convictions. On that 1933 morning in Cairo I did not change my views, but I suddenly discovered what my views were or, perhaps better, were not.[48]

By contrast, Billy Graham described how he met a somewhat similar crisis of faith in a different way. His friend Charles ('Chuck') Templeton had shared with him in some of his early travelling ministry, including their long preaching tour of Europe in the immediate aftermath of the Second World War. Two or three years later Billy Graham writes that his own faith 'was under siege'. He had found that his friend (then at Princeton Theological Seminary) was undergoing serious theological misgivings over the authority of Scripture. 'My respect and affection for Chuck were so great that whatever troubled him troubled me also ... [49] Matters came to a head one night when Graham, with his largest-ever Crusade looming up on him, found himself asking 'Can I trust the Scriptures?'

I had to have an answer. If I *could not* trust the Bible, I could not go on. I would have to quit the school presidency. I would have to leave pulpit evangelism. I was only thirty years of age. It was not too late to become a dairy farmer. But that night I believed with all my heart that the God who had saved my soul would never let go of me.

I got up and took a walk. The moon was out. The shadows were long in the San Bernardino Mountains surrounding the retreat center. Dropping to my knees there in the woods, I opened the Bible at random on a tree stump in front of me. I could not read it in the shadowy moonlight, so I had no idea what text lay before me. Back at Florida Bible Institute, that kind of woodsy setting had given me a natural pulpit for proclamation. Now it was an altar where I could only stutter into prayer.

The exact wording of my prayer is beyond recall, but it must have echoed my thoughts: 'O God! There are many things in this book I do not understand. There are many problems with it for which I have no solution. There are many seeming contradictions. There are some areas in it that do not seem to correlate with modern science. I can't answer some of the philosophical and psychological questions Chuck and others are raising.'

I was trying to be on the level with God, but something remained unspoken. At last the Holy Spirit freed me to say it. 'Father, I am going to accept this as Thy Word – by *faith!* I'm going to allow faith to go beyond my intellectual questions and doubts, and I will believe this to be Your inspired Word.'

When I got up from my knees at Forest Home that August night, my eyes stung with tears. I sensed the presence and power of God as I had not sensed it in months. Not all my questions were answered, but a major bridge had been crossed. In my heart and mind, I knew a spiritual battle in my soul had been fought and won. [50]

To read the full account is to see that this was not simply a blind abdication of reason, nor the betrayal of the God-given powers of mind and thought. Billy Graham had done much study, reading, thinking and praying. The experience of that night (commemorated by a bronze tablet which marks the 'Stone of Witness' at Forest Home where Billy Graham sat, 'his Bible spread open on a tree stump'[51]) was the culmination of a long search for a place where mind and heart could rest which was at once spiritually satisfying and intellectually honest.

John Stott has certainly looked more closely into the intellectual issues; and would be more guarded about any misplaced surrender of the mind: a First in theology is witness to that. But he takes the position, nevertheless, of

> ... both the rightness and the reasonableness of submitting to the authority of Scripture.
>
> First, to accept the authority of the Bible is a Christian thing to do. It is neither a religious eccentricity, nor a case of discreditable obscurantism, but the good sense of Christian faith and humility. It is essentially 'Christian' because it is what Christ himself requires of us. The traditional view of Scripture (that it is God's word written) may be called the 'Christian' view precisely because it is Christ's view.[52]

This, he has always believed and taught, is the clinching argument:

> ... the ultimate issue in the question of authority concerns the Lordship of Christ. 'You call me "Teacher" and "Lord",' he said, 'and rightly so, for that is what I am' (John 13:13). If Jesus Christ is truly our teacher and our Lord, we are under both his instruction and his authority. We must therefore bring our mind into subjection to him as our teacher and our will into subjection to him as our Lord. We have no liberty to disagree with him or to disobey him. So we bow to the authority of Scripture because we bow to the authority of Christ.[53]

But this position, simple as it sounds, was not reached without something of the same painful questionings described by Billy Graham in the quotation above. Nor, because it concerned truth, could it ever be regarded as finally closed. As late as 1960, writing to a friend and colleague, he opened his heart to describe 'two problems' with which he was continuously wrestling:

> I am not sure how far my 2 problems are related – panic from time

to time and the more continuous nagging fear that our conservative position is untenable. But whether they are related or not, I'm sure you are right that the devil is in them both. And I am seeking to resist him. Yet I need help and advice as to what weapons to employ in self-defence. I wonder very much whether a disciple of Him who is the Truth should dismiss his doubts as temptations without examining them at all. Not that I imagine I (or anyone else) will ever get a complete answer to every problem, but that I think I should by study and prayer grasp more firmly the general and positive principles on which our view of the Bible rests. To this end I've been greatly helped this holiday by reading carefully Geldenhuys' 'Supreme Authority'. I expect you know it. I think his 2nd main chapter on the unique authority of the apostles properly so-called (*i.e.* the Twelve and Paul) is first class and very helpful …

I have often thought that these 2 problems *were* allowed as my 'thorn in the flesh'. McCheyne (whom I've been enjoying) writes 'No pain, no palm; no cross, no crown; no thorn, no throne; no gall, no glory!' In this I rejoice, because I do not suffer in any other way – except temptation and being a despised evangelical. I am gladly willing to bear this thorn, so long as it doesn't make me 'a house divided against itself' or (as you say) a 'double-minded man'. – But more when we meet![54]

By the 1980s, the 'submissive spirit' of the Christian heart to Scripture was one of his definitive marks of evangelicalism in his 'response' to David Edwards in their published dialogue, *Essentials*:[55]

I think I would characterise Evangelicals as those who, because they identify Scripture as God's word, are deeply concerned to submit to its authority in their lives (whatever their precise formulation of the doctrine of Scripture may be). In other words, the hallmark of Evangelicals is not so much an impeccable set of words as a submissive spirit, namely their *a priori* resolve to believe and obey whatever Scripture may be shown to teach. They are committed to Scripture in advance, whatever it may later be found to say. They claim no liberty to lay down their own terms for belief and behaviour. They see this humble and obedient stance as an essential implication of Christ's lordship over them.

But this is to leap forward over many years of continuing theological and biblical studies. Perhaps the last word on the Fundamentalist controversy of the 1950s should lie with John Stott's mischievous quotation almost twenty years afterwards of a *jeu d'esprit* from the editor of *Crusade*, published at the time. 'By the mid-nineteen-fifties,' John Stott wrote, 'ecclesiastical authority became aware of the growing strength of evangelicalism, and was alarmed by it.' He continued:

> In August 1955 Canon H. K. Luce of Durham wrote a letter to *The Times* deploring the fact that Dr. Billy Graham had been invited to lead a mission in the sacred precincts of Cambridge University. Billy Graham's approach ('which pays no heed to the work of modern scholarship') would, he declared, be 'unthinkable before a University audience'. If it were made, 'it would be laughed out of court'. This provoked a long and lively correspondence, and the following verse by Timothy Dudley-Smith:

> > O, hang your head for Cambridge
> > Where, deluded in their youth,
> > There are students who would still regard
> > The Word of God as truth;
> > Who in spite of current catchwords
> > And the Modern Churchman's creed,
> > Hold a fundamental gospel
> > For a fundamental need.

> > > How right that someone should reprove
> > > These heresies and crimes
> > > By a cannonade from Durham
> > > In the columns of *The Times*.

> > O, hang your head for Cambridge;
> > She is sorely led astray
> > For we know that Dr. Graham
> > Will have nothing new to say.
> > Let him preach his obscurantist views
> > Of what salvation means
> > At Wembley or at Windsor
> > But not to *King's* or *Queens'*.

> > > For a Sovereign and her subjects
> > > He is simple and sincere;
> > > But to preach to modern scholars
> > > Is a laughable idea!

O, hang your head for Cambridge
That such things are now condoned
Where the *White Horse Inn* was jeered at
And where Simeon was stoned;
Will you lay aside your learning
And demean your ancient name
To consider what the Bible said
Before the critics came?

You cannot preach to men in gowns
What passed with men in skins;
You must have modern scholarship
To save from modern sins.[56]

4

Though Billy Graham had preached in the New England universities in 1950[57] and in Oxford in 1954, and had been for four years the President of Northwestern Schools, comprising a Bible school, a liberal arts college and a theological seminary, the prospect of conducting a full-scale university mission under the auspices of the CICCU began to appear more and more daunting. His name had inevitably been linked both with theological controversy over the fundamentalism issue, and with criticism of transatlantic techniques of evangelism. William Martin in his massive account of Billy Graham's ministry takes up the story:

Graham, ever insecure about his lack of advanced theological education, dreaded the meetings and feared that a poor showing might do serious harm to his ministry and affect 'which way the tide will turn in Britain.' Had he been able to do so without a complete loss of face, he would have canceled the meetings or persuaded some better-qualified man to replace him. 'I am scared stiff about preaching at Cambridge,' he told Stephen Olford, who counselled him 'not to get involved in a philosophical approach or to try to do something that was out of his depth, lest he be discredited for inaccuracies,' and to remember that he was preaching not to students but to sinners, and should keep things simple.[58]

Writing in his autobiography forty years later, Billy Graham quoted from his letter to 'my trusted friend, John Stott', written not many weeks before he was booked to arrive in Cambridge:

'I have been deeply concerned and in much thought about our Cambridge mission this autumn,' I wrote John candidly. 'I do not know that I have ever felt more inadequate and totally unprepared for a mission. As I think over the possibility for messages, I realize how shallow and weak my presentations are. In fact, I was so overwhelmed with my unpreparedness that I almost decided to cancel my appearance, but because plans have gone so far perhaps it is best to go through with it ... However, it is my prayer that I shall come in the demonstration and power of the Holy Spirit, though I am going to lean heavily on you, Maurice, and the others.'[59]

A copy of this letter went to Hugh Gough, Bishop of Barking, the only bishop in England willing to identify himself with Billy Graham before Harringay. He too had proved a staunch friend and adviser and from on board ship, about to sail for Canada, he wrote a reply full of counsel and encouragement:

... I can well understand your feelings of apprehension about Cambridge, but Billy do *not* worry. God has opened up the way so wonderfully and has called you to it and so all will be well. If I may be bold enough to give one suggestion, I would say 'keep to the simplicity of your message'. Do not regard these men as 'intellectuals'. Appeal to their *conscience*. They are sinners, needing a Saviour. *Conviction of sin*, not intellectual persuasion, is the need. So many preachers fail at this point when they speak to university men. So, Billy, keep to the wonderful clear simple message God has qualified you to preach and which He honoured wonderfully in London and Glasgow.[60]

The opening night of the Cambridge mission was Sunday, November 6th. The previous evening was Guy Fawkes day – the traditional night for bonfires and fireworks – and also Poppy Day, when students were out in force collecting for Earl Haig's Fund. As Billy Graham spoke to the CICCU in the Debating Hall of the Union, a fire-cracker was thrown through an open window in spite of a strong police presence outside. *Varsity*, the student newspaper, reported that 'threats to kidnap him did not materialize' and that Billy had told reporters 'I shall be disappointed if I am not kidnapped. I have been looking forward to it.'[61]

There was in fact a little cloak-and-dagger activity, with a pre-arranged change of cars and clandestine signals from one of the university Proctors to forewarn of possible trouble ahead. All went smoothly, however, and Billy Graham met first with a group of Senior Members on the Saturday afternoon before the mission began.[62] John Stott arranged that Graham should have a chance to talk privately with C. S. Lewis, then a Fellow of Magdalene, who had migrated from Oxford a year before to be the first holder of a new Chair as Professor of Medieval and Renaissance English. Lewis himself had suffered hostility in Oxford for what he himself called his 'hot-gospelling', which may have contributed to his being passed over for Professorships there. The three of them met in Magdalene. Billy Graham recalled how –

> ... we talked for an hour or more. I was afraid I would be intimidated by him because of his brilliance, but he immediately put me at my ease. I found him to be not only intelligent and witty but also gentle and gracious; he seemed genuinely interested in our meetings. 'You know,' he said as we parted, 'you have many critics, but I have never met one of your critics who knows you personally.'[63]

Nevertheless, Billy Graham felt that he was taking on a task for which he was 'inadequate and unqualified and in need of prayer'. The university 'loomed as a den of intellectual and theological lions.'[64]

The mission itself began on the Sunday evening in the University Church. Mervyn Stockwood, the Vicar, very recently appointed, had been unsure whether to make his church available, being no respecter of the CICCU or their message:

> The CICCU wanted to take possession of the church for a week and during that week to exclude the Bishop of Ely and myself from their services. The majority view was to refuse the request as it was thought that it would not be appropriate to hold a hot-gospel mission within the precincts of the University Church. The Bishop and the Vice-Chancellor took a different view. If I was in Great St. Mary's each evening and if all the arrangements were approved by me, the evangelistic temperature might be reduced and the gospel became less 'hot'. I did as they required and the CICCU grudgingly accepted the compromise. It was a relief to turn from their committee, most of whom were narrow-minded enthusiasts, to Billy Graham himself.[65]

In keeping with these opinions, Mervyn Stockwood sought to identify Great St. Mary's with Billy Graham personally, and to disassociate it from the CICCU. Basil Atkinson, that experienced if hardly impartial observer of the Cambridge scene, was well aware of these undercurrents and confided to his *Recollections:*

The impact of all this upon the Billy Graham mission was substantial. It occupied two Sundays out of the Great Saint Mary's series. Although it was a CICCU mission, it was incorporated into the Great St. Mary's card and announced as the personal message of the Gospel – or perhaps 'the Gospel for the individual' – as opposed to other sermons in the series which proclaimed the 'social Gospel' etc. The incumbent insisted not only on taking part in the service, but on giving the blessing from the pulpit each night, so that Billy Graham had to come down from it to make room for this anti-climax.[66]

On the first evening of the mission undergraduates and their friends queued, sometimes for forty-five minutes, in a long line stretching back up King's Parade, and round the corner by St. Benet's Church. An eye-witness account captures something of the scene inside the church:

At half-past eight there were some 1,200 people in the church, filling the nave, the great galleries, and the tiny West gallery by the great organ. Some seventy counsellors sat in the choir stalls and on the chairs in the chancel. The pulpit (which moves on rails in the floor) was now standing in the centre of the church, just below the chancel steps.

The organ was playing softly when Dr. Graham made his appearance. With him was the Rev. J. R. W. Stott, his Chief Assistant Missioner, and the Vicar of the University Church who introduced the Mission with a few words and welcomed Dr. Graham to Great St. Mary's.

Mr. Stott led the congregation in a hymn, and then prayed for the Mission, and especially for those who were seeking God. After a reading of Scripture there was a second shorter hymn, during which Billy Graham, in his preaching gown and doctor's hood, climbed into the pulpit and surveyed his congregation. He began with a personal word of gratitude for his welcome, and spoke of the sense of weakness with which he approached his Cambridge Mission. Then, not without humour, he began to enlarge on his theme of the previous afternoon – the critical world situation in which we stand. He quoted authors, journalists, statesmen, divines; almost imperceptibly the first authoritative declaration 'The Bible says ...' sounded through the church.

Graham preached for something over thirty-five minutes, and at the conclusion of his address he invited men who wished either there and then to receive Christ, or to set themselves during the week to seek for Him, to remain behind as the church emptied. He promised that in ten minutes he would return, to explain simply the way to Christ, and with that he concluded his address with prayer. The Vicar gave the blessing, and the three ministers filed into the vestry.

All over the church men and women began to move, thronging the too-small aisles and gangways, drifting home. For some little time it seemed that very few were accepting Graham's invitation to remain. But when he returned and asked all those who were in church to make their way to the front pews, over a hundred people gathered below the pulpit.[67]

While Billy Graham's manifest sincerity earned him respect and a fair hearing from the great majority of those present, it was not surprising that there should be opposition. Tam Dalyell, Old Etonian and future Labour Member of Parliament, was at that time an undergraduate of King's College, following National Service as a Trooper with the Royal Scots Greys. Mervyn Stockwood's biographer, Michael De-la-Noy, quotes Dalyell as saying that he went to Great St. Mary's with the express purpose of heckling the preacher: 'I dared to interrupt Billy Graham, and all hell was let loose on my unsuspecting head. I don't think this had happened to Billy Graham before and the Vicar (*sic*) of All Souls, Langham Place, who also happened to be there, said there was evil – me, presumably! – in the house.'[68] According to the recollections of others present at the time this is a highly fanciful reconstruction. Billy Graham was well used to dealing with hecklers, and though John Stott remembers that there was a heckler one night sitting prominently in the North Gallery, his recollection is that Billy Graham took no notice and he is certain that he himself made no attempt to intervene.[69] Tam Dalyell was to become in parliament an inveterate heckler of party leaders on both sides of the House.

Better authenticated is the clear recollection of an Australian Rector, Lance Shilton, who was at Tyndale House spending part of his honeymoon in post-graduate study. He recounts in his autobiography how in the course of one of Billy Graham's addresses, when he was emphasizing human sinfulness, someone shouted at him from the gallery, 'What about the love of God, Billy?' – to which Billy Graham replied 'I'm coming to that' and continued with his sermon.[70]

In spite of good attendances and serious enquirers, Billy Graham himself, while thankful for every sign that God was honouring the mission, was far from comfortable. It was his first university mission in England (though he told reporters that he hoped to do many more).[71] Inevitably he had heard striking accounts of the John Stott mission three years before. John Stott was his closest adviser in Cambridge, his Chief Assistant Missioner, and a man who had gained his respect and friendship. Indeed, it was during this time that he felt he first got to know him, though they had often met before.[72] Billy Graham was humbly aware that John Stott was equipped for a ministry to Cambridge in ways that he was not. There is a typical story of the time recalling what was an almost daily joke, of the two men going round and round in the revolving door of the University Arms Hotel, each trying to accord the other precedence, and unwilling to be the first out! Inevitably, as Billy Graham prepared his addresses with such an audience in mind, he tried, in his biographer's words, 'to turn himself into a John Stott':

> 'I was really feeling boxed in and inadequate,' comments Billy. 'I felt that John ought to be the preacher, and I should have been his assistant. John is one of my dearest friends, but he can also be a critic. And I felt in the first two or three nights I was preaching to please John rather than the Holy Spirit.'
>
> To Stott himself it did not seem that Billy Graham at Cambridge pandered to the intellect of his hearers. Dons who, on those first three nights in the ancient University Church, detected Billy's unease presumed it arose from his being confined to a pulpit and a geneva gown, without Barrows or Shea or a thousand voice choir. When they mentally appraised his sermons as theological exercises the marks awarded were low. Though undergraduates listened hungrily Billy knew that he was not getting through to their hearts.

Then came the break-through:

> Following the third sermon, the day after his thirty-seventh birthday, he wrestled with this desire to make an appeal to the intellect. He threw aside the prepared sermons and on the Wednesday night preached once again as if before the most ordinary audience in the world.[73]

David Watson, an undergraduate at St. John's College and destined himself to be a well-known evangelist, was one of those who was quick to learn from Billy Graham's experience. In his autobiography he recorded his personal impressions:

> In sweeping contrast to the dithering caution of most academic theologians, who were efficiently undermining the faith of some of my friends, Billy Graham led a mission to the university in

November 1955. Interestingly, when he tried, somewhat unsuc-
cessfully, to be academic, his preaching lacked power. But when
he accepted the apparent foolishness of the message of 'Christ
crucified' and preached it with simplicity and integrity, the power of
God's Spirit was manifestly at work, changing the lives of many
undergraduates. It was a lesson I have never forgotten.[74]

By the end of the week very large numbers – one unofficial estimate said
five hundred – had sought counselling and made or renewed a
commitment to Christ. 'History will begin to show,' John Stott wrote to
his own praying congregation, 'but only eternity will finally reveal, how
much was accomplished during that week.'[75]

He also wrote personally to Billy Graham immediately after the
mission and received this reply:

Kensington Palace Hotel
De Vere Gardens
London, W. 8

November 21, '55

My dear John,
This is the first free moment I have had in a week – please forgive
the delay in answering your wonderful letter. I think I will frame it
and hang it in my study. It was about the finest letter I have ever
received from any of my personal friends.

The Cambridge Mission of November 1955 will live in my
memory for ever as one of the highlights of my ministry! I learned a
great deal about how to conduct University Missions that I can use
profitably in the States ... but John I learned more from you than
all the rest ...

We are both young with most of our ministry before us. It is my
prayer that our friendship will grow and deepen.. and be used of
God as was the friendship of Wesley and Whitfield. There are few
men that I have met and known for so short a time whom I have
grown to love and appreciate as I have you, John ...

Thank you for all you meant to me at Cambridge –

God Bless You
Billy [76]

5

The Cambridge mission was in November 1955. In February of the following year John Stott was in Durham for his first visit as missioner for the DICCU, the Durham Inter-Collegiate Christian Union. It was this prospect which precipitated Michael Ramsey's attack in *The Bishoprick*, 'The Menace of Fundamentalism'. Ramsey wrote: 'It sweeps schoolboys into its camps and undergraduates into its revival missions', which suggests that he was well informed about the DICCU's missioner. In the article he sought to discredit the doctrine of 'penal substitution' as taught by the IVF, and to drive a wedge between Billy Graham's teachings – 'a man of utter humility and simplicity' – and what he called 'our English fundamentalism' which he denounced as at once heretical and sectarian. More, he arranged a series of lectures on the Christian faith to coincide with the mission services.[77] With such a publication circulating in Durham over the signature of the diocesan bishop, and with the mission under attack in the cathedral on the Sunday morning from Canon Stanley Greenslade, Van Mildert Professor of Divinity, the first of the mission services took place on the Sunday evening. There could be no doubt in the minds of anyone that it was unwelcome to the authorities of diocese, cathedral and university. 'The pressure on a missioner in such circumstances can be enormous,' writes Geraint Fielder. 'Does he "answer" the critics or does he go straight ahead with his direct task?' Michael Griffiths, also an assistant missioner, remembers John Stott's Wednesday evening address in particular:

> He preached magnificently from the second half of 1 Peter 2 on the death of Christ: expounding it first as exemplary 'that we might follow his steps' but then pointedly that Peter could not leave it there and went on to show it was also substitutionary. In the post-mortem the following morning some of us expressed the view that he was possibly over-conscious of the critical hearers from the theological faculty, and that he should 'take the gloves off'. This he did on the Thursday night in a superb exposition of Revelation 3:20: 'Who is it standing at the door?' – One whose face shines as the sun in its strength. 'What is he doing?' – Not kicking the door down with feet like burnished bronze, or deafening them with a voice like the sound of many waters, but knocking and counselling. 'What does he want to do?' – Come in. 'What must we do?' – Not pass our collection under the door or pray through the keyhole, but open the door!
>
> It was a great mission: probably the best of all those I went to during my three years as an IVF Travelling Secretary.[78]

One of those who attended every night of the mission was J. P. Hickinbotham, the new Principal of St. John's College, Durham, and one of Ramsey's examining chaplains. John Martin, President of the DICCU at the time, noted how 'St. John's College took on a much more pronouncedly evangelical character from that time – both staff and students.'[79] Hickinbotham's appointment to St. John's had come as a great relief to evangelicals in Durham, following a theologically liberal regime: 'he certainly began the process of stronger evangelical commitment from the first.'[80] This in turn was felt at Wycliffe Hall, Oxford, when Hickinbotham became Principal in 1970. Twenty-five years later, so had the climate changed, the DICCU held the closing meeting of their 1979 mission in Durham Cathedral, 'between the bones of Bede and the tomb of Cuthbert.'[81]

6

The second half of the 1950s saw John Stott undertaking overseas missions in the universities of North America and then of Australia and South Africa. In Great Britain he led a second OICCU mission in November 1957, a second CICCU mission in November 1958, and a second Durham mission in February 1959. Out of these experiences was born MUTS, an acronym for 'Ministers in University Towns'. John Stott convened the first meeting, little more than a gathering of a few friends in Oxford, where the Rector of St. Ebbe's, Basil Gough, acted as host. Gradually it grew in membership to include churches not only in London, Durham, Oxford and Cambridge, but in Newcastle, York, Leeds, Manchester and Birmingham, in Bristol and Exeter, Reading and Norwich. Bertie Lewis from Aberystwyth was a Welsh member: Philip Hacking from St. Thomas, Edinburgh, and George Duncan from St. George's, Tron were a link with Scotland. As membership grew it began to include non-Anglican churches (as St. George's, Tron) and soon a considerable representation attended from Free and Independent churches: a shared concern, and so a perennial topic for discussion, was 'Preaching for a Student Congregation'. In due course Oliver Barclay, on the staff of IVF/UCCF, took over the administration; and soon a few Brethren Assemblies sent delegates. This began to raise questions over the initial M for Ministers; and when some large Polytechnics were added it was no longer appropriate to think only of 'University Towns'. So MUTS became CLISS, 'Church Leaders in Student Situations', and added a 'Broadsheet' to its annual day conference.

All this, like the Eclectic Society, was part of John Stott's conviction that informal 'networking' was a key means to encourage, to disseminate good practice, and to forward the strategic vision of a student generation for Christ. He has always been concerned to try to see that in any appointment to an evangelical church in a 'student situation', a minister or leader should be chosen likely to attract, and be able to exercise a biblical ministry among, the student population. This in turn has done something to help members of student Christian Unions to know what it is to belong to an active local church; and to seek such continuing membership when they graduate.

Early in 1958 John Stott widened his own student ministry, which until then had been largely Oxbridge, Durham and London, with a mission to Loughborough College, strong in engineering and teacher training, with a considerable number of overseas students. The Christian Union had been founded only fourteen years earlier; but in that short time had become one of the strongest in the Technical Colleges. Something like half the college came to one or more of the mission addresses.[82]

Returning to Oxford in 1957 it was heartening to see that both the Chairman and the Treasurer of the student Mission Committee were converts from the John Stott mission of three years before. In reporting on the 1957 mission to his own congregation he added:

I was again impressed by the careful and thorough organization undertaken by the undergraduates themselves. No stone was left unturned. Every detail had been planned. 3,500 prayer partners from all over the world had been enrolled, and of the £1,200 budget, £1,191 had been received by the time the mission began. I was particularly touched by the thoughtfulness of the students who equipped my study next to the bedroom in the hotel where I was staying, supplying me not only with a telephone, a duly-ruled engagement book and vases of flowers, but with a shelf of Christian books to keep me on the straight and narrow, and a little box of shillings for the electricity meter![83]

The main mission meetings were to be held in St. Aldate's, where once again Keith de Berry was showing himself to be a staunch friend of evangelism and of the OICCU; and on Sundays in the Wesley Memorial Church. The general title was still the familiar 'What think ye of Christ?', and the eight main addresses posed other biblical questions: 'What is Man?', 'Ought not Christ to have suffered?', 'How can a man be born when he is old?' Perhaps to many Cambridge graduates, Oxford is always something of an enigma. Certainly 'The Rector's Letter' in *All Souls* asking for the prayers of the congregation in the month of the mission confessed to some anxiety, even while acknowledging that 'the contemporary movement of the Spirit of God in the student world is one of the most encouraging signs of our generation.' He continued:

I should greatly value your prayers as I go from November 9 to 18 to Oxford to lead for the second time the OICCU's triennial mission in the University. The detached, philosophical atmosphere of this University I find both cramping and oppressive. The Oxford undergraduate is ready to be interested, but reluctant to be committed. To him life often seems a drama, of which he is a spectator; he tends to scorn the enthusiast who insists on jumping on to the stage to play a part himself. So I shall go to Oxford, as Paul went to Corinth, 'nervous and rather shaky' (J. B. Phillips' translation of 1 Cor. 2:3), knowing that only the power of the Holy Spirit can enlighten the blind and awaken the dead.[84]

It was no surprise then when (predictably, as the editor admitted) the report of the mission in *The Isis,* the student journal, was implacably hostile. In the familiar currency of juvenile polemics it compared the missioner to 'some Scoutmaster addressing his troop before a hike':

The mission had nothing to tell us which we cannot read in any text-book on the meaning of the Protestant faith. The method in which the sermons were delivered did not excite the audience to a new pitch of religious devotion. They merely reaffirmed a faith which we did or did not have. The University, with its schools of philosophy and theology, history and the rest, all of which have dealt with the problems presented by Christianity during the last few hundred years was totally ignored ... To show oneself to be so completely out of touch either with modern Christian thought (no modern theologian believes it to be necessarily true that God created the moral order) or with modern philosophy as Mr. Stott has done is to show oneself to be utterly unfit to address a University. However O.I.C.C.U. is to be congratulated on choosing this preacher: because it shows how little the University means to them, and how desperately bad English education must be that so many people can take such ideas seriously without having the means to question them ... If God exists, a possibility which one cannot logically quite disregard, we can only hope that Mr. Stott is quite wrong in limiting, defining, and branding him as he does.[85]

Among the letters the following week was one signed FRESHMAN:

Your correspondent writes that Mr. Stott succeeded in making Christianity sound unattractive; I wonder if he stayed on for the continuation services. If so, he would have seen the edifying sight of people as educated, critical and intelligent as himself going forward as a witness to the fact that they had that evening accepted Christ.[86]

The OICCU reported attendances of 600–900 each night, with a high proportion remaining each night to the continuation service. Over one hundred students made a profession of faith during the week.[87]

Experience in university missions had often demonstrated their value as a training ground to the younger 'assistant missioners' who took part. The OICCU mission of 1957 produced further evidence of this in a letter written more than thirty years afterwards:

> Many years ago, in 1957, I was one of the missioners, sharing in a mission which you led at Oxford University. For me it was a memorable experience as a young Methodist Minister home on my first furlough from Ghana. I was assigned to University College. I think I received far more than I was able to give during that mission. Your presentation of the Gospel certainly helped me to express the message more clearly in my ministry. My reason for writing to you now relates to that time. A few months ago, late last year in fact, I met a keen and active Christian named John Tyman – for many years Professor of Geography at Brisbane University in Australia, and now Religious Education Advisor to the Schools in Queensland. When I asked him how he came to know Christ, he told me it was during that Mission to Oxford University that he made his response to the Lord.[88]

By 1958, the year of the second Stott mission at Cambridge, the long-awaited fruits of an evangelical resurgence were beginning to be felt. The mission was held in Holy Trinity, Simeon's old church, since no one wanted to return to Great St. Mary's even if Stockwood had been willing to have them. To Basil Atkinson, it was the fruit of many prayers:

> John had more experience now than in 1952. His exposition of the Gospel was as near perfect in clarity and power as anything can be, and many were brought to the Lord. I remember sitting in Holy Trinity spell-bound and rejoicing. My satisfaction was both spiritual and intellectual.[89]

John Stott had with him a remarkable group of young assistants. Oliver Barclay, from his vantage point on the staff of the IVF, reflected on the progress of the last decade:

> Such a team could not have been found ten years before. Many of

them were the fruits of the evangelism and teaching in the CICCU and OICCU during the previous fifteen years. They brought to light one important side-effect of the evangelistic preaching and the Missions of these years. A growing number of students had received a call to the ministry and a major factor in this had been that they had been given a new vision for a preaching ministry. In this the examples of John Stott and Dr Martyn Lloyd-Jones in London had probably played a key part. The ministry was seen in a new way as an opportunity to preach the Word of God with the authority of God. Evangelical theological colleges, especially in the Church of England, had begun to fill up again and to expand with numerous young graduates, including not a few who had been converted in the CICCU and the OICCU since the war. Churches long in the hands of those with other outlooks began to be recaptured for a more biblical ministry. The Principal of Ridley Hall (a liberal evangelical) lamented that the impetus had gone out of the liberal evangelical tradition and that nearly all the men coming to Ridley were now from a conservative evangelical background with experience in the evangelical youth movements or in the University CUs. No-one could really doubt that the evangelical movement was gaining ground fairly rapidly and this was obviously so as far as Cambridge was concerned.[90]

Though the title was again 'What think ye of Christ?', the individual addresses had shorter titles: 'The Deity of Jesus', 'The New Birth', 'The Two Ways'. *Varsity,* the undergraduate newspaper, reported in terms very different from *The Isis* a year before: 'Both gracious and courteous', was the assessment given of him, during an interview following one of the mission meetings: 'He makes any consideration of personal enmity seem ridiculous ... one senses in him the working of a penetrating analytical mind.' The report continued with a reference to his overseas missions, and his impressions of Christian work among students:

> The most marked characteristics of undergraduate spiritual life are the growth of religious feeling in colleges during the past decade and a paradoxically contradictory refusal on the part of undergraduates to commit themselves truly to their faith. That refusal is perhaps the consequence of the student's awareness of the cost of the true Christian commitment.[91]

John Stott's private records of those who came forward after the mission addresses, or those he counselled during his day-time interviews, contain more than 150 names, from what was clearly a remarkable week.

'I wish that you could have witnessed a number of the scenes which remain most vividly in my mind', he told his congregation:

> I think you would have been astonished and delighted by the signs of a growing movement of the Spirit of God in the universities of the world. Nothing is more encouraging in the Church today. I wish you could have seen over 400 students in the Union society debating hall, on the Saturday night before the mission began, engaged in solid study for three-quarters of an hour, with open Bibles. I wish you could have attended the Sunday morning prayer meeting, with every seat taken in the chapel of Corpus Christi College and students earnestly interceding with God for their friends. I wish you could have been present each evening during the week in Holy Trinity Church, until about 900 students filled it on the last night, with 150 or more in the relay service, and watched the eager, thoughtful, serious reception which was given to the proclamation of the gospel. Finally, I wish you could have risen early and come to Holy Trinity Church this morning to see at 7.45 over 300 students assembled for a half-hour talk on 'How to succeed in the Christian Life,' before we all moved across to a near-by cafe for a farewell breakfast. I have been impressed by the extremely efficient organization of the mission by the student committee; by the hunger for the gospel which is apparent in the university; by the sober and resolute response which many have made; and by the sad phenomenon of those who understand and believe the gospel, and have grasped the issues, but have so far turned away from Christ. Thank you so much for your prayers. Please continue to pray both for the new Christians and for those who are still seeking or hesitating.[92]

January 1959 saw a brief visit to Co. Wicklow to be the speaker at a conference of the Evangelical Fellowship of Irish Clergy; and the following month he returned to Durham for his second mission for the DICCU. He was aware that throughout the 1950s such missions had taken him from the parish with what to some was alarming regularity, and took this opportunity to reassure them:

> I myself am spending the first week of February in Durham, leading a mission in the University, and shall be grateful for your prayers. When it is over, I shall have had the privilege, in the course of the last seven years, of visiting Oxford, Cambridge and Durham, leading a mission twice in each University, not to mention other universities at home and abroad. Apart from the visit to South

Africa which I mentioned in my letter last month, I thought you would like to know that I have decided not to take part in any more University missions for some time.[93]

At Durham the official opposition of three years before was no longer in evidence. James Hickinbotham, Principal of St. John's, continued his staunch support. Six students responded to the invitation on the opening night; and many more throughout the week, or in personal interview. John Stott had asked his congregation (as he always did) to support him:

I ask you most earnestly to pray for me. My experience is that so often a person's life is shaped by decisions made in student days. Durham is full of ordinands and future teachers, and our heart's desire is that they may be won to an intelligent and uncompromising allegiance to the Lord Jesus. This can only be accomplished by the power of the Holy Spirit. Please pray daily throughout the week of the mission that we who have been asked to lead it may be vehicles of His power.[94]

Looking over the names recorded in his diary, at a distance of forty years, it is not difficult to see that their prayers for Durham, as for Cambridge, Oxford and other student missions, were clearly answered.

THIRTEEN

University Missioner: America, Australia and South Africa

1

In Britain the Inter-Varsity Fellowship of Evangelical Unions had begun in 1919, the year following the end of World War I.[1] Its American counterpart, the Inter-Varsity Christian Fellowship (IVCF) was not formally launched until early in 1939, on the eve of the Second World War. It rapidly made progress across much of the States, but 'the older universities of the east seemed immune or disdainful of the Evangelical Movement. Places such as Harvard and Yale, in sporting terms at least, belonged to the "Ivy League" and the "Big-Ten" and might consider themselves above other people in religious matters as well.'[2]

In 1951–52 four British graduates, two from Cambridge (Harvard was founded by a Cambridge man) and two from Oxford (favoured by Yale) had crossed the Atlantic to spend six months on behalf of IVCF in the New England universities. Small Christian Unions had been strengthened or established, and were soon flexing their muscles, ready for a more public witness. In September 1953 John Stott was therefore approached by the Inter-Varsity Christian Fellowships of Canada and of the United States about the possibility of conducting a series of missions in Canadian and American Universities including Harvard and Yale. Wilber

Sutherland, General Secretary of the IVCF in Canada, had visited All Souls following the remarkable 1952 CICCU mission to discuss with John Stott such an invitation. It was more than three years, however, before he was free to accept, and then only after consulting the Bishop of Willesden (on behalf of the Bishop of London) and his church wardens and PCC. George Cansdale, warden at the time, remembers that they encouraged their Rector to seize this opportunity, believing that it might be the first of many:

> It was in the early Fifties that his overseas travels began and I recall clearly the evening that he reported to the Wardens that he had had a request to visit the U.S.A. Should he accept? We insisted that he should go, but we imposed several simple conditions. First, that he should leave in charge a Curate able to preach in the All Souls tradition. Second, that he must be prepared to make a habit of such visits. Third, that the time should not be regarded as part of his holiday entitlement but he should take a few days off for bird-watching before returning to duty refreshed. Little did we realise where that decision would lead![3]

Such an opportunity for ministry overseas was not only unsought, but, in John Stott's mind at least, seemed unlikely to occur again. He was asked twenty-five years later in a student interview whether he had foreseen, and indeed had early ambitions for, a worldwide ministry, or whether he was taken by surprise. 'Yes, I was surprised,' he told the interviewer:

> When I was first invited to lead a series of seven university missions in Canada and the United States in 1956–57, which took me away for four months, I accepted the invitation to be away for so long because it didn't occur to me that I would ever be invited to do it again. Otherwise I would have been away a much shorter period.[4]

His itinerary was sent out individually to members of the Congregational Register and published in the November 1956 issue of *All Souls*. It showed a demanding series of university visits or missions, planned for up to ten days at a time in a total of nine universities including McGill, Harvard and Yale. This was the programme:

4 November	Sail from Southampton
10 to 20 November	University of Toronto, Ontario
24 November to 4 December	University of Western Ontario, London, Ontario

8 to 14 December	University of Michigan, Ann Arbor, Michigan
5 to 15 January	University of Manitoba, Winnipeg
19 to 29 January	University of British Columbia, Vancouver, B.C.
30 January to 3 February	McGill University, Montreal, Quebec
9 to 17 February	Harvard Unversity, Cambridge, Massachusetts
18 to 21 February	Yale University, New Haven, Connecticut
23 to 28 February	University of Illinois, Urbana, Illinois
6 March	Return to London

'I shall miss you all very much indeed,' he told the readers of *All Souls*, 'but I honestly believe that it will be good both for the congregation and for me!' He went on to give his impressions of what he might expect.

> The Christian situation in the American universities, and to a lesser extent the Canadian universities too, appears to be different from that in British universities in several important respects. I shall know more about it when I can see things for myself, but two matters have many times been mentioned to me. There are two reasons why the influence of the I.V.C.F. in Canada and especially the States is smaller than the influence of the I.V.F. in England. The first is that many Christian parents, fearful of exposing their sons and daughters to the influences of a large, secular and 'humanistic' university, send them to the smaller evangelical Christian universities which have no parallel in this country. The result is that the number of evangelical students coming up to the big secular universities is very small. The salt stays snugly in the salt-cellar, if you know what I mean, and this is a great tragedy. Secondly, the great denominations maintain their own student organisations which are active in many of the universities, with the result that students have no time for membership of an interdenominational Christian movement like the I.V.C.F. as well.[5]

In spite of these differences, the position of evangelicalism among the mainstream churches was not wholly dissimilar on the two sides of the Atlantic. Both had begun to emerge from a period of difficulty and obscurity, the war years proving 'a nadir for the movement'.[6]

John Stott left London after 'several days of feverish top-pressure preparation ... my desk was clear, and all letters answered.'[7] There was trouble in the Middle East, and demonstrators in the streets of London were calling for Anthony Eden's resignation over his handling of the Suez crisis. John Stott's parents came with Frances Whitehead to Southampton to see him aboard the *S.S. United States*, 'the world's fastest liner'. Since it was a Sunday, he had written offering to conduct a service, and as soon as the ship sailed he sought out the Chief Purser to confirm the arrangements:

> The service was held in the First Class Theatre, but available to all classes. I stood in front of the stalls, while behind the dropped curtain a small orchestra (piano, fiddle and what sounded like a xylophone!) led the singing. The purser read the lesson. The service was poorly attended. I spoke on the variety of causes responsible for our crossing the Atlantic, the opening of a new chapter of life for many of us, the opportunity of taking stock, and (from St Paul's experience in Philippians 3) the possibility of (1) knowing Christ as Friend, (2) trusting Christ as Saviour, and (3) gaining Christ as Treasure. The small congregation listened attentively, and about 8 later asked for the booklet which I had offered to anybody interested.[8]

November in mid-Atlantic brought heavy seas. Early on the Tuesday morning, the diary records,

> I awoke with a start when the complete array of toilet accessories littering the dressing table beside my bed slid across on top of me, including a glass of water! A little later in the night everything parked on the writing table slithered gracefully onto the floor. The motion was painfully slow, 10 full seconds elapsing from the roll on one side to the roll on the other ... In the morning every public room was criss-crossed with velvet covered ropes, and the most dignified passengers staggered around as if drunk. People absented themselves from meals; and those of us who came to the dining room found ourselves roped in. Taking a walk onto the open 'Sun Deck', the terrific wind blew biting salt spray into one's face, and the tops of breaking waves were glacial green. Looking overboard I watched a Puffin flying fast and fussily alongside, keeping pace with the ship (31 knots). Fulmars wheeled effortlessly in the wind, skimming the crests of the waves while silent Kittiwakes swam in small flocks or flew away alone, masters of the ocean, 1500 miles from the nearest land![9]

The ship docked early under a dull and overcast sky, and Wilber Sutherland was at the foot of the gangplank to meet his guest. During a busy day in New York, John Stott met with members of the Billy Graham New York Crusade Committee, recorded a radio message for a future broadcast, paid a flying visit to see the United Nations headquarters, watched the sunset from the Empire State building, and finally caught the night train to Canada.

2

The first mission of the tour was in Toronto. Here John Stott was welcomed by the familiar faces of Tony Tyndale and his wife Penelope, at whose wedding he had officiated in England less than a year before. Penelope had been a member of All Souls following her conversion at Harringay. Captain Tony Tyndale had come to faith through Iwerne Minster during John Stott's time as camp secretary, and after eleven years in the Royal Dragoon Guards had recently joined the staff of the Canadian IVCF. When Wilber Sutherland had asked him to accompany John Stott on his long mission tour, Tony Tyndale reminded him of Deuteronomy 24:5 – and it was agreed that Penelope should go with him.[10] They not only acted as aides and escorts but as assistant missioners, counselling students and speaking in dormitories, fraternities and student clubs – sometimes until the early hours of the morning.[11]

In Toronto, as in every university, a local committee had gathered a strong team of associate missioners, and arranged a programme of talks and meetings throughout the week, to complement the main mission addresses. Under the theme 'Christianity is Christ' there followed a now familiar pattern: 'Jesus of Nazareth', 'The Fact of Sin', 'The Death of Christ', 'The Necessity of Decision', 'The Cost of Discipleship' and 'The Goal of Life'. Some 500 students gathered on the first evening at 5.00 p.m. in the large Convocation Hall. By Wednesday 900 were attending: 'SIN BOOSTS ATTENDANCE AS FOUR RECEIVE CHRIST' was the headline in the student daily newspaper.[12] At the conclusion, the paper reported John Stott as pleased with the response to the mission, adding that 'Only a small number of students had come to him to "receive Christ", but Mr Stott said this was probably due to the fact that he had made the cost seem difficult. "I did not want irresponsible enthusiasts to come," he said, "and so I made the decision hard." '[13]

Writing home to the people of All Souls, John Stott described one such student:

One Ukrainian girl, who started by writing me anonymous letters because she was too shy to say who she was, and had been disillusioned ever since the Bolsheviks had torn their family Bible into cigarette paper and smoked it, finally disclosed her identity and wrote 'I have committed myself to Jesus. I feel that I have begun to find myself' and later 'How wonderful it is to be a child of God and know it!'.[14]

Among those confronted with the need for decision were some members of the Christian Union who had never committed themselves fully. One man had been putting off the issue for two years 'until on the Thursday of the Mission he wandered into the meeting at five o'clock. The subject was "The Necessity of Decision". There and then he gave his life to Christ.'[15] As in all such missions, the work continued to bear fruit after the missioners had moved on:

> During the week following the Mission another recent convert attended one of the faculty Bible studies. At the beginning of the meeting he introduced himself not only by name but also by family – 'the family of Christ – I was converted at the Mission last week.' He went on to say that he felt that he could now contribute to the discussion because Christ was such a living experience to him.[16]

While in Toronto John Stott was guest at two breakfasts for local ministers, speaking to about 100 of them on his familiar theme of 'Parochial Evangelism by the Laity'; and every morning at 8.15 he had been at the CBC studios to broadcast their 'morning devotions'. Listeners were quick to correspond:

> I have been taking a series of the titles by which Jesus is described in the N.T. – Lord, Saviour, Friend etc. I've had many letters of appreciation, including several with such sentences as 'I was prepared for my confirmation by the late Rev. F. S. Webster', 'I attended All Souls between 1884 and 1888 ... I am in my 89th year', 'one of my relatives was married in All Souls'; and 'a former choirboy of All Souls (1908–13)'! Many people have also introduced themselves after church services as former All Souls members, not least Freddie Geoghegan, former organist ...[17]

Two or three rest days followed, close by the Niagara Falls, which revealed 'thirteen different species of duck, several of which are not recorded in the British List'. The diary recounts how:

> One afternoon, in the snow and biting wind, I determined to go off on a bird watching expedition on my own. Several telephone calls to

the local library, tourist information bureau and high school had failed to enlighten me on a good place to visit, so I walked down to the track leading to the water's edge. The gorge is about 350 feet deep. I reached the jetty from which the boat called 'The Maid of the Mist' sails in the summer to sightsee the falls, but she was on the stocks being repaired and painted. Opposite me were the thunderous American falls. The current along the centre of the river was exceedingly swift. But between the main stream and the shore on which I stood was a small expanse of more slowly moving water which I found to be alive with duck! In the icy green swell Redbreasted Mergansers, their wild crest wet and bedraggled, looked warily this way and that, and dived deep into the foam. Oldsquaws which are really sea-water ducks, black and white pied birds with a long black tail, were also diving hilariously but looked comic and dissolute in their moult plumage. White-winged Scoters in full winter dress, revealing a white wing patch and double light face patches, were a new species for me, and I was thrilled also to get an excellent view of a pair of Buffle Heads, a pair of American Golden-Eye, and one drake Pintail, not to mention a Common Loon, Redheads, Horned Grebe galore, Mallard, Gadwell, and Scaup. It was one of the most exciting birding expeditions I can remember, and I stayed watching this galaxy of beauties and rarities until my hands were numb with cold and the light had faded.[18]

The second mission of the tour opened at the University of Western Ontario in London, a hundred miles to the west, under several inches of snow. Some of the same team of associate missioners were present. The tradition here was for an annual mission, with the main addresses given at noon each day. The student body was less than 3,000 – as compared with eleven or twelve thousand in Toronto – so attendance was inevitably lower. In addition,

Lectures, classes and lunches appear to continue throughout the middle of the day, so that they reckon less than 1,000 students would be *free* to come to the noon-hour mission 'lecture'. All the same the opening attendance of 60 was disappointing, and we were relieved when on Tuesday our numbers had jumped to 140.[19]

But if attendances were small, personal interviews proved fruitful:

I think of the young philosophy professor who came to two meetings, and has more or less passed from atheism to theism but not yet to Christianity; of a fine, honest young fellow doing a business administration course, who came to see me first with a male friend and then with his girl friend, and does not want to make a decision without her; of the first-year music student who came to most of the meetings and wants to know Christ, but confessed that she would find becoming a Christian very 'upheavaling'; and of another girl who knows she must first put right a deep resentment towards her mother before she can enjoy God's forgiveness. So today, as in the first century, moral and spiritual battles are being fought.[20]

The student newspaper at the end of the week was gracious, if a little patronizing; but (perhaps not surprisingly, with a mission every year) unconvinced by the week's meetings:

> Rev. Stott is an able, intelligent, and sincere personality. We enjoyed listening to him, mainly because he talked instead of preached. He has a difficult job – talking theology without stepping on denominational toes. No doubt he wasn't able to avoid this all the time.
>
> But we can't help feeling that something was missing from the Mission and we find it hard to put our finger on it. If he had been the 'fire and brimstone' type, some people would have gone out of curiosity and a few others for laughs. But as things were, we got the impression we were being sold a car without getting a chance to test drive it. Everything we listened to we recall hearing years ago. In that respect the Mission served only to refresh memories. We feel that there was too much Biblical theory involved and not enough relation to the all-important application of Christian theory to the problem of living from day to day ...
>
> We congratulate the local committee for a job well done – but we still want to drive the car.[21]

For the members of the Christian Fellowship, however, it was 'the outstanding week in our university lives.'[22]

As in Toronto, John Stott spoke at a meeting for ministers arranged by the local Council of Churches on 'recruiting, training and using the laity in evangelism'. Sunday was busy:

> I preached in New St. James's Presbyterian church, as a result of which I have had 2 private talks with a bluff and candid policeman (who sings in their choir) and who, I believe, has really received Christ as his Saviour and Lord. In the evening I preached in St. Paul's Cathedral. The Dean was very amiable, and the only fly in the ointment was that (to my great embarrassment) I found myself

sitting by mistake in the Bishop's throne!! and sidled out of it into a humbler stall as soon as decency permitted and nobody seemed to be looking![23]

The last mission before the Christmas break was in Ann Arbor where the 22,000 students of the University of Michigan formed nearly half the population. Once again the mission was billed as a 'Lecture Series', still under the familiar title 'What think ye of Christ?', and advertised with a picture of the missioner in a clerical collar! John Stott arrived in 'a really thick snowstorm', and in his diary described his impressions:

I have been staying in the Michigan Union, which forms one of the chief social centres of the University, mostly for men ... The Michigan Christian Fellowship is a founding member of the American Inter-Varsity Christian Fellowship, and I've developed a high opinion of the students in the steering committee which has organized this week. They have worked immensely hard and very efficiently. Their budget was $1,300, to which the students contributed $1,000. This is remarkable because many American students seem to be having difficulties in making ends meet. Consequently many do a job to help towards fees ...

I've given the main lectures every evening at 8p. m. in Rackham Hall, a super university auditorium with plush cinema-type seats, seating about 1,200. Impartial observers say that attendance has been good, as there is tremendous competition in leisure hours. We are encouraged that we began with 350 students and increased every night until last night nearly 600 were there. The attention has also been close, and about two-thirds of the audience have stayed each evening after the main lecture, for the short instruction talk in which I try to explain simply what it means to be a real Christian, and how to receive Christ personally.

The faculty ... have shown a certain amount of interest. Each evening one of them has introduced me, beginning with Dr. Harlan Hatcher, the President of the University, and continuing with one of the Regents ... Apart from the main lecture series, no fewer than 72 small discussion sessions have been arranged during the week for 'assistant lecturers' and these have been most profitable. Many students have been asking sincere, direct and personal questions about Christianity. There have been countless personal interviews. I'm impressed by the fine quality of the students on this campus. It has been my privilege to see many of them privately. Many of them are truly seeking after God, and we believe a number have found Him in Christ this week. I could tell many stories ...[24]

Writing in *All Souls* to his praying congregation, John Stott filled in a little more of the stories behind these interviews:

> I think of the Armenian student whose earnestness I shall never forget when he remarked: 'If I were sure that Christ was the Son of God, I would become a Christian and never-ever give it up!' Then there was the Jewish fellow, so delightfully genuine, whose male forbears had for many generations been Rabbis and who had become almost certain of Christ's deity; and the married medical student, almost a qualified doctor, who as soon as he was convinced of the deity of Christ knelt with me and accepted Him like a little child. Then there was the fourth year student, shortly leaving for a seminary prior to entering the Methodist ministry, who only received Christ during this week and is bubbling over with joy. And I cannot omit the quiet lad whose hunger for spiritual reality has led him to offer for the Ministry in the hope that he would in that way find what he was searching for! Now he has found Christ, and is waiting on Him to see if he is really called to the Ministry or not.
>
> So, as always, some mocked, some believed, and some are still weighing the issues. We were specially impressed with the quality and potential for the future of those who did profess conversion. Many of them could be spiritual leaders in future years if they remain true and grow into maturity.[25]

Some years later, broadcasting to American listeners in a series of addresses put out by the Episcopal Radio-TV Foundation, John Stott described how during the University of Michigan mission he had been sitting in the barber's shop of the Students' Union, waiting to have his hair cut. A young mathematics teacher came in and engaged him in conversation, describing some of the intellectual difficulties that he found in accepting the Christian faith. John Stott heard him out, and then 'took the liberty of telling him of the change from self to unself that would have to take place in him if ever he committed his life to Christ, how he'd have to make Christ the centre of his life, and himself move over to the circumference.' The lecturer listened to this with some dismay, and then blurted out, 'Gee, I guess I'm very reluctant for this decentralization!'[26] John Stott seized on this as 'a magnificent modern word for conversion'.

3

From Ann Arbor John Stott flew to New York to join Billy Graham. They went on to Princeton together for a conference on evangelism:

Billy and I had communicating rooms in Princeton Inn. Our
windows looked out over the closely cropped lawns of a golf course,
past a little lake with pinioned duck and a pair of wild Canada
Geese, to the impressive tower of the graduate building. For two
nights I gained a little insight into Billy's pressurized programme.
Telegrams kept arriving all day. As I turned my light out he was
still talking on the telephone, and I woke to hear him called up on a
long-distance call from somewhere else! He certainly carries many
and heavy burdens, but remains wonderfully fresh …[27]

A further flight took John Stott to Chicago in the week before Christmas,
to meet Stacey Woods, General Secretary of the American IVCF; and the
following day he took the train south for a twenty-four-hour journey to
North Carolina, to spend Christmas with Billy and Ruth Graham and
their family at Montreat. The train, heavily overloaded for the Christmas
holiday, was four hours late:

Billy met me at the station (he had mercifully taken the precaution
of phoning the station before coming out!) and drove me the 10
miles or so to their home. Montreat is a village, and their house,
which has no name, is 2 or 3 miles away up the mountain. The
drive is long, very steep and winding, and ends in a couple of
hairpin bends. Their house is most delightful. They had it made in
log-cabin style and it was completed less than a year ago. It is
literally cut out of the mountain side, and it is surrounded by
woods, but commands a superb view across the valley where
Montreat nestles to the mountains beyond. The whole setting is
strongly reminiscent of Scotland …[28]

John Stott found himself the only guest, sharing the home with the
Grahams and their four children, whose ages ranged from nearly twelve
down to Franklin Junior who was four:

They love this isolated country life, and have 3 dogs ('Belshazzar', a
Great Pyrenees, 'Princess', a Great Dane, and 'Slow Pokey' a mon-
grel Beagle of sorts), and 3 lovely mountain sheep with black faces
and legs.[29]

It was a particular pleasure to be spending Christmas among a family of
young children:

A big illuminated Christmas tree occupied a prominent position in
the sitting room, and parcels were heaped underneath it. Otherwise

there were no decorations, and one missed holly and mistletoe. Billy (according to Ruth) had insisted that the adults should hang up stockings as well as the children, so that on Christmas eve 7 stockings were solemnly nailed in a row to the huge beam over the sitting room fireplace, – and each stocking clearly labelled in case Santa Claus forgot his spectacles![30]

When John Stott undid his stocking he was astonished to find, among useful oddments such as sea-sick pills and spare socks, a watch inscribed 'John Stott from Billy Graham' which he was to wear for twenty-five years. But that was not all. There was a strange little plastic bottle. 'DEO', John Stott read on the label: '*Deo*', Latin for God. Then DORANT, a word which was new to him – perhaps something to do with a gift of God? Only when he realised that it was one word, not two, did he know what his present was, 'though even then I had to have it explained to me'. Toiletries for men had barely begun to cross the Atlantic![31] One day Cliff Barrows and Grady Wilson came to record the 'Hour of Decision' radio programme. Following this, they played golf with Billy, 'while I was distracted with Yellow-bellied Sap-suckers on the golf course'. John Stott hugely enjoyed his peaceful Christmas, constantly entertained by the Graham children: 'Franklin was about four or five years old and it was amusing to me that he, like myself in early days, was armed to the teeth with daggers.'

Thirty years later Ruth Jnr. wrote to recall his Christmas visit:

Dear Dr Stott,
    Perhaps you will remember me as a second grader the Christmas you spent with my parents, Ruth and Billy Graham. I remember you as a kind, warm stranger with a lovely accent! I even remember your thoughtful gift to me that Christmas – a funny little wooden goat, when you punched a button underneath him, he would collapse! As a matter of fact, I think it is still with me – tucked away with other childhood treasures!!
    However, I have grown up and have children of my own!
    And the reason for this letter is to tell you how much I have been blessed by *Christian Counter-Culture*. I used it for the basis of my study of the Sermon on the Mount this spring as I taught the women of my church and community ...[32]

John Stott, for his part, retained deep impressions of the genuineness of the Grahams' personal and family life, away from the media spotlights and the demands of ministry:

It was very moving for me to see this world-renowned evangelist leading family prayers and instructing his own children in the gospel. And not only that: I remember that on the hills round Montreat are what they call the hillbillies, impoverished farmers; and I was impressed to see Billy taking Christmas gifts round to the hillbillies in his neighbourhood.[33]

But the media could not be kept at bay for long. Four days after Christmas the front page of the local paper was almost entirely given over to a large photograph, *Billy, Belshazzar and Guest*. Belshazzar, Billy's Great Pyrenees dog, posed between the two evangelists who were sitting on a low stone wall in the winter sunshine.[34] With Billy Graham's New York Crusade due to begin in May, the two men had much to talk about; in particular,

> what help can be given to ministers in New York city both in co-operating with the Crusade which begins next May and in bringing new life to their churches *after* the Crusade is over. Billy is humble enough to realise that his Crusade in New York, even if it lasts 3 months, will only be an episode in the spiritual life of the city, and that what matters most is the life and warmth and continuing activity of the local churches.[35]

With Christmas over, John Stott set off for Colorado Springs at the foot of the southern American Rockies, to join Tony and Penny Tyndale at Glen Eyrie, headquarters of the 'Navigators'. Their work was already well known to John Stott for the part they played in the follow-up of the Billy Graham Crusades; and Lorne Sanny, their leader, was a personal friend since the days of Harringay. The mild weather made for some successful bird-watching:

> I greatly enjoyed the opportunity of seeing a number of species which are not seen east of the Rockies. The rich variety of western birds can be appreciated when you know that they boast 19 species of Woodpecker and at least 13 different Hummingbirds! I saw the Canyon Wren, a dapper little creature with chestnut brown belly, dark back, and pure white throat, and also the Redshafted Flicker, a fairly large Woodpecker, the underneath side of whose wings are bright crimson! – I was glad to take out birdwatching one afternoon 12-year-old David Hemery, son of the Navigators' accountant (an Englishman I know quite well), who became greatly enthused as I tried to initiate him. I couldn't help remembering the happy days when Robbie Bickersteth took me out.[36]

In early January it was time to be back at work; three missions were behind him, with six visits still to come. In Winnipeg, where he was to conduct the mission in the University of Manitoba, the temperature was 25° below zero, with Arctic winds. Halfway through the week John Stott went to the Hudson's Bay Company Store and bought what he described as 'an impressive fur hat' with ear pieces: 'I was afraid that otherwise I'd return to England minus an ear or two!'

It proved to be a difficult mission on a split campus. Numbers were not large but there was encouragement from 'the interest shown by senior members of the university. We know of one young professor who has accepted Christ, of several who are on the brink of decision, and of many more whose interest has been aroused.'[37]

Once again the main addresses had to be given midday, and John Stott felt cramped in style by the sense of rush at the weekday meetings; but the mission finished with a profitable and fruitful weekend:

> Several students who had been seriously thinking throughout the week came to a point of commitment. One young science student I shall never forget, who came to me with delightful naiveté to say he wanted to become a Christian and what did he have to do. He told me some of his story, especially that he'd been in trouble with the police for car thefts and housebreaking in Calgary (Alberta), his home town. Two of his friends were serving a 2-year sentence but he had not been caught. When he'd finished, I explained what it meant to be a Christian and what he must do. We prayed and he committed himself to Christ. Later, off his own bat he told me he intended when he got back to Calgary in the Easter holidays to make a clean breast of the past, – even if it meant a sentence. His decision to do this makes me believe his conversion is real.[38]

On Tuesday night, following the final weekend of the mission, John Stott caught the train, the prestigious 'Canadian' of the Canadian Pacific Railways, to travel from Winnipeg to Vancouver, 1,473 miles in thirty-six hours, some of it through the heart of the Rockies. Perhaps it was on this train journey that, according to Tony Tyndale, 'the three of us were chatting. Penelope or I suggested that we were still feeling very tired, and John chided us that it was not surprising since we made love too often! Penelope exploded, declaring that with getting to bed at 2 a.m., and struggling to get to prayer meetings by 6 a.m., we had no time.'[39] John Stott wrote home:

> From Vancouver, the Tyndales and I flew across to Vancouver Island for two days' rest. That evening I went down to the sea

alone, sat on some lonely rocks, watched the sun set over the Pacific, and prayed for God's blessing on the mission in the University of British Columbia. The following morning I was up early, missed breakfast and spent three hours watching birds near the harbour. It was a special treat to see the beautiful Harlequin Duck in its native habitat.

We had an uproarious reception at Vancouver airport. About 20 students came to meet us, and I was first invested with a bright, yellow and blue striped U.B.C. scarf, and then lifted bodily into the air and carried shoulder-high into the waiting hall![40]

John Stott had been given the opportunity to explain the reason for his visit in *The Ubyssey*, the student journal, and had made good use of it. One student wrote later 'This was the mission at which I became a committed Christian. The article in *The Ubyssey* made a tremendous impression on me.'[41] Writing in the issue published on the day before the mission began, John Stott offered this explanation of why he had come: it can be read as a manifesto of the whole tour:

Perhaps I could put it this way. Every University is proud to be an Areopagus, a forum of discussion, a vast debating chamber. Views and standards previously accepted without question are submitted to vigorous critical examination. Some are thrown overboard. The bath water of old-fashioned ideas flows swiftly down the drain, and sometimes the Christian baby goes with the bath water.

In a word, many people reject Christianity without ever giving it a fair hearing. They dismiss it as a religion of childhood and discard it with childhood's toys, without ever investigating it with the honest impartiality of an adult mind.

Now we believe that the intellectual basis for Christianity is respectable. More than that, it's convincing. It can bear scrutiny. Our purpose therefore in this Mission is to bring before the members of the University who care to come and listen, a reasoned statement of the Christian faith. Under the general title 'What think ye of Christ?' I shall try to marshal the evidence for the unique deity of Jesus Christ and to explain what the early apostles taught about His death on the cross. I shall attempt to show why we need Him, what it means (yes, and what it costs) to follow Him, and how to begin ...

A leading faculty member of Yale University recently described the students of today as a 'singularly uncommitted generation.' I think that may well be true. We all prefer to sit on the fence than to get into the field of battle. But I believe that Jesus Christ is the only

Person, and His cause the only cause, which is worthy of our thoughtful and total commitment.[42]

The campus enjoyed a magnificent situation, with views across the water to snow-capped peaks. Growth had been so fast, however, that many of the buildings were temporary wooden structures. The main meetings were again in the lunch-hour, having to compete with lectures and other student activities. 'But,' he reported:

> the university auditorium was almost filled every day with between 600 and 800 students present – many of them eating sandwich lunches during the early part of the address! They listened with close attention, and the whole university seemed to be talking about the mission. I find I had 40 personal interviews during the week, and many students thoughtfully committed their lives to Christ, one or two being leading students in the university.[43]

In between missions there were occasional rest periods, but also much extra ministry. The day began with 'Morning Devotions' on the radio at 7.30 in the CBC studios. There was a prayer meeting at 9.00 a.m., followed by the daily missioners' meeting. Then came an hour or two for preparation before the main meeting at 12.40. Much of the rest of the day was given to personal interviews, or to extra meetings of ministers, or local groups: 'giving about 30 addresses in 9 or 10 days!'

From Vancouver John Stott again crossed the Rockies to Montreal for a brief mission at McGill University, including a residential weekend with some 45 students at a ski resort in the Lawrentian Mountains, and a broadcast service on the Sunday morning from the Cathedral. This was followed by a visit to Carleton College, at that time a very young university in Ottawa, and then three nights in Chicago. His stay included some bird watching on Lake Michigan ('adding Hooded Merganser and Wood Duck to my list'), and an address to the Founder's Week Conference of the Moody Bible Institute: the pastor of the Moody Memorial Church was an English friend, Alan Redpath, formerly minister of Duke Street Baptist Church in Richmond.

A further flying visit to New York included a little shopping ('I bought 13 ties for some of my curates and male friends!') and breakfast with Billy Graham:

> Together we went to a meeting for which I'd come to New York. It was for 100 New York episcopal clergy who have been a bit cool in their reception of the coming Crusade! The idea was to get me to speak for 20–25 minutes from my experience of the Greater

London Crusades on how a church could benefit. Two bishops were also present, and Billy both spoke briefly and answered questions. It was a most cordial meeting and seems to have been very well received. Many misconceptions were put right. It illustrated again Billy's principle of meeting his critics face to face in friendly discussion and interchange of ideas.[44]

Following this meeting, John Stott contributed a brief section, 'Organize the Membership to reach the Unchurched' to the booklet *Preparing for a Billy Graham Crusade* first used in the New York Crusade. Billy Graham himself was due at Yale for a four-day mission, and John Stott fitted in a single preparatory visit before moving on to Harvard. Harvard, the oldest college in the United States, was likely to prove stony ground. An IVCF worker in the 1940s had said that 'trying to find a Christian at Harvard was like Diogenes going around with a lantern looking for an honest man.'[45]

John Stott was given 'The Preacher's Room' in Lowell House, and was delighted to be in a collegiate university again:

All the other Canadian and American universities I've visited are largely non-residential, and even where they have student residences, there are no 'colleges' or 'houses' with dining halls etc. But Harvard and Yale are of course modelled after Oxford and Cambridge, and Radcliffe College is the girls' house. There are about 4,000 undergraduates, 6,000 graduates and as many as 3,000 faculty members at Harvard which has the reputation of being the most indifferent and apathetic as regards Christian things of all American universities. Dr. Pusey, the President of the university, when approached about the possibility of arranging a faculty reception for me, replied wryly: 'Even if the Apostle Paul himself were to visit Harvard, the faculty would not turn out to meet him'! – The numbers attending the lecture-series were therefore small, averaging 200, but the Deans and Professors who chaired the meetings and introduced me all said that this was 'very good for Harvard'![46]

The attendance of 200 has to be seen against the 13,000 members of the university, each of whom had been sent a leaflet about the mission. But numbers are not everything:

We were particularly encouraged by the number of students who came to the whole series, thought hard during the week and only reached a decision by the end. One fine fourth-year biochemist from a wealthy background, who had been wrestling with the problem of his allegiance to Christ all week, grasped my hand during a tea party on the final Sunday and said 'God wins; but it will cause an earthquake at home!'[47]

Once again, besides the mission addresses and personal talks, the days had been filled with extra engagements: speaking at Park Street Congregational Church in Boston, at the Episcopal Theological School, at Wellesley College for women students, the Harvard Divinity School and the Cambridge Ministerial Association. It was a relief to take Saturday as a free day and to be driven by Peter Haile, the local IVCF staff worker (an Englishman whom John Stott had known when he was up at Oxford) to Plum Island, a narrow spit of land thirty miles north of Boston. Here, accessible only by a causeway, the Parker River National Wildlife Refuge had been established among the marshes, dunes and shoreline:

We walked along a sandy beach on the Atlantic coast, deserted by humans and swept by an invigorating sea wind, searching for rare gulls. The so-called 'White-winged' gulls, because they are pure snowy white all over without the grey mantles of Herring and Common gulls, are Arctic birds during the breeding season and only come south in the winter. There are 3 varieties – the Glaucous, the Iceland and the Ivory. Only rare strays are ever recorded in England. – After a longish search we were delighted to spot one (probably an Iceland), – strikingly white in a flock of grey- and black-backs. These gulls would make a good advertisement for Persil![48]

During the mission John Stott had worked closely with Ladd Fagerson, the undergraduate President of the Christian Fellowship who were sponsoring the mission. Fagerson had entered Harvard in 1953 to study law, at a time when the Fellowship consisted of only five members. Before leaving Harvard, John Stott found time to talk with him about his future, and discovered that Fagerson felt God was calling him to train for the ordained ministry, and in consequence had a place booked for the autumn at London Bible College. Soon after John Stott's return to England, he wrote to invite Fagerson to spend the summer living at the Rectory; he later worked for a year at All Souls as a youth club leader before ordination training at Ridley Hall, Cambridge. Fagerson thus became the first of a number of young Americans nurtured by John Stott in London as friends, helpers and (later) study assistants.[49]

While John Stott had been at Harvard, Billy Graham had been at Yale conducting their annual four-day 'University Christian Mission' – an officially sponsored event with some 2,500 students attending each evening. Writing in his autobiography, Graham retained a clear recollection of his visit:

> Like many of America's older colleges and universities, Yale was founded as a Christian institution. One of its early presidents, Timothy Dwight, was a distinguished Christian leader; and during its first century, I heard, Yale sent 40 percent of its graduates into the ministry. Now that strong spiritual heritage has been largely forgotten …
>
> One day the head of the psychology department invited me to have lunch with about twenty members of his department. They all sat with their box lunches on one side of the room, while I sat on the other; I felt at first as if I were a mental patient undergoing examination! They were especially interested in what I meant by *conversion*; and to our mutual surprise, there was much agreement between us, at least as far as the psychological benefits of authentic conversion was concerned.[50]

Though Graham goes on to quote a student journalist as writing of 'Yale's cultivated general indifference toward religion', nevertheless the Christian Fellowship invited John Stott to Yale as Graham left, to conduct follow-up meetings for the 300 or so who had professed a commitment, or re-commitment, to Jesus Christ. Unlike Billy Graham's visit, this was not sponsored officially by the university. According to student rumour, there had been some suggestion that John Stott should add Yale to his tour for a full-scale mission, but was blackballed by the chaplains. It was said they had consulted Bryan Green about him, to receive in reply a one-word telegram 'Fundamentalist'! Graham's visit was seen as something of a sop to the evangelicals on campus; and as a cause of anxiety to the chaplains,[51] so much so that by way of counterbalance Paul Tillich was invited as missioner the following year.[52] The aim of John Stott's visit was both to challenge those who were still undecided and to help the newly-converted. He spoke in the Yale Law School auditorium on 'Christian Assurance', 'Christian Growth', and 'Christian Responsibility', with many personal interviews and was impressed with the student Christian leadership: 'It was particularly encouraging to see in nearly every college that a spontaneous group of Christian students had sprung up for devotional Bible reading and prayer.'[53]

The President of the Yale Christian Fellowship (the IVCF chapter at Yale) was a twenty-three-old, Peter Moore of Timothy Dwight College, where John Stott had a guest room. Moore describes himself as a 'cradle episcopalian' who had never seen an evangelical Episcopal/Anglican church, and indeed from his experience in the US, doubted whether any such existed. Even as a student he had a vision of reaching for Christ the young people of the New England 'Prep Schools' (comparable to the Public Schools of the UK) and their response to this Billy Graham mission further convinced him of their spiritual need. In their talks together, John Stott was able to tell Peter Moore something of Bash's work, and (as with Ladd Fagerson at Harvard) invited him to come to England that summer 'and see what a real evangelical Anglican church was like'.[54] In the event, it was the summer of 1958 before Peter Moore could take up the invitation. John Stott invited him to make his home at 12 Weymouth Street while he pursued a further degree at Jesus College, Oxford, with a view to ordination:

> ... My parents had been divorced only three years earlier, and my mother (the evangelical Christian of the two) was not pleased with my vision to enter the Episcopal ministry, thinking the Episcopal Church apostate, and so I arrived with a great sense of loss, but was perhaps all the more open to new experiences. I recall Desmond Dugan, John's personal assistant, meeting me at Victoria Station on my arrival, and escorting me in a London cab to 12 Weymouth St. – a welcome I can still remember.
>
> The next two years were spent at Oxford, with vacations at the Rectory. It was there, on Christmas morning, that I had a water-pistol fight with John – who showed a rarely seen playful side. John took me to Lady Stott's for Christmas lunch.

While in England, Peter Moore was able to learn more at first-hand of Bash's ministry through his Iwerne Minster camps, and this bore immediate fruit:

> It was partly through John that the vision for founding FOCUS (the American equivalent of Bash camps) was crystallized. I founded *Focus* in 1961, upon my return from Oxford, and ran *Focus* for 25 years, eventually believing that it should be passed on to younger folks. Today the camps are bursting, and there are 18 full-time staff. God has done a great thing, and Bash and John were a vital part of its early vision.[55]

4

The last of the nine main missions was at the State University of Illinois in late February, a huge campus to which John Stott was to return many times in the future for the great Urbana Missionary Conferences. Here the 'lectures' took place in the University Auditorium, and were advertised under such titles as 'Is the Religious Experience purely a Psychological Phenomenon?' or 'Was Jesus of Nazareth a Dangerous Psychotic?'.

The Illinois student Christian Fellowship had laid careful plans. As in all such missions, associate missioners were kept busy with a large variety of fraternity and sorority meetings, as well as personal interviews. Numbers were consistently high:

> An average of 500 students came to the meetings, growing to 600 for the last lecture. Again, these were augmented by many personal interviews, forty auxiliary meetings in living units and a sizable number of students in new studies on the claims of Christ. Each night a good group of students stayed behind to hear how to become a Christian. Many were born into God's family during the week. Stott wrote in his journal, 'I have found the time exacting, but exciting, strenuous but enriching. We are thankful for many who have [made] a first or a fresh commitment to Christ.'[56]

As on other occasions, the student leaders of the mission wanted to give John Stott a small memento of his time with them. James Nyquist, the local IVCF regional secretary, was consulted about what sort of gift might be appropriate:

> After bouncing around various ideas, one thing we cautiously and rather hilariously settled upon was a mug with the emblem of the university. Back in those days mugs were displayed in a man's study and customarily associated with beer, which was then rather frowned upon as being off limits for Christians. When John opened the gift in front of the assembled Christian students, he responded, as was his habit, most graciously without flinching, but his blushing face revealed his shyness.[57]

Nor did the work of the mission finish with the departure of the team:

> John Stott's ministry continued long after he had returned to England, as students gathered on one campus after another to listen to the tapes of his well-reasoned presentation of the gospel. His

messages modelled the simplicity of the gospel message given with the forcefulness of his intellectual commitment to it, and helped students learn to express truth in fresh ways. In March 1958 Stott's *Basic Christianity* began its phenomenal ministry among American students.[58]

For John Stott it was a unique tour: not until he had retired as Rector would he again be away for so long a time. Tony and Penny Tyndale summed up in retrospect their impressions of four intense and demanding months together as a team: 'We lived close to John, impressed not only with his giftedness, but with his discipline. His gracious relations with us both was an example, and his integrity in so many circumstances, was a lesson. We did not see the "clay feet" that we're told great men have.'[59]

Perhaps a clue to the special quality of that 'giftedness' which so impressed the Tyndales can be found in some words of C. S. Lewis, delivered ten or twelve years earlier. Lewis was addressing an assembly of clergy and youth leaders of the Church in Wales at Carmarthen during Easter 1945, on the subject of apologetics. 'A century ago' he told them, 'our task was to edify those who had been brought up in the Faith: our present task is chiefly to convert and instruct infidels.' In pursuing this theme, Lewis moved the whole business of apologetics from defence to attack. After a powerful discussion on problems of communication, he said –

I turn now to the question of the actual attack. This may be either emotional or intellectual. If I speak only of the intellectual kind, that is not because I undervalue the other but because, not having been given the gifts necessary for carrying it out, I cannot give advice about it. But I wish to say most emphatically that where a speaker has that gift, the direct evangelical appeal of the 'Come to Jesus' type can be as overwhelming today as it was a hundred years ago. I have seen it done, preluded by a religious film and accompanied by hymn singing, and with very remarkable effect. I cannot do it: but those who can ought to do it with all their might. I am not sure that the ideal missionary team ought not to consist of one who argues and one who (in the fullest sense of the word) preaches. Put up your arguer first to undermine their intellectual prejudices; then let the evangelist proper launch his appeal. I have seen this done with great success. But here I must concern myself only with the intellectual attack.[60]

In his university missions, John Stott seemed to combine in one individual the gift of what Lewis calls 'the arguer' and 'the evangelist proper'. He called upon his hearers to use their minds to think through their position. In this way the mind was to become the bridgehead to the citadel of heart and will; and he had the gift of moving convincingly and with evident sincerity from argument to appeal. The appeal was never simply to the emotions – though many were stirred and moved – but to the whole person. He was in himself Lewis's 'ideal missionary team', particularly perhaps for the young men and women of a university audience.

Indeed, the most compelling evidence that the Holy Spirit was at work came in the changed lives of students who had found themselves confronted with the claims of Christ, and had turned to him in repentance and faith. One such, from the University of Michigan, wrote to John Stott a year later on the anniversary of his conversion to report progress:

> Tomorrow will be the 16th of December. It might well be just another day for me had I not accepted a challenge, the greatest challenge of my life. You will remember that last year at this time you had spent the week from December 10 to 14 giving lectures of your series 'What Think Ye of Christ?' at the Rackham Lecture Hall in Ann Arbor, Michigan … I had attended your last two lectures of the series, and had walked out with most of the crowd after you had given the group an opportunity to ask Christ to come in and sup.
>
> During the afternoon discussion session, I met Tony Tyndale. Tony talked with me after the discussion, and asked if I had accepted Christ. I told Tony that I had not. Tony warned me against procrastination if I really did intend to accept Christ as my Saviour. I agreed to come to your last lecture on the 16th.
>
> It was at that time that I asked Jesus to come into my heart as my Lord, Saviour, and Friend. I knew that both you and Tony were very happy for me. I, too, was glad that I had made my decision …
>
> At the end of one year, I cannot say that I have become a good Christian. There is more room for improvement than I dare to admit … How well I have found that, as you mentioned in your letter before returning to England, the Christian life is a battle as well as a banquet.
>
> I only pray that I have made some progress in Him, that He can see me as a better person than I was last week, or last month, or last year. I know that He is true to His word, and that He is with me always, even unto the end of the world. I am glad today that I am a Christian.[61]

This first and prolonged American visit had its effect on John Stott also. Gladys Hunt, who with her husband Keith wrote the story of IVCF in America, reflected on the experience:

> In some ways it must have been a terrific and terrifying jolt to him to come here – and yet his reception and the embrace of the enthusiastic and uninhibited Americans gave him a platform that he extended around the world. I think of how up-tight emotionally he was in those early days – and how he now gives *latino abrazos* so freely. Part of that is the mellowing of aging ... but we think that this trip was a launching point for him personally. To say nothing of his subsequent encounters with students at the Urbana conferences where he modelled the kind of teaching that Americans had seldom heard ... His influence on the American IVCF is a significant one![62]

5

From 1956 to 1959, John Stott was overseas every year for one or more university missions. In the late autumn of 1956 and the spring of 1957 he was in North America, in 1958 Australia, and in 1959 South Africa.

The invitation from the Australian Inter-Varsity Fellowship arrived early in 1956 when John Stott was in the thick of plans for the North American mission tour. In consultation with his churchwardens and PCC he agreed to go in 1959, but almost at once Billy Graham announced his plans to visit Australia that year. John Stott's visit was therefore brought forward to June and July 1958. He was to conduct missions in the Universities of Sydney and Melbourne, together with a variety of public meetings and conferences for ministers under the auspices of the Australian Evangelical Alliance. His itinerary was to take him across the full breadth of southern Australia from Perth in the west, via Adelaide and Melbourne to Canberra, Sydney and Brisbane, with a day in Tasmania, and a brief visit to New Zealand. The two university missions were planned for Sydney, 12–22 June; and Melbourne, 10–20 July. He also hoped to see some birds!

Australia was particularly suitable for a second major overseas visit. In spite of its image as thrusting, secular and materialistic, it was (as, in part, it remains) 'a major centre of evangelicalism ... a bastion of evangelical Christianity.'[63] The origins of this tradition go back to the founding of Australia as a penal colony. William Wilberforce was deeply concerned that the first Chaplain should be a man of lively evangelical faith. Members of the Eclectic Society were firm supporters of Richard Johnson, the Chaplain appointed by William Pitt, the Prime Minister, on Wilberforce's recommendation. Extracts from his journal were read at a meeting of the Society in February, 1789.[64]

John Stott flew from Heathrow to Cairo where an unexpected delay allowed a quick visit to the pyramids. After breakfast at Singapore the plane arrived in Perth twelve hours late, in time for him to go straight from the airport to the first of his meetings. It had already been in progress for over an hour when he arrived and it was after midnight before he was in bed. Next morning, he wrote to his parents, 'One of my first sights as I looked out of the window was a pied Honey-eater – the next best thing to a Hummingbird. Later, out in the woods, I was thrilled to see parrots in their native habitat.'[65] So on to Adelaide: after two hours sleep he preached at the morning service at the Cathedral; and in the evening at Holy Trinity, where the 'Guest Service' was directly modelled on All Souls:

> The church was crowded beyond capacity, with people sitting on chairs all over the chancel floor. There was a most encouraging response. One of those who spoke to me was the young proprietor of one of Adelaide's smart night clubs. I lunched with him the following day, in his inner sanctum surrounded by bottles! He has thoughtfully counted the cost and, he says, committed his life to Christ.

After a brief preliminary visit to Melbourne, he flew on to Sydney, preaching three times on the following Sunday and speaking at several public meetings. He wrote home, 'I've discovered that bird watching is a bit of a joke in Australia and there has been no craze for it among the general public as in England.' But he had been introduced to several new species, 'notably the Swamp Hen (an enormous Moor Hen, two to three times as big as ours) ...

> I am staying all this time in Sydney with Mrs. Loane at Moore Theological College. She (Patricia) is the wife of Marcus Loane, the Principal of Moore. He has just been made a Bishop (Coadjutor), the job I felt I should decline as I expect you remember, and is on his way to attend the Lambeth conference. I have a very nice big bed-sitting room in the Principal's house, next to the college which is at one corner of the university grounds ...
>   On Monday evening I called on Howard Mowll, Archbishop of Sydney and Primate of Australia. He was up at Cambridge with Earnshaw Smith and is Richard's godfather. I met him at 12 Weymouth Street when he was over for the last Lambeth

conference. He is a very dear old boy, a staunch evangelical, perhaps a bit of an autocrat, but very sweet and gracious. He has been in hospital for some weeks and has only just returned home. Illness has prevented him from going to Lambeth. I called on him in his bedroom and found him sitting in his dressing gown ...

Sydney university has immense and very spacious grounds. Many of the ramshackle wartime buildings are being replaced by modern concrete and glass structures, and there are ample playing fields, tennis courts and a central quadrangle. The university now numbers nearly 9,000 students and is steadily growing. The Christian Union is here known as the 'E.U.' (Evangelical Union) and boasts a membership of over 400. It's one of the liveliest groups in the university. The mission began yesterday, and the main mission addresses are being given in the Wallace Theatre (their biggest lecture hall) seating about 600. The sessions last from 1.10 to 1.50, and students are eating their lunches at the beginning. Despite this, both yesterday and today the hall was packed to overflowing, with students sitting along the aisles and crowding in the doorways and standing at the back. It's a great privilege to address such a throng, who seem most attentive and receptive also. I've had a number of discussions and personal interviews too.

Last night I spoke to over 200 theological students on evangelism.

Monday is observed as the Queen's Birthday holiday, so I'm taking that day and tomorrow off ...

Predictably, any free days were spent in bird-watching expeditions to Botany Bay ('several dozen Wandering Albatrosses'), Centennial Park, and a day in the Blue Mountains: the diary rejoices in over sixty varieties of bird, many of them quite new to him.

Preaching in St. Andrew's Cathedral, he found, as he had noted elsewhere on his visits, that All Souls was indeed an international fellowship: 'At the end of every service or meeting, people came up to say "I attended your church when visiting London" or "My parents were married in All Souls" etc. etc. !'

As on other occasions, the mission proved to be a learning experience for the team of assistant missioners. Dudley Foord, later Bishop of the Church of England in South Africa, was one who looked back to the 1958 Sydney Mission as a key point in his ministry when he was able 'to catch the vision of what was possible under God'. He writes:

I shall never forget the University Mission at Sydney in 1958 ... it was the power of John's model plus warm encouragement from

John himself that launched me on university missions in the period 1960–80. I was invited to conduct missions in all Australian universities and also 35 countries overseas, mainly in Asia and the Middle East.[66]

A glimpse of John Stott through African eyes comes from a recollection of Gresford Chitemo, at that time an ordinand studying theology at Moore Theological College, Sydney. He describes how he and a fellow student were one day –

> ... repairing a motor cycle just near the college grounds when there came a taxi, and out of the taxi came John Stott. I looked at him and there was some radiance in his face. It was shining. I told my friend 'Look at a man of God'. He looked at him and he said to me 'You, Gresford, everybody you see, you say he is a man of God', and we left it at that.
>
> The next day, we were going to Sydney University to hear John Stott from England ... we sat together in the hall and when John Stott stood up, my friend surprised me and said, 'How did you know that he was a man of God?' and when he began to speak there was something touching our hearts. We were so much impressed by the way the Spirit of God was moving through this man.[67]

During the spring and early summer of 1958 it had become clear that Sir Arnold Stott was failing. He spent each day in his favourite study chair at Bullens Hill Farm, and seldom if ever went out. Before leaving for Australia John Stott discussed with his mother and sisters what he should do, were his father to deteriorate, or even die, while he was away. Lily agreed that he should fulfil his responsibilities, and only then fly home. Sir Arnold was slowly reading through the book based on his son's mission addresses, just published under the title *Basic Christianity*: 'He was about half-way through when I left, and promised to read the rest while I was away ... he seemed interested and impressed by what he'd so far read.'[68] All his life John Stott retained a vivid memory of the news reaching him that his father had died:

> It was during the morning of the Tuesday, while I was preparing, that a telegram was telephoned through to me, announcing my father's death. Although I had been half expecting it, I felt shocked and helpless to be so many thousands of miles away, and it was difficult to collect my thoughts sufficiently to deliver the next mission address an hour or two later. That evening I telephoned my

mother. The funeral would of course take place the following week, but it was agreed that the memorial service in the Chapel of Westminster Hospital would await my return.[69]

Arnold Stott had been a devoted, but not always an easy father. He had found his son's call to ordination, and especially his firmly-held pacifist convictions a grief to him and a frustration of his most cherished hopes. To medical friends, it seemed as if he regarded John's desire to be ordained as 'a kind of prolonged debilitating fever'.[70] When later David Trapnell was on the staff of the Westminster Hospital and his fellow-consultants heard that he was churchwarden at All Souls, there were still men there who made no bones about their strong antipathy to John Stott, based on the grief he had caused Sir Arnold during the difficult Cambridge years.[71] By contrast, in the offices of the Clerical, Medical and General Insurance Company (of which Sir Arnold was one of the medical directors), the recollection was of the pride that he took in his son's appointment as Rector – 'you wait, he will be a bishop one day.'[72]

Arnold Stott's own career had been one of considerable distinction, both in war and peace. As consulting physician to the Army, for example, he had been asked in October 1943 to examine Rudolph Hess, the imprisoned Nazi leader and friend of Hitler, who had flown alone to Scotland in the second year of the war to plead for a negotiated peace.[73] Perhaps because of a lifetime spent making responsible decisions, and in spite of a love for his home and garden, he had not found retirement easy: 'Never robust, Arnold suffered frequently from attacks of bronchial infection. His last few years were clouded by almost complete disablement endured with great courage and a determination that repeatedly confounded dogmatic prognosis.'[74] One of his contemporaries, a highly distinguished radiologist, summed up his professional achievements in his chosen field: 'He belonged to an era of great clinicians when the transition from empiricism to science was just beginning in cardiology and he was not the least of these.'[75] Despite appearances, he was a man of deep affection where friends and family were concerned, and aware that he could seldom demonstrate this as he would have liked: 'To my especial sorrow', he wrote to John at Rugby before the war, 'people are afraid of me for some reason until they get to know me – I've been told it hundreds of times and I suppose it's because I've got a rather sarcastic manner. But I know in my heart of hearts that I am kind by nature ...'[76]

It was a comfort to John Stott in his grief and isolation to remember that he had visited Bullens Farm House regularly on his day off while his father was deteriorating, opening and dealing with his post, sometimes even giving him a bath: 'He took a lot of interest in All Souls and in my travels: we were on good terms before he died.'

Difficult though some undoubtedly found him, Arnold Stott was a source of healing, strength and comfort to his patients, highly respected by his colleagues, and deeply loved by Lily and his children. When, at the age of seventy, John Stott was asked to look back on those who had influenced his life, he chose his mother and father first.[77]

But, for the moment, he had to put aside his grief and preach that day as usual in the Wallace Theatre, Sydney's biggest lecture hall. He described it later as 'the most difficult address I have ever given in my life';[78] and it was as well that the theme was the very familiar one, 'What think ye of Christ?'. This series of addresses had been constantly revised and hammered into shape during the North American missions. The process was not unlike that practised by C. S. Lewis with his famous lectures, *Prolegomena to Medieval Literature* and *Prolegomena to Renaissance Literature*: 'They did not change much, but he kept a notebook for further illustration of these and other works, which he called "thickening".'[79] In something of the same way, with prayer and on the basis of much experience, John Stott's mission addresses were 'thickened' and refined; so that by the time their substance appeared in book form they were particularly suited to their task. The fact that they had just been published as a paperback under the title *Basic Christianity*[80] presented no problem. Very few who attended the midday main addresses would have seen the book, much less read it; and for any who had, the words would come with the additional force of the preacher's personality behind them. He wrote at the end of the week:

For 6 days the lunch-hour meetings (in which the main mission addresses were given) were packed. The Wallace lecture theatre was full to overflowing. 700–800 students were sitting at the desks and on the floor, and standing at the back. They were attentive and receptive, and I was relieved (among other things) that the British sense of humour was not lost on Australians!

I had lots of personal interviews during the afternoons, with Christian and non-Christian students, and was shown a great deal of kindness. I also spoke at several subsidiary meetings, – to senior medical students, law students, evening students etc. Most valuable were 2 special sessions for theological students, at which I had the privilege of speaking to all the 250 (Protestant) theologs in the university – on evangelism. At one of the 2 meetings I showed my slides again (with taped narrative).[81] I am so thankful I brought these. They've aroused much interest. I have lent them all over the place to various groups, and the E.A. are now considering taking copies of the tape, and getting Kodak to make a filmstrip from the slides, for wholesale distribution.

The final meeting was on Sunday night in the Great Hall. A thousand people were crammed in, sitting all over the platform and standing at the back. 'Unfortunately', he wrote home to his mother,

> I have been having trouble with my voice this weekend. The ENT man says it's not the parson's occupational disease so much as a prevalent Sydney bug. I feared I wouldn't be able to get thro' on Sunday night. I had to speak softly without forcing my voice, and seemed almost to be caressing the mike like Bing Crosby! Anyway, despite my disability, or perhaps because of it, there was a wonderful stillness in that meeting and a sense of God's presence, as hundreds of students were facing the great issues of life. Many had been thoughtfully counting the cost of Christian discipleship all week. I am thankful that those who committed their lives to Christ did so with quiet resolve and without superficial emotion. It was altogether a great mission, and, we believe, a demonstration of the power of God.

It was a 'demonstration' of power through weakness that was to prove an encouragement on other occasions. John Stott had been uncertain and anxious through most of Sunday whether to telephone the mission committee and say he could not preach that night. In the event, he was persuaded not to do so:

> At seven-thirty, half an hour before the final meeting was due to begin, I was waiting in a side room. Some students were with me, and I whispered a request to the mission committee chairman to read the 'thorn in the flesh' verses from 2 Corinthians 12. He did. The conversation between Jesus and Paul came alive.
> *Paul*: 'I beg you to take it away from me.'
> *Jesus*: 'My grace is sufficient for you, for my power is made perfect in weakness.'
> *Paul*: 'I will all the more gladly boast of my weaknesses, that the power of Christ may rest upon me ... for when I am weak, then I am strong.'
> After the reading, he prayed over me and for me, and I walked to the platform. When the time came for the address, all I can say is that I croaked the gospel through the microphone in a monotone. I was utterly unable to modulate my voice or exert my personality in any way. But all the while I was crying to the Lord to fulfil his

promise to perfect his power through my weakness. Then at the end, after a straightforward instruction on how to come to Christ, I issued an invitation and there was an immediate and reasonably large response. I have been back to Australia seven or eight times since then, and on every occasion somebody has come up to me and said, 'Do you remember that final service of the 1958 mission in the University Great Hall, when you had lost your voice? I came to Christ that night.'[82]

From Sydney he flew to Queensland for a busy forty-eight hours in Brisbane, speaking seven times and recording three short broadcasts, while finding a moment to admire the wild pelicans. He squeezed in a brief visit to Tasmania to help inaugurate the first Australian National Scripture Union Week, a cause close to his heart.

The Melbourne University Mission was to begin on Thursday, 10 July, and John Stott was in the city for a week beforehand, the guest of the Langford family. Jack Langford was a Council Member of the Victoria Evangelical Alliance. 'They have a nice modern home,' John Stott wrote home,

> ... with circular front and a big tree by the back door, whose overhanging branches spread themselves over the roof. They have 3 daughters, Myra, Jacqueline and Robyn. Myra has just started nursing (aet. 19) and the other 2 are still at school. One evening we had a delightful time of family music, with Myra at the piano, and Jacqueline and Robyn playing the flute and 'cello respectively. You'll be amused to hear that I was enticed to lay hands on the 'cello, and despite the nearly 20 years since I played properly, found I could still manage to hit more or less the right notes!

Robyn Langford, looking back over nearly forty years, retained a child's vivid memory of their visitor:

> I was the youngest of the family (aged 11), very bouncy, too talkative, and as you can imagine was 'put on my best behaviour' for this important English clergyman whom I was not to bother ...
>
> The impact of our visitor was enormous on us as a family, and is the reason, I am sure, that today I am a member of the ministry team at All Souls. John's humility was stunning and unforgettable to me as a child, as he joined us in the washing up, came on picnics, taught us songs and prayers to sing as a family as we drove up to the bush. I was never treated as a nuisance, but he listened to my interminable riddles, played my 'cello ... he modelled Jesus to

us. None of us has ever forgotten this visit, and I can still sing all those songs, word-perfect, nearly 37 years later.[83]

There was time in Melbourne to fulfil a number of other engagements before the mission in the university began:

> On Sunday I had a busy day being an Anglican in the morning (preaching in the cathedral), a Methodist in the afternoon (speaking at a broadcast service for the Central Methodist Mission) and a Presbyterian in the evening (preaching at Scots Church, the leading Presbyterian church in the heart of the city, to a congregation of about 1,000) ...
>
> This morning I visited two 'Grammar Schools'. These are independent, fee-paying schools like our Public Schools. The first (called 'Caulfield') has 850 boys, and its headmaster is a young parson of 32 whom I had met some years ago when he was doing a course in Cambridge. The other (Melbourne Grammar School) is another C of E foundation. Here I spoke to the 6th form in chapel, and lunched afterwards with about eight school prefects in a room off the Tuck Shop. We had a good dingdong discussion.

By this time John Stott had been away from home for more than six weeks, and a number of factors were beginning to take their toll:

> I did not feel like leading a mission in Melbourne so soon after the mission in Sydney. First, the Sydney mission had been physically and spiritually exacting, and I was feeling drained. Secondly, the Sydney mission had ended on the Sunday night in an inspiring meeting in the University Great Hall. It was packed with students. And although I had lost my voice, there had been a significant response, with many coming forward to profess their commitment to Christ. After this high, the anti-climax was all the more depressing. And thirdly, I wanted to return home to stand by my mother and sisters in our common bereavement. For these three reasons I would dearly have loved to skip the mission and fly back to UK.
>
> But I knew both that I must proceed with the Melbourne mission, and that I could not do so unless I was lifted out of my depression and given a fresh vision, confidence and touch of power from the Lord. I was staying in the home of Jack and Georgie Langford. So that Saturday I locked myself into my bedroom, determined not to emerge until I had been re-commissioned and re-equipped. I read Scripture and prayed. Hour followed hour, until I

came to Psalm 145:18 'The LORD is near to all who call on him, to all who call on him in truth.' I sought to lay hold of this conditional promise. 'Lord,' I said 'I am calling upon you now, and doing so in sincerity and truth.' All I can say is that as I sought to fulfil the conditions, he fulfilled his promise. I experienced his nearness. I rejoiced in his presence. I was assured of his blessing, and was able to go forward into the mission.[84]

Compared to Sydney, the Melbourne mission had a slower start. Some 800 students gathered for the lunch-hour meetings in the Wilson Hall, 'the most fabulous, modern University auditorium ... with glass side walls, plush seats and a dramatic mural behind the platform depicting man's search for truth through the mists of ignorance and doubt.'[85] Nevertheless, there seemed little visible response to the message. But gradually the thaw set in. John Stott found himself constantly in demand for interviews and personal counselling, and the climax came on the last evening:

On Sunday night we had our final service of the mission in the cathedral. I was a bit apprehensive because the university is non-residential, and I feared that students would not come in from their homes and digs in the suburbs for a central service. However, my fears proved to be groundless. As the choir and clergy entered the cathedral, we saw what seemed an immense gathering of about 1,800 people, town and gown fairly evenly distributed. As at the end of the Sydney mission, there was a great hush and stillness which one has come to associate with the manifested presence of God. 3 or 4 hundred stayed to the continuation service in which I gave a simple, instructional talk on personal commitment to Christ, and many came forward after the final prayer. We were kept busy counselling people till nearly 10p.m., when we moved over to the Chapter House for a brief farewell meeting with students who had been helped during the mission.

The visit concluded with more Ministers' conferences, and a busy five days of meetings in New Zealand,[86] followed by a break in the flight home at Waikiki, Honolulu, thanks to the extra day provided by crossing the international date line. After buying 'some postcards, a Hawaiian shirt for John Dugan and some tolerably sober bathing pants for myself', John Stott made for the beach:

The sand is silvery, the water unbelievably warm (tho' still fresh), and American, Chinese and half-caste kids excel themselves in surf riding. I later plucked up courage to hire a board for an hour. Like all sports it looks so easy when you're watching somebody else surfing, and is surprisingly difficult when you try it yourself. I was surprised how big and heavy the board is ... Not content with lying on the board when actually surfing, some kneel and the proficient stand on the board, precariously but gracefully balanced. I was rather a miserable failure, finding it hard enough to keep on the board lying and sitting, let alone kneeling and standing!

Nor was this all. In the novelty of trying to surf, John Stott had overlooked the fact that an overcast sky can still allow severe sunburn. On the plane that night to Los Angeles he became sick, and by the following morning his whole back was a huge blister. But he recovered quickly during a brief holiday with friends, returning home hardly the worse (but considerably the wiser!) for his experience.[87]

6

After America, Canada and Australia, it was no great surprise that John Stott should be invited to South Africa the following year to conduct missions at the Universities of Cape Town and of the Witwatersrand, Johannesburg. He told the All Souls congregation that in both cases the Vice-Chancellor of the University had agreed to be President of the Mission and that the Mission Committee included representatives of all the Protestant Christian student organizations.[88] He made it clear, too, that this would be the last of his University missions 'for some time':

> I have just declined invitations to Edinburgh and McGill. You have been very long-suffering and understanding about my absences from the parish. But on my return from South Africa I believe God means me to concentrate more on the work to which He has called me among you; and I greatly look forward to this.[89]

Organized student witness in South Africa dated back at least to 1896 when, under the chairmanship of Andrew Murray, well-known as a Bible teacher and devotional writer, a conference of 400 student delegates met at Stellenbosch and inaugurated a Student Christian Association.[90] It was at the invitation of the direct successors of these students that John Stott was to conduct the missions. He flew on 21 July from London airport: no sooner had he taken his seat than his immediate neighbour fell into conversation. On hearing that John Stott was a parson, he asked 'You weren't by any chance preaching in St. Paul's Cathedral yesterday afternoon?' Hearing that this was so, he explained that he and his wife had been present, and that he was a Professor at Makerere, the University College of East Africa, South African by birth. He proved a very useful informant.[91]

John Stott had arranged to spend a few days in Ruanda–Burundi meeting All Souls missionaries before travelling south. But he began his stay in Africa with a visit to the Botanical Gardens in Entebbe on the edge of Lake Victoria, 'my first fascinating introduction to African birds: a pair of huge Fish Eagles, black, russet and white, soaring round each other with upturned wing tips; flocks of kites, omnivorous scavengers; pure white Egrets; Glossy Ibis; Pied Kingfishers; Jacanas or "Lily Trotters" with feet flat enough to stalk over lily leaves, etc. etc.' In Kampala he was guest of honour at a tea-party for All Souls people, arranged by the Secretary to Leslie Brown, Bishop of Uganda: the other guests included John Sharp, a young doctor still in his twenties who had lived in the Rectory at Weymouth Street for two or three years, and was now an All Souls missionary building a hospital at his mission station at Kisiizi, 240 miles away. He had come in to Kampala to replenish his stores. Also in the city, living in retirement, was Paul Gibson who had been John Stott's Principal at Ridley Hall, and who duly received a visit. At Makerere, the University College of East Africa, John Stott was a guest of the chaplain:

> That night I spoke to about 120 students, packed like sardines in a stifling lecture theatre, on 'Christian Witness in the Student World'. The Chaplain was in the chair, and several staff members came too. A dozen or so stayed behind for more informal, and (as it transpired) profitable, conversation … The Chaplain says he'd like me back for a mission in Makerere! But I've said not in 1960 or 61!!

He made good use of his brief time in East Africa. The diary tells of long journeys over bad roads, with occasional stops to see the sights: 'we had elevenses at King's College, Budo, a boys' secondary school whose grass quadrangle was deliberately built larger all round by one foot than Trinity Great Court'; he also visited the veteran missionaries, Dr. and Mrs. Stanley Smith who had helped to found the Ruanda Mission.

John Sharp, the young doctor from Kisiizi, had invited John Stott to visit the mission where he and his wife Doreen were living with their two small children, transforming a disused factory into a hospital. Looking back on those days, Doreen wrote later:

> We had been sent out from All Souls and received much encouragement and support from them throughout the building of the hospital, and in 1959 our Rector visited the All Souls

missionaries in the Ruanda Mission area including Kisiizi. It meant a lot to have him with us for a few days and he helped us to see things in spiritual perspective. He had some unscheduled experiences of travel in Africa as twice the steering on our ageing car gave way, and on a journey with another missionary the fan belt broke. I remember particularly his interest in the bird life around us and his calm acceptance of being stranded overnight because of car trouble without even a toothbrush, let alone shaving equipment. He might also still remember the bath at Kisiizi – John [her husband] had constructed it out of cement which was an advantage in that the dimensions could be chosen, but the texture was similar to pumice stone![92]

John Stott's diary gives an account of his visit, not forgetting to mention the abrasive bath:

We arrived after dark at about 8.30 p.m. – John [Sharp] is building a mission hospital in a beautiful wide valley out of buildings which formerly did duty as a flax factory. An overflow channel from a splendid waterfall supplies them with electricity, and the main block of the hospital, comprising a maternity ward and a children's ward, is nearly ready to be opened. So far he only has an outpatients' department. Later there will be a men's ward and a women's ward, with 60 beds altogether. It is a lonely place, with lots of Africans living within easy reach, but no European nearer than 15 miles away. I admire the Sharps very much in their enterprise. They are doing a really pioneer work, planting trees, building a vegetable garden (avocado pears, strawberries, maize, bananas, potatoes etc. already in) and contending with all kinds of problems and discouragements. Between 60 and 100 Africans are employed on the site as bricklayers, carpenters, masons and porters, and their work has to be kept under constant supervision ... , the head hospital boy and other leaders are fine Christians ... it was good to get into a bath tonight, even if the bath was a deep trough hollowed out of a slab of concrete!

The next day, Sunday morning, they crossed the lake to the Leper Island on Lake Bunyoni ('two Golden Crested Cranes – the emblem of Uganda – flew majestically by') to share in the worship of the colony:

At the church Dr. Parry, the medical superintendent, greeted us. The service had started, and as we slipped in I saw that the church was almost full. Infectious and non-infectious cases were segregated on each side of the centre aisle, and there in the south aisle were the children in their brightly coloured shirts and blouses. The service' was in Luchiga, but I was able to follow in an English prayer book, and while the local African evangelist was preaching, the English hospital sister wrote a translated summary for me. Then I was called on to say a few words, which were translated to the congregation.

From Uganda he journeyed south (with various mechanical break-downs on the rough roads) to visit more All Souls missionaries on the way. He was driven from station to station, meeting old friends and making new ones, with occasional bird-watching expeditions. At the weekend he flew down to Nairobi to preach in the Cathedral at a service broadcast throughout East Africa: Geoffrey Lester, the Provost, had been his fellow-curate fourteen years before. A former All Souls member, Bob Howarth, drove him to Nakuru, a hundred miles along the spectacular Rift Valley, where the chaplain, George Swannell, was also an old friend (and would later be an All Souls curate):

After lunch I had a most interesting experience. George Swannell drove me to Nakuru Prison. High mud walls surmounted by a barbed-wire entanglement surround it. Its inmates are largely African, but it has a European section in which there are at present 2 Englishmen. The one George took me to see is an old Harrovian, a middle-aged, married man who is a farmer. He has been convicted of assaulting an African,[93] though George is convinced of his innocence. Anyway, he appears to have been really converted in prison and is doing a lot of Christian reading and study. He found in prison a copy of 'Basic Christianity' (left by a previous prisoner to whom George had given it), which he had read and wanted me to autograph! We had an interesting conversation. I should like to tell the present generation of Harrow boys about him when I preach there in November!

The next day he spent the morning alone on the shore of Lake Nakuru:

It's hard to describe the fabulous wealth of bird life that I saw. Nakuru Lake is famed for its Flamingos, and I saw a flock of between 2 and 3 thousand of them. When they took flight the air seemed full of their symphony of white, black and pink. – I was also able to take some close-up photographs of the big, ungainly Marabou Stork, and saw a pair of the splendid Saddle-bill Stork, whose beak is a brilliant patchwork, with lemon yellow patch, blue-black ring and crimson tip. – Returning in the afternoon with Bob

Howarth we watched a flock of 250 Pink-backed Pelicans approach in formation at immense height, circle round in a gradual descent, and finally land on the lake shore.

They returned to Nairobi, seeing something of the Lesters and their family, and of Bob Howarth's work with the 'Navigators', specializing in lay-leadership training. He had time to visit the Royal National Park:

> We saw large flocks of Zebra, Wildebeest, Eland and various gazelles, and had good views of Giraffe. But everybody visiting the Park is principally looking for Lion. We saw no pride, but were fortunate enough to get close to one male monster. It was digging into the 'earth' of some creature, probably a Wart Hog. We drove within about 35 feet and it paid little attention, as it impatiently pawed away the dry earth and poked its face into the hole.

By now it was August and time to set off for Cape Town. John Stott spent a night in Johannesburg en route to have an advance meeting with the mission committee and his team of assistant missioners. It was not wholly reassuring:

> There is little doubt that the Witwatersrand mission is going to be a tougher proposition than ... Cape Town. The Christian students are not so well prepared, and the university as a whole has over 50% Jewish students, an active Rationalist Society etc.

In Cape Town he stayed with Monica Wilson, Professor of Anthropology, an Englishwoman who had lived in South Africa most of her adult life. She was a widow with two sons, Timothy aged 16 and Francis aged 20 who was reading physics at the University, a prominent student and Christian fellowship member:

> I could not have asked for a nicer home in which to stay. Francis and his mother were kindness itself, and in the course of my ten days with them I became one of the family. They are Anglicans, and keenly liberal in politics. Prof. Monica Wilson is a rare combination of grace and forcefulness, and is a vigorous critic of the Nationalist government's 'Apartheid' policy. She is a woman of great ability and integrity. We talked politics a good deal at mealtimes, especially as the 'Extension of University Education Act' has so recently become law. This is permissive legislation giving the government power, when they desire, to apply 'Apartheid' to the English-speaking universities of Wits and Cape Town. At present

Cape Town University of 5,000 students has about 50 Bantu, and 350 Cape coloureds (of mixed racial origin). These have equal academic opportunity with the whites, but (I was surprised to learn) are socially segregated by university policy. Despite this, the University Senates and Students' Representative Councils at Cape Town and Wits have publicly and outspokenly protested against the E.U.E. Act which (if applied) would remove the natives and coloureds and Asiatics (lumped together as 'non-whites') to separate universities of their own. The English-speaking universities are taking a clear and definite stand on the principle that academic merit alone should be the qualification for university entrance.

The University of Cape Town ('U.C.T.' or, to all students, 'varsity') must be built on the most splendid site of any university in the world. It is situated at the foot of 'Devil's Peak', and is approached by steep roads, while it overlooks the Cape Flats stretching to the Hottentot range of mountains many miles away on the horizon. Below the university playing fields is a seated statue of Cecil Rhodes, chin in hand, gazing north across the valley to the interior.

The main addresses, once again under the title 'What think ye of Christ …?', were held each evening in the University Great Hall, with a subsidiary series of lunch-hour meetings. Under a photograph of an unsmiling John Stott, in gleaming dog-collar (and captioned 'Convertor of Agnostics') the local newspaper described how:

U.C.T. Students Flock To Meetings of Visiting Missioner
Campus talk at the University of Cape Town is of the surprising turn-out of 1,000 students for a meeting called by the students' religious societies, that is the Students' Christian Association and the Y.M.C.A. The visit of the Rev. John Stott has blossomed into the big event of the winter term.

A publicity campaign such as this generation of students has not seen before heralded the coming of the Rev. Mr. Stott, Rector of All Souls, the Anglican church in Langham Place that is drawing the largest congregation in London at present.

Several types of advance publicity were used, and finally an aircraft flew over the university scattering pamphlets …

Since the big inaugural meeting he has been addressing about 700 students every evening. He attacks the 'lukewarm Christians' and he goes for the agnostics but all without any display of forensic pyrotechnics.

Clear enunciation and clear thinking are his two characteristics …[94]

In general John Stott was pleased with both attendances and attention: 'I do not remember a mission in which the audience gave such a quiet and thoughtful reception to the message.' A particular encouragement came from the support of the Vice-Chancellor (and therefore Principal) of the university, J. P. Dunning who 'took the chair both at the introductory meeting for staff members and one night in Jameson Hall. When introducing me on the latter occasion he took the opportunity of publicly declaring himself a Christian and in full support of the mission, which deeply impressed the students present.'

Some eighty members of the congregation stayed behind on the first evening to accept copies of St John's Gospel 'on the clear understanding that they would read it as honest seekers after truth.' Like all missions it took its toll of the missioner (who had arrived in Cape Town with a streaming cold):

> I was seldom in bed before midnight, and, as we had breakfast each morning at 7.45, I suffered from a chronic shortage of sleep! I find I have had to give 19 addresses during the mission's 9 days and have had over 30 interviews!

The mission committee had done a notably successful job with their publicity, though the aeroplane can hardly have been popular with the authorities! Among those attracted to the mission was a young student of architecture from Southern Rhodesia, David Wells, who had been brought to the meeting by one of his lecturers:

> I was an unbeliever at this time and had no Christian friends. I did see the publicity regarding his visit, however, and decided to go along once. I actually came in at the end of the week's series of addresses. That night, John was speaking about the cost of Christian discipleship, a cost he said which should be weighed carefully before a Christian commitment was made ... I listened to about half of John's talk and stumped out, muttering about religious fanatics! However, two weeks later, I was with a group of students who were painting in the mountains outside Cape Town. Pieter Peltzer, who was a lecturer in the School of Architecture, took us. The first night, around the camp fire, he spoke of his own faith in Christ. It was exactly what John had been talking about!
>
> I had been very friendly with a Jewish student who was fascinated by philosophy and he had gotten me immersed in it, too. As I went to bed that night in the mountains, and pondered these things, it became clear that the issues I had been thinking about in philosophy – such as the existence of absolutes and their nature, as

well as the problem of evil – seemed to be answered in Christian faith. So, that night, in a shaky way, I committed myself to Christ.

I had been quite rude to several of the Christian students in my residence, so when I returned the first thing that I did was to go to them and apologise for what I had done and identify myself as a new Christian.[95]

While in Cape Town John Stott fitted in a number of other engagements: to see the Archbishop, Joost de Blank, at Bishopscourt ('most cordial and welcoming'); to preach in a Dutch Reformed Church ('an honour given to few Anglicans') and to address the clergy of Cape Town (Anglican, Dutch Reformed, Congregational, Methodist and Baptist), on 'Evangelism through the Local Church'. Canon Jan Hanekom, the chaplain to students at the local Dutch Reformed Church, was an enthusiastic supporter of the mission, and a day or two afterwards he drove John Stott to Stellenbosch to lecture at the seminary. Thirty-five years later he wrote to recall their drive together ('you admired the arum lilies growing wild in our fields. We stopped to enable you to take photographs') and to describe the far-reaching effects of their conversation in the car:

We were discussing the political situation in our country at that time and, as we stopped, you asked me a question to which I was at a loss to give an adequate answer and that challenged me so that it started a process of intense thinking on the whole system of 'apartheid'.

Your question was: 'How can any government by law prohibit two people from getting married if they love each other?' A simple question it may have seemed to someone from outside, but one that cut deeply into prejudices with which we had grown up and had accepted as natural.[96]

Hanekom went on to describe how it was when he was serving in the presbytery at Stellenbosch that the first move was made in the Dutch Reformed Church to reject apartheid as unscriptural: and he himself proposed to its General Synod in 1986 a similar rejection of Government policy which was carried by an overwhelming majority. His letter of 1994 continues:

To this day I thank the Lord for that beautiful spring day when we not only stopped for you to photograph our lovely arum lilies in their glory, but you also stopped me in my tracks with a challenging question posed in such a spirit of brotherly love that I could not do other than take it very seriously. This letter comes to testify to this and thank you for your influence in my life and ministry.[97]

From Cape Town he went on to Durban for four days to give a short course of lectures on 'The Christian Faith'. (Canon Bryan Green of Birmingham was booked to give a continuation of the series a fortnight later.) Here at last he found a little time to himself for some shopping, some bird-watching, some much-needed rest ('ten or eleven hours in bed each night'). He also managed a meeting with the Bishop of Natal and his wife ('They came to All Souls last September but were disappointed to find themselves listening to the XXXIX Articles!! I told them it must have done them good!').

The second of his two missions was in Johannesburg. It was not until the final Saturday that he found time to write home: 'It has been a most interesting time:

> It is astonishing to think that this vast city of skyscrapers and gold dumps is less than 75 years old, as gold was only discovered on the Rand in 1886. Built in the middle of the gold ridge, with the mines stretching east and west along the Rand, Jo'burg is 6,000 feet high, and one feels the height in a certain lassitude which visitors notice. It is remarkable that the gold mines go down to sea level, and the city often hears and feels considerable earth tremors.
>
> The mission at Wits [University of the Witwatersrand, Johannesburg] has been a good deal more effective than we had anticipated, altho' it has by no means made the impact which was apparent at the Univ. of Cape Town. The difference is only partly that Wits has a 50% Jewish student population and also a small but aggressive Rationalist Society who turned up in force at some of the meetings and even once distributed duplicated leaflets, denying the Resurrection, to people going in to my talk on 'Did Jesus rise from the dead?' !
>
> The other reason seems to be that the Christian community at U.C.T. [University of Cape Town] is larger, more united, more mature and more self-assured than at Wits. The Wits Christians tend to hide away in their own fellowship, while the U.C.T. Christians are in several cases occupying influential student positions 'at Varsity', as they call it. I was thrilled to hear yesterday that at the recent elections to the U.C.T. Students' Representative Council the Chairman and Secretary are both leading Christians, while a third S.R.C. member is someone who accepted Christ during the mission.
>
> Despite this we have had fairly good attendances. I have had to

speak at the lunch-hour as well as in the evening each day, and often at a 3rd meeting also. Between 500 and 600 have come to the midday meetings, but only about 200–300 in the evenings. Some U.C.T. Christians had written to friends of theirs at Wits, urging them to attend, and several came in this way. One of the most encouraging things has been that some leading students, who were invited to an introductory meeting before the mission began, have been coming and thinking hard. One particular fellow ... a teacher-training student and voracious reader, well-known in the college for his violently militant antichristian views, has come to several of the meetings and discussions. His attitude has completely changed, to everyone's amazement, and he is now 'not far from the kingdom of God'. It would indeed be wonderful if, like Saul of Tarsus, he could be brought one day to preach the faith he has tried to destroy.

John Stott's stay in Johannesburg included a visit to a native township ('there are one million Africans in and around Johannesburg and so little is being done for their spiritual welfare, let alone their material well-being'). He had a meeting with some of the leaders of the Church of England in South Africa:

It is a very small body, separate from the 'Church of the Province of S. Africa', consisting of only 12 European congregations in the Union, and seems to me to have no future unless it joins, or comes to some association with, the Church of the Province. The Church of the Province is largely Anglo-Catholic, and because of its monochrome character is not representative of the Anglican Communion. There are a few true evangelicals in it, and it seems to me of the greatest importance that we should pray and work towards the strengthening of this evangelical witness within it. Such evangelical testimony would be greatly enriched if the C.E.S.A. were to join the Church of the Province.

He paid a brief visit to the University of Pretoria to speak on 'The Theology of Evangelism'; and to the Kruger National Park for a farewell 'safari':

Winter is only just ending at this time in the Transvaal, so that many of the streams had dried up, and even wide rivers were reduced to a few sparse pools. But in these we saw a number of evil-looking crocodiles, and watched great galumphing hippos both sunbathing on the sand and disporting in the water. Birds were not very much in evidence, but we spotted 3 stately ostriches together, and saw many Lilac-breasted Rollers disappearing into the distance in a flash of brilliant blue. Quaint, eccentric Hornbills (which plaster their female mate in her nesthole so that she can't escape during incubation!) were often in evidence, and we saw 4 varieties, including the great Ground Hornbill, like a massive black turkey with a bright red bill ...

I have left until last giraffe, lion and elephant, the 3 most sought-after animals in the Reserve. Giraffes are surprisingly difficult to spot, despite their immense size. Their diamond pattern and camouflaged colouring fit so well into their background.

But we saw a number gazing down a little scornfully upon us from their superior height, and we watched half a dozen drinking at a pool. Stooping to the water presents the giraffe with a major problem, and it's really comic to see them gradually doing the splits with their front legs in order to reach water level.

We saw no leopard (nocturnal in its habits) or cheetah, but we were fortunate enough to see lion twice. Once we watched a pride of 7 together, several hundred yards away on the other side of a dry river bed. It was the last hour of daylight. Gradually they stirred their lazy bodies, yawned, stood up, stretched, ambled along a few paces and flopped into the dust again, rolling over on their backs and sides in the heat. But as the sun went down they pulled themselves together and moved off purposefully in single file to hunt the night's kill together. Another morning early we came across 2 young male lions lying in the dust by the roadside. Several cars had collected. Somehow they don't seem to connect cars with human beings, and are not afraid of them. We watched them only a few yards away, and when they eventually got up and walked casually away I could have put my hand out of the window and stroked them (but I didn't!).

It was September by the time John Stott was back in England. Just a year before he had spoken at the IVF Annual Public Meeting on 'Evangelism in the Student World'; and all that he had seen in Africa (as in America and Australia) confirmed his convictions. He had suggested two factors which combined to offer special importance to student evangelism. First,

because the majority of the world's leaders in politics, education, medicine, the law and the church are university graduates. Today's leaders were yesterday's students; today's students will be tomorrow's leaders.

Field Marshal Smuts, who read a chapter of his Greek Testament daily throughout his life, looked back to his Cambridge days in the early 1890's with lasting gratitude for the Christian witness of a fellow student, who is now a senior member of I.V.F. Gandhi at the age of nineteen entered University College London, and studied law. In 1893 at the age of twenty-three he spent a year on a legal case in Pretoria, South Africa, and had many contacts with missionaries of the South Africa General Mission. He must have come very near to conversion to Christ. What if Karl Marx, studying law, history, and philosophy in the Universities of Bonn and Berlin between 1835 and 1841, had met a committed and integrated Christian? Or when he was working in Paris or London later?

But secondly, and hardly less important, student minds and characters are still in process of development: 'They are not yet set in their views or ways. They are open to influence.'

Experience had shown him that there was a direct relationship between the ability of a mission to reach those outside organized religion, and the involvement of Christian students in circles of friendship and student activities unconnected with religion. And this was a test, whether at university or in later life, from which few Christians emerged with flying colours:

> We Christians disengage ourselves too much from the society of non-Christians. We find the company of Christians congenial; we are embarrassed by the presence of non-Christians. In this we are poles apart from the Lord Jesus.
>
> No wonder that evangelistic advance is so painfully slow. We are like soldiers who have lost contact with the enemy. Why is our evangelism so ineffective? Why is one of the criticisms of every modern evangelist that he does not reach the outsider, but only the church member and the fringe member? Why is it that at evangelistic services, the church or hall is not crammed to capacity and bulging at the doors? Why is there this frightening gulf between the churches and the masses? I will tell you. It is because the ordinary Christian is not mixing with non-Christians. From some experience of university missions, I would say that an indispensable condition for the 'success' of a mission is that Christian Union members have large numbers of non-Christian friends.[98]

Perhaps it is a lesson which every generation, whether in university or in local church, needs to learn afresh.

FOURTEEN

The Hookses:
A Writer's Retreat

1

Though born and bred a Londoner, and probably ready to agree with Dr. Johnson that 'when a man is tired of London, he is tired of life',[1] John Stott was always a lover of countryside and coast, with a preference for the wild and the remote. By the time he was twenty he had travelled with his family or with Robbie Bickersteth to Scotland, Wales and Ireland as well as France and Germany; and it was not surprising that on holiday, both as curate and as Rector, he should head for the open spaces. He was well-equipped with tent and ground sheet, stove and cooking pots, sleeping bag and pressure lamp; and these would be bundled into his 'jalopy' when the time came to set off on holiday. For four or five years running he gathered a group of friends to explore some different extremity of Great Britain. One of the first of these expeditions – perhaps before the jalopy was available – was to the west coast of Scotland, at Opinan on the southern entrance to Gair Loch. One or two of the party set off in advance by MG sports car while John Stott and a young medical student, Peter Thompson, followed by motorbike. 'This machine John borrowed', Dr. Thompson wrote later, 'and tried out on one or two trips round Regent's Park.' He continued:

We set off with the bike by train to Carlisle. We then hit the misty road north. All went well until we turned onto a more twisting road, when suddenly we were both thrown onto the grass verge as we rounded a bend. After a moment or two I regained consciousness and saw the bike and John lying beside me. He seemed unhurt but was unconscious. I was much relieved when soon he regained consciousness. It was clear no bones were broken or serious injury sustained. This was confirmed when we managed to get to the doctor in the nearby village. This little event (which could so easily have altered the history of the Anglican Church in the mid-twentieth century) delayed our progress north, and we missed the last Ballachulish ferry and had to find a 'B and B' before con-tinuing the Road to the Isles next morning, having read Psalm 116.We paused for a moment on verse 15, 'Precious in the sight of the LORD is the death of his saints.' Careful exegesis needed there![2]

The West Coast lived up to its reputation and it was a wild holiday for campers, rain beating on the tents and high waves pounding the beach with gannets diving headlong into the breakers. On Sunday they attended the service at the local chapel (doubling the congregation) and were hard put to it to sing hymns in Gaelic at what seemed to southern ears a funereal tempo. Then it was back by motorbike through the rain to Carlisle: 'we sat on newspaper in the corridor of the night train all the way to London.'

On a later holiday in Scotland they camped in Galloway, two hundred miles to the south. John Stott had recently become Rector-designate; it was on this holiday that he wrote the editor's letter for *All Souls* perched on a bollard at the end of Stranraer pier, and was taken for a poet. Their camp was at Ardwell Bay, half way between Stranraer and the lighthouse on the southern tip of the Mull of Galloway. They slept in small tents near the shore, in a meadow belonging to a local farm. The farmer's wife, Mrs. McGinty, cooked them an evening meal, and sometimes a memorable breakfast as well – porridge with thick fresh cream. They tramped the hills and along wide deserted beaches; sometimes they would take a boat and row out into the bay to fish for pollock; and always there were birds in abundance. In the early morning they would swim in the ice-cold sea – naked, as often as not, since no one ever used the path along the shore. One morning, however, they were not so lucky: a couple sauntered by while they were bathing and they had to stay submerged, slowly freezing to the marrow, till the coast was clear.[3]

It was in Galloway that John Stott had a brush with the military. Geoff Rocke was one of the party, and recalled how the two of them had gone off together to walk on Luce Sands at low tide and watch the variety of waders on the shoreline:

> The bay, which is vast, faces south, and we entered at the extreme western end which we subsequently learned was the only place 'unauthorized' folk could possibly enter without going through a guard post. Then, while walking slowly along the tide edge watching through glasses the large number of waders, suddenly there was a small explosion and the birds all took off in a panic. We stopped, wondering what it was, and then heard a distinct 'whistle'. In answer to John's question I said, 'Well, if it had been during the war I would have said it was a bomb!' Hardly were these words out of my mouth when there was a much bigger explosion, far too near to be comfortable.[4]

Horrified, they looked up to see a plane circling overhead. At the same moment they realized that their walk had brought them almost up to a carefully-arranged circle of brightly-painted canisters, obviously a target for bombing practice. Geoff Rocke had only recently discarded sticks and crutches following a war wound, but they moved pretty rapidly towards cover:

> On our way we discussed what other action, if any, we should take. We had hardly decided that if we heard any other unexpected noises it would be wise to lie down flat and provide as small a target as possible when there was a distinct rushing noise very near indeed. Down we went and something landed just behind us. It released a cloud of bright red-coloured gas.

After their first panicky reaction, they guessed that this was a Verey light, presumably to alert the aircraft overhead, or perhaps to warn them that they had entered a danger zone. They continued their dash towards the marshes at the edge of the beach, when an aircraft came in low over their heads – 'we thought we really were about to be strafed':

> When it had passed over we struggled over what seemed to be miles and miles of marsh not designed to be crossed at speed and eventually reached a road. Afterwards it did occur to us that it was hardly a wise thing to have done as the whole area was a range and doubtless littered with unexploded shells and bombs.

Other holidays were spent at Cley in Norfolk, famous as a haunt of bird watchers, at St. Just in Cornwall, in North Devon or in Dorset.

John Stott was drawn to the coast, partly by the bird-life, but mainly because of a life-long fascination for the sea: 'perhaps it is my Viking ancestry!'[5] Naturally enough, his friends who joined him on these holidays, looking back over something like fifty years, remembered mainly the incidents that amused them at the time. John Collins spent a week with him camping near Lynton in North Devon, on the cliff top above Lee Abbey:

> To get to civilization, we had to use a private road which belonged, I imagine, to the Conference Centre. John was very anxious not to be recognized. He wanted to be quiet, and to read. If it was known that he was in the vicinity, he would almost certainly have been invited to visit the Abbey, and asked to speak. One day when we reached the gate of the private land, we were challenged by, presumably, a member of the Lee Abbey staff.
>
> 'Who are you?' he asked.
>
> 'We are two campers' replied John.
>
> 'And what are your names?' said the man, officiously.
>
> With his most roguish smile, John immediately replied. 'I am Mr. Jones, and this (pointing at me) is my friend Mr. Smith.'
>
> The man looked at us suspiciously, but allowed us to go on our way.[6]

John Collins was with him again in 1952 when they decided to explore the coast of Pembrokeshire in South Wales. Studying the map, they hit on the village of Dale, close by the entrance to Milford Haven, twelve miles from the railway station at Haverfordwest, and nearly the most westerly point in Wales. They set off for what in the days before motorways was an eight-hour journey, and arrived under louring skies in gloom and rain. There was no hope of finding anywhere to pitch a tent. John Stott described it all in a long letter to his mother written a few days later:

> We are having an absolutely marvellous time, and I'm sending you these few lines to describe our doings to date. John Collins and I left London in the old jalopy at 8a.m. last Friday morning. We had a pretty hectic last few days; and I'm afraid I had to bring some work away in the end, which I hadn't been able to finish, but we actually left according to schedule. The old jalopy was in very good form ...

With 263 miles on the mileometer they arrived in Dale at 6 p.m. :

> It was raining pretty hard, but we were recommended by the

Postmistress of Dale to a farmer up the hill, and he let us sleep in a Nissen hut which he'd erected for the storage of potato boxes. Quite dry and clean. No rats even to enliven the proceedings! Before turning in John [Collins] and I wandered in the rain to the cliffs ... it was altogether rather miserable.[7]

It was so daunting and uncomfortable that John Collins was more than ready to return to London: but they woke next day to a glorious Pembrokeshire morning, the early sunshine sparkling on West Dale bay. After a morning spent walking the coastal path looking for a camp-site they took the car in the afternoon to St. Anne's Head:

All the time we were on the look out for a sheltered spot for camping, and called at many farmhouses, who were all 'too busy' to feed us. The women folk seem to do the milking and other farm work, which gives them little time for other things. However in the end we found our 2 needs met, the site on Saturday evening and the feeding place on Sunday. Both are ideal. Our tents are pitched in a very sheltered dale. Hills on 3 sides, the 4th opening out to the sea overlooking West Dale Bay. A little stream runs down the valley by our tents, which is ideal for washing and drinking. Behind us in the dale is an uninhabited farmhouse with outbuildings. Beyond these, and above on the flat, is a vast, derelict, wartime aerodrome. To reach our feeding place at Marloes, we tootle in the old jalopy round the perimeter track and down the run-way! The Morgans are most amusing, especially he. They've a boy and girl (teenagers) who both help on the farm. We've had 2 chickens slain in our honour already, plenty of E & B [eggs and bacon], farm salty butter and creamy milk.

The letter continues with details of how the Bishop of London had had a number of requests that the talk John Stott had given to the London Diocesan Conference on 'Evangelism as a continuing obligation on the laity in the parishes' should be published: this indeed was part of the work he had to bring with him on holiday ('but have now done, I'm glad to say').[8] Inevitably, too, he described to his mother what Pembrokeshire could offer to a bird-watcher:

We are keen to visit one of the bird sanctuary islands. Birds are fairly plentiful. Several pairs of mewing Buzzards which we've seen quite close. A few Choughs fly raggedly by from time to time, glossy black with crimson bills, uttering their wild, metallic cry which gives them their name.

Though the letter did not say so, they had taken some trouble to find the owner of the deserted valley with its ramshackle buildings, and obtain permission to camp. It belonged, they were told, to the Dale Castle Estate, so they returned by way of the airfield and boldly rang the bell of Dale Castle. They must have looked a scruffy and doubtful pair, and at first Colonel Hugh Lloyd-Philipps was wary and suspicious. But when they had managed to convince him that they were London clergymen on holiday, permission was given. Here in this little valley John Stott stayed for three weeks, visited by a succession of friends, until there was quite an encampment. They washed in the stream, bathed in the sea below the crumbling cliffs, ate an *al fresco* breakfast and a picnic lunch, and were fed royally in the evenings by Mrs. David Morgan of Glen View. After their meal David Morgan himself would sometimes entertain them from his repertoire of local verse, their favourite being a long saga, 'Over the hills to the poorhouse', about the black sheep of the family, who finally gets converted and rescues his mother from the poorhouse to which his spendthrift ways had condemned her: 'there isn't a dry eye when he recites it!'[9]

They discovered that the semi-derelict building in the little valley where they were camping was once a farmhouse, identified on the old Ordnance Survey map as Hook Vale. Everyone referred to it locally as either 'The Hooks' or 'The Hookses', though nobody knows for certain how the name originated. Guesses include the fact that the valley is in the shape of a hook and the possibility that an early tenant farmer occupying the house was a Mr. Hook. There is an old print which shows the house as originally a farm cottage, with a barn and a lean-to shed adjoining, three buildings in a kind of terrace, side by side. Later, the date 1888 was discovered burned into one beam of the barn loft (beams still joined by wooden pegs, without nails). The house itself is built of local sandstone quarried from a bank behind; and at some time earlier this century one of the buildings attached to it was demolished and the other rebuilt to enlarge the house. Clustered round it, some across the little stream, some nearer the cliff, were outbuildings to serve as cow shed, stable and barn. All were at least semi-derelict: one had enough slates missing to show a gaping hole in the roof. Beyond the buildings was the cliff-edge, and a magnificent seascape. Here John Stott sat in the hot sunshine of that idyllic summer, sheltered in a little nook just below the cliff top, preparing the eight main addresses he was to give three months later at Cambridge in his first university mission. It was therefore the seed-bed of his best-selling book, *Basic Christianity*. Raising his head from Bible and notebook, he was surrounded by bird-life in abundance:

Gannets were fishing in West Dale Bay, dropping in their almost perpendicular dive from a height of up to 100 feet; and Fulmars from St. Anne's Head, stiff-winged and inquisitive, sailed by. There was also a constant traffic of five members of the Crow family: Rooks, Crows, Jackdaws, Ravens and – best of all, those 'cavaliers of the cliffs' – Choughs. Jet black with scarlet bill and legs, expert in aerobatics, probing comically into the turf and calling to one another with raucous abandon, they were a source of constant entertainment and delight.

Moreover, about five miles out lay the off-shore islands of Skomer and Skokholm, with Grassholm beyond, world-famous for their breeding colonies of sea birds.

It was the urgent need to combat the menace of the U-boat in the Second World War which put an end to Hook Vale as a working farm. The level plateau on the top of the cliff was taken over as an airfield, a satellite station of Talbenny, five miles to the north overlooking St. Bride's Bay. Concrete runways were laid across the farmland, hangars and control-buildings hastily erected, and the station was manned and opened on 1 June 1942.[10] Its first aircraft were Wellington medium bombers mainly on anti-submarine patrol, but raids on enemy shipping were carried out over the French coast, certainly as far south as the Gironde estuary on the Bay of Biscay. Returning to base was a hazardous operation in bad weather on the exposed peninsula, since runways were approached low above the top of the cliffs:

A particularly tragic accident as a result of this occurred on August 11, 1942 when Wellington HX384 'T' of 304 Squadron was taking off on an anti-submarine sweep. The runway into wind was unserviceable and the aircraft failed to get airborne in the strong cross-wind and went over the cliff into the sea. Superhuman efforts at rescue were made but there were no survivors in the rough sea.[11]

The following year the Wellingtons departed, and in September 1943 the Royal Navy exchanged its base at Angle on the further shore of Milford Haven for RAF Dale, which became home to a target-towing unit. Next, the Fleet Air Arm took over the airfield, 'an ideal choice', since the length of the runways allowed the use of their larger twin-engined aircraft such as Blenheims and Beauforts and the De Havilland Mosquito. Long after the war John Stott met and talked with William Cross, by then a prominent Christian business man, who had been stationed at Dale as a young RNVR Lieutenant in the Fleet Air Arm for two periods of several months during 1944 and 1945. He was there as a pilot in his early twenties and remembered the station well. In his time it was served by about five hundred service personnel, living mostly in Nissen huts, built of breeze blocks with an asbestos roof, to the north-east of the airfield; the Hookses was much sought-after as accommodation for one or two married couples. Two squadrons, each of twelve Beauforts, were stationed at Dale: heavy, lumbering twin-engined torpedo-bombers, each with one torpedo and several depth-charges. About twenty would go out on patrol each day to protect transatlantic convoys against attacks by U-boats. At the various 'dispersal points' off the perimeter track the aircraft were parked, two to a bay, nose to tail, and securely tethered down. There were a few large hangars between the airfield and the camp where maintenance could be carried out. One unofficial job which fell to the Dale squadrons was dropping supplies to the lighthouse keepers on Skokholm, flying as low as possible, perhaps only fifty feet up, to throw packages out of the window, or drop crates through the torpedo doors.[12] After VE day the station continued in use for a variety of training purposes until it closed down in September 1947. Five years later, when John Stott discovered it, the remains of all this activity were still clearly to be seen. The disused runways criss-crossed the former farmland, grass-grown and scarred by the frosts of five winters; and some of the buildings were being used for storage by a local farmer. The little farmhouse with its out-buildings was untenanted and falling into ruin.

Camped at the foot of the valley in that summer of 1952, John found himself wondering if there was a chance that the property might be for sale. He began to dream dreams of a Pembrokeshire haven for missionaries on furlough, a rural retreat for conferences and reading parties, and a place he himself could return to summer by summer. So before his holiday ended he paid a second visit to the Castle, asking to borrow the keys and look round the property:

> What struck me during my inspection was that although the house had not been occupied since the end of the war, it had been very sturdily built to withstand Atlantic storms, with walls some two and a half feet thick. So when I returned the key to Colonel Lloyd-Philipps I plucked up courage to ask that if ever The Hookses were to come on the market, I would be interested to hear.

On his return to London, John Stott wrote to confirm this conversation; but a year went by and nothing further happened. He therefore put the idea out of his mind, assuming that God did not intend him to become a landowner, and uneasily conscious that he would scarcely have had the money to buy the property, even had it been for sale.

The next summer found him in Cornwall camping near Bude; but at the end of August his post included a letter from a Haverfordwest Estate Agent saying that the owner was considering the sale of Hooks Farm House and asking if he was still interested. He replied at once, enquiring about the price; and a week later was told that an offer of £1,000 had already been refused, but that the owner might be prepared to accept £1,200.[13] There was also, John Stott remembers, a duplicated sheet of particulars suggesting that The Hookses would be very suitable for a café in the National Park: 'I shuddered at the prospect!' It all seemed something of a pipe-dream but he was reluctant to see such an opportunity go by. He therefore had the property surveyed, and was advised to offer no more than £500 for it since, though structurally sound, it was falling into increasing disrepair. This he did, only to be told that it had already changed hands for £800. When he asked why he had not been given the chance to raise his bid, he was told they assumed that a clergyman was too impoverished to do so!

So The Hookses became the property of Peter Conder, Warden of Skokholm Island, who needed somewhere on the mainland to live during the winter. Only a few months later, however, even before he had been able to begin to repair the house, Peter Conder was appointed Director of the Royal Society for the Protection of Birds and moved to Bedfordshire. Moreover, by this time John Stott had completed his first book, *Men with a Message,* and Longmans had just paid him £750. He therefore offered Peter Conder £750 and acquired the entire property. A few months later Peter Conder came to lunch at the Rectory, and in the course of their talk together John Stott told him (from a quixotic sense of honour) that it hardly seemed fair to offer him less than he had paid for The Hookses, and handed over a further £50. It was to be an acquisition whose major importance for his whole life and ministry he barely realized at the time. He has been fond of describing the discovery of The Hookses as 'an outstanding example of serendipity' – a word coined by Horace Walpole in the eighteenth century to describe the faculty of making happy and unexpected discoveries by accident, finding what one was not looking for. And there seems no reason why serendipity should not be part of the workings of Providence.

2

As the new owner of The Hookses John Stott was now faced with the task of putting it all in order. That December of 1954 there were gale-force winds on the peninsula strong enough to lift the roof off one of the outbuildings and carry it the length of the valley and up on to the airfield. Fortunately Peter Conder had insured the property for the few months he owned it, and this insurance was still in force and paid for the re-roofing. That same month just after Christmas John Stott with his sister Joy drove down to examine his purchase. John Barrett (Director of Dale Fort Field Centre, and a well-known marine biologist) together with his wife Ruth took pity on them and, since The Hookses was plainly uninhabitable, invited them to stay. John Barrett himself was a much-respected figure in the small local community, and for many years Secretary of the Parochial Church Council. His reading of the lessons in Dale Church reminded John Stott of an Old Testament prophet!

The property was eligible for a post-war 'Improvement Grant' of £400, provided that certain conditions were met: that it be connected to mains water; that a septic tank be installed; and that the windows be enlarged to represent a certain proportion of each room's cubic capacity. While this work was being done, a Rayburn stove was installed for cooking and hot water; light and warmth depended on paraffin lamps and heaters. These improvements rendered the house habitable, and various 'working parties' of friends were invited to help decorate and make it comfortable.

Access was a particular problem. There had once been another farm, Longlands, in the middle of the airfield, but this had been completely demolished. Plainly there must once have been a proper road, but in John Stott's early days at The Hookses there were only muddy tracks:

> Then one year, some people were down with a baby who needed urgently to be taken to hospital, and they got stuck in the mud ... that was the thing that finally persuaded me to have a running battle with the local authority, claiming that it was part of the Queen's Highway and it was their responsibility to maintain it. My argument was that before the war, obviously, there were public thoroughfares to Longlands Farm and to Hooks Farm.

Eventually the local authority accepted this, and laid a hard surface from the gate at the top of the road to the perimeter track of the airfield, which it is their responsibility to maintain.

Attentive readers of John Stott's book *I Believe in Preaching* will have noticed in the Author's Introduction a sentence of thanks to 'my friends Dick and Rosemary Bird who for many years have accompanied me to my Welsh cottage, The Hookses, and unselfishly created the conditions in which I could write in peace and without distraction.'[14] 'Dickie' Bird as he was generally known, and his wife Rosemary, were long-standing friends of John Stott. Rosemary had been nursing at the London Hospital just after the war when Dick was also working there as a pathologist, and they sometimes came to All Souls together. John Stott married them in 1951 and they served together as CMS and All Souls' missionaries in Jordan until Dickie's health brought them home. After a year in a sanatorium he got a research grant to work for a doctorate at the London School of Tropical Medicine, and they and their young family became staunch members of All Souls.

Dickie and Rosemary were among the first to visit The Hookses. There was now mains water on the site, thanks to the improvement grant, but to only a single outside tap. They slept in their old landrover, prepared impromptu meals, and made themselves useful. Rosemary remembers Joy wielding a paint brush, wearing (partly as a tease) a pair of jeans so disreputable that her brother was affronted by them and was forever trying to get her to replace them. There was much discussion about the colour of the bannisters: as a concession to Joy it was agreed that they should be blue but John Stott wanted light blue for Cambridge and Joy characteristically stuck out for dark blue for Oxford. When John stood his ground, she threatened alternate stripes as a suitable compromise! She had a habit when washing up of emptying the tea-leaves out of the kitchen window. John Stott objected, saying that they attracted flies, but to no avail. The next Sunday in church the first lesson from Ecclesiastes 10 began 'Dead flies cause the ointment of the apothecary to send forth a stinking savour ...' Joy caught Rosemary's eye, and they all began to shake with suppressed laughter. 'Packie', the housemother from the Rectory in the pew behind them, was very properly appalled at their behaviour.[15]

So, little by little and with the help of many friends, the property took shape. The floor of the barn loft, riddled with woodworm, was replaced, and the loft itself partitioned into sleeping quarters for groups of young people who came down from All Souls. One or two members of the church, inspired by the beauty of the place and its potential usefulness, gave or bequeathed modest sums of money to help restore or convert the outbuildings. Late December, before or after Christmas, was a favourite time for John Stott to snatch a few days at The Hookses. He would catch the midnight newspaper train from Paddington, laden with food and supplies, and find a taxi at Haverfordwest to take him (and usually a friend or two) on to Dale. Here they would 'pick up the order' at the village shop – paraffin, candles, bread, butter, bacon and so on – and be driven on across the airfield to make breakfast in The Hookses' kitchen. It was on one of these midnight journeys from Paddington that he met his match in a Welsh Trades Union secretary, as he later recounted with some relish to a group of medical students:

I remember on one occasion I was travelling in a train in South Wales in a sleeping compartment. In the second-class compartment, as the English people here will know, you have a double bunk, one bed above the other. In Cardiff, a rather drunk Welshman got in to share my compartment with me and I discovered that he was a Union official of one of the mining Unions and a Communist. When he discovered that I was a pastor, he was shocked beyond description. He said in his sing-song Welsh voice, 'It is time you became productive, man, you are a parasite on the body politic.'[16]

The Hookses soon acquired a visitors' book. The first entry in April 1955 is from David Pytches, then at Tyndale Hall, Bristol; Michael Botting at Ridley Hall, Cambridge; and Eric Morgan, an undergraduate from Oxford. They were members of a student working party, so the morning was given to their books. In the afternoon they worked on the restoration of the property and in the evening John Stott led them in Bible study. Michael Botting remembered long afterwards 'his absolute conviction of the trustworthiness of God's Word in the Scriptures'. He remembered too, with some vividness, the journey home:

> On 19th April we arose at 4.15am to get away really early. Before we had reached Brecon we met up with David Pytches to discover that David Bishop, who was driving the other car, had had a smash, because he went to sleep at the wheel! Five of us travelled in John's car to Oxford. At one point, possibly as we were on the outskirts of Oxford, we were stopped by the police and John was informed that he had been travelling at 60 mph in a built up area.[17]

Whenever John Stott was at The Hookses the local bird life was a continuing preoccupation. The first hide was built on the little headland at the end of the valley – an extremity of 'Pembroke's pastoral forehead' – using a strip of old corrugated-iron dragged from the wreckage of a hut on the airfield. Turf dug from the cliff-top did something to cover it; and a peculiarly disgusting dead rabbit, also found on the airfield, was laid out within camera-range to attract the various gulls: those less ornithologically-minded were carefully instructed in how to distinguish between them. As the property came slowly into shape the immediate pressures of do-it-yourself repairs and restoration eased a little. There was time for walks about the peninsula, boat trips to the off-shore islands, chilly bathes from Marloes beach. As night fell, the adjoining headland twinkled with the lights of HMS *Harrier*, the shore-based naval meteorological station at Kete: to the eye of the imagination the single storied flat-roofed buildings seemed to have a middle-eastern look about them, and were therefore known to The Hookses as 'Damascus'. One visitor lay awake in the night-sleeper returning to London and (borrowing a little from William Wordsworth and Thomas Gray) wrote an Ode which John Stott had lettered and framed, and which still hangs in the cottage thirty-five years on:

O happy times at Hookses!
  Long hours of leisured ease
On Pembroke's pastoral forehead
  Caressed by winds and seas:
The black-backed and the herring gull
  Soar swiftly o'er the bay;
(The Greater has the blacker back,
  The Lesser's back is grey).

O happy days at Hookses!
  O days of sea and sky!
O peaceful paths of lost content!
  O steak-and-kidney pie!
O hours of exercise and toil
  With long and arduous climbs!
O hours of erudition, with
  The crossword from *The Times!*

O happy nights at Hookses –
  For when the days decline
The lamps of little Eastern homes
  From far Damascus shine.
High in the vault of Hookses sky
  The stars their vigil keep:
For us, in earth's diurnal course,
  Eleven hours of sleep.

O happy stars at Hookses –
  Plough, Pleiads and Orion:
Beneath you lies a mound of turf
  And corrugated iron:
In which, as on a slab nearby
  The birds dismember rabbits,
The Rector notes with all-seeing eye
  Their predatory habits.

O happy times at Hookses!
How fast the moments fly:
To eat and idle, swim and sleep –
And then to say good-bye.
So soon the last long lingering look,
So soon the London train!
O may it bring me swift and soon
To Hookses Vale again![18]

Visitors to Hookses might find themselves turning their hand to any task. From the same pen as 'Happy Days at Hookses' came, by request, a song for the Rector to sing (perhaps with his staff of curates) at the All Souls New Year party. Only a fragment survives:

Of London's fair city
I bring you a ditty
concerning two churches
I think will be known:
You will guess, never erring,
to which I'm referring,
All Souls and St. Peter's
of Marylebone.[19]

Though only briefer references to it will appear in volume two, the Hookses continued to play a major role in the story of John Stott's life. What follows, therefore, offers glimpses well beyond the 1950s up to the present day. For the Hookses has never been simply a private possession: it has always offered hospitality not only to John Stott himself, but to a variety of friends and to their growing families, as well as a host of conferences, reading parties, and groups from All Souls and other churches. Clubhouse helpers and staff, and All Souls missionaries on furlough, were always welcome; and the All Souls Church Day School sometimes used it for their School Journey week. The UCCF Writers and Painters workshop came year after year, and other groups have included Polish theological students, veterinary students, Langham Trust scholars, various college Christian Unions and some local secondary school pupils. On hearing that a group at Trinity College, Carmarthen were having trouble in getting permission from the authorities to meet as a Christian Union on college premises, John Stott offered the use of The Hookses, should they ever want to run a weekend house party. The following October, four weeks into the Autumn term, about twenty of them took up the invitation with a Travelling Secretary as one of the weekend leaders:

I remember with great affection that first time we visited The Hookses, in October 1968. I collected a car-load of students from Carmarthen, en route from Bristol to Pembroke. After the seemingly endless journey from Haverfordwest to Dale, we arrived in the village and followed the instructions for finding the cottage. 'Up the narrow lane that leads to a gate at the top of the hill. Through the gate and turn left on to a wide deserted runway. Along the runway for about 600 yards, until you come to a cart track off to the left' ... and there was the small cottage and outhouses tucked in a little valley, with the Atlantic rollers crashing on the rocks below. We opened the door to the cottage and there was the stove burning brightly, oil lamps had been lit and a meal was on the way. We had arranged with two ex-students from Cardiff who were teaching in the area, to help us with the cooking over the weekend. They had no problems in carrying out the task. A file lay on the table containing careful instructions for every conceivable need that might arise![20]

The Hookses has also played host to several couples on honeymoon, while for David and Jane Wells it holds equally romantic associations: it was at The Hookses, while David Wells was living at the Rectory working for a London BD, that he proposed and was accepted.

The All Souls International Fellowship, led by Robert and Sarah Howarth, regularly brought a 'training group' of potential ASIF Fellowship Group leaders for an annual study week:

We discovered that a week at The Hookses was an ideal way of welding these potential ASIF team members together. It did something that even a year of weekly meetings couldn't do; some deep friendships were formed; numbers of individuals seemed to take fire spiritually whilst we were there. And they then became really effective helpers in ASIF – and hopefully, in their home churches when they finally returned.[21]

A typical house party might contain a student from Pakistan, a couple from China, a Swiss chef, a doctor from Ceylon, a Canadian mathematician, Ghanaians, perhaps an Indian, an Egyptian or an Australian – and two or three from Great Britain:

In those days, The Hookses was still pretty primitive ... the dormitory was draughty – basic even by the standards of most of the visitors; the experience of going to bed with a pressure lamp and the shortage of hot water (especially in April) were quite difficult for some of them. Yet, I believe these supposedly negative features in fact contributed to the good spirit among them. And then there was Sarah's food – great jorums of stew; piles of bread, butter and jam; and tea. Also porridge for breakfast (unknown to the majority).[22]

In addition, ASIF used The Hookses to provide holiday weeks for members of the Fellowship whose time (or budget) in the UK did not really allow for holidays. These were always immensely popular, and the strong sense of community engendered by The Hookses lifestyle helped numbers of lonely and perhaps homesick overseas visitors to feel a sense of belonging. There were Bible Schools, too, led by Julian Charley or by Alan Stibbs, evangelistic barbecues for the students at Dale Fort, and endless games, walks, expeditions, swimming and, of course, bird watching.

Often the Howarths would have their three young boys with them at The Hookses during these times. Many of the ASIF members were young, single students, missing their own families. To be part of a family grouping, even for a week, made England – and Wales – feel more like home. It was not only adults and students who valued the sense of remoteness and isolation, the surrounding sea, the wide skies, and the freedom that Hookses had to offer. Comments in the Visitors' Book, as well as many letters, testify to how popular the place, and 'Uncle John' himself, became to successions of his friends' children: 'Absolutely spiffing ... it was blast ... Hookses is ace, cool and simply radical ... fab, smeg, brill, amazing.' A letter from Toby Howarth reads:

> Dear Uncul John Rector
> This is a lovly plasce ('hookses') we have fond a lot entreses up to the arefelde and hiding plasces Thank-you for buying it. We love going for warkes on the clifs with a grone up. I like your preching and the sivises you take.
>
> Lovwe from Toby[23]

Nor was it only the children of friends who çame but also his own family. In about his third summer at Hookses Joanna stayed there with her three daughters, John Stott's nieces, Caroline, Sarah and Jenny. He recalls sitting with them every day on the cliffs, reading from *Treasures of the Snow*. Caroline would be about nine or ten, and Jenny just old enough to follow the story with its drama and spiritual struggles set against the high green hills and snow-capped mountains above Montreux.[24] A generation later Caroline's son John (John Stott's great-nephew) aged about eight, confidently affirmed; 'I'm going to have my honeymoon at The Hookses'.[25] On one occasion a visitor to Hookses, reading a story to his small son, found his host offering improvements as he went along. Not surprisingly, it was a story about a bird ...

> I remember being at The Hookses with him when our eldest son was eighteen months old. I was reading a children's story called 'The Little Red Hen' to Andy. 'Once upon a time there was a little red hen who lived in a farmyard.' John heard me reading it and said, 'If I had written that I would have described the hen in much more detail. "Once upon a time there was a little red hen. He had a red comb, red feathers, red legs and red feet. In fact he was red all over ... "'[26]

In the evenings, by the soft glow of oil lamps, there would often be reading aloud. Saki was a particular pleasure. John Stott had been introduced to his short stories at Rugby, and though not all are quite to his taste, he never tired of re-reading his favourites, such as 'The Story Teller', 'The Stalled Ox' or 'The Secret Sin of Septimus Brope'. 'The Lumber Room' enjoyed a special place in his affections: a small boy, Nicholas, was not believed when he stated that there was a frog in his bread-and-milk ('he had put it there himself so he felt entitled to know something about it.'):

> The fact that stood out clearest in the whole affair, as it presented itself to the mind of Nicholas, was that the older, wiser, and better people had been proved to be profoundly in error in matters about which they had expressed the utmost assurance.
> 'You said there couldn't possibly be a frog in my bread-and-milk; there *was* a frog in my bread-and-milk,' he repeated, with the insistence of a skilled tactician who does not intend to shift from favourable ground.[27]

Attempts have been made, by Dick Lucas among others, to add some of the P. G. Wodehouse short stories to the nightly list; and visitors are sometimes allowed to read their favourites: but Saki remains unchallenged as the authentic Hookses tradition.[28]

Birds and visitors were allowed to break into the daily routine. Twice John Stott spent a week on Skokholm, three and a half miles due west, 'a patch of red-sandstone in the open Atlantic (for the nearest land to the south-west is South America)'[29] Less than a mile long, smaller than 250 acres in area, it is known by bird lovers the world over. Away to the north-west lies Skomer, which John Stott visits regularly – nearly 100 visits in all – and which is particularly known as the breeding ground of the Manx Shearwater, with over 100,000 pairs mating in a single season. It was on Skomer that some friends drew John Stott's attention to a pair of Manx Shearwaters engaged in frenzied activity and asked if they were mating or fighting. They received the laconic reply of the mischievous bachelor, 'I understand there's not much difference.'

3

In the early years John Stott had no bedroom or study set apart for his own use, but shared the rather cramped accommodation in the main house with whatever visitors happened to be there. But in 1960 Charles Fairweather, the building contractor, who was a member of All Souls, arranged to undertake the necessary construction work to provide John Stott with a permanent room of his own. In the alcove formed by the juxtaposition of two outbuildings nearest to the cliff there was a triangular patch of land, with walls on two sides formed by the ends of the barn and an outbuilding, and the third side open towards the sea. Here Charles Fairweather built an enclosing wall, largely of glass, and added a roof; and this triangular room with its magnificent picture window, known as 'The Hermitage', served as study-bedroom until 1990. Then, with the Church Commissioners' retirement grant and an unexpected windfall (from the sale of what proved to be a valuable Victorian bookcase which had long stood in the basement dining-room of the Rectory),[30] a separate bedroom was constructed, a sitting room-cum-office with kitchenette, and a shower room with lavatory, creating an independent flat. The study contains copies of the main reference books needed for whatever John Stott is writing at the time. Thanks originally to a small generator, and now to mains electricity, it has an electric desk lamp (and an electric drill, and even an electric blanket). Before the mains cable was laid in 1997, the lighting and heating were for many years by calor gas, replacing the original oil lamps which proved too dangerous for visitors unused to paraffin.

Here, at his desk in the Hermitage, John Stott writes in longhand, covering page after page with deliberate speed, drawing on notes made from his reading and study beforehand, with little in the way of corrections and crossings-out. Frances Whitehead reads his handwriting and stock abbreviations with practised ease, typing each MS by word-processor either in London or in her adjoining office at The Hookses. 'Visitors wonder', John Stott comments,

> how I can concentrate when, as I sit at my desk, I look out across West Dale Bay to the open Atlantic beyond and birds of all descriptions fly by. I've seen seventy-five varieties in the immediate

environs and another twenty-five in the Gann Estuary near Dale. I can only say that I find these things an inspiration rather than a distraction ... I can read and write for 10 to 12 hours a day without interruption. At the same time, I always keep my binoculars on my desk within easy reach of my right hand.[31]

It is The Hookses, and the coastal scenery and natural life of Pembrokeshire which evoke in John Stott the latent naturalist and the observer's eye for the wonders of the created order. In a letter to London he described The Hookses in winter, on a visit with Dick and Rosemary Bird:

> It's wild and wet down here. Huge rollers are pounding on the rocks. Great globules of spume are being blown up into the valley. The stream is in spate. The new turf we laid is excellent; already you'd hardly suspect it. Despite the weather, a white and a purple heather are in full flower in the rockery, and the Rowan tree has healthy buds on its lower branches. Dick and I have taken our exercise in continuing the excavation behind the dorm, he working from one end and I from the other: we hope to meet before the week ends! Meanwhile Rosemary is weeding the rockery.

He goes on to say that Sunday found them the only visitors in Dale Church among a handful of local residents, all known to them. After lunch (and the mandatory half-hour's sleep) they called on the Barretts to discover where Jack Snipe, a winter migrant rarer than the Common Snipe, could be seen:

> About 3 pairs of Goldeneye in Pickleridge Pools as we walked by; then across the stream, round the muddy path skirting the salt marsh, then right and left into that huge meadow speckled with patches of reeds. This was where we'd looked before. This time we found them! We flushed about half a dozen, obviously different from Common Snipe: (1) they fly at the last moment when one is only 4–6 feet away, (2) they are silent, (3) they do not 'zigzag' or 'tower' like Common Snipe, but fly fairly low and take cover again within a few yards, and (4) they are noticeably smaller. – I'm very glad to know where they are and how to identify them. They only arrive (from Northern Scandinavia) this month.[32]

Indeed, winter visits had a charm all their own. In the early days, oil lamps lent a comforting glow to the windows of the various buildings. Stars were brilliant in the frosty sky. Though the winds might make it difficult to stand when crossing the airfield or on the cliff top, the valley was in shelter:

> Even during the gales of mid-winter The Hookses is safe and snug. It is well-sheltered from the North, East and West. It is exposed only to the south. Then when a southerly wind brings the great Atlantic rollers pounding against the cliffs, and drives the rain horizontally up the gully, it is wise to stay indoors. Once or twice I have seen the whole valley white – not with frost or with snow, but with spume. Then the following day the bracken has turned brown from the salt. Its powers of regeneration are amazing, however. Few plants can stand the salt air; the most successful are fuchsia, hydrangea, potentilla, buddleia, cotoneaster, honeysuckle, escalonia and hebe; all these flourish at The Hookses.[33]

Visitors today find, tucked below the plateau of the airfield, a considerable estate in miniature. Standing back from the cliffs but nearest the sea, is the barn, now converted to a dormitory and a games room below. Next to that is the Hermitage, the study looking across the cliff-top towards St. Anne's Head: among the few pictures in the small adjoining bedroom is an Indian portrait of Christ. Further up the valley, on the eastern side of the stream and across a plank bridge, are 'Helen's Hut' and 'Jo's Barn', the former stable and byre, provide sleeping quarters for visitors. The 'Hut' takes its name from a Scot, Helen Menzies, a widow in the All Souls congregation and a pioneer in hospitality to overseas students who left a small bequest, which paid for the conversion. In a similar way, 'Jo's Barn' commemorates another All Souls stalwart, Miss Jonas. It contains a photograph of her sitting reading letters and wearing a hat; and a couple of her pen-and-ink sketches of frogs and harvest mice. And there is an inscription in proper lapidary style:

Miss A. M. Jonas
('Jo' to her friends)
1875 – 1961
Servant of Jesus Christ
indefatigable in work and intrepid in witness
by whose generosity
and in whose memory
'Jo's Barn' continues in use today.[34]

Below the main house on the western side of the stream the old pigsty was turned into a tool shed next to a workshop, and there is a garage and a store for Calor gas. In April 1992 John Stott and three friends laid a concrete path thirty feet long outside Frances Whitehead's office 'so that she won't get her feet wet in winter. Because she has just celebrated the 36th anniversary of her becoming All Souls Church Secretary and mine, we are naming the path "The Frances Whitehead Walkway"!'[35] Beyond the fence sheep belonging to Elwyn Bryan, John Stott's neighbour at Dale Hill Farm, wander across the airfield. They are a pleasant reminder of The Hookses' setting, amid a pastoral way of life which is close to the natural order and, in essentials, still unchanged over many centuries. In Spring the valley fills with wild flowers. Yellow flags grow where the stream runs into a little pond beside the Hermitage. There are marsh marigolds, bulrushes, purple loosestrife, and red campion flowering all summer in the damp places by the stream. In the pond itself the water lilies open for the dawn and close at dusk, and marsh trefoil spreads matted rootstocks out into the water.

The main house, whose two red chimneys almost reach the level of the surrounding plateau, is painted pink, slate-roofed with natural hardwood front door and window frames. Upstairs are the two original bedrooms of the farm-cottage, together with two additions. When in 1979 Joy died intestate, John Stott and Joanna were legatees as next of kin. Joy had always loved The Hookses from the earliest days, often visiting it (accompanied by her beagle, Fanny, 'as bad in character as it was good in looks').[36] Her name appeared on the opening page of the visitors' book with her address given in typical Joy style as 'Poste Restante, Purgatory'. With her legacy and in her memory John Stott built a first-floor extension at the back of the main house with a double bedroom known as 'Joy's Room', a single bedroom called 'Fanny's Room', and a separate shower and lavatory. 'Fanny's Room' has a photograph of Fanny (1966–79), and 'Joy's Room' contains family photographs, including one of Bullens Hill Farm, her home for almost twenty years.

At the last count The Hookses boasted more than forty representations of its owner's beloved birds: carved on a door knocker, depicted in tiles and fabrics, woven into rugs and tapestries, illustrated in pictures, prints and calendars – even dangling as a mobile over the dining-table. For life at The Hookses, birds are a continually-recurring theme, and the nearby Gann Estuary is a favourite haunt for bird watching. It provided one of the very rare occasions when John Stott's ornithological judgment all but failed him. Rosemary Bird was walking there with Dickie, her husband, when to their astonishment they saw a Hoopoe with its characteristic crest and plumage: they had met it in the Middle East, but had not known of it in Britain. On their return they hastened to inform John Stott, only to be told firmly, 'Hoopoes are unlikely to be seen on the Gann Estuary'. After church the following day the Hookses' party was invited to coffee at the Vicarage, and in the course of conversation John Stott asked John Barrett, the local naturalist, 'Have you seen anything interesting on the Gann?'

'Yes – there is a Hoopoe.'

But if Rosemary expected an apology she was disappointed: the words 'unlikely to be seen' amply covered this ornithological improbability.[37] It was Rosemary Bird, too, who was among The Hookses party for John Stott's sixtieth birthday in April 1981. He took much pleasure in drawing their attention to his personal devaluation, chapter 27 of Leviticus:

> Your valuation of a male from twenty years old up to sixty years old shall be fifty shekels of silver ... and if the person is sixty years old and upward, then your valuation for a male shall be fifteen shekels ...[38]

In something of the same way, he came up from the Hermitage one day, chuckling about the Greek of Ephesians 3:8, where Paul speaks of himself as 'less than the least of all saints' – or, by coining a word, the 'leaster' of all the saints. What Paul here writes in Greek transliterates as *elachistoteros* – and it seemed to him highly appropriate that 'stoteros' should imply 'leaster', less than the least of all saints. The less respectful among those who were with him at Hookses, claimed to have discovered in this word the secret of his girl friend: 'Ella-kiss-Stoteros'![39]

People sometimes ask whether The Hookses, so isolated in its little valley, is not in danger from arson by Welsh nationalists, a fate which has been suffered elsewhere in Wales by second homes belonging to the English. In fact, however, the southern half of Pembrokeshire is English-speaking, and popularly known as 'Little England beyond Wales'. John Stott has never encountered the smallest hostility, but has found himself and his many visitors constantly made welcome by the local community.[40] Of course at first he was a stranger – a 'Londoner': but it did not take long for his real interest in the village to become apparent and appreciated. He quickly made friends in the locality, not least through the parish church; and when a suitable hostess (not to say cook!) was with him, he would invite local friends in to an evening meal, and perhaps (once the generator was installed) to see slides of his travels and the exotic birds he had photographed. He and Frances, or perhaps Rosemary Bird, would plan the menu: what will they eat? Shall we give them sherry? How long will they want to stay? Shall we read and pray with them before the evening ends?[41]

The local parish in which The Hookses is situated has three churches –

St. James's Dale, St. Peter's Marloes and St. Bride's, and Sunday services alternate between them. Over many years John Stott has become a friend to five successive incumbents and a familiar figure to the congregation. In the early days – perhaps for ten years in succession – he used to arrange a week's study-holiday for ordinands. On Sunday they would sometimes be allowed to take over the Service at Dale Church: one would preach, others conduct morning prayer, read lessons and so on. On Sunday evening they would occasionally lead an open-air gospel service on the Dale waterfront.[42] From time to time when he is at The Hookses John Stott accepts an invitation to preach, sometimes on an occasion when all three churches in the benefice join together. After an 11 a.m. service at Dale, the custom then was for the Vicar, the Revd. Peter Davies, to invite the congregation home for coffee:

> John and his friends would always join us and we had some lively conversations. The floor would usually be held by John Barrett, and occasionally he and John would get on to birds, to our great delight. On one occasion my wife Tiggy and our third son Alan, who was living at home at the time, thought they had seen a Black Winged Stilt over a period of several days in West Dale meadow. The two Johns were sceptical, but John Barrett set off later to check up; he called by at the Vicarage that afternoon to confirm the sighting ...[43]

Occasionally in these conversations even ornithology had to take second place. Peter Davies remembers how, after one Sunday service,

> John took me to task for something I'd said – I think it was at a Baptism when I'd referred to the child 'Being made a Christian' or had underlined that point which is made in our Prayer Book. John picked this up and we discussed it in a most amicable way. It was good to be kept on one's toes; it is so easy to expect and to get no reaction to sermons.[44]

Those who have only known John Stott on the steps of All Souls, dressed in a Sunday suit and very much a Londoner, are surprised at the transformation once he is a local landowner in his beloved Pembrokeshire. 'In Dale he is one of us, content to be one of a small village congregation with all the time in the world to stop and chat about our families and our local concerns.'[45] And as occasion demands, he can be very versatile. 'I recall my amazement', remembers his friend Donald English, 'when, sharing a holiday with him and a number of others, in Pembrokeshire, I attended an evening service in a barn where John, in pullover and cords, played the accordion to accompany the hymns.'[46]

4

Wherever evangelical life and teaching flourished in Wales in the days following the Second World War, it did so largely in free and independent churches; the Anglican Church in Wales seemed notably inhospitable to evangelical theology and enterprise. The IVF had been at work in Welsh universities since the 1920s, and as far as students were concerned they had a ready champion:

> Dr. Martyn Lloyd-Jones proved of key importance in the growth from year to year of the conferences in Wales. Having the confidence of both areas he could give maximum help to the students from north and south Wales. He was also the leader from whom the Welsh theological students and graduates gathered inspiration.[47]

From the 1950s on John Stott, too, was a welcome visitor at these conferences, and one known to have a particular concern for the Principality through his residence at The Hookses. One year he spoke at the Theological Students' Fellowship conference in Bristol, where the Chairman, Geraint Fielder, was from Wales – one of a number of Welshmen to hold this office over the years. When back home after the conference, Fielder went down with German measles:

> Asked by the GP if he had been in touch with any expectant mothers, the thought struck him that it had very recently been announced that the Queen was expecting a child. (Not that Her Majesty had been at the TSF conference, but one of her honorary chaplains had!) 'You'd better play safe,' said the GP, 'and inform the gentleman that he is a German measles contact, just in case!' John Stott, in an amused reply, explained that his royal links were not as close as all that![48]

Dr. Lloyd-Jones, however, decided in the early 1950s to withdraw from the Welsh IVF work:

> He still possessed his initial reservations over the development of conferences in Wales which were restricted to students ... separate youth work had never been traditional in the life of the Welsh churches. By the early 1950s a new alignment was emerging in Wales to which he preferred to give his time.[49]

This 'new alignment' took the form of what became known – at Lloyd-

Jones' own suggestion – as the Evangelical Movement of Wales, established following successive well-attended conferences at Caenarfon in 1953 and at Denbigh in 1955. By the 1960s, however, it was clear that the leadership and membership of the Movement (which was interdenominational) was predominantly free church or independent, and could do little to address some of the pressing concerns of the few remaining evangelical members of the Church in Wales. If these were to influence their denomination, a new structure was needed: and it was to meet something of a similar situation in many different parts of the world that the Evangelical Fellowship in the Anglican Communion had come into being in 1960. Given his special concern both for EFAC (where he was the moving spirit and quickly became secretary) and for Wales, it is not surprising that John Stott should soon set about trying to secure a Welsh group member of EFAC, as he had already done in England and Scotland. Forty years before this would have presented little difficulty:

> Until the 1920s there had been a strong evangelical witness within the Church in Wales. During the 1860s to the 1890s probably one in four of the Welsh clergy would have identified themselves as evangelicals. It was the evangelical clergy who enabled the church to survive after the methodist secession of 1811, and who also enabled the church to maintain its 'national' character throughout the period of the disestablishment debates.[50]

But after disestablishment in 1920 (following the estrangement of the majority of the population from Anglicanism) the influence of evangelicalism suffered a disastrous decline:

> By the early 1950s the number of ordained men who could be described as evangelical would be counted on the fingers of one hand, and as late as 1975 it could be argued that there was hardly one parish in Wales which had retained its evangelical character.[51]

In 1962, therefore, John Stott as Secretary of EFAC suggested to Canon Ivor Phillips, Vicar of St. Paul's Newport (and later Archdeacon) that he should convene a meeting of evangelicals; and this took place on 27 February 1962 in Cardiff. Dr. J. I. Packer, then librarian of Latimer House, Oxford, was the speaker. Nothing was decided, and other inconclusive meetings followed: Anglican evangelicalism in Wales was by this time so generally liberal in theological outlook that no agreement could be reached. Some even wanted to change the EFAC constitution so as to accommodate their broader doctrinal outlook. Eventually, at John

Stott's suggestion, it was agreed to cut the Gordian Knot, and to encourage those (few) individuals in real sympathy with the aims of EFAC to apply for individual membership, from which a Welsh Anglican Evangelical Fellowship might later emerge.

In April 1964 these individual Welsh members of EFAC were invited to spend a day at The Hookses. They were few enough to meet in the sitting-room (later, as numbers increased, moving to the games room, and then to Dale Church); Bertie Lewis,[52] at that time Vicar of Llanddewi Brefi, took the chair, and acted as EFAC Regional Secretary. John Stott wrote to him after the meeting to say it had been good to see him 'surrounded by those eight or nine men, the nucleus, I believe, of a growing fellowship'.[53] By March 1967, still small in numbers, the fellowship was formally affiliated as the EFAC group member for Wales.

From this informal gathering a 'Dale Day' became a regular part of the annual programme of EFCW – the Evangelical Fellowship of the Church in Wales. Year by year John Stott continued to invite the individual EFAC members (and after 1967 the Welsh EFAC group) to Hookses to spend a day with him. Roger Brown described Dale Day in the 1980s:

> The tradition of a summer meeting at The Hookses, Dale, John Stott's Welsh home, has been maintained over the years ... his hospitality and biblical teaching have been much appreciated and have done much to encourage individuals in what can still often be a lonely Christian witness. Members continue to travel down to Dale from every corner of Wales to attend this annual meeting, and down the years have listened to John Stott's exposition of the Pastoral Epistles, the first Epistle to the Thessalonians and the Acts of the Apostles. The afternoon session has taken the form of an open forum when members of the fellowship, or John Stott himself, have led discussions on current issues or about various aspects of world Christianity ... The number attending has outgrown the limited accommodation available – in 1973 over seventy people crammed themselves into a small room, a rather close fellowship to say the least! Consequently, in more recent years the morning session has taken place in Dale parish church, by courtesy of the incumbents of the parish, even though it is standing room only for late comers.[54]

Then followed a considerable migration up the narrow lane and across the airfield to The Hookses for a picnic lunch, followed by an afternoon meeting in the Coronation Hall in Dale, or (numbers and weather permitting) at The Hookses. Outdoors, this could be held in the 'Gorlan'

(Welsh for sheepfold) formed as a natural enclosure hemmed-in by the cliff and one side of the workshop, and on the remaining two sides by a low stone wall. It is well protected from the winds; and in 1977 was paved by an amateur work-force under the direction of Merfyn Phillips, one of the Dale Day regulars, a bachelor farmer from St. Dogmael's.

With much regret the pressure of increasing numbers meant that the Dale Day (retaining the name) eventually moved from Dale parish church and The Hookses to the Church of the Holy Spirit in Hubberston, outside Milford Haven. It continued to attract a wonderfully heterogeneous group of regular attenders: clergy, sometimes from distant parishes; lay people, young and old, hungry for solid Bible teaching; academics and a few students from the colleges of the University of Wales in Aberystwyth, Cardiff and Swansea. Besides the thirteen summers expounding Acts, John Stott led them in succeeding years through 1 Thessalonians and then the early chapters of Romans, while preparing to write his studies on these books for the Bible Speaks Today series. More recently still, in response to increasing numbers and the need for somewhere more central, Dale Day has moved to Carmarthen, though in 1997 it was cancelled at the last moment since the day chosen coincided with the funeral of Diana, Princess of Wales.

5

The Hookses was to become a major factor in John Stott's writing programme for the greater part of his life, but he was an author well before he found it. Speaking to an American audience who had demanded that he say something about himself as a writer, he declared once 'I can honestly say that I had no literary ambitions – it had not occurred to me.'[55] Nevertheless, he had edited the Rugby School magazine (not by choice, but because the head of the school was *ex officio* editor), and during his curacy was the author of a booklet on personal evangelism.[56] As with so much that he would write later, this grew from what was originally a talk to undergraduates, given in a number of universities and hammered into shape by questions and discussion.

But it was in the 1950s, following his institution as Rector, that he began to write in earnest; and it is ironical that the original encouragement for so much evangelical writing should have come from a bishop, William Wand, who is not thought of as a particular friend to evangelicals. Some of this feeling about Wand, less strong now than at the time, centres round a single incident when he refused to ordain in St. Paul's Cathedral a candidate who had conscientious objections to the wearing of a stole, to the distress and embarrassment of the man and his family. He was later ordained privately in Wand's chapel at Fulham

Palace. What was less generally known was that Wand's fellow diocesan bishops did not support his action, and felt that this should not occur again.[57] Wand was in fact a supporter – at least in his own mind – of the diversity and breadth of the Church of England. In his early days, as a butcher's son from Grantham, his father had played the harmonium in a local chapel.[58] As a student he had been influenced by the Keswick Convention and though he claimed 'an aversion to strongly expressed religious emotion', he experienced

> ... a warmness of affection and a strength of personal conviction about the religion one encountered in Keswick that was confessedly the result of conscious conviction such as I have always believed to be fundamental to any adequate religion.[59]

Wand was translated from Bath and Wells in 1945, when the See of London represented the first major episcopal vacancy that awaited Geoffrey Fisher's attention on becoming Archbishop of Canterbury – the choice of his own successor. There was a general expectation in the church that George Bell of Chichester would be nominated – indeed, he expected this himself.[60] But Churchill as Prime Minister remembered Bell's outspoken opposition to aspects of his wartime policy, and that he was known to favour a reform of the Establishment. He wrote to Fisher that he would 'find it difficult to commend to the King Dr. Bell of Chichester'. In the event he commended Dr. Wand of Bath and Wells instead.[61]

If Fisher had had his way and Bell had become Bishop of London, it would have fallen to him (or one of his suffragans) to institute John Stott to All Souls. It seems improbable that he would have encouraged him (as Wand did) to give time to writing; nor given him (as Wand did) the commission which produced the first of his many books.

Wand was already sixty when he came to London (he was previously Archbishop of Brisbane in Australia before Bath and Wells) 'the personification of sanctified toughness'.[62] He ordained John Stott both deacon and priest, and instituted him to All Souls in 1950. Looking back, John Stott recalled how,

> I found him a bit formidable. He was essentially an academic and an able speaker (I believe he always preached extempore and never had notes). He was a definite liberal Catholic. I never doubted his sincere devotion to Christ, although his experience of it seemed largely ceremonial, liturgical and sacramental. His clergy held him in awe. I didn't feel he understood evangelicals ...[63]

It seemed therefore all the more remarkable that Wand should invite John Stott to write his 1954 'Bishop of London's Lent Book' for the diocese. Wand was himself a prolific author, mostly of smaller books. About this time one of his clergy commemorated in four lines of pastiche both Wand's legendary capacity for work, and his many publications:

> The sun that bids us rest is waking
> Our Bishop 'neath the Fulham sky,
> And hour by hour his Lordship's writing
> A little book for us to buy.[64]

With the benefit of hindsight, therefore, perhaps Wand's choice of John Stott is not quite so surprising. Wand and Archdeacon Sharpe got on well together; and Sharpe, an evangelical, would be ready to commend the young Rector of All Souls. Even as curate, John Stott had served on a small diocesan group, probably a committee of the Bishop's Council for the Mission to London in the spring of 1948.[65] Wand respected academic ability, and John Stott's double First would have attracted his attention. Moreover, Wand saw a place for evangelicals (provided they were not too intransigent, angular, insular or abrasive) within the comprehensiveness of the Church of England; and he was a firm believer in a scholarly clergy. He had therefore (to John Stott's surprise) made a point in his sermon at the Institution in St. Peter's of telling the new Rector that he must make time to read and write; and urging the lay leadership of the church to see that he did so. He followed this up with the invitation, three years later, to write his 'Lent Book'. John Stott had recently been giving his mind to the big questions about the inspiration and authority of Scripture; and had come to an insight about the integral relationship between the writer and his message, which he later described as 'the dual authorship' of Scripture. The fact does not come about by accident,[66] and speaking in America nearly fifty years afterwards, John Stott recalled this as the starting point of the book:

> I chose to attempt to introduce the New Testament authors, showing that in the process of inspiration the Holy Spirit chose, prepared and fashioned the personality and experience of each author, in order to convey through each a distinctive and appropriate message. The book was published by Longmans under the title *Men with a Message*, and later Eerdmans and InterVarsity Press under the title *Basic Introduction to the New Testament*.[67]

Wisely, he adopted the practice he was to follow with many of his later books, and wrote what he had first taught. The germ of the book was drawn from a series of addresses delivered at the annual Bible School of the Crusaders' Union in St. Peter's, Vere Street, during the Autumn of 1948; but amplified, developed, and supported by a wealth of biblical references. The opening chapter on 'The Message of Jesus' quotes from eleven books from the Old Testament (including seven psalms) and eight from the New (including many references to each of the four gospels).[68] Wand received the MS in the summer of 1953, and replied in a three-page letter, making a number of suggestions with friendliness and courtesy:

> My dear Stott,
> On a fine day's holiday by the sea I have had the pleasure of reading through the manuscript of your forthcoming Lent book. May I say at once how much I enjoyed the exercise, and how grateful I am to you for giving all the prayer and time and trouble that you obviously expended on the work. The completed book ought in my opinion to be of very great value in introducing people to Bible study. This value should be particularly apparent at the time when we are trying to prepare for the Bible weeks, in which we shall direct people's thoughts once again to the necessity of serious Bible reading.
> I am venturing to make one or two suggestions for your consideration.

The suggestions had to do simply with issues such as technicalities of Greek translation, the exact chronology of the New Testament (Wand had himself written on this, taking a different view), or the disputed meaning of the phrase 'the Lord's brethren' in Mark 6:3. Wand concluded–

> I hope you will forgive my making these suggestions. As this is your first published book I think it is particularly important that you should commend yourself to as wide a circle of readers as possible. I think that the suggestions I have made above will help to that end. Of course from my own point of view it is even more important that I should get our Lent book read by as many people as is possible.[69]

The book was published by Longmans, in Janary 1954. Wand maintained his generous reception of it by contributing a Foreword:

> In the last resort what we desire to hear in the Word of God is the

voice of the Holy Spirit speaking directly to our own souls. It is probable that the more completely we understand the nature of the medium employed the more clearly shall we comprehend the meaning of His message.

and added a reminder that it was not a product of the ivory towers of academia:

It should also have a value of a more personal kind in showing the intellectual basis upon which a specially busy parish priest builds the framework of his pastoral life.

It received favourable, if modest notices; and was the basis of a feature article by Sir Richard Acland in the *Daily Herald*.[70]

The chapter on 'The Message of Revelation' made clear his own position on the various interpretations favoured among evangelicals. 'What a persecuted Church needs,' he wrote, 'is not a detailed forecast of future events which has to be laboriously deciphered, but a vision of Jesus Christ ... John's purpose is practical not academic. He is not just a seer but a pastor.'[71] Basil Atkinson, an admirer and encourager of John Stott since his days as an undergraduate, took a different view. Michael Cassidy, a member of the CICCU when the book was published, recalls how

I used to have Basil come to my digs in College, and I would invite ten or fifteen friends around, and we would have Basil go through one of the books of the Bible such as Romans or Hebrews or Revelation. Basil had some interesting views on the book of Revelation which he saw as a series of prophecies about phases of the Church and its history up to the end times. One day in the Cambridge University Library I saw Basil who greeted me with his usual twinkling eyes, plus the twitch of those enormous eyebrows (which were more like two moustaches than two eyebrows) and his great Cheshire cat grin. 'Hello, Basil,' I said. 'I have been reading John Stott's little book *Men with a Message* and, you know, he takes a completely different line on the book of Revelation to the one you take.' Basil replied: 'Yes, dear John, and a marvellous little book. But when he comes to the book of Revelation, he is of course quite wrong. Yes, quite wrong.' At which he beamed at me seraphically and left me to my theological perplexity ...[72]

Not long after publication, Collins sought to secure the rights to *Men with a Message*, hoping to include it in their early Fontana series, alongside titles by C. S. Lewis and J. B. Phillips (Collins had acquired a controlling interest in Geoffrey Bles in 1953); but Longmans were not ready to part with the book and two reprintings quickly followed.[73]

A year after *Men with a Message* came the pamphlet *Parochial Evangelism by the Laity*; and a variety of small publications followed, mainly based on addresses given on behalf of missionary or church societies (in one case, on behalf of the Golders Green Crematorium). At the same time, John Stott was serving on the IVF and EA Literature Committees (on the latter as chairman) and was contributing articles, generally at the editor's request, to a range of periodicals: the *Life of Faith*, *Inter-Varsity*, the *Nursing Times*, the *Sunday Companion*, the *Churchman*, *World Dominion*, even the *Caterer's Record*. Over fifty such articles were published in the 1950s; including (in the later years) contributions to journals in Australia and in America.[74] *Crusade* published in 1955 and 1956 the two articles which became the influential booklet (in the US, a book rather than a booklet) *Fundamentalism and Evangelism*.[75] Part of its significance lay in demonstrating that John Stott was ready to engage not only in general exposition but, where truth was threatened, in current controversy.

The year 1958 saw three books published. The first was on the Letters to the Seven Churches of Revelation 1–3, in a short series, 'Preaching for Today'. John Stott gave it the title *What Christ Thinks of the Church*.[76] The book consisted of expository addresses, delivered 'in embryo' as a Lent course in All Souls the year before, and there is in print a record of their power to reach one young overseas visitor to All Souls, on his first visit to London. It was Easter Sunday, 1957; John Stott was in the pulpit:

> He was preaching on the Laodicean church, the last in a series of seven expositions of the churches in Revelation. I had only just arrived in England; in fact it was my first Sunday. I was completely bowled over by the clarity and power of his sermon. I remember writing home to my local pastor, giving a rave review of John as a preacher and of the way in which God used the message to rebuke my complacency and lukewarm attitude.[77]

Following the publication of *Men with a Message*, John Stott was approached by Leonard Cutts, doyen of London's religious publishers, to write for Hodder and Stoughton a Confirmation manual. John Stott suggested that it might be one of a short series of popular books designed for particular pastoral occasions. This was readily agreed, and under his editorship the 'Christian Commitment' series was launched. Eight or nine volumes were planned and five eventually written; the first, *Your Confirmation*, by John Stott himself. The *Times Literary Supplement* commended it judiciously: 'He has admirably fulfilled his terms of reference and writes clearly and convincingly.'[78] The *Church Times*, on the other hand, complained of its 'theological prejudice',[79] and a very biased review appeared in the *Canterbury Diocesan Notes* over the initials of the editor, Raymond Clark. It is worth quoting the opening sentences, since they are not untypical of the response of other sections of the church to evangelicals and evangelical writing during the years after the war:

> Mr. Stott is so essentially at home with the protestant revivalist terminology and practice of conversion and commitment to Christ that, despite his claim that he should not be thought to 'belittle the ordinance' of Confirmation he succeeds in robbing the 'Christian ceremonies' which Churchpeople 'undergo' (pp. 18, 19) of most of their decisive significance. This is a workmanlike book from the hand of a skilled teacher. Doubtless the orthodoxy of the chapters on Christian Belief is unimpeachable, though your reviewer would quarrel with the crudely substitutionary theory of Atonement (p. 63) and with the identification of the LORD in the Old Testament with God the Father (p. 70).

The book was summed-up as 'a regrettably one-sided production'.[80] Michael Saward, then a curate in the Canterbury diocese, wrote to his bishop in protest. Geoffrey Fisher, never one to let the grass grow under his feet, secured a copy of the book, read it alongside the review, and replied promptly:

> I think your protest was entirely justified, and the review was one-sided and by no means did justice to Stott's book. As far as I could see the theology of Stott's book was a theology which has an entirely acceptable place in Anglican theology and which deserves respect.[81]

Your Confirmation was based on the preparation that John Stott had been accustomed to give each year, first as curate to youngsters in the parish, and then as Rector. It was written mainly at The Hookses, in company with Dick Lucas and John Collins, both of whom had been enlisted to contribute to the series. John Collins provides a highly impressionistic recollection of the three of them at work:

> John Stott took Dick Lucas and myself to The Hookses to write books. Hodder and Stoughton had asked John to be General Editor of a series. He was to write the first, on *Your Confirmation*; I was to

write on *Your Christian Life* and Dick was to write on something or other (*Reminiscences of a Bachelor*, perhaps?). The plan was that we should write all day and then read our work to each other over supper in the evening. On Monday night, John Stott read to us the first impeccable chapter of *Your Confirmation*, and Dick and I produced a few possible outlines for our chapters, which were mercilessly, but kindly, torn to pieces by the General Editor. On Tuesday night, John read to us the second impeccable chapter, and Dick and I produced a few notes for possible second chapters, which were again kindly, but firmly, demolished. The same happened on Wednesday and Thursday. On Friday, Dick and I decided to sunbathe, and on Friday night the General Editor (now slightly 'grieved') read to us a further chapter. On Saturday we all travelled back to London. On the back cover of *Your Confirmation* appeared advertisements for 'forthcoming books by R. C. Lucas and J. T. C. B. Collins, eagerly awaited by the Christian public.' They are still waiting!⁸²

6

By far the most influential book to come out of the early days of writing at The Hookses was *Basic Christianity*, drawing on the addresses to students given at university missions in different parts of the world during the 1950s. It was not quite his first deliberately evangelistic publication: back in 1950 at the start of the All Souls Training School and the programme of Guest Services, he had written a small booklet, *Becoming a Christian*.⁸³ In a dozen pages he there set out to answer two questions: how Christianity 'is God's solution to man's greatest problem', and how to receive God's gift of salvation. By the 1990s the booklet had been reprinted nearly a hundred times (selling between two and three million copies) and was still being used in a wide range of evangelism.

David Watson was one of very many who was helped to understand the issues, and brought to the point of decision, by this booklet. As an undergraduate at Cambridge he had met John Collins at 'a nondescript tea-party' given by the CICCU, and they had talked further over breakfast the following morning. John Collins gave him the booklet as they parted company:

Off I went, with my mind racing. I had gone to breakfast as a humanist, and now, just an hour or so later, I had the trembling excitement that I could be on the verge of a totally unexpected discovery. Or again, it could be yet another disillusionment which would only deepen my conviction as an atheist.

That evening, alone in my room, I read the booklet *Becoming a Christian* by John Stott, Rector of All Souls, Langham Place, London, where John Collins was a curate. The booklet was largely a summary of our breakfast conversation, but with all its simplicity it was compellingly clear in its logical reasoning. Steadily I realised that, if these things were true, I wanted them to become real in my own life. Awkwardly I slipped onto my knees beside my bed and prayed the prayer at the end of the booklet ...[84]

Basic Christianity, however, was to be a book rather than a booklet. It would seek to explain and commend the faith of the New Testament to both mind and heart so as to face the sincere reader with the need for a personal response. In John Stott's own words, it focuses

> ... on the evidence for the deity of Jesus (his claims, character and resurrection), on our need of him (attempting to re-state the meaning of the old-fashioned words 'sin' and 'salvation'), on the achievement of the cross, and on our necessary response ('counting the cost' and 'making a decision').[85]

A further chapter, 'Being a Christian', on beginning to live the Christian life (published a year earlier as a companion booklet to *Becoming a Christian*), was reprinted to form the conclusion of the book,[86] which was one of the titles chosen by Ronald Inchley to launch a new series of 'IVF Pocket Books'.

The inspired title, *Basic Christianity* – which is repeated four times in the brief Preface – owes something to I. A. Richards' and Charles K. Ogden's development of 'Basic English' in the 1930s,[87] and something to the title *Mere Christianity* which C. S. Lewis gave to the collected edition of his talks on the BBC during the Second World War. They sought to present 'an agreed, or common, or central, or "mere" Christianity'.[88] In the same way John Stott wrote in his Preface, 'No attempt has been made to give a comprehensive introduction either to the Christian faith or to the Christian life. I have simply tried to make a frank statement of basic Christianity.'[89] In the chapter 'Counting the Cost' he reprinted some verses written five years before, which he had used to conclude a sermon in All Souls in March 1953. To many readers they served to emphasize the point that the book was not simply addressed to the intellect but to the whole person, mind and will and heart, and that to accept Christ was self-surrender as well as self-discovery:

Thou callest clear, cold centuries across,
    And bidd'st me follow Thee, and take my cross,
And daily lose myself, myself deny,
    And stern against myself shout 'Crucify'.

My stubborn nature rises to rebel
    Against Thy call. Proud choruses of hell
Unite to magnify my restless hate
    Of servitude, lest I capitulate.

The world, to see my cross, would pause and jeer.
    I have no choice, but still to persevere
To save myself – and follow Thee from far,
    More slow than Magi – for I have no star.

And yet Thou callest still. Thy cross
    Eclipses mine, transforms the bitter loss
I thought that I would suffer if I came
    To Thee, – into immeasurable gain.

I kneel before Thee, Jesus, crucified,
    My cross is shouldered and my self denied;
I'll follow daily, closely – will not flee
    To lose myself, for love of man and Thee.[90]

Basic Christianity rapidly became the definitive evangelistic paperback for at least a generation, especially among student Christian Unions. In a brochure celebrating fifty years of publishing, IVP described it as 'In many ways ... an archetypal IVP book. It is rational and logical, clearly but not racily written, appealing to the heart as well as the mind.' It was listed as probably their best known book: 'First published in 1958, revised and reissued in 1971, it has been translated into twenty-five languages and has sold over 1.3 million copies world-wide.'[91] That was in 1988. Today the number of translations is more than double and reads like a roll-call of the United Nations: *Afrikaans, Albanian, Arabic, Armenian, Azeri, Bangla, Bengali, Bulgarian, Burmese, Chinese, Croatian, Czech* ... down to *Uighur, Urdu, Vietnamese* and *Zulu*.[92]

For many correspondents the world over it was a book that led them to decision. From Australia one describes how he had

... inadvertently become caught up in a university mission led by Dudley Foord at the University of New England, Armidale, in 1960. I was given *Basic Christianity*, which I found inescapably persuasive, and the last few chapters of which I read many times until I had exhausted all possibilities of dodging the issue. A year later, at and following another university 'week of witness', I had some 8 or 10 copies of *Basic Christianity* in circulation among my friends (some have never been returned!).[93]

A former airline pilot wrote from Canada to tell how his mother-in-law had given him a copy of the book, which he accepted because he did not want to hurt her feelings but did not intend to read. Leaving hurriedly one day for work to catch a plane to Europe, he was looking for something to read and took the book with him on his flight.

It was in a little room in Amsterdam that I read your book and fully committed my life to Jesus. I was flooded with unbelievable love and was transformed in character (ferocious temper and foul language immediately ceased). My wife was overwhelmed by the change in me. Two weeks later she wanted to share that love and she also gave her life to Christ. We did not know any other Christians who believed like we did, but were soon led to an excited group of young believers ...

By the time this letter was sent, the writer was in the ordained ministry.[94]

Examples could be multiplied and perhaps two more will be enough, from those whose names will be more widely known. Soon after the publication of the 1971 revised edition, John Stott received this letter from Bexhill-on-Sea:

Dear John,
Thank you for writing *Basic Christianity*. It led me to make a new commitment of my life to Christ. I am old now – nearly 78 – but not too old to make a new beginning.
I rejoice in all the grand work you are doing.

Yours sincerely,
Leslie Weatherhead[95]

In 1985 Major-General Sir Laurence New was appointed Lieutenant Governor of the Isle of Man:

A Manxman by education, General New not only served in the Royal Tank Regiment but became in his generation the Army's most knowledgeable officer on the design of modern tanks. A tour as the Defence Attaché in Israel had quickened this interest as it followed the Yom Kippur War. He was much in demand as a lecturer for his absorbing presentation of the key tank battle on the Golan Heights.[96]

As a young staff officer in the Ministry of Defence, he had been converted to Christ twenty-one years before:

> After my first tour with my Regiment I was sailing back from Hong Kong on the *Empire Windrush* in March 1954 when it suffered an engine room explosion, quickly caught fire and was very quickly abandoned. I went over the side without a life jacket in a flimsy pair of shantung silk pyjamas and swam about for over three hours. During that time I made several promises to the Lord, who I didn't really know, to the effect that if he would save me I would take Him very seriously! For the next ten years I tried to keep my promise but I searched in vain. I remember sitting at the feet of General Sir Arthur Smith and listening to the ABC of Conversion but it didn't take. I had always prayed to God, and I prayed on ...
> After the course in December 1963 I was posted to a super job in the Ministry of Defence and I began to travel extensively all over the Middle East. One day flying back from Africa via Gibraltar in an RAF Andover, I was reading *Basic Christianity* which I reckon Ian Dobbie had prayerfully put into my hands. Chapter 10 was titled 'Making a Decision'. In that chapter John Stott describes the famous painting by Holman Hunt, 'The Light of the World', inspired by verse 20 of chapter 3 of the Book of Revelation which reads 'Behold, I stand at the door and knock; if any one hears my voice and opens the door, I will come in and eat with him, and he with me.' John Stott pointed out that Jesus is knocking gently, waiting, but not willing to force His way in. Indeed the door in Holman Hunt's painting is overgrown with weeds and there is (purposely) no handle on the outside of the door. Then I read (on page 129 of the book) these hugely important words:
>> Are you a Christian? A real and committed Christian? Your answer depends on another question – not whether you go to church or not, believe the creed or not, or lead a decent life or not (important as all these are in their place), but rather this: which side of the door is Jesus Christ? Is he on the inside or the outside? That is the crucial issue.
>
> I realised in a moment of clarity that, although I had been praying to Jesus most of my life it had been, as it were, through the keyhole; I had never invited Him in. There and then in the plane at about 25,000 feet I asked Jesus to come in to my whole house, the

dirty bits as well as the polished public rooms, I surrendered it all to Him. Looking back I can see that this was a matter of command rather than a matter of accepting the cross; but it was not a bad place for a soldier to start and, importantly it was acceptable to the Lord. I had asked Him to be my Commander-in-Chief.

Nor was this all. As the long flight home continued, Laurence New read on, finding a totally new relevance in the concluding pages of the book, 'Being a Christian':

John Stott explained in the next chapter that the Holy Spirit would lead me into all truth (John 16:13). And so He did; for the first time I understood the cross and I claimed 2 Corinthians 5:19 and Isaiah 53:9. I read on with my Bible open in front of me, and understood for the first time the promise of eternal life (John 3:16). By the time we landed I was asking that the fruit of the Spirit (Galatians 5:22) would begin to be manifested in my life; there was no stopping me! I rushed home to tell my wife and in the ensuing confusion nearly put her off for life! But that is another story which mercifully has a wonderfully happy ending ...[97]

Today *Basic Christianity* is still widely used. But if he were writing an evangelistic book for today's student generation, John Stott has said he would adopt a different initial approach, not because his understanding of the faith has changed, but because of the decline in Christian presuppositions and general knowledge:

The British students for whom it was primarily written in the fifties still had a veneer of theism. One could assume belief in God; the deity of Jesus was the issue. Today one can assume nothing; one would need to begin elsewhere, probably with the phenomenon of our perceived humanness, and the experienced paradox of its glory and shame. Because *Basic Christianity*, even in its second edition, still takes too much for granted, it is now used less as an evangelistic book than as a primer for new converts.[98]

So from this remotest corner of West Wales has come a ministry which spans the world. When his first attempt to buy The Hookses, wild and semi-derelict as it was, proved unsuccessful, John Stott told himself 'The Lord doesn't want me to become a landed property owner.' It is not difficult to see that this was premature. The Hookses is the only property he has ever owned and in the late 1990s he passed it by Deed of Gift to the Langham Trust. It has served a unique purpose, not only for the many conferences, and visitors, but as a writer's retreat; and no one is more conscious of this than the man who discovered and rebuilt it for his own and future generations:

> It is impossible to express my sense of gratitude to God for his providential gift of The Hookses. I sometimes say to myself that I'm the luckiest man on earth. The intoxicating Pembrokeshire air, the beauty of seascape and landscape, the stillness and seclusion, and the rich variety of bird life, together make a uniquely satisfying combination of blessings. My favourite nook is a turf ledge a few feet down from the top of a nearby cliff. Here, especially in the early evening, as the declining summer sun paints the sea silver and gold, I love to sit, either alone or with a friend, to read, to think, to dream and to pray. It would be hard to imagine a greater contrast between central London and coastal South West Wales, yet each has its own fascination, and I enjoy them both to the full.[99]

Notes

The reference 'Taped interview', unless otherwise attributed, is to a series of recorded conversations between John Stott and the author, mainly at The Hookses in the autumn of 1992, supplemented by later interviews. The numbers following (e.g. 1/8) indicate interview and page number of transcript; in this case, page 8 of the first interview.

Foreword

[1] Chadwick (1990a), p. 112.

[2] Catherwood, C. (1984). See also, for example, the extended entry by Peter Williams in Elwell (ed.) (1993), pp. 338–352. Other brief published studies are referred to in the chapters following.

[3] JRWS papers. Letter to John Lefroy, 3 January 1985.

[4] Trevelyan (1949), pp. 70, 77.

[5] Stott (1991b), p. 73.

[6] Warren (1974), p. 229; Carpenter (1991), p. xix.

[7] Chadwick (1990b).

[8] *Ibid.*, p. 38.

[9] *Ibid.*, p. 156.

[10] Lewis and Calabria (1989), p. 103.

[11] Chadwick (1990b), p. 157.

[12] For the problems of a biographer over even trivial incidents in the not-too-distant past, see for example Ziegler (1990), p. 204.

[13] Stott (1983), p. 3: the text of his 1982 Presidential Address at the British Isles UCCF Conference.

[14] There is a published bibliography listing all his writings up to the end of 1994. See Dudley-Smith (1995a); and for a wide-ranging anthology of John Stott's writings, see also Dudley-Smith (ed.) (1995b).

[15] See Stott (1961) and Stott (1982b). Preaching is a theme to which he returns in a number of other books: *e.g.* (1992) which has a chapter on 'Expounding the Word'.

[16] Chadwick (1990b), p. 160.

[17] Letter dated 7 August 1991.

[18] See Whistler (1993), p. 331.
[19] Ingrams (1995), p. 180.
[20] Carpenter (1996), p. 3.
[21] Chadwick (1990b), p. 283.
[22] Spalding (1988), p. xviii.
[23] Chadwick (1990b), p. 189.

Chapter 1. Family Background: Between the Wars

[1] JRWS papers. John was in fact aged 8 at the date of the letter.
[2] Stott (1973), p. 27.
[3] Stott (1992), p. 120.
[4] Vol. xix, No. 1: Autumn, 1952.
[5] This is the description of Henry Walmsley in Trail (ed.) (1968), p. 402, the source of much of the information in these paragraphs.
[6] See Peter Kerley, 'Sir Arnold Stott' (obituary), *British Heart Journal*, Vol. 21 (1959), pp. 137–138.
[7] See Haslam (1894), especially chapter 7 and the engraving facing p. 62, 'The parson is converted'.
[8] Drawing on a memorandum from John Stott to the author, 2 February 1996.
[9] London: Shaw and Sons. The second edition *The Mechanism and Graphic Registration of the Heart Beat* (1920), became known as 'the Bible of electrocardiography'.
[10] See his obituary in the *British Medical Journal*, 28 June 1958:

> ... eminent cardiologist as he was, he was also a general physician in the fullest and best sense of the term. He had a calm and kindly approach to patients, who soon felt the greatest confidence in his judgment and treatment. As a teacher he was excellent, and his instruction at the bedside gave students on his firm the very best introduction to clinical medicine. He aimed at developing the students' own powers of observation and he demanded a high standard in the clinical notes taken by his clerks. Although his comments were often critical, and at times even caustic, those who were his clerks will always remember the principles of clinical medicine as taught by their chief.

[11] Dr. J. W. MacLeod. Letter to the author, 11 March 1993.
[12] The Revd. Canon Peter R. Thompson. Letter to the author, 9 February 1996.
[13] See Trail (ed.) (1968); Obituary, *British Medical Journal*, 28 June 1958, p. 1546. Author's personal correspondence and interviews.
[14] Drawing on a memorandum from John Stott to the author, 2 February 1996.
[15] Lily wrote in March 1936 to thank John, then aged 15, for sending them a spray of Rosemary from Rugby. JRWS papers; 25 March 1936.
[16] Taped interview, 2/2.
[17] See Baker (1995).
[18] Austen (1958), p. 182. Though first published in 1811, the book was in draft before the turn of the century.
[19] Pound (1967), p. 12; the source of much of the information in these paragraphs.
[20] *Ibid.*, p. 24.
[21] Luker (1979), the source of most of the information in these paragraphs. All Souls is the last surviving church by John Nash.
[22] Osborne (ed.) (1970), p. 1209.
[23] Stott (1991b), p. 98.
[24] Chadwick (1966), p. 11f.
[25] C. J. E. Lefroy, 'Pieces of the Past, III', *All Souls*, March 1959.
[26] There is a photograph of him c. 1884 in dog-collar and Church Army uniform in

Reynolds (1967), facing p. 230.

[27] Captain P. Prior, one of Webster's early students, later ordained: quoted in Reynolds (1967), p. 231.

[28] G. R. Harding Wood, 'Reminiscences of a Pre-War Curate', *All Souls*, May 1951.

[29] Luker (1979), p. 43.

[30] Wolfe (1984), p. 77.

[31] *Ibid.*, p. 7. St Paul's said they were 'opposed to introducing sensational methods into worship'. See also Roberts (1942), p. 111.

[32] See Smith, A. E. (1991), chs. 1 and 2.

[33] Luker (1979), p. 50.

[34] Smyth (1959), p. 179.

[35] Gere and Sparrow (eds.) (1981), p. 58.

[36] Davies (1965), cited from Book 3 of the William Eerdmans reprint, 1996, p. 302.

[37] Cross (ed.) (1957), p. 318.

[38] Hastings (1991), p. 28.

[39] *Ibid.*, p. 22.

[40] A Royal Commission was set up in 1919. By 1926 'Oxford and Cambridge had new constitutions and the statutes of both universities and all the colleges had been revised'. Cambridge was not to admit women as full members of the university for another twenty years. (Brooke [1993], pp. 341f.)

[41] Iremonger (1948), p. 627. The tribute is from R. H. Hodkin, Provost of Queen's College, Oxford, who added that the college had lost the most distinguished of its Fellows since 1341.

[42] Dudley Baines, 'The Onset of Depression', in Johnson (ed.) (1994), p. 163.

[43] Ziegler (1990), p. 110. The figure was soon to rise to over three million. Since 1921 there have never been less than a million unemployed.

[44] Graves and Hodge (1940) p. 166.

[45] Quoted by Howarth (1978), p. 33.

[46] With the end of the war, civil and even private aviation expanded rapidly. By the time John was born, an Oxford and Cambridge Universities Air Race was being planned:

> The first and last race took place in July 1921 when three SE5 planes with light blue tails and three with dark blue set off from Hendon aerodrome for a race of 140 miles round a triangular course taking in Harrow, Epping and Hertford, whose unsuspecting inhabitants had not been warned. The procedings were conducted at 120 miles per hour at 100 feet. The last circuit was described as a most unpleasant affair, a confused mixture of roaring engines and shrieking wires with everyone's engines 'racing far beyond the safety mark and pouring out hot oil and steam'. Cambridge had the first three past the post ... (Howarth [1978], p. 59.)

[47] Williams (1989), p. 41.

[48] Green (1959), p. 125. The phrase is taken up and applied to the world of the young Walter de la Mare in Whistler (1993), p. 65.

[49] Drabble (ed.) (1985), p. 312.

[50] Howarth (1978), p. 175.

[51] Stott (1982b), pp. 51, 83.

[52] *Ibid.*

Chapter 2. Home in Harley Street: A London Childhood

[1] Taped interview with John Stott's sister Joanna, now Lady Hilton, 1 March 1991. Much of these early family recollections are from this source. CSSM: Children's Special Service Mission; see chapter 6.

[2] Stott (1958c), p. 39.

[3] JRWS MS 'The Four Questions', November 1979.

[4] John Stott, 'People who have influenced me', *All Souls Broadsheet*, Summer 1991. The same story is told in much the same words to various interviewers. See, for example, 'People in Close-Up: John Capon talks to John Stott (2.)' in *Crusade*, June 1974.

[5] Taped interview, 1/8.

[6] Taped interview with Lady Hilton.

[7] Taped interview, 4/31.

[8] JRWS MS 'The Four Questions', November 1979. See also: Stott (1984), p. 158.

[9] From notes of an address in Toronto under the auspices of the IVCF, 28 December 1978; amplified by taped interview 1/12. See also Stott (1992) p. 145.

[10] Taped interview, 1/28.

[11] Taped interview with Elizabeth Evans, 19 May 1995.

[12] Taped interview, 1/30.

[13] Taped interview with Tamara Dewdney, 19 May 1995.

[14] Taped interview with Lady Hilton.

[15] No record of this school appears to exist. John Stott recalls it as being in Phillimore Gardens, north of Kensington High Street; but the Kensington Central Library in Phillimore Walk can find no reference to it in their Local Studies collection. A letter home from Oakley Hall gives the name of the headmistress as Miss Walkerdine.

[16] Taped interview with Tamara Dewdney.

[17] Taped interview with Lady Hilton.

[18] Taped interview, 1/34.

[19] Taped interview, 1/34.

[20] Taped interview, 1/34.

[21] Though written in the year John was born, the first London production was not until 1930. By then *Peter Pan* had been staged regularly for a quarter of a century and *Dick Whittington* since at least 1605.

[22] Taped interview with Tamara Dewdney.

[23] Taped interview with Lady Hilton.

Chapter 3. Oakley Hall: A Love of Birds

[1] Taped interview, 2/1.

[2] See Leinster-Mackay (1984), p. 326.

[3] Taped memorandum from Prebendary J. G. G. C. Irvine, January 1955, on which some of the recollections of Oakley Hall are based.

[4] As, for example, one member of the teaching staff, remembered for his ability to write two different sentences simultaneously, a pen in each hand.

[5] JRWS papers, 1929.

[6] Spelling in letters remained highly personal for a few years after this. Writing home at the age of ten, he confesses 'I don't know how to spell "Funnyly" – I might have spelt it write.' (24 June 1931).

[7] From an address by John Stott, given at the International Tea in his honour during the Christian Booksellers Association Convention, Dallas, Texas, 28 June 1992.

[8] JRWS papers, 1929.

[9] JRWS papers, 29 September 1929.

[10] JRWS papers, 30 June and 2 July 1930.

[11] Taped interview 2/14; and with Lady Hilton.

[12] Taped interview 2/13.

[13] He believes he was watching a cuckoo at the time! Taped interview 2/16.

[14] JRWS papers. Letter undated, Autumn term 1932.

[15] Taped interview, 2/11. J. G. G. C. Irvine went on, like John, to take Holy Orders – as did at least three, perhaps four, other boys from the same generation at this comparatively small school. He was incumbent of St. Matthew's, Westminster through the 1970s, and Prebendary of St. Paul's Cathedral. John Stott describes him as 'all his life as strongly an

Anglo-Catholic as I am an Evangelical'. When, in the school holidays, Irvine stayed with John in Harley Street, the pair were known to Joanna, John's elder sister, as 'Cantuar and Ebor', the ecclesiastical titles of the archbishops of Canterbury and York. Gerard Irvine went on to Haileybury where, as an eighteen-year-old, he invited John Betjeman down to the school Arts society: 'I modelled myself largely upon him thereafter.' Forty-five years later, as a prebendary of St. Paul's Cathedral, he used to bring John Betjeman Holy Communion towards the close of his life. See Lycett Green (1994), p. 199.

[16] Taped interview, 2/11. Gerard Irvine remembers that perhaps thirty years later he was at a church conference at Swanwick at which John Stott spoke. They had hardly met since prep school days, but John recognized him and welcomed him from the platform saying something like 'I want to tell you that it was he who first turned my mind when we were schoolboys together to the reality of God'. Irvine recalls that this came as a complete surprise to him.

[17] Oakley Hall magazine, Christmas and Lent terms, 1932–33.

[18] But more generally referred to, as later in this account, as his 'bird diary'.

[19] London: Oxford University Press, 1927.

[20] The Rt. Rev. John Bickersteth to the author, 1 February 1993.

[21] Oakley Hall magazine, summer 1944.

[22] Mrs. A. P. Williams. Taped interview, 2 October 1995. As Miss W. M. Owens, Mrs. Williams was assistant matron at Oakley Hall in John's time.

[23] Coward, T. A. (1928), *The Birds of the British Isles and their Eggs* (3rd ed., London: Warne). John Stott's copy is inscribed 'John Stott – to remind him always of a really wonderful day spent birding on "The Breck" – April 27 1933 – Robert Bickersteth'.

[24] Grey, Sir Edward (1927), *The Charm of Birds*, London: Hodder and Stoughton.

[25] JRWS papers. Robbie Bickersteth to JRWS, 11 January 1934.

[26] In a letter to the author of 22 June 1995 Alfred Stansfeld writes: 'Dr. [Arnold] Stott was, I believe, chiefly instrumental in getting me a Foundation Scholarship at Epsom College, whereby my entire school education, clothing, uniform, etc., was provided via the Royal Medical Benevolent Fund. My two sisters were assisted too, I believe, in this way.'

[27] *Ibid.*

[28] *Ibid.*

[29] The 'mystery bird' turned out to be a Green Sandpiper.

[30] See, for example, Wallace and Bagnall-Oakeley (1951), pp. 145, 167.

[31] Quoted in Hilary Allison, 'The Watcher's Vigil', *National Trust Magazine* No. 68, Spring 1993, pp. 28f.

[32] *Ibid.* Charles Chestney, who features in John's diary – see below – retired in 1951 to be succeeded by his son Bob. Between them they gave sixty years of service to Scolt Head.

[33] Turner, E. L. (1928), *Bird Watching on Scolt Head*. London: Country Life Ltd.

[34] JRWS papers. Robbie Bickersteth to JRWS, 23 September 1934.

[35] Richard Rhodes-James, 'The Pioneer' in John Eddison (ed.) (1983), p. 17.

Chapter 4. Rugby 1935–37: Growing up

[1] Lockhart (1949), p. 391.

[2] Aldous Huxley had made the phrase a household word when he borrowed it from Shakespeare for the title of his futuristic novel, published 1932.

[3] Hughes (1906), p. vii.

[4] Chadwick (1966), Part 1, p. 38.

[5] Edwards (1984), p. 299.

[6] Harvey (ed.) (1946), p. 387.

[7] Hughes (1906), p. 64.

[8] Cited from the memorial stone on the north side of the Close. Ellis was later ordained, sometime incumbent of St. Clement Danes in the Strand, and died 1872.

[9] Green (1959), pp. 313–314.

[10] McLintock (1993), p. 90. Lyon was the longest-serving Rugby headmaster since Arnold.

[11] Hope Simpson (1967), p. 222; the source of much of the information in these paragraphs.

[12] Kilbracken has moved since John went there and is now to be found in Barby Road. (The story goes that the old Kilbracken 'had become unfit for human habitation and was therefore turned into accommodation for members of the teaching staff.)

[13] Montefiore (1995), p. 27.

[14] Taped interview, 2/18.

[15] JRWS MS 'Jottings for a Biography', 1993/4.

[16] Taped interview with the Revd. David Jenkins, 29 January 1994. He is not to be confused with the Rt. Revd. David E. Jenkins, sometime Bishop of Durham.

[17] JRWS papers, 14 March 1935.

[18] JRWS papers. Letter to Rugby, 19 January 1936.

[19] Taped interview, 2/32.

[20] Taped interview, 2/35.

[21] An interviewer aptly described it as a 'Just William' kind of Society, after Richard Crompton's schoolboy hero. See Terry Lovell, 'The Times and Travels of "an Ordinary Christian"', *The Christian Bookseller*, May/June 1992, p. 8.

[22] Taped interview, 2/26. This, together with the Minute Book, is the source of the information in these paragraphs.

[23] Taped interview, 2/27.

[24] House rules would require boys to be out of the house on summer afternoons; and before the days of the transistor this meant that they had no access to a 'wireless'. 'ABC' would creep back into the house surreptitiously, against the rules.

[25] Taped interview, 2/30.

[26] Taped interview, 2/25.

[27] Hodder (1887), Vol. 1, p. 47.

[28] Ziegler (1990), p. 215. Pathé Gazette newsreels at the time showed the Duke himself leading community singing at camps shared by public school boys and young factory workers. The Duke's personal interest was less in the intractable issues of unemployment than in breaking down class-barriers between the young. His camps continued, attracting some 400 youngsters a year, until the outbreak of World War II. *The Times* (8 August, 1939) carried a detailed account of how, as King, he welcomed 200 lads aged 17–19 to a camp at Abergeldie Castle, and entertained them at Balmoral.

[29] Taped interview, 3/22.

[30] Taped interview with Tamara Dewdney, 19 May 1995.

[31] The cello he brought back from Germany in 1936 he eventually gave to the school – a decision he later half-regretted – having found in his first year at Cambridge that he could not afford the time. See Chapter 6.

[32] Taped interview with the Rt. Revd. John Bickersteth, 3 March 1994.

[33] McLintock (1993), p. 107. Beresford wrote to John, 10th February 1941: 'When are you coming? Do let me know, and bring some songs with you, because I'd awfully like to make a record, before it's too late, of you singing "On the idle hill of summer" again, and perhaps "Envoi" or other more worthy songs. If you could think of a time for fitting it in, I could order the operator to be ready for a recording. I'm so glad that … you like "Envoi". I hoped it would suit you, but I'm not yet satisfied with the end of the second verse …'

[34] JRWS papers, 25 May 1936.

[35] Dr. J. W. MacLeod. Letter to the author, 11 March 1993.

[36] Taped interview, 1/13. The crash was on 14 June 1937.

[37] Elected to membership 1934; President (elected in his absence, while fishing in Ireland), 1949.

[38] Memorandum from Lady Hilton, August 1993.

[39] See below, Chapter 14.

[40] Taped interview, 1/41.

[41] 20 August 1935.

[42] JRWS papers, 6 August 1936. Lily had taken her father to the Royal Hotel, Weymouth for a seaside holiday.

[43] JRWS papers. Letter dated 28 May 1936.

[44] *Dictionary of National Biography*, 1951–1960, p. 1005.

[45] JRWS papers, 4 September 1936.

[46] 29 August 1936.

[47] 28 September 1936.

[48] JRWS papers. Letter home, 22 August 1937.

Chapter 5. Rugby 1938–40: Beginning with Christ

[1] Howarth (1978), p. 233. In fairness one should set against this Lord Hailsham's view of Chamberlain as 'a man unjustly treated by history': *A Sparrow's Flight* (London: Collins, 1990), p. 140.

[2] A letter from his father suggests that this had remained a possible choice until John had to decide, after School Certificate, whether to do Classics, Languages or Science in the Sixth (JRWS papers, 7 May 1937).

[3] JRWS papers. The Report is coded C5C6 and dated 31 January 1938 (based on a visit on 17 January) and is over the signature of H. H. T. Child. Extracts in quotation marks are verbatim.

[4] JRWS papers. 'Autobiography' – brief undated notes of a talk given in the US in the 1980s or 90s.

[5] *E.g.* Stott, in Eddison (ed.) (1983), p. 55f; Stott (1958), p. 131; Stott (1958), p. 23; Stott, 'Ten-to-Eight' broadcast, BBC, 11 November 1969; John Stott, 'People who have influenced me', All Souls Broadsheet, Summer, 1991; JRWS MS, 'The Four Questions', November 1979.

[6] Since increased by a further 350 names from the Second World War. See 'A Chapel Guide' in the *Rugby School Service Book* (1992), p. 154f.

[7] Montefiore (1995), p. 1.

[8] JRWS MS 'The Four Questions', November, 1979.

[9] Stott in Eddison (ed.) (1983), p. 57.

[10] Stott (1967), p. 45.

[11] Taped interview, 2/42.

[12] Stott (1958a), p. 74. The book is based on a series of addresses given in the 1950s in a number of university missions. (See Chapter 14.)

[13] *E.g.* the parable of the sower in Matthew 13, Mark 4 and Luke 8.

[14] *E.g.* Psalm 139.

[15] Stott in Eddison (ed.) (1983), p. 57.

[16] Making 550 runs as captain in his last season and taking 38 wickets as a 'leg-break bowler with a curiously crablike action'. J. D. Coldham, obituary in *The Cricketer*, September 1986.

[17] 'Blues' were not awarded during war time.

[18] Taped interview, 2/40.

[19] John Eddison in Eddison (ed.) (1983), p. viii.

[20] Sylvester (1984), p. 96.

[21] Richard Rhodes-James in Eddison (ed.) (1983), p. 17f.

[22] Eddison (ed.)(1983), p. viii.

[23] R. J. Knight in Eddison (ed.) (1983)., p. 48.

[24] Stott, in Eddison (ed.) (1983), p. 57.

[25] Taped interview, 2/43, 44.

[26] Stott in Eddison (ed.) (1983), p. 58.

[27] JRWS MS, 'The Four Questions', November, 1979.

[28] Now in Keble College, Oxford. A later replica hangs in St. Paul's Cathedral (see DNB on Holman Hunt). See also Stott (1958a), pp. 122f. for John Stott's exposition of Revelation 3:20.

[29] Stott (1991c), p. 23f.

[30] Stott (1958a). The diary extracts appear on p. 131 of the original edition.

[31] Because the Oxford Group spoke of 'the Quiet Time' with a rather different significance (sometimes including mutual confession of sin), the phrase more regularly used at camp and by Bash was 'Time of Quiet'.

[32] *Cf.* Matthew 19:22; Luke 18:18.

[33] Memorandum to the author from C. J. E. Lefroy, who remembered being told this by Bash himself, 31 March 1994.

[34] Possibly this was Bash's booklet *How to Succeed in the Christian Life*, but more likely his well-known booklet *Life at its Best* (both privately published, n.d., reprinted many times over a long period). Michael Green wrote of it in the chapter he contributed to Eddison (ed.) (1983) (p. 88):

> 'Life at its Best' was designed to help people over the threshold into the new life. It had an enormous influence. It began precisely where the schoolboy found himself. It used the appropriate language. It dealt with the most pressing questions. And it made the way to a living faith inescapably clear, even to the point of suggesting a prayer of commitment, and the first steps forward from there. Not only did this booklet bring large numbers of people to Christ, but it lay behind a whole generation of evangelistic approaches that followed. Several of Bash's friends, including some contributors to this biography, have written evangelistic booklets which have been widely used; but all of them show the imprint of 'Life at its Best' and its influence.

It is to be distinguished from the small book of the same title by F. Wilmost Eardley (Edinburgh: Faith Press, n.d.).

[35] Stott in Eddison (ed.) (1983), p. 58.

[36] 'A *HIS* Interview with John R. W. Stott', *HIS Magazine,* October 1975, p. 16.

[37] This was a favourite verse, and one often used by Bash and his circle. Bishop John Bickersteth, John Stott's contemporary at Rugby, affirmed that though Bash had talked straightly with him ('challenging my Christian upbringing – "couldn't be a second-hand Christian"') he had never himself been a member of 'Bridger's Affair'; but added 'I still use the New Testament John Bridger gave me with the text from Philippians, "I can do all things through Christ who strengtheneth me."' Taped interview, 3 March 1994.

[38] Stott (1966), p. 49.

[39] Taped interview, 2/49f.

[40] Stott (1958c), p. 54.

[41] Stott, 'How This Book Speaks', *On Special Service* (Australia), June 1959, p. 10. See also Stott (1978), p. 158.

[42] Stott (1982a), p. 47.

[43] Stott, *ibid.*, p. 48. The book is based on five addresses given at All Souls, Spring, 1980.

[44] Stott (1990b), p. 9.

[45] See *All Souls*, October 1946 for three stanzas, published anonymously ('These verses ... have come into our hands'). The full six verses were published in the parish magazine of Christ Church, Southport, August 1945, but the three stanzas here quoted are the best. They were later set to music and sung at camp as a Scripture chorus.

[46] 1938: Tyser (Divinity) prize; Sixth form Reading prize.

   1939: Vacqueray (French) prize.

1940: Demergue (German) prize.
[47] Believe it   2 Timothy 3:16.
     Imbibe it   Psalm 119:11.
     Bank on it   Romans 4:20, 21.
     Live it   James 1:22
     Examine it   Joshua 1:8.
[48] Taped interview, 3/19. Both Philip Tompson's parents died in 1941, when he and John were at Cambridge. He became a Scripture Union staff worker and the founder of CAREFORCE. He died in 1989. John Stott does not recall the verse in question.
[49] Personal memorandum.
[50] Letter to the author, 12 December 1993.
[51] *Ibid.*
[52] JRWS papers. Letter from John Bridger, 14 May 1939.
[53] Peter Melly, after a career in the Royal Navy, became Secretary to the Officers' Christian Union.
[54] JRWS papers. Letter from John Bridger, 8 August 1939.
[55] JRWS papers, 22 November 1939.
[56] JRWS papers, 12 February 1940.
[57] JRWS papers, 23 February 1940.
[58] JRWS papers, 21 April 1940.
[59] JRWS papers, 23 April 1940.
[60] JRWS papers, 22 February 1941.
[61] Taped interview with the Revd. David Jenkins, 29 January 1994. See Chapter 4, note 16.
[62] Of those who taught at Rugby during the five years John Stott spent there, some fifteen went on to headmasterships of other schools, including Epsom, Malvern, Repton, Stowe and Uppingham. A complete list from 1835 to 1964 appears in Hope Simpson (1967), p. 295f.
[63] JRWS papers. Report for term 1939.2.
[64] Patrick Campbell Rodger, Bishop of Manchester 1970–78; of Oxford 1978–86.
[65] March 1938.
[66] JRWS papers. Letter home, 12 June 1939.
[67] *Rugby Advertiser*, 16 June 1939.
[68] June 1939.
[69] JRWS papers.
[70] Taped interview, 2/38.
[71] JRWS papers. Letter undated. The introduction of food rationing on 8 January 1940 presented Lily with an additional challenge.
[72] JRWS papers. Letter from John Bridger, 21 November 1939 from Clare College: 'I shall be up in Cambridge most of your scholarship week so you can come and take as many meals off me as you like.' Trinity College awarded John an entrance scholarship, and in 1943 (the year of his graduation as BA) a Senior Scholarship.
[73] Hope Simpson (1967), p. 228.
[74] *The Meteor*, 16 October 1939, No. 858.
[75] JRWS papers. Letter dated 11 December 1939, from York.
[76] Taped interview, 3/8.
[77] Stott (1958a), p. 79, quoting Temple's *Christianity and the Social Order*, 1942 (London: SCM Press, 1950), pp. 36–37.
[78] See, *e.g.* his chapter in Wallis (ed.) (1983), p. 54.
[79] Taped interview, 2/54.
[80] JRWS papers. Discharge Certificate dated 31 January 1946.
[81] JRWS papers. Letter from the Revd. J. C. Pollock, dated 24 April 1991. John Pollock was to become a professional writer specializing in Christian biography. See the bibliography; he has also written books on Whitefield (1973), Wilberforce (1977),

Shaftesbury (1985) and Gordon (1993).

[82] JRWS papers.

[83] JRWS papers, 30 June 1940.

[84] Canon R. G. B. Bailey in conversation with the author, 26 July 1996. Canon Bailey recalled meeting John Stott years later, when he joined the congregation for a service at All Souls. 'You won't know me ...' he said to the Rector as he passed through the porch on the way out – and was astonished to find he was well remembered.

[85] Hope Simpson (1967), p. 228. ARP: Air Raid Precautions. LDV, Local Defence Volunteers, was an early name for what soon became the Home Guard. The evacuation by sea of 350,000 British troops from Dunkirk was completed in the first week of June.

[86] Sixth Levée Book, Vol. III, 30 May 1940.

[87] *Ibid.*, 18 February 1940. Though the reference is undated in Hope Simpson (1967) the context suggests an earlier date. But the actual date of the Minute, and the characteristic handwriting, demonstrate beyond doubt that this was during John Stott's chairmanship. The point at issue was the wearing of house caps.

[88] Letter of 23 June 1940. Mrs. Anne Tompson's papers.

[89] Sixth Levée Book, Vol. III, 21 July 1940.

[90] From an address by John Stott, given at the International Tea in his honour during the Christian Booksellers Association Convention, Dallas, Texas, 28 June 1992.

[91] *Rugby School Service Book* (1992) No. 200.

Chapter 6. Cambridge in Wartime: Iwerne Minster

[1] Howarth (1978), p. 234.

[2] *Ibid.*, p. 238.

[3] Willey (1970), p. 101.

[4] Peter Richards, 'Cambridge at War', *CAM*, Easter 1994, p. 10.

[5] Editorial, the *Cambridge Review*, 11 October 1940; quoted in Fowler and Fowler (eds.) (1984), p. 330.

[6] Hastings (1991), p. 355.

[7] Michael Sanderson, in Johnson (ed.) (1994), p. 380.

[8] Peter Richards, *ibid.*, p. 11.

[9] Crutchley (1980), p. 87.

[10] Gow (1945), p. 255.

[11] Letter of 13 October 1940. Mrs. Anne Tompson's papers.

[12] Gow (1945), p. 57.

[13] Willey (1970), p. 100.

[14] Peter Richards, *ibid.*, p. 11.

[15] Inglis (1995), p. 70.

[16] *Ibid.*, p. 70.

[17] JRWS papers, 11 October 1940.

[18] Barwell (n.d.), p. 28.

[19] Brooke (1993), p. 288. He is quoting Sir Maurice Amos, an eminent lawyer, whose career lay mainly in Egypt where he held several leading posts in the Egyptian legal service; he was also for a time professor of law at University College, London. Brooke adds 'I am deeply indebted to his daughter Mrs Janet Whitcut for lending me his "Reminiscences for my children", and allowing me to quote from them'.

[20] Trevelyan (1949), p. 49.

[21] Moorman (1980), p. 230.

[22] Barclay (1997), p. 51. Trevelyan was not Master in 1940, which makes 1941 the probable date: see also Johnson (1979), p. 201. Oliver Barclay graduated that summer.

[23] Obituary, *The Times*, 9 September 1991.

[24] Obituary, *The Daily Telegraph*, 5 September 1991.

[25] JRWS papers, 17 October 1940.

[26] JRWS papers, 11 October 1940.

[27] JRWS papers, 17 and 22 October 1940.

[28] JRWS papers. Letter home, 10 November 1940.

[29] Letter to the author, 12 June 1989. Taped interview, 20 January 1993.

[30] The story of Charles Simeon is told in his own *Memoirs*, Carus (1847); and in two biographies, H. C. G. Moule (1892) and Hopkins (1977).

[31] Brooke (1993), p. 132.

[32] Brooke (1993), p. 132, citing Pollock (1953), pp. 113–114.

[33] Stott (1988), p. 8.

[34] See Loane (1960) especially pp. 43–61. See also Barclay (1977), especially pp. 65–70.

[35] Norman P. Grubb, *Once Caught, No Escape*, p. 56. Quoted by Stott (1988), p. 8.

[36] Dillistone (1980), p. 88.

[37] Pollock (1953), p. 252. Contrast this with the First World War when the CICCU 'was down to one registered member' (p. 193, quoted in Brooke [1993], p. 131).

[38] Stott (1982b), p. 309. See also Stevenson (ed.) (1969), p. 53.

[39] From a letter to UCCF Associates, Autumn 1989. UCCF, the Universities and Colleges Christian Fellowship, is the parent body which links together affiliated Christian Unions such as the CICCU. UCCF was known until 1975 as the IVF, the Inter-Varsity Fellowship.

[40] Quoted in Fielder (1988), p. 92.

[41] Oliver Barclay. Memorandum to the author, 23 February 1989.

[42] Henry Chadwick, the youngest of the distinguished brothers, went to camp as an Eton schoolboy in 1936 and was a leader at John Stott's early camps. He was later to be Regius Professor of Divinity successively at Oxford and Cambridge, Dean of Christ Church and Master of Peterhouse.

[43] Memorandum to the author, 8 June 1995.

[44] Henson (1950), p. 331. 'The singing parson' was not a description Geoffrey Lester relished. He saw it for the first time on a poster, 'Come and hear the Singing Parson' on Cromer railway station when he arrived to preach: 'I thought that was appalling' (taped interview, 31 January 1996).

[45] Memorandum to the author, 8 June 1995.

[46] JRWS papers. Letter from Woodlands Farm House, dated 26 January 1941.

[47] Taped interview with J. T. C. B. Collins, 6 July 1994.

[48] J. D. C. Anderson, memorandum to the author, 24 January 1996. Jock Anderson went on to serve as a medical missionary in Pakistan and Afghanistan.

[49] Taped interview 3/48. See also 'People in Close-up: the Cambridge Nine', an interview with Mary Endersbee, *Crusade*, June 1977.

[50] Barclay (1977), p. 111. John Stott's dates include his time as a post-graduate, in Trinity and at Ridley Hall. 'One of their number' in the passage quoted above was in fact Oliver Barclay himself who was CICCU President from Easter 1941 to Christmas 1942.

[51] Atkinson (1966), p. 46. For Dr. Basil Atkinson, see Chapter 8.

[52] Fielder (1988), p. 72.

[53] Letter from Oliver Barclay to the writer, 1992, the source of much of the information above. Among his CICCU friends in Trinity he refers especially to Donald Eddison and Martin Burch, both campers.

[54] J. W. Wenham, draft of *Autobiography* (unpublished) pp. FH 13–1.

[55] Cyrus I. Scofield (ed.) (New York: Oxford University Press, 1909). Scofield was an American Congregationalist, 1843–1921, whose biblical annotations (following J. N. Darby) were much in vogue in some evangelical circles in the 1920s and 30s.

[56] Taped interview 4/61 and conversation with JRWS, 21 October 1993.

[57] A phrase made popular by David O. Moberg as the title of his study (Moberg, 1972).

See Bebbington (1989), p. 214.

[58] Stott (1990a), p. 8. See also Stott (1978a), pp. 35–36.

[59] Taylor and Taylor (1911, 1918).

[60] J. W. Wenham, *ibid.*, p. FH 4–4.

[61] Fielder (1988), p. 93.

[62] John Stott, 'What I learned from Hudson Taylor', *East Asia Millions*, June/July 1990, p. 55.

[63] From an address by John Stott given at the International Tea in his honour during the Christian Booksellers Association Convention, Dallas, Texas, 28 June 1992.

[64] See Johnson (1979), p. 317. The chapter in question was contributed by Ronald Inchley.

[65] Coggan (ed.) (1934).

[66] Hammond (1936); Guillebaud (1937). A third title in the series was Atkinson (1937) *Valiant in Fight*. *In Understanding be Men*, in its third revision, was still selling widely in the 1980s.

[67] Johnson (1979), p. 317.

[68] See Johnson (1979), pp. 212–213. John Wenham had been instigator of the first IVF theological students' conference in Digswell Park in 1937, the year which one contemporary historian identifies as 'a turning point' towards self-confident evangelical scholarship. See Knoll (1991), pp. 83–84.

[69] Anderson (1985), p. 138.

[70] Taped interview with Sir Norman Anderson, 17 January 1991.

[71] *Cambridge University Reporter*, 14 June 1941, p. 821.

[72] JRWS papers.

[73] John Stott writes in Eddison (ed.) (1983), 'I was myself still at school when he invited me to join his team in the children's beach mission at Borth' (p. 61). Scripture Union records are inconclusive; but John Sheldon's diary kept at the time strongly suggests the summers of 1941 and 1942 and other memories confirm this.

[74] CSSM: Children's Special Service Mission, now the Scripture Union.

[75] Canon M. A. C. Warren, 1904–1977: General Secretary, Church Missionary Society, 1942–1963.

[76] Dillistone (1980), p. 20.

[77] See *Dictionary of National Biography*, 1981–1985, p. 324.

[78] Richard Rhodes-James, in Eddison (ed.) (1983), p. 18.

[79] Richard Rhodes-James, *ibid.*, p. 17. His chapter is entitled 'the Pioneer'.

[80] Richard Rhodes-James, *ibid.*, pp. 19, 20.

[81] Sylvester (1984), p. 97.

[82] Manwaring (1985), p. 58.

[83] Sheppard (1964), p. 51.

[84] Catherwood, F. (1995), p. 30f. H. F. R. Catherwood was knighted in 1971 after a distinguished career in industry and politics, including five years as Director-General of the National Economic Development Council.

[85] John R. W. Stott, *Old Campers' Fellowship Newsletter*, 22 April 1965 (a special commemorative issue to mark Bash's retirement from the Scripture Union staff).

[86] John Eddison, memorandum to the author, 20 January 1993.

[87] JRWS papers.

[88] Dr. A. J. Loveless. Letter to the author, 11 March 1997.

[89] Dr. D. H. Trapnell. Taped interview, 18 February 1993.

[90] Stott, in Eddison (ed.) (1983), p. 61.

[91] Taped interview, 4/16.

[92] John Prince was one such. Taped memorandum to the author, December 1994. After the Fleet Air Arm and Cambridge, John Prince emigrated to Australia where he was a teacher and headmaster.

[93] By William Booth-Clibborn. See *Wings of Praise* by 'The Maréchale' [Catherine Booth-Clibborn] (London: Marshall, Morgan & Scott, n.d.), No. 13.

[94] Ira D. Sankey (London: Marshall, Morgan & Scott, 1873). The collection sold more than 80 million copies.

[95] The idea was presumably borrowed by a devotee of the works of P. G. Wodehouse (perhaps Mark Ruston?) from *Summer Lightning* (London: Herbert Jenkins, 1929), p. 107, where Hugo Carmody, spelling out over the telephone the name of Mario's Restaurant, does so as 'Yes. M for mange, A for Asthma, R for rheumatism ...'

[96] In the summer of 1943, with three camps running consecutively for about ten days each, total numbers ran at about 33 officers and 225 campers.

[97] Philip Tompson to his parents, 2 March 1941. Mrs. Anne Tompson's papers.

[98] E. J. H. Nash to F. P. Tompson. Mrs. Anne Tompson's papers, 17 September 1941.

[99] Watson (1983), p. 39.

[100] Lewis (1949), ch. 5.

[101] King (1969), p. 56.

[102] There is a more intimate and first-hand description of camp in John Laird's autobiography: Laird (1981), p. 119.

[103] Gow (1945), p. 75.

[104] Howarth (1978), p. 241.

[105] Gow (1945), p. 98.

[106] Peter Richards, 'Cambridge at War', *CAM*, Easter 1994, p. 11.

[107] Gow (1945), p. 154.

[108] Harold Nicolson, *Diaries*, Vol. II, ed. N. Nicolson; the entry is for 23 January 1941. Quoted in Fowler and Fowler (ed.) (1984), p. 232.

[109] JRWS papers, 6 May 1942.

[110] Taped interview, 3/40.

[111] JRWS papers. P. W. Duff to John Stott, 24 June 1942.

Chapter 7. Towards Ordination: 'An Instinctive Pacifist'

[1] Stott, in Eddison (ed.) (1983), p. 59. Other references in similar words can be found in various Forewords *etc.* to symposia on nuclear disarmament, and in published interviews.

[2] See Hayes (1949). Fenner Brockway in his Foreword compares the treatment of conscientious objectors in the two World Wars and concludes:

> It is true that on the whole Conscientious Objectors had an easier course in the Second World War than in the First, although ... there were individual cases of long-sustained persecution. Both legislation and administration were less harsh; legislation attempted to avoid the repeated sentences – the 'cat and mouse' treatment – which formed the worst feature of the experience of C.O.s from 1916 to 1919, and the members of the Tribunals were generally more fair-minded. There were exceptions ... (p. xii).

[3] JRWS papers. Letter from Bishop's House, Coventry, 24 January 1940.

[4] Barry (1964), p. 43.

[5] JRWS papers. The above quotation is taken from a draft reply (undated) in John Stott's handwriting, scribbled on the back of Bishop Haigh's letter to him of 24 January.

[6] F. S. Guy Warman, Chairman of CACTM, the Central Advisory Council for Training for the Ministry.

[7] JRWS papers. The original letter was presumably sent on to John's father in France but a copy was made by John's sister, from which the above is transcribed. The letter is dated 8 Feb. 1940 and characteristically concludes 'Joy Stott, pp Bish. Coventry'.

[8] Dr. Alan Dods. Letter and conversation with the author, 16 and 17 March, 1992.

[9] Auxiliary Territorial Service, the women's auxiliary of the army. Joy served originally as a

private, refusing a commission because of her socialist principles. Part of her war-service was spent defending gun-emplacements at Shoeburyness at the mouth of the Thames estuary.

[10] JRWS papers. Lily kept a pencil copy of her letter, dated 11 February 1940, from which the above is transcribed.

[11] JRWS papers. Fulljames writes from *HMS Eaglet*, Liverpool, dated 12 February 1940.

[12] JRWS papers. Letter dated 27 February 1940.

[13] JRWS papers. Letter dated 14 March 1940.

[14] JRWS papers. Letter dated 19 February 1940.

[15] JRWS papers. Draft dated Easter Sunday (24 March) 1940.

[16] JRWS papers. Letter from P. W. Duff, 14 May 1940.

[17] *The Times*, 24 February 1941; *Daily Mail* cutting, undated.

[18] JRWS papers. Letter dated 25 April 1940.

[19] JRWS papers. The letter exists only in draft. Coventry had suffered huge destruction in the worst air raid of the war, when on the night of 14 November 1940 the cathedral, eight churches and most of the medieval city had been destroyed and upwards of 1,000 civilians killed – hence the reference in the letter above to 'terribly distressing times'.

[20] 'People in close-up: John Capon talks to John Stott', *Crusade*, May 1974.

[21] Eddison (ed.) (1983), p. 59.

[22] Terry Lovell, 'The Times and Travels of an Ordinary Christian', *The Christian Bookseller*, May/June, 1992.

[23] Taped interview, 3/32.

[24] Taped interview, 3/4.

[25] JRWS papers. Letter dated 19 January 1941 from Woodlands Farm House.

[26] From a draft headed 'My answer:' dated 22 January 1941, attached in John Stott's papers to his mother's letter.

[27] JRWS papers.

[28] JRWS papers. Letter dated 26 January 1941, from Woodlands Farm House. Either Mrs. Stott was reading rather at random, or else was somehow a fortnight ahead of the date in her printed Bible-reading notes. In 1941 Scripture Union published two sets of Bible reading notes, both following the same passages. It appears that John Stott was using *Daily Notes*, in a slightly smaller format than *Daily Bread* which his mother used. The note in *Daily Bread* for Saturday 8 February on Romans 13:1–14 began:

> The Christian's three duties: (i) TO HIS COUNTRY. 'Be subject unto the higher powers,' says St. Paul, for 'the powers that be are ordained of God' (v. 1). Remember that this injunction was given to Christians living in the heathen Roman empire. Laws must be obeyed (vs. 2–5). Taxes must be paid (vs. 6, 7). Service to the state must be rendered as a matter of conscience (v. 5). The Christian must be a good citizen.

[29] JRWS papers. Draft dated 31 January 1941 from Trinity College, Cambridge.

[30] JRWS papers. Letter dated 3 February 1941, from Woodlands Farm House.

[31] JRWS papers. Letter dated 11 February 1941, from Woodlands Farm House.

[32] JRWS papers. Letter dated 24 January 1941 from Bishopscourt, Manchester on behalf of CACTM.

[33] Letter dated 20 March 1941. Mrs. Anne Tompson's papers.

[34] Terry Lovell, 'The Times and Travels of an Ordinary Christian', *The Christian Bookseller*, May/June, 1992.

[35] Brooke (1993), p. 149. Brooke adds: 'An extraordinary trick of fortune made this eminent pacifist Vice-Chancellor just after the end of the Second World War, from 1947 to 1949, and it fell on him to greet Field-Marshall Smuts as Chancellor in his own and Smuts' college, and to entertain war leaders and Churchill himself as they came collecting

honorary degrees.'
[36] Dillistone (1975), p. 228.
[37] *Ibid.*, p. 290.
[38] The description is John Habgood's. See Peart-Binns (1987a), p. 47. Habgood goes on to describe his concern that Raven was a man 'carried along partly by his own enthusiasm'.
[39] Raven (1928), p. 43. 'Little-Go' was the popular name of the old Previous Examination, then required for Cambridge entrance by those who had not obtained exemption.
[40] Oliver Barclay confirms this impression from his own experience at the time: 'Having been scornful of Conservative Evangelicals, he (Raven) became more friendly during and after the war, when he recognized the quality of some of his Conservative Evangelical theological students.' (Barclay [1997], p. 39.)
[41] JRWS papers. Letter dated 19 February 1941.
[42] JRWS papers. Letter dated 21 February 1941 from Woodlands Farm House.
[43] JRWS papers. Letter dated 19 March 1941 from Colonel K. D. M. Murray, Director in Military Studies.
[44] JRWS papers. Letter dated 28 March 1941 from Trinity College.
[45] JRWS papers. Letter dated 15 April 1941 from Colonel K. D. M. Murray.
[46] JRWS papers.
[47] JRWS papers. The letter survives only in draft.
[48] JRWS papers. Letter dated 7 May 1941 from Woodlands Farm House.
[49] JRWS papers. Letter dated 14 June 1941 from Trinity College.
[50] Taped interview, 6/65.
[51] Hastings (1991), p. 357.
[52] JRWS papers. Letter undated; but John Stott's draft reply dated 23 February 1941. Joy writes: 'Sweat with us! Nobody will listen to you afterwards if you have not shared the agony.'
[53] JRWS papers. Letter dated 4 November 1939.
[54] JRWS papers. Letter dated 14 October 1941 in reply to one from John Stott 'six months before'.
[55] John R. W. Stott, 'Vengeance – human and divine', *Church of England Newspaper*, 23 December 1960.
[56] See, for example his interview with Alex Mitchell, 'Struggling with Contemporary Issues', *Third Way*, February 1982; Stott, 'Nuclear weapons change the possibility of war' in Kirk (ed.) (1988), p. 46. John Stott expounds the theory of the 'Just War' in 'Calling for Peacemakers in a Nuclear Age', *All Souls Papers*, 11 November 1979; but most recently in chapter 5, Stott (1998).

Chapter 8. Reading Theology: Ridley Hall
[1] Interview with Steve Turner, 'Backing the Basics', *Church Times*, 13 February 1995. The phrase 'le mot juste' recognizes the French commitment to 'the precise word'. It was a concept dear to the heart of John Stott's French supervisor at Cambridge.
[2] JRWS papers. Letter from Patrick Duff to John Stott, 24 June 1942.
[3] Montefiore (1995), p. 9. Montefiore also quotes (p. 97) an extract from a diary he kept in the 1950s about an overnight journey from Cambridge to Launde Abbey when John Burnaby was one of his passengers: 'J. B. rather nervous – tendency to clutch with his hands and mutter "The roads are rather slippery, aren't they?".'
[4] Obituary. *The Times*, 8 March 1978.
[5] Anon. 'Close-up: Professor John Burnaby', *Trinity Review*, Michaelmas, 1958.
[6] Memorandum to the author, 18 May 1996.
[7] JRWS MS 'Jottings for a biography', 1993/4.
[8] Barclay (1977), p. 95.
[9] From 1951, Lady Margaret Professor of Divinity.

[10] Edwards and Stott (1988), p. 105.

[11] When the Norrisian and Hulsean professorships were united, the restriction to members of the Church of England was removed. Dodd was the first holder of the reconstructed chair. Even so, university sermons in Cambridge could only be preached by Anglicans until 1941; and he preached his first the following year. See Dillistone (1977), pp. 145, 157.

[12] Brooke (1993), p. 409.

[13] Hastings (1991), p. 297.

[14] Taped interview, 3/41.

[15] David Spence, personal conversation. Derek J. Tidball, Principal of the London Bible College told the story at the Brunel University degree ceremony at which John Stott received an Honorary DD, 14 October 1997. Lord Runcie confirms the anecdote.

[16] Barclay (1997), p. 17. C. S. Lewis was to register his celebrated protest at the liberal theology taught to ordinands nearly twenty years later in a striking paper read to the students of Westcott House, Cambridge: 'Once the layman was anxious to hide the fact that he believed so much less than the vicar: now he tends to hide the fact that he believes so much more.' See Lewis (1975) p. 125; originally published 1967.

[17] Stott (1978b), p. 179.

[18] Saunders and Sansom (1992), p. 27.

[19] Atkinson (1966), p. 64.

[20] Fielder (1988), p. 68. The story is attributed to Roger Forster.

[21] Atkinson (1939), p. 15.

[22] Atkinson (1937).

[23] Lowman (1983), p. 52.

[24] *Ibid.*, p. 53, quoting Laird (1981).

[25] Brooke (1993), p. 139. Westcott and Lightfoot both became Bishops of Durham: Westcott might have gone further, but 'the Conservative Prime Minister scotched the Queen's suggestion in 1890 that Westcott should be made Archbishop of York, by drawing her attention to "the Socialist tendencies of the speeches which he has made since becoming a bishop"'. (Edwards [1982], p. 216.)

[26] *The Times*, 14 December 1991.

[27] Catherwood, F. (1995), p. 124.

[28] Fielder (1988).

[29] *Ibid.*, p. 92. DJ for his part saw in Bash a fear of intellectualism and over-cerebral discipleship; together with too general a view of the value of the single life (JRWS taped interview, B40/4).

[30] Letter to the author from Dr. Ian Lodge-Patch, to whom DJ recounted the incident.

[31] John Stott, 'Tyndale House', *Christian Arena*, September 1992. See also Barclay (1977), p. 109.

[32] Stott, in Houston (ed.) (1986), p. xxvii.

[33] Gow (1945), p. 159.

[34] JRWS papers, 8 June 1945.

[35] Myra Chave-Jones. Memorandum to the author, 18 November 1995.

[36] JRWS papers. Letter dated 3 September 1943. John Stott would occasionally pay hasty visits to the school to speak to the meeting, with no time or inclination to call on his housemaster or anyone else. On this occasion, he seems to have been noticed, and to have become the subject of comment!

[37] JRWS papers. Letter dated 7 November 1943. The wartime pay even of a Major-General would be much less than Arnold Stott must have been earning in Harley Street in 1939; and income tax became punitive as the war progressed.

[38] JRWS papers. Letter dated 10 November 1943.

[39] JRWS papers. Letter dated 21 November 1943.

[40] Hastings (1991), p. 362.

[41] Peter Richards, 'Cambridge at War', *CAM,* Easter, 1994.

[42] Edwards (1971), p. 334.

[43] Commission on Evangelism (1945), p. 1. Temple was not a member of the Archbishops' 'Third Committee of Enquiry', which produced the previous Report, *The Evangelistic Work of the Church* (London: SPCK, 1918), where the quotation appears unattributed on the heading to Part Two (p. 18). There is no evidence in either report that Temple drafted the definition, though he might well have done so.

[44] Gummer (1963), p. 169.

[45] Welsby (1984), p. 46.

[46] The friend was C. J. E. Lefroy. Memorandum to the author, 31 March 1994.

[47] See John Capon, 'People in Close-up: John Capon talks to John Stott (1)', *Crusade,* May 1974.

[48] John Collins. Memorandum to the author, 26 July 1994.

[49] Harford and MacDonald (1923), p. 91.

[50] Brooke (1993), p. 144.

[51] Bullock (1941), p. 119.

[52] Not the daily newspaper, formerly the *Manchester Guardian,* but a weekly church newspaper now discontinued.

[53] Handley Moule moved from Ridley Hall to be Norrisian Professor of Divinity; and then Bishop of Durham. Thomas Drury became Bishop of Sodor and Man.

[54] Howarth (1978), p. 177. The *Dictionary of National Biography* describes Haldane in his socialist essays as 'more interested in taking a swipe at God than at the ruling class' (DNB, 1961–1970, p. 474).

[55] Bullock (1941), p. 173.

[56] *Ibid.,* p. 173. The quotation is from *The Battlement,* the magazine of Ridley Hall, June 1945.

[57] Donald English, 'Profile: John Stott – Christian Communicator Extraordinary', *Epworth Review,* May 1993.

[58] Bullock (1941), quoting *The Battlement,* 1941.

[59] Conversation with Dr. Murray Baker, CICCU Treasurer 1944/5, 17 January 1996.

[60] Memorandum to the author, 18 November 1995.

[61] Fielder (1988), p. 92.

[62] JRWS papers. Circular letter dated 17 October 1945 from Ridley Hall, Cambridge.

[63] Presumably Torrey (1923), a favourite booklet of Bash's.

[64] Timothy Dudley-Smith, in Eden and Wells (eds.) (1991), p. 15.

[65] Stott (1949).

[66] Atkinson (1966), p. 1.

[67] JRWS papers, marked 'Given to President, November 1945'.

[68] J. R. W. Stott, 'Child Conversion', *The CSSM Magazine,* Jan/Feb. 1945.

[69] Watson (1983), paperback edition, 1986, p. 40.

[70] Memorandum to the author, 24 May 1996; taped interview, 4/37.

[71] Taped interview, 4/38.

[72] Taped interview, B35A/2.

[73] *Cambridge University Reporter,* 16 June 1945.

[74] Memorandum to the author, 24 May 1996.

[75] Hastings (1991), p. 363.

[76] Stott (1978a), p. 15.

[77] JRWS papers, 13 May 1945.

[78] JRWS papers, 20 May 1945.

[79] Memoranda to the author, 20 January 1993 and 31 May 1989.

[80] JRWS papers, 26 February 1945.

[81] Cuthbert Dukes had been unfortunate in his experience of the Church of England. He once said to John Stott during his time as curate, 'If you had been Rector of All Souls I

would not have become a Quaker.' (JRWS Taped interview, B40/3.) Later the Dukes would come together to the 'Doctors' Service' held annually at All Souls: but Cuthbert Dukes would be careful, in saying the Creed, to omit all references to Christ's resurrection (J. T. C. B. Collins, taped interview, 6 July 1994).

[82] She had attended the exploratory meeting in 1938 at Westminster Central Hall and was for some years a member of the Committee (Chairman, 1943). Family planning was one of her special concerns. (Donald Godden, formerly Publication Officer, National Marriage Guidance Council. Letter to the author, 25 January 1996.)

[83] JRWS papers. Letter from Ethel Dukes dated 13 August 1945.

[84] JRWS papers. Letter dated 28 June 1945.

[85] JRWS papers. A carbon copy of this letter is dated 24 July 1945. Geoffrey Lester had been Earnshaw-Smith's curate since 1942 and was expecting to move on.

[86] JRWS papers.

[87] JRWS papers. Letter dated 6 November 1945.

[88] JRWS papers. Letter dated 17 December 1945.

[89] JRWS papers. Letter dated 18 December 1945.

[90] JRWS papers. Letter dated 19 November 1945.

[91] JRWS papers. Letter dated 13 December 1945.

[92] JRWS papers. Letter dated 15 December 1945.

[93] JRWS papers. Letter dated 11 December 1945.

[94] JRWS papers. Letter dated 25 November 1945.

[95] From an exposition of Malachi 2:2 (RSV): 'If you will not listen, if you will not lay it to heart to give glory to my name, says the Lord of hosts, then I will send the curse upon you and I will curse your blessings ...' The sermon, 'Lost Leaders', is one of a set of tape-recorded addresses under the general title *What I believe and why: twelve selected sermons by John Stott to commemorate his 70th birthday* (All Souls Tape Library, 1992).

[96] JRWS papers. Letter dated 13 January 1946.

[97] Luke 12:35–36.

Chapter 9. Assistant Curate: All Souls and St. Peter's

[1] Mass-Observation (1947), p. 156. Quoted by John Wolffe, in Johnson (ed.) (1994), p. 427.

[2] Elisabeth Earnshaw-Smith. Letter to the author, 10 March 1996.

[3] Cherry and Pevsner (1983), p. 599.

[4] Between the wars the name changed to the 'Cambridge University Mission'; and in the 1990s to the 'Salmon Youth Centre'.

[5] JRWS papers. Letter sent to him in August 1950, a month before his own institution as Rector, by Mr A. R. James of the Protestant Reformation Society to whose predecessor, the Revd. W. A. Limbrick, the original had been addressed.

[6] Book of Common Prayer: The Order for the Administration of the Lord's Supper or Holy Communion. Concluding sentence of the opening rubric.

[7] Luker (1979), p. 52.

[8] John V. Taylor. Letter to the author, 22 January 1996.

[9] Letter to the author from Michael Smith, Archives and Local Studies Assistant, City of Westminster Archives Centre, 18 January 1996; drawing on Civil Defence records Acc. 523/426.

[10] Sister E. P. Jordan, 'The Damaged Church', *All Souls*, May 1951.

[11] Taped interview with Prebendary Geoffrey Lester, 31 January 1996.

[12] Edwards (1984), p. 197.

[13] 7 April 1867; quoted in Cohan (1995), p. 356.

[14] Most of the above information is from Baker (1995).

[15] Taped interview, 4/1.

[16] Dr D. H. Trapnell. Taped interview, 18 February 1993.

[17] Letter to the author, 16 December 1996.

[18] See the standard edition of *Hymns Ancient and Modern*, 1916, No. 278.

[19] Taped interview, 4/4, on which much of the above is based. See also Barclay (1977), p. 100.

[20] Earnshaw-Smith in Colquhoun (ed.) (1948), p. 47.

[21] Atkinson (1966) p. 29; and Barclay (1977), p. 91.

[22] Coggan (ed.) (1934), pp. 211–212.

[23] For exposition of the meaning of 'evangelical' and 'evangelicalism' in this context, see for example numerous published interviews, and Stott (1970), pp. 27–46; Edwards and Stott (1988), esp. pp. 332–338; Stott (1977), the closing address at the National Evangelical Anglican Congress, Nottingham University, April 1977.

[24] Lowman (1983), p. 70. The address appears in Earnshaw-Smith (1939), pp. 12–13. Oliver Barclay cites this conference as laying the foundations for the creation of the International Fellowship of Evangelical Students (IFES) after the intervening years of war. See Barclay (1997), p. 29.

[25] Toon (1979), p. 76. *The Times* survey was in 1844.

[26] Timothy Dudley-Smith, 'Yesterday and Tomorrow: Evangelical Pointers from the Past', *Churchman*, Vol. 93, No. 3, 1979, p. 199.

[27] Quoted from the Preface of Matthew Arnold, *St. Paul and Protestantism* (1870: only the first edition includes the Preface) in Russell (1915), p. 128.

[28] Chadwick (1983), p. 193. It was in the same connection that Henson is said to have coined the phrase 'the Protestant underworld'. Against this should be set Oliver Barclay's assessment that 'by the 1930s, evangelicals were effectively the only section of the British churches' that held to the Reformation doctrine of the final authority and sufficiency of the Bible. In the eyes of some churchmen (today as then) this was enough to account for the epithet 'illiterate'. See Barclay (1997), p. 10.

[29] Neill (1958), p. 398.

[30] Carpenter, E. (1991), p. 120.

[31] JRWS Papers. Unpublished memorandum 'Evangelicals in the Church of England', August 1983. Colin Craston, to become a leading figure in church circles, was advised by his vicar in 1941 not to contemplate ordination when the war ended because 'Evangelicals are finished in the Church of England.' See Craston (1998), p. 60. The whole of the chapter, 'Evangelicals in the Church of England since World War II' offers a personal account of the period.

[32] Hylson-Smith (1988), p. 247. See also Oliver Barclay's discussion of 'conservative, classic and liberal' evangelicalism, and his analysis of liberal disintegration. Barclay (1997), pp. 12 and 40.

[33] Rogers (ed.) (1923).

[34] Barnes (1947). The book was serialized in the *Sunday Pictorial*.

[35] Carpenter, E. (1991), p. 300.

[36] Stott, in Richter (ed.) (1972), p. 172.

[37] Colquhoun (ed.) (1948), p. vii.

[38] John Stott, 'That word "radical"', *Church of England Newspaper*, 24 February 1967.

[39] Smith, A. E. (1991), p. 71.

[40] The third in the series, at Caister, Norfolk, in 1988 was not a Congress but a 'Celebration'; and though John Stott participated it was not under his direction. Compared to Keele 1967 and Nottingham 1977 it must be reckoned ineffective.

[41] 'I personally do not like the label "conservative evangelical"', John Stott wrote in 1988, 'it conjures up the wrong image.' He preferred 'radical conservative Evangelical'. (Edwards and Stott [1988], p. 88.)

[42] Welsby (1984), p. 212. John Stott was in fact Rector of All Souls from 1950 to 1975 and thereafter Rector Emeritus.

[43] Taped interview, 4/65.

⁴⁴ Taped interview, 4/65.

⁴⁵ Taped interview with Prebendary Geoffrey Lester, 31 January 1996, including the story which follows.

⁴⁶ Latimer House was the vision of Charles Baring Young, the founder of Kingham Hill School. It began in 1894 at No. 1, Fitzroy Square: 'Here, so near to the great business houses of the West End and within easy reach of the City, a young man found a pleasant boarding-house, a good club and a Christian home.' Jarvis (1950), p. 66. The new Latimer House in Hanson Street was opened in 1938.

⁴⁷ For example, in his booklet *Life at its Best*: see chapter 5, note 34.

⁴⁸ Revelation 3:20, RSV.

⁴⁹ Taped interview, 4/70.

⁵⁰ See Endersbee (1977), p. 41.

⁵¹ This was a work of Christian philanthropy 'strictly in accordance with the Protestant and Evangelical Religion'. The Annual Report of 1937–8 (the only one available in JRWS papers) speaks of nightly prayers, and 'Gospel Services to tramps' on Sunday afternoons which were well attended.

⁵² JRWS papers. Letter dated 29 January 1946.

⁵³ This is not, of course, the present 'Waldegrave Hall' in the basement of All Souls Church; but something of the history can be read there in a slate tablet commemorating the earlier premises in Duke Street whose name was changed in the 1940s from the Grays Yard Mission to the Waldegrave Hall. The tablet reads:

The Waldegrave Hall

The original Hall at 23 Duke Street was built in 1888 through the energy and faith of Ada Ruth Habershon. It was called the Grays Yard Mission and served the poor and needy of London. Its name was later changed to Waldegrave Hall to commemorate the devotion of Constance Waldegrave, the Mission's Superintendent, 1920–1935. Proceeds from the sale of the Hall in 1976 were invested in the building of this new Waldegrave Hall as part of the All Souls rebuilding project, 1975–1976, which was also the result of much energy, faith and devotion. The new Hall and the renovated church were opened on All Souls Day, 2 November 1976.

⁵⁴ Elizabeth Evans. Letter to the author, 24 March 1995. Miss Evans had been one of the helpers at Children's Church fifty years before.

⁵⁵ *Ibid.*

⁵⁶ Letter to the author from Mark Tomlinson, Promotion and Development Manager of Covenanters, 17 April 1996, quoting the recollections of R. W. G. Turner. John Stott served for some years on the Council of the Covenanter Union.

⁵⁷ Mrs. Pat King. Letter to the author, 14 January 1996.

⁵⁸ Taped interview, B40/2.

⁵⁹ The Revd. Canon Dr. Peter R. Thompson. Letter to the author, 9 February 1996.

⁶⁰ Timothy Dudley-Smith in Eden and Wells (eds.) (1991), p. 16.

⁶¹ The Revd. David L. Jones. Letter to the author, 18 March 1995.

⁶² 'The Boys go Camping', *All Souls*, October 1949.

⁶³ Taped interview with Elisabeth Earnshaw-Smith, 15 May 1995.

⁶⁴ *All Souls*, April 1946.

⁶⁵ He was part of the team, with F. P. and Arthur Wood, in the 'Faith for the Times' campaign of 1944; and with Lindsay Glegg, Roy Cattell and Tom Rees was one of the organizers of the 'This is the Victory' campaign at the Central Hall, Westminster, for four weeks in the following year. (Taped interview with Geoffrey Lester, 31 January 1996.)

⁶⁶ Taped interview with Canon Gordon Mayo, 3 June 1996.

⁶⁷ JRWS papers: n.d. but from about this period.

Notes 481

68 Taped interview with Gordon Mayo, 3 June 1996.
69 Stott (1982b).
70 *Op. cit.*, p. 12.
71 *Op. cit.*, p. 42.
72 Davies (1965), p. 231.
73 *Ibid.*, p. 232.
74 Howard Sainsbury. Letter to the author, 5 March 1996.
75 Stott (1954).
76 Letter dated 24 April 1946. Mrs. Ellen Waterson's papers.
77 Letter dated 18 October 1946. Mrs. Ellen Waterson's papers.
78 Letter dated 2 July 1947. Mrs. Ellen Waterson's papers.
79 Taped interview with Elizabeth Earnshaw-Smith.
80 *Dictionary of National Biography*, 1961–1970, p. 98.
81 JRWS papers. Draft dated 10 March 1947.
82 JRWS papers. The Christian Commando Campaign was an inter-denominational mission organized primarily through Methodist churches.
83 John R. W. Stott 'Evangelical Hypocrisy', *Life of Faith*, 12 January 1949; 'Belief on Testimony', *Inter-Varsity*, Autumn 1949.
84 Stott (1949) and (1950).
85 Taped interviews, 21/17; 5/75.
86 George Dempster was for forty-two years Welfare Superintendent of the British Sailors' Society and was known as 'The Sailors' Friend'. See G. F. Dempster, *Finding Men for Christ* (London: Hodder & Stoughton, 1935); *The Love that will not let me go* (1937); *Touched by a Loving Hand* (1939); *Lovest Thou Me?* (1944); *Until He Find it* (1956).
87 Taped interview, 21/10f.
88 JRWS papers. Letter dated 1 January 1947. John Stott had visited the college to lecture on Isaiah.
89 C. J. E. Lefroy. Memorandum to the author, 31 March 1994.
90 JRWS papers. Letter dated 22 October 1948.
91 Taped interview, B40/3.
92 JRWS papers. Letter from Phyllis Parsons, 30 April 1949.
93 Letter in possession of Gordon Mayo, n.d.
94 JRWS papers. Letter dated 22 February 1950 from Fulham Palace.
95 JRWS papers. Letter dated 2 March 1950 from Queen Anne Street.
96 Palmer (1992), p. 234.
97 *Ibid.*, p. 235.
98 Baron (1952), p. 158.
99 Palmer (1992), p. 236.
100 Minutes of a meeting of the PCC held in All Souls Church House on Tuesday 21 March 1950.
101 George Cansdale, 'The People's Warden Speaks', *All Souls*, August 1962.
102 Taped interview with George Cansdale, 1 October 1992.
103 *Ibid.*
104 John Cordle, later MP for Bournemouth, was one of these. He was a personal friend of Bevir's and sought through him to see that Attlee was aware of this unease. (Conversation with the author, 18 November 1996.)
105 Timothy Dudley-Smith, in Eden and Wells (eds.) (1991), p. 12. The Bishop of Willesden at the time was E. M. Gresford Jones.
106 Both letters, JRWS papers.
107 PCC Minute Book, 27 June 1950.

Chapter 10. Rector of All Souls: A Strategy for Evangelism
1 Taped interview with Elisabeth-Earnshaw Smith, 15 May 1995.

[2] JRWS papers. Letter dated 23 June 1950.

[3] Hastings (1991), p. 43. The fall was from 4,554 in 1938 to 2,189 in 1948.

[4] Sir Eric Richardson. Letter to the author, 7 January 1998. Director of Education (later, Director) of the 'Poly', 1957–70, and an early supporter of the IVF.

[5] *All Souls*, July 1950.

[6] *Ibid.*

[7] JRWS MS, 'Jottings for a Biography', 1993/4, p. 15.

[8] C. J. E. Lefroy. Memorandum to the author, 31 March 1994. The supposition about Hookses was correct: see chapter 14. The 'Austin' was presumably the 'jalopy'.

[9] *All Souls*, September 1950.

[10] *Ibid.*

[11] JRWS papers. Letter dated 13 October 1950.

[12] Stockwood (1982), p. 151.

[13] *The Times*, 31 May, 1963.

[14] Oliver O'Donovan (Exeter: Paternoster, 1986).

[15] Letter to the author, 31 January 1998. The letter continues: 'It is important to recognise that All Souls evangelism in those days was not simply a matter of "decisions" but of very serious and thorough pastoral catechesis.'

[16] *All Souls*, March 1951.

[17] *Ibid.*

[18] *Ibid.*

[19] All Souls PCC Minute Book, 16 January 1951.

[20] Luker (1979), p. 57.

[21] *All Souls*, June 1951.

[22] Taped interview (with JRWS), 5/69. Tom Rees was a notable British evangelist who filled the Albert Hall many times for his evangelistic rallies; and who founded the conference centre 'Hildenborough Hall'. In 1944 he had been one of a team of six evangelists who took the Royal Albert Hall for sixteen consecutive nights, April 8–23. See Glegg (ed.) (1944).

[23] *All Souls*, November 1951.

[24] Taped interview with John Collins, 6 July 1994.

[25] JRWS papers. Letter from J. I. Packer, 5 May 1951.

[26] Stott in Houston (ed.) (1986), p. xxvii.

[27] See above, Chapter 9.

[28] Letter of invitation to the founder members, dated 14 November 1958.

[29] JRWS papers.

[30] Taped interview with John Collins (who was present at the sermon), 6 July 1994. The original letter, dated 25 March 1951, may well have been written tongue-in-cheek.

[31] R. J. B. Eddison. Letter to the author, 15 March 1995. It is difficult to resist a feeling of *ben trovato*, but John Stott confirms the story.

[32] The term is only used for those gaining high distinction in mathematics at Cambridge.

[33] Wilbur M. Smith, 'In the Study', *Moody Monthly*, October 1955.

[34] J. R. W. Stott 'People who have influenced me', *All Souls Broadsheet*, Summer 1991. The 'traditional clerical nightmare' was, in this instance, more than a figure of speech.

[35] Taped interview, 21/28.

[36] Taped interview, 21/30. This was with a Mrs. Stride and her companion, Miss Tyler.

[37] Dr. D. H. Trapnell. Taped interview, 18 February 1993.

[38] Dr. Ian Lodge-Patch. Memorandum to the author, c. 1994.

[39] J. D. C. Anderson. Memorandum to the author, 24 January 1996.

[40] JRWS. Memorandum to the author, 2 February 1996.

[41] John Lefroy. Memorandum to the author, 31 March 1994.

[42] Luker (1979), p. 59.

[43] J. T. C. B. Collins. Memorandum to the author, 29 June 1989.

[44] Letter to the author, 27 May 1997.

[45] The Revd. R. B. Gorrie. Letter to the author, 31 July 1996. Richard Gorrie was a staff worker for the Scottish Scripture Union, Chaplain of Fettes College, and then Scottish Director of the Inter-Schools Christian Fellowship.

[46] Frank Boggs. Letter to the author, 22 March 1997.

[47] JRWS papers, 29 May 1953.

[48] Memorandum to the author, 26 July 1994.

[49] *Ibid.*

[50] John R. W. Stott, 'The Church's Message'; *All Souls: an illustrated Guide*, 1954.

[51] Information from Prebendary Patrick Dearnley. Letter to the author, 2 December 1997.

[52] Letter from John Stott to Dr. A. P. Waterson, 25 August 1955. Mrs. E. M. Waterson's papers.

[53] R. E. H. Bowdler, 'Reminiscences of the Chaplaincy', *All Souls*, March 1958.

[54] *Dictionary of National Biography*, 1961–1970, p. 654.

[55] Taped interview, 5/45.

[56] R. E. H. Bowdler, 'Chaplaincy in the Stores', *Crusade*, January 1956.

[57] 'Pathfinders' had been started in 1935 in the South London parish of Emmanuel, Tolworth as the brain-child of Herbert Taylor, and was launched nationally in 1953 with some ten parish groups. Sister organizations for other age-ranges were added and growth was rapid in Anglican parishes, reaching well over a thousand groups by the 1980s.

[58] All Souls PCC Minute Book, 25 June 1956.

[59] *All Souls*, September 1956.

[60] Rector's Letter, *All Souls*, August 1956.

[61] The donor, Mrs Florence Wrey, died only six months after the Clubhouse opened. See Luker (1979), p. 62. See also Woodings (1998) which contains a brief article by John Stott, 'The Origins of the Clubhouse'.

[62] He had originally come on a temporary arrangement for a three-month stay. See the 'Rector's Letter', *All Souls*, October 1957. The Clubhouse continues to flourish, forty and more years on, serving both as community centre and as what is almost a local church under the 'Clubhouse vicar'.

[63] Letter to the author, 14 June 1997. At the time of this letter Peter Robinson, Tom and Mary's son, was working at the Clubhouse as assistant pastor.

[64] *All Souls* in the 1950s mentions 80 or 90 church organizations or activities.

[65] Valerie Luff in 1956. Letter to the author, 25 March 1995.

[66] Letter to the author, 14 June 1997.

[67] John Collins. Memoranda to the author, 28 June 1989 and 26 July 1994, from which the following account is also taken.

[68] *Ibid.*, 26 July 1994. In the event, John Stott talked with the sister and John Collins with her brother.

[69] Letter to the author, 13 January 1996.

[70] JRWS papers: names have been removed throughout.

[71] John Collins. Memorandum to the author, 29 June 1989.

[72] Robert Howarth. Memorandum to the author, 1996.

[73] Taped interview with Frances Whitehead, 9 February 1993.

[74] The Revd. Ted Schroder. Memorandum to the author, 2 August 1997.

[75] *Ibid.*

[76] Hastings (1991), p. 452.

[77] *Ibid.*, p. 44.

[78] John Stott, 'A Five Point Manifesto', *All Souls*, July 1950.

[79] Stott (1952), p. 2.

[80] All Souls PCC Minute Book: 19 September 1950.

[81] Stott (1952). An initial print-run of 2,000 copies is suggested by the Minute Book of

the Church Information Board Executive Committee for 24 September 1952 (Church of England Record Centre, CIB/EX) and there were reprints in each of the following few years.
[82] Chad Varah, 'All out for Souls', *Church Illustrated*, February 1955. John Stott later came to believe the methodology of this period over-elaborate.
[83] See *All Souls*, February 1958.
[84] Shilton (1997), p. 62.
[85] *Ibid.*, p. 63.
[86] Bishop of Norwich, 1971–85.
[87] *The Times*, 14 January 1953.
[88] Set out in his book (1955), drawing on his earlier paper of 1953.
[89] JRWS papers. Letter dated 14 January 1953.
[90] Lord Sheppard. Letter to the author, 26 February 1997.
[91] Stott (1967), p. 90.
[92] From 1 John 5:13; 1 Peter 2:9; 1 Peter 2:2.
[93] Geoffrey M. Turner, Bishop of Stockport 1994. Letter to the author, 23 October 1996.
[94] 'This is My Story' by 'a former hospital matron'. *All Souls*, August 1961.
[95] 'This is My Story' by 'a business man'. *All Souls*, May 1961.
[96] Stott (1969), p. 66. (The substance of the Durham Lectures.)
[97] *Ibid.*, p. 66.
[98] *Ibid.*, p. 68.
[99] JRWS papers. Letter from Bernard Gook, 5 November 1958. State-of-the-art technology meant that to make the commentary widely available, it was recorded on a 12" slow-playing gramophone record.
[100] Stott (1952), p. 2.

Chapter 11. A Wider Vision: Evangelical Initiatives
[1] Welsby (1984), p. 98.
[2] Founded as the Evangelical Alliance (British Organization) in 1846, it had adopted an international role, and was legally incorporated in 1912 as 'The World's Evangelical Alliance (British Organisation)'. See J. W. Ewing's history (1946), p. 129 and Howard (1986), pp. 14, 21–22. Following the formation of the World Evangelical Fellowship it reverted in 1953 to its original title. John Stott had become an individual member during his days at Cambridge. One other such invitation which he accepted when still a curate was to be Secretary (later, Chairman) of the London Diocesan Union of Evangelical Clergy, which changed its name to the London Diocesan Evangelical Union on admitting lay members.
[3] Howard (1986), p. 31, amplified in taped interview, 8 March 1993. A. J. Dain was later to become Assistant Bishop of Sydney, Australia.
[4] Bishop Maurice Wood. Conversation with the author, 16 May 1995.
[5] Bishop Wallace Benn, Vicar of St. Peter's, 1987–97. Memorandum to the author, 28 February 1997.
[6] 'Mission at St. Martin's, Gospel Oak', *All Souls*, November 1951.
[7] See *All Souls*, January 1952.
[8] See, for example, John Stott, 'Strategy for Sacrifice', *Today*, January 1986.
[9] See *All Souls*, January 1952.
[10] See *All Souls*, March 1952. The Rector of St. John's Wood, Noel Perry-Gore, was a co-leader.
[11] Martin (1992), p. 92.
[12] *Ibid.*, p. 97.
[13] *Ibid.*, p. 96.
[14] For this, and much background information, see Colquhoun (1955).
[15] Pollock (1966), p. 153.

[16] Stott (1982b), p. 270.

[17] JRWS papers. Interview with Dr. Robert O. Ferm, who was doing research for the Billy Graham Evangelistic Association, August 1971.

[18] Graham (1997), p. 218.

[19] JRWS papers: presumably written for publication; no published source identified. The 'girl of seventeen' was Sylvia Mary Haigh. She later published an account of her experience in Alison (1984), p. 11, 28–29. Her husband, the Rt. Hon. Michael J. H. Alison, was converted to Christ through John Stott's ministry in his first term at Oxford, October 1948. The 'missionary in Kenya' was Robert Howarth.

[20] JRWS papers, 23 May 1954.

[21] Pollock (1966), p. 175. In a footnote John Pollock stresses that this is not a subjective estimate but the official turnstile figure from Wembley Stadium.

[22] Stott (1968), p. 11. Transcript of the Diamond Jubilee Lecture, March 1968. See also Stott (1982b), p. 270.

[23] See Torrey (1923). Writing in 1996 about 'Books which have influenced me' John Stott lists this small pamphlet in one of his seven titles, with the comment 'I was introduced as a new convert to books by both Moody and Torrey. I drank them up. They challenged me to evangelism and to whole-hearted discipleship.' (*Mission and Ministry*, Vol. xi, No. 1). See also John Stott's review of Graham's autobiography, *Church Times*, 17 October 1997.

[24] Lyall (1954).

[25] *Ibid.*, p. x.

[26] Frady (1979), p. 321.

[27] Pollock (1966), p. 180.

[28] Martin (1992), p. 184.

[29] High (1957), p. 228: quoting an article by Priestley in *The New Statesman and Nation*.

[30] *Ibid.*, p. 228.

[31] 3 November 1954.

[32] *Crusade*, June 1955, p. 4.

[33] Once named by John Stott as 'my favourite text' (taped interview, 15/7) especially in the RSV translation.

[34] 'Except a Man be Born Again', *Crusade*, June 1955, p. 16.

[35] John R. W. Stott, 'Fundamentalism', *Crusade*, November 1955, p. 10.

[36] F. Roy Cattell, 'Wembley in the Rain', *Crusade*, July 1955, p. 12.

[37] JRWS papers. Interview with Robert O. Ferm, 31 May 1972.

[38] Quoted in Pollock (1966), p. 203.

[39] Bebbington (1989), p. 258.

[40] Hastings (1991), p. 455.

[41] Taped interview, 9/10.

[42] See Balleine (1908), p. 152. John Stott refers to such Societies in his *I Believe in Preaching* (1982b), p. 190.

[43] The full list of those invited was: Peter Barton, John Bickersteth, Richard Bowdler, Tony Capon, John Collins, Timothy Dudley-Smith, Richard Gorrie, Geoffrey Hart, John Lefroy, Dick Lucas, George May, Hugh Mumford, Bob Otway, Kenneth Prior, Tony Richards, Teddy Saunders, Bill Seaman, John Sertin, Peter Sertin, Donald Service, John Sheldon, David Thompson.

[44] Gavin H. Reid, Bishop of Maidstone, 'John Stott and the Eclectic Society: a Reflection'. Memorandum in support of a submission to the Templeton Foundation, 8 August 1996.

[45] Geoffrey Hart. Letter to the author, 7 August 1996. Canon G. W. Hart was Rector of Cheltenham St. Mary, 1973–93.

[46] See Saward (1987), p. 32. The phrase is attributed to Peter Williams. Michael Saward was appointed Canon Residentiary of St. Paul's Cathedral in 1991.

[47] The Rt. Revd. P. S. Dawes. Letter to the author, 22 January 1998. Peter Dawes was

Archdeacon of West Ham, 1980–88, and Bishop of Derby, 1988–95.

[48] Stott, in King (ed.) (1973), p. 180.

[49] Baughen, in Wright and Sugden (eds.) (1990), p. 7. The book was a *Festschrift* to mark the retirement of John Stott as President of the Evangelical Fellowship in the Anglican Communion (EFAC) (1966–90).

[50] 'People in Close-up: John Capon talks to John Stott (2)', *Crusade*, June 1974.

[51] Paul Welsby, sometime Prolocutor of the Convocation of Canterbury, describes (Welsby, 1984) how the process of revision involved five legislative houses at a time. It became clear at an early stage that revised Canons would require revision of ecclesiastical courts and discipline, another protracted and weary process. He concludes: 'Unfortunately, complicated and cumbersome machinery was dismantled only to be replaced by procedures which were hardly less so,' (pp. 43–44).

[52] Barclay (1997), p. 82. See also, for a detailed account of some of the discussions, Murray (1990), p. 314f.

[53] Carpenter, F. (1991), p. 209.

[54] William Temple, in Bullard (ed.) (1934), p. vi.

[55] Taped interview, 9/21. John Stott has cited this on occasion as an example of how taking a stand on matters of principle can help towards change. Under Canon B15A the Church of England now makes clear that 'There shall be admitted to the Holy Communion: (a) Members of the Church of England ... (b) baptised persons who are communicant members of other Churches which subscribe to the doctrine of the Holy Trinity, and who are in good standing in their own Church.'

[56] John Stott, 'Intercommunion', the *Church of England Newspaper*, 5 January 1962; reprinted in Stott (1963).

[57] *Church Times*, 20 November 1959.

[58] See volume two for further details about this series of books.

[59] Preamble attached to the first Minute Book of the Church of England Evangelical Council, signed by A. T. Houghton, 27 May 1960. The agreement to create a new body only followed careful consideration of whether any grouping already in existence should be the English member of EFAC. Church Society and the Church Pastoral-Aid Society were both considered, but CPAS had a distinctive ministry of its own and Church Society could not be regarded as fully representative of English evangelicals.

[60] Later Archbishop of Sydney (1966–82) and Primate of Australia (1978–81).

[61] *The Lambeth Conference* (1958), Section 2, p. 84.

[62] Archbishop Sir Marcus Loane. Letter to the author, 11 November 1994.

[63] Talbot Greaves Mohan served CPAS from 1932 until his retirement in 1965 (Secretary, 1942–65). In 1956 he became Hon. Canon of Sydney; and from 1959 was Commissary to two Archbishops of Sydney, W. K. Mowll and M. L. Loane.

[64] McGrath (1997), p. 97.

[65] John Stott, from a memorandum to the author of 2 February 1996, 'The Beginnings of EFAC and CEEC', on which some of the above account is based. The account 'The Beginnings of EFAC' in the *EFAC Bulletin*, No. 1, 1994, p. 29 is not an accurate report of a presentation by Bishop John Reid at the EFAC consultation of 1993 (letter from Bishop John Reid to the author, 21 January 1998). CEEC: Church of England Evangelical Council.

[66] Lloyd (1966), p. 499.

[67] Judd and Cable (1987), p. 221. The label 'schismatic', when applied to the CESA, should be treated with disdain. Edward Carpenter, for example, appears to use it simply as a term of disapproval in his life of Archbishop Fisher (1991, pp. 483, 485). Fisher ceased to be Archbishop in 1961; while as late as 1984 Dudley Foord was duly consecrated as bishop for the CESA by Donald Robinson, Archbishop of Sydney. See also the whole-page apology in *Crockford's*, 1965/66 in which the editor, printer and publisher apologize for having quoted in their 1961/62 edition from a work which represented the Church of

England in South Africa in an unfavourable light (p. xvii).

[68] JRWS. Memorandum to the author, 2 February 1996.

[69] JRWS papers. Letter dated 29 May 1959. John Collins left in 1957 to become vicar of St. Mark's, Gillingham; Richard Bowdler in 1958 to become Youth Secretary of the Church Society; Sister Jordan retired; John Lefroy became vicar of Christ Church, Highbury in 1965.

[70] This was Oswin Gibbs-Smith, soon to become Archdeacon of London.

[71] Taped interview with Frances Whitehead, 9 February 1993; from which much of what follows is also taken.

[72] *Ibid.*

[73] I owe all this information, including the quotation, to Palmer (1992), p. 243f.

[74] Pawley (1987), p. 99. CACTM was the Central Advisory Council of Training for the Ministry; now the Advisory Board of Ministry.

[75] *Ibid.*, p. 101.

[76] JRWS papers. Letter dated 12 November 1955.

[77] JRWS papers. Letter dated 11 December 1955.

[78] JRWS papers. Letter dated 24 November 1955.

[79] JRWS papers.

[80] See Loane (1960), p. 245f.

[81] Judd and Cable (1987), p. 263.

[82] JRWS papers. Letter from 12 Weymouth Street, dated 18 November 1958.

[83] Both cables, JRWS papers. Ron Bailey, a layman, was a leader in the Anglican Church League.

[84] *The Times*, 27 November 1958.

[85] JRWS papers. Letter dated 29 November 1958.

[86] JRWS papers.

[87] JRWS papers. Letter from St. James's Palace, dated 15 June 1959. Though the title 'Queen's Honorary Chaplain' (with the initials QHC) continues to be used for Service chaplains, there have been no civilian Honorary Chaplains since 1919. The correct title is Chaplain to the Queen.

[88] JRWS papers. Letter dated 13 June 1959. Percy Mark Herbert was every inch the courtier, and followed Cyril Forster Garbett as Clerk of the Closet in 1942, serving in all for 21 years, even after he was no longer Bishop of Norwich. John Bickersteth (himself Clerk of the Closet 1979–89, and to whom I am indebted for background information) describes him in old age:

> In his retirement Herbert lived in a grace-and-favour house in the Great Park at Windsor and – the old man's prerogative – became increasingly vague. He took services in the Park chapel from time to time when the chaplain was away and, on one occasion taking Matins for the first time in decades (bishops in office celebrate Holy Communion every Sunday but rarely lead Matins in public), he used his own prayer book for the State Prayers, and fell straight into the trap of using an uncorrected prayer for the Royal Family. So he prayed 'for Alexandra the Queen Mother (she had been dead for thirty-five years) … (pause) … What's the boy's name? … (mumble, mumble) … and all the Royal Family.' (Bickersteth [1991], p. 78.)

[89] *All Souls*, February 1960, p. 11. Half-a-crown equalled 12.5 new pence.

[90] It was known that Dr. Billy Graham had an audience with the Queen on his way back from Australia about this time. John Pollock, Dr. Graham's authorized biographer, is aware from his records that they spoke together about the place of conservative evangelicals in the church, and their small representation among the bishops. It would not be difficult to surmise from this that such a conversation played a part in the choice of John Stott as Chaplain to the Queen. Such a suggestion must, however, be mistaken since

the audience was on 10 June 1959 and the letter from the Clerk of the Closet was written on 8 June. Four years before this, in a carefully phrased letter, Billy Graham told John Stott that he had been able to talk to the Queen about him and found her 'most interested in all I had to say about the tremendous work you are doing at All Souls' (JRWS papers. Copy of letter dated 26 August 1955).

[91] *Izvori*, May/June 1994. In Latin America a TV interviewer went one better still. John Stott was asked in the course of the programme, 'We understand you're the Chaplain to the Queen. Do you hear her confession – and *what does she say?*'!

[92] JRWS papers. Note dated 16 October 1963 attached to the Minutes of the meeting of the EFAC Council of 6 May 1963. The rumour was still about in the 1990s.

[93] 9 January, 1983.

[94] Taped interview, 15/32. John Stott remembers replying, 'James, you can't possibly love our Lady in the same way that you love our Lord' – but there the conversation (or any recollection of it) comes to an end.

[95] JRWS. Memorandum to the author, 2 February 1996.

[96] *Church Times*, 16 January 1959.

[97] Stott, in Eddison (ed.) (1983), p. 64.

[98] *Ibid*. The whole passage repays attention as setting out a Christian distinctive, in marked contrast to the spirit of the age prevailing even in some church circles.

[99] Steven Turner, 'Backing the Basics', *Church Times*, 13 October 1995. See also an extended interview, 'John Stott on Singleness' contributed as an appendix to Hsu (1997), p. 176f. As far as John Stott's personal story is concerned, it follows very closely the *Church Times* interview above.

[100] Terry Lovell, 'The Times and Travels of an Ordinary Christian', *Christian Bookseller*, May/June, 1992.

[101] Smyth (1959), p. 453.

[102] Randle Manwaring in a letter to the author, 26 October 1995.

[103] Myra Chave-Jones, Director of 'Care and Counsel' of which John Stott was chairman for some ten years. Letter and memorandum to the author, 18 November 1995.

[104] 'People in Close-up: John Capon talks to John Stott (2)', *Crusade*, June 1974.

[105] 'A *HIS* interview with John Stott', *HIS*, October 1975.

[106] Canon D. C. Moore. Letter to the author, 15 February 1996.

[107] Lady Hilton. Letter to the author, 4 March 1997.

[108] JRWS papers. Letter n.d., perhaps 1956.

[109] JRWS papers. Letter n.d. but thought to be September 1956.

[110] Taped interview, 21/21.

Chapter 12. University Missioner: Cambridge, London, Oxford and Durham

[1] Hastings (1991), p. 454. 'Backhouse' in the text of some editions is a misprint.

[2] Fielder (1988), p. 107.

[3] For this story, see Pollock (1955).

[4] Barclay (1977), p. 128.

[5] *Ibid.*, p. 126.

[6] From the author's vivid recollection.

[7] Barclay (1977), p. 126.

[8] *Ibid.*

[9] Atkinson (1966), p. 65.

[10] *Ibid.*

[11] Pollock (1953), p. 263.

[12] JRWS papers. Copy of the CICCU official report on the mission, from the CICCU files, presented to the missioner.

[13] *Ibid.* The titles of the week's addresses were: Sunday, *What is Man?* Monday, *Who was Jesus Christ?* Tuesday, *How am I concerned?* Wednesday, *Why did Christ die?* Thursday,

What must I do? Friday, *What does it cost?* Saturday, *Where will it end?*

[14] Atkinson (1966), p. 66.

[15] JRWS papers. CICCU official report.

[16] Oliver Barclay. Memorandum to the author, 23 February 1989.

[17] 'Stott on Students', *Southern Cross* (Sydney), March 1986.

[18] *All Souls*, November, 1957. Cambridge was still largely a male university.

[19] Canon G. W. Hart. Letter to the author, 7 August 1996.

[20] JRWS papers. Letter from the Revd. Professor W. Owen Chadwick, KBE, 19 April 1990. Dr. Chadwick was Dean of Trinity Hall at the time of the 1952 mission; Master of Selwyn College, 1956–83; President of the British Academy, 1981–85.

[21] Michael Cassidy. Letter to the author, 26 May 1997. Cassidy became the founder of African Enterprise, an evangelistic agency to help bring the gospel to the cities of Africa.

[22] James R. Parratt, Professor of Cardiovascular Pharmacology at the University of Strathclyde. Letter to the author, 19 November 1996, following a letter to John Stott of 10 August 1996 to thank him for 'introducing me to the Lord' and for his writing ministry.

[23] JRWS papers. Letter from the Revd. R. S. Lee, 30 November 1953. The previous OICCU mission, November 1951, had been a slightly uneasy partnership of Hugh Gough, Bishop of Barking, and Dr. Martyn Lloyd-Jones.

[24] JRWS papers. Letter from the Rector of St. Aldate's, the Revd. O. K. de Berry, 7 December 1953. Quoted by permission of the Revd. Robert de Berry.

[25] JRWS papers. Copy of a letter from J. P. Thornton-Duesbury to Julian Charley, n.d.

[26] Fielder (1988), p. 159.

[27] Walker (1982), p. 63.

[28] The Ven. T. O. Tom Walker. Letter to the author, 2 February 1997.

[29] Walker (1982), p. 63. I owe this reference to Fielder (1988), p. 159. Tom Walker's book, from which this account is taken, is long out of print. He served as Archdeacon of Nottingham, 1991–96.

[30] University Sermon, a resumé in *The Cambridge Review*, 7 May 1955, p. 515.

[31] 14 September 1955. The whole correspondence of 28 letters, together with the leading article, was re-published as a pamphlet, *Fundamentalism: A Religious Problem* (London: The Times Publishing Company, 1955).

[32] J. R. W. Stott, 'Fundamentalism', *Crusade*, November 1955, p. 10. *The Fundamentals* were republished in 4 volumes by Baker, USA, in 1994; and reviewed by Alister McGrath in *Anvil*, Vol. 12, No. 1, 1995, p. 57. He found them, naturally enough, to be 'seriously dated'; but adds 'Yet perhaps the importance of these volumes lies less in the ideas and arguments developed, important though these were at the time, but in the realization of the need to identify, defend and affirm the "fundamentals of the faith"'.

[33] The 'Quarterly official gazette' of the Bishopric of Durham, founded by H. Hensley Henson in 1925. See Henson (1943), pp. ix and xii.

[34] *The Bishoprick*, February 1956.

[35] Bowles (1958), p. 5.

[36] *Op. cit.*, p. 2n.

[37] Hebert (1957), pp. 13, 10.

[38] Packer (1958). The origin of the book 'lay in an address which Packer was asked to give to the Graduates' Fellowship meeting in London in 1957'. See McGrath (1997), p. 82 for a detailed account of how the book came to be written.

[39] Packer (1958), p. 137, quoting Stott (1956), p. 137.

[40] Graham (1997), p. 695.

[41] His biographer, Owen Chadwick, is at pains to indicate that he was not intending to be deceitful. See Chadwick (1990a), p. 181.

[42] Letter to Cecil Roberts, 21 December 1962. See Lycett Green (1995), p. 240.

[43] EFAC Bulletin No. 40, Pentecost 1990. As Archbishop of York, Ramsey chaired the

committee of the 1958 Lambeth Conference on the theme of 'The Holy Bible: Its Authority and Message'. Though the committee had some forty members, their sixteen-page report probably represents Ramsey's own views, briefly summed up in the sentence: 'In the light of the relation of the Bible to Jesus Christ we can affirm that the Bible possesses the authority of God's truth and is the work of God's inspiration, without ascribing inerrancy to every statement which the Bible contains' (*The Lambeth Conference Report* [1958], Section 2, p. 8).

[44] Prestige (1935), p. 366.

[45] J. R. W. Stott, 'Evangelicals and Evangelism', *Crusade*, May 1956, p. 4.

[46] Stott (1956).

[47] Graham (1997), p. 251.

[48] Fison (1950), p. 150.

[49] Graham (1997), p. 139.

[50] *Ibid.*

[51] Martin (1992), p. 112.

[52] Stott (1978), p. 154.

[53] *Ibid.*, p. 155.

[54] JRWS papers. Letter to John Lefroy from Hookses, dated 4 September 1960.

[55] Edwards, and Stott (1988), p. 104.

[56] Stott, in King (ed.) (1973), p. 179.

[57] Graham (1997), p. 165.

[58] Martin (1992), p. 190. John Pollock is able to place this conversation with Olford on board the ship to England.

[59] Graham (1997), p. 256. 'Maurice' in the final line is Maurice Wood, at that time Vicar of Islington, who would be coming to Cambridge as one of the assistant missioners.

[60] Pollock (1966), p. 208.

[61] 'World-wide interest in Graham Mission', *Varsity*, 12 November 1955. Five undergraduates were arrested that evening for assaulting the police in the execution of their duty, but this was not unusual for Guy Fawkes day.

[62] See Graham (1997), p. 258.

[63] See Hooper (1996), pp. 65, 76: and Graham (1997), p. 258.

[64] Pollock (1966), p. 207.

[65] Stockwood (1982), p. 86.

[66] Atkinson (1966), p. 74.

[67] 'Mission in Cambridge' by 'an Assistant Missioner' (in fact, the editor), *Crusade*, January 1956.

[68] De-la-Noy (1996), p. 82. A note cites the source as Tam Dalyell in conversation with De-la-Noy.

[69] JRWS. Letter to the author 12 January 1997. John Stott adds, '"Evil in the house" would not be a characteristic phrase of mine, either then or now!'

[70] Shilton (1997), p. 53. The Very Revd. Lance Shilton was later Dean of St. Andrew's Cathedral, Sydney, 1973–97.

[71] 'World wide interest in Graham mission', *Varsity*, 12 November 1955.

[72] Billy Graham, in Samuel and Sugden (eds.) (1981), p. viii.

[73] Pollock, 1966), p. 208.

[74] Watson (1983), p. 37 of 1986 edition.

[75] *All Souls*, December 1955.

[76] JRWS papers.

[77] John Martin. Letter to the author, 20 February 1996.

[78] Michael Griffiths. Letter to the author, 1 November 1995. Michael Griffiths was at that time an IVF Travelling Secretary, 1954–57; then with the Overseas Missionary Fellowship in Japan and Singapore, 1957–80 (General Director from 1969); Principal of the London Bible College, 1980–89; Professor of Mission Studies, Regent College,

Vancouver, 1990–93. See also Fielder (1988), p. 179.
[79] Letter to the author, 20 February 1996.
[80] G. J. C. Marchant. Letter to the author, 16 August 1996.
[81] Michael Griffiths. Letter to the author, 1 November 1995.
[82] Fielder (1988), pp. 189–190.
[83] *All Souls*, January 1958. He stayed at the Golden Cross Hotel, in the city centre.
[84] *All Souls*, November 1957.
[85] John Calmann, 'What think ye of Christ?', *The Isis*, 20 November, 1957.
[86] *Ibid.*, 27 November 1957.
[87] M. A. Green, 'Oxford', *All Souls*, January 1958, p. 16.
[88] JRWS papers. Letter from the Revd. Noel Warman, 4 October 1991.
[89] Atkinson (1966), p. 85.
[90] Barclay (1977), p. 130.
[91] 'Man with a Mission', *Varsity*, 15 November 1958.
[92] *All Souls*, December 1958.
[93] *All Souls*, February 1959.
[94] *All Souls*, February 1959.

Chapter 13. University Missioner : America, Australia and South Africa

[1] A number of its constituent university Christian Unions had been in existence far longer. The CICCU was formally begun in 1877, following a mission conducted the previous year by the Revd. Sholto D. C. Douglas. The OICCU was founded in 1879.
[2] Johnson (1979), p. 278. Until 1986 IVCF was hyphenated as 'Inter-Varsity'.
[3] Memorandum to the author, 19 June 1989.
[4] 'A HIS interview with John R. W. Stott', *HIS*, October 1975, p. 19.
[5] *All Souls*, November 1956.
[6] David Bebbington, in Noll, Bebbington, and Rawlyk (eds.) (1994), p. 367.
[7] JRWS MS diary, *A Visit to Canada and the United States, November 1956 to March 1957*, p. 1a. Hereafter 'Diary'. These diaries were intended not solely as a personal record but so that (at least in the early days) his parents could follow his doings: either as with this small book, by reading of them on his return; or, on future tours, by receiving pages from his loose-leaf diary, a week or two at a time, to supplement his letters home. See note 65.
[8] Diary, p. 2a.
[9] Diary, p. 4.
[10] 'When a man is newly married, he shall not go out with the army or be charged with any business; he shall be free at home one year, to be happy with his wife whom he has taken.' Deuteronomy 24:5, RSV.
[11] Dr. Tony Tyndale. Letter to the author, 22 April 1996.
[12] *The Varsity*, 14 November 1956.
[13] *Ibid.*, 19 November 1956.
[14] 'A Second Letter from America', *All Souls*, January 1957.
[15] Arthur van Seters, 'John Stott Mission: University of Toronto', *HIS*, May 1957.
[16] *Ibid.*
[17] Diary, p. 7.
[18] Diary, p. 9a.
[19] Diary, p. 11a.
[20] 'A Second Letter from America', *All Souls*, January 1957.
[21] 'Something Missing', *The Gazette*, 1 December 1956.
[22] Dan De Silva, 'John Stott Mission: University of Western Ontario', *HIS*, May 1957.
[23] Diary, p. 11a.
[24] Diary, p. 17; as quoted in Hunt and Hunt (1991), p. 177.
[25] 'A Third Letter from America', *All Souls*, February, 1957.

[26] John R. W. Stott, 'Jesus Christ, His Only Son', Sermon 3 in a series, broadcast 25 February 1962. Published as a leaflet, Atlanta: The Episcopal Radio-TV Foundation, 1962.

[27] Diary, p. 19.

[28] Diary, p. 21.

[29] Diary, p. 21a. Ned, the youngest of the family, was not yet born.

[30] Diary, p. 22a.

[31] Taped Interview, 6/17.

[32] JRWS papers. Letter from Ruth Graham Dienert, 22 May 1987. *Christian Counter-Culture: the Message of the Sermon on the Mount* was an early volume in the 'Bible Speaks Today' series (Stott, 1978a).

[33] Taped interview, 6/20

[34] *The Asheville Citizen*, 29 December 1956.

[35] Diary, p. 23a.

[36] Diary, p. 24. David Hemery, whose father Peter had worked for the Evangelical Alliance in London during the 1950s, was to win the men's 400 metre hurdles for Great Britain at the 1968 Olympic Games in Mexico.

[37] 'A Third Letter from America', *All Souls*, February 1957.

[38] Diary, p. 28.

[39] Letter to the author, 22 April 1996. John Stott has no recollection of this conversation!

[40] 'A Fourth Letter from America', *All Souls*, March 1957.

[41] John G. Cochrane. Letter to the author, n.d., c. 1994.

[42] John Stott, 'UBC A Discussion Forum; Why Not Discuss Christ?', *The Ubyssey*, 18 January 1957.

[43] 'A Fourth Letter from America', *All Souls*, March 1957.

[44] Diary, p. 35.

[45] Hunt and Hunt (1991), p. 125. Admittedly the source quoted, Christy Wilson, was a Princeton man!

[46] Diary, p. 35.

[47] 'Fifth American Letter', *All Souls*, April 1957.

[48] Diary, p. 37.

[49] The Revd. J. L. L. Fagerson; letters and memorandum to the author, January/February 1998. Unusually, Fagerson did not return to America but was ordained to a curacy in the Church of England; and apart from overseas service in Afghanistan has spent all his ministry in the British Isles.

[50] Graham (1997), p. 304.

[51] The Very Revd. Dr. Peter C. Moore. Letter to the author, 20 January 1998. Canon Bryan Green, a liberal evangelical and at that time Rector of St. Martin's, Birmingham, was among the best-known evangelists of his generation.

[52] Professor Paul Tillich, philosophical theologian, is one of three whom John Robinson names as seminal influences on him, and whose thinking he popularized in *Honest to God* (1963). Tillich's visit to Yale as missioner came the year after the publication of the second volume of his major *Systematic Theology*.

[53] 'Fifth American Letter', *All Souls*, April 1957.

[54] The Very Revd. Dr. Peter C. Moore. Letter to the author, 20 Janary 1998.

[55] *Ibid.* Peter Moore went on to be Rector of Little Trinity Church, Toronto; and then Dean of Trinity Episcopal School for Ministry, Pittsburgh (which he had helped to found in the 1970s) from 1997.

[56] Hunt and Hunt (1991), p. 179.

[57] Letter to the author, 7 January 1998. James Nyquist was later for twenty years Director of InterVarsity Press, USA.

[58] *Ibid.* For *Basic Christianity* (Stott 1958a), see chapter 14.

[59] Dr. Tony Tyndale. Letter to the author, 22 April 1996.

[60] Lewis, in Hooper (ed.) (1971), p. 72.

[61] *All Souls*, February 1958.

[62] Letter to the author, 16 June 1997.

[63] Stuart Piggin, in Noll, Bebbington, Rawlyk (eds.) (1994), p. 290. Piggin gives a reference for one estimate that in the 1950s almost one-fifth of the population, both in Australia and in New Zealand, was evangelical (p. 304, n. 4).

[64] Stuart Babbage, 'Evangelicals and the Church in Australia', *The Churchman*, June 1963, p. 114. Babbage adds that though Johnson's sermons were criticized for their weighty theological content, he 'was not indifferent to the claims of morality':

> He obtained from the Society for Promoting Christian Knowledge, for distribution to the members of his convict congregation, in addition to Bibles, Prayer Books, and Catechisms, two hundred copies of *Exercises Against Lying*, fifty *Cautions to Swearers*, a hundred *Exhortations to Chastity*, and a hundred *Dissuasions from Stealing*.

[65] From this tour on, John Stott wrote a loose-leaf diary on his overseas travels, sending it home section by section to his parents so that they could follow his travels. Quotations in the rest of this chapter, unless otherwise attributed, come from this diary.

[66] Bishop Dudley Foord. Letter to the author, 30 November 1996.

[67] Bishop Gresford Chitemo. Letter to the author, 24 March 1995.

[68] John Stott. Letter from Sydney to John Lefroy, 27 June 1958.

[69] Memorandum to the author, 2 February 1996. John Stott was staying with Bishop and Mrs. Marcus Loane when the news reached him.

[70] Dr. J. W. MacLeod. Letter to the author, 11 March 1993.

[71] David Trapnell. Taped interview, 18 February 1993.

[72] Randle Manwaring. Letter to the author, 20 October 1995. Sir Arnold was not alone in this view: a distinguished medical colleague at Guy's Hospital wrote to him not long before his death: 'I have never met your son but he obviously is regarded as a live wire in the Anglican organisation. I am told he is likely to be a bishop one day. I have never got further than being baptised, but I am very interested in the architecture of parish churches and their furnishings.'!

[73] JRWS papers: Sir Arnold Stott's correspondence. Hess was later sentenced to life imprisonment at the Nuremberg trials.

[74] Obituary, *The Lancet*, 28 June 1958.

[75] Peter Kerley, Obituary, *British Heart Journal*, Vol. 21 (1959), pp. 137–8.

[76] Letter dated 19 November 1936.

[77] John Stott, 'People who have influenced me', *All Souls*, summer 1991.

[78] 'Stott on Students', interview in *Southern Cross*, March 1986.

[79] Derek Brewer, in Como (ed.) (1980), p. 54.

[80] Stott (1958a).

[81] 'Mobilizing the Church for Evangelism'.

[82] Stott (1982), p. 333.

[83] Robyn Langford. Letter to the author, 21 March 1994. Robyn Langford became a teacher; and then served with the South American Missionary Society in Argentina, Paraguay and Chile, before joining the staff of All Souls to take charge of the All Souls International Fellowship

[84] Memorandum to the author, February 1996.

[85] 'Final Australian Bulletin', *All Souls*, September 1958.

[86] The director of Scripture Union of Papua New Guinea, Terry Cowland, wrote to John Stott almost thirty years later (10 March 1987): 'I responded to Christ's invitation to become his disciple ... during your mission ... it is some years since that cool Sunday evening at St Matthew's, Dunedin when you spoke very simply on Rev. 3:20 and it is

good to let you know that I'm still walking and learning.' (JRWS papers).
[87] JRWS. Memorandum to the author, 6 January 1998.
[88] Rector's Letter, *All Souls*, January 1959.
[89] Rector's Letter, *All Souls*, February 1959.
[90] See Lowman (1983), p. 28.
[91] As with his Australian tour, this section draws on the diary that John Stott sent home with letters to his family. Quotations not otherwise attributed are from the diary.
[92] Sharp (1996). John Sharp died in 1966, aged 35. *A Vision Fulfilled* is his wife's fascinating account of their pioneer missionary work together.
[93] George Swannell says his crime was punching a policeman, and adds 'John was immediately at home with such a character'. (Letter to the author, 1993).
[94] *The Cape Argus*, 13 August 1959.
[95] David Wells, Andrew Mutch Distinguished Professor of Historial and Systematic Theology, Gordon-Conwell Theological Seminary, Massachusetts. Letter to the author, 21 August 1995. Writing to John Stott two years after the mission, David Wells recalled that he had attended only half an address: 'but in God's grace I was saved to the marrow three weeks later...' Southern Rhodesia became the Republic of Zimbabwe in 1980.
[96] JRWS papers. Letter from the Revd. Jan Hanekom, 24 June 1994.
[97] *Ibid.*
[98] J. R. W. Stott, 'Evangelism in the Student World', *The Christian Graduate*, March 1959. The address was given at the IVF Annual Public Meeting, 26 September 1958. Smuts' fellow student was G. T. Manley, one of the earliest IVF authors and first Chairman of the IVF Literature Committee until his death in 1961. He was Senior Wrangler in 1893 (Bertrand Russell came sixth); ordained while a Fellow of Christ's College, Cambridge; and after working among students in India spent 20 years on the staff of CMS. See Barclay (1997) for a number of references to him.

Chapter 14. The Hookses: A Writer's Retreat
[1] Letter to Boswell, 20 September 1777.
[2] Canon Dr. Peter R. Thompson. Letter to the author, 9 February 1996.
[3] J. E. Trapnell and Canon D. C. Moore. Letters to the author, 9 January and 15 February 1996.
[4] G. F. Rocke. Memorandum to the author, 7 March 1992.
[5] JRWS MS 'Jottings for a biography', 1993/4, p. 24.
[6] J. T. C. B. Collins. Memorandum to the author, 26 July 1994.
[7] JRWS papers. Letter written from c/o Mrs. Morgan, Glen View, Marloes, and dated 22 August 1952.
[8] The pamphlet was published later that year under the title *Parochial Evangelism by the Laity*: see above, chapter 10.
[9] These recollections and much of what follows is based on taped interviews with JRWS at Hookses (tape 7, 8 September 1992), and JRWS MS 'Jottings for a biography', 1993/4.
[10] Smith, D. J. (1990), see 'Dale'. Much of what follows is based on that account.
[11] *Ibid.*
[12] JRWS papers. Memorandum by John Stott of conversation with H. W. Cross, 25 May 1995, the year of Cross's death.
[13] JRWS papers. Letters from R. K. Lucas and Son, dated 28 and 31 August 1953.
[14] Stott (1982b), p. 13.
[15] Taped interview with Rosemary Bird, 26 February 1996.
[16] Stott, in Ng (ed.) (n.d.), p. 19.
[17] Canon Michael H. Botting. Letter to the author, 12 August 1992. David Pytches became Bishop of Valparaiso in 1970; and subsequently Bishop of Chile, Bolivia and Peru.

[18] June 1959, by the author of this book. A further verse, commemorating the nightly inspection of a lobster pot attached to the rocks just off-shore was added ten years later from the pen of a visiting ordinand, Neil Jackson:

> O happy climbs at Hookses!
> With basket and with bait
> We brave the crumbling sandstone
> To seal the lobster's fate.
> The crafty old crustacean
> Knows what the basket's for,
> And grasps the bait from outside
> With armour-plated claw.

[19] To the tune 'Cockles and Mussels' from the Oxford Song Book.

[20] Ian Herring. Letter to the author, 16 November 1997.

[21] The Revd. Robert Howarth. Memorandum to the author, 3 April 1997.

[22] *Ibid.*

[23] JRWS papers. Letter dated 5 April, probably 1969. Toby would be six or seven at the time, and later became one of John Stott's study asisstants.

[24] Patricia M. St. John, *Treasures of the Snow* (London: CSSM, 1950); from a taped interview with JRWS; 2 June 1995.

[25] Taped interview, 19/30.

[26] David Cranston. Letter to the author, 8 May 1995.

[27] Munro (1930), p. 423. Septimus Brope achieved the later distinction of a quotation in *The Contemporary Christian* (1992), p. 376.

[28] 'Dick' is Prebendary R. C. Lucas, for nearly forty years Rector of St. Helen's, Bishopsgate in the City of London, and founder of the Proclamation Trust. In the Foreword John Stott contributed to a Festschrift for Dick Lucas on his seventieth birthday, he described their fifty years of friendship as 'an affirming, liberating and enriching experience'. See Green and Jackman (1995), p. 9.

[29] R. M. Lockley, *Letters from Skokholm* (London: Dent, 1947), p. 2.

[30] It had come from Harley Street where it housed part of Sir Arnold's medical library. At auction John Stott learnt with astonishment that from a reserve of £8,000 bidding had closed at £26,000!

[31] JRWS MS 'Jottings for a biography', 1993/4, p. 33, and memorandum to the author, n.d.

[32] JRWS papers. Letter to Frances Whitehead, 15 December 1982.

[33] JRWS MS 'Jottings for a biography', 1993/4, p. 32.

[34] See her obituary by JRWS, *All Souls*, February 1962. She was described as a 'Florence Nightingale figure', converted to Christ under Prebendary Webster, generous, outspoken and (as the memorial above makes plain) fearless in Christian witness.

[35] JRWS. Letter to the Revd. Robert D. Wismer (study assistant, 1982–84), 12 April 1992.

[36] John Stott's description. JRWS papers, MS 'Jottings for a biography', 1993/4, p. 31.

[37] Taped interview with Rosemary Bird, 26 February 1996 (B41/1), p. 8.

[38] vv. 3, 7. Taped interview B41/5.

[39] David Cranston. Letter to the author, 8 May 1995.

[40] JRWS MS 'Jottings for a biography', 1993/4, p. 33.

[41] Taped interview with Rosemary Bird.

[42] Taped interview, 7/35.

[43] Peter R. Davies. Letter to the author, 16 March 1996.

[44] *Ibid.* The 'taking to task' was originally by letter.

[45] *Ibid.*

[46] Donald English, 'Profile: John Stott – Christian Communicator Extraordinary', *The Epworth Review*, May 1993, p. 35. The Revd. Donald English, CBE was President of the Methodist Conference, 1978–79 and 1990–91, and Moderator of the Free Church Federal Council, 1986–87.

[47] Johnson (1979), p. 228.

[48] Fielder (1983), p. 201.

[49] Murray (1990), p. 274.

[50] Brown (1988), p. 6. Much of what follows is taken from this short history.

[51] *Ibid.*

[52] The Very Revd. Bertie Lewis, later Archdeacon of Cardigan and Dean of St. David's.

[53] Quoted in Brown (1988), p. 7.

[54] Brown, *Ibid.*, p. 10. In his *The Message of Acts* (1990b), p. 13, John Stott pays tribute to those members of EFCW 'who stoically submitted to annual instalments which went on for thirteen years'.

[55] JRWS papers. Notes for a talk headed 'Autobiography', n.d. 1980s?

[56] Stott (1949).

[57] Personal knowledge of the author; in conversation with W. D. L. Greer, Bishop of Manchester, 1947–1970.

[58] Peart-Binns (1987b), pp. 4, 6.

[59] *Ibid.*, p. 15. See also Wand's university sermon, 'In praise of parties', *The Cambridge Review*, 14 May 1955, p. 538.

[60] Carpenter, E. (1991), p. 219.

[61] Palmer (1992), p. 226f.

[62] Peart-Binns (1987), p. 131.

[63] JRWS. Memorandum to the author, 1996.

[64] Peart-Binns (1987), p. 190. Wand wrote about forty books in all. When he resigned his bishopric in 1955, he arranged to become a Canon of St. Paul's Cathedral in the same diocese!

[65] See Peart-Binns, (1987), p. 154. John Stott was not in fact a member of the Council itself.

[66] Taped interview, 7/44.

[67] From an address by John Stott, given at the International Tea in his honour during the Christian Booksellers Association Convention, Dallas, Texas, 28 June 1992.

[68] This opening chapter draws on a Tyndale Lecture which John Stott had recently given on 'The Kingdom of God' (unpublished). In Steve Motyer's 1994 revision it is replaced by chapters on 'Mark and his Message' and 'Matthew and his Message'. Motyer adds that he 'dropped the original first chapter on Jesus, which from the beginning seemed a bit out of place' (p. 9). See note 73 below.

[69] JRWS papers. Letter dated 12 August 1953.

[70] 25 January 1954.

[71] Stott (1954), p. 158.

[72] Michael Cassidy. Abbreviated from a letter to the author, 26 May 1997.

[73] In 1964, when John Stott's name was becoming known in America, Eerdmans and IVP jointly published an American edition under the title *A Basic Introduction to the New Testament* (Stott, 1964a). Forty years after its first publication, it was reissued in a new and illustrated edition, updated and revised by Steve Motyer, who was named as joint author. 'In reality', John Stott wrote in the Preface, 'it is more his book than mine.'

[74] See Dudley-Smith (1995).

[75] See *Crusade*, November 1955 and May 1956. The two articles formed the basis of Stott (1959).

[76] Stott (1958b). In 1989 John Stott successfully sought from the original publishers the reversion of all rights to himself as author: 'Since the contract is now more than thirty-two years old, since the book has been out of print for a very long time, and since the

original payment by Lutterworth was only £75 for 5,000 copies, I feel confident you will agree with the rightness of this step.' (JRWS papers. Letter to Lutterworth Press, dated 7 March 1989.) This opened the way for the enterprising trio (later partnership) 'Three's Company' to design and place with new publishers a revised and illustrated edition under the same title. (Wheaton: Harold Shaw; Milton Keynes: Word, 1990).

[77] Chua (1992), p. 145. Chua Wee Hian was for more than twenty-five years the General Secretary of the International Fellowship of Evangelical Students. The same book tells how his wife, King Ling, was converted to Christ through reading *Basic Christianity* (p. 147).

[78] 5 April 1958.

[79] 12 September 1958.

[80] *Canterbury Diocesan Notes*, May 1958.

[81] From Lambeth Palace, 29 May 1958.

[82] J. T. C. B. Collins. Memorandum to the author, 1989. John Stott's files confirm that these books were projected, with Dick Lucas (at that time Candidates' Secretary of CPAS) writing on *Your Vocation*. Philip Hughes was due to write on *Your Church* and John Stott to contribute a second volume, *Your Creed*, which in the event was subsumed into *Your Confirmation* as part II, 'Christian Belief'. The back cover of the first edition of *Your Confirmation* lists five titles in the series, all of which were published. Perhaps the 'advertisements' John Collins remembers were in earlier advance publicity – or in his fertile imagination? *Your Confirmation* has almost never been out of print. Over the years the 1958 edition sold some 300,000 copies, and the 1991 edition is still selling under the title *Christian Basics*. See Stott (1991a).

[83] Stott (1950).

[84] Watson (1983), p. 21.

[85] JRWS MS 'Jottings for a biography', 1993/4, p. 23.

[86] Stott (1957). Both booklets owe something to Bash's booklets, *Life at its Best* and *How to Succeed in the Christian Life*.

[87] This was intended to be an auxiliary international language of some 850 words. 'Basic' was an acronym for British, American, Scientific, International, Commercial.

[88] Lewis (1952), p. viii. Surprisingly, *Mere Christianity* was one of 'five books which every Christian should read', named by John Stott in response to an American interviewer in 1996. See Russell Levenson, Jr., 'Interview with the Reverend Dr. John R. W. Stott', *The Anglican Digest*, Transfiguration 1996, p. 35.

[89] p. 7, 1958 edition.

[90] Stott (1958a), p. 120. It appears in an updated version in the 1971 revision.

[91] *IVP* (1986). The 1971 revision made a slightly shorter book, lighter in style.

[92] Based on a list by Frances Whitehead of 61 permissions given, December 1997. Some will be still in preparation. Not all will achieve publication.

[93] Ian Hore-Lacy. Letter to the author, 15 March 1995.

[94] JRWS papers. Letter to John Stott from the Revd. J. E. Campbell, Senior Pastor of the Dresden Community Church, Canada, 15 September 1982.

[95] JRWS papers. Letter dated 22 May 1971. A leading Methodist and a prolific writer, the Revd. Leslie Weatherhead was President of Conference, 1955. Perhaps his most influential years were as minister of the (Congregational) City Temple when he was a national figure.

[96] Dobbie (1988), p. 11.

[97] Letter to the author, 6 July 1997. The extract from *Basic Christianity* is here quoted from the second edition, 1971.

[98] JRWS MS 'Jottings for a biography', 1993/4, p. 23.

[99] Memorandum to the author; 'The Hookses', n.d.

Bibliography

The books listed are usually those referred to in the text or notes.

(1958), *The Lambeth Conference, 1958*, London: SPCK.

(1986), *IVP: The First Fifty Years*, Leicester: IVP.

(1992), *Rugby School Service Book and Hymnal*, Henley-on-Thames: Gresham Books.

Alison, Sylvia Mary (1984), *God is Building a House*, London: Marshalls.

Anderson, J. N. D. (1985), *An Adopted Son*, Leicester: IVP.

Atkinson, B. F. C. (1937) *Valiant in Fight*, London: IVF.

—— (1939), *The Christian's Duty in War*, London: S. E. Roberts.

—— (1966), *Basil's Recollections*, Unpublished MS in the possession of UCCF.

Austen, Jane (1811), *Sense and Sensibility*, London: Folio Society edition 1958.

Baker, Betty (1995), *St. Peter's Church*, London: The Institute for Contemporary Christianity.

Balleine, G. R. (1908), *A History of the Evangelical Party*, London: Longmans.

Barclay, Oliver R. (1977), *Whatever Happened to the Jesus Lane Lot?* Leicester: IVP.

—— (1997), *Evangelicalism in Britain 1935–1995: A Personal Sketch*, Leicester: IVP.

Barnes, E. W. (1947), *The Rise of Christianity*, London: Longmans.

Baron, Barclay (1952), *The Doctor*, London: Edward Arnold & Co.

Barry, F. R. (1964), *George Mervyn Haigh*, London: SPCK.

Barwell, Noel (n.d), *Cambridge*, London: Blackie.

Bebbington, D. W. (1989), *Evangelicalism in Modern Britain*, London: Unwin Hyman.

Bickersteth, John (1991), *Clerks of the Closet*, Stroud: Alan Sutton.

Bowles, C. W. J. (1958), *The Many Fundamentalisms*, London: SPCK.

Brooke, G. N. L. (1993), *A History of the University of Cambridge*, Vol. IV, 1870–1990. Cambridge: Cambridge University Press.

Brown, Roger L. (1988*)*, *The Evangelical Fellowship in the Church in Wales: the First Twenty-One Years*, Cardiff: EFCW.

Bullard, J. V. (ed.) (1934), *The Standing Orders of the Church of England*, London: The Faith Press.

Bullock, F. W. B. (1941), *The History of Ridley Hall, Cambridge*, vol. 1, Cambridge: Ridley Hall.

Carpenter, Edward (1991), *Archbishop Fisher: his life and times*, Norwich: Canterbury Press.

Carpenter, Humphrey (1996), *Robert Runcie: The Reluctant Archbishop*, London: Hodder & Stoughton.

Carus, William (ed.) (1847), *Memoirs of the Life of the Rev. Charles Simeon*, London: Hatchard & Son.

Catherwood, Christopher (1984), *Five Evangelical Leaders*, London: Hodder & Stoughton.

Catherwood, Sir Fred (1995), *At the Cutting Edge*, London: Hodder & Stoughton.

Chadwick, Owen (1966), *The Victorian Church*, part 1, London: A & C Black.

—— (1983), *Hensley Henson*, Oxford: Clarendon Press.

—— (1990a), *Michael Ramsey, a life*, Oxford: Clarendon Press.

—— (1990b), *The Spirit of the Oxford Movement*, Cambridge: Cambridge University Press.

Cherry, Bridget and Pevsner, Nikolaus (1983), *The Buildings of England: London 2: South*, Harmondsworth: Penguin.

Chua Wee Hian (1992), *Getting through Customs*, Leicester: IVP.

Coggan, F. D. (ed.) (1934), *Christ and the Colleges*, London: IVF.

Cohan, Morton N. (1995), *Lewis Carroll: A Biography*, London: Macmillan.

Colquhoun, Frank (ed.) (1948), *Evangelicals Affirm*, London: Church Book Room Press.

Colquhoun, Frank, (1955), *Harringay Story*, London: Hodder & Stoughton.

Commission on Evangelism (1945), *Towards the conversion of England: the report of a commission on evangelism appointed by the Archbishops of Canterbury and York*, London: Press and Publications Board of the Church Assembly.

Como, James T. (ed.) (1980), *C. S. Lewis at the Breakfast Table*, London: Collins.

Craston, Colin (1998), *Debtor to Grace*, London: Silver Fish Publishing.

Cross, F. L. (ed.) (1957), *The Oxford Dictionary of the Christian Church*, London: Oxford University Press.

Crutchley, Brooke, (1980), *To Be a Printer*, London: Bodley Head.

Davies, Horton (1965), *Worship and Theology in England, Volume Five, The Ecumenical Century, 1900–1965*, Princeton University Press, repr. William Eerdmans, 1996.

De-la-Noy, Michael (1996), *Mervyn Stockwood: A Lonely Life*, London: Mowbray.

Dillistone, F. W. (1975), *Charles Raven*, London: Hodder & Stoughton.

—— (1977), *C. H. Dodd*, London: Hodder & Stoughton.

—— (1980), *Into All the World*, London: Hodder & Stoughton.

Dobbie, Ian (1988), *Sovereign Service*, Aldershot: The Soldiers' and Airmen's Scripture Readers Association.

Drabble, Margaret (ed.) (1985), *The Oxford Companion to English Literature*, 5th Ed. Oxford: Oxford University Press.

Dudley-Smith, Timothy (1995a), *John Stott – a Comprehensive Bibliography*, Leicester: IVP.

Dudley-Smith, Timothy (ed.) (1995b), *Authentic Christianity*, Leicester: IVP.

Earnshaw-Smith, Harold (1939), *Christ our Freedom*, London: IVF.

Eddison, John (ed.) (1983), *Bash – A Study in Spiritual Power*, Basingstoke / London: Marshalls.

Eden, Martyn and Wells, David (eds.) (1991), *The Gospel in the Modern World*, Leicester: IVP.

Edwards, David L. (1971), *Leaders of the Church of England 1828–1944*, London: Oxford University Press.

—— (1984), *Christian England*, vol. 3, London: Hodder & Stoughton.

Edwards, David L. and Stott, John R. W. (1988), *Essentials: A Liberal-Evangelical Dialogue*, London: Hodder & Stoughton.

Elwell, Walter A. (ed.) (1993), *A Handbook of Evangelical Theologians*, Grand Rapids: Baker Books.

Endersbee, Mary (1977), *Hidden Miracles at All Souls*, London: Lakeland.

Ewing, J. W. (1946), *Goodly Fellowship*, London: Marshall, Morgan & Scott.

Fielder, Geraint (1983), *Excuse me, Mr Davies – Hallelujah!* Bryntirion, Bridgend: Evangelical Press of Wales.

—— (1988), *Lord of the Years*, Leicester: IVP.

Fison, J. E. (1950), *The Blessings of the Holy Spirit*, London: Longmans.

Fowler, Lawrence and Helen (eds.) (1984), *Cambridge Commemorated*, Cambridge: CUP.

Frady, Marshall (1979), *Billy Graham: A Parable of American Righteousness*, London: Hodder & Stoughton.

Gere, J. A. and Sparrow, John (eds.) (1981), *Geoffrey Madan's Notebooks*, 1984 edition, Oxford.

Glegg, Lindsay (ed.) (1944), *The Royal Albert Hall Campaign, 1944*, London: Pickering & Inglis.

Gow, A. S. F. (1945), *Letters from Cambridge, 1939–1944*, London: Jonathan Cape.

Graham, Billy (1997), *Just as I am*, London: HarperCollins.

Graves, Robert and Hodge, Alan (1940), *The Long Week-End*, Sphere Books Cardinal edition, 1991.

Green, Christopher, and Jackman, David (1995), *When God's Voice is Heard*, Leicester: IVP.

Green, Peter (1959), *Kenneth Grahame*, London: John Murray.

Guillebaud, H. E. (1937), *Why the Cross?* London: IVF.

Gummer, Selwyn (1963), *The Chavasse Twins*, London: Hodder & Stoughton.

Hammond, T. C. (1936), *In Understanding Be Men*, London: IVF.

Harford, J. B. and MacDonald, F. C. (1923), *Handley Carr Glyn Moule*, London: Hodder & Stoughton.

Harvey, Paul (ed.) (1946), *The Oxford Companion to English Literature*, 3rd Ed., Oxford: Clarendon Press.

Haslam, W. (1894), *From Death into Life*, London: Jarrold & Son.

Hastings, Adrian (1991), *A History of English Christianity, 1920–1990*, 3rd, Ed. London: SCM Press.

Hayes, Denis (1949), *The Story of the Conscientious Objectors of 1939–1945*, London: Allen & Unwin.

Henson, Herbert Hensley (1943), *Retrospect of an Unimportant Life*, Vol. 2, London: Oxford University Press.

—— (1950), *Retrospect of an Unimportant Life*, Vol 3. Oxford: OUP.

Hebert, Gabriel (1957), *Fundamentalism and the Church of God*, London: SCM Press.

High, Stanley (1957), *Billy Graham*, Kingswood: The World's Work.

Hodder, Edwin (1887), *The Life and Work of the Seventh Earl of Shaftesbury*, London: Cassell.

Hooper, Walter (1996), *C. S. Lewis: A Companion and Guide*, London: HarperCollins.

Hope Simpson, J. B. (1967), *Rugby Since Arnold*, London: Macmillan.

Hopkins, Hugh Evan (1977), *Charles Simeon of Cambridge*, London: Hodder & Stoughton.

Houston, James M. (ed.) (1986), *Evangelical Preaching: An Anthology of Sermons by Charles Simeon*, Portland, Oregon: Multnomah Press.

Howard, David M. (1986), *The Dream That Would Not Die*, Exeter: Pasternoster.

Howarth, T. E. B. (1978), *Cambridge Between Two Wars*, London: Collins.

Hsu, Albert Y. (1997), *Singles at the Cross-roads*, Leicester: IVP.

Hughes, Thomas (1906), *Tom Brown's School Days*, London: J. M. Dent, Everyman edition.

Hunt, Keith and Gladys (1991), *For Christ and the University*, Downers Grove: IVP.

Hylson-Smith, Kenneth (1988), *Evangelicals in the Church of England, 1734–1984*, Edinburgh: T. & T. Clark.

Inglis, Fred (1995), *Raymond Williams*, London: Routledge.

Ingrams, Richard (1995), *Muggeridge: The Biography*, London: HarperCollins.

Iremonger, F. A. (1948), *William Temple*, London: Oxford University Press.

Jarvis, Alfred F. (1950), *Charles Baring Young of Daylesford*, London: Church Book Room Press.

Johnson, Douglas (1979), *Contending for the Faith*, Leicester: IVP.

Johnson, Paul (ed.) (1994), *20th Century Britain*, London: Longmans.

Judd, Stephen and Cable, Kenneth (1987), *Sydney Anglicans*, Sydney: Anglican Information Office.

King, John (1969), *The Evangelicals*, London: Hodder & Stoughton.

King, John (ed.) (1973), *Evangelicals Today*, Guildford: Lutterworth.

Kirk, Andrew (ed.) (1988), *Handling Problems of Peace and War*, London: Marshall Pickering.

Laird, John (1981), *No Mere Chance*, London: Hodder & Stoughton/Scripture Union.

Leinster-Mackay, Donald (1984), *The Rise of the English Prep School*, Lewes: The Falmer Press.

Lewis, C. S. (1949), *Transposition and Other Addresses*, London: Geoffrey Bles.

—— (1952), *Mere Christianity*, London: Bles.

—— (1971), *Undeceptions*, London: Geoffrey Bles.

—— (1975), *Fernseed and Elephants*, London: Fontana/Collins

Lewis, C. S. and Calabria, Don Giovanni (1989), *Letters*, London: Collins.

Lloyd, Roger (1966), *The Church of England, 1900–1965*, London: SCM.

Loane, M. L. (1960), *Archbishop Mowll*, London: Hodder & Stoughton.

Lockhart, J. G. (1949), *Cosmo Gordon Lang*, London: Hodder & Stoughton.

Lowman, Pete (1983), *The Day of his Power*, Leicester: IVP.

Luker, Raymond (1979), *All Souls Langham Place: A History*, London: All Souls Church.

Lyall, Leslie T. (1954), *John Sung*, China Inland Mission: London.

Lycett Green, Candida (1994, 1995), *John Betjeman: Letters*, 2 vols., London: Methuen.

Manwaring, Randle (1985), *From Controversy to Co-existence*, Cambridge: Cambridge University Press.

Martin, William (1992), *The Billy Graham Story*, London: Hutchinson.

Mass Observation (1947), *Puzzled people: a study in popular attitudes to religion, ethics, progress and politics in a London Borough*, London.

McGrath, Alister (1997), *To Know and Serve God: A Life of James I. Packer*, London: Hodder & Stoughton.

McLintock, Alan (1993), *Hugh Lyon 1893–1986: A Memoir*, Berkhamsted: Laurence Niveny.

Moberg, David O. (1972), *The Great Reversal: Evangelism Versus Social Concern*, Philadelphia: Scripture Union.

Montefiore, Hugh (1995), *O God, What Next?* London: Hodder & Stoughton.

Moorman, Mary (1980), *George Macaulay Trevelyan: A Memoir*, London: Hamish Hamilton.

Moule, H. C. G. (1892), *Charles Simeon*, London: Methuen, repr. London: IVF, 1948.

Munro, H. H. (1930), *The Short Stories of Saki*, London: John Lane.

Murray, Iain H. (1990), *D. M. Lloyd-Jones. Vol 2: The Fight of Faith 1939–1981*, Edinburgh: Banner of Truth.

Neill, Stephen (1958), *Anglicanism*, Harmondsworth: Penguin.

Ng, Lee Moy (ed.)(n.d.), *ICMS 80: Proceedings of the International Conference of Christian Medical Students*, Oxford, July/August 1980 (London: ICCMS)

Noll, Mark A. (1991), *Between Faith and Criticism: Evangelical Scholarship and the Bible*, Leicester: IVP Apollos.

Noll, Mark A., Bebbington, David W., Rawlyk, George A. (eds.) (1994), *Evangelicalism: Comparative Studies of Popular Protestantism in North America, the British Isles, and beyond, 1700–1990*, New York: Oxford.

Osborne, Harold (ed.) (1970), *Oxford Companion to Art*, 16th impression, 1995. Oxford: OUP.

Packer, J. I. (1958), *Fundamentalism and the Word of God*, London: IVP.

Palmer, Bernard (1992), *High and Mitred*, London: SPCK.

Pawley, Margaret (1987), *Donald Coggan*, London: SPCK.

Peart-Binns, John S. (1987a), *Living with Paradox*, London: Darton, Longman & Todd.

—— (1987b), *Wand of London*, Oxford: Mowbray.

Pollock, J. C. (1953), *A Cambridge Movement*, London: John Murray.

—— (1955), *The Cambridge Seven*, London: IVF.

—— (1959), *The Good Seed*, London: Hodder & Stoughton.

—— (1966), *Billy Graham: The Authorised Biography*, London: Hodder & Stoughton.

Pound, Reginald (1967), *Harley Street*, London: Michael Joseph.

Prestige, G. L. (1935), *The Life of Charles Gore*, London: Heinemann.

Raven, C. E. (1928), *A Wanderer's Way*, London: Martin Hopkinson.

Reynolds, J. S. (1967), *Canon Christopher*, Abingdon: The Abbey Press.

Richter, Friedmann (ed.) (1972), *Die Kommende Ökumene: Theologische untersuchungen*, Wuppertal: Rolf Brockhaus.

Roberts, R. Ellis (1942), *H. R. L. Sheppard*, London: John Murray.

Rogers, T. Guy (ed.) (1923*)*, *Liberal Evangelicalism: An Interpretation: by Members of the Church of England*, London: Hodder & Stoughton.

Russell, George W. E. (1915), *A Short History of the Evangelical Movement*, London: A. R. Mowbray.

Samuel, Vinay and Sugden, Chris (eds.) (1981), *AD 2000 and Beyond: A Festschrift for John Stott's 70th Birthday*, Oxford: Regnum Books.

Saunders, Teddy and Sansom, Hugh (1992), *David Watson: A Biography*, London: Hodder & Stoughton.

Saward, Michael (1987), *Evangelicals on the Move*, London: Mowbrays.

Sharp, Doreen (1996), *A Vision Fulfilled*, Privately printed.

Sheppard, David (1964), *Parson's Pitch*, London: Hodder & Stoughton.

Shilton, Lance (1997), *Speaking Out: A Life in Urban Mission*, Sydney: Centre for the Study of Australian Christianity.

Smith, A. Eric (1991), *Another Anglican Angle*, Oxford: The Amate Press.

Smith, D. J. (1990), *Action Stations 3: Military Airfields of Wales and the North West*, Sparkford, Somerset: Patrick Stephens.

Smyth, Charles (1959), *Cyril Forster Garbett*, London: Hodder & Stoughton.

Spalding, Frances (1988), *Stevie Smith: A Critical Biography*, London: Faber.

Stevenson, H. F. (ed.) (1969), *The Keswick Week 1969*, London: Marshall, Morgan & Scott.

Stockwood, Mervyn (1982), *Chanctonbury Ring*, London: Hodder & Stoughton.

Stott, John R. W. (1949), *Personal Evangelism*, London: IVF and Downers Grove IVP.

—— (1950), *Becoming a Christian*, London: IVF and Downers Grove: IVP.

—— (1952), *Parochial Evangelism by the Laity*, London: Church Information Board.

—— (1954), *Men with a Message*, London: Longmans.

—— (1956), *Fundamentalism and Evangelism*, London: Crusade booklets.

—— (1957), *Being a Christian*, London: IVF.

—— (1958a), *Basic Christianity*, London: IVF.

—— (1958b), *What Christ Thinks of the Church*, London: Lutterworth.

—— (1958c), *Your Confirmation*, London: Hodder & Stoughton.

—— (1961), *The Preacher's Portrait*, London: Tyndale Press.

—— (1963), *Intercommunion and Prayer Book Revision*, London: Falcon.

—— (1964a), *A Basic Introduction to the New Testament*, Grand Rapids: Eerdmans & Downers Grove: IVP.

—— (1964b), *The Epistles of John*, London: Tyndale Press.

—— (1966), *Men Made New*, London: IVP.

—— (1967), *Our Guilty Silence*, London: Hodder & Stoughton.

—— (1968), *The Call to Preach*, London: London Baptist Preachers' Association.

—— (1969), *One People*, London: Falcon.

—— (1970), *Christ the Controversialist*, London: Tyndale Press.

—— (1973), *Guard the Gospel*, Leicester: IVP.

—— (1977), *What is an Evangelical?* London: Falcon.

—— (1978a), *Christian Counter-Culture: The Message of the Sermon on the Mount*, Leicester: IVP.

—— (1978b), *Understanding the Bible*, London: Scripture Union.

—— (1982a), *The Bible: Book for Today*, Leicester: IVP.

—— (1982b), *I Believe in Preaching*, London: Hodder & Stoughton.

—— (1983), *Make the Truth Known*, Leicester: UCCF booklets.

—— (1988), *The Cross of Christ*, Leicester: IVP.

—— (1990a), *Issues facing Christians Today*, London: Marshall Pickering.

—— (1990b), *The Message of Acts*, Leicester: IVP.

—— (1991a), *Christian Basics: a Handbook of Christian Faith*, London: Hodder & Stoughton.

—— (1991b), *Life in Christ*, Eastbourne: Kingsway.

—— (1992), *The Contemporary Christian*, Leicester: IVP.

—— (1998), *Issues Facing Christians Today*, 3rd ed. revised; London: HarperCollins.

Sylvester, Nigel (1984), *God's Word in a Young World*, London: Scripture Union.

Taylor, Howard and Geraldine (1911, 1918), *Hudson Taylor in Early Years: The Growth of a Soul* and *Hudson Taylor and the China Inland Mission: The Growth of a Work of God*, London: Morgan & Scott (one volume edition 1920).

Temple, William (1950), *Christianity and Social Order*, London: SCM Press.

Toon, Peter (1979), *Evangelical Theology 1833–1856*, London: Marshall, Morgan & Scott.

Torrey, R. A. (1923), *Why God used D. L. Moody*, Chicago: Moody Bible Institute.

Trail, Richard R. (ed.) (1968), *Lives of the Fellows of the Royal College of Physicians*, London: Published by the College.

Trevelyan, G. M. (1949), *An Autobiography and Other Essays*, London: Longmans.

Walker, Tom (1982), *Renew Us By Your Spirit*, London: Hodder & Stoughton.

Wallace, D. and Bagnall-Oakeley, R. P. (1951), *Norfolk*, London: Robert Hale.

Wallis, Jim (ed.) (1983), *Peacemakers: Christian Voices from the New Abolitionist Movement*, New York: Harper & Row.

Warren, Max (1974), *Crowded Canvas*, London: Hodder & Stoughton.

Watson, David (1983), *You are my God*, London: Hodder & Stoughton.

Welsby, Paul A. (1984), A *History of the Church of England, 1945–1980*, Oxford: Oxford University Press.

Whistler, Theresa (1993), *Imagination of the Heart*, London: Duckworth.

Willey, Basil (1970), *Cambridge and Other Memories*, London: Chatto & Windus.

Williams, Betty (1989), *Portrait of a Decade: The 1920s*, London: Batsford.

Wolfe, Kenneth M. (1984), *The Churches and the British Broadcasting Corporation 1922–1956*, London: SCM Press.

Wood, Maurice A. P. (1953), *Lay Leadership Preparation*, London: CPAS Fellowship paper.

—— (1956), *Like a Mighty Army*, London: Marshall, Morgan & Scott.

Woodings, Tim (ed.) (1998), *Forty Love: A Community Reflects*, London: All Souls Clubhouse.

Wright, Christopher and Sugden, Christopher (1990), *One Gospel – Many Clothes: Anglicans and the Decade of Evangelism*, Oxford: EFAC & Regnum Books.

Ziegler, Philip (1990), *King Edward VIII*, London: Collins.

Index